NINTH EDITION

Fundamental Statistics

FOR THE BEHAVIORAL SCIENCES

DAVID C. HOWELL

University of Vermont

CENGAGE
Learning®

Australia • Brazil • Mexico • Singapore • United Kingdom • United States

Fundamental Statistics for the Behavioral Sciences, **Ninth edition**
David C. Howell

Product Director: Jon Goodspeed

Product Manager: Timothy Matray

Content Developer: Tangelique Williams-Grayer

Product Assistant: Adrienne McCrory

Marketing Manager: James Finlay

Art and Cover Direction, Production Management, and Composition: Lumina Datamatics, Inc.

Manufacturing Planner: Karen Hunt

Cover Image: Ajay Bhaskar/Shutterstock.com

For product information and technology assistance, contact us at
Cengage Learning Customer & Sales Support, 1-800-354-9706

For permission to use material from this text or product, submit all requests online at **www.cengage.com/permissions**. Further permissions questions can be e-mailed to **permissionrequest@cengage.com**

Library of Congress Control Number: 2015960736

Student Edition:

ISBN: 978-1-305-65297-2

Loose-leaf Edition:

ISBN: 978-1-305-86316-3

Cengage Learning
20 Channel Center Street
Boston, MA 02210
USA

Cengage Learning is a leading provider of customized learning solutions with employees residing in nearly 40 different countries and sales in more than 125 countries around the world. Find your local representative at **www.cengage.com**.

Cengage Learning products are represented in Canada by Nelson Education, Ltd.

To learn more about Cengage Learning Solutions, visit **www.cengage.com**.

Purchase any of our products at your local college store or at our preferred online store **www.cengagebrain.com**.

Printed in the United States of America
Print Number: 01   Print Year: 2016

*Dedication: To my wife, Donna, who has tolerated,
"I can't do that now, I am working on my book"
for far too long.*

Brief Contents

Contents

Preface

Why Statistics?

Those of us who teach in this area hate to admit it, but statistics is seldom listed as the most sought-after course on campus. A high percentage of students enroll because their department has made this a required course. Under these conditions students have a right to ask, "Why?" and there are at least two good answers to that question. The traditional answer is that we want our students to learn a specific set of skills about data analysis (including formulae and procedures) so that they can understand the experimental literature and conduct analyses on their own data. The broader answer, and one that applies to perhaps a larger number of students, is that some more general facility with numbers and data in general is an important skill that has lifelong and career-related value. Most of us, and not only those who do experimental work, frequently come across numerical data as part of our jobs, and some broad understanding of how to deal with those data is an important and marketable skill. It is my experience that students who have taken a course in statistics, even if they think that they have forgotten every technique they ever learned, have an understanding of numerical data that puts them ahead of their colleagues. And in a world increasingly dominated by quantitative data, that skill is more and more in demand.

Statistics is not really about numbers; it is about understanding our world. Certainly an important activity for statisticians is to answer such questions as whether cocaine taken in a novel context has more of an effect than cocaine taken in a familiar context. But let's not forget that what we are talking about here is drug addiction or the effect of the environment on learning and memory. The results of our experiment have a life beyond the somewhat limited world of the cognitive or behavioral scientist. And let's also remember that the numbers that most people see do not relate to tightly controlled experiments, but to the implications of a traffic study for the development of a shopping center, the density of residential housing and its impact on the local school budget, and a marketing survey for a new product. All of these examples involve many of the basic statistical concepts covered in this book.

Why This Text?

Enough preaching about the value of a course in statistics. Presumably the instructor was convinced before he or she started reading, and I hope that students have become at least a bit more open minded. But the question remains, why should you use this book instead of another of the many available texts? Part of the answer comes down to the matter of style. I have deliberately set out to make this book both interesting and useful for students and instructors. It is written in an informal style, every example is put in the context of an investigation that one might reasonably conduct, and almost all of the examples are taken from the published literature. It does not make much sense to ask people to learn a series of statistical procedures without supplying examples of situations in which those techniques would actually be applied. This text is designed for an introductory statistics course in psychology, education, and other behavioral sciences. It does not presuppose a background in mathematics beyond high-school algebra, and it emphasizes the *logic* of statistical procedures rather than their derivation.

Over the past 25 years the world of data analysis has changed dramatically. Whereas we once sat down with a calculator and entered data by hand to solve equations, we are now much more likely to use a statistical package running on a desktop computer. In fact, for some purposes we are likely to be using an online program written in Java or some similar language that we download free of charge from the Internet. (I sometimes use an app downloaded to my iPhone.) As the mechanics of doing statistics have changed, so too must our approach to teaching statistical procedures. While we cannot, and should not, forego all reference to formulae and computations, it is time that we relaxed our emphasis on them. And by relaxing the emphasis on computation, we free up the time to increase the emphasis on interpretation. That is what this book tries to do. It moves away from simply declaring group differences to be significant or not significant toward an explanation of what such differences mean relative to the purpose behind the experiment. I like to think of it as moving toward an analysis of *data* and away from an analysis of numbers. It becomes less important to concentrate on whether there is a difference between two groups than to understand what that difference means.

In the process of moving away from a calculator toward a computer, I have altered my approach to formulae. In the past I often gave a definitional formula, but then immediately jumped to a computational one. But if I have to worry less about computation, and more about understanding, then I am able to revert to the use of definitional formulae. It is my hope that this will make students' lives a bit easier. Beyond that, in this edition I spend considerably more time on computer solutions, in part because seeing how a computer would solve the problem can actually make it easier to understand what is going on. That is not always true, but it is true enough to suggest the importance of being able to run a computer program to come to an answer. (And then changing things slightly, rerunning the program, and looking at what happens.)

Unique Features

Several features of this book set it apart from other books written for the same audience. One of these was just noted: the use of examples from the research literature. I have attempted to choose studies that address problems of interest to students. Examples include the effect of context on heroin overdose, the relationship between daily stress and psychological symptoms, variables influencing course evaluations, the effect of early parental death on children's feelings of vulnerability, and variables controlling how memory changes as a function of age. I want students to have some involvement in the questions being asked, and I want to illustrate that statistical analyses involve more than just applying a few equations.

In most chapters a section is devoted to an example using SPSS and R. Readers have suggested that I concentrate most on R and less on SPSS. R is becoming a standard of computing, and is a free package that is constantly under development. SPSS is a commercial package for which many colleges and universities have a license. *R* is a bit more difficult to learn, but it really is becoming the package of the future. And being free is nothing to sneer at. My purpose is to familiarize students with the form of computer printouts and the kinds of information they contain. I am not trying to make students an expert on statistical packages, but I am trying to give them the information they need to make modifications to the code and do things on their own. In addition, I use *R*, in particular, to illustrate statistical concepts visually.

But if students are going to be using these computer packages, I would hate to have them buy an SPSS manual or an *R* textbook, just to do their work. I have two SPSS manuals on the Web and encourage students to go to them. They are not as complete as a printed book would be, but they are more than sufficient to allow students to work with SPSS. I recommend the shorter manual, but the longer one is there if additional information is needed. Similarly I have presented chapter by chapter Web documents on the use of *R*, and students should be able to follow along with those; again modifying code to do their own analyses.

Data files for all of the examples and exercises used in the text are available on a website that I maintain for this book. The basic URL for that site is www.uvm .edu/~dhowell/fundamentals9/index.html. A link at that site will take you to the data. These files are formatted in ASCII, so that they can be read by virtually any statistical program. (I also supply copies of data files formulated specifically for SPSS.) The variable names appear on the first line and can be directly imported to your software. The data can be saved to your computer simply by selecting your browser's Save option. The availability of these files makes it easy for students and instructors to incorporate any statistical package with the text.

A Student Manual is also available at the previously mentioned website. It provides complete solutions for half the exercises. This supplements the short answers to those questions at the back of the book. I have included answers only to the odd-numbered questions because many instructors prefer to assign problems (or exam questions) on material that does not have an answer in the back of the book or the Student Solution Handbook. (I am very much aware that this does annoy students, from whom I sometimes receive unhappy mail messages, but it is a balance between the needs of students and the desires of the instructors.) I make available to instructors the answers to all of the questions. Those answers frequently come with comments such as "In class you might point out ..." or "The reason why I asked this question is to get at ..." As I read through them in creating this edition, I realized that many, though not all, of those comments would also be useful to students. So I have included many of them in the Student Manual as well. Some of them may appear unhelpful or out of context, but I think most of them are worth reading.

On my Web pages I have also included many links to other sites, where you can find good examples, small programs to demonstrate statistical techniques, a more extensive glossary, and so on. People have devoted a great deal of time to making material available over the Internet, and it is very worthwhile to use that material.

Why a New Edition?

When an author comes out with a new edition, I think that it is fair to ask what was wrong with the old one, other than the fact that it is widely available in the used book market. Normally I design a new edition to incorporate changes that are going on in the field and to remove things that are no longer needed. And, despite what many people think, there is a lot of new work going on. But in this edition and the previous one I have taken a different approach. While I have added some new material, the major effort has been to read the book as a new student would, and try to find ways to clarify and repeat concepts. For example, I know that the Y axis is the vertical one, but most people don't, and telling them once is not enough. So I often write something like "On the Y (vertical) axis …" And when you start looking at a book that way, you find many places for clarification—especially because I have a wife who has spent most of her life in secondary education and knows more about pedagogy than I do. (She actually read every chapter and made many fruitful suggestions.) I have also begun each chapter with a list of concepts that will be important in the chapter, in hopes that if you aren't sure what they are you will review them.

Where necessary I have inserted important comments in boxes to pull several points together, to highlight material that you really need to understand, or to clarify difficult concepts. I have also inserted short biographies of important statisticians. Especially in the first half of the 20th century there were many interesting (and cantankerous) people in the field and they are worth meeting. Next, I have removed the very brief and weak chapter summaries and replaced them with much more complete ones. My goal was to condense the chapter into a few paragraphs, and you will do well to spend some time on them. A while back I was reading a programming text on Java and came across an author who inserted simple questions, with answers, at the end of each chapter. I discovered that I learned a lot from those simple questions, so I have followed his lead in this edition. The questions are intended to focus your attention on many of the important points in the chapter. I hope that they are useful.

An important feature of this book is the continued increase in emphasis on measures of effect size. Statistics in the behavioral sciences are rapidly shifting away from compete dependence on a statement of statistical significance and toward measures that tell you more about how large, and how important, a finding is. This has been long overdue, and is reflected in changes that I continue to make to the text. Not only is this is in line with trends in the field, but it is also important because it causes the student, and the researcher, to think carefully about what a result means. In presenting effect size measures I have tried to convey the idea that the writer is trying to tell the reader what the study found, and there are different ways of accomplishing that goal. In some situations it is sufficient to talk about the difference between means or proportions. In other situations a standardized measure, such as Cohen's d, is helpful. I have stayed away from correlation-based measures as much as I reasonably can because I don't think that they tell the reader much of what he or she wants to know.

One of the changes taking place in statistics is the movement toward what are called "resampling statistics." Because of the enormous speed of even a simple desktop computer, it is possible to look at outcomes in ways that we could think about before but never really do. One advantage of these procedures is that they call for many fewer assumptions about the data. In some ways they are like the more traditional nonparametric procedures that we have had for years, but more powerful. I have revised the chapter on traditional nonparametric statistics to move almost completely away from hand calculation, and used the freed-up space to introduce resampling. The nice thing is that once I illustrate resampling techniques for one kind of analysis, the student can readily see how some sort of modification of that approach could apply to other experimental designs.

I have maintained from earlier editions a section labeled "Seeing Statistics." These sections are built around a set of Java applets, written by Gary McClelland at the University of Colorado. These allow the students to illustrate for themselves many of the concepts that are discussed in the book. Students can open these applets, change parameters, and see what happens to the result. A nice illustration of this is the applet illustrating the influence of heterogeneous subsamples in a correlation problem. See Chapter 9, p. 217. These applets are available directly from my website referred to earlier.

An important addition to this edition is the inclusion of a chapter on meta-analysis. Meta-analysis is an analysis of multiple studies at the same time. There have been many research studies on the treatment of depression, for example. A meta-analytic study of depression would bring all of those studies together and attempt to draw conclusions on the basis of their similar or differing findings. The current emphasis on evidence-based medicine is an excellent example. If I am to be treated for cancer, for example, I want that treatment to be based on more than the most recent study that came out last week or on my oncologist's favorite study. What we really have here is the extension of the behavioral science's emphasis on effect sizes along with statistical significance. This inclusion of meta-analysis of multiple studies probably would not have appeared in any introductory statistics text 20 years ago.

In addition to the features already described, the website linked to this book through the publisher's pages (there is a link on my pages) contains a number of other elements that should be helpful to students. These include a Statistical Tutor, which is a set of multiple-choice questions covering the major topics in the chapter. Whenever a student selects an incorrect answer, a box appears explaining the material and helping the student to see what the correct answer should be. I did not write those questions, but I think that they are very well done. There are also links to additional resources, a review of basic arithmetic, and links to other examples and additional material.

Organization and Coverage

This section is meant primarily for instructors, because frequent reference is made to terms that students cannot yet be expected to know. Students may wish to skip to the next section.

- The first seven chapters of the book are devoted to standard descriptive statistics, including ways of displaying data, measures of central tendency and variability, the normal distribution, and those aspects of probability that are directly applicable to what follows.

- Chapter 8 on hypothesis testing and sampling distributions serves as a nontechnical introduction to inferential statistics. That chapter was specifically designed to allow students to examine the underlying logic of hypothesis testing without simultaneously being concerned with learning a set of formulae and the intricacies of a statistical test.

- Chapters 9, 10, and 11 deal with correlation and regression, including multiple regression.

- Chapters 12–14 are devoted to tests on means, primarily t tests.

- Chapter 15 is concerned with power and its calculation and serves as an easily understood and practical approach to that topic.

- Chapters 16–18 are concerned with the analysis of variance. I have included material on simple repeated-measures designs, but have stopped short of covering mixed designs. These chapters include consideration of basic multiple comparison procedures by way of Fisher's protected t, which not only is an easily understood statistic but has also been shown to be well behaved, under limited conditions, with respect to both power and error rates. At the request of several users of the earlier editions, I have included treatment of the Bonferroni test, which does a very commendable job of controlling error rates, while not sacrificing much in the way of power when used judiciously. Also included are measures of magnitude of effect and effect size, a fairly extensive coverage of interactions, and procedures for testing simple effects. The effect size material, in particular, is considerably expanded from earlier editions.

- Chapter 19 deals with the chi-square test, although that material could very easily be covered at an earlier point if desired.

- Chapter 20 covers the most prominent distribution-free tests, including resampling statistics.

- Chapter 21 was a completely new chapter in the last edition. It deals with meta-analysis. Along with an increased emphasis on effect sizes for individual studies, meta-analysis takes us in the direction of combining many similar studies though the use of those effect sizes. This field is becoming much more important, and follows in the footsteps of those in medicine who espouse what is called Evidence Based Medicine. If you are going to be treated for cancer, wouldn't you like that treatment to be based on a solid analysis of all of the literature surrounding your form of cancer? The same is true for our interests in the behavioral sciences.

Not every course would be expected to cover all these chapters, and several (most notably multiple regression, power, and distribution-free statistical methods) can be omitted or reordered without disrupting the flow of the material. (I cover chi-square early in my courses, but it is late in the text on the advice of reviewers.)

MindTap for Howell's Fundamental Statistics for the Behavioral Sciences

MindTap is a personalized teaching experience with relevant assignments that guide students to analyze, apply, and improve thinking, allowing you to measure skills and outcomes with ease.

- **Personalized Teaching:** Becomes yours with a Learning Path that is built with key student objectives. Control what students see and when they see it. Use it as-is or match to your syllabus exactly—hide, rearrange, add and create your own content.

- **Guide Students:** A unique learning path of relevant readings, multimedia, and activities that move students up the learning taxonomy from basic knowledge and comprehension to analysis and application.

■   **Promote Better Outcomes:** Empower instructors and motivate students with analytics and reports that provide a snapshot of class progress, time in course, engagement and completion rates.

Supplements

Online Instructor's Manual with Test Bank and Electronic Lecture Notes includes the complete answers to exercises, suggestions on different ways to present the material and engage the students' attention, additional examples that can be used to supplement the text for lecture purposes, Internet links to additional resources, and added material chosen by the author, David Howell. Also included are electronic transparencies for use as lecture notes or worksheets.

Acknowledgments

Many people have played an important role in the development of this book. My product team, was supportive of this revision, including Product Manager, Tim Matray; Product Assistant, Adrienne McCrory; Content Developer, Tangelique Williams-Grayer; and Lumina Program Manager, Kailash Rawat. Diane Giombetti Clue did an excellent job of editing of the manuscript and was always supportive on those few occasions when I insisted that quaint spellings and my positioning of prepositions were better than the ones preferred by style manuals. My daughter, Lynda, did extensive work on aligning and formatting the Instructor and Student manuals and spotting the occasional error.

A number of reviewers made many helpful suggestions in earlier editions, especially Dr. Kevin J. Apple (Ohio University), Eryl Bassett (University of Kent at Canterbury), Drake Bradley (Bates College), Deborah M. Clauson (Catholic University of America), Jose M. Cortina (Michigan State University), Gary B. Forbach (Washburn University), Edward Johnson (University of North Carolina), Dennis Jowaisas (Oklahoma City University), David J. Mostofsky (Boston University), Maureen Powers (Vanderbilt University), David R. Owen (Brooklyn College CUNY), Dennis Roberts (Pennsylvania State University), Steven Rogelberg (Bowling Green State University), Deborah J. Runsey (Kansas State University), Robert Schutz (University of British Columbia), N. Clayton Silver (University of Nevada), Patrick A. Vitale (University of South Dakota), Bruce H. Wade (Spelman College), Robert Williams (Gallaudet University), Eleanor Willemsen (Santa Clara University), Pamela Zappardino (University of Rhode Island), and Dominic Zerbolio (University of Missouri–St. Louis). For years Dr. Karl Wuensch (East Carolina University) has filled pages with suggestions, disagreements, and valuable advice. He deserves special recognition, as does Dr. Kathleen Bloom (University of Waterloo) and Joan Foster (Simon Fraser University). Gary McClelland, at the University of Colorado, graciously allowed me to use some of his Java applets, and was willing to modify them when necessary to meet my needs.

I want to thank all of those users (instructors and students alike) who have written me with suggestions and who have pointed out errors. I don't have the space to thank them individually, but many are listed along with the errors they found, on the Web pages labeled "Errata."

I owe thanks to my past colleagues at the University of Vermont. I retired from there in May of 2002, but still consider the University to be my intellectual home. I most certainly want to thank colleagues at the University of Bristol, England, where part of a sabbatical leave was devoted to completing the first edition of the book. Most of all, however, I owe a debt to all of my students who, over the years, have helped me to see where problems lie and how they can best be approached. Their encouragement has been invaluable. And this includes students who have never met me but have submitted questions or comments through the Internet. (Yes, I do read all of those messages, and I hope that I respond to all of them.).

David C. Howell
St. George, Utah
December, 2015
Internet: David.Howell@uvm.edu

NINTH EDITION

Fundamental Statistics

FOR THE BEHAVIORAL SCIENCES

## CHAPTER 1

Introduction

Students usually come to any course with some doubt about just what will be involved and how well they will do. This chapter will begin by laying out the kinds of material that we will, and will not, cover. I will then go on to make a distinction between statistics and mathematics, which, for the most part, really are not the same thing at all. As I will point out, all of the math that you need for this course you learned in high school—though you may have forgotten a bit of it. I will then go on to lay out why we need statistical procedures and what purpose they serve, and to provide a structure for all of the procedures we will cover. Finally, the chapter will provide an introduction to computer analyses of data.

For many years, when I was asked at parties and other social situations what I did for a living, I would answer that I was a psychologist (now retired). Even though I quickly added that I was an experimental psychologist, people would make comments about being careful what they said and acted as if I were thinking all sorts of thoughts that would never occur to me. So finally I changed tactics and started telling people that I taught statistics—an answer that is also perfectly true. That answer solved one problem—people no longer look at me with blatant suspicion—but it created another. Now they tell me how terrible they are in math, and how successful they were in avoiding ever taking a statistics course—not a very tactful remark to make to someone who spent his professional life teaching that subject. Now I just tell them that I taught research methods in psychology for 35 years, and that seems to satisfy them. Perhaps they don't know that research methods involve statistics. I won't tell them.

Let's begin by asking what the field of statistics is all about. After all, you are about to invest a semester in studying statistical methods, so it might be handy to know what you are studying. The word *statistics* is used in at least three different ways. As used in the title of this book, *statistics* refers to a set of procedures and rules (not always computational or mathematical) for reducing large masses of data to manageable proportions and for allowing us to draw conclusions from those data. That is essentially what this book is all about.

A second, and very common, meaning of the term is expressed by such statements as "statistics show that the number of people applying for unemployment benefits has fallen for the third month in a row." In this case *statistics* is used in place of the much better word *data*. For our purposes *statistics* will never be used in this sense.

A third meaning of the term is in reference to the result of some arithmetic or algebraic manipulation applied to data. Thus the mean (average) of a set of numbers is a statistic. This perfectly legitimate usage of the term will occur repeatedly throughout this book.

We thus have two proper uses of the term: (1) a set of procedures and rules and (2) the outcome of the application of those rules and procedures to samples of data. You will always be able to tell from the context which of the two meanings is intended.

The term *statistics* usually elicits some level of math phobia among many students, but mathematics and mathematical manipulation do not need to, and often don't, play a leading role in the lives of people who work with statistics. (Indeed, Jacob Cohen, one of the clearest and most influential writers on statistical issues in the behavioral sciences, suggested that he had been so successful in explaining concepts to others precisely because his knowledge of mathematical statistics was so inadequate. People could actually understand what he was saying.) Certainly you can't understand any statistical text without learning a few formulae and understanding many more. But the required level of mathematics is not great. You learned more than enough in high school. Those who are still concerned should spend a few minutes going over Appendix A. It lays out some very simple rules of mathematics that you may have forgotten, and a small investment of your time will be more than repaid in making the rest of this book easier to follow. I know—when I was a student I probably wouldn't have looked at it either, *but you really should!* A more complete review of arithmetic, which is perhaps more fun to read, can be found by going to the website for this book at

 https://www.uvm.edu/~dhowell/fundamentals9/ArithmeticReview/review_of_arithmetic_revised.html

There is a lot of stuff on that website, and most of it is useful for understanding the material in this book.

Something far more important than worrying about algebra and learning to apply equations is thinking of statistical methods and procedures as ways to tie the results of some experiment to the hypothesis that led to that experiment. Several editions ago I made a major effort to remove as much mathematical material as possible when that material did not contribute significantly to your understanding of data analysis. I also simplified equations by going back to definitional formulae rather than present formulae that were designed when we did everything with calculators. This means that I am asking you to think a bit more about the logic of what you are doing. I don't mean just the logic of a hypothesis test. I mean the logic behind the way you approach a problem. It doesn't do any good to be able to ask if two groups have different means (averages) if a difference in means has nothing to say about the real question you hoped to ask. And it does no good to say that a difference is not due to chance without also giving me some idea of how large the difference is and whether it makes an important difference. When we put too much emphasis on formulae, there is a tendency to jump in and apply those formulae to the data without considering what the underlying question really is.

Another concern that some students have, and I may have contributed to that concern in the preceding paragraph, is the belief that the only reason to take a course in statistics is to be able to analyze the results of experimental research. Certainly your instructor hopes many of you will use statistical procedures for that purpose, but those procedures and, more importantly, the ways of thinking that go with them have a life beyond standard experimental research. This is my plea to get the attention of those, like myself, who believe in a liberal arts education. Much of the material we will cover here will be applicable to whatever you do when you finish college. People who work for large corporations or small family-owned businesses have to work with data. They even have to use computers to work toward some sort of solution to a problem. People who serve on a town planning commission have to be able to ask how various changes in the town plan will lead to changes in residential and business development. They will have to ask how those changes will in turn lead to changes in school populations and the resulting level of school budgets, and so on. Those people may not need to run an analysis of variance (Chapters 16 through 18), though some acquaintance with regression models (Chapters 9 through 11) may be helpful, but the logical approach to data required in the analysis of variance is equally required when dealing with town planning. (And if you mess up town planning, you have everybody angry with you.)

A course in statistics is not something you take because it is required and then promptly forget. (Well, that probably is why many of you are taking it, but I hope you expect to come away with more than just three credits on your transcript.) If taught well, knowledge of statistics is a job skill you can use (and market). That is largely why I have tried to downplay the mathematical foundations of the field. Those foundations are important, but they are not what will be important later. Being able to think through the logic and the interpretation of an experiment or a set of data is an important skill that will stay with you; being able to derive the elements of a regression equation is not. That is why most of the examples used in this book relate to work that people actually do. Work of that type requires thought. It may be easier to understand an example that starts out, "Suppose we had three groups labeled A, B, and C" than it is to understand an actual experiment. But the former is boring and doesn't teach you much. A real-life example is more interesting and has far more to offer.

1.1   A Changing Field

People are often puzzled when I say that I am working on a revision of a text. They assume that statistical procedures stay pretty much constant over time. Fortunately that is not the case—we do actually learn more as time goes on. Not only do methods for carrying out more complex and interesting analyses continue to develop, but over the years we have changed the way we look at the results of experimental research. When I was in graduate school and for quite a few years beyond, researchers in the behavioral sciences were primarily concerned with whether a difference that they found between experimental groups (or the relationship they found between two or more variables) was *reliable*. If they ran the study over again would they still be likely to find that the experimental group outperformed a control group? After a while the field slowly began to change by going further and asking if a difference was *meaningful*. Perhaps the groups really were different, but the difference was too small to matter to anyone. That led to the development of a number of different indices of importance, or *effect size*. Along with effect sizes are *confidence limits*, or *confidence intervals*, which are designed to give you information about how confident you can be about the likely values of some measure on a whole population of observations. That was a very important step forward for the field. A number of people have begun to refer to "the new statistics" to emphasize the importance of going beyond a simple statistical test. Some disciplines were ahead of us in that transition, while other fields are slower to ask that question about meaningfulness.[1]

In the late 1980s, which really is a lot closer to us than you might imagine, a few people in psychology began asking a slightly different question. If the results we found are reliable, and if they are meaningful, what have other people found? Perhaps there are 20 studies on a particular theoretical question, but people are finding different results. Or perhaps most studies agree, at least in a general sense. This idea of looking at multiple studies on a topic has been extremely important in medicine, where we now speak of "evidence-based practice." Let's combine all of the studies on dealing with a particular type of cancer and see if there is agreement on the best form of treatment. This approach is called "meta-analysis," and I have added a non-technical discussion of it later in the book. It is time that we stopped acting as if the study we ran is the only study of interest. As you can see, the field has moved from "Is this difference reliable?" to "Is this difference meaningful?" to "Is this what other people are finding as well?"

This edition differs in significant ways from prior editions of this book. As I have said, I spend much more time on effect sizes and confidence limits than I did in the past. And, as I said earlier, over the past years I have greatly reduced the emphasis on statistical equations and have presented the equations in a different form, which are more difficult to compute with a hand-held calculator but are much truer to the logic of what you are doing. In this edition I am going further by including considerably more material on the use of computer software to come to conclusions. I have done that for years in another book that I write, but I decided that it was important to move in that direction for this edition of this book. I will deliberately present the computer material in ways that do not detract from the discussion and which could be skipped over if your instructor prefers to go that way. I certainly do not want people to stop using this book because they don't want to play with a computer language. Computers are ubiquitous and nearly everyone either has one or has ready access to one. Most people are familiar with the idea of downloading software, music files, videos, etc., so downloading statistical software should not be a big obstacle. The software that we will use is free, so that is a big plus. In addition, some of the computer functions that we will need can even be downloaded directly to your cell phone, either free of charge or at little cost. Seeing the answers come out on your computer screen, especially when they are the right answers, makes the underlying material more meaningful.

---

[1]An excellent discussion by an undergraduate named Staci Weiss (2014) at SUNY Geneseo does an excellent job of discussing the role of the New Statistics and of *R* and how she went about mastering them. It is an excellent article, and puts the new developments in perspective. It is in the December 2014 issue of the Association of Psychological Sciences' *Observer*.

1.2   **The Importance of Context**

Let's start with an example that has a great deal to say in today's world. It may be an old study, but it is certainly an important one and one that is still cited in the literature on drug use. Drug use and abuse is a major problem in our society. Heroin addicts die every day from overdoses. Psychologists should have something to contribute to understanding the problem of drug overdoses, and, in fact, we do. I will take the time to describe an important line of research in this area because a study that derives from that line of research can be used to illustrate a number of important concepts in this chapter and the next. Many of you will know someone who is involved with heroin, and because heroin is a morphine derivative, this example may have particular meaning to you.

We will take as an example a study similar to an important experiment on morphine tolerance by Shepard Siegel way back in 1975. Morphine is a drug that is frequently used to alleviate pain. Repeated administrations of morphine, however, lead to morphine tolerance, in which morphine has less and less of an effect (pain reduction) over time. (You may have experienced the same thing if you eat spicy food very often. You will find that the more you eat it, the hotter you have to make it in order for it to taste the way it did when you first started eating it.) A common experimental task that demonstrates morphine tolerance involves placing a rat on an uncomfortably warm surface. When the heat becomes too uncomfortable, the rat will lick its paws, and the latency of the paw-lick is used as a measure of the rat's sensitivity to pain. A rat that has received a single morphine injection typically shows a longer paw-lick latency, indicating a reduced pain sensitivity. The development of morphine tolerance is indicated by a progressive shortening of paw-lick latencies (indicating increased sensitivity, or decreased insensitivity) with repeated morphine injections.

Siegel noted that there are a number of situations involving drugs other than morphine in which *conditioned* (learned) drug responses are opposite in direction to the unconditioned (natural) effects of the drug. For example, an animal injected with atropine will usually show a marked decrease in salivation. However if physiological saline (which should have no effect whatsoever) is suddenly injected (*in the same physical setting*) after repeated injections of atropine, the animal will show an *increase* in salivation. It is as if the animal was compensating for the anticipated effect of atropine. In such studies, it appears that a learned compensatory mechanism develops over trials and counterbalances the effect of the drug. (You experience the same thing if you leave the seasoning out of food that you normally add seasoning to. It will taste unusually bland, though the Grape Nuts you eat for breakfast do not taste bland—and I hope that you don't put seasoning on Grape Nuts.)

Siegel theorized that such a process might help to explain morphine tolerance. He reasoned that if you administered a series of pretrials in which the animal was injected with morphine and placed on a warm surface, morphine tolerance would develop as the drug has less and less of an effect. Thus, if you again injected the subject with morphine on a subsequent test trial, the animal would be as sensitive to pain as would be a naive animal (one who had never received morphine) because of that tolerance that has fully developed. Siegel further reasoned that if on the test trial you instead injected the animal with physiological saline, which should have no effect, *in the same test setting* as the normal morphine injections, the conditioned (learned) hypersensitivity that results from the repeated administration of morphine would not be counterbalanced by the presence of morphine, and the animal would show very short paw-lick latencies and heightened sensitivity.

You may think that an experiment conducted more than 40 years ago, which is before most of the readers of this book were born, is too old to be interesting. But a quick Internet search will reveal a great many recent studies that have derived directly from Siegel's early work. A particularly interesting one by Mann-Jones, Ettinger, Baisden, and Baisden (2003) has shown that a drug named dextromethorphan can counteract morphine tolerance. That becomes interesting when you learn that dextromethorphan is an important ingredient in cough syrup. This suggests that heroin addicts don't want to be taking cough syrup any more than they want to be administering heroin in novel environments. The study can be found at www.eou.edu/psych/re/morphinetolerance.doc

But what do mice on a warm surface have to do with drug overdose? First, heroin is a derivative of morphine. Second, heroin addicts show clear tolerance effects with repeated use and, as a result, often increase the amount of each injection to what formerly would have been lethal levels. By Siegel's theory, they are protected from the dangerous effects of the large (and to you and me, lethal) dose of heroin by the learned compensatory mechanism associated with the context in which they take the drug. But if they take what has come to be their standard dose in an entirely new setting, they would not benefit from that protective compensatory mechanism, and what had previously been a safe dose could now be fatal. In fact, Siegel noted that many drug overdose cases occur when an individual injects heroin in a novel environment. We're talking about a serious issue here, and drug overdoses often occur in novel settings.

If Siegel is right, his theory has important implications for the problem of drug overdose. One test of Siegel's theory, which is a simplification of studies he actually ran, is to take two groups of mice who have developed tolerance to morphine and whose standard dosage has been increased above normal levels. One group is tested in the same environment in which it previously has received the drug. The second group is treated exactly the same, except that it is tested in an entirely new environment. If Siegel is correct, the animals tested in the new environment will show a much higher pain threshold (the morphine will have more of an effect) than the animals injected in their usual environment. This is the basic study we will build on.

Our example of drug tolerance illustrates a number of important statistical concepts. It also will form a useful example in later chapters of this book. Be sure you understand what the experiment demonstrates. It will help if you think about what events in your own life or the lives of people around you illustrate the phenomenon of tolerance. What effect has tolerance had on behavior as you (or they) developed tolerance? Why is it likely that you probably feel more comfortable with comments related to sexual behavior than do your parents? Would language that you have come to not even notice have that same effect if you heard it in a commencement speech?

1.3 Basic Terminology

Statistical procedures can be separated into roughly two overlapping areas: descriptive statistics and inferential statistics. The first several chapters of this book will cover descriptive statistics, and the remaining chapters will examine inferential statistics. We will use my simplified version of Siegel's morphine study to illustrate the differences between these two terms.

Descriptive Statistics

Whenever your purpose is merely to *describe* a set of data, you are employing descriptive statistics. A statement about the average length of time it takes a normal mouse to lick its paw when placed on a warm surface would be a descriptive statistic, as would be the time it takes a morphine-injected mouse to do the same thing. Similarly, the amount of change in the latency of paw-licks once morphine has been administered and the variability of change among mice would be other descriptive statistics. Here we are simply reporting measures that describe average latency scores or their variability. Examples from other situations might include an examination of dieting scores on the Eating Restraint Scale, crime rates as reported by the Department of Justice, and certain summary information concerning examination grades in a particular course. Notice that in each of these examples we are just describing what the data have to say about some phenomenon.

Inferential Statistics

All of us at some time or another have been guilty of making unreasonable generalizations on the basis of limited data. If, for example, one mouse showed shorter latencies the second time it received morphine than it did the first, we might try to claim clear evidence of morphine tolerance. But even if there were no morphine tolerance, or environmental cues played no role in governing behavior, there would still be a 50-50 chance that the second trial's latency would be shorter than that of the first, assuming that we rule out tied scores. Or you might hear or read that tall people tend to be more graceful than short people, and conclude that that is true because you once had a very tall roommate who was particularly graceful. You conveniently forget about the 6' 4" klutz down the hall who couldn't even put on his pants standing up without tripping over them. Similarly, the man who says that girls develop motor skills earlier than boys because his daughter walked at 10 months and his son didn't walk until 14 months is guilty of the same kind of error: generalizing from single (or too limited) observations.

Small samples or single observations may be fine when we want to study something that has very little variability. If we want to know how many legs a cow has, we can find a cow and count its legs. We don't need a whole herd—one will do, unless it is a very weird cow. However, when what we want to measure varies from one individual to another, such as the amount of milk a cow will produce or the change in response latencies with morphine injections in different contexts, we can't get by with only one cow or one mouse. We need a bunch. This relates to an important principle in statistics—variability. The difference between how we determine the number of legs on a cow, versus the milk production of cows, depends critically on the degree of variability in the thing we want to measure. Variability will follow you throughout this course.

When the property in question varies from animal to animal or trial to trial, we need to take multiple measurements. However, we can't make an unlimited number of observations. If we want to know whether morphine injected in a new context has a greater effect, how much milk cows generally produce, or when girls usually start to walk, we must look at more than one mouse, one cow, or one girl. But we cannot possibly look at all mice, cows, or girls. We must do something in between—we must draw a *sample* from a *population*.

POPULATIONS, SAMPLES, PARAMETERS, AND STATISTICS:

A **population** can be defined as the entire collection of events in which you are interested (e.g., the scores of all morphine-injected mice, the milk production of all cows in the country, the ages at which every girl first began to walk, etc.). Thus if we were interested in the stress levels of all adolescent Americans, then the collection of all adolescent Americans' stress scores would form a population, in this case a population of more than 50 million numbers. If, on the other hand, we were interested only in the stress scores of the sophomore class in Fairfax, Vermont (a town of approximately 2,300 inhabitants), the population would contain about 60 numbers and could be obtained quite easily in its entirety. If we were interested in paw-lick latencies of mice, we could always run another mouse. In this sense the population of scores theoretically would be infinite.

The point is that a population can range from a relatively small set of numbers, which is easily collected, to an infinitely large set of numbers, which can never be collected completely. The populations in which we are interested are usually quite large. The practical consequence is that we can seldom, if ever, collect data on entire populations. Instead, we are forced to draw a **sample** of observations from a population and to use that sample to infer something about the characteristics of the population.

When we draw a sample of observations, we normally compute numerical values (such as averages) that summarize the data in that sample. When such values are based on the sample, they are called **statistics**. The corresponding values in the population (e.g., population averages) are called **parameters**. The major purpose of inferential statistics is to draw inferences about parameters (characteristics of populations) from statistics (characteristics of samples).[2]

- ■ Descriptive statistics: Simply describe the set of data at hand
- ■ Inferential statistics: Use statistics, which are measures on a sample, to infer values of parameters, which are measures on a population.

We usually act as if a sample is a truly **random sample**, meaning that each and every element of the population has an equal chance of being included in the sample. If we have a true random sample, not only can we estimate parameters of the population, but we can also have a very good idea of the accuracy of our estimates. To the extent that a sample is not a random sample, our estimates may be meaningless, because the sample may not accurately reflect the entire population. In fact, we rarely take truly random samples because that is impractical in most settings. We usually take samples of convenience (volunteers from Introductory Psychology, for example and *hope* that their results reflect what we would have obtained in a truly random sample.

---

[2]The word *inference* as used by statisticians means very much what it means in normal English usage—a conclusion based on logical reasoning. If three-fourths of the people at a picnic suddenly fall ill, I am likely to draw the (possibly incorrect) inference that something is wrong with the food. Similarly, if the average social sensitivity score of a random sample of fifth-grade children is very low, I am likely to draw the inference that fifth graders in general have much to learn about social sensitivity. Statistical inference is generally more precise than everyday inference, but the basic idea is the same.

A problem arises because one person's sample might be another person's population. For example, if I were to conduct a study into the effectiveness of this book as a teaching instrument, the scores of one class on an exam might be considered by me to be a sample, though a nonrandom one, of the population of scores for all students who are or might be using this book. The class instructor, on the other hand, cares only about her own students and would regard the same set of scores as a population. In turn, someone interested in the teaching of statistics might regard my population (the scores of everyone using this book) as a nonrandom sample from a larger population (the scores of everyone using *any* textbook in statistics). Thus the definition of a population depends on what you are interested in studying. Notice also that when we speak about populations, we speak about populations of *scores*, not populations of *people* or *things*.

The fact that I have used nonrandom samples here to make a point should not lead the reader to think that randomness is not important. On the contrary, it is the cornerstone of much statistical inference. As a matter of fact, one could define the relevant population as the collection of numbers from which the sample has been *randomly* drawn.

INFERENCE: We previously defined inferential statistics as the branch of statistics that deals with inferring characteristics of populations from characteristics of samples. This statement is inadequate by itself because it leaves the reader with the impression that all we care about is determining population parameters such as the average paw-lick latency of mice under the influence of morphine. There are, of course, times when we care about the exact value of population parameters. For example, we often read about the incredible number of hours per day the average high-school student spends sending text messages, and that is a number that is meaningful in its own right. But if that were all there were to inferential statistics, it would be a pretty dreary subject, and the strange looks I get at parties when I admit to teaching statistics would be justified.

In our example of morphine tolerance in mice, we don't really care what the average paw-lick latency of mice is. By itself it is a pretty useless piece of information. But we do care whether the average paw-lick latency of morphine-injected mice tested in a novel context is greater or less than the average paw-lick latency of morphine-injected mice tested in the same context in which they had received previous injections. And for this we need to estimate the corresponding population means. In many cases inferential statistics is a tool used to estimate parameters of two or more populations, more for the purpose of finding if those parameters are different than for the purpose of determining the actual numerical values of the parameters.

Notice that in the previous paragraph it was the population parameters, not the sample statistics, that I cared about. It is a pretty good bet that if I took two different *samples* of mice and tested them, one sample mean (average) would be larger than another. (It's hard to believe that they would come out absolutely equal.) But the real question is whether the sample mean of the mice tested in a novel context is sufficiently larger than the sample mean of mice tested in a familiar context to lead me to conclude that the corresponding *population* means are also different.

And don't lose sight of the fact that we really don't care very much about drug addiction in mice. What we do care about are heroin addicts. But we probably wouldn't be very popular if we gave heroin addicts overdoses in novel settings to see what would happen. That would hardly be ethical behavior on our part. So we have to make a second inferential leap. We have to make the *statistical* inference from the sample of mice to a population of mice, and then we have to make the *logical* inference from mice to heroin addicts. Both inferences are critical if we want to learn anything useful to reduce the incidence of heroin overdose.

In this edition I am putting much more emphasis on the fact that we not only want to know whether a difference that we find is unlikely to be due to chance, but we also want to know just how meaningful that difference is. Two population means could be different, but the difference could be so small that it is really inconsequential. In the past behavioral sciences focused primarily on whether a difference could be due to chance. But in recent years we have begun to emphasize the importance of the size of an effect—does it really matter that the population means are slightly different? Especially in the second half of this book there is noticeably more emphasis on what are called "effect sizes," though it is still important to first convince ourselves that what we see is not just some chance difference.

I think that this newer emphasis makes the field of statistics much more meaningful. In some cases we can focus on "meaningfulness" in just a sentence or two. In other cases it takes more work and more discussion. And to go one step further, in the last chapter of the book I will discuss meta-analysis. This refers to drawing conclusions from a whole set of similar experiments on a given phenomenon. Not only do we want to know if an effect is reliable and important, but we want to know if several different studies on the same phenomenon agree on what the effect is. This tells us a great deal more about some phenomenon than the results of one particular study.

1.4 Selection among Statistical Procedures

As we have just seen, there is an important distinction between descriptive statistics and inferential statistics. The first part of this book will be concerned with descriptive statistics because we must describe a set of data before we can use it to draw inferences. When we come to inferential statistics, however, we need to make several additional distinctions to help us focus the choice of an appropriate statistical procedure. On the inside back cover of this book is what is known as a **decision tree**, a scheme used for selecting among the available statistical procedures to be presented in this book. This decision tree not only represents a rough outline of the organization of the latter part of the text, it also points up some fundamental issues that we should address at the outset. In considering these issues, keep in mind that at this time we are not concerned with which statistical test is used for which purpose. That will come later. Rather, we are concerned with the kinds of questions that come into play when we try to treat the data statistically, whether we are talking about descriptive or inferential procedures. These issues are listed at the various branching points of the tree. I will discuss the first three of these briefly now and leave the rest to a more appropriate time.

Types of Data

Numerical data generally come in two kinds; there are measurement data and categorical data. By **measurement data** (sometimes called **quantitative data**) we mean the result of any sort of measurement, for example, a score on a measure of stress, a person's weight, the speed at which a person can read this page, or an individual's score on a scale of authoritarianism. In each case some sort of instrument (in its broadest sense) has been used to measure something.

Categorical data (also known as **frequency data** or **count data**) consist of statements such as, "Seventy-eight students reported coming from a one-parent family, while 112 reported coming from two-parent families" or "There were 238 votes for the new curriculum and 118 against it." Here we are counting things, and our data consist of totals or frequencies for each category (hence the name categorical data). Several hundred members of the faculty might vote on a proposed curriculum, but the results (data) would consist of only two numbers—the number of votes for, and the number of votes against, the proposal. Measurement data, on the other hand, might record the paw-lick latencies of dozens of mice, one latency for each mouse.

Sometimes we can measure the same general variable to produce either measurement data or categorical data. Thus, in our experiment we could obtain a latency score for each mouse (measurement data), or we could classify the mice as showing long, medium, or short latencies and then count the number in each category (categorical data).

The two kinds of data are treated in two quite different ways. In Chapter 19 we will examine categorical data. We might, for example, want to determine whether there are reliable differences among the number of tumors rejected by rats living under three different levels of stress. In Chapters 9 through 14, 16 through 18, and 20 we are going to be concerned chiefly with measurement data. But in using measurement data we have to make a second distinction, not in terms of the type of data, but in terms of whether we are concerned with examining differences among groups of subjects or with studying the relationship among variables.

Differences Versus Relationships

Most statistical questions fall into two overlapping categories: differences and relationships. For example, one experimenter might be interested primarily in whether there is a difference between smokers and nonsmokers in terms of their performance on a given task. A second experimenter might be interested in whether there is a relationship between the number of cigarettes smoked per day and the scores on that same task. Or we could be interested in whether pain sensitivity decreases with the number of previous morphine injections (a relationship) or whether there is a difference in average pain sensitivity between those who have had previous injections of morphine and those who have not. Although questions of differences and relationships obviously overlap, they are treated by what appear, on the surface, to be quite different methods. Chapters 12 through 14 and 16 through 18 will be concerned primarily with those cases in which we ask if there are differences between two or more groups, while Chapters 9 through 11 will deal with cases in which we are interested in examining relationships between two or more variables. These seemingly different statistical techniques turn out to be basically the same fundamental procedure, although they ask somewhat different questions and phrase the answers in distinctly different ways.

Number of Groups or Variables

As you will see in subsequent chapters, an obvious distinction between statistical techniques concerns the number of groups or the number of variables to which they apply. For example, you will see that what is generally referred to as an independent *t* test is restricted to the case of data from at most two groups of subjects. The analysis of variance, on the other hand, is applicable to any number of groups, not just two. The third decision in our tree, then, concerns the number of groups or variables involved.

The three decisions we have been discussing (type of data, differences versus relationships, and number of groups or variables) are fundamental to the way we look at data and the statistical procedures we use to help us interpret those data. One further criterion that some textbooks use for creating categories of tests and ways of describing and manipulating data involves the scale of measurement that applies to the data. We will discuss this topic further in the next chapter, because it is an important concept with which any student should be familiar, although it is no longer considered to be a critical determiner of the kind of test we may run.

1.5 Using Computers

In the not too distant past, most statistical analyses were done on calculators, and textbooks were written accordingly. Methods have changed, and most calculations are now done almost exclusively by computers. In addition to performing statistical analyses, computers now provide access to an enormous amount of information via the Internet. We will make use of some of this information in this book.

As I said earlier, I will be including computer material in each chapter, along with printouts for one of several main computing packages. For the most part I am going to focus on a free software system called *R* (R Core Team (2014). R: A language and environment for statistical computing. R Foundation for Statistical Computing, Vienna, Austria. URL http://www.R-project.org/.) and a well-known commercial package called SPSS (IBM Corp. Released 2013. IBM SPSS Statistics for Apple Macintosh, Version 22.0. Armonk, NY: IBM Corp.) *R* has become more and more common over the last 10 years and has drawn some attention away from the old-line software like SPSS and SAS/STAT® software. Calling them old-line is not a derogatory label. That software is excellent and highly popular, but it is expensive and, in general, you need to hope that your school has a license and a way to use that license in a convenient environment. I do present material on SPSS, but there is somewhat greater emphasis on *R*, which you can download free of charge to almost any computer. Chernick and LaBudde (2011) have stated, "Over the last decade *R* has become the statistical environment of choice for academics, and probably is now the most used such software system in the world." That may be an exaggeration, but even if you don't want to learn to be an expert in *R*, you can derive an enormous benefit from reproducing the results that I present and then looking at what happens if you vary your instructions slightly. I have developed many Web pages of material on the use of *R*. I have even more coverage of SPSS on the book's website, so I would not expect that you would have much trouble working with either piece of software. Well, the first day might be a little frustrating, but those frustrations quickly disappear as you go on. The main address for the website associated with this book is at www.uvm.edu/~dhowell/fundamentals9/index.html.

I need to say that there are different ways of approaching *R*. To explain, let me start with SPSS. SPSS has a very good graphical user interface (GUI). Using the interface, you operate through a set of drop-down menus and tabs. You specify what files to upload and what procedures to run simply by clicking on various buttons and variable names. There is a GUI for R, written by John Fox at McMaster University, but I am not going to use it for this book. The GUI is just fine, but I want you to see the underlying code so that you have a sense of what analyses are like. I don't expect you to learn a great deal of the R language (this is a book on statistics, not on R), but I give you enough of the code that you can paste it into R and experiment with what results. R has many functions that will do the work for you, and you could carry out a multiple regression, for example, just by entering a simple line to read the data and type in some variable names to the "lm()" function. You can actually learn quite a lot that way, and I think that it will make learning the material in this book easier. I hope that you will go on to learn a lot more about R, but even cutting and pasting my code, and making appropriate changes in variable names, will teach you a lot. And varying the code slightly and rerunning the analysis will teach you even more. That doesn't mean that I don't have to teach some things about R so that you can recognize what it is doing, but I am trying to present a happy medium so as to teach the material without overwhelming the reader.

In addition to what I present in the text, I provide Web pages that represent an introduction to R so that you have a sense of what it does and what it looks like. I also provide Web pages containing R code and other material for each chapter. You can find those pages simply by going to https://www.uvm.edu/~dhowell/fundamentals9/index.html. I have provided pages so that you can go to the appropriate one, copy the code for R, and paste it into a program. You can then modify it, if you wish, to see what happens. That page also leads you to other material that will be helpful as you go along, as well as copies of all data files used in the book.

A word for those who have no desire to use a computer to analyze data: I have tried to write so that you could read this book without reading any of the material on R or SPSS and still learn a great deal about statistics. I hope that you make use of the code, but the world will not collapse if you don't.

For most of the history of statistics, people had to have available statistical tables that translated the results they computed into probability values. Fortunately, we no longer have to rely on such tables. I continue to place them in the appendices, but you can very easily download software that will immediately perform those calculations for you. In fact, some of those programs can be loaded onto your cell phone. It doesn't get much easier than that.

Leaving statistical programs aside for the moment, one of the huge advances in the past decades has been the spread of the World Wide Web. This has meant that many additional resources are available to expand on the material to be found in any text. I will make frequent reference to websites throughout this book, and I encourage you to check out those sites for what they have to offer. I have mentioned a site specifically for this book at

https://www.uvm.edu/~dhowell/fundamentals9/index.html

and I hope that you will make use of it. It contains all of the data used in this book, more fully worked out answers to odd-numbered exercises (instructors generally want some answers to be unavailable), two primers on using SPSS and information on using the online packages mentioned above, material on getting started with R, computer code for all examples using R, computer applets that illustrate important concepts, and a host of other things. These Web pages even contain a list of errors for this book. (Yes, I'm sure there will be some, and the list will expand as I, or other people, find them.) But that is nowhere near all that the Web has to offer.

Not long ago very few students would have any idea how to gain access to the World Wide Web; in fact, most people had never heard of it. Today most people have had considerable experience with the Web and link to Web pages on a regular, even daily, basis. This has become even more important in recent years because of the enormous amount of information that is available. If you do not understand something in this book, remember that search engines are your friend. Just type in your question and you are bound to get an answer. For example, "What is a standard deviation?" or "What is the difference between a parameter and a statistic?" I try to explain things as clearly as I can, but what is clear to me may not always be clear to you. I encourage you to go to your favorite search engine when you want a better explanation. A question such as "Why do we divide by n-1 instead of n to calculate a standard deviation?" will give you a wide range of good answers, and I'm sure that some of them will strike you as better than the answer that I gave. (In 0.73 seconds, Google came up with 12,400 references, the first bunch of which is really quite good.) And don't forget to use a search engine when you want to do something new in R. For example, "How do I correlate two variables in R? r-project." (I added "r-project" to the end of that merely to focus the search on sites related to the R computer language rather than to just any word with an "R" in it. After a while, your computer and the search engine will get the idea of what you mean when you include "R" in a search, and you can drop that.)

Aside from the Web pages that I maintain, the publisher also has ancillary material available for your use. The URL is too complicated to put here, but if you just do an Internet search for "Cengage Howell Fundamental" you will find the page for this book, and if you click on "Student Companion Site" you will find material to help you learn the material.

1.6 Summary

In this chapter we saw the distinction between descriptive and inferential statistics. Descriptive statistics deal with simply describing a set of data by computing measures such as the average of the scores in our sample or how widely scores are distributed around that average. Inferential statistics, on the other hand, deals with making an inference from the data at hand (the sample) to the overall population of objects from which the sample came. Thus we might use a sample of 50 students to estimate (infer) characteristics of all of the students in the university from which that sample was drawn, or even all college students or all people between the ages of 18 and 22. When we have a measure that is based on a sample, that measure is called a statistic. The corresponding measure for the whole population is referred to as a parameter.

We also saw two other important concepts. One was the concept of random sampling, where, at least in theory, we draw our sample randomly from the population, such that all elements of the population have an equal opportunity of being included in the sample. We will discuss this again in the next chapter. The other important concept was the distinction between measurement data, where we actually measure something (e.g., a person's level of stress as measured by a questionnaire about stress) and categorical data, where we simply count the number of observations falling into each of a few categories. We will come back to each of these concepts in subsequent chapters. For those students who are worried about taking a course that they think will be a math course, the point to keep in mind is that there is a huge difference between statistics and mathematics. They both use numbers and formulae, but statistics does not need to be seen as a mathematical science, and many of the most important issues in statistics have very little to do with mathematics.

Key Terms

Population, 8	Random sample, 8
Sample, 8	Decision tree, *10*
Statistics, 8	Measurement (quantitative) data, *10*
Parameters, 8	Categorical (frequency, count) data, *11*

1.7 A Quick Review

I was recently working my way through a textbook on computer programming, and I noticed that the author inserted a set of very basic questions (with answers) about the material at the end of the chapter. I thought that it was such a good learning device that I am copying that idea. At the end of each chapter you will see about 10 questions that serve as review. They are not difficult questions; they are there to highlight important points in the chapter. I hope that you can answer all of them correctly, but, if not, the answers are there as well. They are simply meant to pull the basic material together.

1. What are important ways that the field of statistics has changed over time?
   Ans: A movement toward the meaningfulness of a result, a movement toward combining the results of multiple studies, and a movement away from hand calculation.

2. What is the difference between a statistic and a parameter?
   Ans: A statistic refers to a measure (e.g., average) based on a sample of data and a parameter refers to that measure on a whole population of objects.

3. Inferential statistics are used to draw conclusions about a whole population (T or F).
   Ans: True

4. Our ability to draw meaningful conclusions based on a sample statistic depends, in part, on the _____ of our sample.
   Ans: variability

5. In the ideal situation our sample should be a _____ sample from some population.
   Ans: random

6. A random sample is one in which _____.
   Ans: every member of the population has an equal chance of being included.

7. When we are engaged in drawing conclusions about a population we are using inferential statistics. (T or F)
   Ans: True

8. List three things that partly determine the specific analysis that we will use to analyze a data set.
    Ans: Type of data, number of groups or variables, differences versus relationships.

9. A scheme for distinguishing and choosing among statistical procedures is called a
    Ans: decision tree.

1.8 Exercises

1.1   To gain a better understanding of the morphine example that we have been using in this chapter, think of an example in your own life in which you can see the role played by tolerance and context. How would you go about testing to see whether context plays a role?

1.2   In testing the effects of context in the example you developed in Exercise 1.1, to what would the words "population" and "sample" refer?

1.3   Give an example in everyday life wherein context affects behavior.

For Exercises 1.4–1.6 suppose that we design a study that involves following heroin addicts around and noting the context within which they inject themselves and the kind of reaction that results.

1.4   In this hypothetical study what would the population of interest be?

1.5   In this study how would we define our sample?

1.6   For the heroin study identify a parameter and a statistic in which we might be interested.

1.7   Drawing from a telephone book has always been used as an example of bad random sampling. With the rapid expansion of Internet use, why would a standard telephone book be an even worse example than it used to be?

1.8   Suggest some ways in which we could draw an approximately random sample from people in a small city. (The Census Bureau has to do this kind of thing frequently.)

1.9   Give an example of a study in which we don't care about the actual numerical value of a population average, but in which we would want to know whether the average of one population is greater than the average of a different population.

1.10   I mentioned the fact that variability is a concept that will run throughout the book. I said that you need only one cow to find out how many legs cows have, whereas you need many more to estimate their average milk production. How would you expect that variability would contribute to the size of the sample you would need? What would you have to do if you suspected that some varieties of cows gave relatively little milk, while other varieties gave quite a lot of milk?

1.11   To gain a better understanding of the role of "context" in the morphine study, what would you expect to happen if you put decaf in your mother's early-morning cup of coffee?

1.12   Give three examples of categorical data.

1.13   Give three examples of measurement data.

1.14   The Mars Candy Company actually keeps track of the number of red, blue, yellow, etc. M&Ms™ there are in each batch. (These make wonderful examples for discussions of sampling.)

a)   This is an example of _____ data. The company used to publish the percentage of each color in a bag, but it no longer does so—at least not in a place that I can find. However, you can find the percentages as of 2008 at

 https://www.exeter.edu/documents/mandm.pdf

I have put a copy of that page on my own website, under the material for this chapter, but I do not deserve the credit for collecting it. The interesting M&M site itself keeps being moved around, so you may have to hunt for it.

b) How do the words "population," "sample," "parameter," and "statistic" apply to the example at this link?

c) Believe it or not, there is a whole Web page devoted to how the colors of M&Ms have changed over the years. You can find it at http://en.wikipedia.org/wiki/M&M's. It's a fun article, though I can't think of a question to go with it.

1.15 Give two examples of studies in which our primary interest is in looking at relationships between variables.

1.16 Give two examples of studies in which our primary interest is in looking at group differences.

1.17 How might you redesign our study of morphine tolerance to involve three groups of mice to provide more information on the question at hand?

1.18 Connect to

 https://www.uvm.edu/~dhowell/fundamentals9/index.html

What kinds of material can you find there that you want to remember to come back to later as you work through the book?

1.19 Connect to any search engine on the Internet and search for the word "statistics."

a) How would you characterize the different types of sites that you find there?

b) You should find at least one electronic textbook in addition to Wikipedia. Note its address and go to it when you need help.

c) Many statistics departments have links to statistics-related pages. What kinds of things do you find on those pages?

1.20 An interesting Web source contains a collection of Web pages known as "SurfStat" created by Keith Dear when he was at the University of Newcastle in Australia. The address is

 http://surfstat.anu.edu.au/surfstat-home/surfstat-main.html

Go to these pages and note the kinds of pages that are likely to be useful to you in this course. (I know that this text isn't in Dear's list of favorites, but I'm sure that was just an oversight, and so I will forgive him.) **Note:** I will check all addresses carefully just before this book goes to press, but addresses do change, and it is very possible that an address that I give you will no longer work when you try it. One trick is to shorten the address progressively by deleting elements from the right, trying after each deletion. You may then be able to work your way through a set of links to what you were originally seeking. Or you could do what I just did when I found the old address didn't work. I entered "surfstat" in a search engine, and the first response was what I wanted. One final trick is to select the name of the file you want (e.g., the file "surfstat-main.html") and search on that name. Some sites just disappear off the face of the earth, but more commonly they move to a new location.

## CHAPTER 2

Basic Concepts

For the rest of the book each chapter will start with a box entitled "Concepts you will need to recall from previous chapters." These are important concepts that will be referred to in the chapter. Some of them will have been developed in the previous chapter and some will come from several chapters back. Others will be repeated at the beginning of several chapters. I have tried to identify those concepts that students find confusing ("Is the X axis on a graph the horizontal or vertical one?"), and these sometimes need to be repeated. In fact, some of the simplest ones, such as "which is the X axis?" are among the hardest to keep straight.

We will begin the chapter by looking at different *scales of measurement*. Some measurements carry more meaning than others (e.g., measuring people in inches rather than classifying them as "short" or "tall.") and it is important to understand the ways in which we refer to measurements. The things that we measure are going to be called "*variables*" (e.g., paw-lick latency,) so it is important to know what a variable is. We will then bring up the distinction between *dependent variables* (the scores or outcomes that we obtain) and *independent variables* (the things that we generally manipulate). For example, we could sort people in terms of age group (independent variable) and then measure their text messaging frequency (dependent variable). Next we have to consider where our samples come from. Do we *randomly sample* from some large population or do we draw a selected sample? Do we *randomly assign* participants to groups, or do we take what we can get? Finally I will lay out some basic information about how we represent variables

CONCEPTS YOU WILL NEED TO RECALL FROM THE PREVIOUS CHAPTER

Population:	The collection of all events in which you are interested
Sample:	The set of observations that you have made or the individuals who you measured
Parameter:	A measure based on the population
Statistic:	A measure based on the sample

notationally (e.g., subscripted symbols) and cover a few simple rules about *summation notation*. None of this is particularly difficult.

Measurement is frequently defined as the *assignment of numbers to objects*, with the words *numbers* and *objects* being interpreted loosely. That looks like a definition that only a theoretician could love, but actually it describes what we mean quite accurately. When, for example, we use paw-lick latency as a measure of pain sensitivity, we are measuring sensitivity by assigning a number (a time) to an object (a mouse) to assess the sensitivity of that mouse. Similarly, when we use a test of authoritarianism (e.g., the Adorno Authoritarianism Scale) to obtain an authoritarianism score for a person, we are measuring that characteristic by assigning a number (a score) to an object (a person). Depending on what we are measuring and how we measure it, the numbers we obtain may have different properties, and those different properties of numbers often are generally discussed under the specific topic of scales of measurement.

2.1 Scales of Measurement

Spatz (1997) began his discussion of this topic with such a nice example that I am going to copy it, with modifications. Consider the following three questions and answers:

1. What was your bib number in the swimming meet? (Ans: 18)
2. Where did you finish in the meet? (Ans: 18)
3. How many seconds did it take you to swim a lap? (Ans: 18)

The answer to each question was 18, but those numbers mean entirely different things and are entirely different kinds of numbers. One just assigns a label to you, one ranks you among other contenders, and one is a continuous measure of time. We will elaborate on each of these kinds of numbers in this section.

Scales of measurement is a topic that some writers think is crucial and others think is irrelevant. Although this book tends to side with the latter group, it is important that you have some familiarity with the general issue. (You do not have to agree with something to think that it is worth studying. After all, evangelists claim to know a great deal about sin, but they certainly don't endorse it.) An additional benefit of this discussion is that you will begin to realize that statistics as a subject is not merely a cut-and-dried set of facts but rather a set of facts put together with a variety of interpretations and opinions.

Probably the foremost leader of those who see scales of measurement as crucially important to the choice of statistical procedures was S. S. Stevens. Basically, Stevens defined four types of scales: nominal, ordinal, interval, and ratio.[1] These scales are distinguished on the basis of the relationships assumed to exist between objects having different scale values. Later scales in this series have all the properties of earlier scales and additional properties as well.

Zumbo and Zimmerman (2000) have discussed measurement scales at considerable length and remind us that Stevens's system has to be seen in its historical

---

[1]SPSS and much other software use only three types of scales, namely "nominal," "ordinal," and "scale," where the last one lumps together interval and ratio scales. R refers to nominal variables , and sometimes ordinal variables, as "factors."

Who was S. S. Stevens?

Stanley Smith Stevens (1906–1973) was an extremely influential psychologist. He was born in Utah, raised in a polygamous family by his grandfather, spent three years in Europe as a missionary (without even learning the language), did poorly at the University of Utah, where he failed an algebra course, and finally graduated from Stanford. He could have gone to medical school at Harvard, but that would have required that he take a course in organic chemistry, which he did not find appealing. So he enrolled in Harvard's School of Education, which he didn't like much either. (You can see that he wasn't off to a very promising start.) By luck he managed to establish an academic relationship with E. G. Boring, the only professor of psychology at Harvard and a very important pioneer in the field. He began working with Boring on perception, did a dissertation in two years on hearing, did more work on hearing, and published what was for a long time the major work in psychoacoustics. In the 1950s Stevens jumped into psychophysics and developed the idea of the four scales mentioned earlier. He never left Harvard, where he held the title of Professor of Psychophysics. Along the way he managed to publish *The Handbook of Experimental Psychology* (Stevens, 1951), which sat on almost every experiment psychologist's bookshelf well into the 1970s. (I still have my copy.) In his day he was one of the most influential psychologists in the country.

context. In the 1940s and 1950s, Stevens was attempting to defend psychological research against those in the "hard sciences" who had a restricted view of scientific measurement. He was trying to make psychology "respectable." Stevens spent much of his very distinguished professional career developing measurement scales for the field of psychophysics. However, outside of that field there has been little effort in psychology to develop the kinds of scales that Stevens pursued, nor has there been much real interest. The criticisms that so threatened Stevens have largely evaporated, though our data remain far more variable than those in the physical sciences, and with them much of the belief that measurement scales critically influence the statistical procedures that are appropriate. But debates over measurement have certainly not disappeared, which is why it is important for you to know about scales of measurement.

Nominal Scales

In a sense a **nominal scale** is not really a scale at all, because it does not scale items along any dimension; but rather, it labels items. One example is the number that you wore on your bib during the race. Another classic example of a nominal scale is the set of numbers assigned to football players. Frequently these numbers have no meaning whatsoever other than as convenient labels that distinguish the players, or their positions, from one another. We could just as easily use letters or pictures of animals. In fact, gender is a nominal scale that uses words (male and female) in place of numbers, although when we code gender in a data set we often use 1 = male and

2 = female. Nominal scales generally are used for the purpose of *classification*. Categorical data, which we discussed briefly in Chapter 1, are often measured on a nominal scale because we merely assign category labels (e.g., Male or Female, Same context group or Different context group) to observations. Quantitative (measurement) data are measured on the other three types of scales.

Ordinal Scales

The simplest true scale is an **ordinal scale**, which orders people, objects, or events along some continuum. One example is the 18 that was assigned to you as your finishing position (rank) in the swim meet. Here the scale tells us who in the race was the fastest, who was second-fastest, and so on. Another example would be a scale of life stress. Using this scale you simply count up (sometimes with differential weightings) the number of changes in the past six months of a person's life (e.g., marriage, moving, new job, etc.). A person with a score of 20 is presumed to have experienced more stress than someone with a score of 15, who is presumed to have experienced more stress than someone with a score of 10. Thus we order people, in terms of stress, by the changes in their lives.

Notice that these two examples of ordinal scales differ in the numbers that are assigned. In the first case we assigned the rankings 1, 2, 3, . . . , whereas in the second case the scores represented the number of changes rather than ranks. Both are examples of ordinal scales, however, because no information is given about the *differences* between points on the scale. This is an important characteristic of ordinal scales. The difference in time between runners ranked 1 and 2 in a marathon may be as much as a minute. The difference in time between runners ranked 256 and 257 may be on the order of a tenth of a second.

Interval Scales

An **interval scale** is a scale of measurement about which we can speak legitimately of differences between scale points. A common example is the Fahrenheit scale of temperature, in which a 10-point difference has the same meaning anywhere along the scale. Thus, the difference in temperature between 10°F and 20°F is the same as the difference between 80°F and 90°F. Notice that this scale also satisfies the properties of the two preceding scales (nominal and ordinal). What we do not have with an interval scale, however, is the ability to speak meaningfully about ratios. Thus we cannot say, for example, that 40°F is one-half as hot as 80°F or twice as hot as 20°F, because the zero point on the scale is arbitrary. For example, 20°F and 40°F correspond roughly to −7° and 4° on the Celsius scale, respectively, and the two sets of ratios are obviously quite different and arbitrary. The Kelvin scale of temperature *is* a ratio scale, but few of us would ever think of using it to describe the weather.

The measurement of pain sensitivity is a good example of something that is probably measured on an interval scale. It seems reasonable to assume that a difference of 10 seconds in paw-lick latency may represent the same difference in sensitivity across most, but not all, of the scale. I say "not all" because in this example, very long latencies probably come from a situation in which the animal doesn't notice pain and therefore leaves his or her foot on the surface for an arbitrary amount of time. I would not expect the difference between a one-second latency and an 11-second latency to be equivalent to the difference between a 230-second latency and a 240-second latency.

Notice that I said that our measure of pain sensitivity can *probably* be taken as an interval measure over much of the scale. This is another way of suggesting that it is rare that you would find a true and unambiguous example of any particular kind of scale. I can think of several reasons why I might argue that paw-lick latencies are not absolutely interval scales, but I would be willing to go along with considering them to be that for purposes of discussion. (I might have considerable reluctance about saying that the scale is interval at its extremes, but our experimenter would not work with a surface that is extremely hot or one that is at room temperature.)

I would be extremely reluctant, however, to suggest that an animal that takes 25 seconds to lick its paw is *twice* as sensitive as one that takes 50 seconds. To be able to make those types of statements (statements about ratios), we need to go beyond the interval scale to the ratio scale.

Ratio Scales

A **ratio scale** is one that has a true zero point. Notice that the zero point must be a *true* zero point, and not an arbitrary one, such as 0°F or 0°C. A true zero point is the point that corresponds to the absence of the thing being measured. (Because 0°F and 0°C do not represent the absence of electron motion, they are not true zero points.) The time it took you to finish the race referred to earlier, 18 seconds, is an example of a ratio scale of time because 0 seconds really is a true zero point. Other examples of ratio scales are the common physical ones of length, volume, weight, and so on. With these scales not only do we have the properties of the preceding scales, but we also can speak about ratios. We can say that in physical terms 10 seconds is twice as long as five seconds, 100 lbs is one-third as heavy as 300 lbs, and so on.

But here is where things get tricky. One might think that the kind of scale with which we are working would be obvious to everyone who thought about it. Unfortunately, especially with the kinds of measures that we collect in the behavioral sciences, this is rarely the case. Let's start with your time (18 seconds) in the swim meet. It is true that your teammate who came in at 22 seconds took 1.222 times as long as you did, but does that really mean that you are 1.22 times better than she is? Here time is a ratio measure of how long something takes, but I doubt very much if it is a ratio measure of ability. For a second example, consider the temperature of the room you are in right now. I just told you that temperature, measured in degrees Celsius or Fahrenheit, is a clear case of an interval scale. In fact, it is one of the classic examples. Well, it is and, then again, it isn't. There is no doubt that to a physicist the difference between 62° and 64° is exactly the same as the difference between 72° and 74°. But if we are measuring temperature as an index of comfort rather than as an index of molecular activity, the same numbers no longer form an interval scale. To a person sitting in a room at 62°F, a jump to 64°F would be distinctly noticeable and probably welcome. The same cannot be said about the difference in room temperature between 82°F and 84°F. This points to the important fact that it is the underlying variable being measured (e.g., comfort), not the numbers themselves, that defines the scale.

Because there is usually no unanimous agreement concerning the scale of measurement, it's up to you, as an individual user of statistical procedures, to make the best decision you can about the nature of the data. All that can be asked of you is that you think about the problem carefully before coming to a decision and not simply assume that the standard answer is necessarily the best answer. It seems a bit unfair to dump that problem on you, but there really is no alternative.

A review:

- Nominal scales: Name things
- Ordinal scales: Order or rank things
- Interval scales: Equal intervals represent equal differences
- Ratio scales: Allow us to use phrases such as "half as much."

The Role of Measurement Scales

I made the statement earlier that there is a difference of opinion as to the importance assigned to scales of measurement. Some authors have ignored the problem completely, but others have organized whole textbooks around the different scales. It seems to me that the central issue is the absolute necessity of separating in our minds the numbers we collect from the objects or events to which they refer. If one student in a memory study recalled 20 items and another participant recalled 10 items, the number of words recalled was twice as large for the first participant. However, we might not be willing to say that the first student remembered twice as much about the material studied. Certainly if you get a 100 on an exam and I get a 50, few people would be willing to suggest that you know twice as much as I do.

A similar argument was made for the example of room temperature, wherein the scale (interval or ordinal) depended on whether we were interested in measuring some physical attribute of temperature or its effect on people. In fact, it is even more complicated than that, because whereas molecular activity continues to increase as temperature increases, comfort at first rises as the temperature rises, levels off briefly, and then starts to fall. In other words, the relationship is shaped like an inverted U.

Because statistical tests use numbers without considering the objects or events to which those numbers refer, we can carry out standard mathematical operations (e.g., addition, multiplication, etc.) regardless of the nature of the underlying scale. An excellent and highly recommended reference on this point is an old but entertaining paper by Lord (1953) entitled "On the Statistical Treatment of Football Numbers." Lord argues that you can treat these numbers in any way you like. His often quoted statement on this issue is "The numbers do not remember where they came from." You don't need a course in statistics to know that the average of 8 and 15 is 11.5, regardless of whether that average has any sensible interpretation in terms of what we are measuring.

The problem comes when it is time to *interpret* the results of some form of statistical manipulation. At that point we must ask if the statistical results bear any meaningful relationship to the objects or events in question. Here we are no longer dealing with a statistical issue, but with a methodological one. No statistical procedure can tell us whether the fact that one group received higher grades than another on a history examination reveals anything about group differences in knowledge of the subject matter. (Perhaps they received specific coaching on how to take multiple-choice exams. Perhaps they cheated.) Moreover, to be satisfied because the examination provides grades that form a ratio scale of correct items (50 correct items is twice as many as 25 correct items) is to lose sight of the fact that we set out to measure knowledge of history, which may not increase in any orderly way with increases in scores. Statistical tests can be applied only to the numbers we obtain, and the validity of statements about the objects or events that we think we are measuring hinges primarily on our knowledge of those objects or events, not on the scale of measurement. We do our best to ensure that our measures bear as close a relationship as possible to what we want to measure, but our results are ultimately only the numbers we obtain and our faith in the *relationship* between those numbers and the underlying objects or events.

To return for a moment to the problem of heroin overdose, notice that in addressing this problem we have had to move several steps away from the heroin addict sticking a needle in his arm under a bridge. Because we can't use actual addicts, we used mice. We assume that pain tolerance in mice under morphine is a good analogue to the tolerance we see in human heroin addicts, and it probably is. But then to measure pain tolerance we measure changes in sensitivity to pain, and to measure sensitivity we measure paw-lick latency. And finally, to measure changes in sensitivity, we measure changes in paw-lick latencies. All these assumptions seem reasonable, but they are assumptions nonetheless. When we consider the scale of measurement, we need to think about the relationships between these steps. That does not mean that paw-lick latency needs to be an interval measure of heroin tolerance in human addicts—that wouldn't make any sense. But it does mean that we need to think about the whole system and not just one of its parts.

2.2 Variables

Properties of objects or events that can take on different values are referred to as **variables**. Hair color, for example, is a variable because it is a property of an object (hair) that can take on different values (e.g., brown, yellow, red, and, in recent years, blue, green, and purple). Properties such as height, length, and speed are variables for the same reason. Bib numbers, position in the race, and the time it takes to swim a lap are all variables, and in our example they just happen to be the same number. We can further discriminate between **discrete variables** (such as gender, marital status, and the number of television sets in a private home), in which the variable can take on only a relatively few possible values, and **continuous variables** (such as speed, paw-lick latency, amount of milk produced by a cow, and so on), in which the variable could assume—at least in theory—any value between the lowest and highest points on the scale. (Note that nominal variables can never be continuous because they are not ordered along any continuum.)

As you will see later in this book, the distinction between discrete and continuous variables plays a role in some of our procedures, but mostly in the extreme cases of discreteness. Often a variable that is actually discrete, such as the number of items answered correctly on an exam, will be treated as if it were continuous because there are so many different values of that variable that its discreteness is irrelevant. For example, we might score students as 1, 2, 3, or 4 depending on their year in college. That is a discrete variable and we normally would not calculate the mean value, but rather would focus on how many fell in each year. On the other hand, we could score courses by the number of students who were enrolled in each, and an average of class sizes would seem a reasonable thing to compute even though the numbers themselves are discrete because you cannot have 23.6 students in a class.

In statistics we also distinguish between different kinds of variables in an additional way. We speak of **independent variables** (those that are manipulated by the experimenter) and **dependent variables** (those that are not under the experimenter's control—the data). In psychological research the experimenter is interested in measuring the effects of independent variables on dependent variables. Common examples of independent variables in psychology are schedules of reinforcement, forms of therapy, placement of stimulating electrodes, methods of treatment, and the distance of the stimulus from the observer. Common examples of dependent variables are running speeds, depression scores, behavioral response of a subject, number of aggressive behaviors, and apparent size.

Basically what the study is all about is the independent variable, and the results of the study (the data) are measurements of the dependent variable. For example, a psychologist may measure the number of aggressive behaviors in depressed and non-depressed adolescents. Here the state of depression is the independent variable, and the number of aggressive acts is the dependent variable. Independent variables can be either qualitative (e.g., a comparison of three different forms of psychotherapy) or quantitative (e.g., a comparison of the effects of one, three, or five units of caffeine), but dependent variables are generally—but certainly not always—quantitative.[2] What are the independent and dependent variables in our study of morphine tolerance in mice?

To be honest, although it is usually clear what a dependent variable is (it is the number or observation that we write down when we record the data), independent variables are harder to tie down. If we assign participants to three groups and treat the groups differently, groups is clearly the independent variable. However, if I take males and females and measure them, gender is not something that I actually manipulated (I took it as I found it), but it is what I am studying and it is also called an independent variable. If I ask how much time people spend texting and what their GPA is, both of those are, in a way, dependent variables, but I am most interested in GPA as dependent on texting, the independent variable. As I said, the distinction is a bit squishy.

---

[2]Hint: The next time you come across the independent/dependent-variable distinction on a test, just remember that *dependent* and *data* both start with a d. You can figure out the rest from there.

2.3 | Random Sampling

In the first chapter I said that a sample is a random sample if each and every element of the population has an equal chance of being included in the sample. I further stated that the concept of a random sample is fundamental to the process of using statistics calculated on a sample to infer the values of parameters of a population. It should be obvious that we would be foolish to try to estimate the average level of sexual activity of all high-school students on the basis of data on a group of ninth graders who happen to have a study hall at the same time. We would all agree (I hope) that the data would underestimate the average value that would have been obtained from a truly random sample of the entire population of high-school students.

There are a number of ways of obtaining random samples from fairly small populations. We could assign every person a number and then use a table of random numbers to select the numbers of those who will be included in our sample. Or, if we would be satisfied with a nearly random sample, we could put names into a hat and draw blindly. The point is that every score in the population should have an approximately equal chance of being included in the sample.

It is often helpful to have a table of random numbers to use for drawing random samples, assigning subjects to groups, and other tasks. Such a table can be found in Appendix E (Table E.9). This table is a list of uniform random numbers. The adjective *uniform* is used to indicate that every number is equally (uniformly) likely to occur. For example, if you counted the occurrences of the digits 1, 5, and 8 in this table, you would find that they all occur about equally often.

Table E.9 is quite easy to use. If you wanted to draw random numbers between 0 and 9, you would simply close your eyes and put your finger on the table. You would then read down the column (after opening your eyes), recording the digits as they come. When you came to the bottom of the column, you would go to the next column and continue the process until you had as many numbers as you needed. If you wanted numbers between 0 and 99, you would do the same thing, except that you would read off pairs of digits. If you wanted random numbers between 1 and 65, you again would read off pairs of digits, but ignore 00 and any number greater than 65.

If, instead of collecting a set of random data, you wanted to use the random-number table to assign subjects to two treatment groups, you could start at any place in the table and assign a participant to Group I if the random number was odd and to Group II if it was even. Common-sense extrapolations of this procedure will allow you to assign participants randomly to any number of groups.

With large populations most standard techniques for ensuring randomness are no longer appropriate. We cannot put the names of all U.S. women between 21 and 30 into a hat (even a very big hat). Nor could we assign all U.S. women a number and then choose women by matching numbers against a random-number table. Such a procedure would be totally impractical. Unless we have substantial resources, the best we can do is to eliminate as many potential sources of bias as possible (e.g., don't estimate level of sexual behavior solely on the basis of a sample of people who visit Planned Parenthood), restrict our conclusions with respect to those sources of bias that we could not feasibly control (e.g., acknowledge that the data came only from people who were willing to complete our questionnaire), and then hope a lot. Any biases that remain will limit the degree to which the results can be generalized to the population as a whole. A large body of literature is concerned with sampling methods designed to ensure representative samples, such as techniques used in conducting the decennial census, but such methods are beyond the scope of this book.

Random numbers don't always look as random as you and I might expect. Try writing down the results you think might be reasonable from five coin flips—e.g., H (heads) T (tails) H H H. Then go to the July 1997 issue of *Chance News* on the Internet for an interesting discussion of randomness (Item 13). The address is

 http://www.dartmouth.edu/~chance/chance_news/recent_news/chance_ news_6.07.html#randomness

This could form the basis of an interesting class discussion. (If you have a minute, snoop around at this site. They have all sorts of cool things. I particularly like the page about Barney the dinosaur. But the article on the genetics of breast cancer is now out of date. Chance News has been around since 1992 and publishes some excellent material on statistics and experimental design. Unfortunately, it seems to keep moving.)

Two paragraphs back I spoke about using random numbers to assign subjects to groups. This is called **random assignment**, and I would argue that it is even more important than random sampling. We like to have a random sample because it gives us confidence that our results apply to a larger population. You aren't going to draw a truly random sample from the population of all college sophomores in the United States, and no one would fault you for that. But you certainly would not want to compare two methods of teaching general survival skills by applying one method in a large urban school and the other in a small rural school. Regardless of the effectiveness of the teaching methods themselves, pre-existing differences between the two samples would greatly influence the results, though they are not what we intended to study.

Random sampling is an important consideration primarily in the generalizability from the sample to the population. Random assignment, on the other hand, is necessary to ensure that the differences between the groups reflect the differences in the experimental treatments, and nothing more. Where possible, you should always aim for random assignment.

2.4 Notation

Any discussion of statistical techniques requires a notational system for expressing mathematical operations. It is thus perhaps surprising that no standard notational system has been adopted. Although there have been several attempts to formulate a general policy, the fact remains that different textbooks do not use exactly the same notation.

The notational systems that we do have range from the very complex to the very simple. The more complex systems gain precision at the loss of easy intelligibility, and the simpler systems gain intelligibility at the loss of some precision. Because the loss of precision is usually minor when compared with the gain in comprehension, this book will use an extremely simple system of notation.

Notation for Variables

The general rule for our purposes is that a variable will be represented by an upper-case letter, often X or Y. An individual value of that variable will be represented by the letter and a subscript. Suppose, for example, that we have the following five scores on the length of time (in seconds) that third-grade children can sit absolutely still:

$$45 \quad 42 \quad 35 \quad 23 \quad 52$$

This set of scores will be referred to as X. The first number of this set (45) can be referred to as X_1, the second (42) as X_2, and so on. To refer to a single score without specifying which one, we will refer to X_i, where i can take on any value between 1 and 5. The use of subscripts is essential to precise description of statistical procedures. In practice, however, the use of subscripts is often more of a distraction than an aid. In this book subscripts will generally be omitted where the meaning is clear without them.

Summation Notation

One of the most common symbols in statistics is the uppercase Greek letter **sigma** (**Σ**), the standard notation for summation, which means "add up, or sum, what follows." Thus, ΣX_i is read "Sum the X_is." To be precise, if we have 25 cases (denoted as $N = 25$) the notation for summing all N values of X is

$$\sum_{1}^{N} X_i$$

which translates to, "Sum all the X_is from $i = 1$ to $i = N$." There is seldom any need in practice to specify what is to be done in such detail; ΣX_i, or even ΣX, will do. In most cases in this book subscripts will be dropped, and the notation for the sum of the values of X will be simply ΣX.

There are several extensions of the simple case of ΣX, and you need to understand them. One of these is ΣX^2, which is read, "Sum the squared values of X" (i.e., $45^2 + 42^2 + 35^2 + 23^2 + 52^2$). Another common expression is ΣXY, which means, "Sum the products of the corresponding values of X and Y." The use of these terms is illustrated in the following example.

Imagine a simple experiment in which we record the number of major and minor life events in an adolescent's life and a measure of behavior problems. For the sake of our example, we will use only five adolescents (i.e., $N = 5$). The data and simple summation operations on them are illustrated in Table 2.1. Some of these operations have been discussed already; others will be discussed in the next few chapters. Examination of Table 2.1 reveals a set of operations involving parentheses, such as $(\Sigma X)^2$.

The rule that always applies is to perform operations within parentheses before performing operations outside parentheses.

Table 2.1 Illustration of operations involving summation notation

	Life Events	Behavior Problems				
	X	Y	X^2	Y^2	$X{-}Y$	XY
	10	3	100	9	7	30
	15	4	225	16	11	60
	12	1	144	1	11	12
	9	1	81	1	8	9
	10	3	100	9	7	30
Sum	56	12	650	36	44	141

$$\Sigma X = (10 + 15 + 12 + 9 + 10) = 56$$

$$\Sigma Y = (3 + 4 + 1 + 1 + 3) = 12$$

$$\Sigma X^2 = (10^2 + 15^2 + 12^2 + 9^2 + 10^2) = 650$$

$$\Sigma Y^2 = (3^2 + 4^2 + 1^2 + 1^2 + 3^2) = 36$$

$$\Sigma(X-Y) = (7 + 11 + 11 + 8 + 7) = 44$$

$$\Sigma XY = (10*3 + 15*4 + 12*1 + 9*1 + 10*3) = 141$$

$$(\Sigma X)^2 = 56^2 = 3136$$

$$(\Sigma Y)^2 = 12^2 = 144$$

$$(\Sigma(X-Y))^2 = 44^2 = 1936$$

$$(\Sigma X)(\Sigma Y) = 56*12 = 672$$

For $(\Sigma X)^2$ we would sum the values of X and *then* square the result, as opposed to ΣX^2, in which we would square the Xs *before* we sum. Confirm that ΣX^2 is not equal to $(\Sigma X)^2$ by using simple numbers such as 2, 3, and 4.

You need a thorough understanding of notation if you are to learn even the most elementary statistical techniques. Given what we already know, we can go one step further and lay out three additional rules. I leave it to you to illustrate their correctness by taking a few simple numbers and applying the rules to them.

Rules of Summation:

1. $\Sigma(X - Y) = \Sigma X - \Sigma Y$. The sum of a set of differences is the same as the sum of the first set minus the sum of the second set.

2. $\Sigma CX = C\Sigma X$. The notation ΣCX means to multiply every value of X by the constant C and then sum the results. A **constant** is any number that does not change its value in a given situation (as opposed to a variable, which does). Constants are most often represented by the letters C and k, but other symbols may be used.

3. $\Sigma(X + C) = \Sigma X + NC$. Where N represents the number of items that are being summed and C is a constant.

2.5 | Summary

In this chapter we examined briefly the concept of measurement and considered four different levels, or scales, of measurement. Nominal scales simply name things, and we can use either numbers or letters or names to do that. Ordinal scales put items in increasing or decreasing order but don't go beyond that. With interval scales we can meaningfully speak of the differences between points on a scale. (The difference between 20 and 30 is the same as the difference between 30 and 40.) Finally, with ratio scales we can speak about something being twice as much as something else.

We also discussed the different types of variables. Continuous variables can take on any value between the lowest and highest points on the scale, whereas discrete variables can take on only a limited number of values with nothing in between those values. (Even if a variable is technically discrete, such as the number of students in a class, we treat it as continuous if there are many possible values.) Also remember that dependent variables are variables that we measure, whereas independent variables are *usually* under the control of the experimenter and are the things that we are studying, such as different methods of teaching reading.

Random sampling refers to how we select individuals or objects to be measured, whereas random assignment refers to the way participants are assigned to different treatment groups. The latter is generally more important.

It is very important that you understand the rules of notation, and we will refer back to these throughout the book. At this point you have the basic terminology you will need to begin looking at data. Now we can get started.

Key Terms

Measurement, 19	Discrete variables, 24
Scales of measurement, 19	Continuous variables, 24
Nominal scale, 20	Independent variables, 25
Ordinal scale, 21	Dependent variables, 25
Interval scale, 21	Random assignment, 27
Ratio scale, 22	Sigma (Σ), 28
Variables, 24	Constant, 29

2.6 | A Quick Review

A. Name the four common scales of measurement.
Ans: Nominal, ordinal, interval, ratio

B. Why was Stevens more concerned about scales of measurement than we are?
Ans: Stevens was trying to make psychology respectable to people in the physical sciences who complained that the measurements we make are sloppy. We no longer have

that same perspective and have learned to live with less precise measurement. But we continue to refer to such scales by name.

C. What is the difference between an interval and a ratio scale?
Ans: In the latter we can meaningfully speak of the ratio between numbers (e.g., "twice as big"). But we will generally apply the same statistical procedures to both kinds of data.

D. The most important characteristics behind using different scales is to keep in mind the numbers themselves. (T or F)
False. What is important is the underlying variable that we hope we are measuring.

E. What is the practical distinction between discrete and continuous variables?
Ans: Discrete variables take on only a few different values, but continuous variables can take on any value between the lowest and highest score.

F. What is the independent variable?
Ans: This is the variable that we are trying to study, as opposed to the score that we obtain.

G. To oversimplify, random selection is useful to _____ while random assignment is useful to _____.
Ans: "assure that we can generalize to the population from which we sampled"; "assure that differences between groups are not due to extraneous variables"

H. When we refer to X_i we are referring to ____.
Ans: any specific value of the variable X

I. What is the general rule about what to do with parentheses in an equation?
Ans: Perform the operation within the parentheses before you perform the operation outside of the parentheses.

J. The notation "Σ" refers to _____.
Ans: summation

2.7 Exercises

2.1 Give one example each of a nominal, ordinal, interval, and ratio measure.

2.2 At the beginning of the chapter I gave three examples of different meanings for the number 18 in terms of the underlying scale of measurement. Give an example where the number 18 would be on an interval but not on a ratio scale. (Do not use temperature, as that has been used several times in the chapter.)

2.3 We trained rats to run a straight-alley maze for food reinforcement. All of a sudden one of the rats lay down and went to sleep halfway through the maze. What does this say about the scale of measurement when speed is used as an index of learning? What does this say about speed used as an index of motivation?

2.4 If you have access to SPSS, go to the website for this book

🌐 **https://www.uvm.edu/~dhowell/fundamentals9/**

select the link for the short SPSS manual, and read the brief introduction. Download the "apgar.sav" file referenced in that document and open it in SPSS. To download the file, left click on the file name in the third paragraph. That will open the file. Then right click on the page and select a location to store it. After you have done that, double click on the icon for that file and it will open in SPSS. What can you tell about the data? How would you describe the scale of measurement of the 10 variables given there?

2.5 In Section 2.1 I talked about the chain of assumptions that take us from a human heroin addict under a bridge to a mouse on a warm surface. List those assumptions.

2.6 Write a sentence describing the morphine tolerance experiment in terms of an independent variable and a dependent variable.

Exercises 2.7–2.10 relate to a study conducted by Pliner and Chaiken (1990). In their study about the social desirability of behavior, they examined the amount of food eaten by male and female participants in the presence of a person of the same gender, or a person of the opposite gender.

2.7 What are the independent variables in the study just described?

2.8 What is the dependent variable in that study?

2.9 Experiments like this are usually done with some hypothesis in mind. What would you expect was the experimenter's hypothesis?

2.10 Describe the chain of assumptions underlying the measurement issues in this study.

2.11 We saw that we often treat a discrete variable as if it were continuous. Under what conditions would we be likely to do so?

2.12 Give three examples of discrete variables and three examples of continuous variables.

2.13 Most people assume that random numbers are actually more orderly than they really are. For example, they assume that if you draw 50 random numbers, Nature will somehow almost ensure that you have 25 even numbers and 25 odd ones, or very close to that. Draw 50 random numbers from Table E.9 in Appendix E and calculate the proportion of even numbers. Then do this two more times and record the proportion of even numbers that you obtained each time. Do these data look the way you would expect them to look?

2.14 First write down any six sequences of heads and tails that you might expect to occur on five coin flips (e.g., HTHHT). Then take an actual coin and create another six sequences by flipping the coin five times for each sequence. Next go to the following link at *Chance News* given below and read the article on randomness. How does it compare with the sequences you predicted and the sequences you actually obtained? (In that article don't get too hung up on the idea of writing the shortest computer program; I don't know what he's talking about either.)

 https://www.dartmouth.edu/~chance/chance_news/recent_news/chance_news_6.07.html

2.15 In a study of the moon illusion that we will discuss in Chapter 5, Kaufman and Rock (1962) tested an earlier hypothesis about reasons for the moon illusion by comparing how observers performed when they were able to look at the moon with their eyes level, and again with their eyes elevated. The data for the Eyes Level condition follow:

| 1.65 | 1.00 | 2.03 | 1.25 | 1.05 | 1.02 | 1.67 | 1.86 | 1.56 | 1.73 |

Using X to represent this variable,
(a) What are X_3, X_5, and X_8?
(b) Calculate ΣX.
(c) Write the summation notation for (b) in its most complex form.

2.16 With reference to Exercise 2.15, the data for the Eyes Elevated condition are

| 1.73 | 1.06 | 2.03 | 1.40 | 0.95 | 1.13 | 1.41 | 1.73 | 1.63 | 1.56 |

Using Y for this variable,
(a) What are Y_1 and Y_{10}?
(b) Calculate ΣY.

2.17 Using the data from Exercise 2.15,
(a) Calculate $(\Sigma X)^2$ and ΣX^2.
(b) Calculate $\Sigma X/N$, where N = the number of scores.
(c) What do you call what you just calculated?

2.18 Using the data from Exercise 2.16,
(a) Calculate $(\Sigma Y)^2$ and ΣY^2.
(b) Given the answers to (a), calculate

$$\frac{\Sigma Y^2 - \dfrac{(\Sigma Y)^2}{N}}{N-1}$$

(c) Calculate the square root of the answer to (b). (You will come across these calculations again in Chapter 5.)

2.19 The data from Exercises 2.15 and 2.16 come from the same 10 (N) observers. In other words, the same person had a score of 1.65 in the Eyes Level condition and 1.73 in the Eyes Elevated condition. Therefore the data form pairs of scores.
(a) Multiply the scores in each pair together to get a variable called XY.
(b) Calculate ΣXY.
(c) Calculate $\Sigma X \Sigma Y$.
(d) Do ΣXY and $\Sigma X \Sigma Y$ differ, and would you normally expect them to?
(e) Calculate

$$\frac{\Sigma XY - \dfrac{\Sigma X \Sigma Y}{N}}{N-1}$$

(You will come across these calculations again in Chapter 9. The result is called the covariance. Very few of the calculations in this book will be any more complex than this one.)

2.20 Use the previous data to show that
(a) $\Sigma (X + Y) = \Sigma X + \Sigma Y$
(b) $\Sigma XY \neq \Sigma X \Sigma Y$
(c) $\Sigma CX = C \Sigma X$
(d) $\Sigma X^2 \neq (\Sigma X)^2$

2.21 Make up five data points and show that $\Sigma (X + C) = \Sigma X + NC$, where C is any constant (e.g., 4) and N is the number of data points.

2.22 I have been (correctly) criticized for using "the number of hairs on a goat" as an example of a continuous variable in an earlier edition of this book. Why is this really a discrete variable? Would this alter how you treat the data?

2.23 Can an ordinal variable be measured on a continuous scale?

2.24 I have argued that paw-lick latencies can reasonably be taken to be an interval scale of pain sensitivity in mice. Suppose that someone else felt that the square root of paw-lick latency was more appropriate. How might we decide between these two competing measures?

2.25 The *Chicago Tribune* of July 21, 1995 reported on a study by a fourth-grade student named Beth Peres. In the process of collecting evidence in support of her campaign for a higher allowance from her parents, she polled her classmates on what they received as an allowance. She was surprised to discover that the 11 girls who responded reported an average allowance of $2.63 per week, but the seven boys reported an average of $3.18, 21% more than for the girls. At the same time boys had to do fewer chores to earn their allowance than did girls. The story achieved considerable national prominence, as you would expect, and raised the question of whether the income disparity for adult women relative to adult men may actually have its start very early in life. (Good for Beth!)

(a) What are the dependent and independent variables in this study, and how are they measured?

(b) What kind of a sample are we dealing with here?

(c) How could the characteristics of the sample influence the results she obtained?

(d) How might Beth go about "random sampling"? How would she go about "random assignment"?

(e) If random assignment is not possible in this study, does that have negative implications for the validity of the study?

(f) What are some of the variables that might influence the outcome of this study separate from any true population differences between boys' and girls' income?

(g) Distinguish clearly between the descriptive and inferential statistical features of this example.

2.26 The *Journal of Public Health* published data on the relationship between smoking and health (see Landwehr and Watkins (1987). They reported the cigarette consumption per adult for 21 mostly Western and developed countries, along with the coronary heart disease rate for each country. The data clearly show that coronary heart disease is highest in those countries with the highest cigarette consumption.

(a) Why might the sampling in this study have been limited to developed countries?

(b) How would you characterize the two variables in terms of what we have labeled "scales of measurement"?

(c) If our goal is to study the health effects of smoking, how do these data relate to that overall question?

(d) What other variables might need to be taken into consideration in such a study?

(e) It has been reported that tobacco companies are making a massive advertising effort in Asia. A few years ago only 7% of Chinese women smoked (compared to 61% of Chinese men). How would a health psychologist go about studying the health effects of likely changes in the incidence of smoking among Chinese women?

(f) Do a search of the Internet using Google to find articles relating secondhand smoke to coronary heart disease. What do these articles suggest?

2.27 There has recently been discussion on the Internet concerning whether the Shuffle feature on your iPod is truly random. (Well, some things really are more important than others!) How would you go about deciding whether the playing sequence is random? What would actually constitute randomness? An item about this issue can be found at

 http://ipodusers.tribe.net/thread/9c5fe30c-728a-44cf-9b6f-9ad426641d12

If it is gone by the time you search for it, it is highly likely that an Internet search would bring up closely related items.

2.28 Go to the Internet link at

http://www.stat.ucla.edu/cases/yale/

and read the very short case study there. Answer the questions on sampling and compare your answer with the explanation given in an accompanying link labeled "Explain" in the lower left.

2.29 Do an Internet search for someone else's explanation of scales of measurement. (Don't be terribly surprised if that person uses different terminology than is used here, though my terminology has pretty much become standard.)

## CHAPTER 3

Displaying Data

We begin this chapter with a simple example to illustrate that plotting data can reveal a great deal more than simply looking at the numbers themselves. We start with histograms, which are some of the simplest plots, and learn how to create them. While we are at it, we look at how to set up and use the computing environment *(R)* to do the plotting and other analyses that we will want. But histograms are not the only way to look at data, nor are they even the preferred way in some situations, so we continue by looking at alternative methods, including stem-and-leaf displays, bar graphs, line graphs, and related methods. We will also look at terms that we use to describe distributions, such as symmetry and skewness. Finally, we will use SPSS and *R* to make graphs quickly and easily.

A collection of raw data, taken by itself, is no more exciting or informative than junk mail before election day. Whether you have neatly arranged the data in rows on a data collection form or scribbled them on the back of an out-of-date announcement you tore from the bulletin board, a collection of numbers is still just a collection of numbers. To be interpretable, they first must be organized in some sort of logical order.

Psychologists interested in sensory perception have long wondered how people compare two things mentally. For example, suppose that I presented you with two visual images in different orientations. Either they are identical images that have been rotated with respect to each

CONCEPTS THAT YOU WILL NEED TO REMEMBER FROM PREVIOUS CHAPTERS

Continuous variable:	One that can take on many possible values
Discrete variable:	One that takes on only a few possible values
Dependent variable:	The variable that you are measuring
Independent variable:	The variable that you manipulate

other (e.g., a normal uppercase R and an uppercase R lying on its back) or they are mirror images of each other (e.g., R and Я). Your task is to tell me as quickly as possible whether they are the same image or mirror images. This may sound easy, but it is not. I can measure both the accuracy of your response and its speed. I can also ask if the time it takes you to respond depends on how far the images have been rotated from one another.

There is an excellent website maintained by John Kranz at Hanover College that allows you to collect your own data on this question. Kranz and his students have put together a number of interesting experiments, and these can be found at

 http://psych.hanover.edu/JavaTest/CLE/Cognition/Cognition.html

(While you are there, take a look at all the other great stuff the department's website has to offer, much of which is produced by students. If you want to try one of their experiments, first look at http://www.uvm.edu/~dhowell/fundamentals9/SeeingStatisticsApplets/Applets .html and carefully read the third paragraph.) The experiment that we are going to consider deals with mental rotation of oddly shaped objects.

Below is an example of two stimuli presented on a computer screen. The cross in the center is the fixation point on which you should focus between trials.

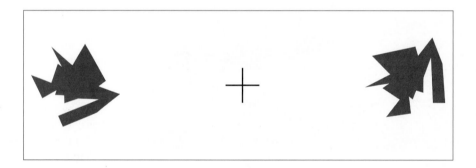

The observer's task is to press the letter S or the letter M as quickly as possible, depending on whether you think these are the Same stimulus or Mirror images of each other. Then another pair of figures appears with the same instructions. (If you should choose to participate in this experiment you can vary the size of the stimuli, the number of different levels by which they can be rotated, and several other independent variables.) I collected my own data from 600 trials that allowed for 10 different degrees of rotation in 20° steps. But having collected the data I now need to make sense of what I have. There are a number of interesting questions that I could ask of the data. For example, I could ask whether it takes longer for incorrect answers than for correct answers. I could also ask if objects that have been rotated many degrees from each other take longer to judge than objects that have been rotated only a few degrees, or perhaps none. Before I can look at questions like that I will begin by looking at all of the data without regard to the levels of the independent variables and without regard to the accuracy of my choices.

The data that we will use were originally recorded to the nearest millisecond. The computer can measure that precisely, so that is the way they were recorded. However, I have rounded the data to hundredths of a second for our convenience. Doing so does not distort the results in any way.

An example of the data file is shown in Table 3.1, and you can download the full set of data from

 https://www.uvm.edu/~dhowell/fundamentals9/DataFiles/Tab3-1.dat

Table 3.1 Sample reaction time data from the mental rotation experiment

Trial	Angle	Stimulus	Response	Accuracy 1 = correct	RxTime
1	140	Same	Same	1	4.42
2	60	Same	Same	1	1.75
3	180	Mirror	Mirror	1	1.44
4	100	Same	Same	0	1.74
5	160	Mirror	Mirror	1	1.94
6	180	Mirror	Mirror	1	1.42
7	180	Mirror	Mirror	1	1.94
8	0	Same	Same	1	1.24
9	40	Mirror	Mirror	1	3.30
10	140	Same	Same	1	1.98
11	60	Mirror	Mirror	1	1.84
12	160	Same	Same	1	3.45
13	40	Mirror	Mirror	1	3.00
14	180	Mirror	Mirror	1	4.44
15	140	Mirror	Mirror	1	2.92
…	…	…	…	…	….
600	40	Mirror	Mirror	1	1.12

The independent variables are Trial, Angle of rotation, and Stimulus (were the stimuli the same or mirror images?). The dependent variables are Response (what key did I press?), Accuracy, and RxTime (in seconds). Notice that on some trials it took me more than four seconds to make a response, and even then I wasn't always correct.

3.1 Plotting Data

As you can imagine, with 600 responses times it is not possible for us to be able to interpret them at a glance. One of the simplest methods to reorganize data to make them more intelligible is to plot them in some sort of graphical form. Data can be represented graphically in several common ways. Some of these methods are frequency distributions, histograms, and stem-and-leaf displays, which we will discuss in turn.

Frequency Distributions and Histograms

As a first step we can make a **frequency distribution** of the data as a way of organizing them in some sort of logical order. For our example of reaction times, we would count the number of times that each possible reaction time occurred. However, the data are recorded to the nearest 100th of a second, which would make for a very long table. In Table 3.1 I have collapsed the data into 10th-of-a-second intervals and shown the center of the interval as well as the bounds on the interval. The upper and lower bounds for an interval are known as the **real lower limit** and the **real upper limit**. Any value that falls within these limits is classed as being in the interval. For example, a score equal to or greater than 1.895000 and less than 1.995000 would fall in the 1.90–1.99 interval.[1] The center of the interval is referred to as the **midpoint** of the interval.

---

[1] A word about rounding! This book adopts the rule that when you want to round a number that ends in five, you round up or down, whichever will make the result even. Thus 1.895 would round up to 1.90, whereas 1.885 would round down to 1.88.

Table 3.2   Frequency distribution of reaction times (in 10ths of seconds)

Reaction Time	Midpoint	Freq	Reaction Time	Midpoint	Freq	Reaction Time	Midpoint	Freq
.50–.59	.55	0	2.00–2.09	2.05	21	3.50–3.59	3.55	0
.60–.69	.65	0	2.10–2.19	2.15	19	3.60–3.69	3.65	0
.70–.79	.75	7	2.20–2.29	2.25	10	3.70–3.79	3.75	1
.80–.89	.85	18	2.30–2.39	2.35	6	3.80–3.89	3.85	2
.90–.99	.95	39	2.40–2.49	2.45	11	3.90–3.99	3.95	2
1.00–1.09	1.05	45	2.50–2.59	2.55	11	4.00–4.09	4.05	0
1.10–1.19	1.15	45	2.60–2.69	2.65	7	4.10–4.19	4.15	2
1.20–1.29	1.25	43	2.70–2.79	2.75	7	4.20–4.29	4.25	1
1.30–1.39	1.35	46	2.80–2.89	2.85	4	4.30–4.39	4.35	0
1.40–1.49	1.45	45	2.90–2.99	2.95	5	4.40–4.49	4.45	2
1.50–1.59	1.55	50	3.00–3.09	3.05	5			
1.60–1.69	1.65	42	3.10–3.19	3.15	2			
1.70–1.79	1.75	34	3.20–3.29	3.25	1			
1.80–1.89	1.85	37	3.30–3.39	3.35	3			
1.90–1.99	1.95	23	3.40–3.49	3.45	4			

The frequency distribution for these data is presented in Table 3.2, which reports how often each time occurred. The data will be plotted as a histogram in Figure 3.1.

From the distribution shown in Table 3.2, it is clear that there is a wide distribution of reaction times, with times as low as about 0.75 seconds and as high as 4.5 seconds. The data tend to cluster around about 1.5 seconds, with most of the scores between 0.75 and 3.00 seconds. This tendency was not apparent from the unorganized data shown in Table 3.1. Notice that the reaction times seem to tail off to the right. This is not surprising, because there is a limit on how quickly a participant can respond to a stimulus, but there is no limit on how long it will take that participant to respond.

It is usually far easier to see what is going on when we plot the data than when we just look at a table. In this case we can graph the data in the form of a **histogram**. (We will use *R* to create our histogram, and the accompanying box on Obtaining *R* and RStudio describes how to download and install *R*. A more complete version of getting started with *R* can be found at this chapter's website: www.uvm.edu/~dhowell /fundamentals9/Supplements/DownloadingR.html. (If you read the box, you probably won't need more direction.) But even before you download and install *R*, you can get a sense of what it can do with graphics and what the commands look like by going to an excellent introductory *R* Graphics tutorial at http://flowingdata.com/2012/05/15/ how-to-visualize-and-compare-distributions/) I point to that page merely to illustrate what the code actually looks like and what kinds of graphs we can produce. I want you to have a visual experience of what *R* is all about, but there is no need for you to memorize anything or even understand everything. That can come later.

In what follows, you will see sections containing code for *R*. I strongly urge you to install and start *R*. Then paste in and run that code as you go along. I even suggest that you modify that code and see what happens—if your change doesn't work, no one will slap you with a ruler, and you may learn stuff.

Obtaining R and RStudio

In order to make use of *R* you need to download it from the Web. I go into more detail on this process, with screen shots, at www.uvm.edu/~dhowell/fundamentals9 /Supplements/DownloadingR.html, and you may want to look at that page. But installing and running *R* really is quite simple. Start up your browser and go to r-project.org, click on "CRAN," select the file you need for your operating system, and download that file. (Along the way you can read any of the links on that page that look interesting, but unless you are running Windows Vista, you probably don't need to do that and may find some of them confusing.) When the file has downloaded, click on the file and it will install. You can do the same for RStudio at http:// www.rstudio.com/products/rstudio/download/. RStudio is an editor that works very nicely with *R*. You type your code in RStudio, click on the "Run" button, and see your results. As a matter of fact, whenever you start RStudio it automatically starts *R* at the same time. While you are at it, I suggest that you also go to www.uvm .edu/~dhowell/fundamentals9/DataFiles/DataFiles.zip and download that file to a directory named StatisticsData—or whatever you want to name it—so that you can easily bring up data for all of the examples and homework exercises in the book. (If you do this, you can download data files either from your own hard drive or from the Web. I will generally show each data file as coming from my website, but that is because I don't know if you have copied the data to your hard drive. If you have, simply ignore my link and go to yours. That way you can even run the examples when you are wandering around in a place without a wireless connection. That assumes that you are doing your homework in such a place rather than studying dutifully in your room.) You can use the file menu, either on RStudio or *R*, to set the appropriate default directory to make it easy to load data without a lot of hunting around for the file. That way the StatisticsData folder will open whenever you try to load a file. See the example in the code, lines 3 and 4 of Figure 3.1. The "#" at the beginning of a line turns that line into a comment, which is not executed unless you remove the #.

For our data perceptual rotation, the *R* code and the resulting histogram are shown in Figure 3.1. Notice how much easier it is to see the pattern in the data than it was in a table. Notice particularly how the distribution trails off on the right. I strongly suggest that you read through the code to get a general sense of what *R* is doing and how it does it. I don't expect you to learn many *R* commands that way.

```
### - - - - - - { Plotting a histogram for the reaction time data.
- - - - - -

# setwd("C:/Users/Dave/Dropbox/Webs/Fundamentals8/DataFiles")
# An example of "set working directory."
# data1<- read.table("Tab3-1.dat", header = TRUE)
# Now you just need to give the file name.
data1 <- read.table("http://www.uvm.edu/~dhowell/fundamentals9/Data-
Files/Tab3-1.dat", header = TRUE)
names(data1)      #Tells me the names of those variables
```

```
attach(data1)                      # Make the variables available for use
par(mfrow = c(2,1))                #Just to make things pretty--
                                   uses only half the screen
hist(RTsec, breaks = 40, xlim = c(0,5), xlab = "Reaction Time (in
sec.)")
# For Figure 3.1
stem(RTsec, scale = 2)             # Not used discussed in text
# More useful stuff
install.packages("psych")          # Only use this the first time you
                                   install a library
library(psych)                     # Assumes lpsych library has been
                                   installed
describe(data1)                    # Extra stuff that we come back to
                                   later
```

Figure 3.1 *R code and plot of reaction times against frequency*

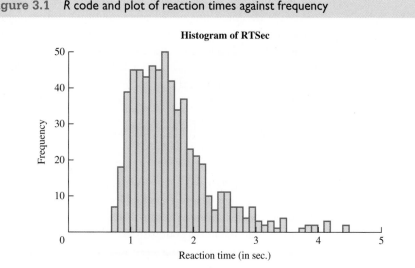

Histogram of RTSec

Things to keep in mind about reading the R code

1. If you set the working directory, then you don't have to specify it again in that session—just give the file name. I have commented out those two lines

2. The line that begins "data1 <- read.table . . ." is a common method of reading files from the Web.

3. The install.packages command finds the appropriate library (psych) and installs it. You will never have to install it again, though you do load it each time with "library(psych)."

Histograms generally collapse the data into intervals, just as we did in Table 3.2, though the width of the intervals (e.g., 1.00–1.09 versus 1.00–1.19) may be selected by the computer program that does the plotting. In the current case I forced the histogram to use the same interval widths as those in Table 3.2. (That's what the "breaks = 40" command does.)

The optimal number of intervals to use when grouping data usually follows the Goldilocks principle—neither too many nor too few. (In R you can roughly control the number of intervals with the "breaks =" command.) You want to illustrate the overall nature of the distribution without excessive detail. In general and when practical it is best to use natural breaks in the number system (e.g., 0–9, 10–19 or 100–119, 120–139, etc.) rather than to break up the range into some arbitrarily defined number of intervals. However, if another kind of limit makes the data more interpretable, then use those limits. Remember that you are trying to make the data meaningful—don't try to follow a rigid set of rules made up by someone who has never seen your problem. Most software uses one of many available algorithms for determining the number of intervals, but you can generally override that choice to obtain something that better serves your purpose.

A few more comments about R

- The code and histogram are computed within RStudio, which automatically starts R and then handles the code and output in its own windows. You could just use R and paste the code into its own editor, but that is not much of an editor.

- To run the code, just enter it into the RStudio editor, select all of it, or as much as you want to run, and click "Run." The printed output, such as the names of the variables, will appear in the lower left. You won't have any trouble finding the plots.

- R is case sensitive, so if you type "names(Data1)," when the file is named "data1," it won't have any idea what you are talking about.

- When you read in a data file, whether it contains one or several variables, it is stored as a data frame. To have access to those variables, use the "attach" command—e.g. attach(data1).

- There is a lot of controversy over the "attach" command. When you read your data, R stores it in a data frame, which is in effect a safe. If you ask for a histogram of RTsec it will tell you that there is no such variable. If you type "attach(data1)," it will take the variables out of the data frame, make copies of them, and then let you use those copies. There are other ways around this problem, but "attach" is the simplest, and that's what I will use here.

- When you have a question about a command (e.g., hist) just type ?hist. If you aren't exactly sure what the command is, type ??histogram and it will find various possibilities.

- There are graphical interfaces for running R. The best known is RCommander. Your instructor may suggest that you use one, but I have chosen to provide the direct R code because it makes it clear what you are doing. Instructions for installing Rcmdr can be found on the DownloadingR Web page, should you desire it, but I will not discuss its use—which you can probably figure out on your own with a bit of trial and error.

3.2 | Stem-and-Leaf Displays

Frequency distributions tell you how many times each value occurs, and the associated histogram gives you a visual representation of the data. A very nice way of retaining both the individual values and the frequency of those values is by creating what John Tukey devised and called a **stem-and-leaf display**, to be discussed next.

Who was John Tukey?

John Tukey was one of the most influential statisticians of the second half of the 20th century. Tukey was born in 1915 and by the age of three he could reportedly read a newspaper. Colleagues have said that he could sit through an entire meeting reading a book, and at the end of the faculty meeting he could report everything that had been said—poor guy. He went to Brown University and received a master's degree in chemistry. He then went on to Princeton intending to get a PhD in chemistry, but instead he took a PhD in mathematics. A few years later he had drifted into statistics, where he remained. He was a brilliant man and there are many anecdotes about his life, his work, and his interactions with others. Tukey spent his entire professional life at Princeton and at the nearby Bell Labs. He worked in many fields, but in this book we are going to see his contribution to what he named "Exploratory Data Analysis" and his work on multiple comparison procedures, where he developed one of the best-known statistical tests. You will see that there are not a lot of fixed rules and procedures in Tukey's exploratory data analysis. One of his most quoted statements is to the effect that it is better to have a fuzzy answer to the right question than a precise answer to the wrong question.

John Tukey (1977), as part of his general approach to data analysis known as **exploratory data analysis (EDA)**, developed a variety of methods for displaying data in visually meaningful ways. One of the simplest of these methods is a stem-and-leaf display. I can't start with the reaction-time data here because that would require a slightly more sophisticated display due to the large number of observations. Instead, I'll use a real set of data on the number of intrusive thoughts experienced by newly diagnosed breast cancer patients (Epping-Jordan, Compas, & Howell, 1994). As you might expect, some women are troubled a great deal by thoughts that keep coming to mind about their cancer. On the other hand, some women report very few such thoughts.

The data are given in Figure 3.2. On the left side of the figure are the raw data, and on the right is the complete stem-and-leaf display that results.

From the raw data in Figure 3.2, you can see that there are several scores below 10, many scores in the teens, some in the 20s, and three in the 30s. We refer to the tens' digits—here 0, 1, 2, and 3—as the **leading digits** (sometimes called the **most significant digits**) for these scores. These leading digits form the **stem**, or vertical axis, of our display. (There are times when we will need a two-digit stem, as you will soon see with the reaction time data.) Within the set of scores that were in the 20s,

Figure 3.2 Stem-and-leaf display of data on intrusive thoughts

Raw Data	Stem	Leaf
0 1 1 2 2 3 4 4 4 5 5 5 6 6 7 7 7 7 8 8 9 9	0 |	0112234445556677778899
	1 |	0111222333334445555556666 666666777888899
10 11 11 11 12 12 12 13 13 13 13 13 14 14 14 15 15 15 15 15 15 16 16 16 16 16 16 16 16 16 16 17 17 17 18 18 18 18 19 19	2 |	00112233444455667889
	3 |	005
20 20 21 21 22 22 23 23 24 24 24 24 25 25 26 26 27 28 28 29	|	
30 30 35		

you can see that there were two 20s, two 21s, two 22s, two 23s, four 24s, two 25s, two 26s, one 27, two 28s, and one 29. The units' digits 0, 1, 2, 3, 4, and so on, are called the **trailing** (or **less significant**) **digits**. They form the **leaves**—the horizontal elements—of our display.[2]

On the right side of Figure 3.2 you can see that next to the stem entry of 2 you have two 0s, two 1s, two 2s, two 3s, four 4s, two 5s, two 6s, one 7, two 8s, and one 9. These leaf values correspond to the units' digits in the raw data. Similarly, note how the leaves opposite the stem value of 1 correspond to the units' digits of all responses in the teens. From the stem-and-leaf display you could completely regenerate the raw data that went into that display. For example, you can tell that one person reported no intrusive thoughts, two people each reported one intrusive thought, and so on. Moreover, the shape of the display looks just like a sideways histogram, giving you all of the benefits of that method of graphing data as well.

One apparent drawback of this simple stem-and-leaf display is that for some data sets it will lead to a grouping that is too coarse for our purposes, thus including too many leaves for each stem. In fact, that is why I needed to move away from the reaction time example temporarily. If I tried to use the reaction time data, one second would have 410 leaves opposite it, which would be a little silly. Not to worry; Tukey was there before us and figured out clever ways around this problem.

If we have a problem when we try to lump together everything between 50 and 59, perhaps what we should be doing is breaking that interval into smaller intervals. We could try using the intervals 50–54 and 55–59, and so on. But then we couldn't just use 5 as the stem, because it would not distinguish between the two intervals. Tukey suggested that we use "5*" to represent 50–54, and "5." to represent 55–59. But that won't solve our problem here, because the categories still are too coarse. So Tukey suggested an alternative scheme, whereby "5*" represents 50–51, "5t" represents 52–53, "5f" represents 54–55, "5s" represents 56–57, and "5." represents 58–59. (You might

---

[2]It is not always true that the tens' digits form the stem and the units' digits the leaves. For example, if the data ranged from 100 to 1000, the hundreds' digits would form the stem, the tens' digits the leaves, and we would ignore the units' digits.

wonder why he chose those particular letters, but "two" and "three" both start with a "t," and you can figure out the rest. I lived for nearly 50 years without noticing that pattern in number names, but I'm not John Tukey.) If we apply the scheme to the data on reaction times, we obtain the results shown in Figure 3.3. In Figure 3.3 the complete stem-and-leaf display is there, allowing you to reproduce the complete data set.

Figure 3.3 Stem-and-leaf display for the mental rotation data

The decimal point is one digit(s) to the left of the "|"

Stem	Leaves
07	2222233
08	111113333333333333
09	2222222222222222222222222222222224444
10	111111111122222222222233333333333333333333333333
11	22222222222222222222222222222222222222222222244
12	222222222222222222222333333333333344444444448
13	333333333333333333333333333333333333333333333344
14	2222222222222222222244444444444444444444444444
15	1122222233333333333333333333333333333333333333333333335
16	222222222222222222222222244444444444444444444
17	22222223333333333334444444444444458
18	333333333333333333333333334444444444489
19	2444444444444444444448
20	3333333333333355555555
21	2222444444444444444444
22	3333335555
23	334444
24	24444444445
25	22235555559
26	4444446
27	3555555
28	4446
29	22555
30	00555
31	79
32	7
33	004
34	5557
35	
36	
37	5
38	36
39	18
40	
41	26
42	0
43	
44	24

Sometimes the extreme values in our data file may be very high or low, For example, one trial might have a score of 6.8 and another trial might have a score of 8.3. In this case the bottom entry for the stem might be the word "High," and the leaves opposite it might be 6.8 and another trial might have a score of 8.3. I could do a similar thing for low values by writing "Low" on the first line and then fill in the leaves with the actual values. Otherwise the display would get out of hand.

Graphing the mental rotation data will take a bit more work. Part of the problem is that we just have too many observations to fit neatly in a table. (In fact, stem-and-leaf displays are most often used for smaller data sets.) Here we are just going to have to break down and use two-digit stems. That is not really breaking a rule, because with exploratory data analysis there are very few firm rules. The goal is to display data in the most meaningful way. This stem-and-leaf display is shown in Figure 3.3. Notice the legend at the top that indicates that the decimal place in the stems is one digit to the left of the vertical line. In other words, the stem for the first row is actually 0.7.

The appropriate command in R would be
stem(RTsec, scale = 1)
Try that out and then experiment by setting scale to .5, 2, or 3.

One reason why I wanted to present these data in a stem-and-leaf display is that the display reveals something interesting about our data. Notice that the leaves for most of the stems contain very few values greater than five. This is not an error on my part; it reflects the data themselves. My guess would be that the timing function in the reaction-time program interacts in some way with the cycling rate of the computer to produce this anomaly. This will not have any material effect on our interpretation of the data, but it does point out that stem-and-leaf displays can show you things that you would not see in other types of displays.

Back-to-Back Stem-and-Leaf Displays

Do you attend class reliably? Does it matter? I think it matters, and the data to support that belief can best be presented by plotting two distributions on opposite sides of the stem in a stem-and-leaf display. In a course that I once taught we asked the laboratory assistants, at the end of the course, to indicate which of their students came to class regularly (3), occasionally (2), or rarely (1).[3] We will ignore those who came occasionally, leaving us with the data on two groups. Figure 3.4 shows the distribution of total points in the course for the two groups. These are actual data. We have put the stem down the center and the leaves for the two separate categories (missed often and attended regularly) on either side of the center. So we read the stem-and-leaf for those who attended regularly by looking at the stem and right side of the figure, and we read the data for those who missed class often by looking at the stem and the left side of the figure. Notice the code at the bottom of the table that indicates how entries translate to raw scores. With a stem of 25 and a leaf of 6, for example, you can't tell whether an entry represents a score of 25.6, of 256, or even of 2.56. The code at the bottom of the figure tells you that a stem of 25 and a leaf of 6 actually represent 256.

---

[3]The laboratory assistants came to each lecture and were in a position to make an informed judgment on attendance.

Figure 3.4	Total points in an actual course on psychological methods plotted separately for those who missed class often or attended regularly	
Missed Class Often	**Stem**	**Attended Regularly**
8	18	
5 5	19	
	20	
	21	
8 5	22	
9 7 3 2	23	
0	24	1 3 6 9
6 6 6 0	25	0 2 4 4 5 6
8 4 4 1	26	1 2 3 4 4 4 5 7 7
7 4 4 0 0	27	0 1 2 3 6 6 7 8 8
	28	0 1 2 4 8 8
	29	0 1 1 2 3 4 6 6 7 8
8	30	
	31	0
	32	0 1 8
Code |25| 6 = 256		

Finally, notice that the figure nicely illustrates the difference in performance between those students who attend class regularly and those who came when they couldn't think of anything better to do. A few got away with it, but most people who skipped got into trouble. (The folks who came to class sporadically fell in the middle in terms of total points.) As you will see throughout the book, we want to be able to tell not only whether a difference is not just due to chance, but we also want to have a sense of just how big or important a difference is. You can see here that the back-to-back stem-and-leaf display does a nice job of illustrating just how large the difference is. (The code for doing this in *R* follows. ("file.choose()" will open a window and let you hunt on your hard disk for the file.) Look at it to see how the code works, and then paste it into the RStudio window. One interesting feature emerges in the code. The base code for *R* does not handle back-to-back displays, but someone wrote a library of functions named "aplpack," and we can load that library and use their "stem. leaf.backback()" function.

```
data <- read.table(file.choose(), header = TRUE) # Then select Fig3-4.dat
attach(data)
poorAttend <- Points[Attend == 1]
goodAttend <- Points[Attend == 2]
install.packages("aplpack")                       # Use only the first time.
library(aplpack)
stem.leaf.backback(poorAttend,goodAttend, m = 2) # m controls bin size
```

3.3 Reading Graphs

In recent years I have heard more and more comments from my colleagues to the effect that students are having trouble understanding graphs. It is hard to tell whether this is just an example of the fact that my colleagues are getting older and "students aren't like they were in my day," or if interpretation of graphs has become more difficult for students. This section is my attempt at addressing the problem.

One difficulty stems from the fact that we can't make any dogmatic statement about whether the dependent variable goes on the Y (vertical) axis or the X (horizontal) axis. Clear rules make life so much simpler, but they don't apply here. If you take the histograms that we have been looking at, you will see that the dependent variable (e.g., Reaction time) is placed along the X axis, and the frequency with which each value occurred is on the Y axis. That is true for any histogram that I can think of. On the other hand, consider the graph shown in Figure 3.5. This is called a **bar graph**, because it uses vertical bars to represent the average reaction time. The graph shows the average response time as a function whether or not the participant was correct in his or her choice of "Same" or "Mirror." Notice that the independent variable (Accuracy) is presented on the horizontal, or X, axis, and the dependent variable (Reaction Time) is on the vertical, or Y, axis. You will notice that the participant seems to respond a bit faster on those trials in which his or her choice is correct. I don't know whether or not this difference is reliable, but even if it is, it appears to be a small difference. Not all reliable differences are important. (The R code for this can be found at https://www.uvm.edu/~dhowell/fundamentals9/Supplements /Chapter3R.html along with other Chapter 3 material.)

A second graph, with Time on the X axis, is shown in Figure 3.6. Here we see the frequency of video game sessions as a function of age.[4] The data came from Gentile (2009). In R the code would be

---

Figure 3.5 Average reaction time as a function of whether or not the judgment was correct

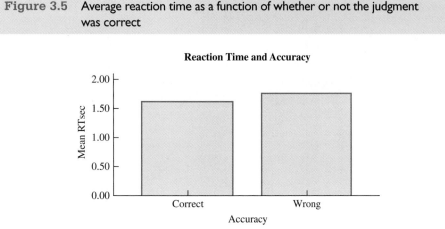

---

[4]Here is an example in which the dependent variable is an ordinal measure (0 = never, 1 = less than once/ month, 2 = about once/month, . . . , 7 = at least once per day), but it nevertheless seems reasonable to average those values.

```
# Plotting Video Game data from Gentile(2009)

videoData <- c(4.8, 4.8, 4.9, 4.4, 5.4, 4.8, 3.6, 4.1, 3.4, 3.7, 2.9)
age <- c(8,9,10,11,12,13,14,15,16,17,18)
    ## You could also use age <- c(8:18)
plot(videoData  ~  age, type = "l", ylim = c(2,6), ylab = "Mean
  Frequency", col = "red", lwd = 3)  #lwd = line width   "~" is read as
  "as a function of", "l" = "line"
```

This graph can be reproduced in SPSS by selecting `Graphs/Legacy Dia-logs/Line`, specifying that `Data in Chart` represents values of individual cases, and then setting `Line Represents` to Frequency and `Category Labels` to Age. The data are at www.uvm.edu/~dhowell/fundamentals9/DataFiles/Fig3-6.dat (or "Fig3-6.sav" for a SPSS system file). The data for hours spent on video games are also in that file.

In creating this graph I have connected the data points with a line, making it a **line graph**, rather than bars, which would be a bar graph. I did this because it seems appropriate given the ordinal nature of the independent variable (Age). Notice that this graph nicely illustrates the decrease in the frequency of use as players age. The interesting thing is that if you drew a similar graph for the mean hours per week of video game play, the line would be relatively flat. Apparently the *frequency* of play declines with age, but the amount of time spent on each occasion increases.

It may seem rather obvious to say so, but the most important thing in making sense of a graph is to first identify what is plotted on each axis. Then identify the

Figure 3.6 Frequency of video game sessions as a function of age

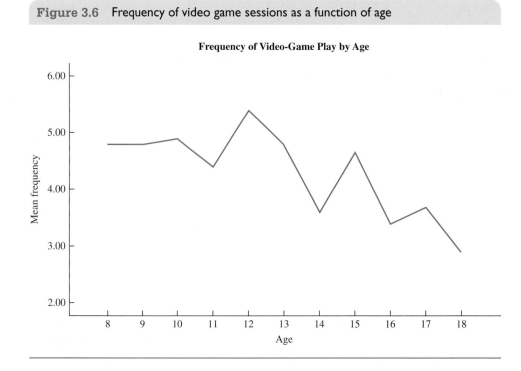

Frequency of Video-Game Play by Age

dependent and independent variables, and, finally, look for patterns in the data. In histograms we are looking for the shape of the distribution and usually hoping to see that it is at least highest toward the center. For bar graphs (Figure 3.5) and line graphs (Figure 3.6) we are generally looking for differences between groups and/or trends in the data. Often, the choice between a bar graph and a line graph is a matter of preference, though there are many people with strongly held views on this topic. If one of them is your instructor, you should pay close attention to what he or she says.

Axes on graphs

Vertical axis, Y axis, ordinate: All ways of naming the vertical axis
Horizontal axis, X axis, abscissa: All ways of naming the horizontal axis

In a histogram, the X axis represents the scores on the dependent variable
In a line graph or bar graph, the independent variable generally goes on the X axis.

3.4 | Alternative Methods of Plotting Data

The previous sections dealt with only a few ways of plotting data. Data can be represented in an almost unlimited number of other ways, some of which are quite ingenious and informative, and some of which obscure what the data have to say.

Two comments are in order about how we plot data. First, the point of representing data graphically is to communicate to an audience. If there is a better way to communicate, then use it. Rules of graphical presentation are intended as guides to clearer presentation, not as prescriptive rules that may never be broken. This point was made earlier in the discussion about the number of intervals that should be used for a histogram, but it goes beyond histograms. So the first "rule" is this: *If it aids understanding, do it; if it doesn't, please don't.* A great reference for plotting data is a paper by Howard Wainer (1984) entitled "*How to display data badly.*" You can learn a lot from that paper, and many other papers by Wainer. It is available as a pdf file on the Web at https://www.rci.rutgers.edu/~roos/Courses/grstat502/wainer.pdf

The second rule is to keep things simple. Generally, the worst graphics are those that include irrelevant features that only add to the confusion. Tufte (1983) calls such material "chart junk," and you should avoid it. Perhaps the worst sin, in the opinion of many, is plotting something in three dimensions that could be better plotted in two. (I think that is even worse than using a pie chart.) There are occasionally legitimate reasons for three-dimensional plots, but three dimensions are more likely to confuse the issue than to clarify it. Unfortunately, most graphics packages written for corporate users (often called "presentation graphics") encourage the addition of unnecessary dimensions. Graphics should look utilitarian, neat, and orderly; they should rarely look "pretty." If you think you need three dimensions to represent the material, ask yourself if the reader is going to be able to understand what you're trying to show. Often the third dimension either makes the figure visually uninterpretable or it adds a level of complexity that many of us are not prepared to handle. If you have taken a psychology course on perception, you will know that the eye is great at handling three-dimensional objects in three-dimensional space. But our eyes (and brains) play tricks on us when they try to handle three-dimensional

Figure 3.7 Disposition of those under correctional supervision

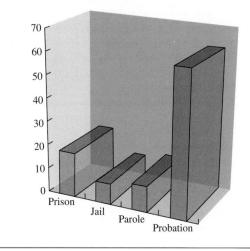

objects in two-dimensional space. Figure 3.7 is a deliberately poorly constructed version of a graph that purports to show the disposition of people under correctional supervision. Can you tell whether there are more people in jail than on parole? What percentage of those in the correctional system are on parole? Glance ahead to Figure 6.2 (p. 110) to see a much clearer way of presenting these data.

Figure 3.8 is a back-to-back display of the distribution, by age and gender, of the populations of Mexico, Spain, the United States, and Sweden. This figure clearly portrays differences between countries in terms of their age distributions (compare Mexico and Sweden, for example). By having males and females plotted back to back, we can also see the effects of gender differences in life expectancy. The older age groups in three countries contain more females than males. In Mexico, it appears that men begin to outnumber women in their early 20s. This type of distribution was common in the past, when many women died in childbirth, and we might start looking there for an explanation. The purpose in presenting graphs such as these is to illustrate that simple graphs can tell a compelling story.

Guidelines for plotting data

- Supply a main title

- Always label the axes

- Try to start both the X and Y axis at 0. If you can't, break the axis with —⋀— if that makes sense

- Pie charts: Don't! Please! They are very difficult to read accurately

- Try not to plot in more than two dimensions

- Avoid adding nonessential material

Figure 3.8   Population for selected countries by sex and age; 1970

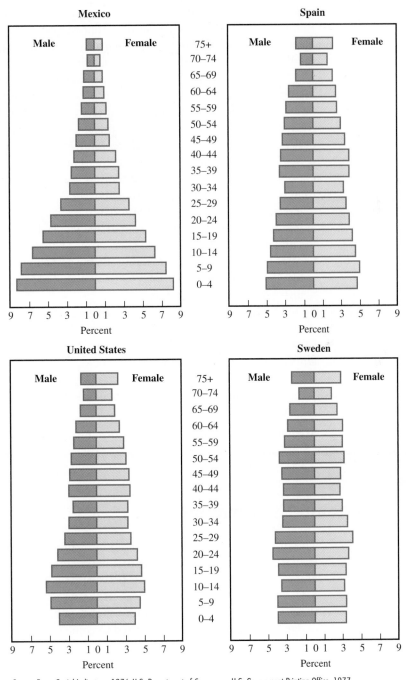

Source: From *Social Indicators: 1976*, U.S. Department of Commerce, U.S. Government Printing Office, 1977.

I thought that she was a nurse!

One of the most important contributors to the early use of graphics was someone that you probably never thought of in that way—but the early use of graphs by Florence Nightingale (1820–1910) showed the power of graphics and led to a number of ways of presenting data visually.

When the Crimean War broke out in 1854, the British government sent Nightingale to Turkey with a team of nurses. She was disturbed by the lack of sanitary conditions and fought the military establishment for years to improve the quality of care. Most importantly to statistics, she collected data on the causes of death among soldiers, and used her connections to publicize her results. She was able to show that soldiers were many times more likely to die from illnesses contracted as a result of poor sanitation in the hospitals, or wounds left untreated, than to die from enemy fire. She created a complicated graphic using polar area diagrams whose areas were proportional to the cause of deaths. Among other graphics, Nightingale created a simple line graph showing the death rates of civilian and military personnel during peacetime. The data were further broken down by age. The implications were unmistakable and emphasize the importance of controlling confounding variables. Her work led to significant improvements in health care within the military.

For the rest of her life, Florence Nightingale fought for improved health standards and was not afraid to take on the British government on almost any topic. Though she had no formal training in statistics, she was elected the first female fellow of the Royal Statistical Society in 1858 and an honorary member of the American Statistical Association a few years later.

You can read more about Florence Nightingale in Howell (2005) and an interesting biography of her at

http://www.biographyonline.net/humanitarian/florence-nightingale.html

3.5 Describing Distributions

The distributions of scores illustrated in Figures 3.1 and 3.2 were more or less regularly shaped distributions, rising to a maximum and then dropping away smoothly. Not all distributions are like that, however (see the stem-and-leaf display in Figure 3.4), and it is important to understand the terms used to describe different distributions. Consider the two distributions shown in Figure 3.9(a) and (b). These plots are of data that were computer-generated to come from populations with specific shapes. They, and the other two in Figure 3.9, are based on samples of 1,000 observations, and the slight irregularities are just random variability. The distributions in Figures 3.9(a) and (b) are called **symmetric** because they have the same shape on both sides of the center. The distribution shown in Figure 3.9(a) came from what we will later refer to as a normal distribution. The distribution in Figure 3.9(b) is referred to as **bimodal**, because it has two peaks. The term *bimodal* is used to refer to any distribution that has two predominant peaks, whether or not those peaks are of exactly the

> **Figure 3.9**   Shapes of frequency distributions: (a) Normal; (b) Bimodal; (c) Negatively skewed; (d) Positively skewed

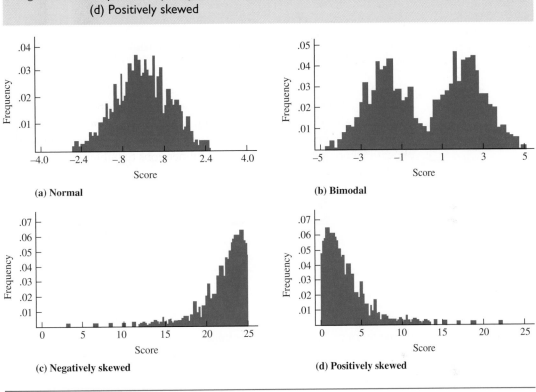

same height. If a distribution has only one major peak, it is called **unimodal**. The term used to refer to the number of major peaks in a distribution is **modality**.

Next consider Figure 3.9(c) and (d). These two distributions obviously are not symmetric. The distribution in Figure 3.9(c) has a tail going out to the left, whereas that in Figure 3.9(d) has a tail going out to the right. We say that the former is **negatively skewed** and the latter **positively skewed**. (*Hint*: To help you remember which is which, notice that negatively skewed distributions point to the negative, or small, numbers, and that positively skewed distributions point to the positive end of the scale.) There are statistical measures of the degree of asymmetry, or **skewness**, but they are not commonly used in the behavioral sciences. You have previously seen one positively skewed distribution in Figure 3.1.

An interesting real-life example of a positively skewed distribution is shown in Figure 3.10. These data were generated by Bradley (1963), who instructed subjects to press a button as quickly as possible whenever a small light came on. Most of the data points are smoothly distributed between roughly 7 and 17 hundredths of a second, but a small but noticeable cluster of points lies between 30 and 70 hundredths, trailing off to the right. This second cluster of points was obtained primarily from trials on which the subject missed the button on the first try and had to try again. Their inclusion in the data significantly affects the distribution's shape. An experimenter who had such a collection of data might seriously consider treating times greater than

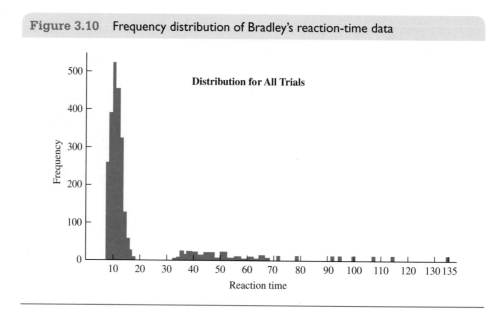

Figure 3.10   Frequency distribution of Bradley's reaction-time data

some maximum separately, on the grounds that those times were more a reflection of the *accuracy* of a psychomotor response than a measure of the *speed* of that response.

Nearly every textbook author feels the need to discuss another measure of the shape of a distribution, called its kurtosis. But very few people know what it really measures, and even fewer have ever used it. We will skip it here, but if you are really curious, enter "kurtosis Wuensch" as search terms in a search engine. Karl Wuensch knows much more about kurtosis than I even want to know.

It is important to recognize that relatively large samples of data are needed before we can have a good idea about the shape of a distribution. With sample sizes of around 30, the best we can reasonably expect to see is whether the data tend to pile up in the center of the distribution or are markedly skewed in one direction or another.

3.6   Using SPSS to Display Data

As I said earlier, almost all statistics texts once assumed that simple data analyses will be carried out by hand with the help of a standard calculator. This may be the best approach to teaching, though I don't think so, but today computer programs carry out more and more analyses. Thus you need to know how to read and interpret the results of computer printouts. We have already seen examples of plotting data using *R* and SPSS. Most chapters in this book will include samples of computer solutions for examples previously analyzed by hand. I will focus primarily on *R* and SPSS. As I have said elsewhere, I chose *R* because it is freely available for download to any computer, it is becoming an important data analysis tool in psychology and other disciplines, and it is the kind of software you can use along with your reading. I chose SPSS because it is the most commonly available "heavy-duty" program and is often requested by instructors. But anything that I do here can probably be done with any program you can get your hands on. We have already seen what *R* can do, so I will focus here on SPSS.

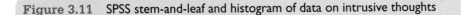

Figure 3.11 SPSS stem-and-leaf and histogram of data on intrusive thoughts

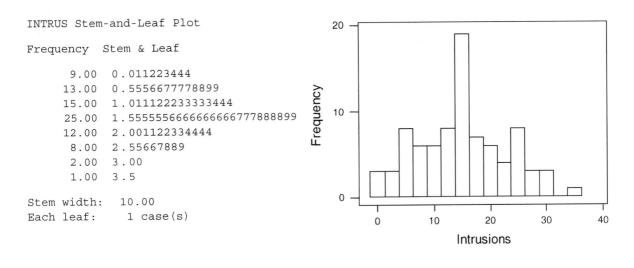

```
INTRUS Stem-and-Leaf Plot

Frequency   Stem & Leaf

     9.00   0 . 011223444
    13.00   0 . 5556677778899
    15.00   1 . 011122233333444
    25.00   1 . 5555556666666666777888899
    12.00   2 . 001122334444
     8.00   2 . 55667889
     2.00   3 . 00
     1.00   3 . 5

Stem width:    10.00
Each leaf:      1 case(s)
```

Figure 3.11 shows a histogram and a stem-and-leaf display produced by SPSS for the data on intrusive thoughts shown in Figure 3.2. (In SPSS the stem-and-leaf plot is found under *Analyze/Descriptives/Explore*.) These plots are somewhat different from the ones that we obtained earlier, owing to the amount of grouping that was done.

So far in our discussion almost no mention has been made of the numbers themselves. We have seen how data can be organized and presented in the form of distributions, and we have discussed a number of ways in which distributions can be characterized. These are symmetry or its lack (skewness) and modality. As useful as this information might be in certain situations, it is inadequate in others. We still do not know the average speed of a simple mental rotation reaction time nor how alike or dissimilar are the reaction times for individual trials. Nor do we know the mean scores for students who did, and who did not, attend my class. To obtain this knowledge, we must reduce the data to a set of measures that carry the information we need. The questions to be asked refer to the location, or central tendency, and to the dispersion, or variability, of the distributions along the underlying scale. Measures of these characteristics will be considered in the next two chapters.

3.7 Summary

In this chapter we discussed ways of describing distributions. We began by taking data in a table and condensing them to combine observations falling within an interval, such as 1.90–1.99. In doing so, we recorded the number of observations in each interval. We designated the lower and upper limits as those points cutting off the ends of the intervals (e.g., 1.895 and 1.995) and the midpoint as the center of the interval (e.g., 1.95). We then represented those data in a histogram, with the different values of our dependent variable (e.g., reaction time) along the X, or horizontal, axis and the frequency for each interval along the Y, or vertical, axis.

We next spent time discussing stem-and-leaf displays and their uses. In a stem-and-leaf display the most significant (or perhaps the two most significant) digit(s) form the stem, the next most significant digit forms the leaf, and any other less significant digits are discarded. Such displays are particularly good when drawn back to back, allowing us to compare data from two different groups or categories. We briefly touched on bar graphs and line graphs. For these, the levels of the independent variable are placed on the X axis. Some outcome measure, such as the group averages or the value of some other variable (such as life expectancy) is plotted on the Y axis. I made the point that a graph should be as plain and simple as possible so as not to confuse the reader with irrelevant dimensions or other information.

Finally, we examined some of the terms that are used to describe distributions. A symmetric distribution is one that has the same shape around the center of the distribution, while a skewed distribution is asymmetric. A positively skewed distribution has a tail going off to the right, while a negatively skewed distribution has a tail to the left.

Key Terms

Frequency distribution, 37	Outliers, 45
Real lower limit, 37	Bar graph, 47
Real upper limit, 37	Line graph, 48
Midpoint, 37	Symmetric, 52
Histogram, 38	Bimodal, 52
Stem-and-leaf display, 42	Unimodal, 53
Exploratory data analysis (EDA), 42	Modality, 53
Leading digits (most significant digits), 42	Negatively skewed, 53
Stem, 42	Positively skewed, 53
Trailing digits (less significant digits), 43	Skewness, 53
Leaves, 43	

3.8 A Quick Review

A. The primary purpose of plotting data is to make them _____.
   Ans: interpretable

B. The endpoints of an interval are called _____.
   Ans: the real upper (and lower) limits

C. A figure that plots various values of the dependent variable on the X axis and the frequencies on the Y axis is called a _____.
Ans: histogram—though some people also refer to it as a frequency distribution

D. The optimal number of intervals for a histogram (and for a stem-and-leaf display) is _____.
Ans: whatever makes the figure show the most useful description of the data without creating too many or too few intervals

E. List three important things about a stem-and-leaf display.
Ans: It can be used to present both the shape of a distribution and the actual values of the scores; it can be used back-to-back to compare two related distributions; it can be adjusted to handle different sized values for the dependent variable

F. List three different terms for describing the shape of a distribution.
Ans: Symmetry, modality, and skewness

G. A positively skewed distribution has a tail stretching out to the right. (T or F)
Ans: True

H. A major characteristic of a good graphic is _____.
Ans: simplicity

I. In the next two chapters we are going to extend our description of data to _____.
Ans: describing the center of a distribution and its variability or spread

3.9 Exercises

3.1 Have you ever wondered how you would do on the SATs if you didn't even bother to read the passage you were asked about?[5] Katz, Lautenschlager, Blackburn, and Harris (1990) asked students to answer SAT-type questions without seeing the passage on which the questions were based. This was called the NoPassage group. Data closely resembling what they obtained follow, where the dependent variable was the individual's score on the test.

54 52 51 50 36 55 44 46 57 44 43 52 38 46

55 34 44 39 43 36 55 57 36 46 49 46 49 47

a) Plot a histogram for these data—either by hand or by using R or SPSS.
b) What is the general shape of the distribution?

3.2 Make a stem-and-leaf display for the data in Exercise 3.1 using a reasonable number of intervals.

3.3 Use R to reproduce the stem-and-leaf display of the data in Figure 3.3. The code can be found in Section 3.2.

3.4 If students had just guessed in the Katz et al. study, they would have been expected to earn a score of approximately 20. Do these students appear to do better than chance even when they haven't read the passage?

3.5 As part of the study described in Exercise 3.1, the experimenters obtained the same kind of data from a smaller group who had read the passage before answering the questions (called the Passage group). Their data follow.

66 75 72 71 55 56 72 93 73 72 72 73 91 66 71 56 59

---

[5]For those readers outside the United States, SAT exams are exams taken by many, though by no means all, students seeking admission to American universities. There is a Math and a Verbal section to this exam, and scores typically range from 200 to 800 for each section, with an average somewhere around 500. We will refer to SAT scores occasionally throughout this book.

a) What can you tell just by looking at these numbers? Do students do better when they have read the passage?

b) Plot these data by hand on one side of a stem-and-leaf display and the NoPassage data on the other side of the same stem-and-leaf display.

c) What can you see by looking at this stem-and-leaf display?

d) A further discussion of this example can be found at

https://www.uvm.edu/~dhowell/fundamentals9/Chapters/Chapter3/Katzfolder/katz.html

although it also covers material that we will discuss later in this book.

3.6 In Chapter 2, Exercise 2.4, I asked those with access to SPSS to go to the book's website, find the short SPSS manual, and download the apgar.sav file. If you have SPSS but did not do that exercise, go back and read the manual to see how to download the file and then open it in SPSS. The introduction to that Web page describes the data. Read the first three chapters (they are *very* short) and then read Chapter 4 on describing and graphing data. (That chapter is a bit longer, but most of that is taken up with graphics.) Recreate the frequency distributions and graphs that are shown there, varying the coarseness of the display.

3.7 Use SPSS or *R* to load and plot the data on mental rotation reaction times that were presented (in part) in Table 3.1. These data can be found in the data files of this book's website as Tab3-1.dat, and you will probably have to read the material in Chapter 3 of the manual on how to import text data.

3.8 Go to the Web pages at http://www.uvm.edu/~dhowell/fundamentals9/Supplements/IntroducingR.html. Skim that page for information on *R* and then read the section on "Simple Examples," referenced at the bottom of the page.

The next two exercises refer to a large data set in Appendix D. The data can also be downloaded from the Web at

https://www.uvm.edu/~dhowell/fundamentals9/DataFiles/Add.dat

These data come from a research study by Howell and Huessy (1985), which is described at the beginning of the appendix. We will refer to them throughout the book.

3.9 Create a histogram for the data for GPA in Add.dat, using reasonable intervals. You can do this by hand or by using any available software.

3.10 Create a stem-and-leaf display for the ADDSC score in Add.dat, again using any available software.

3.11 What three interesting facts about the populations of Mexico and Spain can be seen in Figure 3.10?

3.12 In some stem-and-leaf displays with one or two unusually low values, the first stem is often written as LOW, with the complete values in the leaf section. Why and when might we do this?

3.13 How would you describe the distributions of the grades of students who did, and did not, attend class in Figure 3.4? Why would you have expected this kind of distribution even before you saw the data?

3.14 In Table 3.1 the reaction-time data are broken down by the degrees of rotation separating the objects. (You may want to sort the data by this variable.) Use SPSS or another computer program to plot separate histograms of these data as a function of the Angle of rotation. (You can do it in *R*, but it requires things you don't yet know. See the Web page for this chapter.) These data are available at

Figure 3.12 From Cohen, Kaplan, et al. (1992)

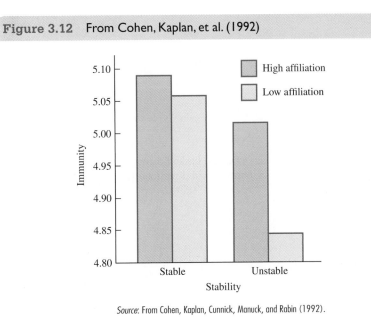

Source: From Cohen, Kaplan, Cunnick, Manuck, and Rabin (1992).

https://www.uvm.edu/~dhowell/fundamentals9/DataFiles/MentalRotation.dat

3.15 When Krantz devised the experiment that produced the data in Table 3.1, he was interested in seeing whether the required degree of mental rotation influenced reaction time. From the answer to Exercise 3.14, what would you conclude about this question?

3.16 In addition to comparing the reaction times as a function of rotation, how else might you use these data to draw conclusions about how people process information?

3.17 One frequent assumption in statistical analyses is that observations are independent of one another (knowing one response tells you nothing about the magnitude of another response). How would you characterize the reaction time data in Table 3.1, just based on what you know about how it was collected? (A lack of independence would not invalidate anything we have done with these data in this chapter, though it might have an effect on more complex analyses.)

3.18 Figure 3.12 is adapted from a paper by Cohen, Kaplan, Cunnick, Manuck, and Rabin (1992), which examined the immune response of nonhuman primates raised in stable and unstable social groups. In each group animals were classed as high or low in affiliation, measured in terms of the amount of time they spent in close physical proximity to other animals. Higher scores on the immunity measure represent greater immunity to disease. Write two or three sentences describing what these results would seem to suggest.

3.19 Rogers and Prentice-Dunn (1981) had 96 White male undergraduates deliver shocks to their fellow subjects as part of a biofeedback study. They recorded the amount of shock that the subjects delivered to White participants and Black participants when the subjects had and had not been insulted by the experimenter. Their results are shown in Figure 3.13. Interpret these results. (One of my earlier guidelines said to start each axis at zero or break the axis. Why does that not make sense here?)

Figure 3.13 From Rogers and Prentice-Dunn (1981)

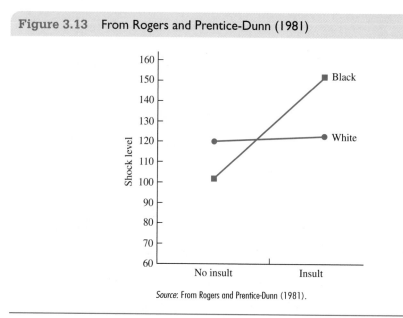

Source: From Rogers and Prentice-Dunn (1981).

3.20 The following data represent U.S. college enrollments by census categories as measured in 1982, 1991, and 2005. (The 2005 data are approximate.) Plot the data in a form that represents the changing enrollment patterns of college students in the United States from 1982 to 2005. (The data entries are in 1,000s, and the 1991 data are shown simply for your information.)

Ethnic Group	1982	1991	2005
White	9,997	10,990	11,774
Black	1,101	1,335	2,276
Native American	88	114	179
Hispanic	519	867	1935
Asian	351	637	1,164
Foreign	331	416	591

You can find additional longitudinal data at

 http://trends.collegeboard.org/education-pays/figures-tables/immediate-enrollment-rates-race-ethnicity-1975-2008

3.21 The *New York Times* (March 16, 2009) reported that approximately 3% of the population of Washington, D.C., was living with HIV/AIDS. Search the Web for worldwide statistics that would put that number in context.

3.22 The following data represent the total number of U.S. households, the number of households headed by women, and family size from 1960 to 1990. Present these data in a way that reveals any changes in U.S. demographics. What do the data suggest about how a social scientist might look at the problems facing the United States? (Households are given in 1,000s.) (For more recent data to 2011, see http://www.pewsocialtrends.org/2013/05/29/breadwinner-moms/, which points out that the median family income for families led by a single mom is $23,000.)

Year	Total Households	Households Headed by Women	Family Size
1960	52,799	4,507	3.33
1970	63,401	5,591	3.14
1975	71,120	7,242	2.94
1980	80,776	8,705	2.76
1985	86,789	10,129	2.69
1987	89,479	10,445	2.66
1988	91,066	10,608	2.64
1989	92,830	10,890	2.62
1990	92,347	10,890	2.63

3.23 Modify the *R* code given for Figure 3.6 to reproduce the figure in the previous exercise.

3.24 Repeat Exercise 3.23, but this time plot changes in family size.

3.25 Moran (1974) presented data on the relationship, for Australian births, between maternal age and Down syndrome (a serious handicapping condition on which psychologists have done a lot of work). The data follow, though in a form that may require some minor calculations on your part to be meaningful. What can you conclude from these results?

Age of Mother	Total Number of Births	Number of Births with Down Syndrome
20 or less	35,555	15
20–24	207,931	128
25–29	253,450	208
30–34	170,970	194
35–39	86,046	197
40–44	24,498	240
45 or more	1,707	37

3.26 Further information on Down Syndrome and maternal age can be found at

 https://www.aafp.org/afp/20000815/825.html

3.27 Does the month in which you were born relate to your later mental health? Fombonne (1989) took all children referred to a psychiatric clinic in Paris with a diagnosis of psychosis and sorted them by birth month. (There were 208 such children.) He had a control group of 1,040 children referred with other problems. The data are given below, along with the percentage in the general population born in that month.

	Jan	Feb	Mar	Apr	May	Jun	Jul	Aug	Sep	Oct	Nov	Dec	Total
Psychosis	13	12	16	18	21	18	15	14	13	19	21	28	208
Control	83	71	88	114	86	93	87	70	83	80	97	88	1040
% General Population	8.4	7.8	8.7	8.6	9.1	8.5	8.7	8.3	8.1	8.1	7.6	8.0	100%

a)   How will you adjust (transform) the Psychosis and Control groups' data so that all three data sets can fit on the same graph?

b)   How will you plot the data?

c)   Plot the data.

d)   Do those diagnosed with psychosis appear to differ from the general population?

e)   What purpose does the Control group play?

f)   What do you conclude?

3.28 Psychologists concerned about self-injurious behaviors (e.g., smoking, eating fatty diets, drug abuse, etc.) worry about the effects of maternal smoking on the incidence of low birth weight babies, who are known to be at risk for developmental problems. The Centers for Disease Control and Prevention has published statistics relating maternal smoking to low birth weight. The data follow in terms of the percentage of birth weights < 2,500 grams. Find a way to present these data that illustrates this relationship clearly. Why is this relationship not likely to be a statistical fluke?

	1989	1990	1991	1992	1993
Smokers	11.36%	11.25	11.41	11.49	11.84
NonSmokers	6.02	6.14	6.36	6.35	6.56

3.29 Additional (and more recent) data on smoking and low birthweight (in Switzerland) can be found at

 http://www.smw.ch/docs/pdf200x/2005/35/smw-11122.pdf

Plot those data (and/or other data that you can find on the Web) and draw the appropriate conclusions.

3.30 The *Journal of Statistics Education* maintains a fairly extensive collection of data on a wide variety of topics. Each data set is accompanied by a description of the data and how they might be used. These data are available at

 http://www.amstat.org/publications/jse/jse_data_archive.htm

Go to this Internet link, find a set of data that interests you, and display those data in a way that makes their meaning clear. For most of these data sets you will want to use some sort of computer software, although that is not a requirement. (It might be easier to use SPSS at this point, but *R* will work fine when you know a bit more.) There are many things that could be done with the data that we have not yet covered, but displaying the data will reveal much that is of interest.

3.31 The following graph plots the data on life expectancy of White and Black females. What conclusions would you draw from this graph? (Comparable data for men can be found at

http://www.elderweb.com/book/appendix/1900-2000-changes-life-expectancy-united-states)

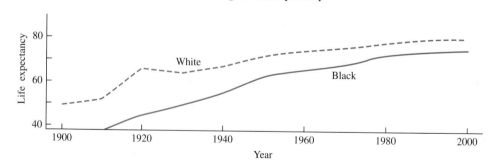

3.32 Using the data on men found at the website given above, plot that line graph in *R*. To get both lines on the same graph, draw one plot, enter "par = new", and then draw the second plot.

3.33 In 1970, at the height of the Vietnam War, the U.S. government held a lottery to determine which individuals would be drafted. Balls representing the 366 possible birthdays were drawn from an urn, and the order in which the days were drawn represented the order in which young males would be drafted. (If your birthday was one of those selected early, you would have a low selection number and a very high probability of being drafted, and if it was one of those with a high selection number, you probably would not be called.) That particular lottery received considerable criticism because people born late in the year appeared much more likely to receive a low number. (The average selection number for those born in December was 121.5, while the average selection number for those born in January was 201.2.)

The results appear below. Graph these data and draw appropriate conclusions. There is every reason to believe that those who carried out the lottery did their best to be fair, but if you were one of those eligible to be drafted, would you be satisfied with the result? How might you explain these results? More complete data are available at

 http://www.amstat.org/publications/jse/v5n2/datasets.starr.html

Jan	Feb	Mar	Apr	May	June	July	Aug	Sept	Oct	Nov	Dec
201.2	203.0	225.8	203.7	208.0	195.7	181.5	173.5	157.3	182.5	148.7	121.5

3.34 Use R to reproduce display Figure 3.4 as a boxplot instead of back-to-back stem-and-leaf displays. The command is boxplot(y ~ x), where "~" is read "as a function of" and x and y are the relevant variables. Just experiment.

3.35 Use R to produce the back-to-back stem-and-leaf display in Figure 3.4—stored as Fig3-4.dat. This is a tricky one, and it is more of a puzzle to work on. Can you get it to work? I suggest that you look at

http://exploredata.wordpress.com/2012/08/28/back-to-back-stemplots/

Ignore his reference to LearnEDA—it no longer exists. Instead, use "install.packages(aplpack)" and then "library(aplpack)." The data file is available at www.uvm.edu/~dhowell/fundamentals9/DataFiles/Fig3-4.dat. The data are tab separated, so use sep = "\t"

(The Web page on R for this chapter contains the necessary code for a different data set, but see if you can work it out for yourself. It's fun when it finally works. The code using the dropbox feature is also there.)

## CHAPTER 4

Measures of Central Tendency

In this chapter we look at measures of what is called **central tendency**, a term which refers to measures that relate to the center of a distribution of scores. The most common measures are the mean, which is what we usually mean by average; the median, which is the middle score; and the mode, which is the most common score. We will consider the advantages and disadvantages of each, because no one measure is universally better than another. We will then look at how we can use computer software to calculate these measures and will look at printout from SPSS and R. In the next chapter we will go a step further and look at measures that deal with how the observations are scattered around that central tendency, but first we must address identifying the center of the distribution.

In Chapter 3 you saw how to display data in ways that allow us to begin to draw some conclusions about what the data have to say. Plotting data shows the general shape of the distribution and gives a visual sense of the general magnitude of the numbers involved. Some of the graphs in Chapter 3 had "averages" plotted on the *Y* (vertical) axis, and those averages play a central role in this chapter.

CONCEPTS THAT YOU WILL NEED TO REMEMBER FROM PREVIOUS CHAPTERS

Independent variable:	The variable you manipulate or are studying
Dependent variable:	The variable that you are measuring—the data
Modality:	The number of meaningful peaks in a distribution
Σ	The symbol for summation of what follows
Symmetric distribution:	A distribution that has the same shape on either side of the center

Variables are often labeled with a single letter, frequently *X* or *Y*

4.1 The Mode

The **mode (Mo)**, which is the least used (and least useful) measure, can be defined simply as the most common score, that is, the score obtained from the largest number of subjects. Thus the mode is that value of X, the dependent variable that corresponds to the highest point on the distribution. In the example in Chapter 3 that dealt with reaction times in a mental rotation task (see Table 3.2), the values in the interval 1.50 to 1.59 occurred 50 times, making that interval the modal interval. (If you want a single number as the mode, take the midpoint of that interval, which is 1.55. This can be seen clearly in Figure 3.1)

If two *adjacent* times occur with equal (and greatest) frequency, a common convention is to take an average of the two values and call that the mode. If, on the other hand, two *nonadjacent* reaction times occur with equal (or nearly equal) frequency, we say that the distribution is bimodal and would most likely report both modes. You can see in Figure 3.1 that several intervals were nearly as frequent as the one mentioned earlier. In reporting your results you should probably make reference to that fact and mention that the most common responses fell between 1.00 and 1.60 or 1.70. That is more informative to your audience than stating that the mode was 1.55. When we are speaking of the modality of a distribution, we are speaking of prominent characteristics of the distribution, not the results of minor fluctuations in our particular sample.

4.2 The Median

The **median (Mdn)** is most easily defined as the middle score in an ordered set or data. By this definition the median is also called the 50th percentile.[1] For example, consider the numbers (5, 8, 3, 7, 15). If the numbers are arranged in numerical order (3, 5, 7, 8, 15), the middle score is 7, and it would be called the median. Suppose, however, that there were an even number of scores, for example (5, 11, 3, 7, 15, 14). Rearranging, we get (3, 5, 7, 11, 14, 15), and there is no middle score. That point actually falls between the 7 and the 11. In such a case, the average (9) of the two middle scores (7 and 11) is commonly taken as the median.[2]

A term that we will need shortly is the **median location**, which is the position in an ordered distribution occupied by the median. The median location of N numbers is defined as

$$\text{Median location} = (N + 1)/2$$

---

[1]The specific percentile is defined as the point on a scale at or below which a specified percentage of the scores fall.

[2]The definition of the median is another one of those things over which statisticians love to argue. The definition given here, in which the median is defined as a *point* on a distribution of numbers, is the one most critics prefer. It is also in line with the statement that the median is the 50th percentile. On the other hand, there are many who are perfectly happy to say that the median is either the middle *number* in an ordered series (if N is odd) or the average of the two middle *numbers* (if N is even). Reading these arguments is a bit like going to a faculty meeting when there is nothing terribly important on the agenda. The less important the issue, the more there is to say about it.

Thus, for five numbers the median location $= (5 + 1)/2 = 3$, which simply means that the median is the third number in an ordered series. For 12 numbers the median location $= (12 + 1)/2 = 6.5$; the median falls between, and is the average of, the sixth and seventh numbers.

For the data on reaction times in Table 3.1, the median location $= (600 + 1)/2 = 300.5$. When the data are arranged in order, the 300.5th score is in the interval of 1.50–1.59, and so we take the midpoint of that interval (1.55) as our median. For the data on intrusive thoughts in the breast cancer patients presented in Figure 3.13, there are 85 scores, and the median location is $(85 + 1)/2 = 43$. We can tell from the stem-and-leaf display that the 43rd score is 15, which is the median.

4.3 The Mean

The most common measure of central tendency is the mean, or what people generally have in mind when they use the word *average*. The **mean** $(\overline{X})$ is the sum of the scores divided by the number of scores and is usually designated $\overline{X}$ (read "X bar"). (Almost everyone in statistics uses the "bar" notation, but the American Psychological Association (2010) prefers to use the letter M, though they will allow $\overline{X}$. I go along with most of their notation, but am not giving up the use of the bar notation—although I will use M in sections that discuss how to report the results of a study.) It is defined (using the summation notation given in Chapter 2) as

$$\overline{X} = \frac{\Sigma X}{N}$$

where ΣX is the sum of all values of X, and N is the number of X values. Therefore the mean of the numbers 3, 5, 12, and 5 is

$$(3 + 5 + 12 + 5)/4 = 25/4 = 6.25$$

You will see the notation $\overline{X}$, and often $\overline{Y}$, used throughout the text. You need to remember that they refer to the mean of that variable. That will always be the case when we put a bar over the name or abbreviation of a variable.

For the reaction time data illustrated in Table 3.1, the sum of the observations is 975.60 (in 10th-of-a-second units). When we divide that by $N = 600$, we get $975.60/600 = 1.626$. Notice that this answer is somewhat higher than the mode and the median, which we found to be about 1.55. The mean and the median will be close whenever the distribution is nearly symmetric (i.e., falls off symmetrically on either side of the mean). When the distribution is nearly symmetric and unimodal, the mode will also be in general agreement with the mean and median. But for asymmetric distributions, the mean, median, and mode can all be quite different from one another. The fact that Figure 3.1 is positively skewed is what gives us a somewhat larger mean.

We could calculate the mean for the intrusive-thoughts data by obtaining the raw data values from the stem-and-leaf display in Figure 3.11, summing those values, and dividing by 85. For that example, the sum of the values would be 1,298, and there are $N = 85$ values. Therefore, the mean would be $1{,}298/85 = 15.27$. Later in this chapter you will see how to use R and SPSS to save yourself considerable work in calculating the mean for large data sets.

- ■   Mode: Most common value; highest region of a distribution
- ■   Median: Middle value or mean of two middle values
- ■   Mean: What we normally mean by "average"; sum of observations divided by the number of observations

---

4.4   Relative Advantages and Disadvantages of the Mode, the Median, and the Mean

Only when the distribution is symmetric will the mean and the median be equal, and only when the distribution is symmetric and unimodal (having one modal point) will all three measures be the same. In all other cases—including almost all situations with which we will deal—some measure of central tendency must be chosen. A set of rules governing when to use a particular measure of central tendency would be convenient, but there are no such rules. Some idea of the strengths and weaknesses of each statistic is required to make intelligent choices among the three measures.

The Mode

The mode is the most commonly occurring score. By definition, then, it is a score that actually occurred, whereas the mean and sometimes the median may be values that never appear in the data. The mode also has the obvious advantage of representing the largest number of people having the same score. There has been a great deal of discussion recently of the salaries earned by people on Wall Street. If you told me the mean salary of everyone who works at Goldman Sachs, and I don't know what that is, it probably would not tell me very much. There are people earning huge salaries and many people, such as secretaries, earning more ordinary salaries. Similarly, I don't think that the median would tell me very much either. But if you gave me the modal salary, you are telling me something like "Most people at Goldman Sachs earn about \$ . . . ," and that I would find informative.

By definition, the probability that an observation drawn at random (X_i) will be equal to the mode is greater than the probability that it will be equal to any other specific score. Expressing this algebraically, we can say

$$p(X_i = mode) > p(X_i = any \ other \ score)$$

Finally, the mode has the advantage of being applicable to nominal data, which is obviously not true of the median or the mean.

The mode has its disadvantages, however. We have already seen that the mode depends on how we group our data. Moreover, it may not be particularly representative of the entire collection of numbers. This is especially true when the modal value is 0, such as would occur if we calculated the number of cigarettes each person in a group smokes in a day. Here the mode would be 0 because of the preponderance of nonsmokers, but it would tell us nothing about the behavior of smokers. You might consider the modal value for only the smokers, though you need to make clear what you did. (Note that the mean or median would be a lot more informative, but they, too, would be biased by the nonsmokers.)

The Median

The major advantage of the median, which it shares with the mode, is the fact that it is unaffected by extreme scores. Thus the medians of both (5, 8, 9, 15, 16) and (0, 8, 9, 15, 206) are 9. Many experimenters find this characteristic to be useful in studies in which extreme scores occasionally occur but have no particular significance. For example, the average trained rat can run down a short runway in approximately one to two seconds. Every once in a while this same rat will inexplicably stop halfway down, scratch himself, poke his nose at the photocells, and lie down to sleep. In that instance it is of no practical significance whether he takes 30 seconds or 10 minutes to get to the other end of the runway. It may even depend on when the experimenter gives up and pokes him with a pencil. If we ran a rat through three trials on a given day and his times were (1.2, 1.3, and 20 seconds), that would have the same meaning to us—in terms of what it tells us about the rat's knowledge of the task—as if his times were (1.2, 1.3, and 136.4 seconds). In both cases the median would be 1.3. Obviously, however, his daily *mean* would be quite different in the two cases (7.5 versus 46.3 seconds). In situations like this, experimenters often work with the median score over a block of trials. Similarly, when speaking of salaries and home prices, we often use the median in place of the corresponding means, although my Wall Street example was an exception. The median has the advantage of eliminating the influence of extreme scores.

A major disadvantage of the median is that it does not enter readily into equations and is thus more difficult to work with than the mean. It is also not as stable from sample to sample as is the mean, as we will see in the next chapter, and this often presents problems when we use the sample statistics to estimate parameters.

The Mean

Of the three principal measures of central tendency, the mean is by far the most common. It would not be too much of an exaggeration to say that for many people statistics is (unfortunately) nearly synonymous with the study of the mean.

As we have already seen, certain disadvantages are associated with the mean. It is influenced by extreme scores, its value may not actually exist in the data, and its interpretation in terms of the underlying variable being measured requires at least some faith in the interval properties of the data. You might be inclined to suggest politely that if the mean has all the disadvantages I have just ascribed to it, then maybe it should be quietly forgotten and allowed to slip into oblivion along with statistics like the "critical ratio," a statistical concept that hasn't been heard from in years. The mean, however, is made of sterner stuff.

The mean has several important advantages that far outweigh its disadvantages. Probably the most important of these from a historical point of view (though not necessarily from your point of view) is that the mean can be manipulated algebraically. In other words, we can use the mean in an equation and manipulate it through the normal rules of algebra, specifically because we can write an equation that defines the mean. Since you cannot write a standard equation for the mode or the median, you have no real way of manipulating those statistics using standard algebra. Whatever the mean's faults, this accounts in some part for its widespread application. The second important advantage of the mean is that it has several desirable properties with respect to its use as an estimate of the population mean. In particular, if we drew many samples from some population, the sample means that resulted would be more stable (less variable) estimates of the central tendency of that population than would the sample medians or modes. The fact that the sample mean (a statistic) is in general a better estimate of the population mean (a parameter) than is the mode or the median is a major reason that it is so widely used by statisticians.

Trimmed Means

We are going to go back for a moment and look at an old idea that has begun to take on a new life. When I discussed the mean I implied that one of our criteria for selecting a good statistic was how well it estimated the population parameter. Although the sample mean is generally a good estimate of the population mean, there are times when it doesn't do as well as we would like. Suppose that we have a badly skewed distribution, for example, or a heavy-tailed distribution—one with an unusual number of large or small values. Repeated samples from that population would have sample means that vary a great deal from one another. If in one sample you had one or more large values, its mean would be pulled in a positive direction. If the next sample didn't have an extreme value, its mean would be more centered on the distribution. Thus from sample to sample we would have quite different estimates of the population mean. One way around this problem is to use what are called **trimmed means**. To calculate a trimmed mean we take one or more of the largest and smallest values in the sample, set them aside, and take the mean of what remains. For a 10% trimmed mean, for example, we would set aside the largest 10% of the observations and the lowest 10% of the observations. The mean of what remained would be the 10% trimmed mean. (We always discard the same percentage of the scores from each end of the distribution.)

A number of people (e.g., Wilcox, 2003) have argued that we should make much more use of trimmed means. They claim that doing so would overcome some of the problems of overly wide populations and improve the conclusions we draw from experiments. (The general suggestion is to trim 10% or 20% from each end, but it depends on how variable the data are.) I will return to this problem later in the book and illustrate an advantage of trimmed means. For now, all you need to know is how a trimmed mean is defined.

> Trimmed means discard equal numbers of scores at each end of the distribution and take the mean of what remains. They are becoming more common in treating particularly skewed data.

4.5 | Obtaining Measures of Central Tendency Using SPSS and *R*

For small sets of data it is perfectly reasonable to compute measures of central tendency by hand. With larger sample sizes or data sets with many variables, however, it is much simpler to let a computer program do the work. SPSS is ideally suited to this purpose since it is easy to use, versatile, and widely available at many colleges and universities. (For instructions on the commands we would use in SPSS to obtain descriptive statistics as well as graphs, go to this book's website, navigate to the Short SPSS Manual, and look at Chapter 4.)

In Exercise 3.1 we had data from a study by Katz et al. (1990) on the performance of students who were asked to answer multiple-choice questions about a passage they had not read. These data are illustrated in Figure 4.1. We can obtain the

Figure 4.1 Score on items when passage not read

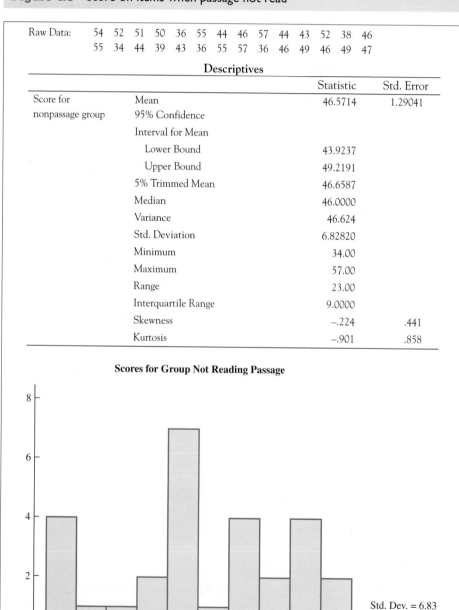

| Raw Data: | 54 52 51 50 36 55 44 46 57 44 43 52 38 46 |
| | 55 34 44 39 43 36 55 57 36 46 49 46 49 47 |

Descriptives

		Statistic	Std. Error
Score for nonpassage group	Mean	46.5714	1.29041
	95% Confidence Interval for Mean		
	Lower Bound	43.9237	
	Upper Bound	49.2191	
	5% Trimmed Mean	46.6587	
	Median	46.0000	
	Variance	46.624	
	Std. Deviation	6.82820	
	Minimum	34.00	
	Maximum	57.00	
	Range	23.00	
	Interquartile Range	9.0000	
	Skewness	–.224	.441
	Kurtosis	–.901	.858

Scores for Group Not Reading Passage

Std. Dev. = 6.83
Mean = 46.6
N = 28.00

> **Figure 4.2** *R* output of measures of central tendency

```
NumCorrect <- c(54, 52, 51, 50, 36, 55, 44, 46, 57, 44,43, 52, 38, 46,
                55, 34, 44, 39, 43, 36, 55, 57, 36, 46, 49, 46, 49, 47)
xbar <- mean(NumCorrect)
xbar.trim <- mean(Numcorrect, trim = .10)
med <- median(NumCorrect)
cat("The mean is = ", xbar,
    "\nThe 10% trimmed mean is ", xbar.trim, "\nThe median is = ", med)
hist(NumCorrect, main = "Number of Items Correct", breaks = 10, col =
"green")

    # For a more complete description of a variable or data frame
install.packages("psych")      # Needed only first time
library(psych)
describe(NumCorrect)

############################################################################
The mean is =  46.57143
The 10% trimmed mean is  46.66667
The median is =  46

>  vars n mean sd median trimmed mad min max range skew kurtosis se
   1 28 46.57 6.83 46 46.67 8.15 34 57 23 -0.2 -1.1 1.29
```

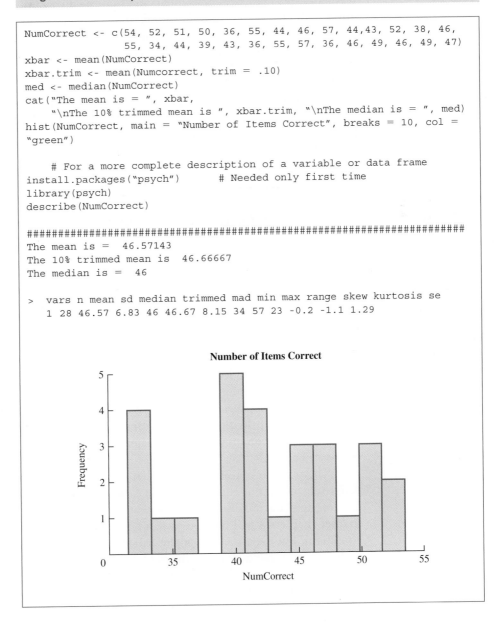

mean and the median directly, but to get the mode we need to produce a histogram (or a stem-and-leaf display) and then look for the most frequently appearing interval. The commands for SPSS are `Analyze/Descriptive Statistics/Explore`. You then move the variable in question (Score) to the Dependent Variable box, select whatever statistics you need, and examine the results. For the histogram you simply select `Graphs/Legacy Dialogs/Histogram`.

From the figure you can see that the mean (46.6), the median (46), and the mode (44) are approximately equal, and that the distribution is fairly smooth. We don't really have enough data to talk about skewness. We can also see from the histogram that there is variability in the scores of our 28 subjects. This dispersion on either side of the mean is discussed in the next chapter. There are many statistics in Figure 4.1 that we haven't discussed, but they will come up later in the book.

The basic measures of central tendency are also easily obtained using R. The code is shown in Figure 4.2, including the command to read the data. Notice that the histogram differs slightly from the one that SPSS produced simply because of minor differences in the way that they choose cut-points. Notice also that these data are an example of a case in which no measure of central tendency does a good job of describing the data—they are far too dispersed around any measure of central tendency.

4.6 | A Simple Demonstration—Seeing Statistics

Before we end this chapter, I think that you will find it interesting to make use of a small computer program (called a Java applet) produced by Gary McClelland at the University of Colorado. Dr. McClelland has produced a large number of applets and packaged them under the title *Seeing Statistics*. An overview can be found at

 http://www.seeingstatistics.com

though you would need to subscribe to view all of the applets. Many of those applets have been included on the website established for this book and are available free of charge. Simply go to https://www.uvm.edu/~dhowell/fundamentals9 /SeeingStatisticsApplets/Applets.html. We will refer to them many times throughout the text. **But as of the time of this writing, you need to make a small change to allow Java to function properly. See the note in the third paragraph on my Web page referenced above.**

The purpose of using these applets is to give you an opportunity to play an active role in learning this material and to allow you to illustrate for yourself many of the concepts that are discussed in the text. For example, when we come to the *t* test in later chapters, I will tell you what a *t* distribution would look like under certain conditions. But the associated applet will allow you to vary those conditions and actually see what that does to the distribution of *t*. I suspect that you will learn far more from what you do than from what I tell you.

It is my expectation that the applets will also assist in preparing for exams. Having worked through the short activities associated with each applet, you will have access to yet another way of retrieving information you have stored in memory. The more methods of access, the better the retrieval.

The first applet that we will use produces a set of meaningful data and illustrates an important principle of visual perception. To see this applet, simply go to

 https://www.uvm.edu/~dhowell/fundamentals9/SeeingStatisticsApplets /Applets.html

and follow the instructions. The applet you want is named Brightness Matching. Be sure to read the instructions on the opening page about Java applets. You may need to download free software (but probably won't), and sometimes the applets take a bit of time to load.

This Brightness Matching applet allows you to manipulate the brightness of a gray circle centered within a larger circle of a lighter or darker color. An example is shown in the accompanying figure. Your task is to adjust the center of the circle on the right to be the same shade of gray as the center of the circle on the left. That is surprisingly difficult to do accurately.

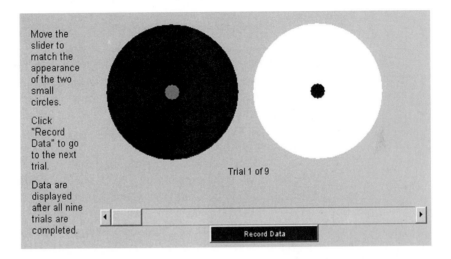

As you move the slider to the right, the center of the right circle will lighten. When you think that you have a match, click on the button labeled "Record Data." At this point another set of circles will appear and you will repeat the process. When you have made nine settings, the applet will present your data, showing you how accurate you were. (Write these data down or print them out, because you can't retrieve them once you move on.)

When I performed that task, I produced the following data.

Move the slider to match the appearance of the two small circles.	Trial	BG1	BG2	FG1	Match	Diff
	1	1.0	0.0	0.5	0.43	0.07
	2	0.25	0.75	0.4	0.7	-0.3
	3	0.5	0.5	0.6	0.62	-0.02
	4	0.75	0.25	0.5	0.37	0.13
	5	0.0	1.0	0.6	0.78	-0.18
Click "Record Data" to go to the next trial.	6	0.25	0.75	0.6	0.74	-0.14
	7	0.0	0.0	0.4	0.5	-0.1
	8	1.0	0.0	0.4	0.31	0.09
	9	1.0	1.0	0.5	0.53	-0.03

Data are displayed after all nine trials are completed.

Table 4.1 Results of nine trials of color matching

Left Background	Trials	Differences	Mean	Median
Lighter	2, 5, 6	−.30, −.18, −.14	−.21	−.18
Darker	1, 4, 8	.07, .13, .09	.10	.09
Equal	3, 7, 9	−.02, −.10, −.03	−.05	−.03

The headings "BG1" and "BG2" refer to the grayness of the left and right backgrounds (0 = White, 1 = Black). "FG1" refers to the grayness of the foreground (the center dot) on the left. "Match" refers to my setting for the dot on the right, and "Diff" is the difference in the setting for the two dots. A positive difference means that my setting was less gray than it should have been to match the dot on the left.

A general principle of human visual perception is that a dark background will cause a spot in the center to appear lighter than it actually is. Thus, in the example shown above, we would expect you to err by setting the center spot at the right lighter than it really should be. This means that the *difference* in brightness between the two center dots will be positive. This would apply to trials 1, 4, and 8. The reverse should happen on trials 2, 5, and 6, where the background on the left is lighter than the one on the right—here the differences should be negative. Finally, trials 3, 7, and 9 were control conditions, where the two backgrounds were the same, and we would expect the most accurate settings, and relatively small (positive or negative) differences.

For your own data calculate the mean and median differences under each of the three conditions described earlier. Create a table similar to Table 4.1.

- What do your data show with respect to the hypothesis outlined earlier?

- Would you have a preference for the mean over the median as the important statistic here?

- Why would the mode not be a useful measure?

- Why do you suppose that the three differences within any one line are not all the same? (This will be a very important point later when we refer to this variability of scores obtained under similar conditions as "random error.")

I chose to use this applet here because it serves several purposes. First, it gives you something active to do, rather than just to plod through what I have written. Second, it gives you a chance to collect real data on a real phenomenon. Third, it will allow you to examine those data in light of a set of reasonable hypotheses about human perceptions. Finally, although there are too few data points to get too excited about the actual measures of central tendency, you can make some interesting observations about the role of the mean and median, although the actual observations you make will depend, at least in part, on your personal data.

But going one step further, which will set us up for later material, I repeated this experiment five more times. The combined data, now with 18 observations (three observations for each of six replications) for each of our three conditions are given in Table 4.2.

You will notice that the means and medians have not changed very much, but, as we will see later, we have more faith in the stability of these new means as estimates of the population mean. We will come back to these data shortly.

Table 4.2   Results of 54 trials of color matching

Left Background	Replication	Trials	Differences	Mean	Median
Lighter	I	2, 5, 6	−.30, −.18, −.14	−.20	−.225
	2	2, 5, 6	−.27, −.22, −.28		
	3	2, 5, 6	−.22, −.12, −.25		
	4	2, 5, 6	−.27, −.25, −.10		
	5	2, 5, 6	−.27, −.19, .10		
	6	2, 5, 6	−.31, −.23, −.13		
Darker	I	1, 4, 8	.07, .13, .09	.09	.075
	2	1, 4, 8	.17, .03 −.02		
	3	1, 4, 8	.08, .03, .04		
	4	1, 4, 8	.05, .08, .12		
	5	1, 4, 8	.23, .06, .15		
	6	1, 4, 8	.16, .03, .07		
Equal	I	3, 7, 9	−.02, −.10, −.03	−.05.	−.045
	2	3, 7, 9	−.03, .05, −.06		
	3	3, 7, 9	.00, .00, −.11		
	4	3, 7, 9	.01, −.04, −.12		
	5	3, 7, 9	.01, −.14, −.12		
	6	3, 7, 9	−.05, −.13, −.10		

4.7   Summary

In this chapter we considered several measures used to describe the center of a distribution. The most frequently used measure is the mean, often represented by the symbol $\overline{X}$, which is simply what most of us learned in elementary school as the "average." You add up all of the scores and then divide by the number of scores, which is usually denoted as N. We went a bit further with the mean and discussed the trimmed mean, which is simply the mean of the data you have left when you drop some percentage of values at each end of the distribution. Trimming 10% at each end often proves useful. A third very useful measure of central tendency is the median, which is the middle value when you arrange your data in ascending or descending order. (If there are an even number of values, the median is the average of the two middle values.) Finally, we have the mode, which is that value (or set of values) that occurs most frequently in the distribution of outcomes.

The mean is the most commonly used measure of central tendency, but the median is very useful when you want to minimize the effect of extreme scores. When speaking about the salaries of sports figures, for example, the median salary is a more meaningful measure of how much players make, because, unlike the mean, it is not influenced by the huge salaries that a few players receive.

Key Terms

Central tendency, 64	Median location, 65
Mode (Mo), 65	Mean ($\overline{X}$ or M), 66
Median (Mdn), 65	Trimmed mean, 69

4.8 A Quick Review

A. Which of the measures of central tendency are you most likely to see reported in the popular press?
Ans: The mean

B. What do we report when a distribution has two distinct, and nonadjacent, modes?
Ans: You should report both. Similarly, you should report the mode of nonzero scores if zero more appropriately means "non-applicable."

C. When is the median most useful?
Ans: When we don't want extreme scores to influence the result.

D. Give two advantages of the mean relative to the other measures.
Ans: The mean gives a more stable estimate of the central tendency of a population over repeated sampling. The mean can be used algebraically.

E. Why do we use trimmed samples?
Ans: To eliminate the influence of extreme scores.

F. What is a good percentage to trim from a sample?
Ans: 10% or 20% from each end.

G. Do the data from the Seeing Statistics example support what perceptual psychology would expect us to see?
Ans: Yes

4.9 Exercises

4.1 As part of the Katz et al. (1990) study that examined test performance on a passage that a group of students had not read, the experimenters obtained the same kind of data from a smaller group of students who had read the passage (called the Passage group). Their data follow.

66 75 72 71 55 56 72 93 73 72 72 73 91 66 71 56 59

Calculate the mode, median, and the mean for these data.

4.2 The measures of central tendency for the data on Katz's study who did not read the passages were given in the SPSS printout in Figure 4.1. Compare those answers with the answers to Exercises 4.1. What do they tell you about the value of reading the passage on which questions are based?

4.3 If a student in Katz's study simply responded at random (even without reading the questions), she would be expected to get 20 items correct. How does this compare to the measures we found in Section 4.5? Why should this not surprise you?

4.4 Make up a set of data for which the mean is greater than the median.

4.5 Make up a positively skewed set of data. Does the mean fall above or below the median?

4.6 Plot the data for each of the three conditions in Table 4.2 and describe the results.

4.7 A group of 15 rats running a straight-alley maze required the following number of trials to perform to a predetermined criterion. The frequency distribution follows.

Trials to reach criterion	18	19	20	21	22	23	24
Number of rats (frequency)	1	0	4	3	3	3	1

Calculate the mean and median number of trials to criterion for this group. (You can either write out the 15 numbers or you can think about how you could incorporate the frequencies directly into the formula for the mean.)

4.8 Given the following set of data, demonstrate that subtracting a constant (e.g., 5) from every score reduces all measures of central tendency by that amount.

8   7   12   14   3   7

4.9 Given the following data, show that multiplying each score by a constant multiplies all measures of central tendency by that constant.

8   3   5   5   6   2

4.10 Create a sample of 10 numbers that has a mean of 8.6. Notice carefully how you did this—it will help you later to understand the concept of degrees of freedom.

4.11 Calculate the measures of central tendency for the data on ADDSC and GPA in Appendix D—also available at this book's website as Add.dat.

4.12 Why would it not make any sense to calculate the mean for SEX or ENGL in Appendix D? If we did go ahead and compute the mean for SEX, what would the value of $(\overline{X} - 1)$ really represent?

4.13 In Table 3.1 the reaction time data are broken down separately according to whether we are looking at the same stimulus or whether the stimuli are mirror images of one another. The data can be found by going to this book's website and obtaining the data labeled as Tab3-1.dat. Using SPSS or similar software, calculate the mean reaction time under the two conditions. Does it take longer to respond to stimuli that are mirror images? This question requires some thought. You can either go to the menu labeled Data and ask it to split the data on the basis of the variable "Stimulus" and then use the `Analyze/Descriptive Statistics/ Descriptives` analysis, or you cannot split the data but go to `Analyze/Descriptive Statistics/Explore` and enter the variable "Stimulus" in the Factor List.

4.14 With reference to Exercise 4.13, if people take longer to process an image that has been both reversed and rotated, then the mean reaction time should depend on whether or not the comparison stimulus has been reversed. If reversal does not alter the difficulty of processing information, then the means should be similar. What do the answers to Exercise 4.13 suggest about how we process information?

4.15 Why is the mode an acceptable measure for nominal data? Why are the mean and the median not acceptable measures for nominal data?

4.16 In the exercises in Chapter 2 we considered the study by a fourth-grade girl who examined the average allowance of her classmates. Recall that seven boys reported an average allowance of $3.18, while 11 girls reported an average allowance of $2.63. These data raise some interesting statistical issues. This fourth-grade student did a meaningful study (well, it was a lot better than I would have done in fourth grade), but let's look at the data more closely.

The paper reported that the highest allowance for a boy was $10, while the highest for a girl was $9. It also reported that the two lowest girls' allowances were $0.50 and $0.51, while the lowest reported allowance for a boy was $3.00.

a) Create a set of data for boys and girls that would produce these results. (No, I didn't make an error.)
b) What is the most appropriate measure of central tendency to report in this situation?
c) What does the available information suggest to you about the distribution of allowances for the two genders?
d) What do the data suggest about the truthfulness of little boys?

4.17 In Chapter 3 (Figure 3.4) we saw data on grades of students who did and did not attend class regularly. What are the mean and median scores of those two groups of students? (The data are reproduced here for convenience.) What do they suggest about the value of attending class?

Attended class	241	243	246	249	250	252	254	254	255	256
	261	262	263	264	264	264	265	267	267	270
	271	272	273	276	276	277	278	278	280	281
	282	284	288	288	290	291	291	292	293	294
	296	296	297	298	310	320	321	328		
Skipped class	188	195	195	225	228	232	233	237	239	240
	250	256	256	256	261	264	264	268	270	270
	274	274	277	308						

4.18 Why do you think that I did not ask you to calculate the mode? (*Hint:* If you calculate the mode for those who skipped class frequently, you should see the problem.)

4.19 Search the Internet for sources of information about measures of central tendency. What do you find there that was not covered in this chapter?

4.20 Use *R* to calculate the mean and median of the data in Exercise 4.1. (Hint: the commands are of the form xbar <- mean(variableName) and med <- median(variableName). You can review how to read the data by looking at the *R* code in Chapter 3.

4.21 The Internet is a great resource when you don't know how to do something. Search the Internet to find out how to use SPSS to calculate the mode of a set of data. You can just go to any search engine and enter "How do I calculate the mode in SPSS?"

4.22 The bases package for *R* does not have a command such as "a <- mode(variableName)." Search the Web to find a way to get the mode using *R*.

4.23 a) Calculate the 10% trimmed mean for the data on test performance in Figure 4.1. (Remember that 10% trimming means removing the 10% of the scores at *each* end of the distribution.)

b) Assume that you collected the following data on the number of errors that participants made in reading a passage under distracting conditions.

10 10 10 15 15 20 20 20 20 25 25 26 27 30 32 37 39 42 68 77

Calculate the 10% trimmed mean for these data.

c) Trimming made more of a difference in (b) than it did in (a). Can you explain why this might be?

4.24 Seligman, Nolen-Hecksema, Thornton, and Thornton (1990) classified participants in their study (who were members of a university swim team) as Optimists or Pessimists. They then asked them to swim their best event, and in each case they reported times that were longer than the swimmer actually earned, disappointing everyone. Half an hour later they asked them to repeat the event again. The dependent variable was $Time_1/Time_2$, so a ratio greater than 1.0 indicates faster times on the second trial. The data follow.

Optimists

0.986	1.108	1.080	0.952	0.998	1.017	1.080	1.026	1.045	0.996
0.923	1.000	1.003	0.934	1.009	1.065	1.053	1.108	0.985	1.001
0.924	0.968	1.048	1.027	1.004	0.936	1.040			

Pessimists

0.983	0.947	0.932	1.078	0.914	0.955	0.962	0.944	0.941	0.831
0.936	0.995	0.872	0.997	0.983	1.105	1.116	0.997	0.960	1.045
1.095	0.944	1.069	0.927	0.988	1.015	1.045	0.864	0.982	0.915
1.047									

Use R or SPSS to calculate the mean for each group. Seligman et al. thought that optimists would try harder after being disappointed. Does it look as if they were correct?

4.25 In Exercise 4.22 women did not show much difference between Optimists and Pessimists. The first 17 scores in the Optimist group are for men and the first 13 scores in the Pessimist group are for men. What do you find for men?

4.26 I have suggested that if you don't understand something I write, go to any search engine and find something better. In Chapter 2 I admitted that it was pretty easy to define a dependent variable, but the definition of an independent variable is a bit more complicated. Go to the Internet and type in "What is an independent variable." Read at least five of the links that come up (not necessarily the first five) and write down the best definition that you find—the one that is clearest to you.

[CHAPTER 5

Measures of Variability

Understanding measures of central tendency is important, but we need to go further. This chapter will take up the topic of variability of scores and explain why variability is such a central concept in statistical analysis. We will see a number of different ways to measure variability. Each has its strengths and weaknesses, but we will focus primarily on two of them. What makes one measure of variability better than another? We will discuss this under the heading of estimation and we will see how variability can be represented graphically. Finally, we will cover what most people see as the odd fact that when we want to average quantities to obtain our measure we don't just divide by the number of quantities, but we divide by one less than the number of quantities. That seems weird.

In Chapter 3 we looked at ways to characterize and display the shape of a distribution. In Chapter 4 we considered several measures related to the center of a distribution. However, the shape and average value for a distribution (whether it be the mode, the most common value, the median, the middle value, or the mean) fail to give the whole story. We need some additional measure (or measures) to indicate the degree to which individual observations are clustered about or, equivalently, deviate from that average value. The average may reflect the general location of most of the scores, or the scores may be distributed over a wide range of values, and the "average" may not be very representative of most of the observations. Probably everyone has had experience with examinations on which all students received approximately

CONCEPTS THAT YOU WILL NEED TO REMEMBER FROM PREVIOUS CHAPTERS

Independent variable:	The variable you manipulate or are studying
Dependent variable:	The variable that you are measuring—the data
Mean:	The sum of the values divided by the number of values
Trimmed sample:	A sample with a fixed percentage of scores deleted from each end
$\overline{X}$:	A common symbol for the mean
Σ:	The symbol for summation of what follows
N:	The number of observations
Median location:	The position of the middle score in an ordered list

the same grade and with examinations on which the scores ranged from excellent to dreadful. Measures that refer to the differences between these two types of situations are what we have in mind when we speak of **dispersion**, or **variability**, around the median, the mode, or any other point we wish. In general we will refer specifically to dispersion around the mean.

As an example of a situation in which we might expect differences in variability from one group to another, consider the example in the previous chapter in which some students answered questions about passages they had read, and other students answered questions about the same passages, but without reading them. It is likely that those who did not read the passage simply guessed, and their performance would differ from each other only by chance—some people who guessed were luckier in their guesses than others even though both could sort out the silly answers. But for those who read the passage, there might be more substantial differences among people. Not only would there be chance differences, depending on how lucky they were when they didn't know the answer, but there would be real differences reflecting how much more of the passage one person understood than did another. Here the means of the two groups would most likely differ, but that is irrelevant. The difference in variability is our focus. The groups could have different levels of variability even if their means were comparable. Do my hypotheses correspond with your experience? If not, what would you expect to happen? Does your expectation lead to differences in means, variances, both, or neither?

For another illustration we will take some interesting data collected by Langlois and Roggman (1990) on the perceived attractiveness of faces. This study was one of several conducted by those authors examining attractiveness and its importance in life. It generated a great deal of discussion, and you can easily find extensive reference to that and related studies by an Internet search for "Langlois and Roggman." A valuable discussion of their work can be found at Langlois's website at the University of Texas at Austin, where you can see good examples of what is meant by the computer averaging of faces. A Recent study (Sofer et al., 2015) found that rated attractiveness does increase as "typicality" decreased, as Langlois and Rogmann have shown. But when the judgment was for "trustworthiness," stimuli with more typical faces were judged as more trustworthy. This was true whether the faces were more attractive or less attractive than normal.

Think for a moment about some of the faces you consider attractive. Do they tend to have unusual features (e.g., prominent noses or unusual eyebrows), or are the features rather ordinary? Langlois and Roggman were interested in investigating what makes faces attractive. Toward that end they presented students with computer-generated pictures of faces. Some of these pictures had been created by averaging together actual snapshots of four different people to create a composite. We will label these photographs Set *X*, where the *X* stands for averaging over four faces. Other pictures (Set *Y*) were created by averaging across snapshots of 32 different people. As you might suspect, when you average across four people, there is still room for individuality in the composite. For example, some composites show thin faces, while others show round ones. However, averaging across 32 people usually gives results that are very "average." Noses are neither too long nor too short, ears don't stick out too far nor sit too close to the head, and so on.

Students were asked to examine the resulting pictures and rate each one on a five-point scale of attractiveness. The authors were primarily interested in determining whether the *mean* rating of the faces in Set *X* was less than the mean rating of the faces in Set *Y*. The data came out as they expected, though not as I would have expected, suggesting that faces with distinctive characteristics are judged as less attractive than more ordinary faces. In this chapter, however, we are more interested in the degree of *similarity* in the ratings of faces than in the mean. We expect that composites of many faces will be more homogeneous, and thus would be rated more similarly, than composites of only a few faces.

The data are shown in Table 5.1, where the scores are the consensus across several judges rating the images on a five-point scale, with "5" as the most attractive.[1] From the table you can see that Langlois and Roggman were correct in predicting that Set *Y* faces would be rated as more attractive than Set *X* faces. (The means were 3.26 and 2.64, respectively.) But notice also that the ratings for the composites of 32 faces are considerably more homogeneous than the ratings of the composites of four faces. We can plot these two sets of data as standard histograms, as in Figure 5.1.

Although it is apparent from Figure 5.1 that there is much greater variability in the rating of composites of four photographs than in the rating of composites of 32 photographs, we need some sort of measure to reflect this difference in variability. A number of measures could be used, and they will be discussed in turn, starting with the simplest.

Table 5.1 Data from Langlois and Roggman

	Set *X*		Set *Y*	
Picture	Composite of Four Faces	Picture	Composite of 32 Faces
1	1.20	21	3.13
2	1.82	22	3.17
3	1.93	23	3.19
4	2.04	24	3.19
5	2.30	25	3.20
6	2.33	26	3.20
7	2.34	27	3.22
8	2.47	28	3.23
9	2.51	29	3.25
10	2.55	30	3.26
11	2.64	31	3.27
12	2.76	32	3.29
13	2.77	33	3.29
14	2.90	34	3.30
15	2.91	35	3.31
16	3.20	36	3.31
17	3.22	37	3.34
18	3.39	38	3.34
19	3.59	39	3.36
20	4.02	40	3.38
	Mean = 2.64		Mean = 3.26

[1]These data are not the actual numbers that Langlois and Roggman collected, but they have been generated to have exactly the same mean and standard deviation as the original data. Langlois and Roggman used six composite photographs per set. I have used 20 photographs per set to make the data more applicable to my purposes in this chapter. The conclusions that you would draw from these data, however, are exactly the same as the conclusions you would draw from theirs.

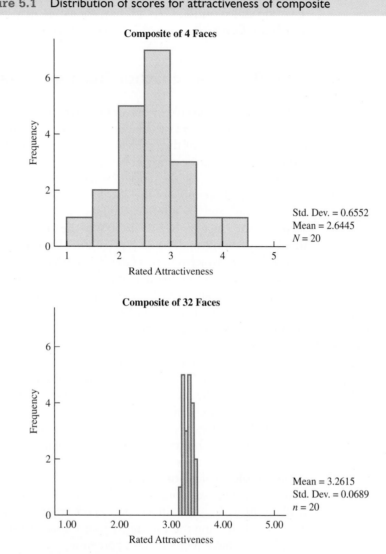

Figure 5.1 Distribution of scores for attractiveness of composite

5.1 Range

The **range** is a measure of distance, namely the distance from the lowest to the highest score. For our data the range for Set X is $(4.02 - 1.20) = 2.82$ units; for Set Y it is $(3.38 - 3.13) = 0.25$ unit. The range is an exceedingly common measure and is illustrated in everyday life by such statements as "The price of hamburger fluctuates over a 70¢ range from \$1.29 to \$1.99 per pound." (Although in common statements like this we specify the end points of the distribution, the range is really the difference or distance between the points. Here the range is 0.70.) The range suffers, however, from a total reliance on extreme values, or, if the values are *unusually* extreme, or what are called **outliers**. As a result, the range may give a distorted picture of the variability. One really unusual value could change the range drastically.

5.2 Interquartile Range and Other Range Statistics

If the range is too affected by one or two extreme scores, perhaps we should just get rid of those extremes before we compute the range. The **interquartile range** represents an attempt to circumvent the problem of the range being heavily dependent on extreme scores. An interquartile range is obtained by discarding the upper and lower 25% of the distribution and taking the range of what remains. You may recognize that cutting off the upper and lower ends of the distribution is what we referred to in the last chapter as "trimming," and the interquartile range is the range of a 25% trimmed sample. As such, it is the range of the middle 50% of the observations, or the difference between the 75th percentile and the 25th percentile. We can calculate the interquartile range for the data on attractiveness of faces by omitting the lowest five scores and the highest five scores and determining the range of the remainder. In this case, the interquartile range for Set X would be 0.58 and the interquartile range for Set Y would be only 0.11.

The interquartile range plays an important role in a useful graphical method known as a boxplot. This method will be discussed in Section 5.8.

In many ways the interquartile range suffers from problems that are just the opposite of those found with the range. Specifically, it may discard too much of the data. Trimming off 25% of the scores at each end of the distribution may give us a good estimate of the mean, but it usually does not yield a very good estimate of overall variability. If we want to know if one set of photographs is judged more variable than another, it does not make much sense to toss out the half of those scores that are most extreme and thus vary the most from the mean.

There is nothing sacred about eliminating the upper and lower 25% of the distribution before calculating the range. In fact we could eliminate any percentage we wanted as long as we could justify that number to ourselves and to others. What we really want to do is eliminate those scores that are likely to be accidents or errors without eliminating the variability that we seek to study. As we saw in Chapter 4, samples that have had a certain percentage (e.g., 10%) of the values in each tail removed are called **trimmed samples**, and statistics calculated on such samples are called **trimmed statistics** (e.g., trimmed means or trimmed ranges). Statisticians seem to like trimmed samples a lot more than psychologists do. That is unfortunate, because trimmed samples, and their associated trimmed statistics, have a lot to offer and can make our analyses more meaningful. As I said earlier, trimmed samples are beginning to make a comeback, though it will take time. It is nice to see trimmed statistics beginning to appear in research articles, because it means that our techniques are constantly, though slowly, improving.

Ranges and interquartile ranges look at the extreme scores of a distribution or the extreme scores of a 25% trimmed sample. The measures to be discussed next make use of all of the data points.

5.3 | The Average Deviation

At first glance it would seem that if we want to measure how scores are dispersed around the mean $(\overline{X})$ (i.e., deviate from the mean), the most logical thing to do would be to obtain all the deviations (i.e., $X_i - \overline{X}$) and average them. The more widely the scores are dispersed, the greater the deviations of scores from their mean and therefore the greater the average of the deviations—well, not quite. Common sense has led us astray here. If you calculate the deviations from the mean, some scores will be above the mean and have a positive deviation, while others will be below the mean and have negative deviations. In the end, the positive and negative deviations will exactly balance each other out, and the sum of the deviations will be zero. This will not get us very far.

To illustrate what I mean by deviations balancing each other out, consider the numbers 1, 4, and 5. The mean is

$$\frac{\Sigma X}{N} = \frac{(1 + 4 + 5)}{3} = 3.333$$

and the sum of the deviations from the mean is

$$\frac{\Sigma(X - \overline{X})}{N} = \frac{(1 - 3.333) + (4 - 3.333) + (5 - 3.333)}{3}$$

$$= \frac{-2.333 + 0.667 + 1.667}{3} = \frac{0}{3} = 0$$

5.4 | The Variance

One way to eliminate the problem of the positive and negative deviations balancing each other out would be to use absolute deviations, where we simply eliminate the sign. Although that produces a legitimate measure of variability (the mean absolute deviation, m.a.d.), that measure is seldom used, and so we will not say more about it here. The measure that we will consider in this section, the **sample variance (s^2)**, represents a different approach to the problem that the deviations themselves average to zero. (When we are referring to the **population variance**, we use σ^2 [sigma squared] as the symbol.) In the case of the variance, we take advantage of the fact that the square of a negative number is positive. Thus we sum the *squared* deviations rather than the deviations themselves.

Because we want an average, we next divide that sum by a function of N, the number of scores. Although you might reasonably expect that we would divide by N, we actually divide by $(N-1)$. We use $(N-1)$ as a divisor *for the sample variance* (s^2) because, as I will explain shortly, it leaves us with a sample variance that is a better estimate of the corresponding population variance. For now, just accept that we need to use $(N-1)$ for the sample variance. (The population variance (σ^2) is calculated by dividing the sum of the squared deviations, for each value in the population, by N rather than $(N-1)$, but we rarely actually calculate a population variance. Other than in writing textbooks, I don't think that I can recall a time that I calculated a *population* variance, though there are countless times when I have estimated them with a *sample* variance.) If it is important to specify more precisely the variable to which s^2 refers, we can subscript it with a letter representing the variable. Because we have denoted the sample using only the images averaged over four faces as X, the variance could be denoted as s_X^2.

$$s_X^2 = \frac{\Sigma(X - \overline{X})^2}{N - 1}$$

For our example, we can calculate the sample variances of Set X and Set Y as follows:[2]

Set X
The mean of X is

$$\overline{X} = \frac{\Sigma X}{N} = \frac{52.89}{20} = 2.64$$

then

$$s_X^2 = \frac{\Sigma(X - \overline{X})^2}{N - 1}$$

$$= \frac{(1.20 - 2.64)^2 + (1.82 - 2.64)^2 + \cdots + (4.02 - 2.64)^2}{20 - 1}$$

$$= \frac{8.1567}{19} = 0.4293$$

Set Y
The mean of Y is

$$\overline{Y} = \frac{\Sigma Y}{N} = \frac{65.23}{20} = 3.26$$

then

$$s_Y^2 = \frac{\Sigma(Y - \overline{Y})^2}{N - 1}$$

$$= \frac{(3.13 - 3.26)^2 + (3.17 - 3.26)^2 + \cdots + (3.38 - 3.26)^2}{20 - 1}$$

$$= \frac{0.0902}{19} = 0.0048$$

From these calculations we see that the difference in variances reflects the differences we see in the distributions. The variance of Set Y is very much smaller than the variance of Set X.

Although the variance is an exceptionally important concept and one of the most commonly used statistics, it does not have the direct intuitive interpretation we would like. Because it is based on *squared* deviations, the result is in terms of squared

---

[2]In these calculations and others throughout the book, my answers may differ slightly from those that you obtain for the same data. If so, the difference is most likely due to rounding. If you repeat my calculations and arrive at a quite similar answer, that is sufficient.

units. Thus Set X has a mean attractiveness rating of 2.64 and a variance of 0.4293 *squared* unit. But squared units are awkward things to talk about and have little intuitive meaning with respect to the data. Fortunately, the solution to this problem is simple: Take the square root of the variance.

5.5 The Standard Deviation

The **standard deviation (s or σ)** is defined as the positive square root of the variance and, for a sample, is symbolized as *s* (with a subscript identifying the variable if necessary). When used in a publication in psychology to report results, the symbol SD is often used. (The notation σ is used only in reference to a *population* standard deviation.) The following formula defines the standard deviation:

$$s_X = \sqrt{\frac{\Sigma(X - \overline{X})^2}{N - 1}}$$

For our example,

$$s_X = \sqrt{s_X^2} = \sqrt{0.4293} = 0.6552$$

$$s_Y = \sqrt{s_Y^2} = \sqrt{0.0048} = 0.0689$$

For convenience I will round these answers to 0.66 and 0.07, respectively.

If you look at the formula, you will see that the standard deviation, like the mean absolute deviation, is basically a measure of the average of the deviations of each score from the mean. Granted, these deviations have been squared, summed, and so on, but at heart they are still deviations. And even though we have divided by $(N - 1)$ instead of N, we still have obtained something very much like a mean or an "average" of these deviations. Thus we can say without too much distortion that attractiveness ratings for Set X deviated positively or negatively, on the average, 0.66 unit from the mean, whereas attractiveness ratings for Set Y deviated, on the average, only 0.07 unit from the mean. This means that the variability of estimates of attractiveness based on images that are an average of four faces is about 10 times greater than estimates based on averages of 32 faces. That strikes me as quite a difference.

This rather loose way of thinking about the standard deviation as a sort of average deviation goes a long way toward giving it meaning without doing serious injustice to the concept.

These results tell us two interesting things about attractiveness. The fact that computer averaging of many faces produces similar composites would be reflected in the fact that ratings of pictures in Set Y do not show much variability—all those images are judged to be pretty much alike. Second, the fact that those ratings have a higher mean than the ratings of faces in Set X reveals that averaging over many faces produces composites that seem more attractive. Does this conform to your everyday experience? I, for one, would have expected that faces judged attractive would be those with distinctive features, but I would have been wrong. Go back and think again about those faces you class as attractive. Are they really distinctive? If so, do you have an additional hypothesis to explain the findings?

We can also look at the standard deviation in terms of how many scores fall no more than a standard deviation above or below the mean. For a wide variety of reasonably symmetric and mound-shaped distributions, we can say that approximately two-thirds of the observations lie within one standard deviation of the mean (for a normal distribution, which will be discussed in Chapter 6, it is almost exactly two-thirds). Although there certainly are exceptions, especially for badly skewed distributions, this rule is still useful. If I told you that for traditional jobs the mean starting salary for liberal arts college graduates in 2014 was expected to be $45,445 with a standard deviation of $4,000, you probably would not be far off to conclude that about two-thirds of graduates who take these jobs will earn between about $41,500 and $49,500.

Measures of Variability

- **Range:**   Distance from lowest to highest score

- **Interquartile Range:**   The range remaining after we delete the highest and lowest 25% of the scores. The range of the middle 50% of the scores

- **Mean Absolute Deviation:**   Sum of the absolute deviations from the mean divided by the sample size

- **Variance:**   Sum of the squared deviations from the mean ($\overline{X}$) divided by one less than the sample size

$$s_X^2 = \frac{\Sigma(X - \overline{X})^2}{N - 1}$$

- **Standard Deviation:**   Square root of the variance

$$s_X^2 = \sqrt{\frac{\Sigma(X - \overline{X})^2}{N - 1}}$$

5.6   Computational Formulae for the Variance and the Standard Deviation

The previous expressions for the variance and the standard deviation, although perfectly correct, are unwieldy if you are doing the calculations by hand for any reasonable amount of data. They are also prone to rounding errors, since they usually involve squaring fractional deviations. They are excellent definitional formulae, but we will now briefly consider a more practical set of calculational formulae. These formulae are algebraically equivalent to the ones we have seen, so they will give the same answers but with much less effort. (Interestingly, in earlier editions of this book I emphasized the computational formulae that I'm about to produce over the definitional ones. But as people rely more and more on computers, and less and less on calculators, I find myself swinging more in the direction of definitional formulae. If you want to understand what the standard deviation is, concentrate on the formula we just used. If you have to carry out a calculation with more than a few numbers, then move to the formula that follows.)

The definitional formula for the sample variance was given as

$$s_X^2 = \frac{\Sigma(X - \overline{X})^2}{N - 1}$$

A more practical computational formula, which is algebraically equivalent, is

$$s_X^2 = \frac{\Sigma X^2 - \dfrac{(\Sigma X)^2}{N}}{N - 1}$$

Similarly, for the sample standard deviation

$$s_X = \sqrt{\frac{\Sigma(X - \overline{X})^2}{N - 1}}$$

$$= \sqrt{\frac{\Sigma X^2 - \dfrac{(\Sigma X)^2}{N}}{N - 1}}$$

Applying the computational formula for the sample variance for Set X, with $N = 20$ observations, we obtain

$$s_X^2 = \frac{\Sigma X^2 - \dfrac{(\Sigma X)^2}{N}}{N - 1}$$

$$= \frac{1.20^2 + 1.82^2 + \cdots + 4.02^2 - \dfrac{52.89^2}{20}}{19}$$

$$= \frac{148.0241 - \dfrac{52.89^2}{20}}{19} = 0.4293$$

You should notice that to use this formula we summed all of the scores. That gave us ΣX. Then we squared all of the scores and summed those squares, which gave us ΣX^2. N is just the number of scores. We substituted each of those values in the equation, carried out the necessary arithmetic, and had our answer. Note that the answer we obtained here is exactly the same as the answer we obtained by the definitional formula. Note also, as pointed out in Chapter 2, that $\Sigma X^2 = 148.0241$ is quite different from $(\Sigma X)^2 = 52.89^2 = 2797.35$. Summing squared terms and squaring a sum are two very different things. I leave the calculation of the standard deviation for Set Y to you, but the answer is 0.0689.

You might be somewhat reassured that the level of arithmetic required for the previous calculations is about as much as you will need anywhere in this book. (I told you that you learned it all in high school.)

5.7 The Mean and the Variance as Estimators

In Chapter 1 I mentioned that we generally calculate measures such as the mean and the variance as *estimates* of the corresponding values in the populations. Characteristics of samples are called *statistics* and are designated by Roman letters (e.g., $\overline{X}$ and s_x). Characteristics of populations, on the other hand, are called *parameters* and are designated by Greek letters. Thus the population mean is symbolized by μ (lowercase mu) and the population standard deviation as σ (lowercase sigma). In general, then, we use statistics as estimates of parameters.

If the purpose of obtaining a statistic is to use it as an estimator of a population parameter, it should come as no surprise that our choice of a statistic (and even how we define it) is partly a function of how well that statistic functions as an estimator of the parameter in question. In fact, the mean is usually preferred over other measures of central tendency precisely because of its performance as an estimator of μ. The sample variance (s^2) is defined as it is specifically because of the advantages that accrue when s^2 is used to estimate the population variance, signified by σ^2.

The Sample Variance as an Estimator
of the Population Variance

The sample variance offers an excellent example of a property of estimators known as **bias**. A biased sample statistic is one whose long-range average is not equal to the population parameter it is supposed to estimate. An unbiased statistic, as you might guess, is one whose long-range average is equal to the parameter it estimates. Unbiased statistics, like unbiased people, are nicer to have around. If you calculate the sample variance in the right way, it is unbiased.

Earlier I sneaked in the divisor of ($N - 1$) instead of N for the calculation of the variance and the standard deviation. The quantity ($N - 1$) is referred to as the **degrees of freedom (df)** and represents an adjustment to the sample size to account for the fact that we are working with sample values. To be a bit more specific, in estimating the sample standard deviation we first had to calculate and use $\overline{X}$ to estimate the population mean (μ). Because we did that we need to adjust the sample size accordingly. Now is the time to explain why we do this. You need to have a general sense of the issues involved, but you don't need to worry about the specifics. Whenever you see a variance or a standard deviation, it will have been computed with ($N - 1$) in the denominator. You can say, "It's probably because of some obscure statistical argument," and skip this section, or you can read this section and see that ($N - 1$) makes a good deal of sense.

The reason why sample variances require ($N - 1$) as the denominator can be explained in a number of ways. Perhaps the simplest is in terms of what has been said already about the sample variance (s^2) as an unbiased estimate of the population variance (σ^2). Assume for the moment that we had an infinite number of samples (each containing N observations) from one population and that we knew the population variance (σ^2). Suppose further that we were foolish enough to calculate sample variances as $\Sigma(X - \overline{X})^2/N$ (note the denominator). If we took the average of these sample variances, we would find

$$average\left(\frac{\Sigma(X - \overline{X})^2}{N}\right) = E\left(\frac{\Sigma(X - \overline{X})^2}{N}\right) = \frac{(N - 1)\sigma^2}{N}$$

where $E(\ )$ is read as "the **expected value** of" whatever is in parentheses. Here we see that the expected value of the variance, when calculated with N in the denominator, is not equal to σ^2, but to $(N-1)/N$ times σ^2. Well, that doesn't seem like such a good thing!

But we can easily get out from under this problem. If

$$average\left(\frac{\Sigma(X-\overline{X})^2}{N}\right) = E\left(\frac{\Sigma(X-\overline{X})^2}{N}\right) = \frac{(N-1)\sigma^2}{N}$$

then with a small amount of algebra we can see that

$$average\left(\frac{\Sigma(X-\overline{X})^2}{N}\right)\left(\frac{N}{N-1}\right) = E\left(\frac{\Sigma(X-\overline{X})^2}{\cancel{N}}\right)\left(\frac{\cancel{N}}{N-1}\right)$$

$$= E\left(\frac{\Sigma(X-\overline{X})^2}{N-1}\right) = \sigma^2$$

In other words, when we use $(N-1)$ as the divisor instead of N, our result is an unbiased estimate of σ^2.

Degrees of freedom

Throughout this book you will come across the concept of degrees of freedom. Degrees of freedom (df) come into play whenever we use sample statistics to estimate population parameters. Often, the degrees of freedom will be $N-1$, but in some situations (e.g., Chapters 9–11) they will be $N-2$ or $N-3$. But in all cases they are an adjustment that we apply to the sample size. In cases when we have five groups or three categories, the degrees of freedom for groups will be $5-1=4$, and the degrees of freedom for categories will be $3-1=2$. You will do best if you just think of degrees of freedom as an adjustment to some other value, such as the sample size, the number of groups, the number of pairs of observations, and so on. In each case where you need to use the degrees of freedom, I will be careful to tell you how to calculate them.

5.8 | Boxplots: Graphical Representations of Dispersion and Extreme Scores

In Chapter 3 you saw how stem-and-leaf displays can represent data in several meaningful ways at the same time. Such displays combine data into something very much like a histogram, while retaining the individual values of the observations. In addition to the stem-and-leaf display, John Tukey developed other ways of looking at data, one of which gives greater prominence to the dispersion of the data. This method is known as a **boxplot**, or sometimes, **box-and-whisker plot**. Tukey's method of calculating the ingredients of a boxplot is more complicated than it really needs to be, and in recent years most people have adopted a somewhat simpler approach that produces nearly the same plot with more easily understood steps. That is the approach that I will adopt in this edition.

Table 5.2 Data and stem-and-leaf display on length of hospitalization for full term newborn infants (in days)

Data			Stem-and-Leaf
2	I	7	1 | 000
I	33	2	2 | 000000000
2	3	4	3 | 00000000000
3	*	4	4 | 0000000
3	3	10	5 | 00
9	2	5	6 | 0
4	3	3	7 | 0
20	6	2	8 |
4	5	2	9 | 0
I	*	*	10 | 0
3	3	4	HI | 20, 33
2	3	4	
3	2	3	Missing = 3
2	4		

The data and the accompanying stem-and-leaf display in Table 5.2 were taken from normal- and low-birth weight infants participating in a study at the University of Vermont (Nurcombe et al., 1984), and they represent preliminary data on the length of hospitalization of 38 normal-birth weight infants. Data on three infants are missing for this particular variable and are represented by an asterisk (*). (They are included to emphasize that we should not just ignore missing data.) Because the data are integers between 1 and 10, with two exceptions, all the leaves are zero because there are no "less significant" digits to serve as leaves. The zeros really just fill in space to produce a histogram-like distribution. Examination of the data as plotted in the stem-and-leaf display reveals that the distribution is positively skewed with a median stay of three days. Near the bottom of the stem you will see the entry HI and the values 20 and 33. These are extreme values, or outliers, and are set off in this way to highlight their existence. Whether they are large enough to make us suspicious is one of the questions a boxplot is designed to address. The last line of the stem-and-leaf display indicates the number of missing observations.

To help understand the next few points, I have presented the boxplot of the data listed in Table 5.3. This is shown in Figure 5.2. It was constructed using R, and the code is given below. Different software often gives slightly different plots, but the differences are minor.

To understand how a boxplot is constructed, we need to invoke a number of concepts we have already discussed and then add a few more. In Chapter 4 we defined the median location of a set of N scores as $(N + 1)/2$. When the median location is a whole number, as it will be when N is odd, then the median is simply the value that occupies that location in an ordered arrangement of data. When the median location is a decimal number (i.e., when N is even), the median is the average of the two values on either side of that location. For the data in Table 5.3, the median location is

```
### Boxplot of data on days of hospitalization of normal-birth weight infants
    days <- c(2, 1, 7, 1, 33, 2, 2, 3, 4, 3, NA, 4,
              3, 3, 10, 9, 2, 5, 4, 3, 3, 20, 6, 2,
              4, 5, 2, 1, NA, NA, 3, 3, 4, 2, 3, 4,
              3, 2, 3, 2, 4)     # NA represents missing ("not available") data

    xbar <- mean(days, na.rm = TRUE)      # na.rm tells it to first remove
                                                missing data.
    stdev <- sd(days, na.rm = TRUE)
    cat("xbar = ",xbar, "  st. dev = ", stdev) # Print out mean and st dev.
    boxplot(days, border = "red", boxwex = .5, col = "blue", main =
        "Length of Hospitalization", ylab = "Days of Hospitalization")
          ### boxwex governs width of box, col = color of box
```

Figure 5.2   Boxplot of data on length of hospitalization from Table 5.2

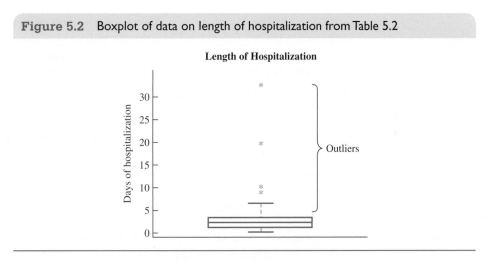

$(38 + 1)/2 = 19.5$, and the median is 3. Notice that the horizontal line in the middle of the small box in Figure 5.2 is drawn at the median. The next step in constructing a boxplot is to take what amounts to the medians of each half of the ordered distribution. These are the locations of the first and third quartiles (i.e., the 25th and 75th percentiles), which Tukey referred to as "hinges." To calculate the quartiles, we first need to obtain the **quartile location**, which is defined as

$$\text{Quartile location} = \frac{\text{Median location} + 1}{2}$$

If the median location is a fractional value, the fraction should be dropped from the numerator before you compute the quartile location. The quartile location is to a quartile what the median location is to the median. It tells us where, in an ordered

Table 5.3 Calculation and boxplots for data from Table 5.2

Median location	$(N + 1)/2 = (38+1)/2 = 19.5$
Median	3
Quartile location	(Median location[†] $+ 1)/2 = (19 + 1)/2 = 10$
Lower quartile	10th lowest score = 2
Upper quartile	10th highest score = 4
Interquartile range	Third quartile − First quartile = 4 − 2 = 2
Interquartile range × 1.5	2 × 1.5 = 3
Maximum lower whisker	(First quartile − 1.5 × Interquartile range) = 2 − 3 = −1
Maximum upper whisker	(Third quartile + 1.5 × Interquartile range) = 4 + 3 = 7
End lower whisker	Smallest value ≥ −1 = 1
End upper whisker	Largest value ≤ 7 = 7

[†]Drop any fractional value

series, the quartile values are to be found. For the data on hospital stay, the quartile location is $(19 + 1)/2 = 10$. Thus the quartiles are going to be the tenth scores from the bottom and from the top of the ordered values. These values are 2 and 4, respectively. For data sets without tied scores, or for large samples, the first and third quartiles will bracket the middle 50% of the scores. Notice that the top and bottom of the box in Figure 5.2 are at 2 and 4, and correspond to the first and third quartiles.

The next concept we need goes back to our interquartile range, which is simply the range of values remaining after we cut off the lower and upper quartiles. Tukey called it the "H–spread," but that terminology seems to be dropping by the wayside. For our data the interquartile range (or H-spread) is $4 - 2 = 2$. The next step in drawing the boxplot, then, is to draw a line (**whisker**) from the top and bottom of the box to the farthest point that is *no more than* 1.5 times the interquartile range. Because the interquartile range is 2 for our data, the whisker will be no farther than $2 \times 1.5 = 3$ units out from the box. (It won't be a full three units unless there is an obtained value at that point. Otherwise it will go as far as the most extreme value that is not more than three units from the box.) Three units below the box would be at $2 - 3 = -1$, but the smallest value in the data is 1, so we will draw the whisker to 1. Three units above the box would be at $4 + 3 = 7$. There is a 7 in the data, so we will draw that whisker to 7. The calculations for all the terms we have just defined are shown in Table 5.3.

The steps above were all illustrated in Figure 5.2. The only question is "where did those asterisks come from?" The asterisks in that plot represent values that are so extreme that they lie outside the whiskers. They are commonly referred to as outliers. They could be correct values that are just extreme, or they could be errors. The nice thing about that boxplot is that it at least directs our attention to those values. I will come back to them in just a minute.

From Figure 5.2 we can see several important things. First, the central portion of the distribution is reasonably symmetric. This is indicated by the fact that the median lies in the center of the box and was apparent from the stem-and-leaf display. We can also see that the distribution is positively skewed, because the whisker on the top is substantially longer than the one on the bottom. This also was apparent from the stem-and-leaf display, although not so clearly. Finally, we see that we have four outliers, where an outlier is defined here as any value more extreme than the whiskers. The stem-and-leaf display did not show the position of the outliers nearly so graphically as does the boxplot.

Outliers deserve special attention. An outlier could represent an error in measurement, in data recording, or in data entry, or it could represent a legitimate value that just happens to be extreme. For example, our data represent length of hospitalization, and a full-term infant might have been born with a physical defect that required extended hospitalization. Because these are actual data, it was possible to go back to hospital records and look more closely at the four extreme cases. On examination, it turned out that the two most extreme scores were attributable to errors in data entry and were readily correctable. The other two extreme scores were caused by physical problems of the infants. Here a decision was required by the project director as to whether the problems were sufficiently severe to cause the infants to be dropped from the study (both were retained). The two corrected values were 3 and 5 instead of 33 and 20, respectively. If you are using *R* you can go back and change the code by entering the correct values and produce a corrected boxplot.

From what has been said, it should be evident that boxplots are extremely useful tools for examining data with respect to dispersion. I find them particularly useful for screening data for errors and for highlighting potential problems before subsequent analyses are carried out. Boxplots are presented in the remainder of this book as visual guides to the data.

There are a number of sites on the Web that either illustrate useful ways in which boxplots can be used or allow you to draw your own. A particularly good one is http://onlinestatbook.com/2/graphing_distributions/boxplots.html by David Lane at Rice. (Any site by David Lane is worth reading.) But if you have trouble with your computer allowing you to run his applets, go to http://www.uvm.edu/~dhowell/fundamentals9/SeeingStatisticsApplets/Applets.html and read the discussion in the third paragraph. The fault is not David's; the change was made by Sun Microsystems. You may need to reboot your computer to have the change take effect.

For People in a Hurry

A boxplot really doesn't take all that long to draw, but some people just don't have any patience. For those who don't want to fuss too much and just want a general sense of the data, the simplest thing is to find the median and the first and third quartile. Then draw your box. Assuming that you have a large number of scores, you can set aside the largest 2.5% and the smallest 2.5% and draw the whiskers to the largest and smallest values that remain. Then put those extreme values in as outliers. In fact, some computer programs look as if that's exactly the way they construct boxplots.

5.9   A Return to Trimming

As you should recall from Chapter 4, one technique for dealing with outliers that distort the mean is to trim the sample, meaning that we lop off a certain number of values at each end of the distribution. We then find the mean of the observations that remain. You might logically think that we should do the same thing when examining the variance or standard deviation of that sample. But, instead, we are going to modify the procedure slightly.

Winsorized Variance

For a 20% trimmed mean we set aside the 20% of the highest and lowest values and find the mean of what remains. There is also a statistic called the **Winsorized mean**, which replaces the extreme observations with the highest (and lowest) value remaining after trimming. (Charles P. Winsor had a huge influence on John Tukey, whom we have met already. Tukey was the one who coined the term "Winsorizing.") For example, suppose that we had the following observations.

12 14 19 21 21 22 24 24 26 27 27 27 28 29 30 31 32 45 50 52

With 20 values, 20% trimming would remove the lowest and highest four observations, giving us

21 22 24 24 26 27 27 27 28 29 30 31

which gives a trimmed mean of 316/12 = 26.33. (The original mean was 28.05.)

When we Winsorize the data we replace the lowest scores that we have eliminated with 21 (the lowest value remaining) and the highest scores with 31 (the highest value remaining.) This gives us

21 21 21 21 21 22 24 24 26 27 27 27 28 29 30 31 31 31 31 31

Then the Winsorized mean would be 524/20 = 26.2, which is actually quite close to the trimmed mean.

For technical reasons that I won't elaborate, we rarely use the Winsorized mean; we use the trimmed mean instead. However, when it comes to calculating a variance or standard deviation, we fall back on Winsorizing. When we work with a trimmed mean we find that the **Winsorized variance** or **Winsorized standard deviation** is a more useful statistic. And to compute a Winsorized variance we simply compute the variance of the Winsorized sample. So we want the variance of

21 21 21 21 21 22 24 24 26 27 27 27 28 29 30 31 31 31 31 31

which is 16.02. (The variance of the trimmed sample would have been only 9.52.)

We will return to Winsorized variance and standard deviations later in the book, but for now you simply need to understand what they are. And if you know that, you will be ahead of most people around you.

5.10 Obtaining Measures of Dispersion Using SPSS & R

We will use SPSS to calculate measures of dispersion on the reaction time data discussed in Chapter 3 (see page 38.). In Figure 5.3 I calculated the output using **Descriptive Statistics/Explore** and broke the data down by whether I made the correct or incorrect choice. In that figure you can see the descriptive statistics calculated separately for those trials on which the response was correct and for those on which it was wrong. You will notice that in the upper right of each section is a statistic called the Standard Error. For now you can ignore that statistic, but in case you are curious it refers to how variable the *mean* would be over repeated samples, whereas the standard deviation refers to the variability of the individual observations. In Figure 5.3b are the corresponding boxplots.

From Figure 5.3a you can see that the mean reaction time was slightly longer on those trials in which my choice was incorrect, but the median values are identical. The boxplot in Figure 5.3b shows that the data for wrong choices were positively skewed (the median is not centered in the box). SPSS also labeled the outliers by their ID number. For example, responses 179 and 202 were two of the outliers. There are noticeably more outliers on correct trials, which indicates that sometimes it took me a long time to figure out what the correct response would be. But when I did figure it out I was more often correct. I point this out because it illustrates again that boxplots are useful for making clear the meaning of the data, not simply whether two means are equal or not.

You can accomplish much the same thing in R by installing and then loading the "psych" library. The simple function that you would want is named "describe" and the only argument for that function is the name of the variable that you want to analyze. The code follows in Figure 5.4, where I first break the data down by whether the response was correct or wrong. I have included a slightly edited version of the results. We saw how to obtain the boxplot earlier in the chapter.

Figure 5.3a   Distribution and measures of central tendency and dispersion on reaction time data set

Descriptives			Statistic	Std. Error
RTsec	Correct	Mean	1.6128	.02716
		95% Confidence Interval for Mean		
		Lower Bound	1.5595	
		Upper Bound	1.6662	
		5% Trimmed Mean	1.5549	
		Median	1.5300	
		Variance	.402	
		Std. Deviation	.63404	
		Minimum	.72	
		Maximum	4.44	
		Range	3.72	
		Interquartile Range	.73	
		Skewness	1.522	.105
		Kurtosis	3.214	.209
	Wrong	Mean	1.7564	.08906
		95% Confidence Interval for Mean		
		Lower Bound	1.5778	
		Upper Bound	1.9349	
		5% Trimmed Mean	1.7192	
		Median	1.5300	
		Variance	.436	
		Std. Deviation	.66052	
		Minimum	.72	
		Maximum	3.45	
		Range	2.73	
		Interquartile Range	.60	
		Skewness	1.045	.322
		Kurtosis	.444	.634

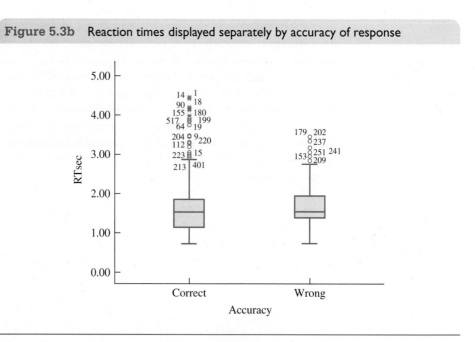

Figure 5.3b   Reaction times displayed separately by accuracy of response

Figure 5.4   Results of applying *R* to the reaction time data

```
### Reaction Time Data
rxData <- read.table(file.choose(), header = TRUE) # Load Tab3-1.dat
attach(rxData)
Accuracy <- factor(Accuracy) # Convert Accuracy to a factor with levels 0 and 1
library(psych)   # Necessary because "describe" is not part of base package
correct <- RTsec[Accuracy == 1]
cat("Results for Correct trials \n")
describe(correct)
incorrect <- RTsec[Accuracy == 0]
cat("Results for Incorrect trials \n")
describe(incorrect)
```

Results for Correct trials

	vars	n	mean	sd	median	trimmed	mad	min	max	range	skew	kurtosis	se
1	1	545	1.61	0.63	1.53	1.53	0.61	0.72	4.44	3.72	.51	3.14	0.03

Results for Incorrect trials

	vars	n	mean	sd	median	trimmed	mad	min	max	range	skew	kurtosis	se
1	1	55	1.76	0.66	1.53	1.69	0.44	0.72	3.45	2.73	0.99	0.18	0.09

5.11 | **The Moon Illusion**

I'm sure that you all experience nights when you drive along and see this absolutely huge moon sitting just above the horizon. How did it get that way? Did someone just blow it up like a balloon? Hardly! Then why does the moon appear to be so much larger when it is near the horizon than when it is directly overhead? This simple question has produced a wide variety of theories from psychologists and for many years was very involved in the literature on the psychology of perception. Kaufman and Rock (1962) carried out a complete series of studies. They proposed that the moon illusion is caused by the greater *apparent distance* of the moon when it is at the horizon than when it is at its zenith (something along the idea that "if it is really that far away, it must be really big").[3] When we discuss the *t* test in Chapters 12 through 14, we will examine Kaufman and Rock's data in more detail, but first we have to ask if the apparatus they used really produced a moon illusion in the first place. Table 5.4 gives the actual measures of the moon illusion collected by Kaufman and Rock. For these data a score of 1.73, for example, means that the moon appeared to the subject to be 1.73 times larger when on the horizon than when overhead. Ratios greater than 1.00 are what we would expect if the apparatus works correctly (producing an illusion). Ratios close to one would indicate little or no illusion. Moreover, we hope that if the task given the subjects is a good one, there would not be much variability in the scores.

As a review of the material in this chapter we can illustrate the procedures by performing the relevant calculations on these data.

Table 5.4 Moon illusion data

Illusion (X)	X^2
1.73	2.9929
1.06	1.1236
2.03	4.1209
1.40	1.9600
0.95	0.9025
1.13	1.2769
1.41	1.9881
1.73	2.9929
1.63	2.6569
1.56	2.4336
$\Sigma X = 14.63$	$\Sigma X^2 = 22.4483$

---

[3] For an interesting discussion of the recent work by Kaufman and his son, go to carlkop.home.xs4all/moonillu .html. The brief historical section near the end of that page is interesting, and shows that the moon illusion has been around for a very long time, as has what has now come to be the dominant theory used to explain it.

Mean:

$$\overline{X} = \frac{\Sigma X}{N} = \frac{14.63}{10} = 1.463$$

Variance:

$$s^2 = \frac{\Sigma X^2 - \dfrac{(\Sigma X)^2}{N}}{N-1} = \frac{22.4483 - \dfrac{(14.63)^2}{10}}{9} = 0.1161$$

Standard deviation:

$$s = \sqrt{0.1161} = 0.3407$$

So we have a mean illusion of 1.46, which tells us that the horizon moon looked almost one and a half times the size of the moon overhead (the zenith moon). With a standard deviation of .34, we can estimate that about two-thirds of the observations fell between 1.12 and 1.97, which is just the mean plus and minus a standard deviation. Now let's see what this looks like graphically.

Boxplots:

We can go about calculating the boxplot by systematically working through a number of steps. I broke things down this much to make it clear that there is a logical ordering for what we do.

First rearrange the observations in ascending order:

0.95 1.06 1.13 1.40 1.41 1.56 1.63 1.73 1.73 2.03

Calculate the median location so that we can get the median:

Median location = (N + 1)/2 = 11/2 = 5.5
Median = (1.41 + 1.56)/2 = 1.485

Now get the quartile locations so that we can find the first and third quartile:

Quartile location = (Median location + 1)/2 = (5 + 1)/2 = 3
(Drop fraction from median location if necessary.)
Quartiles = The third observations from the top and the bottom of the
ordered series
= 1.13 and 1.73

Now work on the whiskers

Interquartile range = Distance between third and first quartiles
= 1.73 – 1.13 = 0.60
1.5 × Interquartile range = 1.5(0.60) = 0.90
Maximum whisker length = Quartiles ± 1.5 × (Interquartile range)
Maximum of upper whisker = 1.73 + 0.90 = 2.63
Maximum of lower whisker = 1.13 – 0.90 = 0.23
Values closest to *but not exceeding* whisker lengths:
Lower whisker end = 0.95
Upper whisker end = 2.03

Resulting boxplot:

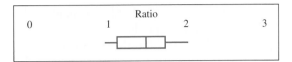

From these results we can see that the average moon illusion is well above 1.00; in fact only one measurement was less than 1. With a mean of 1.46, we can say that, on average, the horizon moon appears to be about half again as large (46% more) as the zenith moon. More important for our purposes here, the variability of the illusion is reasonably small; the standard deviation (s) = 0.34, meaning that the measurements are in pretty good agreement with one another, and there are no outliers. It looks as if Kaufman and Rock's apparatus works well for their purpose.

5.12 Seeing Statistics

Earlier I told you that we use the divisor of $N - 1$ in calculating the variance and standard deviation because it leads to a less biased estimate of the population variance. I largely left it to you to accept my statement on faith. However, using one of McClelland's applets from *Seeing Statistics*, you can illustrate this for yourself. You will see that while $N - 1$ does not *always* produce the better estimate, it certainly does on average.

The applet can be found at

 www.uvm.edu/~dhowell/fundamentals9/SeeingStatisticsApplets/Applets.html

and is named "Why divide by $N - 1$?" In this applet we have created a population consisting of each of the numbers between 0 and 100. Because we have the whole population, we know that the true mean is $\mu = 50$, and the variance is $\sigma^2 = 850$. The population standard deviation (σ) is thus 29.2. (You could calculate those for yourself if you are compulsive.) The applet itself, before any samples have been collected, looks like the one shown.

You can draw individual samples of size 3 from this population and display the results using both N and $N - 1$ as the denominator by clicking on the New Sample button. First, draw individual samples and note how they vary. Note that sometimes one denominator produces the closer estimate, and sometimes the other denominator does so. Now click on the "10 samples" button. This will draw 10 samples of $N = 3$ at once, and will give you the average values for these 10 samples. Such a display is illustrated next.

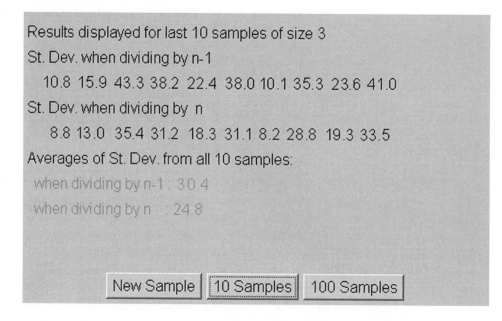

Results displayed for last 10 samples of size 3
St. Dev. when dividing by n-1
   10.8 15.9 43.3 38.2 22.4 38.0 10.1 35.3 23.6 41.0
St. Dev. when dividing by n
   8.8 13.0 35.4 31.2 18.3 31.1 8.2 28.8 19.3 33.5
Averages of St. Dev. from all 10 samples:
when dividing by n-1 : 30.4
when dividing by n   : 24.8

New Sample | 10 Samples | 100 Samples

Usually, though not always, with 10 samples you can see that the divisor of $N - 1$ produces the better average estimate. (Remember that the true population standard deviation is 29.2.) For this example, I have drawn 10 samples. The display shows you the estimated standard deviations for those 10 samples, as computed by using both $(N - 1)$ and N as the denominator. It also shows you the averages of the 10 values for each of those two estimates.

If you keep clicking on this button you will be adding 10 new samples to your collection each time. Clicking on the next button will add 100 samples at a time. I drew a total of 500 samples. Using $(N - 1)$ as the denominator, our average estimate was 31.8, which is too high by 2.6 units. Using N as the denominator, we were off, on average, by $29.2 - 26 = 3.2$ units. Clearly $(N - 1)$ was more accurate.

Click on the "100 Samples" button until you have accumulated about 5,000 samples. What is your average estimate of the population standard deviation using the two different divisors? (I found 29.1 and 23.8.)

It should be evident that as N, the size of an individual sample, increases, the relative difference between N and $N - 1$ will decrease. This should mean that there will be less of a difference between the two estimates. In addition, with larger sample sizes, the average sample standard deviation will more closely approximate σ. The second applet on your screen allows you to repeat the process above using a sample size of 15. What effect does this have on your results?

5.13 | **Summary**

In the last three chapters we have learned how to plot data, how to calculate sensible measures of the center of the distribution, and how to calculate measures of dispersion. In the rest of the book you will learn more about plotting data, but you basically have the information you will need about descriptive statistics, such as the mean and standard deviation.

We began with the simplest measure of dispersion, the range, which is just the difference between the lowest and highest scores. We built on the range to cover the interquartile range, which is the range after you remove the lowest and highest 25% of the scores. The interquartile range can also be thought of as the range of a 25% trimmed sample, because a 25% trimmed sample would discard the lowest and highest 25%. In fact, there is nothing uniquely important about the interquartile range, and we can take the range of a sample that has been trimmed of any specific percentage of cases.

The most commonly used measures of dispersion are the sample variance (s^2) and the sample standard deviation (s). The variance is essentially the average of the squared distances between each observation and the sample mean. To compute the variance, we "average" by dividing by one less than the sample size (i.e., $N - 1$), rather than by the full sample size. This gives us an unbiased estimate of the population variance (σ^2). The sample standard deviation (s) is simply the square root of the variance. An unbiased estimator is one whose long-term average is equal to the population parameter that it is intended to estimate. We also saw that when it comes to working with trimmed samples, we calculate our sample variance and standard deviation by creating a Winsorized sample, which is just a trimmed sample with the elements that were dropped being replaced by the lowest and highest elements that remain.

We looked at computational formulae for the variance and standard deviation. Unless you are doing calculations by hand, these formulae are not particularly important, though in the past they were very important and saved a great deal of time.

Boxplots were presented as an excellent way of creating a visual representation of our data. We draw a horizontal line at the median, then draw a box around the data from the first quartile to the third quartile, and then draw whiskers from each end of the box. The whiskers are equal in length to no more than 1.5 times the interquartile range. (They actually extend to the observation that is no more than that distance from the box.) Anything that lies beyond the end of the whiskers is considered an outlier and deserves serious attention.

Key Terms

Dispersion (variability), 81	Trimmed samples, 84
Range, 83	Trimmed statistics, 84
Outlier, 84	Sample variance (s^2), 85
Interquartile range, 84	Population variance (σ^2), 85

Standard deviation (s or σ), 87	Box-and-whisker plot, 91
Bias, 90	Quartile location, 93
Degrees of freedom (df), 90	Whisker, 94
Expected value, 91	Winsorized mean, 96
Boxplot, 91	Winsorized variance and standard deviation, 96

5.14 | A Quick Review

A. An outlier is
   Ans: An unusually extreme score.

B. What is a major problem with the interquartile range?
   Ans: It deletes so many observations that it eliminates much of the interesting variability in addition to the variability due to plan old extreme scores.

C. How would you describe the interquartile range with respect to trimmed samples?
   Ans: It is a 25% trimmed sample.

D. What is wrong with the average deviation from the mean?
   Ans: The average deviation will always be 0.0.

E. Why is the standard deviation a better measure than the variance when we are trying to *describe* data?
   Ans: The variance is a measure presented in terms of squared units, whereas the standard deviation is presented in terms of the units of measurement themselves.

F. Why do we divide by $N - 1$ instead of N when we are computing the variance and the standard deviation?
   Ans: This gives us an unbiased estimate of the population variance or standard deviation.

G. What do we mean by an "unbiased" estimate of a parameter?
   Ans: An unbiased estimate is one whose long-range average is equal to the parameter it is estimating.

H. We refer to quantities like $N - 1$ as _____.
   Ans: the degrees of freedom.

I. What is the "quartile location?"
   Ans: They are the points that cut off the first and third quartiles.

J. How do we determine the values that will be the end of the whiskers in a boxplot?
   Ans: They are the values that are *no more than* 1.5 times the interquartile range from the top and bottom of the box.

K. What is a Winsorized sample?
   Ans: One in which the trimmed values are replaced by the largest and smallest values that remain.

5.15 | Exercises

5.1 Calculate the range, the variance, and the standard deviation for data that Katz et al. collected on SAT performance without reading the passage. The data follow.

54 52 51 50 36 55 44 46 57 44 43 52

38 46 55 34 44 39 43 36 55 57 36 46

49 46 49 47

5.2 Calculate the range, the variance, and the standard deviation for the Katz et al. data on SAT performance after reading the passage.

66 75 72 71 55 56 72 93 73 72 72 73

91 66 71 56 59

5.3 Repeat exercises 5.1 and 5.2 using R. (It is easiest if you use the "describe" command from the "psych" library.)

5.4 In Exercise 5.1, what percentage of the scores fall within two standard deviations from the mean?

5.5 In Exercise 5.2, what percentage of the scores fall within two standard deviations from the mean?

5.6 Create a small data set of about seven scores and demonstrate that adding or subtracting a constant to each score does not change the standard deviation. What happens to the *mean* when a constant is added or subtracted?

5.7 Given the data you created in Exercise 5.6, show that multiplying or dividing by a constant multiplies or divides the standard deviation by that constant. How does this relate to what happens to the *mean* under similar circumstances?

5.8 Using what you have learned from Exercises 5.6 and 5.7, transform the following set of data to a new set with a standard deviation of 1.00.

5 8 3 8 6 9 9 7

5.9 Use the answers to Exercises 5.6 and 5.7 to modify the answer to Exercise 5.8 to have a mean of 0 and a standard deviation of 1.00. (*Note:* The solution to Exercises 5.8 and 5.9 will be important in Chapter 6.)

5.10 Create two sets of scores with equal ranges but different variances.

5.11 Create a boxplot for the data in Exercise 5.1.

5.12 Create a boxplot for the data in Exercise 5.2 using R or SPSS if possible.

5.13 Create a boxplot for the variable ADDSC in Appendix D. These data are available at

🌐 **https://www.uvm.edu/~dhowell/fundamentals9/DataFiles/Add.dat**

5.14 Using the data for the variable ENGG in Appendix D

(a) Calculate the variance and the standard deviation for ENGG.

(b) These measures should be greater than the corresponding measures on GPA. Can you explain why this should be? (We will come back to this later in Chapter 12, but see if you can figure it out.)

5.15 The mean of the data used in Exercise 5.1 is 46.57. Suppose that we had an additional subject who had a score of 46.57. Recalculate the variance for these data. (You can build on the intermediate steps used in Exercise 5.1.) What effect does this score have on the answers to Exercise 5.1?

5.16   Instead of adding a score equal to the mean (as in Exercise 5.15), add a score of 40 to the data used in Exercise 5.1. How does this score affect the answers to Exercise 5.1?

5.17   Use SPSS, R, or other software to draw a set of boxplots (similar to Figure 5.3b) to illustrate the effect of increase in the angle of rotation in the Mental Rotation data set. The data can be found at https://www.uvm.edu/~dhowell/fundamentals9/DataFiles/MentalRotation.dat (A file with the "sav" extension is the SPSS file itself, and you can load that file if you want to use SPSS.)

5.18   Given the following data:

1 3 3 5 8 8 9 12 13 16 17 17 18 20 21 30

(a) Draw a boxplot.
(b) Calculate the standard deviation of these data and divide every score by the standard deviation.
(c) Draw a boxplot for the data in (b).
(d) Compare the two boxplots.

5.19   The following graph came from the JMP statistical package applied to the data in Table 5.3 on length of hospitalization. Notice the boxplot on the top of the figure. How does that boxplot compare with the ones we have been using? (*Hint:* The mean is 4.66.)

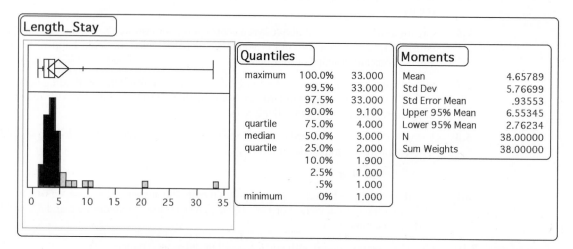

5.20   In Section 5.10, statistics were computed from the reaction time data in Chapter 3. What would you conclude from these data about the relationship between accuracy and reaction time?

5.21   Everitt, as reported in Hand et al. (1994), presented data on the amount of weight gained by 72 anorexic girls under one of three treatment conditions. The conditions were Cognitive Behavior Therapy, Family Therapy, and a Control group who received no treatment. The data follow, and are available on the Web as Ex5.21.dat:

Cog.	1.7	0.7	−0.1	−0.7	−3.5	14.9	3.5	17.1	−7.6	1.6	11.7	6.1	1.1	−4.0
Behav.	20.9	−9.1	2.1	−1.4	1.4	−0.3	−3.7	−0.8	2.4	12.6	1.9	3.9	0.1	15.4
	−0.7													
Family	11.4	11.0	5.5	9.4	13.6	−2.9	−0.1	7.4	21.5	−5.3	−3.8	13.4	13.1	9.0
	3.9	5.7	10.7											
Control	−0.5	−9.3	−5.4	12.3	−2.0	−10.2	−12.2	11.6	−7.1	6.2	−0.2	−9.2	8.3	3.3
	11.3	0.0	−1.0	−10.6	−4.6	−6.7	2.8	0.3	1.8	3.7	15.9	−10.2		

a) What would you hypothesize about central tendency and variability?

b) Calculate the relevant descriptive statistics and graphics for each condition separately.

c) What kind of conclusions would you feel comfortable in drawing, and why? (We haven't covered hypothesis testing, but you are doing an elementary hypothesis test here. Think carefully about how you are doing it—it may help you in Chapter 8.)

5.22 Compare the mean, standard deviation, and variance for the data in Exercise 5.1 with their trimmed and Winsorized counterparts.

5.23 Compare the mean, standard deviation, and variance for the data for the Cognitive Behavior condition in Exercise 5.21 with their 20% trimmed and Winsorized counterparts. Why is the Winsorized variance noticeably smaller than the usual variance? (You can do this using *R* by loading the "psych" library and using the "describe" command.)

## CHAPTER 6

The Normal Distribution

In this chapter we will look at the normal distribution, which is a distribution that is very important to statisticians. I assume that the word "normal" came from the fact that at one time people thought that the distribution was extremely common and applied to such things as weight, intelligence, level of self-confidence, and so on. Because there are an unlimited number of normal distributions, one for each combination of mean and variance, we are going to look at ways to rein them in and work with a common scale. We will then show that we can use the normal distribution to derive probabilities of events and will see how to do that. We will also see that there are many other distributions that are similar to the normal distribution and are used in many applications. Finally, we will use applets to demonstrate how to work with the normal distribution.

From the preceding chapters it should be apparent that we are going to be very much concerned with distributions—distributions of data, hypothetical distributions of populations, and sampling distributions. Of all the possible forms that distributions can take, the class known as the **normal distribution** is by far the most important for our purposes.

Before elaborating on the normal distribution, however, it is worth a short digression to explain just why we are so interested in distributions in general. The critical factor is that there is an important link between distributions and probabilities. If we know something about the distribution of events (or of sample statistics), we know something about the probability that

CONCEPTS THAT YOU WILL NEED TO REMEMBER FROM PREVIOUS CHAPTERS

Independent variable:	The variable you manipulate or are studying
Dependent variable:	The variable that you are measuring—the data
X axis:	The horizontal axis, also called the abscissa
Y axis:	The vertical axis, also called the ordinate
Histogram:	A plot of data with the values of the dependent variable on the X axis and the frequency with which those occurred on the Y axis
Bar chart:	A graph with the independent variable on the X axis and the mean or other measure on the Y axis
$\overline{X}$:	A common symbol for the mean
s^2:	A common symbol for the variance
Σ:	The symbol for summation of what follows
N:	The number of observations

one of those events (or statistics) is likely to occur. To see the issue in its simplest form, take the lowly pie chart. (This is the only time you will see a pie chart in this book. They are very difficult to interpret accurately, and there are much better choices. We shouldn't be using graphics whose message isn't obvious.)

The pie chart shown in Figure 6.1 is taken from a U.S. Department of Justice report on probation and parole. It shows the status of all individuals convicted of a criminal offense. From this figure you can see that 9% were in jail, 19% were in prison, 61% were on probation, and the remaining 11% were on parole. You can also see that the percentages in each category are directly reflected in the percentage of the area of the pie that each wedge occupies. The area taken up by each segment is directly proportional to the percentage of individuals in that segment. Moreover, if we declare that the total area of the pie is 1.00 unit, the area of each segment is equal to the proportion of observations falling within that segment.[1]

It is easy to go from speaking about areas to speaking about probabilities. The concept of probability will be elaborated on in Chapter 7, but even without a precise definition of probability we can make an important point about areas of a pie chart. For now, simply think of probability in its common everyday usage, referring to the likelihood that some event will occur. From this perspective it is logical to conclude that, because 19% of those convicted of a federal crime are currently in prison, if we were to draw at random the name of one person from a list of convicted individuals, the probability is .19 that the individual would be in prison. To put this in slightly different terms, if 19% of the area of the pie is allocated to prison, then the probability that a randomly chosen person would fall into that segment is .19.

This pie chart also allows us to explore the addition of areas. It should be clear that if 19% are in prison and 9% are in jail, $19 + 9 = 28\%$ are incarcerated. In other words,

Figure 6.1   Pie chart showing persons under correctional supervision, by type of supervision in 1982[2]

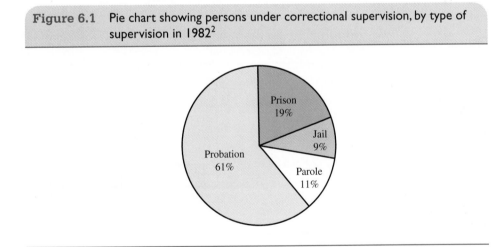

---

[1]Some students think that it is rather cavalier to just decide on your own that the area of the pie is 1.0 unit. If you have that problem, just imagine redrawing the pie chart, to scale, so that its total area is one square inch. Then a slice of the pie that represents 25% of the incarcerations, will actually measure 0.25 square inch.

[2]For 2004, the figures were Jail = 10%, Prison = 20%, Probation = 60%, and Parole = 10%. What does this tell us about changes in how we deal with convictions? A search of the Internet under the words "correctional supervision" reveals all sorts of interesting statistics, which seem to vary with the politics of the person reporting them. In particular, you might try http://www.ojp.usdoj.gov/bjs/glance/corr2.htm. (Just double click on the graphic to see the raw data.) The alarming thing is that the percentages haven't changed all that much but the total numbers have gone up drastically.

we can find the percentage of individuals in one of several independent categories just by adding the percentages for each category. The same thing holds in terms of areas, in the sense that we can find the percentage of incarcerated individuals by adding the areas devoted to prison and to jail. And finally, if we can find percentages by adding areas, we can also find probabilities by adding areas. Thus the probability of being incarcerated is the probability of being in one of the two segments associated with incarceration, which we can get by summing the two areas (or their associated probabilities). I hope that I haven't really told you anything that you didn't already know. I'm just setting the stage for what follows.

There are other, and better, ways to present data besides pie charts. One of the simplest is a bar chart, where the height of each bar is proportional to the percentage of observations falling in that category. (We saw a bar chart in Figure 3.5, where the Y axis represented the mean reaction time and the X axis represented the correctness of the choice.) Figure 6.2 is a redrawing of Figure 6.1 in the form of a bar chart. Although this figure does not contain any new information, it has two advantages over the pie chart. First, it is easier to compare categories because the only thing we need to look at is the height of the bar, rather than trying to compare the lengths of two different arcs in different orientations. The second advantage is that the bar chart is visually more like the common distributions we will deal with, in that the various levels or categories are spread out along the horizontal dimension, and the percentages in each category are shown along the vertical dimension. Here again you can see that the various areas of the distribution are related to probabilities. Further, you can see that we can meaningfully sum areas in exactly the same way that we did in the pie chart. When we move to other distributions, particularly the normal distribution, the principles of areas, percentages, probabilities, and the addition of areas or probabilities carry over almost without change.

Figure 6.2   Bar chart showing persons under correctional supervision, by type of supervision[3]

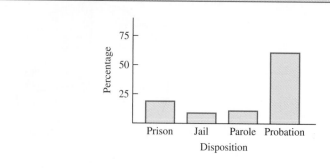

---

[3]This plot can be created with the following *R* code

```
# Bar chart for correctional supervision
areas <- c(.61, .19, .09, .11)
name <- names(areas) <- c("Probation","Prison","Jail", "Parole")
barplot(height = areas, ylab = "Percentage", main = "Form of
Supervision", density = 10, col = "darkgreen")
```

6.1 The Normal Distribution

Now let's move closer to the normal distribution. I stated earlier that the normal distribution is one of the most important distributions we will encounter. There are several reasons for this:

1. Many of the dependent variables with which we deal are commonly assumed to be normally distributed in the population. That is to say, we frequently assume that if we were to obtain the whole population of observations, the resulting distribution would closely resemble the normal distribution. Such assumptions are often necessary to justify the computation of a probability value that we will develop as a result of the data.

2. If we can assume that a variable is at least approximately normally distributed, then the techniques that are discussed in this chapter allow us to make a number of inferences (either exact or approximate) about values of that variable.

3. The theoretical distribution of the hypothetical set of sample *means* obtained by drawing an infinite number of samples from a specified population can be shown to be approximately normal under a wide variety of conditions. Such a distribution is called the sampling distribution of the mean and is discussed and used extensively throughout the remainder of this book.

4. Most of the statistical procedures we will employ have, somewhere in their derivation, an assumption that a variable is normally distributed.

To introduce the normal distribution, we will look at one additional data set that is approximately normal (and would be closer to normal if we had more observations). The data we are going to look at were collected using the Achenbach Youth Self-Report form (Achenbach[4], 1991). This is one of the most frequently used measures of childhood behavior problems, and it produces scores on a number of different dimensions. The one we are going to look at is the dimension of Total Behavior Problems, which represents the total number of behavior problems reported by the child's parent (weighted by the severity of the problem). (Examples of Behavior Problem categories are "Argues," "Impulsive," "Shows off," and "Teases.") Figure 6.3 is a histogram of data from 289 junior high-school students. A higher score represents more behavior problems. (For the moment, ignore the smooth curve that is superimposed on the figure.) You can see that this distribution has a center very near 50 and is fairly symmetrically distributed on either side of that value, with the scores ranging between about 25 and 75. The standard deviation of this distribution is approximately 10. The distribution is not perfectly even—it has some bumps and valleys—but overall it is fairly smooth, rising in the center and falling off at the ends. (The actual mean and standard deviation for this particular sample are 49.13 and 10.56, respectively.)[5]

---

[4]Tom Achenbach has developed several extremely important scales for looking at behavior problems in children, and these scales are widely used in clinical work.
[5]The R code for superimposing this normal distribution is available on the Web page for this chapter.

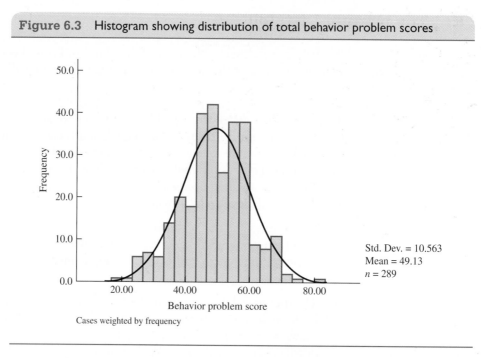

Figure 6.3 Histogram showing distribution of total behavior problem scores

Std. Dev. = 10.563
Mean = 49.13
$n = 289$

Behavior problem score

Cases weighted by frequency

One thing that you might note from this distribution is that if you add the frequencies of subjects falling into the intervals 52–53, 54–55, and 56–57, you will find that 64 students obtained scores between 52 and 56. Because there are 289 observations in this sample, 64/289 = 22% of the observations fell in this interval. This illustrates the comments made earlier on the addition of areas.

If we take this same set of data and represent it by a line graph rather than a histogram, we obtain Figure 6.4. There is absolutely no information in this figure that was not in Figure 6.3. I merely connected the tops of the bars in the histogram and then erased the bars themselves. Why, then, waste an artist's time by putting in a figure that has nothing new to offer? The reason is simply that I want to get people to see the transition from a histogram, which you often see when you open a newspaper or a magazine, to a line graph. The next transition from there to the smoothed curves you will often see in the rest of the book. You can see that smoothed curve in Figure 6.3, where I instructed SPSS to superimpose the best-fitting normal distribution on top of the histogram. The major difference between the line graph (frequency polygon) and the smoothed curve is that the latter is a stylized version that leaves out the bumps and valleys. If you would prefer, you can always think of the smoothed curve as sitting on top of an invisible histogram (with very narrow bars).

Now we are ready to go to the normal distribution. First, we will consider it in the abstract, and then we will take a concrete example, making use of the Achenbach Youth Self-Report Total Behavior Problem scores that we saw in Figures 6.3 and 6.4.

The distribution shown in Figure 6.5 is a characteristic normal distribution. It is a symmetric, unimodal distribution, frequently referred to as "bell shaped," and

Figure 6.4 Frequency polygon showing distribution of total behavior problem scores

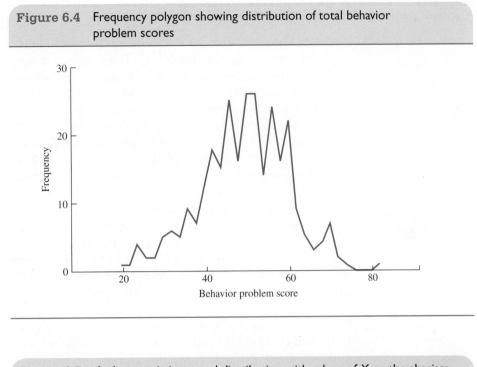

Figure 6.5 A characteristic normal distribution with values of X on the abscissa and density on the ordinate

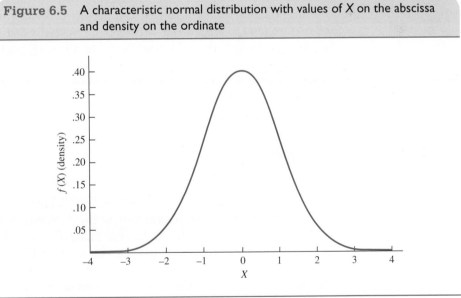

has limits of ±∞. The **abscissa**, or horizontal axis, represents different possible values of X, while the **ordinate**, or vertical axis, is referred to as the **density**, often denoted $f(x)$, and is related to (but not the same as) the frequency or probability of occurrence of X. The concept of density is discussed in further detail in the next chapter.

The normal distribution has a long history. It was originally investigated by Abraham DeMoivre (1667–1754), who was interested in its use to describe the results of games of chance (gambling). The distribution was defined precisely by Pierre-Simon Laplace (1749–1827) and put in its more usual form by Carl Friedrich Gauss (1777–1855), both of whom were interested in the distribution of errors in astronomical observations. In fact, the normal distribution often is referred to as the Gaussian distribution and as the "normal law of error." Adolphe Quetelet (1796–1874), a Belgian astronomer, was the first to apply the distribution to social and biological data. He collected chest measurements of Scottish soldiers and heights of French soldiers. (I can't imagine why—he must have had too much time on his hands.) He found that both sets of measurements were approximately normally distributed. Quetelet interpreted the data to indicate that the mean of this distribution was the ideal at which nature was aiming, and observations to either side of the mean represented error (a deviation from nature's ideal). (For 5'8" males like me, it is somehow comforting to think of all those bigger guys as nature's errors, although I don't imagine they think of themselves that way.) Although we no longer think of the mean as nature's ideal, this is a useful way to conceptualize variability around the mean. In fact, we still use the word *error* to refer to deviations from the mean. Francis Galton (1822–1911) carried Quetelet's ideas further and gave the normal distribution a central role in psychological theory, especially the theory of mental abilities. Some would insist that Galton was *too* successful in this endeavor, and that we tend to assume that measures are normally distributed even when they are not. I won't argue the issue here, but it is very much a point of debate among statisticians.

Mathematically the normal distribution is defined as

$$f(X) = \frac{1}{\sigma\sqrt{2\pi}}(e)^{-\frac{(X-\mu)^2}{2\sigma^2}}$$

where π and e are constants ($\pi = 3.1416$ and $e = 2.7183$), and μ and σ are the mean and the standard deviation, respectively, of the distribution. Given that μ and σ are known, $f(X)$, the height of the curve, or ordinate, for any value of X is obtained simply by substituting the appropriate values for μ, σ, and X and solving the equation. This is not nearly as difficult as it looks, but in practice you will probably never have to make the calculations. The cumulative form of this distribution is tabled, and we can simply read the information we need from the table.

Those of you who have had a course in calculus may recognize that the area under the curve between any two values of X (say, X_1 and X_2), and thus the probability that a randomly drawn score will fall within that interval, could be found by integrating the function over the range from X_1 to X_2—although that is not a simple task. Those of you who have not had such a course can take comfort from the fact that tables are readily available in which this work has already been done for us or by use of which we can easily do the work ourselves. Such a table appears in Appendix E (Table E.10), and an abbreviated version of that table is shown later in the chapter in Table 6.1.

Most people are happy to take this formula on faith, especially because they will never have to use it. But for those who like formulae or don't take things on faith, assume that we had a population with a mean (μ) = 0 and a standard deviation (σ) = 1. We want to know how high the curve will be (its density) at a score of X = 1, where mu = 0 and sigma = 1. Then

$$f(X) = \frac{1}{\sigma\sqrt{2\pi}}(e)^{-\frac{(X-\mu)^2}{2\sigma^2}} = \frac{1}{1\sqrt{2\pi}}e^{-\frac{(X-0)^2}{2(1)}}$$

$$= \frac{1}{\sqrt{2(3.1416)}}e^{-\frac{X^2}{2}} = \frac{1}{2.5066}e^{-\frac{1}{2}} = 0.3989 * (2.7183)^{-.5} = .2420$$

For those who think that paper and pencil tables and calculations went out in the very dim past before instant messaging and the iPod, you can go to the Web and find sites that will do the calculations for you. One of the best is at http://www.danielsoper .com/statcalc3/, although the pop-up ads that sometimes take over make me prefer the calculators at vassarstats.net or the simpler, but less complete, ones at http://statpages.org/ pdfs.html.

If you are using R, the calculation can be made simply by invoking the command

```
dnorm(x = 1, mean = 0, sd = 1)
```

You might be excused at this point for wondering why anyone would want to table, or compute, such a distribution in the first place. Just because a distribution is common (or at least commonly assumed) doesn't automatically suggest a reason for having an appendix that tells all about it. But there is a reason. By using Table E.10, we can readily calculate the probability that a score drawn at random from the population will have a value lying between any two specified points (X_1 and X_2). Thus by using statistical tables we can make probability statements in answer to a variety of questions. You will see examples of such questions in the rest of this chapter and in many other chapters throughout the book. You can also use a site such as Soper's to do these calculations easily.

6.2 The Standard Normal Distribution

A problem arises when we try to table the normal distribution, because the distribution depends on the values of the mean (μ) and the standard deviation (σ) of the population. To do the job right, we would have to make up a different table for every possible combination of the values of μ and σ, which certainly is not practical. What we actually have in Table E10 is what is called the **standard normal distribution**, which has a mean of 0 and a standard deviation and variance of 1. Such a distribution is often designated as $N(0, 1)$, where N refers to the fact that it is normal, 0 is the value of μ, and 1 is the value of σ^2. The more general expression is $N(\mu, \sigma^2)$. Given the standard normal distribution in the appendix and a set of rules for transforming any normal distribution to standard form and vice versa, we can use Table E.10 or any statistical calculator to find the areas under any normal distribution.

You might think about what we are doing here by converting values to a standard normal distribution as vaguely similar to letter grades that you get on an exam. You might take a 100-question exam and get 90 questions right. I might take a 50-item exam and get 45 items right. Someone else may take a 10-question exam and get nine questions correct. We all have different numbers correct, but we will all probably get an A on the exam. What we are doing with both z and the letter grade is essentially adjusting for the different scales on which those numbers are measured.

Consider the distribution shown in Figure 6.6, with a mean of 50 and a standard deviation of 10 (variance of 100). It represents the distribution of *an entire population* of Total Behavior Problem scores from the Achenbach Youth Self-Report form, of which the data in Figures 6.3 and 6.4 are a sample. If we knew something about the areas under the curve in Figure 6.6, we could say something about the probability of various values of Behavior Problem scores and could identify, for example, those scores that are so high that they are obtained by only 5% or 10% of the population.

The only printed tables of the normal distribution that are readily available are those of the *standard* normal distribution. Therefore, before we can answer questions about the probability that an individual will get a score above some particular value, we must first transform the distribution in Figure 6.6 (or at least specific points along it) to a standard normal distribution. That is, we want to be able to say that a score of X_i from a normal distribution with a mean of 50 and a variance of 100—often denoted $N(50,100)$—is comparable to a score of z from a distribution with a mean of 0 and a variance, and standard deviation, of 1—denoted $N(0,1)$. Then anything that is true of z_i is also true of X_i, and z and X are comparable variables.

Figure 6.6 A normal distribution with various transformations on the abscissa

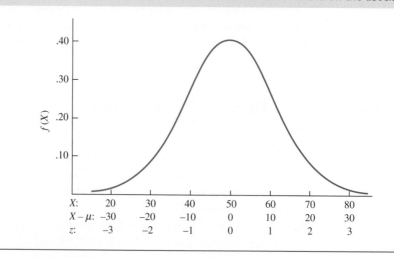

From Exercise 5.6 we know that subtracting a constant from each score in a set of scores reduces the mean of the set by that constant. Thus if we subtract 50 (the mean) from all the values for X, the new mean will be 50 − 50 = 0. (More generally, the distribution of [X − μ] has a mean of 0.) The effect of this transformation is shown in the second set of values for the abscissa in Figure 6.6. We are halfway there, because we now have the mean down to 0, although the standard deviation (s) is still 10. We also know from Exercise 5.7 that if we divide all values of a variable by a constant (e.g., 10), we divide the standard deviation by that constant. Thus after dividing the deviations from the mean by 10 the standard deviation will now be 10/10 = 1, which is just what we wanted. We will call this transformed distribution z and define it, on the basis of what we have done, as

$$z = \frac{X - \mu}{\sigma}$$

Notice that we subtract the mean before we divide by the standard deviation.

For our particular case, where μ = 50 and σ = 10,

$$z = \frac{X - \mu}{\sigma} = \frac{X - 50}{10}$$

The third set of values (labeled z) for the abscissa in Figure 6.6 shows the effect of this transformation. Note that aside from a **linear transformation**[6] of the numerical values, the data have not been changed in any way. The distribution has the same shape and the observations continue to stand in the same relation to each other as they did before the transformation. It should not come as a great surprise that changing the unit of measurement does not change the shape of the distribution or the relative standing of observations. Whether we measure the quantity of alcohol that people consume per week in ounces or in milliliters really makes no difference in the relative standing of people. It just changes the numerical values on the abscissa. (The town drunk is still the town drunk, even if now his liquor is measured in milliliters.)

If we had a score of 43, the value of z would be

$$z = \frac{(X - \mu)}{\sigma} = \frac{(43 - 50)}{10} = \frac{-7}{10} = -.70$$

It is important to realize exactly what converting X to z has accomplished. A score that used to be 60 is now 1. That is, a score that used to be one standard deviation (10 points) above the mean remains one standard deviation above the mean,

---

[6]A linear transformation involves only multiplication (or division) of X by a constant and/or adding or subtracting a constant to or from X. Such a transformation leaves the relationship among the values unaffected. In other words, it does not distort values at one part of the scale more than values at another part. Changing units from inches to centimeters is a good example of a linear transformation.

but now is given a new value of 1. A score of 43, which was 0.7 standard deviation *below* the mean, now is given the value of −0.7, and so on. In other words, a **z score** represents the number of standard deviations that X_i is above or below the mean—a positive z score being above the mean and a negative z score being below the mean.

The equation for z is completely general. We can transform any distribution to a distribution of z scores simply by applying this equation. Keep in mind, however, the point that was just made. The *shape* of the distribution is unaffected by the transformation. That means that *if the distribution was not normal before it was transformed, it will not be normal afterward.* Some people believe that they can "normalize" (in the sense of producing a normal distribution) their data by transforming them to z. It just won't work.

The standard normal distribution is a normal distribution with a mean of 0 and a standard deviation of 1. It serves as the basis for much that follows and values along that distribution are often referred to as z scores. A z score represents the number of standard deviations an object is above or below the mean.

Using the Tables of the Standard Normal Distribution

As I have mentioned, the standard normal distribution is extensively tabled. Although I hope that most students will use a software program to make calculations—for $2.99 I have the Statsmate© app on my cell phone—describing the use of tables makes the underlying process a bit clearer. Such a table can be found in Table E.10, part of which is reproduced in Table 6.1.[7] To see how we can make use of this table, consider the normal distribution represented in Figure 6.7. This might represent the standardized distribution of the Behavior Problem scores as seen in Figure 6.6. Suppose we want to know how much of the area under the curve is above one standard deviation from the mean if the total area under the curve is taken to be 1.00. (We care about areas because they translate directly to probabilities.) We already have seen that z scores represent standard deviations from the mean, and thus we know that we want to find the area above $z = 1$.

Only the positive half of the normal distribution is tabled. Because the distribution is symmetric, any information given about a positive value of z applies equally to the corresponding negative value of z. From Table 6.1 (or Table E.10) we find the row corresponding to $z = 1.00$. Reading across that row, we can see that the area from the *mean to z = 1* is 0.3413, the area in the *larger portion* is 0.8413, and the area in the *smaller portion* is 0.1587. (If you visualize the distribution being divided into the segment below $z = 1$ [the unshaded part of Figure 6.7] and the segment above $z = 1$ [the shaded part], the meanings of the terms *larger portion* and *smaller portion*

---

[7]Later in this chapter we will use McClelland's *Seeing Statistics* applets to explore the normal distribution further.

Table 6.1 The Normal Distribution (Abbreviated Version of Table E.10)

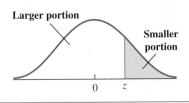

z	Mean to z	Larger Portion	Smaller Portion	z	Mean to z	Larger Portion	Smaller PorHon
0.00	0.0000	0.5000	0.5000	0.45	0.1736	0.6736	0.3264
0.01	0.0040	0.5040	0.4960	0.46	0.1772	0.6772	0.3228
0.02	0.0060	0.5080	0.4920	0.47	0.1808	0.6808	0.3192
0.03	0.0120	0.5120	0.4880	0.48	0.1844	0.6844	0.3156
0.04	0.0160	0.5160	0.4840	0.49	0.1879	0.6879	0.3121
0.05	0.0199	0.5199	0.4801	0.50	0.1915	0.6915	0.3085
...	...	...	...	...	...	...	...
0.97	0.3340	0.8340	0.1660	1.42	0.4222	0.9222	0.0778
0.98	0.3365	0.8365	0.1635	1.43	0.4236	0.9236	0.0764
0.99	0.3389	0.8389	0.1611	1.44	0.4251	0.9251	0.0749
1.00	0.3413	0.8413	0.1587	1.45	0.4265	0.9265	0,0735
1.01	0.3438	0.8438	0.1562	1.46	0.4279	0.9279	0.0721
1.02	0.3461	0.8461	0.1539	1.47	0.4292	0.9292	0.0708
1.03	0.3485	0.8485	0.1515	1.48	0.4306	0.9306	0.0694
1.04	0.3508	0.8508	0.1492	1.49	0.4319	0.9319	0.0681
1.05	0.3531	0.8531	0.1469	1.50	0.4332	0.9332	0.0668
...	...	...	...	...	...	...	...
1,95	0.4744	0.9744	0.0256	2.40	0.4918	0.9918	0.0082
1.96	0.4750	0.9750	0.0250	2.41	0.4920	0.9920	0.0080
1.97	0.4756	0.9756	0.0244	2.42	0.4922	0.9922	0.0078
1.98	0.4761	0.9761	0.0239	2.43	0.4925	0.9925	0.0075
1.99	0.4767	0.9767	0.0233	2.44	0.4927	0.9927	0.0073
2.00	0.4772	0.9772	0,0228	2.45	0.4929	0.9929	0.0071
2.01	0.4778	0.9778	0,0222	2.46	0.4931	0.9931	0.0069
2.02	0.4783	0.9783	0.0217	2.47	0.4932	0.9932	0.0068
2.03	0.4788	0.9788	0.0212	2.48	0.4934	0.9934	0.0066
2.04	0.4793	0.9793	0.0207	2.49	0,4936	0.9936	0.0064
2.05	0.4798	0.9798	0.0202	2.50	0.4938	0.9938	0,0062

become obvious.) Thus the answer to our original question is 0.1587. Because we already have equated the terms *area* and *probability* (see Chapter 3), we now can say that if we sample a child at random from the population of children, and if Behavior Problem scores are normally distributed with a mean of 50 and a standard deviation of 10, then the probability that the child will score *more than* one standard deviation

Figure 6.7 Illustrative areas under the normal distribution

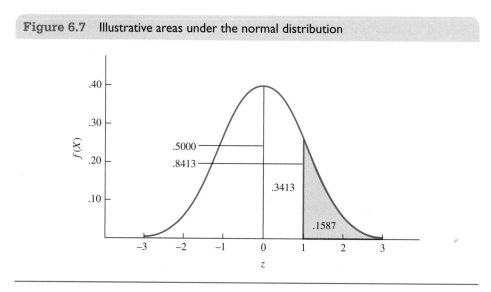

above the mean of the population (i.e., above 60) is .1587. Because the distribution is symmetric, we also know that the probability that a child will score more than one standard deviation *below* the mean of the population is also .1587.

Now suppose that we want the probability that the child will be more than one standard deviation (10 points) from the mean *in either direction*. This is a simple matter of the summation of areas. Because we know that the normal distribution is symmetric, then the area below $z = -1$ will be the same as the area above $z = +1$. This is why the table does not contain negative values of z—they are not needed. We already know that the areas in which we are interested are each 0.1587. Then the total area outside $z = \pm 1$ must be 0.1587 + 0.1587 = 0.3174. The converse is also true. If the area outside $z = \pm 1$ is 0.3174, then the area between $z = +1$ and $z = -1$ is equal to 1 − 0.3174 = 0.6826. Thus the probability that a child will score between 40 and 60 is .6826. This is the origin of an earlier statement that for many distributions approximately two-thirds of the scores fall within a standard deviation of the mean.

To extend this procedure, consider the situation in which we want to know the probability that a score will be between 30 and 40. A little arithmetic will show that this is simply the probability of falling between 1.0 standard deviation below the mean and 2.0 standard deviations below the mean. This situation is diagrammed in Figure 6.8.

It is always wise to draw simple diagrams such as Figure 6.8. They eliminate many errors and make clear the area(s) for which you are looking.

From Table E.10 we know that the area from the mean to $z = -2.0$ is 0.4772 and from the mean to $z = -1.0$ is 0.3413. The difference in these two areas must represent the area between $z = -2.0$ and $z = -1.0$. This area is 0.4772 − 0.3413 = 0.1359. Thus the probability that Behavior Problem scores drawn at random from a normally distributed population will be between 30 and 40 is .1359.

> **Figure 6.8** Areas between 1.0 and 2.0 standard deviations below the mean

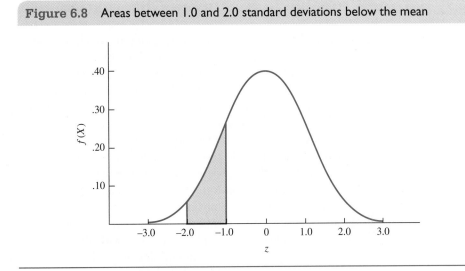

I Don't Like Tables—Using Online Calculators

Last summer I had a high-school student down the street stop by and ask me for statistical advice. After we did the necessary calculation, I said that we could find the answer by looking in the table. She looked at me as if I were crazy, and said that she had been taught to find the probability on her calculator. I felt a little foolish saying, "Well, I don't use the appendices either. I do the calculation using R." It's hard not to look foolish when a high-school student knows a better way.

As I said, you can make these calculations using an online calculator such as the one found at http://www.danielsoper.com/statcalc3. Select the Normal Distribution from the menu and then try out various calculators from the choices given. If you were to select the z-score calculator, for example, you could specify a percentage of the area under the normal curve (e.g., 0.85) and the calculator will give you the z score that cuts off that percentage (1.0364). See Figure 6.9 for an example. [You can find the same result in R using $z = $ qnorm(0.85, 0, 1).]

> **Figure 6.9** Calculation of z using an online calculator

> **Standard Normal Distribution Z-Score Calculator**
>
> ▼ 🖩
>
> 🐦 Tweet 👍 +1 f Recommend 8
>
> This calculator will tell you the normal distribution Z-score associated with a given cumulative probability level.
>
> Please supply the necessary parameter value, and then click 'Calculate'.
>
> Cumulative probability level: [0.85] ⓘ
>
> [Calculate!]
>
> Z-score: **1.03643339**

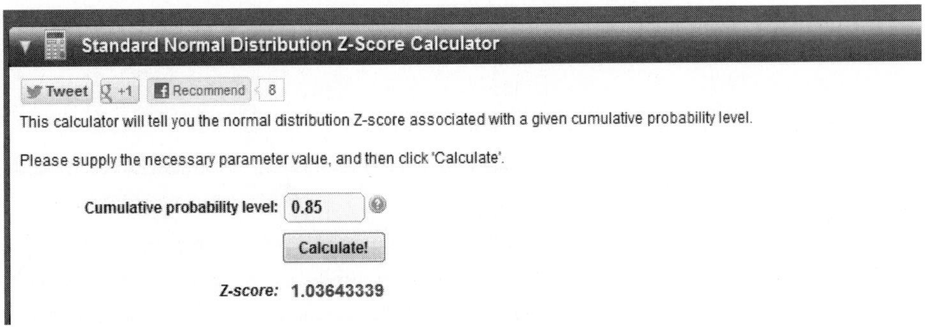

6.3 Setting Probable Limits on an Observation

For a final example, consider the situation in which we want to identify limits within which we have some specified degree of confidence that a child sampled at random will fall. In other words, we want to make a statement of the form, "If I draw a child at random from this population, 95% of the time her score will lie between _____ and _____." From Figure 6.10 you can see the limits we want—the limits that include 95% of the scores in the population.

If we are looking for the limits within which 95% of the scores fall, we also are looking for the limits beyond which the remaining 5% of the scores fall. To rule out this remaining 5%, we want to find that value of z that cuts off 2.5% at each end, or "tail," of the distribution. (We do not need to use symmetric limits, but we typically do because they usually make the most sense and produce the shortest interval.) From Table E.10 we see that these values are $z \pm 1.96$. Thus we can say that 95% of the time a child's score sampled at random will fall between 1.96 standard deviations above the mean and 1.96 standard deviations below the mean. (Using the online calculator mentioned earlier, select the "Standard Normal Distribution Z-score calculator and enter 0.025 or 0.975 to get the appropriate cutoffs.)

Because we generally want to express our answers in terms of raw Behavior Problem scores, rather than z scores, we must do a little more work. To obtain the raw score limits, we simply work the formula for z backward, solving for X instead of z. Thus if we want to state the limits within which 95% of the population falls, we want to find those scores that are 1.96 standard deviations above or below the mean of the population. This can be written as

$$z = \frac{X - \mu}{\sigma}$$

$$\pm 1.96 = \frac{X - \mu}{\sigma}$$

$$X - \mu = \pm 1.96\sigma$$

$$X = \mu \pm 1.96\sigma$$

Figure 6.10   Values of z that enclose 95% of the behavior problem scores

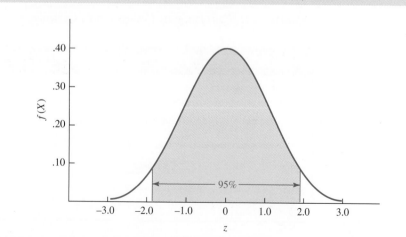

where the values of X corresponding to $(\mu + 1.96\sigma)$ and $(\mu - 1.96\sigma)$ represent the limits we seek. For our example the limits will be

$$\text{Limits} = 50 \pm (1.96)(10) = 50 \pm 19.6 = 30.4 \text{ and } 69.6$$

So the probability is .95 that a child's score (X) chosen at random would be between 30.4 and 69.6. We may not be interested in low scores because they don't represent behavior problems. But anyone with a score of 69.6 or higher is a problem to someone. Only 2.5% of children score that high.

Although we do not use what I have called "probable limits" very often, I have introduced them here because they are a great introduction to what we will later see as "confidence limits." With probable limits, we know the mean and standard deviation of a population and want to make an intelligent guess where individual observations would fall. With confidence limits, we have individual observations and want to make an intelligent guess about probable values of the population mean. You don't need to know anything about confidence limits at this point, but remember this discussion when we come to them in Chapter 12.

6.4   Measures Related to *z*

We already have seen that the *z* formula given earlier can be used to convert a distribution with any mean and variance to a distribution with a mean of 0 and a standard deviation (and variance) of 1. We frequently refer to such transformed scores as **standard scores**, and the process of computing these standard scores is called **standardization**. Every day, people use other transformational scoring systems with particular properties without realizing what they are.

A good example of such a scoring system is the common IQ. Raw scores from an IQ test are routinely transformed to a distribution with a mean of 100 and a standard deviation of 15 (or 16 in the case of the Binet). Knowing this, you can readily convert an individual's IQ (e.g., 120) to his or her position in terms of standard deviations above or below the mean (i.e., you can calculate the *z* score). Because IQ scores are more or less normally distributed, you can then convert *z* into a percentage measure by use of Table E.10. (In this example, a score of 120 would be 1.33 standard deviations above the mean, and would have approximately 91% of the scores below it. This is known as the 91st **percentile**.)

Another common example is a nationally administered examination such as the SAT. The raw scores are transformed by Educational Testing Service, the producer of the test, and reported as coming from a distribution with a mean of 500 and a standard deviation of 100 (at least, it meant this back in the old days when I took them—the mean and standard deviation are no longer exactly those values). Such a scoring system is easy to devise. We start by converting raw scores to *z* scores (on the basis of the raw score mean and standard deviation). We then convert the *z* scores to the particular scoring system we have in mind. Thus

$$\text{New score} = \text{New SD}(z) + \text{New mean}$$

where *z* represents the *z* score corresponding to the individual's raw score. For the SAT

New score $= 100(z) + 500$

Scoring systems such as the one used on Achenbach's Youth Self-Report checklist, which have a mean set at 50 and a standard deviation set at 10, are called **T scores** (the *T* is always capitalized). These tests are useful in psychological measurement because they have a common frame of reference. For example, people become accustomed to seeing a cutoff score of 63 as identifying the highest 10% of the subjects. (The true cutoff would be 62.8, but the test scores come as integers.)

6.5 Seeing Statistics

When you open the applet named Normal Distribution from www.uvm.edu/~dhowell/fundamentals9/SeeingStatisticsApplets/Applets.html and click on the applet for this chapter, you will see a display that looks like the display in Figure 6.11.

This applet will allow you to explore the normal distribution by changing values of the mean, the standard deviation, the observation, or *z* itself, and examining the areas under the curve. When you change any value, you must press the Enter (or Return) key to have that value take effect.

On the left of the display are the definitions of the way the different tails of the distribution can be displayed. Make selections from the box that is currently labeled "Two-Tailed" to illustrate these various choices.

Next change the entry in the box labeled "prob:" to 0.01. Notice that the entry in the box for "*z*" changes accordingly, and is the two-tailed critical value for *z* to cut off the extreme 1% of the distribution.

Figure 6.11 An applet illustrating various aspects of the normal distribution and z scores

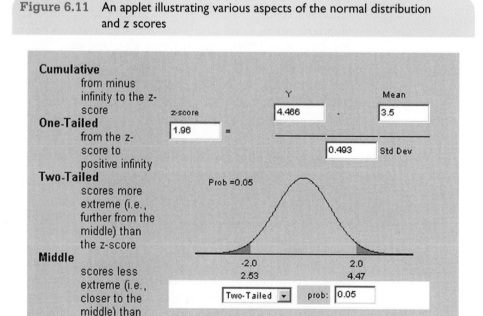

Take an example of a year in which the mean Graduate Record Exam score was 489 and the standard deviation was 126. Use this display to calculate the percentage of students who would be expected to have a score of 500 or higher. (You simply enter the appropriate numbers in the boxes and press the Return key after each entry.) What about the percentage expected to score over 700? (Be sure that you select the proper tail of the distribution in computing your percentages.)

6.6 Summary

In this chapter we examined the normal distribution. The normal distribution is a very common distribution in statistics, and it is often taken as a good description of how observations on a dependent variable are distributed. We very often assumed that the data in our sample came from a normally distributed population.

This chapter began by looking at a pie chart representing people under correctional supervision. We saw that the area of a section of the pie is directly related to the probability that an individual would fall in that category. We then moved from the pie chart to a bar graph, which is a better way of presenting the data, and then moved to a histogram of data that have a roughly normal distribution. The purpose of those transitions was to highlight the fact that area under a curve can be linked to probability.

The normal distribution is a symmetric distribution with its mode at the center. In fact, the mode, median, and mean will be the same for a variable that is normally distributed. We saw that we can convert raw scores on a normal distribution to z scores by simply dividing the deviation of the raw score from the population mean (μ) by the standard deviation of the population (σ). The z score is an important statistic because it allows us to use tables of the standard normal distribution (often denoted $N(\mu, \sigma^2)$). Once we convert a raw score to a z score we can immediately use the tables of the standard normal distribution to compute the probability that any observation will fall within a given interval.

We also saw that there are a number of measures that are directly related to z. For example, data are often reported as coming from a population with a mean of 50 and a standard deviation of 10. IQ scores are reported as coming from a population with a mean of 100 and a standard deviation of 15, and, at least originally, the SAT

Key Terms

Normal distribution, 108	z score, 118
Abscissa, 113	Standard scores, 123
Ordinate, 113	Standardization, 123
Density, 113	Percentile, 123
Standard normal distribution, 115	T scores, 124
Linear transformation, 117	

college entrance exam scores were once reported as coming from a distribution with a mean of 500 and a standard deviation of 100.

6.7 A Quick Review

A. The "ordinate" is what we have previously called the _____ axis.
   Ans: Y

B. What is special about a standard normal distribution?
   Ans: Its mean is 0 and its standard deviation is 1.0.

C. What does $N(\mu, \sigma^2)$ represent?
   Ans: A normal distribution with a mean of μ and a variance of σ^2.

D. A linear transformation is one in which _____.
   Ans: We only multiply or divide by a constant and add or subtract a constant. It does not change the shape of the distribution in the slightest.

E. A _____ represents the number of standard deviations above or below the mean.
   Ans: z score

F. Probable limits are used to _____.
   Ans: give us limits within which we have a specified probability (e.g., .95) that a randomly chosen observation will fall.

G. How do we go from z back to the corresponding X?
   Ans: $z = \dfrac{X - \mu}{\sigma}$ therefore $X = \mu + z * \sigma$

H. What do we mean by "standardization?"
   Ans: The process of transforming a raw score to a scale with a specified mean and variance, usually 0 and 1.

I. What is the 32nd percentile?
   Ans: It is the point below which 32% of a distribution falls.

J. What are the mean and standard deviation of T scores?
   Ans: 50 and 10

6.8 Exercises

6.1 Assuming that the following data represent a population of X values with $\mu = 4$ and $\sigma = 1.58$:

$$X = 1 \; 2 \; 2 \; 3 \; 3 \; 3 \; 4 \; 4 \; 4 \; 4 \; 5 \; 5 \; 5 \; 6 \; 6 \; 7$$

a) Plot the distribution as given.
b) Convert the distribution in (a) to a distribution of $X - \mu$.
c) Go the next step and convert the distribution in (b) to a distribution of z.

6.2 Using the distribution in Exercise 6.1, calculate z scores for $X = 2.5$, 6.2, and 9. Interpret these results.

6.3 Most of you have had experience with exam scores that were rescaled so that the instructor could "grade on a curve." Assume that a large Psychology 1 class has just taken an exam with 300 four-choice multiple-choice questions. (That's the kind of Psych 1 exam I took when I was a student—honest. And then professors recruited students to grade them.) Assume that the distribution of grades is normal with a mean of 195 and a standard deviation of 30. Use the software by Soper (http://www.danielsoper.com/statcalc3/) or similar widely available software, to calculate the answers to the following questions.

a) What percentage of the counts will lie between 165 and 225?
b) What percentage of the counts will lie below 195?
c) What percentage of the counts will lie below 225?

6.4 Using the example from Exercise 6.3:

a) What two values of X (the count) would encompass the middle 50% of the results?
b) 75% of the counts would be less than _____.
c) 95% of the counts would be between _____ and _____.

6.5 Do you remember the earlier study by Katz et al. that had students answer SAT-type questions without first reading the passage? (If not, look at Exercises 3.1 and 4.1.) Suppose that we gave out the answer sheets for our Psychology 1 exam mentioned in Exercise 6.3 but forgot to hand out the questions. If students just guessed at random, they would be expected to have a mean of 75 and a standard deviation of 7.5. The exam was taken by 100 students.

a) Among those who guessed randomly, what would be the cutoff score for the top 10 students?
b) What would be the cutoff score for the top 25% of the students?
c) We would expect only 5% of the students to score below _____.
d) What would you think if 25% of the students got more than 225 questions correct?

6.6 Students taking a multiple-choice exam rarely guess randomly. They usually can rule out some answers as preposterous and identify others as good candidates. Moreover, even students who have never taken Psychology 1 would probably know who Pavlov was, or what we mean by sibling rivalry. Suppose that the exam in question was our Psychology 1 exam, where each question had four alternative choices.

a) What would you conclude if the student got a score of 70?
b) How high a score would the student have to get so that you were 95% confident that the student wasn't just guessing at random?

6.7 A set of reading scores for fourth-grade children has a mean of 25 and a standard deviation of 5. A set of scores for ninth-grade children has a mean of 30 and a standard deviation of 10. Assume that the distributions are normal.

a) Draw a rough sketch of these data, putting both groups in the same figure.
b) What percentage of fourth graders score better than the average ninth grader?
c) What percentage of the ninth graders score worse than the average fourth grader? (We will come back to the idea behind these calculations when we study power in Chapter 15.)

6.8 Under what conditions would the answers to (b) and (c) of Exercise 6.7 be equal?

6.9 Many diagnostic tests are indicative of problems only if a child scores in the upper 10 percent of those taking the test (at or above the 90th percentile). Many of these tests are scaled to produce T scores, with a mean of 50 and a standard deviation of 10. What would be the diagnostically meaningful cutoff?

6.10 A dean must distribute salary raises to her faculty for next year. She has decided that the mean raise is to be $2,000, the standard deviation of raises is to be $400, and the distribution is to be normal. She will attempt to distribute these raises on the basis of merit, meaning that people whose performance is better get better raises.

a) The most productive 10% of the faculty will have a raise equal to or greater than $____.
b) The 5% of the faculty who have done nothing useful in years (and there are those people) will receive no more than $____ each.

6.11 We have sent out everyone in a large introductory course to check whether people use seat belts. Each student has been told to look at 100 cars and count the number of people wearing seat belts. The number found by any given student is considered that student's score. The mean score for the class is 44, with a standard deviation of 7.

a) Diagram this distribution, assuming that the counts are normally distributed.

b) A student who has done very little work all year has reported finding 62 seat belt users out of 100. Do we have reason to suspect that the student just made up a number rather than actually counting?

6.12 Several years ago a friend of mine in the Communication Sciences department produced a diagnostic test of language problems that is still widely used. A score on her scale is obtained simply by counting the number of language constructions (e.g., plural, negative, passive, etc.) that the child produces correctly in response to specific prompts from the person administering the test. The test has a mean of 48 and a standard deviation of 7. Parents have trouble understanding the meaning of a score on this scale, and my friend wanted to convert the scores to a mean of 80 and a standard deviation of 10 (to make them more like the kinds of grades parents are used to). How could she have gone about her task?

6.13 Unfortunately, the whole world is not built on the principle of a normal distribution. In the preceding exercise the real distribution is badly skewed because most children do not have language problems and therefore produce all constructions correctly.

a) Diagram how this distribution might look.

b) How would you go about finding the cutoff for the bottom 10% if the distribution is not normal?

6.14 We have referred several times to data on reaction times in a mental rotation task. These data can be found on this book's website as Ex6-14.dat. Using SPSS, read in the data and plot a histogram of reaction times in seconds. Click on the appropriate box to superimpose a normal distribution on the graph. What does this suggest about the normality of these data and why might you not expect them to be normal?

6.15 Use the R code given on the Web page for this chapter to plot the data on mental rotation that we have seen in Chapter 3.

6.16 The data in Appendix D (available at www.uvm.edu/~dhowell/fundamentals9/DataFiles/Add.dat) are actual data on high-school students. What is the 75th percentile for GPA in these data? (This is the point below which 75% of the observations are expected to fall.)

6.17 Assuming that the Behavior Problem scores discussed in this chapter come from a population with a mean of 50 and a standard deviation of 10, what would be a diagnostically meaningful cutoff if you wanted to identify those children who score in the highest 2% of the population? (Diagnostic cutoffs like this are a major reason for converting raw scores to T scores on such tests.)

6.18 In Section 6.4 I said that T scores are designed to have a mean of 50 and a standard deviation of 10 and that the Achenbach Youth Self-Report measure produces T scores. The data in Figure 6.3 do not have a mean and standard deviation of exactly 50 and 10. Why do you suppose that this is so?

6.19 On December 13, 2001, the Associated Press reported a story titled "Study: American kids getting fatter at disturbing rate."

> By 1998, nearly 22 percent of Black children ages 4 to 12 were overweight, as were 22 percent of Hispanic youngsters and 12 percent of Whites. . . . In 1986, the same survey showed that about 8 percent of Black children, 10 percent of Hispanic youngsters and 8 percent of Whites were significantly overweight. . . . Overweight was defined as having a body-mass index higher than 95 percent of youngsters of the same age and sex, based on growth charts from the 1960s to 1980s. . . . Disturbing trends also were seen in the number of children who had a body-mass index higher than 85 percent of their peers. In 1986, about 20 percent of Blacks, Hispanics and Whites alike were in that category. By 1998, those figures had risen to about 38 percent of Blacks and Hispanics alike and nearly 29 percent of Whites.

This report drew a lot of attention from a statistics list server that is populated by statisticians. Why do you think that a group of professional statisticians would be so excited and annoyed by what they read here? Do these data seem reasonable?

6.20 You can use SPSS to create normally distributed variables (as well as variables having a number of other shapes). Start SPSS, and under `Data/Go To Case`, tell it to go to case 1000 and then enter any value in that cell. (That just sets the size of the data set to 1000.) Then click on `Transform/Compute` and create a variable named X with the formula (rv. normal(15, 3)). That will sample from a normally distributed population with mean = 15 and standard deviation = 3. Then plot the histogram, instructing the software to superimpose a normal distribution. Experiment with other means and standard deviations. Then use the `Functions` menu on the `Transform/Compute` dialog box to try other distributions.

6.21 You can generate normally distributed variables in R by using the function

$$X <- rnorm(1000, 15, 3)$$

Where $1000 = N$, $15 = \mu$, and $3 = \sigma$. This will produce essentially the same result as for Exercise 6.20. Plot these data using

$$hist(X, main = \text{"Normally Disrupted Data"}, xlab = \text{"Score"}, ylab = \text{"Frequency"})$$

6.22 Suppose that we are collecting a large data set of emotional reactivity in adults. Assume that for most adults emotional reactivity is normally distributed with a mean of 100 and a standard deviation of 10. But for people diagnosed with bipolar disorder, their scores are all over the place. Some are temporarily depressed and they have low reactivity scores. Others are temporarily in a manic phase and their scores are quite high. As a group they still have a mean of 100, but they have a standard deviation of 30. Assume that 10% of the population is bipolar. (The actual percentage is closer to 1%, but 10% will lead to a better example.) This is a case of what is called a mixed normal distribution. Sketch what you think that this distribution might look like. What would happen if we made the means very different?

6.23 Use any Internet search engine to find a program, or "app," that will calculate areas under the normal distribution. (Don't use the ones referred to in this chapter.)

## CHAPTER 7

Basic Concepts of Probability

I n this chapter we will look at a number of aspects of the theory of probability. It probably isn't nice to say it, but probability theory rarely comes at the top of the list of students' favorite topics. But you really do need to know a bit about probability in order to have the basic material for the rest of the book. There is not a lot of material that is essential, but there is some. One of the things that you will see is that there is a fundamental difference between probability theory for discrete variables and for continuous variables. That will not represent a major stumbling block, but we need to pay attention.

In Chapter 6 we began to make use of the concept of probability. For example, we saw that about 68% of children have Behavior Problem scores between 40 and 60 and thus concluded that if we choose a child at random, the probability that he or she would score between 40 and 60 is .68. When we begin concentrating on inferential statistics in Chapter 8, we will rely heavily on statements of probability. There we will be making statements of the form, "If this hypothesis were true, the probability is only .015 that we would have obtained a result as extreme as the one we actually obtained." If we are to rely on statements of probability, it is important to understand what we mean by probability and to understand a few basic rules for computing and manipulating probabilities. That is the purpose of this chapter.

130

CONCEPTS THAT YOU WILL NEED TO REMEMBER FROM PREVIOUS CHAPTERS

Discrete variable:	A variable that can take on only a limited number of values
Continuous variable:	A variable that can take on an infinite number (or at least a great many) values between the lowest and highest values
X axis:	The horizontal axis, also called the abscissa
Y axis:	The vertical axis, also called the ordinate
Frequency distribution:	A plot showing the values of the dependent variable on the X axis and their frequency on the Y axis
Bar chart:	A graph with the independent variable on the X axis and the mean or other measure on the Y axis
$\overline{X}$:	A common symbol for the mean
s:	A common symbol for the variance
Σ:	The symbol for summation of what follows
N:	The number of observations

As I said, my colleagues will probably chastise me for saying it, but probability is one of those topics that students try to avoid. Probability is scary to many, and it can be confusing to even more. Add to this the fact that most instructors, myself included, have a weak background in probability theory, and you have a bad situation. However, just because people are anxious about a topic doesn't constitute grounds for avoiding all mention of it. There are some things you just have to know, whether you want to or not. To avoid slurping your soup in a restaurant is one, and probability is another. But soup can be good even if eaten properly, and probability can be manageable, even if you hated it in high school.

The material covered in this chapter has been selected for two reasons. First, it is directly applicable to an understanding of the material presented in the remainder of the book. Second, it is intended to allow you to make simple calculations of probabilities that are likely to be useful to you. Material that does not satisfy either of these qualifications has been deliberately omitted. For example, we will not consider such things as the probability of drawing the queen of hearts, given that 14 cards, including four hearts, have already been drawn. Nor will we consider the probability that your desk light will burn out in the next 25 hours of use, given that it has already lasted 250 hours. Both of those topics may be important in some situations, but you can go miles in statistics and have a good understanding of the methods of the behavioral sciences without having the slightest idea about either of those probability questions.

7.1 Probability

The concept of probability can be viewed in several different ways. There is not even general agreement as to what we mean by the word *probability*. The oldest and perhaps the most common definition of a probability is what is called the **analytic view**. One of the examples that is often drawn into discussions of probability is that of one of my favorite candies, M&M's®. M&M's are a good example because everyone is familiar with them, they are easy to use in class demonstrations because they don't get your hand all sticky, and you can eat them when you're done. The Mars Candy Company is so fond of having them used as an example that they keep lists of the percentage of colors in each bag—though they seem to keep moving the lists around, making it a challenge to find them on occasion. The data on the milk chocolate version is shown in Table 7.1.

Table 7.1 Distribution of Colors in an Average Bag of M&M's	
Color	Percentage
Brown	13
Red	13
Yellow	14
Green	16
Orange	20
Blue	24
Total	**100**

Suppose that you have a bag of M&M's in front of you and you reach in and pull one out. Just to simplify what follows, assume that there are 100 M&M's in the bag, though that is not a requirement. What is the probability that you will pull out a blue M&M? You can probably answer this question without knowing anything more about probability. Because 24% of the M&M's are blue, and because you are sampling randomly, the probability of drawing a blue M&M is .24. This example illustrates one definition of probability:

Analytic view of probability

If an event can occur in A ways and can fail to occur in B ways, and if all possible ways are equally likely (i.e., each M&M in a bag has an equal chance of being drawn), then the probability of its occurrence is $A/(A + B)$, and the probability of its failing to occur is $B/(A + B)$.

Because there are 24 ways of drawing a blue M&M (one for each of the 24 blue M&M's in a bag of 100 M&M's) and 76 ways of drawing a different color, $A = 24$, $B = 76$, and $p(A) = 24/(24 + 76) = .24$.

An alternative view of probability is the **frequentist view**. Suppose that we keep drawing M&M's from the bag, noting the color on each draw. In conducting this sampling study we **sample with replacement**, meaning that each M&M is replaced before the next one is drawn. If we made a very large number of draws, we would find that (very nearly) 24% of the draws would result in a blue M&M. Thus we might define probability as the limit[1] of the relative frequency of occurrence of the desired event that we approach as the number of draws increases.

Frequentistic view of probability

Here, probability is defined in terms of past performance. If we have drawn green M&M's 160 times out of the last 1,000 draws, the probability of drawing a green M&M is estimated as 160/1000 = .16.

Yet a third concept of probability is advocated by a number of theorists. That is the concept of **subjective probability**. By this definition, probability represents an individual's subjective belief in the likelihood of the occurrence of an event. We make all sorts of decisions based on our subjective belief in the occurrence of something. Often we don't have any other way to set a probability of an event. Subjective probabilities may in fact have no mathematical basis whatsoever. We could ask, "What is the probability that Bob and May's marriage will end in divorce?" Of course,

---

[1]The word *limit* refers to the fact that as we sample more and more M&M's, the proportion of blue will get closer and closer to some value. After 100 draws, the proportion might be .23; after 1,000 draws it might be .242; after 10,000 draws it might be .2398, and so on. Notice that the answer is coming closer and closer to $p = .2400000...$. The value that is being approached is called the limit.

we could find out what percentages of marriages end in divorce, but there are so many unique things about Bob and Mary that we would probably not be willing to base our probability on that. If we knew that they fought all the time, we might be better off taking the percentage of divorces for the population and adding perhaps 10 points to that. This would be a subjective probability. This is not to suggest that such a view of probability has no legitimate claim for our attention. Subjective probabilities play an extremely important role in human decision making and govern all aspects of our behavior. We will shortly discuss what is called Bayes' theorem, which is essential to the use of subjective probabilities. Statistical decisions as we will make them here generally will be stated with respect to frequentist or analytical approaches, although, even so, the *interpretation* of those probabilities has a strong subjective component.

Although the particular definition that you or I prefer may be important to each of us, any of the definitions will lead to essentially the same result in terms of hypothesis testing, effect sizes, and confidence intervals, the discussion of which runs through the rest of the book. (It should be said that those who favor subjective probabilities often disagree with the general hypothesis-testing orientation.) In actual fact, most people use the different approaches interchangeably. When we say that the probability of losing at Russian roulette is 1/6, we are referring to the fact that one of the gun's six cylinders has a bullet in it. When we buy a particular car because *Consumer Reports* says it has a good repair record, we are responding to the fact that a high proportion of these cars has been relatively trouble free. When we say that the probability of the Colorado Rockies winning the pennant is high, we are stating our subjective belief in the likelihood of that event (or perhaps engaging in wishful thinking). But when we reject some hypothesis because there is a very low probability that the actual data would have been obtained if the hypothesis had been true, it may not be important which view of probability we hold.

7.2 Basic Terminology and Rules

Here's where you have to start learning some probability stuff. There isn't much, and it isn't hard or painful, but you have to learn it.

The basic bit of data for a probability theorist is called an **event**. The word *event* is a term that statisticians use to cover just about anything. An event can be the occurrence of a king when we deal from a deck of cards, a score of 36 on a scale of likability, a classification of "female" for the next person appointed to the Supreme Court, or the mean of a sample. Whenever you speak of the probability of something, the "something" is called an event. When we are dealing with a process as simple as flipping a coin, the event is the outcome of that flip—either heads or tails. When we draw M&M's out of a bag, the possible events are the various possible colors. When we speak of a grade in a course, the possible events are the letters A, B, C, D, and F.

Two events are said to be **independent events** when the occurrence or nonoccurrence of one has no effect on the occurrence or nonoccurrence of the other. The voting behaviors of two randomly chosen citizens in different parts of the country normally would be assumed to be independent, especially with a secret ballot, because how one person votes could not be expected to influence how the other will vote. However, the voting behaviors of two members of the same family probably would not be independent events, because those people share many of the same beliefs and attitudes. The events would probably not be independent even if those two people were careful not to let the other see their ballot.

Two events are said to be **mutually exclusive** if the occurrence of one event precludes the occurrence of the other. For example, the standard college classes (under the U.S. university system) of first year, sophomore, junior, and senior are mutually exclusive because one person cannot be a member of more than one class. A set of events is said to be **exhaustive** if it includes all possible outcomes. Thus the four college classes in the previous example are exhaustive with respect to full-time undergraduates, who have to fall into one or another of those categories—if only to please the registrar's office. At the same time, they are not exhaustive with respect to total university enrollments, which include graduate students, medical students, nonmatriculated students, hangers-on, and so forth.

Important probability concepts

- Independent events: The outcome for one event does not depend on the outcome for another event.

- Dependent events: The outcome of one event is related to the outcome for another event.

- Mutually exclusive: If something happens one way, it cannot also happen in another way. With one flip of a coin you can either get a head or a tail, but not both.

- Exhaustive: The list of all possibilities. Head and tail are the only ways a coin can come up unless you consider landing on its edge is possible, in which case the three events are exhaustive

---

As you already know—or could deduce from our definitions of probability—probabilities range between .00 and 1.00. If some event has a probability of 1.00, then it *must* occur. (Very few things have a probability of 1.00, including the probability that I will be able to keep typing until I reach the end of this paragraph.) If some event has a probability of .00, it is certain *not* to occur. The closer the probability comes to either extreme, the more likely or unlikely is the occurrence of the event.

Basic Laws of Probability

To illustrate the additive rule, we will use our M&M's example and consider all six colors. From Table 5.1 we know from the analytic definition of probability that $p(\text{blue}) = 24/100 = .24$, $p(\text{green}) = 16/100 = .16$, and so on. But what is the probability that I will draw a blue or green M&M instead of an M&M of some other color? Here we need the **additive law of probability**.

Additive law of probability: Given a set of *mutually exclusive* events, the probability of the occurrence of one event *or* another is equal to the sum of their separate probabilities.

Thus, p(blue or green) = p(blue) + p(green) = .24 + .16 = .40. Notice that we have imposed the restriction that the events must be mutually exclusive, meaning that the occurrence of one event precludes the occurrence of the other. If an M&M is blue, it can't be green. This requirement is important. About one-half of the population of this country are female, and about one-half of the population have traditionally feminine names. But the probability that a person chosen at random will be female *or* will have a feminine name is obviously not .50 + .50 = 1.00. Here the two events are *not* mutually exclusive. However, the probability that a girl born in the United States in 2005 was named Emily or Madison, the two most common girls' names in that year, equals p(Emily) + p(Madison) = .013 + .011 = .024. Here the names are mutually exclusive because you can't have both Emily *and* Madison as your first name (unless your parents got carried away and combined the two with a hyphen).

The Multiplicative Rule

Let's continue with the M&M's, where p(blue) = .24, p(green) = .16, and p(other) = .60. Suppose I draw two M&M's, replacing the first before drawing the second. What is the probability that I will draw a blue M&M on the first trial *and* a blue one on the second? Here we need to invoke the **multiplicative law of probability**.

The multiplicative law of probability: The probability of the joint occurrence of two or more independent events is the product of their individual probabilities.

Thus

p(blue, blue) = p(blue) × p(blue) = .24 × .24 = .0576.

Similarly, the probability of a blue M&M followed by a green one is

p(blue, green) = p(blue) × p(green) = .24 × .16 = .0384.

Notice that we have restricted ourselves to independent events, meaning the occurrence of one event can have no effect on the occurrence or nonoccurrence of the other. Because gender and name are not independent, it would be wrong to state that p(female with feminine name) = .50 × .50 = .25. However, it most likely would be correct to state that p(female, born in January) = .50 × 1/12 = .50 × .083 = .042, because I know of no data to suggest that gender is dependent on birth month. (If month and gender were related, my calculation would be wrong.)

In Chapter 19 we will use the multiplicative law to answer questions about the independence of two variables. An example from that chapter will help illustrate a specific use of this law. In a study to be discussed in that chapter, Geller, Witmer, and Orebaugh (1976) wanted to test the hypothesis that what someone did with a supermarket flier depended on whether the flier contained a request not to litter. Geller et al. distributed fliers as people entered the store. Approximately half of these fliers included the request not to litter, and half did not. At the end of the day they searched the store to find where the fliers had been left. Testing their hypothesis involves, in part, calculating the probability that a flier would contain a message about littering *and* would be found in a trashcan. We need to calculate what this probability would be if the two events (contains message about littering and flier in trash) are independent. *If* we assume that these two events are independent (people don't pay any attention to messages), the multiplicative law tells us that p(message, trash) = p(message) $\times$ p(trash). In their study, 49% of the fliers contained a message, so the probability that a flier chosen at random would contain the message is .49. Similarly, 6.8% of the fliers were later found in the trash, giving p(trash) = .068. Therefore, if the two events are independent,

$$p(\text{message, trash}) = .49 \times .068 = .033,$$

we would expect 3.3% of the fliers with the message would be in the trash. (In fact, 4.5% of the fliers with messages were found in the trash, which is a bit higher than we would expect if the ultimate disposal of the flier were independent of the message. Assuming that this small difference between 3.3% and 4.5% is reliable, what does this suggest to you about the effectiveness of the message?)

Finally, we can take a simple example that illustrates both the additive and the multiplicative laws. What is the probability that over two trials (sampling with replacement) I will draw one blue M&M and one green one, *ignoring the order in which they are drawn?* First, we use the multiplicative rule to calculate

$$p(\text{blue, green}) = .24 \times .16 = .0384,$$
$$p(\text{green, blue}) = .16 \times .24 = .0384,$$

Because these two outcomes satisfy our requirement (and because they are the only ones that do), we now need to know the probability that one or the other of these outcomes will occur. Here we apply the additive rule:

$$p(\text{green, blue}) + p(\text{green, blue}) = .0384 \times .0384 = .0768$$

Thus the probability of obtaining one M&M of each of those colors over two draws is approximately .08—that is, it will occur a little less than 8% of the time.

Students sometimes get confused over the additive and multiplicative laws because they almost sound the same when you hear them quickly. One useful idea is to realize the difference between the situations in which the rules apply. In those situations in which you use the additive rule, you know that you are going to have *one* outcome. An M&M that you draw may be blue or green, but there is only going to be one of them. In the multiplicative case, we are speaking about at least *two* outcomes (e.g., the probability that we will get one blue M&M *and* one green one). For single outcomes we add probabilities; for multiple independent outcomes we multiply them.

Joint and Conditional Probabilities

Two types of probabilities play an important role in discussions of probability: joint probabilities and conditional probabilities.

A **joint probability** is defined simply as the probability of the co-occurrence of two or more events. For example, in Geller's study of supermarket fliers, the probability that a flier would *both* contain a message about littering *and* be found in the trash is a joint probability, as is the probability that a flier would both contain a message about littering and be found stuffed down behind the Raisin Bran®. Given two events, their joint probability is denoted as $p(A, B)$, just as we have used p(blue, green) or p(message, trash). *If those two events are independent,* then the probability of their joint occurrence can be found by using the multiplicative law, as we have just seen. If they are *not* independent, the probability of their joint occurrence is more complicated to compute. We won't compute that probability here.

A **conditional probability** is the probability that one event will occur, *given* that some other event has occurred. The probability that a person will contract AIDS, given that he or she is an intravenous drug user, is a conditional probability. The probability that an advertising flier will be thrown into the trash, given that it contains a message about littering, is another example. A third example is a phrase that occurs repeatedly throughout this book: "If the null hypothesis is true, the probability of obtaining a result such as this is. . . ." Here I have substituted the word *if* for *given*, but the meaning is the same. (I'll define the phrase *null hypothesis* in Chapter 8.)

With two events, A and B, the conditional probability of A, given B, is denoted by use of a vertical bar, as in $p(A \mid B)$, for example, p(AIDS | drug user) or p(trash | message).

We often assume, with some justification, that parenthood breeds responsibility. People who have spent years acting in careless and irrational ways somehow seem to turn into different people once they become parents, changing many of their old behavior patterns. Suppose that a radio station sampled 100 people, 20 of whom had children. They found that 30 of the people sampled used seat belts, and that 15 of those people had children. The results are shown in Table 7.2.

The information in Table 7.2 allows us to calculate the simple, joint, and conditional probabilities. The simple probability that a person sampled at random will use a seat belt is $30/100 = .30$. The joint probability that a person will have children *and* will wear a seat belt is $15/100 = .15$. The conditional probability of a person using a seat belt given that he or she has children is $15/20 = .75$. Do not confuse joint and conditional probabilities. As you can see, they are quite different. You might wonder why I didn't calculate the joint probability here by multiplying the appropriate simple probabilities. The use of the multiplicative law requires that parenthood and seat belt use be independent. In this example they are not, because the data show that whether people use seat belts depends very much on whether or not they have children. (If I had assumed independence, I would have predicted the joint probability to be $.30 \times .20 = .06$, which is less than half the size of the actual obtained value.)

To take another example, the probability that you have been drinking alcohol and that you have an automobile accident is a joint probability. This probability is not very high, because relatively few people are drinking at any one time and relatively few people have automobile accidents. However, the probability that you have an accident *given* that you have been drinking, or, in reverse, the probability that you have been drinking *given* that you have an accident, are both much higher. At night, the conditional probability of p(drinking | accident) approaches .50, since nearly half

Table 7.2 The Relationship Between Parenthood and Seat Belt Use

Parenthood	Wears Seat Belt	Does Not Wear Seat Belt	Total
Children	15	5	20
No children	15	65	80
Total	30	70	100

of all automobile accidents at night in the United States involve alcohol. I don't know the conditional probability of $p(\text{accident} \mid \text{drinking})$, but I do know that it is much higher than the **unconditional probability** of an accident, that is, $p(\text{accident})$.

Joint probability:

You have two friends who can't stand each other. You are having a party and feel obligated to invite each of them. You then worry about the *joint* probability that they will both show up.

Conditional probability:

You have two friends that you have invited to a party. They have started hanging around together, so you know that if Mary comes, Bob is very likely to come as well. You are talking about a conditional probability—the probability of Bob *given* Mary.

7.3 The Application of Probability to Controversial Issues

A number of studies have looked at the imposition of the death sentence in the United States as a function of the race of the defendant and the victim. (Data on the role of the victim will be presented in the Exercises at the end of this chapter.) A report on the influence of the race of the defendant was compiled by Dieter (1998) can be found at

 http://www.deathpenaltyinfo.org/article.php?scid=45&did=539.

To oversimplify the issue, but not to distort the findings, we can look at the breakdown of death sentence by race of defendant. The data are shown in Table 7.3.

The row percentages are computed by dividing the frequency of "Yes" or "No" by the number of cases in that row. The column percentages are calculated by dividing Black or NonBlack by the column totals. The cell percentages are simply the number of observations in that cell divided by the total sample size (667).

Table 7.3   The Relationship Between Death Sentence and Race of the Defendant

Defendant's race	Death Sentence		Total
	Yes	No	
Black	95	425	520
Row %	18.3%	81.7%	78.0%
Col %	83.3%	76.8%	
Cell %	14.2%	63.7%	
Nonblack	19	128	147
Row %	12.9%	87.1%	22.0%
Col %	16.7%	23.1%	
Cell %	2.8%	19.2%	
Total	114	553	667
Col %	17.1%	82.9%	

The information in Table 7.3 allows us to calculate the simple, joint, and conditional probabilities. The simple probability that a defendant will be given the death penalty is

$$114/667 = .171,$$

the proportion of the total cases that receive that sentence. The probability that a defendant is Black is

$$520/667 = .780.$$

The joint probability that a person is Black and is sentenced to death is

$$95/667 = .142,$$

the proportion of the total observations that fell in the Black/Yes cell.

If sentencing has nothing to do with race, then the two events would be independent. In that case we would expect that the probability of being Black and of being sentenced to death is $p(\text{Black}) \times p(\text{Death}) = .780 \times .171 = .134$. Do you think that the two events are independent?

What is most interesting in this table are the conditional probabilities. The probability that a defendant will be sentenced to death *given* that he or she is Black is

$$95/520 = .183.$$

The conditional probability that a defendant will be sentenced to death given that he or she is nonBlack is

$$19/147 = .129.$$

There is a considerable disparity between the sentencing of Black and nonBlack defendants. The death sentence rate for Black defendants is nearly 50% higher than for nonBlacks.

Odds and Risk

This is a good place to introduce a few terms that you need to know and be able to work with. Even if you did not need them for a statistics course, you would need to know them in everyday life. Unfortunately, they are easily confused and often used incorrectly.

I will start with **risk**, which is simply the probability that something will happen. For a Black defendant in the previous example, the risk of being sentenced to death was $95/520 = .183$. For a nonBlack defendant the risk of a death sentence was $19/147 = .129$, which we also saw before. But we can go one step further and compute what is called the **risk ratio**, which is just the ratio of the two risks. In this case, that is $.183/.129 = 1.42$. This tells us that the risk of being sentenced to death is 1.42 times greater for Black than for nonBlack offenders. That's quite a difference.

Now let's move to **odds**. On the surface they look almost like risks, but here we take the number of Black defendants who were sentenced to death divided by *the number who were not* sentenced to death. Notice that the denominator has changed from the total number of Blacks to the number of Blacks who did not receive a death sentence. In this case, the odds are $95/425 = .224$. For nonBlacks the odds are $19/128 = .148$. Just as we did with the risk ratio, we can create an **odds ratio**, as the ratio of the two odds. In this case, the odds ratio is .224/.148 = 1.51, which is a bit higher than the risk ratio. We would interpret this to say that your odds of being sentenced to death are 1.51 times higher if you are Black.

Why do we need both odds and risk? Won't one of them be sufficient and less confusing? Well, no. One answer is that some people feel more comfortable speaking in terms of odds, and their ratio, rather than risks and their ratio. (I am certainly not one of them, but I can dimly see their reasoning.) For others, risk seems like a more reasonable statistic, because it speaks directly to the probability that a person will fall in one category or another. When it comes to the ratios, there is a very good technical reason for using odds ratios. Depending on how the study was designed, there are many situations when it is not possible to compute a risk ratio. But we can always compute an odds ratio, and when we are speaking of very unlikely events (e.g., being diagnosed with tuberculosis), the odds ratio is an excellent estimate of what the risk ratio would be if we could derive it for our sample.

To calculate risk, we divide by the total row frequency, whereas to calculate odds we divide by the number of observations in the other cell of that row. Both risk ratios and odds ratios appear to address the very same question, but for technical reasons we can often not compute a risk ratio. For low frequency events, an odds ratio is a very good estimate of what the risk ratio would be if we could calculate it.

In spite of the fact that for low probability events an odds ratio is a reasonable estimate of what a risk ratio could be if it could be computed, that is not a ringing endorsement for odds ratios. Many people, particularly in medicine, have argued that odds ratios can be misleading. A very interesting Web page by Mark Liberman (2007), titled *Thou shalt not report odds ratios,* can be found at http://itre.cis.upenn.edu/~myl/languagelog/archives/004767.html. It is an excellent example of this issue. This does not mean that odds ratios should necessarily be avoided, but it is probably best to restrict their use to low probability events.

7.4 Writing Up the Results

Throughout the remainder of this book I will insert sections describing how to write up the results of a statistical analysis. The write-ups will be quite brief and will not necessarily conform to the requirements of various journals. They are intended to show the kinds of things that you need to cover. In this chapter we have not seen a full-blown experiment with tests of statistical hypotheses, but I can at least write up the results of the study on the death penalty as if I had shown that the differences were reliable. (They actually are.)

I will start by listing the things that need to go into such a report. We want to say something about what the problem is, how we approached the problem, and where, and how, we collected the data. Don't forget to mention how many observations were involved. Then we would want to mention the important unconditional probabilities, such as the overall probability that a person will be sentenced to death, and perhaps the probabilities for each race. The conditional probabilities and/or the odds are important to include, and then we need to create and report the risk or odds ratio. Because the probabilities are not very low, I would stick with risk ratios. Finally, we need to draw conclusions and put the study in a context of other work that has been done on the topic. To include all of this I would write:

The Death Penalty Information Center issued a report edited by Dieter (1998) on the application of death penalties as a function of race. The report examined the outcomes of cases in Philadelphia between 1983 and 1993. The fundamental purpose was to ask whether the death penalty was applied evenly for defendants of different races. The authors surveyed 667 instances when a defendant faced the possibility of the death penalty and broke the data down by the race of the defendant and the sentence that was given.

The results revealed that in 17.1% of the cases the defendant was sentenced to death. However, sentencing was statistically related to race. When the defendant was Black the risk of being sentenced to death was .183, whereas for nonBlack defendants the risk was only .129. These are probabilities conditional on race, and directly address the problem. These conditional probabilities produce a risk ratio of 1.42, indicating that Blacks are approximately 40% more likely to be sentenced to death than nonBlack. This disparity held even when the data were split on the basis of the severity of the offense. There would appear to be racial bias in the assignment of death penalties.

These are data from the period 1983–1993, and it is possible that the results would be different if more current data were used. However, that question deserves separate study. The results were a replication of very similar results by Radelet and Pierce (1991). The discussion continues in both the popular press and the scientific community. As recently as 2008, Justices John Paul Stevens and Clarence Thomas strongly disagreed over the role that race had played in a Georgia case.[2]

7.5 | Discrete Versus Continuous Variables

We have covered several terms that are used with probability, and we have looked at two rules that allow us to calculate probabilities in simple, but very real and common, situations. Now we need to go a bit further and look at the variables to which these probabilities apply. It turns out that we do different things, depending on the kind of variable we have.

In Chapter 2 I made a distinction between discrete and continuous variables. As mathematicians view things, a discrete variable is one that can take on a countable number of different values, whereas a continuous variable is one that can take on an infinite number of different values. For example, the number of people participating in an experiment on interpersonal space is a discrete variable because we literally can

---

[2]See the *Washington Post* for October 21, 2008. The study can be found at http://www.washingtonpost.com/wp-dyn/content/article/2008/10/20/AR2008102003133.html

count the number of people in the experiment, and there is no such thing as a fractional person. However, the distance between two people in a study of personal space is a continuous variable because the distance could be 2', or 2.8', or 2.8173754814'. Although the distinction given here is technically correct, common usage is somewhat different.

In practice, when we speak of a discrete variable, we *usually* mean a variable that takes on one of a relatively small number of possible values (e.g., a five-point scale of socioeconomic status, or a three-point scale of preference [e.g., like, neutral, or dislike]). A variable that can take on one of many possible values is generally treated as a continuous variable if the values represent at least an ordinal scale. Thus we usually think of an IQ score as a continuous variable, even though we recognize that IQ scores come in whole units and we will not find someone with an IQ of 105.317.

The distinction between discrete and continuous variables is reintroduced here because the *distributions* of the two kinds of variables are treated somewhat differently in probability theory. With discrete variables we can speak of the probability of a specific outcome. With continuous variables, on the other hand, we need to speak of the probability of obtaining a value that falls within a specific *interval*.

To elaborate on this point, assume that we have 25 M&M's of each of four colors and we drop them in a bag. The probability that we will draw exactly one blue M&M is 25/100 = .25. But the probability that that M&M will weigh exactly 1.000000000 grams is infinitely small, although there is some reasonable probability that it will fall *in the interval between* 1 gram and 1.25 grams. With discrete variables we can talk about the probability of a specific event, but with continuous variables we have to talk about the probability of the event falling within some interval.

7.6 Probability Distributions for Discrete Variables

An interesting example of a discrete probability distribution is seen in Figure 7.1. The data plotted in this figure come from a Scottish government survey of environmental attitudes, collected in 2009. Researchers were interested in studying environmental issues, but in the process collected data on general life satisfaction using the Satisfaction With Life Scale (SWLS) by Edward Diener at the University of Illinois.[3] Figure 7.1 presents the distribution of responses for the question that asked respondents to rate the sentence "In most ways my life is close to ideal." The possible values of X (the rating) are presented on the abscissa or X axis, and the relative frequency (or proportion) of people choosing that response is plotted on the ordinate or Y axis. It is interesting to see how satisfied people are with their lives—I would not have expected such responses. Proportions translate directly to probabilities for

---

[3]You can find out more about this scale at http://internal.psychology.illinois.edu/~ediener/SWLS.html. You might have a use for such a scale in the next few years in conjunction with one or more of your courses. The particular study cited here can be found at http://www.scotland.gov.uk/Publications/2009/03/25155151/0.

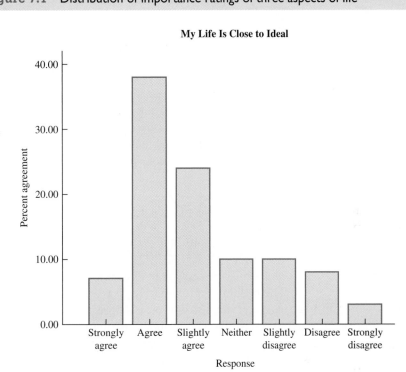

Figure 7.1   Distribution of importance ratings of three aspects of life

the sample, and the probability that a person chosen at random will "Agree" that his or her health is close to ideal is .38. Adding together the three positive categories, as we did with the criminal data earlier, we have 69% of the sample at least slightly agreeing that their life is close to ideal.

7.7   Probability Distributions for Continuous Variables

When we move from discrete to continuous probability distributions, things become more complicated. We dealt with a continuous distribution when we considered the normal distribution in Chapter 6. You may recall that in that chapter we labeled the ordinate of the distribution "**density**." We also spoke in terms of intervals rather than in terms of specific outcomes. Now we need to elaborate somewhat on those points.

Figure 7.2 shows the approximate distribution of the maternal age at first birth, from data supplied by Martin, et al. (2012), in National Vital Statistics Reports, Vol. 62, No. 9, December 30, 2013, by the Centers for Disease Control and Prevention (CDC, 2013). It is available at http://www.cdc.gov/nchs/data/nvsr/nvsr62/nvsr62_09 .pdf. Adjustments have been made to interpolate across age groups. The curve that has been drawn on the graph is called a kernel density curve and is an estimate of the best fitting line to the data. (Data from 2002 can be found at http://www.cdc.gov/ nchs/data/nvsr/nvsr52/nvsr52_10.pdf)

Figure 7.2 Age of mother at birth of first child

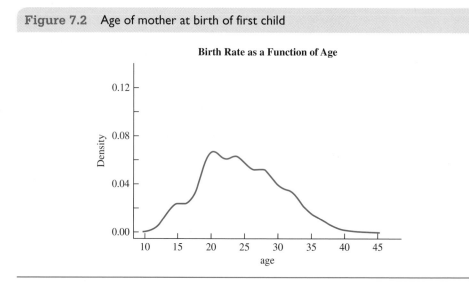

The mean is approximately 25 years, the standard deviation is approximately five years, and the distribution is surprisingly symmetrical. Because the smooth line fitted to the data is a continuous distribution, the ordinate is labeled "density." Density is not synonymous with probability, and it is probably best thought of as merely the height of the curve at different values of X. At the same time, the fact that the curve is higher near 25 years than it is near 15 years tells us that children are more likely to be born when their mother is in her mid-20s than when she is in her mid-teens. That is not a particular surprise. The reason for changing the label on the ordinate is that we now are dealing with a continuous distribution rather than a discrete one. If you think about it for a moment, you will realize that although the highest point of the curve is at 20 years, the probability that a mother picked at random will give birth at *exactly* 20 years (i.e., 20.00000000 years) is infinitely small—statisticians would argue that it is in fact 0. Similarly, the probability that the mother gave birth at 20.00001 years also is infinitely small. This suggests that it does not make any sense to speak of the probability of any *specific* outcome, although that is just what we did with discrete distributions. On the other hand, we know that many mothers give birth at *approximately* 20 years, and it does make considerable sense to speak of the probability of obtaining a score that falls within some specified *interval*. For example, we might be interested in the probability that an infant will be born when mom is between 24.5 and 25.5 years old. Such an interval is shown in Figure 7.3. If we arbitrarily define the total area under the curve to be 1.00, then the shaded area in Figure 7.3 between points 24.5 and 25.5 years will be equal to the probability that a mother will give birth at age 25. Those of you who have had calculus will probably recognize that if we knew the form of the equation that describes this distribution (i.e., if we knew the equation for the curve), we would simply need to integrate the function over the interval from 24.5 to 25.5. But you don't need calculus to solve this problem, because the distributions with which we will work are adequately approximated by other distributions that have already been tabled. In this book we will never integrate functions, but we will often refer to tables of distributions. You have already had experience with this procedure with regard to the normal distribution in Chapter 6.

Figure 7.3   Probability of giving birth at ages 15 and 25 years

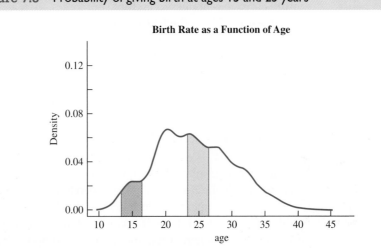

We have just considered the area of Figure 7.3 between 24.5 and 25.5 years, which is centered near the mean. However, the same things could be said for any interval. In Figure 7.3 you can also see the area that corresponds to the period that is half a year on either side of 15 years (denoted as the shaded area between 14.5 and 15.5 years). Although there is not enough information in this example for us to calculate actual probabilities, it should be clear by inspection of Figure 7.3 that the interval around 25 years has a higher probability (greater shaded area) than the area around 15 years.

A good way to get a feel for areas under a curve is to take a piece of transparent graph paper and lay it on top of the figure (or use a regular sheet of graph paper and hold the two up to a light). If you count the number of squares that fall within a specified interval and divide by the total number of squares under the whole curve, you will approximate the probability that a randomly drawn score will fall within that interval. It should be obvious that the smaller the size of the individual squares on the graph paper, the more accurate the approximation.

7.8 | Summary

In this chapter we examined the various definitions of the term *probability* and saw that probabilities can be based on a logical analysis of the problem (analytic probability), on a history of past experience (frequentistic probability), or on a subjective belief in the likelihood that an event will occur (subjective probability). We considered the difference between independent and nonindependent events and saw that "mutually exclusive" refers to the situation where the occurrence of one event precludes the occurrence of another. Similarly, an "exhaustive" set of events is one that includes all possible outcomes.

We considered two fundamental laws of probability, which were the additive and the multiplicative laws. The additive law concerns the situation where our focus is on the occurrence of one outcome, where we would use the word "or" in describing it.

For example, what is the probability that your one grade will be an A *or* a B? The multiplicative law applies to multiple outcomes, such as "What is the probability that you will earn an A on the first test *and* a B on the second?"

Next we looked at joint and conditional probabilities. A joint probability is the probability of two or more things occurring, such as in the example of an A on one test and a B on another. A conditional probability is the probability that something will occur *given* that something else occurs. What is the probability that you will earn a B on the second exam *given* (or *if*) you earned an A on the first?

We then saw two new terms, "risk" and "odds." A risk is essentially a probability—"What is the risk (probability) that you will have an accident on the way home from class?" We just divide the number of people who have accidents by the total number of people—or some similar kind of calculation. Odds are a bit different. There we divide the number of people who have an accident by the number of people that *don't* have an accident. Both odds and risk are legitimate ways of speaking of the likelihood that something will occur. Odds are most commonly seen in horse racing and other forms of gambling, and are frowned upon in medical research unless the odds are very low, and thus are a good estimate of the risk ratio.

With risk or with odds we can form a ratio. In our example, the risk ratio was the risk of being sentenced to death if you were Black divided by the risk of being sentenced to death if you were White. The odds ratio is similar except that we divide odds rather than risks. The advantage of the odds ratio is that we can compute it almost regardless of the design of our study, whereas we can only compute a risk ratio under specific experimental conditions. For low probability events the odds ratio is a good estimate of what the risk ratio would be. However if we are not dealing with quite low probability events, the odds ratio will be misleadingly high compared to the risk ratio.

Finally, we saw that there is an important difference between discrete and continuous variables, and with the latter we generally use the term density. We will see throughout the book that discrete variables are usually dealt with in ways that are different from the way we treat continuous variables.

Key Terms

Analytic view, *131*	Multiplicative law of probability, *135*
Frequentist view, *132*	Joint probability, *136*
Sample with replacement, *132*	Conditional probability, *137*
Subjective probability, *132*	Unconditional probability, *138*
Event, *133*	Risk, *139*
Independent events, *133*	Risk ratio, *139*
Mutually exclusive, *134*	Odds, *139*
Exhaustive, *134*	Odds ratio, *139*
Additive law of probability, *134*	Density, *143*

7.9 A Quick Review

A. Name three types of definitions of probability.
  Ans: Frequentistic, analytic, and subjective

B. What does it mean to "sample with replacement?"
  Ans: After we draw an observation we replace it before the next draw.

C. Why would we sample with replacement?
  Ans: This keeps the probabilities constant over trials.

D. What are mutually exclusive events?
  Ans: The occurrence of one event precludes the occurrence of the other. You have one outcome or the other, *but not both.*

E. What is the multiplicative rule?
  Ans: The probability of one event followed by another is the probability of the first event times the probability of the second event, assuming that the events are independent.

F. What is the additive rule?
  Ans: The probability of the occurrence of one or another of two mutually exclusive events is the sum of the two probabilities.

G. Give an example of a conditional probability.
  Ans: The probability that it will snow *given that* the temperature is below 32 degrees is .20.

H. How do we signify conditional probabilities?
  Ans: We place a vertical bar between the two events. For example, p(snow | below 32°).

I. What is a risk ratio, also known as "relative risk"?
  Ans: It is the ratio of one risk over another. Put differently, it is the probability of depression for females divided by the probability of depression for males.

J. What is the difference between odds and risks?
  Ans: The odds are the number of occurrences of event divided by the number of occurrences of the other event. Risk is the number of occurrences of one event divided by the total number of occurrences of any event.

K. What do we mean by density?
  Ans: The height of the curve representing the distribution of events measures on a continuous scale.

7.10 Exercises

7.1 Give one example each of an analytic, a relative frequency, and a subjective view of probability.

7.2 Suppose that neighborhood soccer players are selling raffle tickets for $500 worth of groceries at a local store, and you bought a $1 ticket for yourself and one for your mother. The children eventually sold 1,000 tickets.

a) What is the probability that you will win?
b) What is the probability that your mother will win?
c) What is the probability that you *or* your mother will win?

7.3 Now suppose that because of the high level of ticket sales, an additional $250 second prize will also be awarded.

a) Given that you don't win first prize, what is the probability that you will win second prize? (The first-prize ticket is not put back into the hopper before the second-prize ticket is drawn.)
b) What is the probability that your mother will come in first and you will come in second?

c) What is the probability that you will come in first and she will come in second?

d) What is the probability that the two of you will take first and second place?

7.4 Which parts of Exercise 7.3 dealt with joint probabilities?

7.5 Which parts of Exercise 7.3 dealt with conditional probabilities?

7.6 Make up a simple example of a situation in which you are interested in joint probabilities.

7.7 Make up a simple example of a situation in which you are interested in conditional probabilities. Frame the issue in terms of a research hypothesis.

7.8 In some homes a mother's behavior seems to be independent of her baby's and vice versa. If the mother looks at her child a total of two hours each day, and if the baby looks at the mother a total of three hours each day, and if they really do behave independently, what is the probability that they will look at each other at the same time?

7.9 In Exercise 7.8 assume that both mother and child sleep from 8:00 P.M. to 7:00 A.M. What would be the probability now?

7.10 I said that the probability of alcohol involvement, given an accident at night, was approximately .50, but I don't know the probability of an accident, given that you had been drinking. How would you go about finding the answer to that question if you had sufficient resources?

7.11 In a study of the effectiveness of "please don't litter" requests on supermarket fliers, Geller, Witmer, and Orebaugh (1976) found that the probability that a flier carrying a "do not litter" message would end up in the trash, *if what people do with fliers is independent of the message that is on them*, was .033. I also said that 4.5% of those messages actually ended up in the trash. What does this tell you about the effectiveness of messages?

7.12 Give an example of a common continuous distribution for which we have some real interest in the probability that an observation will fall within some specified interval.

7.13 Give an example of a continuous variable that we routinely treat as if it were discrete.

7.14 Give two examples of discrete variables.

7.15 A graduate admissions committee has finally come to realize that it cannot make valid distinctions among the top applicants. This year the committee rated all 500 applicants and randomly chose 10 from those at or above the 80th percentile. (The 80th percentile is the point at or below which 80 percent of the scores fall.) What is the probability that any particular applicant will be admitted (assuming you have no knowledge of his or her rating)?

7.16 With respect to Exercise 7.15, determine the conditional probability that the person will be admitted, given the following:

a) That he or she has the highest rating

b) That he or she has the lowest rating

7.17 In Appendix D (or the Add.dat data set on the website), what is the probability that a person drawn at random will have an ADDSC score greater than 50?

7.18 In Appendix D, what is the probability that a male will have an ADDSC score greater than 50?

7.19 In Appendix D, what is the probability that a person will drop out of school, given that he or she has an ADDSC score of at least 60?

7.20 How might you use conditional probabilities to determine if an ADDSC cutoff score in Appendix D of 66 is predictive of whether or not a person will drop out of school?

7.21 Compare the conditional probability from Exercise 7.20 with the unconditional probability of dropping out of school.

7.22 People who sell cars are often accused of treating male and female customers differently. Make up a series of statements to illustrate simple, joint, and conditional probabilities with respect to such behavior. How might we begin to determine if those accusations are true?

7.23 Assume you are a member of a local human rights organization. How might you use what you know about probability to examine discrimination in housing?

7.24 A paper by Fell (1995) has many interesting statistics on the relationship between alcohol, drugs, and automobile accidents in the United States. The paper is available at

 http://raru.adelaide.edu.au/T95/paper/s14p1.html

With the author's permission, a copy of the paper is also available at

http://www.uvm.edu/~dhowell/StatPages/More_Stuff/Fell.html

From the statistics in this paper create several questions illustrating the principles discussed in this chapter. (These might make good exam questions if collected by the instructor.)

7.25 In 2000 the U.S. Department of Justice released a study of the death penalty from 1995 to 2000, a period during which U.S. Attorneys were required to submit to the Justice Department for review and approval all cases in which they sought the death sentence. (The report can be found at http://www.usdoj.gov/dag/pubdoc/_dp_survey_final.pdf.) The data were broken down by whether the U.S. attorney recommended seeking the death penalty and by the race of the *victim* (not the defendant). These data are summarized below.

| | Death Sentence Recommendation | | |
Victim's race	Yes	No	Total
Non-White	388	228	616
Row proportion	.630	.370	1.000
White	202	76	278
Row proportion	.726	.274	1.000
Total	590	304	894
Col %	.660	.340	

What would you conclude from looking at this table?

7.26 Using the data from Exercise 7.25, compute the risk and odds ratios of punishment as a function of race.

7.27 Recently I had a call from a friend who is a lawyer in Vermont. He was representing an African-American client who was challenging the fairness of a jury selection. His concern was that African-Americans were not proportionately represented in the pool from which jurors are selected. In Vermont, 0.43% of the adult population is African-American. The pool of 2,124 names from which juries are drawn contained only four African-Americans. It is straightforward to calculate that if the jury pool was fairly selected the probability that the pool would have four or fewer African-Americans is almost exactly .05. (You do not yet know how to make that calculation). My friend was asking me to explain "all of this hypothesis-testing stuff that the expert witnesses are talking about." Write a short answer to his question.

7.28 Using the *R* code available on the Web page for this chapter, compare the birthrates by age for data from 2002 and 2012. I would expect that we would see more babies born to older women in 2012 because many of them have put off having a child for many years. Does my expectation hold up?

CHAPTER 8

Sampling Distributions and Hypothesis Testing

This is a transitional chapter. In the preceding chapters we examined a number of different statistics and how they might be used to describe a set of data or present the probability of the occurrence of some event. You now have covered the groundwork that underlies the more interesting questions that statisticians are asked to answer. Starting in the next chapter we will begin to look at specific statistical techniques and their applications. Although the description of data is important and fundamental to any analysis, it is not sufficient to answer many of the most interesting problems we encounter. And although it is nice to be able to perform various statistical tests, we need to know what to do with those tests once we have done the arithmetic. In this chapter we are going to examine the general procedure for going from sample statistics to conclusions about population parameters.

CONCEPTS THAT YOU WILL NEED TO REMEMBER FROM PREVIOUS CHAPTERS

Sample statistics:	Here I refer to mainly the mean $(\overline{X})$ and standard deviation (s) computed on a sample
Population statistics:	Mainly the mean (μ) and standard deviation (σ) of a population
N:	The number of observations in a sample
Conditional probability:	The probability of an event occurring given that some other event has occurred

8.1 | Sampling Distributions and the Standard Error

There is considerable evidence in the literature that taller people tend to be more powerful than shorter people. They tend to earn higher salaries, to be found in higher status occupations, to more likely be leaders, and so on. (During the huge oil spill in the Gulf of Mexico in 2010, the president of BP claimed that BP cared about the "small people," which did not make him popular with those people. Perhaps it was a language problem.) Duguid and Goncola (2012) asked the question backward. They asked if perceived power affects whether people under-estimate or over-estimate their own height. They randomly assigned one group of people to play the role of manager and another group of people to play the role of employee in a paired situation. It is worth noting that the participants never actually played that role—they were simply told that they would be assigned that role. Shortly after the assignment, the participants were asked to report their own height. Although the true mean heights of the two groups were no different (the sample means differed by less than 3/8 of an inch), those who were told that they would act the role of managers, the high-power group, over-estimated their actual height by 0.66 inches, while those in the low-power group underestimated their actual height by an average of −0.21 inches. Thus the difference in the reported sample means was 0.87 inches. You would probably agree that no matter how trivial the intervention, the two groups would almost certainly differ to some small degree in their mean estimates. You would probably like to ask if the simple assignment of a more powerful role really makes people over-estimate their height, or if this is just some sort of chance difference. Is a difference of more than three-quarters of an inch more than just "some small degree" that could be attributed to chance?

This example illustrates the general kinds of questions we will be concerned with. We will ask if a mean, or a difference between means, or a correlation coefficient (a measure of the degree of relationship between variables) is small enough to be attributed to chance, or is it so large that we will conclude that it reflects a real underlying difference between groups or relationship between variables? And in subsequent chapters we will go further, asking not only if the difference or relationship is real, but also if it is meaningful and worth worrying about.

To understand hypothesis testing we need to understand the concepts of **sampling distributions** and **sampling error**. The former represents the distribution of sample statistics that we would see if we calculated some statistic (such as the mean) from multiple samples from some population. The latter represents the variability of those statistics from one sample to another. Sampling error refers to the fact that the value of a sample statistic probably will be in error (i.e., will deviate from the parameter it is estimating) as a result of the particular observations that are included in the sample. In this context "error" does not imply carelessness or a mistake. If we are studying behavior problems, one random sample might just happen to include an unusually obnoxious child, whereas another sample might happen to include an unusual number of relatively well-behaved children. If we are studying height estimations, one sample may just happen to have more people who over-estimate their height. Please remember that in statistics "error" does not usually mean what it means in standard English; it simply means random variability.

I can illustrate this concept of sampling error by returning to the study by Duguid and Goncola. For now we will work with just the group members who were told that they were going to be managers. (We will come back to directly comparing the two groups later.) Suppose that we have a set of heights from a hypothetical population of people with a mean over-estimated height of 0.66 inches. The standard deviation was estimated from their data to be 0.88 inches. (Remember, these are the population scores of over-estimates in height, not height itself. In other words, the difference between a person's true height and his or her estimate of that.) These are approximately the mean and standard deviation that Duguid and Goncolo found in their "high-power" sample. They had 50 participants in each group, so I will draw 50 scores from this hypothetical population, compute the sample mean of those 50 scores, and store that result. I will repeat this 10,000 times and record each sample mean so that we can see the spread of the sample means that we obtain. The results that I obtained when I went through this procedure are shown in Figure 8.1. (R code that will generate a distribution like this can be found in the footnote. You might try changing the sample size or the mean and see what happens.[1] If you cut

Figure 8.1   Distribution of sample means of over-estimation of heights drawn from a population with $\mu = 0.66$, $\sigma = 0.88$, and $N = 50$

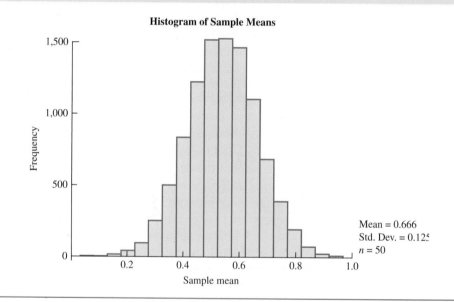

```
 # Sampling distribution of the mean
par(mfrow = (c(1,1)))
nreps = 10000; n = 50   #Semicolons allow you to save space by putting
                        several lines on one line.
xbar <- numeric(nreps)
for (i in 1:nreps) {
 x <- rnorm(n = 50, mean = .667, sd = 0.88)
 xbar[i] <- mean(x)
}
meanxbar <- round(mean(xbar), digits = 3); semean <- round(sd(xbar),
digits = 3)
cat("The mean of the sampling distribution is ",meanxbar, "\n")
cat("The standard error of the mean is ", semean, "\n")
hist(xbar, col = "#22748A", xlab = "Sample Mean",
   main = "Histogram of Sample Means" )
legend(0.85, 800, paste("Mean = ", meanxbar, "\nSt. Dev = ", semean,"\nn = ", n),
bty = "n")
```

and paste this code into R you may get a slightly different figure because of the random sampling and the fact that R chooses its own bar width.) We will have more to say about such distributions shortly, but for now all that I want you to see is that sampling error represents differences between one sample statistic (in this case a mean) and another. Notice how a few means of the over-estimates are below 0.40 and a few are above 1.0. However, most means fall pretty much in the middle. If people in the higher-power population really resemble those that we found in our sample of 50 cases, the majority of the time a sample of 50 cases from that population would have a sample mean somewhere between 0.40 and 1.0. (I could come up with more precise values, but these approximate values are easy to see and make the same point.)

This distribution illustrates what we mean by sampling error, and it also illustrates something that we will call the **standard error of the mean**. A standard error is just the standard deviation of the sampling distribution. You can see that in this example the standard error of the mean is 0.125.

You may object that you don't want to go out and repeat your experiment 10,000 times just to see what kinds of means you would get. That is not a problem. As we will see shortly, we can predict quite well on the basis of one sample what you would find if you drew all 10,000 samples. The point here is just to show what kinds of results we can expect.

8.2 Two More Examples Involving Course Evaluations and Human Decision Making

Before continuing, let's look at some other examples that make a similar point. One example that we will investigate near the end of the next chapter looks at the relationship between how students evaluate a course and the grade they expect to receive in that course. This is a topic that many faculty members feel strongly about, because even the best instructors turn to the semiannual course evaluation forms with some trepidation—perhaps the same amount of trepidation with which many students open their grade report form. Some faculty think that a course is good or bad independent of how well a student feels he or she will do in terms of a grade. Others feel that a student who seldom came to class and who will do poorly as a result will also (unfairly?) rate the course as poor. Finally, there are those who argue that students who do well and experience success take something away from the course other than just a grade and that those students will generally rate the course highly. But the relationship between course ratings and student performance is an empirical question and, as such, can be answered by looking at relevant data. (I chose this example because it involves a measure of relationship rather than a measure of differences between means.)

Suppose that in a random sample of 50 courses we find a general upward trend—in those courses in which students expect to do well, they tend to rate the course highly; and in those courses in which students expect to do poorly, they tend to rate the overall quality of the course as low. How do we tell whether this trend in our small data set is representative of a trend among students in general or just a fluke that would disappear if we ran the study again? Here our statistic will be a correlation coefficient, which is simply a number between 0 and 1.0 reflecting the degree to which two variables are related.

A second example comes from a study by Strough, Mehta, McFall, and Schuller (2008). They were examining what is called the "sunk-cost fallacy." They define the fallacy as "a decision-making bias that reflects the tendency to invest more future resources in a situation in which a prior investment has been made, as compared with a similar situation in which a prior investment has not been made." For example, suppose that you paid $10 to watch a movie on pay TV. After a few minutes you find that the movie is pretty awful. Are you more likely to continue watching that movie (i.e., invest more cost in terms of your time and/ or boredom or discomfort) having paid $10 than you would be if the movie were free? (I suspect that I would keep watching; not only would I be out $10, which I wouldn't get back anyway, but I would also have to suffer through an awful movie.) The phrase "sunk costs" refers to costs that cannot be recovered once they are incurred. (You are out $10 no matter what you do.) Strough et al. asked whether older participants were more or less likely than younger participants to keep watching. Their measure was the sunk-cost-fallacy score that they calculated based on the participants' behavior. A higher score means that a participant was more likely to keep watching. They found that for 75 younger participants (college students) the sample mean ($\overline{X}_Y$) was approximately 1.39, while for 73 older participants (ages 58–91) the mean ($\overline{X}_O$) was 0.75. (The subscripts "Y" and "O" stand for "young" and "old," respectively.) For both groups the estimated standard deviation was approximately 0.50. These results could be explained in one of two ways:

- The difference between 1.39 in one sample and 0.75 in the other sample is simply attributable to sampling error (random variability among samples); therefore, we cannot conclude that age influences the sunk-cost fallacy.

- The difference between 1.39 and 0.75 is large. The difference is not just sampling error; therefore, we conclude that older people are less likely to buy into the sunk-cost fallacy and continue watching the movie.

Although the statistical calculations required to answer this question are different from those used to answer the one about course evaluations (because the first deals with relationships and the second deals with differences between means), the underlying logic is fundamentally the same.

The most basic concept underlying all statistical tests is the sampling distribution of a statistic. It is fair to say that if we did not have sampling distributions, we would not have any statistical tests. Roughly speaking, sampling distributions tell us what values we might (or might not) expect to obtain for a particular statistic under a set of predefined conditions (e.g., what the obtained mean of five children might be *if* the true mean of the population from which those children come is 50). Notice that I'm talking about a *conditional probability* here; the probability of something happening *if* something else is true. You have already seen one sampling distribution in Figure 8.1, where we asked about the distribution of the overestimation of mean heights of groups of people assigned to the "powerful" condition.

These examples of the effects of (1) power, (2) the relationship between grades and course evaluations, and (3) the sunk-cost fallacy are the kinds of questions that fall under the heading of **hypothesis testing**. This chapter is intended to present the theory of hypothesis testing in as general a way as possible, without going into the specific techniques or properties of any particular test. I will focus largely on the situation involving differences instead of the situation involving relationships, but the logic is basically the same. You will see additional material on examining relationships when we discuss correlation in the next chapter.

The theory of hypothesis testing is so important in all that follows that you really need a thorough understanding of it. This chapter is designed to separate the logic of hypothesis testing from the technical aspects of actually running a statistical test. You can learn formulae later, after you understand *why* you might want to use them. Professional statisticians might fuss over the looseness of the definitions, but that will be set right in subsequent chapters. The material covered here cuts across all statistical tests and can be discussed independently of them. By separating the material in this way, you are free to concentrate on the underlying principles without worrying about the mechanics of calculation.

The important issue in hypothesis testing is to find some way of deciding whether, in the sunk-costs study for example, we are looking at a small chance fluctuation in differences between the two age groups or at a difference that is sufficiently large for us to believe that older people are much less likely to "throw good after bad" than younger people.

To answer the question about sunk-costs, we not only need to know what kind of value to expect for a mean sunk-cost-fallacy score, but we also have to know something about how variable those mean values might be if we had many of them. We only have one mean, but we know that if we repeated the study our next mean would be somewhat different. We need to know just how much different it is likely to be. One estimate of how variable a set of means would be can be derived from the standard deviation of our sample. We can convert this standard deviation to an estimate of the **standard error**, as that was defined above—in other words, the standard deviation of means. Such a standard error, for overestimation of heights, was reported in Figure 8.1 where you see that the standard deviation *of the means* was 0.125. Sampling distributions provide the opportunity to evaluate the likelihood of an obtained sample statistic, given that such predefined conditions actually exist. In addition, the standard error tells us how variable such distributions are. Although sampling distributions are almost always derived mathematically, it is easier to understand what they represent if we consider how they could, in theory, be derived empirically with a simple sampling experiment.

Look at Figure 8.2. Here I drew samples from the same population as in Figure 8.1, except that this time I drew samples of size 10, rather than size 50. (To obtain this figure, I generated 10,000 samples of random data, wherein each result was the mean of 10 random observations from a $N(0.667, 0.88^2 = 0.774)$ population. Notice that the distribution in Figure 8.2 is more spread out than the one in Figure 8.1. The means of each distribution of means are virtually the same to three decimal points, but the standard deviation rose from 0.125 to 0.278. That is because means based on fewer scores are, not surprisingly, less consistent.) As we will see throughout this book, the size of the sample plays an important role.

Referring to Figure 8.2, we see that sample means between about 0.25 and 1.40, for example, are quite likely to occur when we sample 10 participants chosen at random. We also can see that it is extremely unlikely that we would draw from this population a sample of 10 observations with a sample mean as low as −0.25, although there is some small probability of doing so. The fact that we know the

> **Figure 8.2** Distribution of sample means of over-estimation of heights, each based on $n = 10$ scores

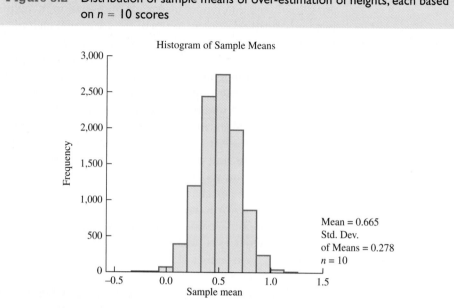

Histogram of Sample Means

Mean = 0.665
Std. Dev.
of Means = 0.278
$n = 10$

kinds of values to expect for the mean of a sample drawn from this population is going to allow us to turn the question around and ask if an obtained sample mean can be taken as evidence in favor of the hypothesis that we actually are sampling from this population.

There are two important points to keep in mind as we go forward. A sampling distribution is the distribution of *any* statistic. For example, the **sampling distribution of the mean** is the distribution of means that we would obtain from repeated random samples from a specific population, while the sampling distribution of the variance would be the distribution of those sample variances. Also, the standard error, which we will frequently refer to, is simply the standard deviation of a sampling distribution. Thus the standard error of the mean is the standard deviation of means from repeated sampling. For samples of size 10, the standard error of the mean was 0.278, which is shown in Figure 8.2.

8.3 Hypothesis Testing

In Chapter 6 we considered the distribution of Total Behavior Problem scores from the Achenbach Youth Self-Report form. Total Behavior Problem scores (because of the way that the instrument was developed) are nearly normally distributed in the population (i.e., the complete population of such scores would be normally distributed) with a population mean (μ) of 50 and a population standard deviation (σ) of 10. We know that different children show different levels of problem behaviors and therefore have different scores. Similarly, different samples of children are not likely to have exactly the same mean score. If we took a sample of children their mean would probably not equal exactly 50. One sample of children might have a mean of 49.1, while a second sample might have a mean of 53.3. The actual sample means would depend on the particular children who happened to be included in the sample. This expected variability that we see from sample to sample is what is meant when we speak of "variability due to chance." We are referring to the fact that statistics (in this case, means) obtained from samples naturally vary from one sample to another. This is the same issue we face in the study of height and power. We know that the mean of the two treatment conditions (managers and employees) are almost certain to differ simply because of the particular participants who happened to be in the two groups. But we want to know if the difference we found is actually greater than the small chance differences we expect.

We do not go around obtaining sampling distributions, either mathematically or empirically, simply because they are interesting to look at. We have important reasons for doing so. The usual reason is that we want to test some hypothesis. Let's consider the random sample of five highly stressed children with a mean behavior problem score of 56. We want to test the hypothesis that such a sample mean could reasonably have arisen had we drawn our sample from a population in which $\mu = 50$ and $\sigma = 10$. This is another way of saying that we want to know whether the mean of stressed children is different from the mean of normal children. The only way we can test such a hypothesis is to have some idea of the probability of obtaining a sample mean as extreme as 56 *if* we actually sampled observations from a population in which the children are *normal* ($\mu = 50$). The answer to this question is precisely what a sampling distribution is designed to provide.

Suppose we obtained (constructed) the sampling distribution of the mean for samples of five children from a population whose mean (μ) is 50 and $\sigma = 10$. (I have done this by drawing 10,000 observations from a specified population. This is just a minor modification of the R code found in footnote 1.) This distribution is plotted in Figure 8.3. Suppose further we then determined from that distribution the probability of a sample mean of 56 *or higher*. For the sake of argument, suppose this probability is .094. Our reasoning could then go as follows: "If we did sample from a population with $\mu = 50$, the probability of obtaining a sample mean as high as 56 is .094—not a result that will occur frequently, but certainly not an unusual one. Because a sample mean that high is obtained about 9% of the time from a population with a mean of 50, we don't have a very good reason to doubt that this sample came from such a population."

Alternatively, suppose we obtained a sample mean of 62 and calculated from the sampling distribution that the probability of a sample mean as high as 62 was only .0038. Our argument could then go like this: "*If we did sample from a population with $\mu = 50$ and $\sigma = 10$, the probability of obtaining a sample mean as high as 62 is only .0038*—a highly unlikely event. Because a sample mean that high is unlikely to be obtained from such a population, it would be reasonable to conclude that this sample probably came from some other population (one whose mean is higher than 50)."

It is important to realize what we have done in this example, because the logic is typical of most tests of hypotheses. The actual test consisted of several stages:

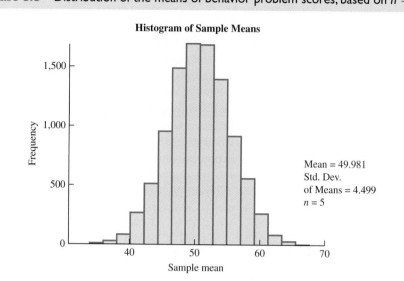

Figure 8.3 Distribution of the means of behavior problem scores, based on $n = 5$

1. We wanted to test the hypothesis, often called the **research hypothesis, H_1,** that children under the stress of divorce are more likely than normal children to exhibit behavior problems.

2. We set up the hypothesis (called the **null hypothesis, H_0**) that the sample was actually drawn from a population whose mean, denoted μ_0, equals 50. This is the hypothesis that stressed children do not differ from normal children in terms of behavior problems.

3. We obtained a random sample of children under stress.

4. We then obtained the sampling distribution of the mean under the assumption that H_0 (the null hypothesis) is true (i.e., we obtained the sampling distribution of the mean from a population with $\mu_0 = 50$ and $\sigma = 10$).

5. Given the sampling distribution, we calculated the probability of a mean *at least as large* as our actual sample mean.

6. On the basis of that probability, we made a decision: either to reject or fail to reject H_0. Because H_0 states that $\mu = 50$, rejection of H_0 represents a belief that $\mu > 50$, although the actual value of μ remains unspecified.

If you remember nothing else from this chapter, be sure that you thoroughly understand the logic of the steps listed in this shaded box. It is the basic principle behind statistical hypothesis tests, no matter how complicated they look.

The preceding discussion is oversimplified in several ways. First, we are not going to have to sit down with our computer and actually draw 10,000 samples and calculate their mean to get the sampling distribution of the mean, although that approach would certainly work and, because of the availability of high-speed computing, now represents a viable approach to statistical tests, and one that is very likely to become prevalent in the future. We have simple ways to calculate what it would be. Also, we generally would prefer to test the research hypothesis that children under stress are *different from* (rather than just *higher than*) other children, but we will return to that point shortly. It is also oversimplified in the sense that in practice we also would need to take into account (either directly or by estimation) the value of σ^2, the population variance, and N, the sample size. But again, those are specifics we can deal with when the time comes. The logic of the approach is representative of the logic of most, if not all, statistical tests. In each case we follow the same steps: (1) specify a research hypothesis (H_1), (2) set up the null hypothesis (H_0), (3) collect some data, (4) construct, or more often imagine, the sampling distribution of the particular statistic on the assumption that H_0 is true, (5) compare the sample statistic to that distribution, and find the probability of exceeding the observed statistic's value, and (6) reject or retain H_0, depending on the probability, under H_0, of a sample statistic as extreme as the one we have obtained.

8.4 The Null Hypothesis

As we have seen, the concept of the null hypothesis plays a crucial role in the testing of hypotheses. People frequently are puzzled by the fact that we set up a hypothesis that is directly counter to what we hope to show. For example, if we hope to demonstrate the research hypothesis that college students do not come from a population with a mean self-confidence score of 100, we immediately set up the null hypothesis that they do. Or if we hope to demonstrate the validity of a research hypothesis that the means (μ_1 and μ_2) of the populations from which two samples are drawn are different, we state the null hypothesis that the population means are the same (or, equivalently, $\mu_1 - \mu_2 = 0$). (The term "null hypothesis" is most easily seen in this example, in which it refers to the hypothesis that the difference between the two population means is zero, or *null*. Some people refer to that hypothesis as the "nil null," but I see absolutely no advantage to such a distinction.) We use the null hypothesis for several reasons. The philosophical argument, put forth by Fisher when he first introduced the concept, is that we can never prove something to be true, but we can prove something to be false. Observing 3,000 cows with only one head does not prove the statement "All cows have only one head." However, finding one cow with two heads does disprove the original statement beyond any shadow of a doubt. While one might argue with Fisher's basic position—and many people have—the null hypothesis retains its dominant place in statistics. You might also draw the parallel between the null hypothesis that we usually test and the idea that someone is innocent until proven guilty, which is the basis for our system of justice. We begin with the idea that the defendant is innocent, and agree to convict only if the data are sufficiently inconsistent with that belief. You can't push that idea very far, but it has considerable similarity with the way we test hypotheses.

A second and more practical reason for employing the null hypothesis is that it provides us with the starting point for any statistical test. Consider the case in which you want to show that the mean self-confidence score of college students is greater than 100. Suppose further that you were granted the privilege of proving the truth of some hypothesis. What hypothesis are you going to test? Should you test the hypothesis that $\mu = 101$, or maybe the hypothesis that $\mu = 112$, or how about $\mu = 113$? The point is that we do not have a *specific* alternative (research) hypothesis in mind (and I can't recall any experiment that did), and without one we cannot construct the sampling distribution we need. However, if we start off by assuming H_0: $\mu = 100$, we can immediately set about obtaining the sampling distribution for $\mu = 100$ and then, with luck, reject that hypothesis and conclude that the mean score of college students is greater than 100, which is what we wanted to show in the first place.

Sir Ronald Alymer Fisher 1890–1962

Having mentioned Fisher's name in connection with statistical hypothesis testing, I should tell you something about him. In a discipline with many interesting characters, Fisher stands out as extraordinary, and he probably made greater contributions to the early field of statistics than any other person, with the possible exception of his archrival Karl Pearson.

Fisher started life with very poor eyesight and required special tutoring early on. He won a scholarship to Cambridge, where he studied mathematics and then physics and was at the top of his class. Because of his poor eyesight he had to imagine problems geometrically rather than working through problems with pencil and paper. This greatly influenced the way he thought about statistics and often set him off from his colleagues. He developed strong interests in genetics and eugenics and helped to form the Cambridge Eugenics Society. During World War I his notoriously bad eyesight kept him from military service, and he bounced around among several jobs. After the war he took a position at a small agricultural experiment station named Rothamsted, which would probably not be remembered by anyone if it weren't for Fisher's connection to it. While there, Fisher worked with the mounds of agricultural data that had been collected but never analyzed, and this work formed the basis for many of his contributions to the field. He developed the concept of the analysis of variance, which is today one of the most important techniques in statistical analysis. He also developed the theory of maximum likelihood, without which many areas of statistics would not even exist. He put forth the idea of the null hypothesis and is noted for saying that, "Every experiment may be said to exist only in order to give the facts a chance of disproving the null hypothesis."

In later years, he quarreled for at least a decade with Jerzy Neyman and Egon Pearson, Karl Pearson's son, who argued for a different approach to hypothesis testing. What we now teach as "hypothesis testing" is an amalgam of the two approaches, which would probably not satisfy either side in that debate. No scientist today could get away with saying to others in print the kind of remarks that went back and forth between the two groups. Statistics in England in the first half of the 20th century was certainly interesting. (Good [2001] has pointed out that one of the speakers who followed a presentation by Fisher referred to Fisher's presentation as "the braying of the Golden Ass." You can be sure that Fisher had something equally kind to say in reply.) But despite the animosities, statistics in England at that time was incredibly fruitful.

Fisher was very active in the eugenics movement and was the Galton Professor of Eugenics at University College London and then the Arthur Balfour Professor of Genetics at Cambridge, two of the most prestigious universities in the world. Though neither of those departments was a department of statistics, their work was highly statistical, and it is statistical work for which Fisher is known.

8.5 | **Test Statistics and Their Sampling Distributions**

We have been discussing the sampling distribution of the mean, but the discussion would have been essentially the same had we dealt instead with the median, the variance, the range, the correlation coefficient (as in our course evaluation example), proportions, or any other statistic you care to consider. (Technically the shape of these distributions would be different, but I am deliberately ignoring such issues in this chapter.) The statistics just mentioned usually are referred to as **sample statistics**, because they describe samples. A whole different class of statistics called **test statistics** is associated with specific statistical procedures and has its own sampling distributions. Test statistics are statistics such as t, F, χ^2, which you may have run across in the past. If you are not familiar with them, don't worry—we will consider them separately in later chapters. This is not the place to go into a detailed explanation of any test statistic (I put this chapter where it is because I didn't want readers to think that they were supposed to worry about technical issues.) This chapter *is* the place, however, to point out that the sampling distributions for test statistics can be obtained and used in essentially the same way as the sampling distribution of the mean.

As an illustration, consider the sampling distribution of the statistic t, which will be discussed in Chapters 12 through 14. For those who have never heard of the t test, it is sufficient to say that the t test is often used, among other things, to determine whether two samples were drawn from populations with the same means. For example, is the mean error of height estimation the same for participants who are told that they will play the role of managers as it is for those told that they will play the role of employees? Suppose that μ_1 and μ_2 represent the means of the populations from which the two samples were drawn. The null hypothesis is the hypothesis that the two population means (μ_1 and μ_2) are equal, in other words, H_0: $\mu_1 = \mu_2$ (or $\mu_1 - \mu_2 = 0$). If we were patient, we could empirically obtain the sampling distribution of t when H_0 is true by drawing an infinite number of pairs of samples, all from one population, calculating t for each pair of samples (by methods to be discussed later), and plotting the resulting values of t. In that case, H_0 must be true because the samples came from the same population. The resulting distribution is the sampling distribution of t *when H_0 is true*. If we had a sample of two groups that produced a particular value of t, we would test the null hypothesis by comparing that sample t to the sampling distribution of t. We would reject the null hypothesis if our obtained t did not look like the kinds of t values that the sampling distribution told us to expect when the null hypothesis is true.

I could rewrite the preceding paragraph substituting χ^2, or F, or any other test statistic in place of t, with only minor changes dealing with how the statistic is calculated. Thus you can see that all sampling distributions can theoretically be obtained in basically the same way (calculate and plot an infinite number of statistics by sampling from a known population). Once you understand that fact, much of the remainder of the book is an elaboration of methods for calculating the desired statistic and a description of characteristics of the appropriate sampling distribution. And don't worry. We have simple techniques to calculate what those sampling distributions would be without drawing thousands of samples.

Keep in mind the analogy to our legal system that I used. The null hypothesis is roughly analogous to the idea that someone is innocent until proven guilty. The idea of rejecting the null hypothesis is analogous to the idea that we convict someone when we believe him or her to be guilty "beyond a reasonable doubt." We don't have to "prove" that the person is innocent; we have to conclude only that the test of "reasonable doubt" fails in this instance. To say this another way, Fisher (1935) wrote, "In relation to any experiment we may speak of this hypothesis as the 'null hypothesis,' and it should be noted that the null hypothesis is never proved or established, but is possibly disproved, in the course of experimentation." I will keep coming back to this point because it is critical to understanding what a test of significance is.

8.6   Using the Normal Distribution to Test Hypotheses

Much of the discussion so far has dealt with statistical procedures that you do not yet know how to use. I did this deliberately to emphasize the point that the logic and the calculations behind a test are two separate issues. You now know quite a bit about how hypothesis tests are conducted, even if you may not have the slightest idea how to do the arithmetic. However, we now can use what you already know about the normal distribution to test some simple hypotheses. In the process we can deal with several fundamental issues that are more easily seen by use of a concrete example.

An important use of the normal distribution is to test hypotheses, either about individual observations or about sample statistics such as the mean. Here we will deal with individual observations, leaving the question of testing sample statistics until later chapters. Note, however, that in the general case we test hypotheses about sample statistics such as the mean rather than hypotheses about individual observations. I am starting with an example of an individual observation because the explanation is somewhat clearer. Because we are dealing with only single observations, the sampling distribution invoked here will be the distribution of individual scores (rather than the distribution of means). The basic logic is the same, and we are using an example of individual scores only because it simplifies the explanation and is something with which you have had experience. I should point out that in fields such as neurology and occasionally clinical psychology testing using individual scores is reasonably common. For example, neurologists often use simple measurements, such as two-point sensitivity[2], to diagnose disorders. For example, someone might be classified as having a particular disorder if his or her two-point sensitivity or visual response time is significantly greater than that of normal responders.

For a simple example assume that we are concerned with the rate at which people can tap their fingers. That may seem like an odd thing to worry about, but neuropsychologists and neurologists frequently use finger tapping as a diagnostic tool. Christianson and Leathem (2004) developed a computerized finger-tapping test that produces scores from nonclinical participants with a mean of 59 and a standard deviation of 7 (rounded) over a 10-second trial. It is known that Alzheimer's patients show decreased tapping speed, as do those suffering from a variety of neurological disorders. (Interestingly, a full year after being exposed to very high altitudes, climbers of Mt. Everest also continued to show depressed tapping performance. Just thought you'd like to know.)

---

[2]If I poke you with either one or two needles, the two-point sensitivity is the distance between the two points before you can tell that I have two needles and not one.

We will assume that we know that the mean rate of finger tapping of normal healthy adults is 59 taps in 10 seconds, with a standard deviation of 7, and that tapping speeds are normally distributed in the population. Assume further that we know that the tapping rate is slower among people with certain neurological problems. To take an extreme example, suppose that you use Christianson and Leathem's test on your grandfather and he gets a score of 20. You would probably say something like, "Wow, Grandpa certainly isn't normal." But if his score had been 52 you might have said "A trifle low, better keep an eye on the old guy, but for now he seems fine.[3]" Finally, to take a more reasonable example, suppose that we have just tested an individual who taps at a rate of 45 taps in 10 seconds. Is his score sufficiently below the mean for us to assume that he did not come from a population of neurologically healthy people? This situation is diagrammed in Figure 8.4, in which the arrow indicates the location of our piece of data (the person's score).

The logic of the solution to this problem is the same as the logic of hypothesis testing in general. We begin by assuming that the individual's score does come from the population of healthy scores. This is the null hypothesis (H_0). If H_0 is true, we automatically know the mean and the standard deviation of the population from which he was supposedly drawn (59 and 7, respectively). With this information we are in a position to calculate the probability that a score *as low as* his would be obtained from this population. If the probability is very low, we can reject H_0 and conclude that he did not come from the healthy population. Conversely, if the probability is not particularly low, then the data represent a reasonable result under H_0, and we would have no reason to doubt its validity and thus no reason to doubt that the person is

Figure 8.4   Location of a person's tapping score on a distribution of scores of neurologically healthy people

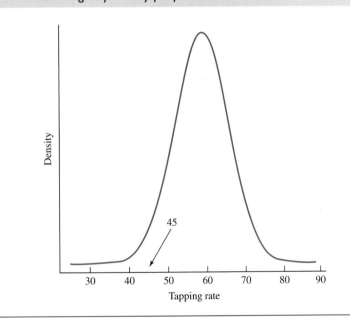

---

[3] I just tried the test and got a 52, and I know that I am perfectly fine—well, aren't I?

healthy. Keep in mind that we are not interested in the probability of a score *equal* to 45 (which, because the distribution is continuous, would be infinitely small) but rather in the probability that the score would be at least as low as (i.e., less than or equal to) 45.

The individual had a score of 45. We want to know the probability of obtaining a score *at least as low as* 45 if H_0 is true. We already know how to find this—it is the area below 45 in Figure 8.4. All we have to do is convert 45 to a z score and then refer to Table E.10. Or you can go to http://www.danielsoper.com/statcalc3/ and calculate it directly[4].

$$z = \frac{X - \mu}{\sigma} = \frac{45 - 59}{7} = \frac{-14}{7} = -2.00$$

From Table E.10 we can see that the probability of a z score of −2.00 or below is .0228. (Locate $z = 2.00$ in the table and then read across to the column headed "Smaller Portion." Remember that the distribution is symmetric, so the probability of $z \leq -2.00$ is the same as the probability of $z \geq +2.00$.)

At this point we have to become involved in the **decision-making** aspects of hypothesis testing. We must decide if an event with a probability of .0228 is sufficiently unlikely to cause us to reject H_0. Here we will fall back on arbitrary conventions that have been established over the years. The rationale for these conventions will become clearer as we go along, but for the time being keep in mind that they are merely conventions. One convention calls for rejecting H_0 if the probability under H_0 is less than or equal to .05 ($p \leq .05$), while another convention calls for rejecting H_0 whenever the probability under H_0 is less than or equal to .01. The latter convention is more conservative with respect to the probability of rejecting H_0. These values of .05 and .01 are often referred to as the **rejection level**, or **significance level**, of the test. Whenever the probability obtained under H_0 is less than or equal to our predetermined significance level, we will reject H_0.

Another way of stating this is to say that any outcome whose probability under H_0 is less than or equal to the significance level (i.e., the probability provides "more than a reasonable doubt"), falls into the **rejection region**, because such an outcome leads us to reject H_0. In this book we will use the .05 level of significance, keeping in mind that some people would consider this level to be too lenient. For our particular example, we have obtained a probability value of .0228, which obviously is less than .05. Because we have specified that we will reject H_0 if the probability of the data under H_0 is less than .05, we will conclude that we have a person whose score does not come from a population of healthy people. More specifically, we conclude that a finger-tapping rate of 45 is inconsistent with results for a nonclinical population with a mean equal to 59 and a standard deviation equal to 7. It is important to note that we have not proven that this person is not healthy, but we have shown that he does not look like a healthy person. On the other hand, if the person had tapped at a rate of 52 taps per 10 seconds, the probability of 52 taps or lower would be .1587, which

---

[4]If you go to that website and enter $z = 2.00$, you will get an answer of .9772. That is because it is giving you the probability of all outcomes *below* 2.00. What you want is the probability of values less than −2.00, which is .0228. Often you will have to think about which tail of the distribution you want and act accordingly—or subtract .9772 from 1.00. In Soper's calculator you can enter −2.00, but with printed tables you have to work with positive values and then reverse the probability for negative values.

would not lead to rejection of the null hypothesis. This does not necessarily mean that the person is healthy; it just means that we do not have sufficient evidence to reject the null hypothesis that he is. It may be that he is just acquiring a disorder and therefore is not quite as different from normal as is usual for his condition. Or maybe he has the disease at an advanced stage but just happens to be an unusually fast tapper. Remember that we can never say that we have proved the null hypothesis. We can conclude only that this person does not tap sufficiently slowly for a disorder, if any, to be statistically detectable.[5]

It is important to remember that the rejection level (usually .05 or .01) is a probability, and it is the probability that an observation will fall in the rejection region. The rejection region represents those outcomes that are so unlikely under the null hypothesis that we reject the null hypothesis based on the reasoning that we would not reasonably expect such results if the null hypothesis were true.

The theory of significance testing as just outlined was popularized by R. A. Fisher in the first third of the 20th century. The theory was expanded and cast in more of a decision framework by Jerzy Neyman and Egon Pearson between 1928 and 1938, often against the loud and abusive objections of Fisher. Current statistical practice more closely follows the Neyman-Pearson approach, which emphasizes more than did Fisher the fact that we also have an **alternative hypothesis (H_1)** that is contradictory to the null hypothesis (H_0). (There is yet a third position put forth in recent years by Jones and Tukey, and we will come to that later in the chapter.) If the null hypothesis is

$$H_0: \mu = 100$$

then the alternative hypothesis could be

$$H_1: \mu \neq 100$$

or

$$H_1: \mu > 100$$

or

$$H_1: \mu < 100$$

We will discuss alternative hypotheses in more detail shortly.

There is some controversy about how to report significance levels. In the past it was standard to report simply whether the probability was less than .05 (or .01), without reporting the exact level. The American Psychological Association

---

[5]The particular approach used here is designed for situations where the "population" on which our "normal" sample parameters are based is sufficiently large to give us solid faith in the values of the mean and standard deviation we use. Crawford and Howell (1998) noted that in many cases, especially in neuropsychology, the sample on which the norms are based is quite small, and they proposed an alternative approach in those situations. To further understand that approach, see Crawford, Garthwaite, and Howell (2009).

now requires that the exact p level be reported, although not all of their journals follow this proscription. On the other hand, Boos and Stefanski (2011) have argued that the precision and reproducibility of exact p values is questionable and conclude that "our findings shed light on the relative value of exact p-values vis-a-vis approximate p-values, and indicate that the use of *, **, and *** to denote levels 0.05, 0.01, and 0.001 of statistical significance in subject-matter journals is about the right level of precision for reporting p-values when judged by widely accepted rules for rounding statistical estimates." My advice would be to report the p level, to three decimal places, mainly because that is what the APA requires, but to not put too much faith in its exact value. That is what I will do in what follows.

The argument over whether to make a statement such as "$p < .05$" as opposed to "$p = .032$" becomes important to me, and thus to you, because it influences how I set up and use this book. Ever since the beginning days of statistics, statisticians have employed tables of statistical distributions. And that's the way courses have been taught and textbooks have been written for years and years. For example, suppose that I calculate some statistic from data—call it $t = 2.53$ for a study with 25 cases. I want to reject the null hypothesis if the probability of that t value is less than .05. What I would do in the past was to go to a table, such as those in the back of this book, and discover that, given the sample size of my study, any t value greater than 2.06 would occur less than 5% of the time. Because $2.53 > 2.06$, I can reject the null hypothesis.

But, having rejected the null hypothesis, I still don't know the actual probability of $t = 2.53$—only that it is less than .05. For a very long time that was OK—I didn't need to know the exact probability, and calculating it was so involved that it was easier just to look in a table and be satisfied with an approximate answer.

Finally, that approach is changing. Because most statistical tests are handled using statistical software such as R, SPSS, SAS, or SYSTAT, and because that software can immediately print out the exact probability, we can report that probability and do away with statements such as "$p < .05$" in favor of statements such as "$p = .032$." But what about poor me, writing a text for students who may not have instant access to software that will provide them with exact probability values? Do I go with a more modern approach and say to those that don't have software that they are out of luck? Or do I go with the old approach that very few practitioners still use and rely exclusively on statistical tables? Like most people faced with two alternatives, I want to have it both ways. So what I will do is to describe how to use each table, giving specific examples, but also ask that you calculate and report exact probabilities if you can. And it really isn't all that hard. If you use standard statistical software, you will have the answer automatically. If you do the calculations by hand, you can go to the Web, to a site such as http://www.danielsoper.com/statcalc3/ or http://www.statpages.org/pdfs.html, and very easily calculate the probability value you seek. The former site is more complete, but the latter is much easier to use. (I just computed such a probability from a $0.99 app named 89-in-1 Statistics Calculator on my iPhone. I really like that one.) To make such calculations using SPSS, see the site by Karl Wuensch at East Carolina University. The link is http://core.ecu.edu/psyc/wuenschk/SPSS/P-SPSS.docx And if you are in a place where you don't have access to the Web, you can fall back on a table and report that at least the probability is less than .05, even if you don't know its exact value.

To illustrate how easy it is to obtain probability values from the Web, go to your PC or Mac and log into one of the two sites I have mentioned. All that I want you to see is that you can simply click on the test statistic you have calculated, enter two or three numbers, and it will do the calculation for you. For Soper's site, choose Cumulative Area under the Standard Normal Curve Calculator. Enter $z = 2$, click "Calculate!" and you will get a probability of 0.97725, which is the probability below $z = 2$. For the probability above $z = 2$, simply subtract from 1.00. For the "statpages" site, enter $z = 2$, and click "Calc p." It will report 0.0455, which is the probability of exceeding ±2.0 in either direction. Half of that is 0.0228, which is the probability in each tail. And 1.00 – 0.0228 = 0.97725, the probability less than 2.0. For "89-in-1" just let mu = 0 and sd = 1 as the default. Finally, using R the command is simply pnorm(2,0,1), or, because 0 and 1 are the defaults, pnorm(2) is sufficient.

8.7 Type I and Type II Errors

Whenever we reach a decision with a statistical test, there is always a chance that our decision is the wrong one. While this is true of almost all decisions, statistical or otherwise, the statistician has one point in her favor that other decision makers normally lack. She not only makes a decision by some rational process, but she can also specify the conditional probabilities of a decision's being in error. In everyday life we make decisions with only subjective feelings about what is probably the right choice. The statistician, however, can state quite precisely the probability that she erroneously rejected H_0 in favor of the alternative (H_1). This ability to specify the probability of error follows directly from the logic of hypothesis testing.

Consider the finger-tapping example, this time ignoring the score of the individual sent to us. The situation is diagrammed in Figure 8.5, in which the distribution is the distribution of scores from healthy subjects, and the shaded portion represents the lowest 5% of the distribution. The actual score that cuts off the lowest 5% is called the **critical value**. Critical values are those values of X (the variable), or a test statistic, that describe the boundary or boundaries of the rejection region(s). For this particular example, the critical value is 47.48.

If we have a decision rule that says to reject H_0 whenever an outcome falls in the lowest 5% of the distribution, we will reject H_0 whenever an individual's

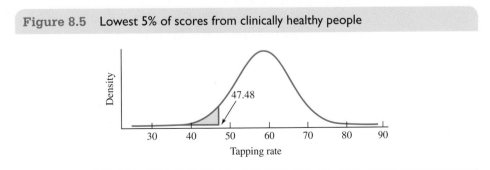

Figure 8.5 Lowest 5% of scores from clinically healthy people

Where did that 47.48 come from?

We are looking to reject the hypothesis that a person taps at a normal speed if that person's speed falls in the lowest 5% of the distribution of normal tapping scores. A z score of -1.645 cuts off the lowest 5%. We then solve for the raw score that corresponds to a z score of -1.645.

$$z = \frac{X - \mu}{\sigma} = \frac{X - 59}{7} = -1.645$$

$$X - 59 = -1.645 \times 7 = -11.515$$

$$X = -11.515 + 59 = 47.48$$

score falls into the shaded area; that is, whenever a score as low as his has a probability of .05 or less of coming from the population of healthy scores. Yet by the very nature of our procedure, 5% of the scores from perfectly healthy people will themselves fall into the shaded portion. Thus if we actually have sampled a person who is healthy, we stand a 5% chance of his or her score being in the shaded tail of the distribution, causing us erroneously to reject the null hypothesis. This kind of error (rejecting H_0 when, in fact, it is true) is called a **Type I error**, and its conditional probability (the probability of rejecting the null hypothesis given that it is true) is designated as α **(alpha)**, the size of the rejection region. In the future, whenever we represent a probability by α, we will be referring to the probability of a Type I error.

Keep in mind the "conditional" nature of the probability of a Type I error. I know that sounds like jargon, but what it means is that you should be sure you understand that when we speak of a Type I error, we mean the probability of rejecting H_0, *given that it is true*. We are not saying that we will reject H_0 on 5% of the hypotheses we test. We would hope to run experiments on important and meaningful variables and, therefore, to reject H_0 often. But when we speak of a Type I error, we are speaking only about rejecting H_0 in those situations in which the null hypothesis happens to be true.

You might feel that a 5% chance of making an error is too great a risk to take and suggest that we make our criterion much more stringent, by rejecting, for example, only the lowest 1% of the distribution. This procedure is perfectly legitimate, but you need to realize that the more stringent you make your criterion, the more likely you are to make another kind of error—failing to reject H_0 when it is actually false and H_1 is true. This type of error is called a **Type II error**, and its probability is symbolized by β **(beta)**.

The major difficulty in terms of Type II errors stems from the fact that if H_0 is false, we almost never know what the true distribution (the distribution under H_1) would look like for the population from which our data came. We know only the distribution of scores under H_0. Put in the present context, we know the distribution of scores from healthy people but not from people who are not healthy.[6] It may be that people suffering from some neurological disease tap, on average, considerably more slowly than healthy people, or it may be that they tap, on average, only a little more slowly. This situation is illustrated in Figure 8.6, in which the distribution labeled H_0 represents the distribution of scores from healthy people (the set of observations expected under the null hypothesis), and the distribution labeled H_1 represents our hypothetical distribution of nonhealthy scores (the distribution under H_1). Remember that the curve H_1 is only hypothetical. We really do not know the location of the nonhealthy distribution. I have shifted the distribution of nonhealthy patients to the left of the distribution of healthy patients because we know that nonhealthy patients tap more slowly—we just don't know how much more slowly. (I have arbitrarily drawn that distribution with a mean of 50 and a standard deviation of 7.)

The shaded portion in the top half of Figure 8.6 represents the rejection region. Any observation falling into that area (i.e., to the left of about 47.48) would lead to rejection of the null hypothesis. If the null hypothesis is true, we know that our observation will fall into this area 5% of the time. Thus we will make a Type I error 5% of the time.

The shaded portion in the bottom half of Figure 8.6 represents the probability (β) of a Type II error. Notice that the whole distribution is displaced to the left because I am assuming that the value of μ under H_1 is 50 rather than 59. This is the situation of a person who was actually drawn from the nonhealthy population but

Figure 8.6   Areas corresponding to α and β for tapping-speed example

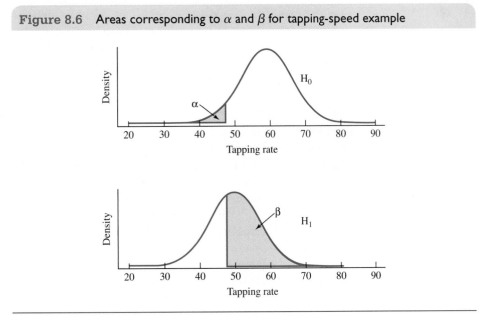

---

[6]You might say, "Well, go out and get some sick people and make them tap." Well, how sick would you like them to be? Very sick, with very slow speeds, or just a little sick, with slightly slow speeds? We aren't so much interested in classifying people as very sick or a little sick. And how sick is "a little sick"? We want to classify them as healthy or not healthy, and in that situation the only thing we can do is to compare a patient against healthy people.

whose score was not sufficiently low to cause us to reject H_0. You would only reject the null here if the score were less than 47.48, the cutoff point under the null.

In the particular situation illustrated in Figure 8.6, we can, in fact, calculate β for this combination of μ and σ by using the normal distribution to calculate the probability of obtaining a score *greater than* 47.48 if $\mu = 50$ and $\sigma = 7$—the mean and standard deviation of our hypothetical population on patients who are not healthy. The actual calculation is not important for your understanding of β; this chapter was designed specifically to avoid calculation. I will simply state that this probability (i.e., the area labeled β) is .64. Thus for this example, 64% of the time when we have a person who is actually nonhealthy (i.e., H_1 is actually true), we will make a Type II error by failing to reject H_0 when it is false (as medical diagnosticians, we leave a lot to be desired)[7].

From Figure 8.6 you can see that if we were to reduce the level of α (the probability of a Type I error) from .05 to .01 by moving the rejection region to the left, it would reduce the probability of Type I errors but would increase the probability of Type II errors. Setting α at .01 would give us a cutoff under the null hypothesis of 42.72. This would raise β to .85. Obviously, there is room for debate over what level of significance to use. The decision rests primarily on your opinion concerning the relative seriousness of Type I and Type II errors for the kind of study you are conducting. If it is important to avoid Type I errors (such as telling someone that he has a disease when he does not), then you would set a stringent (i.e., low) level of α. If, on the other hand, you want to avoid Type II errors (telling someone to go home and take an aspirin when, in fact, he or she needs immediate treatment), you might set a fairly high level of α. (Setting $\alpha = .20$ in this example would reduce β to .33.) Unfortunately, in practice most people choose an arbitrary level of α, such as .05 or .01, and simply ignore β. In many cases, this may be all you can do. (In fact, you will probably use the alpha level that your instructor recommends.) In other cases, however, there is much more you can do, as you will see in Chapter 15.

I should stress again that Figure 8.6 is purely hypothetical. I was able to draw the figure only because I arbitrarily decided that speeds of nonhealthy people were normally distributed with a mean of 50 and a standard deviation of 7. In most everyday situations we do not know the mean and the standard deviation of that distribution and can make only educated guesses, thus providing only crude estimates of β. In practice, we can select a value of μ under H_1 that represents the *minimum* difference we would like to be able to detect, because larger differences will have even smaller βs.

From this discussion of Type I and Type II errors we can summarize the decision-making process with a simple table. Table 8.1 presents the four possible outcomes of an experiment. The items in this table should be self-explanatory, but there is one concept—power—that we have not yet discussed. The **power** of a test is the probability of rejecting H_0 when it is actually false. Because the probability of *failing* to reject a false H_0 is β, then the power must equal $1 - \beta$. Those who want to know more about power and its calculation will find the material in Chapter 15 relevant.

---

[7]The R code for this is simply

```
beta <- 1-pnorm(x = 47.48, mean = 50, sd = 7)
Print(beta) # Subtract from 1.00 because pnorm(47.48, 50, 7) gives the probability below 47.48.
[1] 0.6405764
# To get cutoff at 1%
qnorm(.01, 50, 7)
```

Table 8.1 Possible Outcomes of the Decision-Making Process

	True State of the World	
Decision	H_0 True	H_0 False
Reject H_0	Type I error	Correct Decision
	$p = \alpha$	$p = 1 - \beta$ = Power
Fail to Reject H_0	Correct Decision	Type II error
	$p = 1 - \alpha$	$p = \beta$

8.8 One- and Two-Tailed Tests

The preceding discussion brings us to a consideration of one- and two-tailed tests. In our tapping example we knew that nonhealthy subjects tapped more slowly than healthy subjects; therefore, we decided to reject H_0 only if a subject tapped too slowly. However, suppose our subject had tapped 180 times in 10 seconds. Although this is an exceedingly unlikely event to observe from a healthy subject, it would not fall into the rejection region, which consists *solely* of low rates. As a result we find ourselves in the unenviable position of not rejecting H_0 in the face of a piece of data that is extremely unlikely, but not in the direction expected. (The probability is so small that R presents it as just plain 0.)

The question then arises as to how we can protect ourselves against this type of situation (if protection is thought necessary). The answer is to specify before we run the experiment that we are going to reject a given percentage (say 5%) of the *extreme* outcomes, both those that are extremely high and those that are extremely low. But if we reject the lowest 5% and the highest 5%, then we would, in fact, reject H_0 a total of 10% of the time when it is actually true, that is, $\alpha = .10$. We are rarely willing to work with α as high as .10 and prefer to see it set no higher than .05. The only way to accomplish our goal is to reject the lowest 2.5% and the highest 2.5%, making a total of 5%.

The situation in which we reject H_0 for only the lowest (or only the highest) tapping speeds is referred to as a **one-tailed**, or **directional, test**. We make a prediction of the direction in which the individual will differ from the mean and our rejection region is located in only one tail of the distribution. When we reject extremes in both tails, we have what is called a **two-tailed**, or **nondirectional, test**. It is important to keep in mind that while we gain something with a two-tailed test (the ability to reject the null hypothesis for extreme scores in either direction), we also lose something. A score that would fall into the 5% rejection region of a one-tailed test may not fall into the rejection region of the corresponding two-tailed test, because now we reject only 2.5% in each tail.

In the finger-tapping example, the decision between a one- and a two-tailed test might seem reasonably clear-cut. We know that people with a given disorder tap more slowly; therefore we care only about rejecting H_0 for low scores—high scores have no diagnostic importance. In other situations, however, we do not know which tail of the distribution is important (or if both are), and we need to guard against extremes in either tail. The situation might arise when we are considering a campaign to persuade young people not to smoke. We might find that the campaign leads to a decrease in the rate of smoking. Or, we might find that the campaign actually is taken by young adults as a challenge, making smoking look more attractive instead of less. (In fact, there is some evidence that this is exactly what happens.) In either case we would want to reject H_0.

In general, two-tailed tests are far more common than one-tailed tests for several reasons. One reason for this is that the investigator may have no idea what the data will look like and therefore has to be prepared for any eventuality. Although this situation is rare, it does occur in some exploratory work.

Another common reason for preferring two-tailed tests is that the investigators are reasonably sure the data will come out one way but want to cover themselves in the event that they are wrong. This type of situation arises more often than you might think. (Carefully formed hypotheses have an annoying habit of being phrased in the wrong direction, for reasons that seem so obvious after the event.) One question that arises when the data may come out the other way around is, "Why not plan to run a one-tailed test and then, if the data come out the other way, just change the test to a two-tailed test?" However, there is a problem with this approach. If you start an experiment with the extreme 5% of the left-hand tail as your rejection region and then turn around and reject any outcome that happens to fall into the extreme 2.5% of the right-hand tail, you are working at the 7.5% level. In that situation you will reject 5% of the outcomes in one direction (assuming that the data fall into the desired tail), and you are willing also to reject 2.5% of the outcomes in the other direction (when the data are in the unexpected direction). There is no denying that 5% + 2.5% = 7.5%. To put it another way, would you be willing to flip a coin for an ice cream cone if I choose "heads" but also reserve the right to switch to "tails" after I see how the coin lands? Or would you think it fair of me to shout, "Two out of three!" when the coin toss comes up in your favor? You would object to both of these strategies, and you should. For the same reason, the choice between a one-tailed test and a two-tailed one is made *before* the data are collected. It is also one of the reasons that two-tailed tests are usually chosen.

Although the preceding discussion argues in favor of two-tailed tests, and although in this book we generally confine ourselves to such procedures, there are no hard-and-fast rules. The final decision depends on what you already know about the relative severity of different kinds of errors. It is important to keep in mind that with respect to a given tail of a distribution, the difference between a one-tailed test and a two-tailed test is that the latter just uses a different cutoff. A two-tailed test at $\alpha = .05$ is more liberal than a one-tailed test at $\alpha = .01$.

We have just covered a great deal of information, and it will be helpful to pull it together in a paragraph or two. We are engaged in a process of decision making, trying to decide whether one of two hypotheses is true. One is the null hypothesis (H_0), which states that a person did come from a specific population, or that the mean of several people came from a specific population, or that two samples came from populations with the same mean, or that there is no correlation between two variables, and so on. This hypothesis, put most generally, says that "there are no differences." The other hypothesis is the alternative hypothesis (H_1), which states that the person did not come from a specific population, or that the mean of several people did not come from a specific population, or that two group means are not from the same population, or that the correlation between two variables is not zero, and so on. In making decisions we set up a specific rejection level (e.g., 5%) and reject the null hypothesis if the probability of the obtained result, when the null hypothesis is true, is less than that rejection level. Associated with a rejection level is a critical value, which is that value of the statistic that is exceeded with a probability of 5%, for example. In making our decision we can make two kinds of errors. We make a Type I error when we reject the null hypothesis when it is true, and the probability of that error is denoted as α. The other kind of error is a Type II error, and that is the probability of not rejecting the null hypothesis when we should. Its probability is denoted as β.

Finally, we considered one- and two-tailed tests. The most common approach is to use a two-tailed test and reject the null hypothesis whenever the result is either too high or too low. Using .05 as the rejection level, this means rejecting it when the result is in either the upper or lower 2.5% of the outcomes when the null hypothesis is true. This is a two-tailed test. An alternative approach is to specify that we are interested in rejecting the null only if the result is too low or, alternatively, only if the result is too high. Here we would reject it if the result has a probability of .05 and the direction is as we predicted.

An alternative view by Jones and Tukey (2000)

But here is where things now start getting interesting. What I have just described is the standard treatment of null hypothesis testing, and it is something that you really need to know. And I have told you that I am a strong proponent of two-tailed tests. But in 2000, Jones and Tukey (the same Tukey you have already read about) came out with a somewhat different proposal. They argued that, first of all, the null hypothesis is almost certainly false if you look hard enough. (Does anyone really believe that the mean height of people west of the Mississippi is *exactly* the same as the mean height of people east of the Mississippi? I don't, though I don't know which group has the larger mean.) So Jones and Tukey reasoned that we can set the null hypothesis aside. Now the only mistake that we can make is saying that people in the East are taller when, in fact, people in the West really are, or vice versa. They argue that failing to find a significant difference may be unfortunate, but it is not an error. So, they recommend only using a one-tailed test without specifying in advance which tail we will use.

To take a simple example, Adams, Wright, and Lohr (1996) showed a group of homophobic heterosexual males ($Group_h$) and a group of nonhomophobic heterosexual males ($Group_{nh}$) a videotape of erotic homosexual behavior and recorded their level of sexual arousal. They wanted to see if there was a difference between the two groups. Jones and Tukey (2000) and Harris (2005) have argued that, while there are three possible outcomes ($\mu_h < \mu_{nh}$; $\mu_h = \mu_{nh}$; and $\mu_h > \mu_{nh}$), the second of those is a nonstarter. So we really have two choices. If ($\mu_h < \mu_{nh}$) but we erroneously conclude that ($\mu_h > \mu_{nh}$), we have made an error, but the probability of that happening is at most .025 (assuming that we are working with a two-tailed test at the .05 level). The same probability holds for the opposite state of affairs. Because only one state of affairs can be true, the probability of an error is only .025, not .05. If we can't reject either of those hypotheses, we simply declare that we don't have enough data to make a choice, and this is not an error.

So, Jones and Tukey suggest that we always do one-tailed tests, that we don't specify a direction beforehand, and that we put 5% in each tail. If it wasn't for the stature of Jones and Tukey, that idea might not have gotten off the ground, but sensible people generally do not ignore advice from John Tukey. As I said at the beginning, the approach that I first discussed is the traditional one that most people follow and you have to know, but the approach given here is a very sensible one based on a realistic assessment of hypothesis testing approaches.

Unfortunately it seems as if sensible people *have* ignored John Tukey, which is a real surprise. The literature, at least in psychology, continues to go on as before. That might lead me to delete this discussion, but the point is far too important to delete. Even if you follow traditional approaches, it is important for you to understand the point that they have made. That is why it is still there. But another reason for not removing it is to note, as I will throughout the book, that what is sometimes called the "New Statistics" is a movement away from a primary focus on straight null hypothesis testing and toward an increased emphasis on the combination of hypothesis testing and confidence limits. The former says something like "the null hypothesis is false," whereas the latter says something like "reasonable values for the true value of μ are between 39.6 and 48.8." As we continue to move in the direction of confidence limits, the distinction that Jones and Tukey make is less central to our work.

Perhaps I can re-express the Jones and Tukey suggestion by quoting from a suggestion by Robinson and Wainer (2001) to take the approach that

> "If p is less than 0.05, researchers can conclude that the direction of a difference was determined ... If p is greater than 0.05, the conclusion is simply that the sign of the difference is not yet determined. This trinary decision approach (either $\mu_1 > \mu_2$, $\mu_2 > \mu_1$, or do not know yet) has the advantages of stressing that research is a continuing activity and of never having to 'accept' a null hypothesis that is likely untrue."

That is a less specific statement than Jones and Tukey's, but it points to the same approach.

We have covered a lot of material here, but if you have a sound grasp of the logic of testing hypotheses by use of sampling distributions, the remainder of this course will be relatively simple. For any new statistic you encounter, you will need to ask only two basic questions:

1. How and with which assumptions is the statistic calculated?
2. What does the statistic's sampling distribution look like under H_0?

If you know the answers to these two questions, your test is accomplished by calculating the test statistic for the data at hand and comparing the statistic to the sampling distribution. Because the relevant sampling distributions are readily available over the Web, and are included in the appendices, all you really need to know is which test is appropriate for a particular situation and how to calculate its test statistic. (Keep in mind, however, there is a great deal more to understanding the field of statistics than how to calculate, and evaluate, a specific statistical test.)

Before I leave this topic, it is important to point out that I have addressed only half the problem. Certainly hypothesis testing is important, which is why I spent a chapter on it. But as you will see, other measures, such as confidence intervals and effect sizes, are also important. One could argue that they are even more important than traditional hypothesis testing. A discussion of them builds on what we have just covered, and you will see much more about such measures as you move through the book. I just don't want you to think that hypothesis testing is the beginning and ending of statistical analyses, which it used to be. There is much more to be said.

8.9 Seeing Statistics

You can easily practice manipulating probabilities, one- and two-tailed tests, and the null hypothesis by opening SeeingStatistics at

 https://www.uvm.edu/~dhowell/fundamentals9/SeeingStatisticsApplets/ Applets.html

and going to the applets for Chapter 8. Because this applet allows you to change any values within a problem, and to choose between one- and two-tailed tests, you can reproduce the statistics behind the discussion of finger tapping in Section 8.6. The output of the applet is shown here.

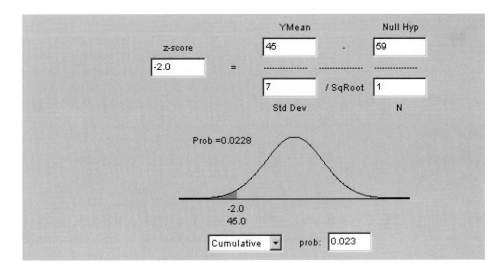

Remember that we are working with individual observations, not sample means, so we can enter our individual score of 45 in the box labeled "Y Mean." The mean under the null hypothesis would be 59, with a standard deviation of 7.0. If you enter an "Enter" or "Return" after changing the value in any cell, the value of z will be recomputed. We saw earlier that our individual score fell below the 5% cutoff in the lower tail. The null hypothesis is given by the problem, as is the standard deviation. The sample size (N) is one because this is a single observation.

You can see that in my example the probability came out to be 0.0228, leading us to reject the null hypothesis that this score came from a population of normal tapping scores. You should now try varying the observed score, and note how the probability, and the shaded portion of the graphic, change. You can select a two-tailed test by clicking on the box in the lower left and choosing "two-tailed." You may be surprised by what happens if you select "one-tailed" in that box. Why is the right half of the curve shaded rather than the left half?[8] Finally, read the next section (Section 8.10), and use the applet to reproduce the values found there. Again, remember that we are substituting a single observation for a mean, and the sample size is 1.

8.10 A Final Example

We began the chapter with a study by Duguid and Goncalo (2012) looking at the difference in *reported* height for two groups of participants, one of which was told that it was to play the role of managers and the other of which was told that it was to play the role of employees. The participants actually never played either of these roles. The dependent variable was the difference between actual and reported height for each participant. The "management" group overestimated its true height by an average of 0.66 inches. On the other hand, the "employee" group actually underestimated its mean height by an average of −0.21 inches. Therefore the mean over- or under-estimates of the two groups differed by 0.87 inches, and yet the only thing that distinguished the groups was the role each was told it would play, but never actually played.

The question is whether the roles that participants were assigned, even though they never actually played them, influenced their estimates of their own height. Following the logic of Jones and Tukey (2000), we have three alternatives. We can decide that, in the population, people who are assigned a powerful rule overestimate their own heights relative to others, or we can decide that they underestimate their heights, or we can conclude that we cannot tell which alternative is true. Using more traditional language, we can conclude that $\mu_m < \mu_e$ or $\mu_m > \mu_e$, or we can fail to reject the null hypothesis.

Following the traditional model, we now need to choose between a one-tailed and a two-tailed test. Because the difference could fall in either direction, we will choose a two-tailed test, rejecting the null hypothesis if the absolute value of the difference is greater than would be expected by chance. Before we can apply our statistical procedures to the data at hand, we must make one additional decision. We have to decide on a level of significance for our test. In this case I have chosen to run the test at the 5% level because I am using $\alpha = .05$ as a standard for this book.

We have not yet discussed the kind of test that is needed in this situation (a t test for two independent groups), but we can at least use a computer to imitate the kind of approach that we will take. We know that people in general are not likely to give a completely accurate answer when asked their height, and we can tell from the data of Duguid and Goncola that, *averaged across treatment groups*, people in general overestimate their heights by 0.225 inches. That sounds reasonable. The standard deviation of such differences between true and estimated height is approximately 0.88 inches, based on the data presented in the paper.

So what if we set up a simple sampling study to draw two sets of scores (one for the managers and one for the employees) representing the difference between

---

[8]Because the applet was created to run a one-tailed test in the opposite direction.

true and estimated heights? We will draw both of these samples from a population whose mean difference in height is 0.225 inches, with a standard deviation of 0.88 inches. Note that both of these samples are drawn from the same population, so the null hypothesis is true by definition. Further suppose that we calculate the difference between the means of the two groups, and then go on to repeat this process 9,999 more times, each time recording the mean difference. The distribution of those 10,000 mean differences would be the distribution of outcomes that we would expect if the null hypothesis is true—that is, if both groups overestimate their heights to the same degree. That distribution looks like the one in Figure 8.7. You can tell from this figure that under the null hypothesis the distribution of differences between means will be centered at 0.00, and almost all of the values will fall between about −0.5 and +0.5. But Duguid and Goncola found an actual difference between the group means of 0.87. That is indeed a rare event if the null hypothesis is true. In fact, it would have a probability of occurrence of only $p = .0003$. We should certainly feel confident in rejecting the null hypothesis. Simply telling people that they are in a high- or low-power group affects even their estimates of their own height. See the Duguid and Goncola (2012) paper for two other experiments confirming the general finding.

As I said at the beginning of this example, this is not the way that we will actually run a test when we come to the t test in Chapter 14. But it is a legitimate approach that would be considered appropriate by almost any journal, and which may end up replacing the t test some years from now. I chose to do this here because it

Figure 8.7 The distribution of outcomes of differences in sample means when the null hypothesis is true

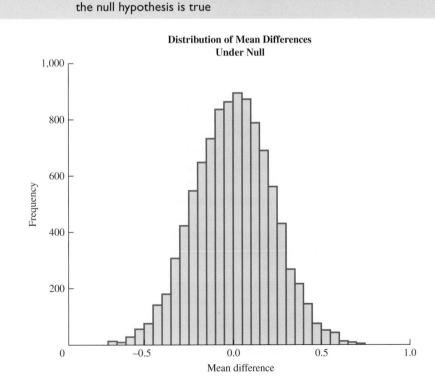

points out clearly the kind of decisions and procedures that go into testing a hypothesis. Keep this idea in mind even when we are looking at what appear to be different kinds of tests. The basic idea of resampling a population many times and looking at the result, while different from the arithmetic of the tests we will study, actually underlies the general concept.

8.11 Back to Course Evaluations and Sunk Costs

Early in this chapter we looked an example of the relationship between how students evaluate a course and the grade they expect to receive in that course. A second example looked at age differences in the tendency to endorse the sunk-costs fallacy. As you will see in the next chapter, the first example uses a correlation coefficient to represent the degree of relationship. The second example simply compares two means. Both examples can be dealt with using the techniques discussed in this chapter. In the first case, if there is no relationship between the two variables, we would expect that the true correlation in the population of students is 0.00. We simply set up the null hypothesis that the population correlation is 0.00 and then ask about the probability that a sample of 15 observations would produce a correlation as large as the one we obtained. In the second case we set up the null hypothesis that there is no difference between the mean sunk-costs fallacy scores *in the population* of younger and older participants. Then we ask, "What is the probability of obtaining a difference in means as large as the one we obtained (in our case 0.64) if the null hypothesis is true?" I do not expect you to be able to run these tests now, but you should have a general sense of the way we will set up the problem when we do learn to run them.

8.12 Summary

The purpose of this chapter has been to examine the general theory of hypothesis testing without becoming involved in the specific calculations required to carry out such a test. Hypothesis testing and related procedures are at the heart of how we analyze data from most experiments, though there are those who do not think that is a good state of affairs. We first considered the concept of the sampling distribution of a statistic, which is the distribution that the statistic in question would have if it were computed repeatedly from an infinite number of samples drawn from one population under certain specified conditions. (The statistic could be anything you want, such as a mean, a median, a variance, a correlation coefficient, and so on.) The sampling distribution basically tells us what kinds of values are reasonable to expect for the statistic if the conditions under which the distribution was derived are met.

We then examined the null hypothesis and the role it plays in hypothesis testing. The null hypothesis is usually the hypothesis of no difference between two or more groups or no relationship between two or more variables. We saw that we can test any null hypothesis by asking what the sampling distribution of the relevant statistic would look like if the null hypothesis were true and then comparing our particular statistic to that distribution. We next saw how a simple hypothesis actually could be tested using what we already know about the normal distribution.

Finally, we looked at Type I and Type II errors and one- and two-tailed tests. A Type I error refers to rejecting the null hypothesis when it is actually true, whereas a Type II error refers to failing to reject a false null hypothesis. A one-tailed test rejects the null hypothesis only when the obtained result falls in the extreme of that tail of the distribution that we have designated. A two-tailed test rejects the null hypothesis whenever the result falls in the extreme of either tail.

After considering one-and two-tailed tests, we briefly looked at the proposal by Jones and Tukey that suggests that we ignore the null hypothesis because it is virtually never exactly true and focus instead on seeing if we can decide which of two groups (for example) has a mean that is larger than the mean for the other group. They suggest a one-tailed test without the requirement to specify in advance which tail you will use.

Key Terms

Sampling error, *151*	Rejection region, *164*
Standard error of the mean, *153*	Alternative hypothesis (H_1), *165*
Hypothesis testing, *154*	Critical value, *167*
Sampling distribution of the mean, *156*	Type I error, *168*
Research hypothesis, *158*	α (alpha), *168*
Null hypothesis (H_0), *158*	Type II error, *168*
Sample statistics, *161*	β (beta), *168*
Test statistics, *161*	Power, *170*
Decision making, *164*	One-tailed test (directional test), *171*
Rejection level (significance level), *164*	Two-tailed test (nondirectional test), *171*

8.13   A Quick Review

A. What is a sampling distribution?
    Ans: The distribution of a statistic over repeated sampling.

B. What is sampling error?
    Ans: The variability of sample estimates of some statistic such as the mean.

C. What is the standard error of the mean?
    Ans: The standard deviation of the sampling distribution of the mean.

D. What do we mean by hypothesis testing?
    Ans: We are referring to testing some hypothesis about the relationships between population parameters.

E. What is a research hypothesis?
Ans: This is usually the hypothesis that there is a true difference or a true relationship between variables.

F. What is the null hypothesis?
Ans: This is the hypothesis that the apparent difference or relationship is due to chance.

G. Why do we test the null hypothesis instead of the alternative hypothesis?
Ans: The alternative hypothesis is too vague, whereas the null hypothesis is specific and, if we can reject it, we can argue that the alternative hypothesis is true.

H. What is another term for the "rejection level"?
Ans: The "significance level."

I. What is a Type I error?
Ans: It refers to rejecting the null hypothesis when the null hypothesis is actually true.

J. What is a critical value?
Ans: It is the value of the test statistic beyond which you reject the null hypothesis.

K. We often reject the null hypothesis if the conditional probability of the data given that the null hypothesis is true is less than. 05. What symbol do we often use to represent .05?
Ans: The Greek letter α: alpha

L. If we will reject the null hypothesis only if the difference between groups is too large (positive), we are using a _____ tailed test.
Ans: one-tailed

8.14 Exercises

8.1 Suppose I told you that last night's NHL hockey game resulted in a score of 26 to 13. You would probably decide that I had misread the paper, because hockey games almost never have scores that high, and I was discussing something other than a hockey score. In effect you have just tested and rejected a null hypothesis.

a) What was the null hypothesis?
b) Outline the hypothesis-testing procedure that you have just applied.

8.2 For the past year I have spent about $4 a day for lunch, give or take a quarter or so.

a) Draw a rough sketch of this distribution of daily expenditures.
b) If, without looking at the bill, I paid for my lunch with a $5 bill and received $.75 in change, should I worry that I was overcharged?
c) Explain the logic involved in your answer to (b).

8.3 What would be a Type I error in Exercise 8.2?

8.4 What would be a Type II error in Exercise 8.2?

8.5 Using the example in Exercise 8.2, describe what we mean by the rejection region and the critical value.

8.6 Why might I want to adopt a one-tailed test in Exercise 8.2, and which tail should I choose? What would happen if I choose the wrong tail?

8.7 Using the *R* code given for Figure 8.1, reproduce Figure 8.2 as closely as possible.

8.8 What would happen in Exercise 8.7 if we doubled the size of the standard deviation?

a) What happens if you change each sample's size from 10 to 100?

8.9 It is known that if people are asked to make an estimate of something, for example, "How tall is the University chapel?" the average guess of a group of people is more accurate than an individual's guess. Vul and Pashler (2008) wondered if the same held for multiple guesses by the same person. They asked people to make guesses about known facts. For example, "What percentage of the world's airports is in the United States?" Three weeks later the researchers asked the same people the same questions and averaged each person's responses over the two sessions. They asked whether this average was more accurate than the first guess by itself. We will come back to this example later in the book.

    a) What are the null and alternative hypotheses?
    b) What would be a Type I and Type II error in this case?
    c) Would you be inclined to use a one-tailed or a two-tailed test in this case?

8.10 Define "sampling error."

8.11 What is the difference between a "distribution" and a "sampling distribution"?

8.12 How would decreasing α affect the probabilities given in Table 8.1?

8.13 Magen, Dweck, and Gross (2008) asked participants to choose, for example, between $5 today or $7 next week. In one condition, the choices were phrased exactly that way. In a second condition, they were phrased as "$5 today and $0 next week or $0 today and $7 next week," which is obviously the same thing. Each person's score was the number of choices in which the smaller but sooner choice was made. The mean for the first group was 9.24 and the mean for the second group was 6.10.

    a) What are the null and alternative hypotheses?
    b) What statistics would you compare to answer the question? (You do not yet know how to make that comparison.)
    c) If the difference is significant with a two-tailed test, what would you conclude?

8.14 For the distribution in Figure 8.6 I said that the probability of a Type II error (β) is .64. Show how this probability was obtained.

8.15 Rerun the calculations in Exercise 8.14 for $\alpha = .01$.

8.16 In the example in Section 8.10, what would we have done differently if we had chosen to run a two-tailed test?

8.17 Describe the steps you would go through to flesh out the example given in this chapter about the course evaluations. In other words, how might you go about determining if there truly is a relationship between grades and course evaluations?

8.18 Describe the steps you would go through to test the hypothesis that people are more likely to keep watching a movie if they have already invested money to obtain that movie.

8.19 In the exercises in Chapter 2, we discussed a study of allowances in fourth-grade children. We considered that study again in Chapter 4, where you generated data that might have been found in such a study.

    a) Consider how you would go about testing the research hypothesis that boys receive more allowance than girls. What would be the null hypothesis?
    b) Would you use a one-tailed or a two-tailed test?
    c) What results might lead you to reject the null hypothesis, and what might lead you to retain it?
    d) What might you do to make this study more convincing?

8.20 Simon and Bruce (1991), in demonstrating an approach to statistics called "resampling statistics," tested the null hypothesis that the price of liquor (in 1961) for the 16 "monopoly" states, where the state owned the liquor stores, was different from the mean price in the 26 "private" states, where liquor stores were privately owned. (The means were $4.35 and $4.84, respectively, giving you some hint at the effects of inflation.) For technical reasons, several states don't conform to this scheme and could not be analyzed.

a) What is the null hypothesis that we are actually testing?
b) What label would you apply to $4.35 and $4.84?
c) If these are the only states that qualify for our consideration, why are we testing a null hypothesis in the first place?
d) Identify a situation in which it does make sense to test a null hypothesis here.

8.21 Several times in this chapter I have drawn a parallel between hypothesis testing and our judicial system. How would you describe the workings of our judicial system in terms of Type I and Type II errors and in terms of power?

## CHAPTER 9

Correlation

I n this chapter we are going to look at the relationship between two variables. We will begin by seeing how we can plot the data in a way that makes sense of it. We will then move on to develop the concept of *covariance* to measure that relationship numerically, and then turn that covariance into a *correlation* coefficient and see why that is a better measure. Having developed the correlation coefficient for raw data, we will take a look at what happens when those data are in the form of ranks. You will be pleased to see that not a lot happens. Correlation coefficients can be influenced by a number of factors, and we will next take a look at what those factors might be. Then we will develop and use a statistical test to see if the correlation is sufficiently different from 0 to lead us to conclude that there is a true relationship between two variables. That is a straightforward extension of what we have just covered in Chapter 8. We will next briefly look at a few other correlation coefficients that we might want to calculate and then see how we can use software to compute our correlations.

The previous chapters have dealt in one way or another with describing data on a single variable. We have discussed the distribution of a variable and how to find its mean and standard deviation. However, some studies are designed to deal with not one dependent variable, but with two or more. In such cases we often are interested in knowing the relationship between two variables, rather than what each variable looks like on its own. To illustrate the kinds of studies that might involve two variables (denoted X and Y), consider the following, quite different, research questions:

CONCEPTS THAT YOU WILL NEED TO REMEMBER FROM PREVIOUS CHAPTERS

Independent variable:	The variable you manipulate or are studying
Dependent variable:	The variable that you are measuring—the data
X axis:	The horizontal axis, also called the abscissa
Y axis:	The vertical axis, also called the ordinate
$\overline{X}, \overline{Y}, s_X, s_Y$:	The mean and standard deviation of two variables labeled X and Y

- Does the incidence of breast cancer (Y) vary with the amount of sunlight (X) in a particular location?

- Does life expectancy (Y) for individual countries vary as a function of the per capita consumption of alcohol (X)?

- Does the rating of an individual's "likability" (Y) have anything to do with physical attractiveness (X)?

- Does degree of hoarding behavior in hamsters (Y) vary as a function of level of deprivation (X) during development?

- Does the accuracy of performance (Y) decrease as speed of response (X) increases?

- Does the average life span (Y) in a given country increase as the country's per capita health expenditure (X) increases?

In each case we are asking if one variable (Y) is related to another variable (X). When we are dealing with the relationship between two variables, we are concerned with **correlation**, and our measure of the degree or strength of this relationship is represented by a **correlation coefficient**. We can use a number of different correlation coefficients, depending primarily on the underlying nature of the measurements, but we will see later that in many cases the distinctions among these different coefficients are more apparent than real. For the present we will be concerned with the most common correlation coefficient—the **Pearson product-moment correlation coefficient (r)**.

9.1   Scatter Diagrams

When we collect measures on two variables for the purpose of examining the relationship between these variables, one of the most useful techniques for gaining insight into this relationship is a **scatterplot** (also called a **scatter diagram** or **scattergram**). In a scatterplot, every experimental subject or unit or observation in the study is represented by a point in two-dimensional space. The coordinates of this point (X_i, Y_i) are the individual's (or object's) scores on variables X and Y, respectively. Examples of three such plots appear in Figures 9.1–9.3.

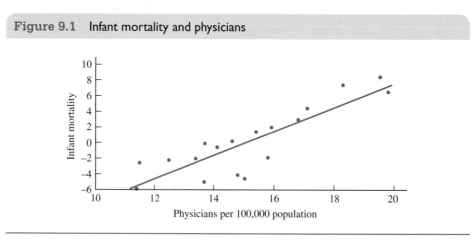

Figure 9.1   Infant mortality and physicians

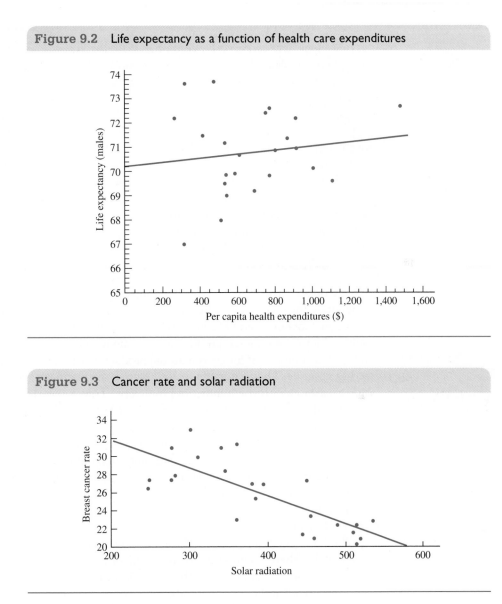

Figure 9.2 Life expectancy as a function of health care expenditures

Figure 9.3 Cancer rate and solar radiation

In preparing a scatter diagram the **predictor variable**, or independent variable, is traditionally presented on the X (horizontal) axis, and the **criterion variable**, or dependent variable, on the Y (vertical) axis. If the eventual purpose of the study is to predict one variable from knowledge of the other, the distinction is obvious: The criterion variable is the one to be predicted, whereas the predictor variable is the one from which the prediction is made. If the problem is simply one of obtaining a correlation coefficient, the distinction may be obvious (incidence of cancer would be dependent on amount smoked rather than the reverse, and thus incidence would appear on the ordinate). On the other hand, the distinction may not be obvious (neither running speed nor number of correct choices—common dependent variables in an animal learning study—is obviously in a dependent position relative to the other). Where the distinction is not obvious, it is irrelevant which variable is labeled X and which Y.

Terminology here can get a bit confusing. If I tell you that I am going to survey a group of people and measure depression and stress, we would think of both of those variables as dependent variables because they are the data that I will collect. However, if we wanted to know if depression varies as a function of stress, we would think of stress as an independent variable and depression as a dependent variable—we want to know if depression *depends* on stress. So the use of the terms "independent" and "dependent" get a bit sloppy. Perhaps it is better to fall back on predictor variable and criterion variable as descriptive terms. But even here things get a bit messy, because if I want to know if there is a relationship between height and weight, neither one of them is clearly the predictor variable—or they both are. I mention this because you are going to have to be a bit tolerant of the terminology we use. Don't pound your head trying to decide which, if either, variable should be called the independent variable.

Consider the three scatter diagrams in Figures 9.1–9.3. These all represent real data—they have not been contrived. Figure 9.1 is plotted from data reported by St. Leger, Cochrane, and Moore (1978) on the relationship between infant mortality, adjusted for gross national product, and the number of physicians per 10,000 population. (The adjustment for gross national product is what leaves some infant mortality scores negative. That is not a problem.) Notice the fascinating result that infant mortality *increases* with the number of physicians. That is clearly an unexpected result, but it is almost certainly not due to chance. (As you look at these data and read the rest of the chapter you might think about possible explanations for this surprising result.[1] In a sample of 31 developed or developing countries in the world, the United States ranked 30th in the rate of infant mortality, right ahead of Slovakia.)

The lines superimposed on these figures represent those straight lines that "best fit the data." How we determine that line will be the subject of much of the next chapter. I have included the lines in each of these figures because they help to clarify the relationships. These lines are what we will call the **regression lines** of Y predicted on X (abbreviated "Y on X"), and they represent our best prediction of Y_i for a given value of X_i, where i represents the ith value of X or Y. Given any specified value of X, the corresponding height of the regression line represents our best prediction of Y (designated $\hat{Y}$ and read "Y hat"). In other words, we can draw a vertical line from X_i to the regression line and then move horizontally to the Y axis and read off $\hat{Y}_i$. Again, regression is covered in the next chapter.

The degree to which the points cluster around the regression line (in other words, the degree to which the actual values of Y agree with the predicted values) is related to the correlation (r) between X and Y. Correlation coefficients range between 1 and -1. For Figure 9.1, the points cluster very closely about the line, indicating that there is a strong linear relationship between our two variables. If the points fell exactly on the line, the correlation would be $+1.00$. As it is, the correlation is actually .81, which represents a high degree of relationship for real variables. The complete data file for Figure 9.1 can be found at

 **https://www.uvm.edu/~dhowell/fundamentals9/DataFiles/Fig9-1.dat**

---

[1]See Young (2001) for a reasonable explanation of this phenomenon.

In Figure 9.2 I have plotted data on the relationship between life expectancy (for males) and per capita expenditure on health care for 23 developed (mostly European) countries. These data are from Cochrane, St. Leger, and Moore (1978). At a time when there is considerable discussion nationally about the cost of health care, these data give us pause. If we were to measure the health of a nation by life expectancy (certainly not the only and admittedly not the best measure), it would appear that the total amount of money we spend on health care bears no relationship to the resultant quality of health (assuming that different countries apportion their expenditures in similar ways). Several hundred thousand dollars spent on transplanting an organ from a nonhuman primate into a 57-year-old male, as was done several years ago, may increase the man's life expectancy by a few years, but it is not going to make a dent in the nation's life expectancy. A similar amount of money spent on the prevention of malaria in young children in sub-Saharan Africa, however, has the potential to have a very substantial effect. Notice that the two countries in Figure 9.2 with the longest life expectancy (Iceland and Japan) spend nearly the same amount of money on health care as the country with the shortest life expectancy (Portugal). The United States has nearly the highest rate of expenditure but ranks well below most developed countries in terms of life expectancy. Figure 9.2 represents a situation in which there is no apparent relationship between the two variables under consideration. If there were absolutely no relationship between the variables, the correlation would be 0.0. As it is, the correlation is only .14, and even that can be shown not to be reliably different from 0.0. The complete data file for Figure 9.2 can be found at

 https://www.uvm.edu/~dhowell/fundamentals9/DataFiles/Fig9-2.dat

Finally, Figure 9.3 presents data from a 1991 article in *Newsweek* on the relationship between breast cancer and sunshine. For people like me who love the sun, it is encouraging to find that there may be at least some benefit from additional sunlight—though that is probably a short-sighted interpretation of the data. Notice that as the amount of solar radiation increases, the incidence of deaths from breast cancer decreases. (There has been considerable research on this topic in recent years, and the reduction in rates of certain kinds of cancer is thought to be related to the body's production of vitamin D, which is increased by sunlight. An excellent article, which portrays the data in a different way, can be found in a study by Garland et al. [2006].) This graphic is a good illustration of a **negative relationship**, and the correlation here is −.76. The complete data file for Figure 9.3 can be found at

 https://www.uvm.edu/~dhowell/fundamentals9/DataFiles/Fig9-3.dat

It is important to note that the *sign* of the correlation coefficient has no meaning other than to denote the direction of the relationship. The correlations of .75 and −.75 signify exactly the same *degree* of relationship. It is only the *direction* of that relationship that is different. For this reason the relationships shown in Figures 9.1 and 9.3 are approximately equally strong, though of the opposite sign.

We will look a little more closely at what produces a high or low correlation by examining one further example. Researchers in the behavioral sciences often work on the problem of behavioral change and health. There are interesting data on the relationship between red wine consumption and coronary artery disease

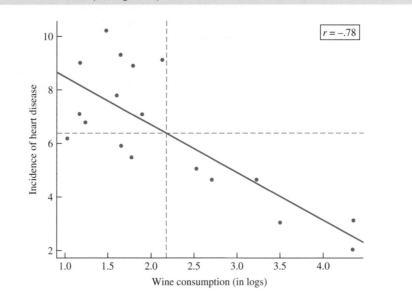

Figure 9.4 Relationship between death rate due to heart disease and consumption of wine (on log scale). The dashed lines are at $\overline{X}$ and $\overline{Y}$.

(or heart disease). This example is presented in Figure 9.4, and it shows the relationship between the incidence of death due to heart attacks in various European countries and the consumption of wine in those countries. These data were taken from a paper by St. Leger, Cochrane, and Moore (1979).

There are several things that I can point out with respect to this example that are important in your understanding of correlation and regression.

■ Notice that on the X axis I have plotted the logarithm of consumption, rather than consumption itself. This was because consumption was heavily skewed to the right, and taking logs helps to correct this. (The data file on the Web contains both Wine and Logwine, so you can plot either way.)

■ Notice that, for this example, deaths due to heart disease actually decline with an increase in consumption of wine. This was originally a controversial finding, but there is now general agreement that it is a real (though not necessarily causal) effect. This might be taken by some as a license for university students to drink even more. However, heart disease is only rarely a problem for college students, and no protection is needed. In addition, alcohol has many negative effects that are not examined here. It doesn't seem sensible to increase the very real danger of alcohol abuse to ward off a problem that is highly unlikely to arise. Killing yourself by driving into a tree or developing liver problems is a very bad, but effective, way to reduce your risk of dying of heart disease.

■ A third point to be made is that in this figure, and the previous figures, the data points represent countries rather than individuals. That just happens to be a characteristic of the data sets that I chose to use. We could, in theory, select a large sample of people, record each person's age at death (admittedly not the same as incidence of heart disease), and then plot each person's age at death against his or her level of wine consumption. It would not be an easy study to run (We would have to call each person up monthly and ask, "Are you dead yet?") but it could be done. But individuals' age at death varies all over the place, as does wine consumption, whereas a *country's* mean age at death and a *country's* mean wine consumption are quite stable. So we need very many fewer points when each refers to a country than when each point refers to a person. (You saw something about the stability of aggregated data in the last chapter when we saw that the sampling distribution of the mean had a smaller standard error with increased sample size.)

■ In Figure 9.4 I have drawn horizontal and vertical (dashed) lines corresponding to $\overline{Y}$ and $\overline{X}$. Notice that in the upper left quadrant there are nine observations with an $\overline{X}$ value less than $\overline{X}$ and a $\overline{Y}$ value more than $\overline{Y}$. Similarly in the lower right quadrant there are six instances where the value is greater than $\overline{X}$ and less than $\overline{Y}$. There are only three cases that break this pattern by being above the mean on both variables or below the mean on both variables.

■ An interesting discussion of studies relating wine consumption and heart disease can be found at the *Chance News* site, which always offers an entertaining way to spend time and frequently teaches me something. (Unfortunately, it moves sites periodically, but an Internet search can always find it.) The most recent link is

 http://test.causeweb.org/wiki/chance/index.php/Chance_News_16#Does_a_ glass_of_wine_a_day_keep_the_doctor_away.3F

If there were a strong negative relationship between wine drinking and heart disease, we would expect that most of the countries that were high (above the mean) on one variable would be below the mean on the other. Such an idea can be represented by a simple table in which we count the number of observations that were above the mean on both variables, the number below the mean on both variables, and the number above the mean on one and below the mean on the other. Such a table is shown in Table 9.1 for the data in Figure 9.4.

With a strong negative relationship between the two variables, we would expect most of the data points in Table 9.1 to fall into the "Above-Below" and "Below-Above" cells with only a smattering in the "Above-Above" and "Below-Below" cells. Conversely, if the two variables are not related to each other, we would expect to see approximately equal numbers of data points in the four cells of the table (or quadrants of the scatter diagram). And for a large positive relationship we would expect

Table 9.1 Examining Scatterplots by Division into Quadrants in Relation to the Means

| | | Heart disease | |
		Above	Below
	Above	0	6
Wine consumption	Below	9	3

a preponderance of observations falling in the "Above-Above" and "Below-Below" Cells. From Table 9.1, we see that for the relationship between wine consumption and heart disease, 15 out of the 18 participants fall into the cells associated with a negative relationship between the variables. In other words, if a country is below the mean on one variable it is most likely to be above the mean on the other, and vice versa. Only three countries break this pattern. This example, then, illustrates in a simple way the interpretation of scatter diagrams and the relationship between variables.[2] For Figure 9.4 the correlation is −.78.

Other variables may affect results

But things are not always simple. Other variables can influence the results. Wong (2008) noted that just as wine consumption varies across Europe, so does solar radiation. He presents data to argue that not only could red wine and Mediterranean diet be explanations for variability in rates of coronary heart disease, but so could solar radiation, in ways that we saw in Figure 9.3 with breast cancer.

9.2 An Example: The Relationship Between the Pace of Life and Heart Disease

The examples that we have seen in the previous pages have either been examples of very strong relationships (positive or negative) or of variables that are nearly independent of each other. Now we will turn to an example in which the correlation is not nearly as high, but is still significantly greater than 0. Moreover, it comes closer to the kinds of studies that behavior scientists do frequently.

There is a common belief that people who lead faster-paced lives are more susceptible to heart disease and other forms of fatal illness. (Discussions of "Type A" personality come to mind.) Levine (1990) published data on the "pace of life" and age-adjusted death rates from ischemic heart disease. In his case, he collected data from 36 cities, varying in size and geographical location. He was ingenious when it came to measuring the pace of life. He surreptitiously used a stopwatch to record the time that it took a bank clerk to make change for a $20 bill, the time it took an average person to walk 60 feet, and the speed at which people spoke. Levine also recorded the age-adjusted death rate from ischemic heart disease for each city. The data follow, where "pace" is taken as the average of the three measures. (The units of measurement are arbitrary. The data on all pace variables are included in the data set on the Web.) Here is an example where we have two dependent measures, but one is clearly the predictor (Pace goes on the X (horizontal) axis and Heart disease goes on the Y (vertical) axis).

The data are plotted in Figure 9.5.

---

[2]In the days before computers and electronic calculators, many textbooks showed how to estimate the correlation coefficient by breaking the scatterplot into squares and counting the number of observations in each square. The breakdown was finer than the four quadrants used here, but the idea was the same. Fortunately, we no longer need to compute correlations that way, though the approach is instructive.

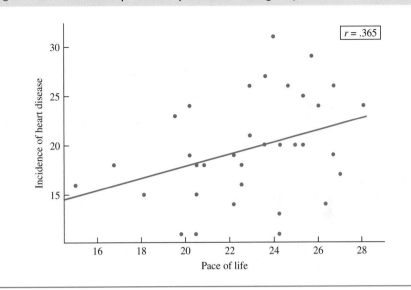

Figure 9.5 Relationship between pace of life and age-adjusted rate of heart disease

As you can see from this figure, there is a tendency for the age-adjusted incidence of heart disease to be higher in cities where the pace of life is faster—where people speak more quickly, walk faster, and carry out simple tasks at a faster rate. The pattern is not as clear as it was in previous examples, but it is similar to patterns we find with many psychological variables.[3]

From an inspection of Figure 9.5 you can see a strong positive relationship between the pace of life and heart disease—as pace increases, deaths from heart disease also increase, and vice versa. It is a **linear relationship** because the best fitting line is straight. (We say that a relationship is linear if the best (or nearly best) fit to the data comes from a straight line. If the best fitting line was not straight, we would refer to it as a **curvilinear relationship**.) I have drawn in this line to make the relationship clearer. Look at the scatterplot in Figure 9.5. If you just look at the people with the highest pace scores and those with the lowest scores, you will see that the death rate is nearly twice as high in the former group.

9.3 The Covariance

The correlation coefficient that we want to compute on these data is itself based on a statistic called the **covariance**. The covariance is basically a number that reflects the degree to which two variables vary together. If, for example, high scores on one variable tend to be paired with high scores on the other, the covariance will be large and positive. When high scores on one variable are paired about equally often with both high and low scores on the other, the covariance will be near zero, and when high scores on one variable are generally paired with low scores on the other, the covariance is negative.

---

[3]Levine and Norenzayan (1999) found very similar results when they examined this relationship for 31 different countries. There the correlation was $r = .35$.

To define the covariance mathematically we can write

$$\text{cov}_{XY} = \frac{\Sigma(X - \overline{X})(Y - \overline{Y})}{N - 1}$$

From this equation it is apparent that the covariance is similar in form to the variance. If we changed each Y in the equation to X, we would have s_X^2.

It is possible to show that the covariance will be at its positive maximum whenever X and Y are perfectly positively correlated ($r = +1.00$) and at its negative maximum whenever they are perfectly negatively correlated ($r = -1$). When there is no relationship ($r = 0$), the covariance will be zero.

9.4 The Pearson Product-Moment Correlation Coefficient (r)

You might expect that we could use the covariance as a measure of the degree of relationship between two variables. An immediate difficulty arises, however, in that the absolute value of cov_{XY} is also a function of the standard deviations of X and Y. For example, $\text{cov}_{XY} = 20$ might reflect a high degree of correlation when each variable contains little variability, but a low degree of correlation when the standard deviations are large and the scores are quite variable. To resolve this difficulty, we will divide the covariance by the standard deviations and make the result our estimate of correlation. (Technically, this is known as *scaling* the covariance by the standard deviations because we basically are changing the scale on which it is measured.) We will define what is known as the **Pearson product-moment correlation coefficient (r)** as[4]

$$r = \frac{\text{cov}_{XY}}{s_X s_Y}$$

The maximum value of cov_{XY} turns out to be $\pm s_X s_Y$. (This can be shown mathematically, but just trust me.) Because the maximum of cov_{XY} is $\pm s_X s_Y$, it follows that the limits on r are ± 1.00. One interpretation of r, then, is that it is a measure of the degree to which the covariance approaches its maximum.

An equivalent way of writing the preceding equation would be to replace the variances and covariances by their computational formulae and then simplify by cancellation. If we do this, we will arrive at

$$r = \frac{N\Sigma XY - \Sigma X \Sigma Y}{\sqrt{[N\Sigma X^2 - (\Sigma X)^2][N\Sigma Y^2 - (\Sigma Y)^2]}}$$

This formula is useful if you are calculating correlations by hand, and I am including it because several reviewers asked to have it here. Those students who have computer software available, and that includes spreadsheets like Excel, will prefer to let the software do the calculation. (Many hand calculators will also compute correlations.) Since most calculators produce some or all of the needed statistics

---

[4]This coefficient is named after its creator (Karl Pearson). Deviations of the form $(X - \overline{X})$ and $(Y - \overline{Y})$ are called "moments," hence the phrase "product-moment."

automatically, it is usually much simpler to work with deviation scores and use the first formula in this section. That one at least has the advantage of making it clear what is happening. Both equations for *r* will produce exactly the same answer; the choice is up to you. I prefer the expression in terms of the covariance and the standard deviations, but historically the second one has appeared in most texts.

The covariance and the two standard deviations for the pace of life data are given in Table 9.2. Applying the first equation to the data in Table 9.2, we have

$$r = \frac{\text{cov}_{XY}}{s_X s_y} = \frac{5.74}{(3.015)(5.214)} = .365$$

I leave the calculations using the second formula to you. You will find that it will give the same result.

The code for calculating the correlation using *R* follows. The lower part of the code involves fitting a regression line named "reg", which I will expand on in the next chapter. It is here because we need that calculation in order to draw the line in the next statement. You can ignore it for now if you like.

```
#  Pace of Life
Pace.life <- read.table("https://www.uvm.edu/~dhowell/fundamentals9/
DataFiles/Fig9-5.dat", header = TRUE)
attach(Pace.life)
head(Pace.life)     # Just to find the variable names
correl <- cor(Heart, Pace)
correl <- round(correl, 3)
plot(Pace, Heart, xlab = "Pace of Life", ylab = "Incidence of Heart Disease")
reg <- lm(Heart~Pace)
abline(reg = reg)
legend(16, 28, paste("r = ",correl), bty = "n")
```

Table 9.2 Pace of Life and Death Rate Due to Heart Disease in 36 U.S. Cities

Pace (X)	27.67	25.33	23.67	26.33	26.33	25.00	26.67	26.33	24.33	25.67
Heart (Y)	24	29	31	26	26	20	17	19	26	24
Pace (X)	22.67	25.00	26.00	24.00	26.33	20.00	24.67	24.00	24.00	20.67
Heart (Y)	26	25	14	11	19	24	20	13	20	18
Pace (X)	22.33	22.00	19.33	19.67	23.33	22.33	20.33	23.33	20.33	22.67
Heart (Y)	16	19	23	11	27	18	15	20	18	21
Pace (X)	20.33	22.00	20.00	18.00	16.67	15.00				
Heart (Y)	11	14	19	15	18	16				

$\Sigma X = 822.333$ $\Sigma Y = 713$ $\Sigma XY = 16,487.67$
$\Sigma X^2 = 19,102.33$ $\Sigma Y^2 = 15,073$ $N = 36$
$\overline{X} = 22.84$ $\overline{Y} = 19.81$ $\text{cov}_{XY} = 5.74$
$s_X = 3.015$ $s_Y = 5.214$

The correlation coefficient must be interpreted cautiously. Specifically, $r = .36$ should *not* be interpreted to mean that there is 36% of a relationship (whatever that might mean) between pace of life and heart disease. The correlation coefficient is simply a point on the scale between -1.00 and $+1.00$, and the closer it is to either of those limits, the stronger is the relationship between the two variables. For a more specific interpretation we will prefer to speak in terms of r^2, which is discussed in Chapter 10.

Karl Pearson

Karl Pearson was one of the most influential people in statistics during the early 20th century. He developed the Pearson product-moment correlation coefficient, which is the subject of this chapter, and the chi-square statistic, which is the subject of Chapter 19. (Unfortunately he got the latter slightly wrong, Fisher corrected him, and the two feuded loudly ever after. Field (2009) refers to them as "a bunch of squabbling children.") Pearson also developed a number of other statistical techniques that we are not going to see.

Karl Pearson was born in 1857 and was an amazing polymath; he knew a great deal about a great many things. He was a historian, he wrote passion plays about religion, he was admitted to the bar, he studied mathematics and held a chair in applied mathematics, and then founded the world's first department of statistics at University College, London. He also directly influenced Einstein with his writings on anti-matter, wrinkles in time, and the fourth dimension. When he retired, his statistics department was split into two departments, with his son, Egon, as Professor of Statistics and R. A. Fisher as Professor of Genetics. You have to admit that he was a pretty accomplished person. At the time, the journal *Biometrika* was perhaps the most prestigious journal in the field, and you can probably guess that he was its editor until his death. The fact that he refused to publish Fisher's papers stirred the pot of their rivalry even more.

Pearson's correlation coefficient was hugely influential, and along with linear regression in the next chapter, was one of the most popular data analysis techniques, at least until Fisher published his work on the analysis of variance in the 1930s. It is still one of the most used statistical techniques, and we owe a debt to Pearson even if he was nasty to our buddy Fisher.

9.5 Correlations with Ranked Data

In the previous example the data points for each subject were recorded in everyday units such as the time to do three tasks and the incidence of deaths due to heart disease. Sometimes, however, we ask judges to rank items on two dimensions; we then want to correlate the two sets of ranks. For example, we might ask one judge to rank the quality of the "statement of purpose" found in 10 applications to graduate school in terms of clarity, specificity, and apparent sincerity. The weakest would be assigned a rank of 1, the next weakest a rank of 2, and so on. Another judge might rank the overall acceptability of these same 10 applicants based on all other available information, and we might be interested in the degree to which well-written statements of purpose are associated with highly admissible applicants. When we have such ranked data, we frequently use what is known as **Spearman's correlation coefficient for ranked data**, denoted r_S. (This is not the only coefficient that can be calculated from ranked data, nor even the best, but it is one of the simplest and most common.[5])

In the past when people obtained correlations by hand, they could save time by using special formulae. For example, if the data are ranks of N objects, you can either add up all the ranks, or you can calculate $\Sigma X = N(N + 1)/2$. The answers will be the same. That was fine when we had to do our calculations using pencil and paper, but there is little to be gained now by doing so. But that kind of formula is exactly where Spearman's formula came from. He just took Pearson's formula and made substitutions. (For example, he replaced ΣX by $N(N-1)/2$.) But if you apply Pearson's formula to those ranks instead of Spearman's, you will get the same answer—without memorizing another formula. In fact, no matter how you calculate it, Spearman's r_s is a plain old Pearson product-moment correlation coefficient, only this time it is calculated on ranks rather than on measured variables. If there are tied ranks we have to adjust Spearman's coefficient, but that just brings it back in line with Pearson's r. The interpretation, however, is not quite the same as the usual Pearson correlation coefficient.

Why Rank?

It is one thing to think of Spearman's r_s when the data naturally occur in the form of ranks. (For example, when the participant is asked to "Rank these cookies in terms of preference.") But why would someone want to rank values on a continuous variable? The main reason for ranking is that you either do not trust the nature of the underlying scale or you want to down-weight extreme scores. As an example of the former, we might measure a person's social isolation by the number of friends he or she claims to have and measure his or her physical attractiveness by asking an independent judge to assign a rating on a 10-point scale. Having very little faith in the underlying properties of either scale, we might then simply convert the raw data on each variable to ranks (e.g., the person reporting the fewest friends is assigned a rank of 1, and so on) and carry out our correlations with those ranks. But what about the case where you might want to down-weight extreme values? In Exercise 9.10 you will see data on the incidence of Down syndrome as a function of age of the mother. Incidence differences due to age in younger mothers are quite small, but among older ages incidence increases sharply. Ranking will rein in those later increases and keep them at the same general level of magnitude as increases for younger ages. Whether this is a smart thing to do is a different question, and it is one you would need to consider.

The Interpretation of r_S

Spearman's r_S and other coefficients calculated on ranked data are slightly more difficult to interpret than Pearson's r, partly because of the nature of the data. In the example that I have described concerning rankings of statements of purpose, the data

---

[5]Kendall's tau coefficient has better properties in many cases, but we are not going to discuss that statistic here.

occurred naturally in the form of ranks because that is the task that we set our judges. In this situation, r_S is a measure of the linear (straight line) relationship between one set of ranks and another set of ranks.

In cases where we convert the obtained data to a set of ranks, r_S is a measure of the linearity of the relationship between the ranks, but it is a measure only of the **monotonic relationship** between the original variables. (A monotonic relationship is one that is continuously rising or continuously falling—the line does not need to be straight; it can go up for a while, level off, and then rise again. It just can't reverse direction and start falling.) This relationship should not surprise you. A correlation coefficient, regardless of whether it is a Pearson correlation or a Spearman correlation, tells us directly only about the variables on which it is computed. It cannot be expected to give very precise information about variables on which it was not computed. As discussed in Chapter 2, it is essential to keep in mind the similar distinction between the variables that you have actually measured (e.g., number of friends) and the underlying property that you want to examine (e.g., social isolation).

9.6   Factors That Affect the Correlation

The correlation coefficient can be importantly affected by characteristics of the sample. Three of these characteristics are the restriction of the range (or variance) of X and/or Y, nonlinearity of the relationship, and the use of heterogeneous subsamples.

The Effect of Range Restrictions and Nonlinearity

A common problem that arises in many instances concerns restrictions on the range over which X and Y vary. The effect of such **range restrictions** is to alter the correlation between X and Y from what it would have been if the range had not been so restricted. Depending on the nature of the data, the correlation may either rise or fall as a result of such restrictions, although most commonly r is reduced.

With the exception of very unusual circumstances, restricting the range of X will increase r only when the restriction results in eliminating some curvilinear relationship. For example, if we correlated reading ability with age, where age ran from 0 to 70, the data would be decidedly curvilinear (level for a few years, rising to about 17 years of age, and then leveling off or even declining), and the correlation, which measures linear relationships, would be quite low. If, however, we restricted the range of ages to 4 to 17, the correlation would be quite high, because we have eliminated those values of Y that were not varying linearly with X.

An excellent example of a curvilinear relationship, which at first glance would appear to run counter to Figure 9.2, is shown in Figure 9.6, again plotting health care expenditures versus life expectancy. You can see that this relationship is distinctly curvilinear, rising with expenditures. However if you look only at the data points for countries spending more than about $2,000 per capita, there is no clear relationship. (See area bounded by the red rectangle.) The best fitting straight line would be essentially flat. I show this figure to illustrate the fact that curvilinearity may depend on only a small portion of the data and may be a misleading, though accurate, label.

Figure 9.6   Life expectancy as a function of per capita health expenditure

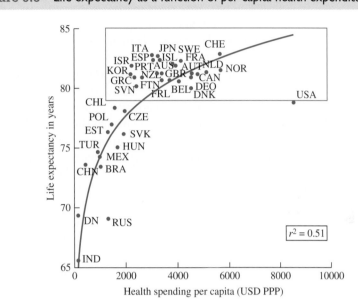

Source: OECD Health Statistics 2013. Available at http://dx.doi.org/10.1787/health-data-en Obtained from http://www.oecd.org/health/health-systems/health-at-a-glance.htm

The more usual effect of restricting the range of X or Y is to reduce the correlation. This problem is especially important in the area of test construction, because in that area the criterion measure (Y) may be available for only the higher values of X. Consider the hypothetical data in Figure 9.7.

This figure represents the hypothetic relationship between college grade point averages and scores on a standard achievement test for a sample of students. In the

Figure 9.7   Hypothetical data illustrating the effect of restricted range

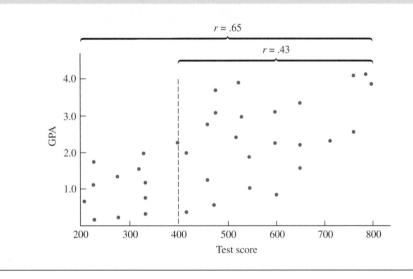

ideal world of the test constructor, all people who took the exam would then be sent to college and receive a grade point average, and the correlation between test scores and grade point averages would be computed. As can be seen from Figure 9.6, this correlation would be reasonably high ($r = .65$).

In the real world, however, not everyone is admitted to college. Colleges take only those who they think are the more able students, whether this ability is measured by achievement test scores, high school performance, or whatever. That means college grade point averages are available mainly for students having relatively high scores on the standardized test. This has the effect of allowing us to evaluate the relationship between X and Y for only those values of, say, X greater than 400.

The effect of range restrictions must be taken into account whenever we see a coefficient based on a restricted sample. The coefficient might be quite inappropriate for the question at hand. Essentially what we have done is to ask how well a standardized test predicts a person's suitability for college, but we have answered that question by reference only to those people who were actually admitted to college. At the same time, it is sometimes useful to deliberately restrict the range of one of the variables. For example, if we wanted to know the way in which reading ability increases linearly with age, we probably would restrict the age range by using only subjects who are at least four years old and younger than 20 years old (or some other reasonable limits). We presumably would never expect reading ability to continue to rise indefinitely.

The Effect of Heterogeneous Subsamples

Another important consideration in evaluating the results of correlational analyses deals with **heterogeneous subsamples**. This point can be illustrated with a simple example involving the relationship between height and weight in male and female subjects. These variables may appear to have little to do with psychology, but considering the important role both variables play in the development of people's images of themselves, the example is not as far afield as you might expect. In addition, these relationships play a role in the debate over the appropriateness of the Body Mass Index (BMI), which is used in many studies of diet and health. The data plotted in Figure 9.8 come from sample data from the Minitab manual (Ryan et al., 1985). These are actual data from 92 college students who were asked to report height, weight, gender, and several other variables. (Keep in mind that these are self-report data, and there may be systematic reporting biases.) The complete data file can be found at

 https://www.uvm.edu/~dhowell/fundamentals9/DataFiles/Fig9-8.dat

When we combine the data from both males and females in the bottom figure, the relationship is strikingly good, with a correlation of .78. When you look at the data from the two genders separately, however, the correlations fall to .60 for males and .49 for females. The important point is that the high correlation we found when we combined genders is not due purely to the relation between height and weight. It is also due largely to the fact that men are, on average, taller and heavier than women. In fact, a little doodling on a sheet of paper will show that you could create artificial, and improbable, data where within each gender weight is negatively related to height, while the relationship is positive when you collapse across gender. (There is an example of this kind of relationship Exercises 9.25.)

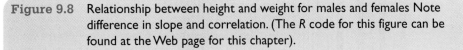

Figure 9.8   Relationship between height and weight for males and females Note difference in slope and correlation. (The *R* code for this figure can be found at the Web page for this chapter).

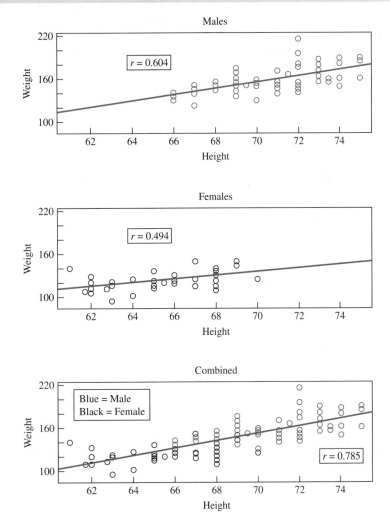

The point I am making here is that experimenters must be careful when they combine data from several sources. The relationship between two variables may be obscured or enhanced by the presence of a third variable. Such a finding is important in its own right.

A second example of heterogeneous subsamples that makes a similar point is the relationship between cholesterol level and cardiovascular disease in men and women. If you collapse across both genders, the relationship is not impressive. But when you separate the data by male and female, there is a distinct trend for cardiovascular disease to increase with increased level of cholesterol. This relationship is obscured in the combined data because men, regardless of cholesterol level, have an elevated level of cardiovascular disease compared to women.

9.7 | Beware Extreme Observations

An interesting data set on the relationship between smoking and drinking can be found at the Data and Story Library website (DASL). The data are from a British government survey of households in Great Britain on household spending on tobacco products and alcohol. The data are given in Table 9.3 for 11 regions in Great Britain, where I have recorded the average amount of household income spent on each item.

I would expect that these two variables would tend to be related, just based on common observation. But if we compute the correlation, it is only .224, and the p value is .509, meaning that we should not be surprised by a correlation at least that high from 11 pairs of observations even if the null hypothesis is true. Perhaps my intuition is wrong, or maybe there is some other explanation.

The first thing that we should do with any data, even before we jump in and calculate the correlation, is to look at the distributions. If you do, you will see that no region is particularly unusual on either variable. Expenditures on alcohol in Northern Ireland are lower than elsewhere, but not dramatically so. Similarly, the people of Northern Ireland spend a bit more on tobacco than others, but not unduly so. However, if you create a scatterplot of these data you see a problem. The plot is given in Figure 9.9.

Notice that everything looks fine except for the data point for Northern Ireland. Though it is not unusually extreme on either of the variables taken alone, the combination of the two is indeed extreme, because it is unusual to have an observation be so high on one variable *and* so low on the other. If we remove Northern Ireland from the data, we find that the remaining points show a correlation of .784, and an associated two-tailed p value of .007. This is more like what I would have expected.

So, can we just toss out observations that we don't like? Not really. At least you can't just pretend they are not there. It is appropriate to leave out Northern Ireland if we make clear what we have done, and either offer a reasonable excuse for omitting that data point or else make clear to our reader that the point is aberrant for unknown reasons, and also report the result of including that point.

Table 9.3 Household Expenditures on Tobacco and Alcohol Products in Great Britain

Region	Alcohol	Tobacco
North	6.47	4.03
Yorkshire	6.13	3.76
Northeast	6.19	3.77
East Midlands	4.89	3.34
West Midlands	5.63	3.47
East Anglia	4.52	2.92
Southeast	5.89	3.20
Southwest	4.79	2.71
Wales	5.27	3.53
Scotland	6.08	4.51
Northern Ireland	4.02	4.56

Figure 9.9 Scatterplot of expenditures on alcohol and tobacco

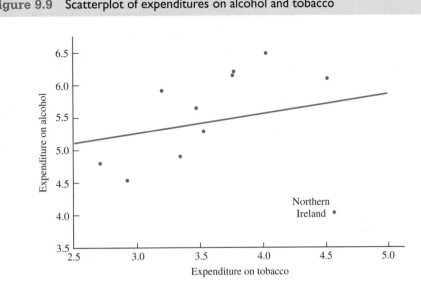

9.8 | Correlation and Causation

A statement that you will find in virtually every discussion of correlation is that correlation does not imply causation. Just because two variables are correlated doesn't mean that one caused the other. In fact, I would guess that most of the time that is not the case. Textbook authors usually make this statement, give one extreme example, and move on. But I think that we need to dwell on this point a bit longer.

I have shown you several examples of correlated variables in this chapter. We began with the case of infant mortality and number of physicians in the area, and I assume everyone is willing to agree that there is no way that having more physicians causes an increase in mortality. Doctors try very hard not to kill people. Then we had the case of life expectancy and health care expenditures, and we really didn't have to even consider causation because there was clearly no relationship. (We might, however, wonder what causes our variables to appear so completely unrelated.) Then we saw the relationship between solar radiation and breast cancer, and the relationship between wine consumption and heart disease. There we have to be a great deal more careful. In both cases it would be tempting to think in terms of causation, and actually causation might be a logical explanation. Solar radiation does increase the production of vitamin D, and that might play a protective role against breast cancer. Similarly, compounds in wine might actually reduce the bodily processes that lead to heart disease. How are we to know whether we are talking about causation or something else?

Utts (2005) presents an excellent list of possible explanations of a significant correlation between two variables. I am unabashedly following her lead in what follows. She suggested seven possible reasons for two variables to be correlated, and only one of them is causal.

1. The relationship actually could be causal. Sunlight does increase the production of vitamin D, and vitamin D might very well protect the body against breast cancer.

2. We may have the relationship backward, and the response variable could actually cause the explanatory variable. It might appear that happiness leads to better social relationships, but it is just as plausible that having good social relationships leads to people feeling happier about their lives.

3. The relationship may be only partially causal. The predictor variable may be a necessary cause, but changes in the dependent variable either only occur, or are accentuated in the presence of some other variable. Increased wealth may lead to increased happiness, but only if other conditions (e.g., a supportive family, good friends, etc.) are present.

4. There may be a third, confounding, variable present. The changing size of the population of the United States is correlated with changes in infant mortality, but no one believes that having more people around reduces the number of infants who die. Both of those variables are related to time and the other changes in health care that have occurred over that time. Similarly, as we saw earlier, Wong (2008) pointed to the fact that areas of Europe that drink a lot of red wine also have more sunlight, and solar radiation has been shown to also be associated with decreases in heart disease. So is it solar radiation or wine that is responsible for reduced hard disease, or both, or neither?

5. Both variables may be related to a third, causal, variable. Family stability and physical illness may be correlated because both are themselves a function of outside stresses on the individual.

6. Variables may be changing over time. Utts (2005) gives the nice example of the high correlation between divorce rate and incidence of drug offenses. Those variables are correlated mainly because they both are increasing over time.

7. The correlation may be due to coincidence. Your father-in-law moves in on you and your marriage goes down the tubes. It could be that your father-in-law is truly a disruptive influence, but it could also be that those two things just happened to occur at the same time. We often see causal relationships when no cause exists.

It is very difficult to establish causal relationships, and we need to be careful about any assertions of cause. One important consideration is that in order for A to cause B, A must occur before, or at the same time as B. Causation cannot work backward in time. Second, we need to rule out other variables. If we can show that A leads to B in both the presence and the absence of other possible causal factors, we have strengthened our argument. That is one reason that science is so concerned with randomization, and especially with random assignment. If we take a large group of people, *randomly* split them into three groups, expose the three groups to different conditions, and show that the three groups subsequently behave reliably differently, we have a good argument for causation. The random assignment makes it highly unlikely that there are systematic differences between the groups that were responsible for whatever differences occurred. Finally, before we declare that one variable causes another, we need to come up with some reasonable explanation of how this could be. If we can't explain why we found what we did, the best that we can say is that this is a relationship worth exploring further to see if an explanation for the correlation can be found. This leads nicely to the next section.

9.9   If Something Looks Too Good to Be True, Perhaps It Is

Not all statistical results mean what they seem to mean; in fact, not all results are meaningful. This is a point that will be made repeatedly throughout this book, and it is particularly appropriate when we are speaking about correlation and regression.

In Figure 9.1 we saw a plot of data collected by Cochrane, St. Leger, and Moore (1978) on the relationship between a country's infant mortality rate and the number of physicians per 10,000 population. This correlation ($r = .88$) was not only remarkably high, but positive. The data indicate that as the number of physicians increases, the infant mortality rate also increases. What are we to make of such data? Are physicians really responsible for deaths of children? In the previous section I said that I strongly doubted that the relationship was causal, and I hope that everyone would agree with that.

No one has seriously suggested that physicians actually do harm to children, and it is highly unlikely that there is a causal link between these two variables. For our purposes, the data are worth studying more for what they have to say about correlation and regression than what they have to say about infant mortality, and it is worth considering possible explanations. In doing so, we have to keep several facts in mind. First, these data are all from developed countries, primarily but not exclusively in Western Europe. In other words, we are speaking of countries with high levels of health care. Although undoubtedly there are substantial differences in infant mortality (and the number of physicians) among these countries, these differences are nowhere near as large as we would expect if we took a random sample of all countries. This suggests that at least some of the variability in infant mortality that we are trying to explain is probably more meaningless random fluctuation in the system than meaningful variability.

The second thing to keep in mind is that these data are selective. Cochrane et al. did not simply take a random sample of developed countries—they chose carefully what data to include, but did so for reasons having little or nothing to do with this peculiar relationship. We might, and probably would, obtain somewhat less dramatic relationships if we looked at a more inclusive group of developed countries. (I am not in any way suggesting that the authors fudged their data.) A third consideration is that Cochrane et al. selected this particular relationship from among many that they looked at because it was a surprising finding. (If you look hard enough, you are likely to find something interesting in any set of data, even when there is nothing really important going on.) They were looking for predictors of mortality, and this relationship popped out among other more expected relationships. In their paper they give possible explanations, and their article is a good example of the need to look beyond the numbers.

In terms of explanations for the finding shown in Figure 9.1, let's consider a few possible—though not terribly good—ones. In the first place, it might be argued that we have a reporting problem. With more physicians we stand a better chance of having infant deaths reported, causing the number of reported deaths to increase with increases in physicians. This would be a reasonable explanation if we were speaking of underdeveloped countries, but we are not. It is probably unlikely that many deaths would go unreported in Western Europe or North America even if there weren't so many physicians. Another possibility is that physicians go where the health problems are. This argument implies a cause-and-effect relationship, but in the opposite direction—high infant mortality causes a high number of physicians. A third possibility is that high population densities tend to lead to high infant mortality and also tend to attract physicians. In the United States both urban poverty and physicians tend to congregate in urban centers. (How would you go about testing such a hypothesis?) Interestingly, the relationship we have been looking at is much weaker if we limit "doctors" to pediatricians and obstetricians, who are much more likely to have a direct effect, though it is still positive.

9.10 Testing the Significance of a Correlation Coefficient

The fact that a sample correlation coefficient is not exactly zero does not necessarily mean that those variables are truly correlated in the population. For example, I wrote a simple program that drew 25 numbers from a random number generator and arbitrarily named that variable "income." I then drew another 25 random numbers and named that variable "musicality." When I paired the first number of each set with the first number of the other set, the second with the second, and so on, and calculated the correlation between the two variables, I obtained a correlation of .278. That seems pretty good. It looks as if I've shown that the more musical a person is the greater his or her income (and vice versa). But we know these data are just random numbers, and there really isn't any true correlation between two sets of random numbers. I just happened to get a reasonably large value of r by chance.

The point of this example is *not* to illustrate that statistics lie. (I hear too many comments to that effect already!) The point is that correlation coefficients, like all other statistics, suffer from sampling error. They deviate from the true correlations in the population (in this case zero) by some amount. Sometimes they are too high, sometimes too low, and sometimes, but rarely, right on. If I drew a new set of data in the previous example, I might get $r = .15$, or maybe $r = .03$, or maybe even $r = -.30$. But I probably would not get $r = .95$ or $r = -.87$. Small deviations from the true value of zero are to be expected; large deviations are not.

But how large is large? When do we decide that our correlation coefficient is far enough from zero that we can no longer believe it likely that the true correlation in the population is zero? This is where we come to the issue of hypothesis testing developed in Chapter 8.

First, let's look at an empirical sampling distribution of the correlation coefficient based on 1,000 samples, each with 50 pairs of X and Y. I simply drew 1,000 pairs of samples of the random numbers I mentioned in the preceding paragraph and calculated r for each. In this case the data were random numbers, so the true correlation in the population (denoted as ρ [rho]) is 0. The distribution is shown in Figure 9.10.

Notice the range of values that we obtain. Even with 50 pairs of observations or random numbers, we obtain some reasonably large correlations once in a while.

Earlier in this chapter I used the relationship between the pace of life and the incidence of heart disease. There the correlation was 0.365 based on 36 pairs of observations. Now I want to know whether those variables are truly correlated in the whole population of courses. In order to arrive at some decision on this question, I will set up my null hypothesis that the **population correlation**

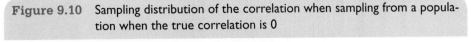

Figure 9.10 Sampling distribution of the correlation when sampling from a population when the true correlation is 0

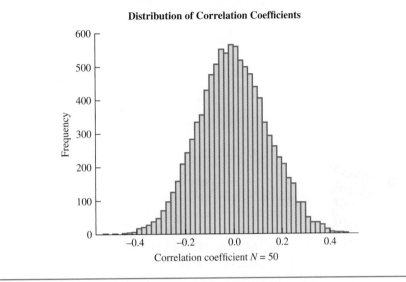

coefficient **rho** (denoted ρ) is 0 (i.e., H_0: $\rho = 0$). If I am able to reject H_0, I will be able to conclude that the pace of life in a given city does have an influence on the rate of heart disease in that same city. If I cannot reject H_0, I will have to conclude that I have insufficient evidence to show whether or not these variables are related and the direction of that relationship, and I will treat them as linearly independent.

I prefer to use two-tailed tests, so I will choose to reject H_0 if the obtained correlation is too large in either a positive or a negative direction. In other words, I am testing

$$H_0: \rho = 0$$

against

$$H_0: \rho \neq 0$$

But we are still left with the question, "How big is too big?"

In the past we often evaluated the statistical significance of a correlation coefficient by use of tables of correlations. However we no longer need to do that because we can very easily compute another statistic and evaluate that statistic for significance. The statistic that we will compute is called Student's t, and can be computed very simply.

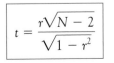

$$t = \frac{r\sqrt{N-2}}{\sqrt{1-r^2}}$$

For our example this becomes

$$t = \frac{r\sqrt{N-2}}{\sqrt{1-r^2}}$$

$$= \frac{.365\sqrt{36-2}}{\sqrt{1-.365^2}}$$

$$= \frac{.365 * \sqrt{34}}{\sqrt{.8667}} = 2.286$$

When we are predicting one variable from one other variable, as we are in this chapter, the degrees of freedom $= N - 2$, where N is the size of our sample (the number of pairs, not the number of individual data points, which will be 2 times N). We are using an example where $N = 36$, so our degrees of freedom for evaluating this statistic is $36 - 2 = 34$. We can evaluate the probability of a t on 34 degrees of freedom by going to any of the probability calculators that we have been using from the Web. I solved this using the calculator at vassarstats.net. I selected **utilities/Statistical Tables Calculator/r to P**. The resulting screen, with the calculation included, can be seen below in Figure 9.11.

I can state all this in terms of a rule. First, calculate the sample correlation and compute $df = N - 2$, where N is the number of pairs of observations. Then calculate t and use a probability calculator to calculate its (two-tailed) probability under the null hypothesis. Vassarstats calculates t for you given N and r. We then reject H_0: $\rho = 0$ whenever that probability is less than .05. This means that if H_0 is true, the probability that we would obtain a sample correlation at least as large (positive or negative) as the one we obtained is .029.

As another example, look at Table 9.3, where you will see the output from SPSS for the same problem. To obtain that output I simply loaded the data in Fig 9-5. sav, selected **Analyze/Correlate**, filled in the appropriate variables, and clicked "OK."

You can run the same analysis in R by loading the data and simply typing cor. test(Heart, Pace). That will also give us the 95% confidence interval on ρ, to be discussed next.

```
cor.test(Heart, Pace, alternative = two.sided)
  # We are using Pearson's product-moment correlation

data:  Heart and Pace
t = 2.2869, df = 34, p-value = 0.02855
alternative hypothesis: true correlation is not equal to 0
95 percent confidence interval:
 0.04158114      0.61936671
sample estimates:
   cor
0.3651289
```

Figure 9.11 Calculation of the probability for a correlation coefficient using Vassarstats

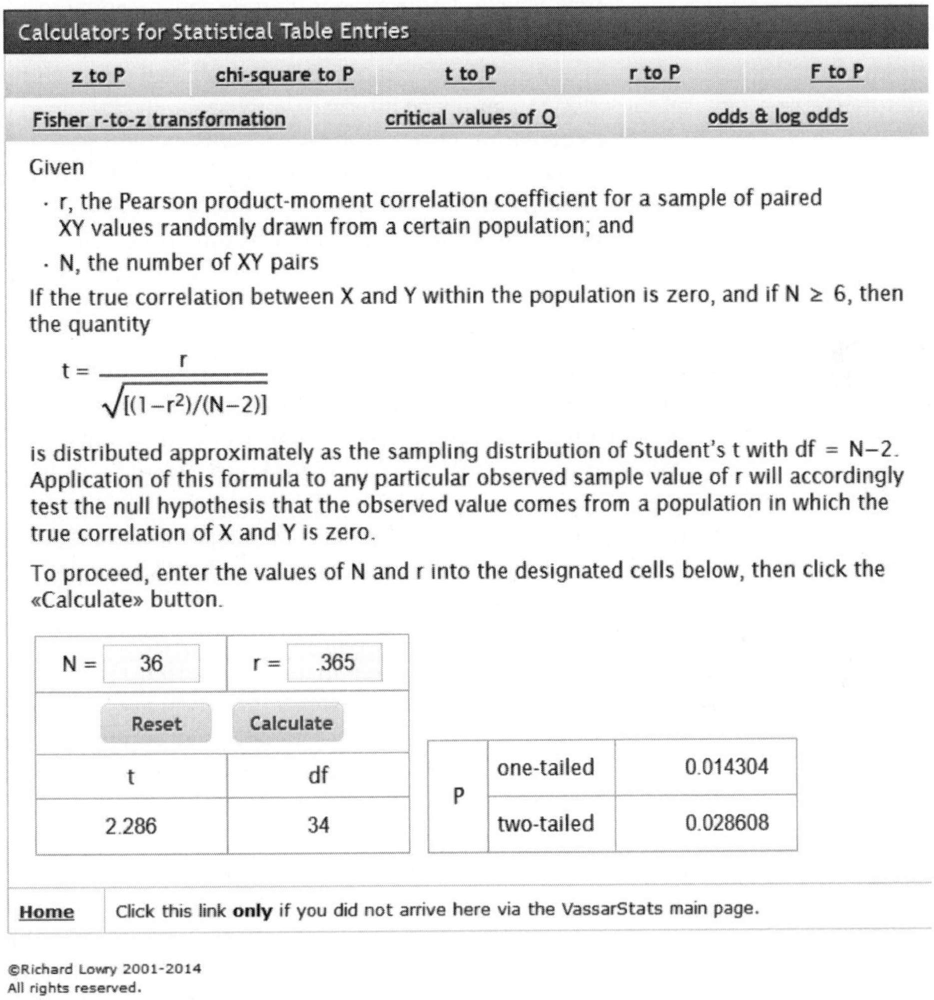

Calculators for Statistical Table Entries

z to P	chi-square to P	t to P	r to P	F to P

Fisher r-to-z transformation	critical values of Q	odds & log odds

Given

· r, the Pearson product-moment correlation coefficient for a sample of paired XY values randomly drawn from a certain population; and

· N, the number of XY pairs

If the true correlation between X and Y within the population is zero, and if $N \geq 6$, then the quantity

$$t = \frac{r}{\sqrt{[(1-r^2)/(N-2)]}}$$

is distributed approximately as the sampling distribution of Student's t with df = N−2. Application of this formula to any particular observed sample value of r will accordingly test the null hypothesis that the observed value comes from a population in which the true correlation of X and Y is zero.

To proceed, enter the values of N and r into the designated cells below, then click the «Calculate» button.

N =	36		r =	.365

Reset	Calculate

t	df
2.286	34

P	one-tailed	0.014304
	two-tailed	0.028608

Home   Click this link **only** if you did not arrive here via the VassarStats main page.

That result may be a bit more than you asked for, but you will soon see where the unfamiliar parts come from. The important result for us at this point is the line that gives $p = 0.02855$.

9.11 Confidence Intervals on Correlation Coefficients

A significance test tells us whether or not we have reason to believe that the true correlation in the population between two variables is different from 0.00, However it doesn't tell us very much about what the true correlation in the population actually is. For that we want a confidence interval. If you look at the R printout that you saw in the last paragraph, you will see that it gives a 95% confidence interval of $0.042 - 0.619$ (rounded to three decimal places). But how do we interpret this interval?

Let us assume that over your lifetime you are going to compute 1,000 95% confidence intervals on some statistic. (I know that you would need to have strange interests to do that, but you can pretend.) I can tell you with reasonable certainty that of those 1,000 confidence intervals, approximately 950 are likely to include (bracket) the true population correlation and 50 of them will not. That is basically what we mean by a confidence interval. (Note that I can't tell you which 50, but only that there will be about 50 of them.)

Now assume that you are about to run an experiment in which you will compute a correlation coefficient on some data. I can tell you right now that you have a probability of .95 of bracketing the true correlation with your interval when you do run that experiment.

But now let's take it one tiny step further. I just gave an example related to the pace of life and the incidence of heart attacks. I computed that the 95% confidence interval on ρ was $.042 - .619$. You would probably want to say that you are 95% certain that this interval includes ρ. I would not complain too loudly if you said that, but strict probability theorists most definitely would. They would argue that once you have run the experiment and computed your statistic, the confidence interval either does include ρ or it does not, and it is inappropriate to assign it a probability of .95.

For a very long time I, and others who write textbooks on statistics, have said that you should go with the purists and say that an interval calculated *in the way we have calculated this one* will have a probability of .95 of including ρ, but that you cannot tie that statement to the numbers we computed in this study. Well, technically that is true, but it is such a convoluted way of speaking about confidence intervals that I would be perfectly happy to hear you say that "the probability is .95 that the interval $.042 - .619$ includes ρ." No, that is not strictly true, but there are many other "errors" that you could make that are far more serious. I want you to phrase the interval in a way that makes sense to you, and I think that my last statement of it makes a great deal of sense. Go for it![6] Some people that I respect may be upset with my statement, (e.g., Smithson (2000)), but insisting that the probability refers to the procedure, not the numbers, while true, confuses students more than it helps them.[7]

---

[6] Bayesian statisticians, who think of probability in terms of personal belief, would use the phrase "credible interval" to describe what I have called "confidence interval." Others might use the term "plausible interval." An excellent discussion of this whole point can be found in Dracup (2005).

[7] At the risk of appearing to beat this issue to death, let me quote from a chapter by two highly respected medical statisticians. (Gardner & Altman (2002), p. 17–18.) They had just calculated a confidence interval of 1.1 – 10.9mmHg. They wrote, "Put simply, this means that there is a 95% chance that the indicated range includes the 'population' difference in mean blood pressure level … More exactly, in a statistical sense, the confidence interval means that if a series of identical studies were carried out repeatedly on different samples from the same population, and a 95% confidence interval … calculated in each sample, then, in the long run, 95% of these confidence intervals would include the population difference between means." If Gardner and Altman can have it both ways, so can we.

Calculation

But how do we calculate the confidence interval? Well, we have some simple formulae that use a transformation attributable to R. A. Fisher (sometimes called Fisher's r'). However you are very unlikely to need to calculate this by hand, and there are a number of sources which will do it for you. You have just seen that R gives you the confidence interval if you use the function cor.test(). For some reason SPSS does not report confidence limits. But the website at http://vassarstats.net/rho.html will calculate it very easily, as will the code in the R page for this chapter. (Go to vassarstats. net, select Correlation and Regression from the panel on the left, and then select 0.95 and .99 confidence limits for r.)

9.12 | **Intercorrelation Matrices**

So far we have largely been speaking about the relationship between two variables. Often, however, we have a whole set of variables and want to know how they relate to each other in a pairwise fashion. In Figure 9.12 I plotted, in one table, the correlations among several variables concerned with expenditures for education, by state, and academic performance as measured by the SAT and ACT (two tests often used in student selection for U.S. colleges and universities). The raw data are available at

http://www.uvm.edu/~dhowell/fundamentals9/DataFiles/SchoolExpend.dat

In Figure 9.12 I first requested what is known as an **intercorrelation matrix**. It is simply a matrix in which each cell contains the correlation, and related information, between the variables on the rows and columns. These data are slightly modified from a paper by Guber (1999), who was interested in asking whether academic performance was positively correlated with state education budgets.

I have also plotted what is called a scatterplot matrix, which is just a matrix in whose cells are the scatterplots of the row and column variables. The variables appear in the order Expenditures (by state), Pupil-Teacher ratio, Salary, SAT, ACT combined score, and the percentage of students in each state taking the SAT or the ACT.

If you look closely at this table you will see an example of reporting probability values for tests of significance. If we test each of these correlations for statistical significance, it would be very cumbersome to report the exact p value next to each correlation. So SPSS falls back on the older convention and follows each correlation that is significant at $p < .05$ with a single asterisk. One that is significant at $p < .01$ gets two asterisks. We sometime use three asterisks for probabilities less than .001. (There is considerable sentiment among behavioral scientists that such an approach is not really a good thing, but we have it.) This table came from SPSS and includes the exact probability under the null on the line below the correlation. R does not give us such a neat result without more work than you want to do.

We will have much more to say about these variables in Chapter 11, but I should point out here the interesting anomaly that SAT scores are negatively correlated with expenditures. This would *appear* to suggest that the more a state

Figure 9.12 Matrix of intercorrelations and scatterplot matrix among course evaluation variables

Correlations

		Expend	PT ratio	Salary	SAT	ACT comp	Pct ACT	Pct SAT
Expend	Pearson Correlation	1	−.371**	.870**	−.381**	.380**	−.512**	.593**
	Sig. (2-tailed)		.008	.000	.006	.007	.000	.000
	N	50	50	50	50	50	50	50
PT ratio	Pearson Correlation	−.371**	1	−.001	.081	−.004	.120	−.213
	Sig. (2-tailed)	.008		.994	.575	.977	.406	.137
	N	50	50	50	50	50	50	50
Salary	Pearson Correlation	.870**	−.001	1	−.440**	.355**	−.566	.617**
	Sig. (2-tailed)	.000	.994		.001	.012	.000	.000
	N	50	50	50	50	50	50	50
SAT	Pearson Correlation	−.381**	.081	−.440**	1	.169	.877**	−.887**
	Sig. (2-tailed)	.006	.575	.001		.240	.000	.000
	N	50	50	50	50	50	50	50
ACT comp	Pearson Correlation	.380**	−.004	.355*	.169	1	−.143	.106
	Sig. (2-tailed)	.007	.977	.012	.240		.323	.465
	N	50	50	50	50	50	50	50
Pct ACT	Pearson Correlation	−.512**	.120	−.566**	877**	−.143	1	−.959**
	Sig. (2-tailed)	.000	.406	.000	.000	.323		.000
	N	50	50	50	50	50	50	50
Pct SAT	Pearson Correlation	.593**	−.213	.617**	−.887**	.106	−959**	1
	Sig. (2-tailed)	.000	.137	.000	.000	.465	.000	
	N	50	50	50	50	50	50	50

**Correlation is significant at the 0 .01 level (2-tailed).
*Correlation is significant at the 0 .05 level (2-tailed).

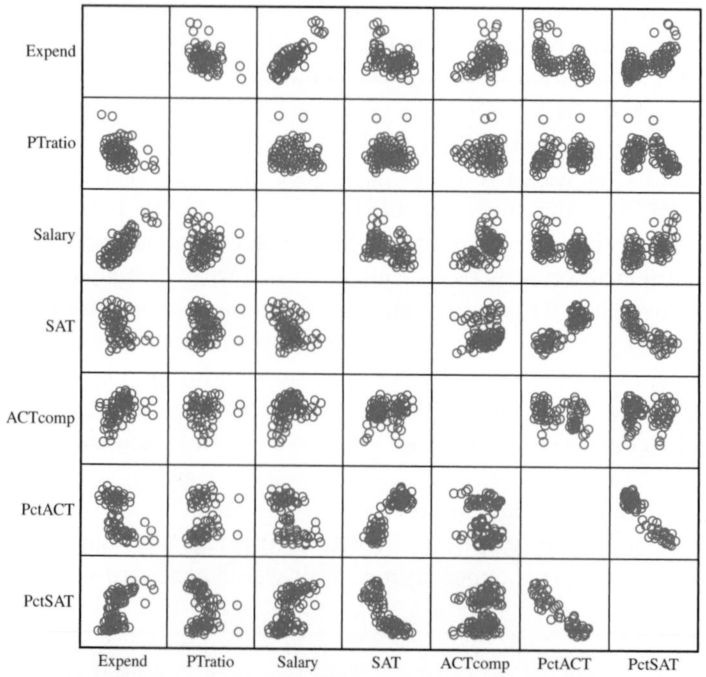

spends on education, the worse its students do. We will see in Chapter 11 that this does not mean what we would at first think that it means.

9.13 | Other Correlation Coefficients

The standard correlation coefficient is Pearson's r, which applies primarily to variables distributed more or less along interval or ratio scales of measurement. We also have seen that the same formula will produce a statistic called Spearman's r_S when the variables are in the form of ranks. You should be familiar with two other correlation coefficients, although here again there is little that is new.

When we have one variable measured on a continuous scale and one variable measured as a dichotomy (i.e., that variable has only two levels), then the correlation coefficient that we produce is called the **point biserial correlation (r_{pb})**. For example, we might perform an analysis of test items by correlating the total score on the test (X) with "right/wrong" on a particular item (Y). (We might do this to see how well that particular item discriminates between those students who appear, from their final grade, to really know that material, and those who appear not to. What would you suggest doing when such a correlation is very low?) In this case X values might run from roughly 60 to 100, but Y values would be either 0 (wrong) or 1 (right). Although special formulae exist for calculating r_{pb}, you can accomplish exactly the same thing more easily by computing r. The only difference is that we call the answer r_{pb} instead of r to point out that it is a point biserial correlation computed from data for which one variable was a dichotomy. Don't let the point about the calculation of r_{pb} pass by too quickly. I belong to several electronic mail discussion groups dealing with statistics and computing, and once every few weeks someone asks if a particular statistical package will calculate the point biserial correlation. And every time the answer is, "Yes it will, just use the standard Pearson r procedure." In fact, this is such a frequently asked question that people are beginning to be less patient with their answers.

A point is in order here about **dichotomous variables**. In the preceding example I scored "wrong" as 0 and "right" as 1 to make the arithmetic simple for those who are doing hand calculations. I could just as easily score them as 1 and 2 or even as 87 and 213—just as long as all the "right" scores receive the same number and all the "wrong" scores receive the same (but different) number. The correlation coefficient itself, with the possible exception of its sign, will be exactly the same no matter what pair of numbers we use.

A slightly different correlation coefficient, ϕ **(phi)**, arises when both variables are measured as dichotomies. For example, in studying the relationship between gender and religiosity we might correlate gender (coded Male = 1, Female = 2) with regular church attendance (No = 0, Yes = 1). Again it makes no difference what two values we use to code the dichotomous variables. Although phi has a special formula, it is again just as easy and correct to use Pearson's formula but label the answer phi.

A number of other correlation coefficients exist, but the ones given here are the most common. All those in this text are special cases of Pearson's r, and all can be obtained by using the formulae discussed in this chapter. These coefficients are the ones that are usually generated when a large set of data is entered into a computer

Table 9.4 SPSS Printout for the Correlation Between Pace of Life and Heart Disease

Correlations

		Pace	Heart
Pace	Pearson Correlation	1	.365*
	Sig. (2-tailed)		.029
	N	36	36
Heart	Pearson Correlation	.365*	1
	Sig. (two-tailed)	.029	
	N	36	36

*Correlation is significant at the .05 level (2-tailed).

data file and a correlation or regression program is run. Table 9.5 shows a diagram that illustrates the relationships among these coefficients. The empty spaces of the table reflect the fact that we do not have a good correlation coefficient to use when we have one ranked variable and one continuous or dichotomous variable. In each case you could use the standard Pearson correlation coefficient, but remember the kinds of variables you have when it comes to interpreting the result. Keep in mind that all the correlations shown in this table can be obtained by using the standard Pearson formula.

9.14 Using SPSS to Obtain Correlation Coefficients

The printout in Figure 9.13 looks back to the data in Table 9.2 on the relationship between the pace of life and incidence of heart disease. I have used SPSS to produce these results. (Instructions on using SPSS to compute correlations can be found on this book's website as Chapter 6 in the *Short SPSS Manual*.) Notice that in the second line of each row SPSS prints out the probability that we would have obtained this correlation if the true correlation in the population is 0. In this case that probability is .029, which, because it is less than .05, will lead us to reject the null hypothesis.

9.15 r^2 and the Magnitude of an Effect

Earlier in the book I referred to a class of measures that we call "effect sizes." These are very important, and we will see a number of different ones as we go along, but this

Table 9.5 Various Correlation Coefficients

		Continuous	Variable X Dichotomous	Ranked
Variable Y	Continuous	Pearson	Point Biserial	
	Dichotomous	Point Biserial	Phi	
	Ranked			Spearman

Figure 9.13   SPSS analysis of the relationship between pace of life and heart disease

Descriptive Statistics			
	Mean	Std. Deviation	N
Pace	22.8422	3.01462	36
Heart	19.8056	5.21437	36

Correlations		Pace	Heart
Pace	Pearson Correlations	1.000	.365*
	Sig. (2-tailed)		.029
	N	36.000	36
Heart	Pearson Correlation	.365*	1.000
	Sig. (2-tailed)	.029	
	N	36	36.000

*Correlation is significant at the 0.05 level (2-tailed).

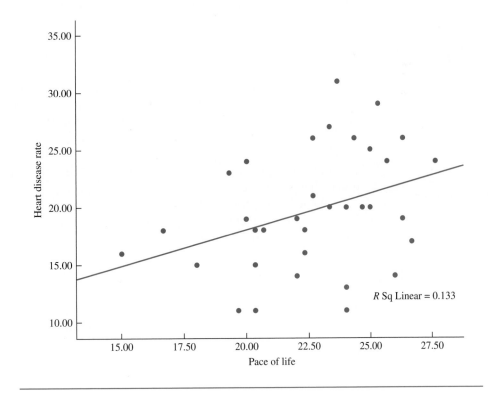

is the place to introduce one of the better known measures. This measure is simply the square of the correlation coefficient, and I will have more to say about that measure in the next chapter.

Suppose that we looked at the incidence of heart disease across our 36 cities. If we calculated the variation of that variable, we would have a measure of how different the cities are in the incidence of heart disease. (Notice that I used the wishy-washy word "variation" instead of a more precise word like "variance." The measure that we will use will be very similar to the variance, but is not quite there, which is why I use a less precise term.) Now suppose that I devised some way, to be discussed in the next chapter, to calculate predicted heart disease scores based only on the city's score on the Pace variable. High heart disease predictions will tend to go with high Pace scores and vice versa. Now I calculated my measure of the variation in those *predicted* scores. The variation would be smaller than it was before because I have taken Pace into account, but there would still be variation remaining because of the differences in heart disease that Pace would not predict. The variation remaining is error variation—variation that cannot be explained by the city's Pace score. But suppose that the remaining variation is quite small. You could say, "Notice that after you take into account differences from one city to another in terms of Pace, there really isn't a lot of error variance left in the variation of heart disease!" That's a good thing. The ideal case, which we will never reach in practice, is for one variable (Pace) to explain almost all of the variation in heart disease.

If we take the correlation coefficient that we have calculated and square it, the result can be interpreted as the percentage of variation in heart disease that we could predict just knowing the pace of life in that city. In other words, r^2 is the percentage of explained variation. In our case, $r = .365$, and $r^2 = .133$. That can be interpreted to mean that about 13% of the differences among cities in terms of the incidence of heart disease can be explained by their differences in the pace of life they exhibit. Now you may think that 13% sounds pretty small, but in practice for many of the variables we study, 13% is a respectable amount. We would love to be able to explain 75% of the variation in some variable, but in practice with meaningful variables that doesn't happen very often.

We will come back to r^2 in the next chapter, but for now just make a note that it represents the percentage of explainable variation. As such, it gives us at least some idea how "important" or "influential" out predictor is.

9.16 Seeing Statistics

A number of applets will help you to see the important concepts that were developed in this chapter. These are found on the book's website at

https://www.uvm.edu/~dhowell/fundamentals9/SeeingStatisticsApplets/ Applets.html

The first applet allows you to enter individual data points by clicking with your mouse and then displays the resulting correlation. The following graphic shows sample output.

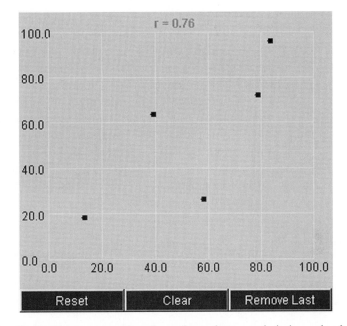

Start the Seeing Statistics applets from the website, and click on the first applet in Chapter 9, which is labeled Correlation Points. Now add points to the plot to see what happens to the correlation. Try to produce data with very low, low, medium, and high correlations, and then reverse those to produce negative correlations.

The next applet draws a scatterplot of a set of data and allows you to examine the correlation as you remove or replace a data point. This is illustrated in the following printout, using the data on alcohol and tobacco consumption in Great Britain that we saw in Table 9.3.

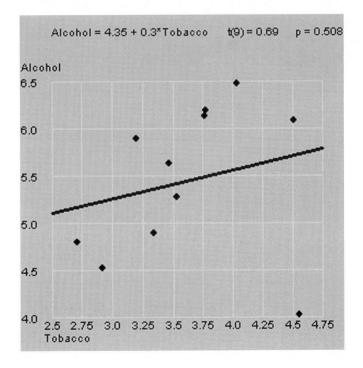

The purpose of the data in Table 9.3 was to illustrate the dramatic influence that a single data point can have. If you click on the point for Northern Ireland, in the lower right, you will remove that point from the calculation, and will see a dramatic change in the correlation coefficient. Next, try clicking on other points to see what effect they have.

Another way to illustrate the relationship between a scatterplot and a correlation is shown in the applet named Correlation Picture. This applet allows you to move a slider to vary the correlation coefficient and then see associated changes in the scatterplot. Two scatterplots are shown, one with the regression line (to be discussed in Chapter 10) superimposed. The line often makes it easier to see the relationship between the variables, especially for low correlation. An example of the output of the applet follows.

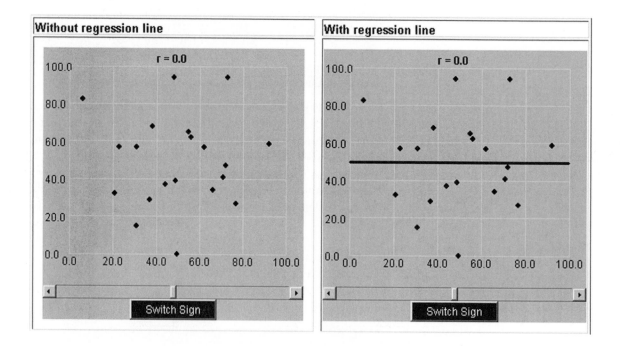

Practice moving the slider to vary the correlation coefficient. Then click on the button labeled "Switch Sign" to see the same degree of correlation in a negative relationship.

One of the important points made in this chapter was the influence of the range of values on the correlation coefficient. The applet labeled RangeRestrict allows you to move sliders to restrict the range of either variable and then see the resulting effect on the correlation coefficient. This is illustrated below.

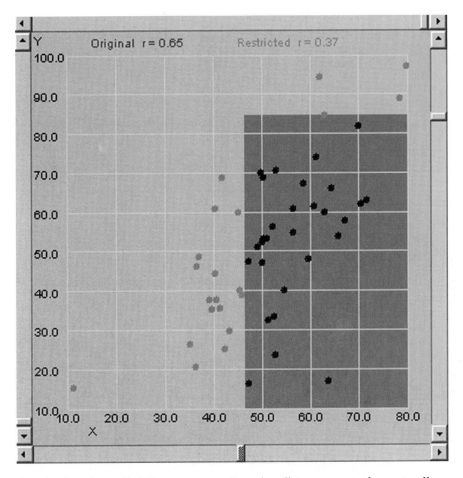

One final applet, called Heterogeneous Samples, illustrates some dramatic effects that you can see with heterogeneous subsamples of data. An illustration follows.

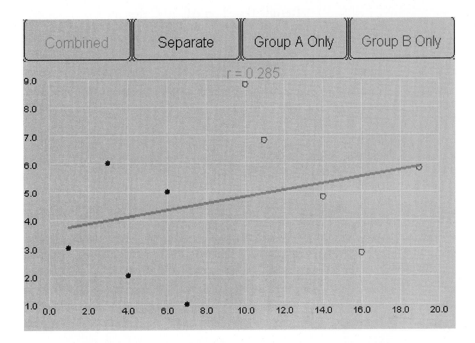

By clicking on the buttons at the top of the display, you can plot the data for all cases combined, for the combined data but with separate regression lines, or for each group alone. The applets on the website also allow you to investigate the data plotted in Figure 9.7 in similar ways.

9.17 A Review: Does Rated Course Quality Relate to Expected Grade?

We have used an example in this chapter and in Chapter 8 of the relationship between course evaluations and students' anticipated grades, but we never actually saw data or the calculation of the correlation. The following set of observations represents actual data on 50 courses taken from a large data set on the evaluation of several hundred courses. (I have shown only the first 15 cases on two variables to save space, but the statistics given below the data were calculated for all 50 cases.) The raw data are available at

 http://www.uvm.edu/~dhowell/fundamentals9/DataFiles/albatros.dat

All six variables appear there, in the order Overall, Teach, Exam, Knowledge, Grade, and Enroll.

Expected Grade (X)	Overall Quality (Y)	Expected Grade (X)	Overall Quality (Y)
3.5	3.4	3.0	3.8
3.2	2.9	3.1	3.4
2.8	2.6	3.0	2.8
3.3	3.8	3.3	2.9
3.2	3.0	3.2	4.1
3.2	2.5	3.4	2.7
3.6	3.9	3.7	3.9
4.0	4.3		

Results Based on All 50 Cases

$$\Sigma X = 174.3$$

$$\Sigma X^2 = 613.65$$

$$\Sigma Y = 177.5$$

$$\Sigma Y^2 = 648.57$$

$$\Sigma XY = 621.94$$

Our first step is to calculate the mean and the standard deviation of each variable, as follows:

$$\overline{X} = \frac{174.3}{50} = 3.486$$

$$s_X = \sqrt{\frac{613.65 - \frac{174.3^2}{50}}{49}} = 0.3511$$

$$\overline{Y} = \frac{177.5}{50} = 3.550$$

$$s_Y = \sqrt{\frac{648.57 - \dfrac{177.5^2}{50}}{49}} = 0.6135$$

The covariance is given by

$$\mathrm{cov}_{XY} = \frac{621.94 - \dfrac{(174.3)(177.5)}{50}}{49} = 0.0648$$

Finally, the correlation is given by

$$r = \frac{\mathrm{cov}_{XY}}{s_X s_Y} = \frac{0.0648}{(0.3511)(0.6135)} = .3008$$

This is a moderate correlation, one that would lend support to the proposition that courses that have higher mean grades also have higher mean ratings. As we saw in Section 9.9, this correlation is significant. You should realize that this correlation does not necessarily mean higher grades cause higher ratings. It is just as plausible that more advanced courses are rated more highly, and it is often in these courses that students do their best work.

Additional Examples

I have pulled together a few additional examples and useful material at https://www.uvm.edu/~dhowell/StatPages/More_Stuff/CorrReg.html

These are more complex examples than we have seen to date, involving several different statistical procedures for each data set. However, you can get a good idea of how correlation is used in practice by looking at these examples, and you can just ignore the other material that you don't recognize. Keep in mind that even with the simple correlational material, there may be more advanced ways of dealing with data that we have not covered here, but what we have will answer a lot of questions.

Writing up the Results of a Correlational Study

If you were asked to write up the study on course evaluations concisely but accurately, how would you do it? Presumably you would want to say something about the research hypothesis that you were testing, the way you collected your data, the statistical results that followed, and the conclusions you would draw. The two paragraphs that follow are an abbreviated form of such a report. A regular report would include a review of the background literature and considerably more information on data collection. It would also include an extensive discussion of the results and speculate on future research.

Abbreviated Report

It is often thought by course instructors that the way in which students evaluate a course will be related, in part, to the grades that are given in that course. In an attempt to test this hypothesis we collected data on 50 courses in a large state university located in the Northeast, asking students to rate the overall quality of the course (on a five-point scale) and report their anticipated grade (A = 4, B = 3, etc.) in that course. For each of the 50 courses we calculated the overall mean rating and the mean anticipated grade. Those means were the observations used in the analysis.

A Pearson correlation between mean rating and mean anticipated grade produced a correlation of $r = .30$, and this correlation, though small, was significant at $\alpha = .05$, $p = .034$). From this result we can conclude that course ratings do vary with anticipated grades, with courses giving higher grades having higher overall ratings. The interpretation of this effect is unclear. It may be that students who expect to receive good grades have a tendency to "reward" their instructors with higher ratings. But it is equally likely that students learn more in better courses and rate those courses accordingly.

9.18   Summary

In this chapter we dealt with the correlation coefficient as a measure of the relationship between two variables. We began by seeing three distinctly different scatterplots of data. All of the relationships were linear, meaning the relationship did not change in form as we increased the value of either variable. The chapter briefly introduced the concept of the covariance, pointing out that it increases in absolute value as the relationship increases. We then used the covariance and the two standard deviations to define the correlation coefficient, commonly referred to as the Pearson product-moment correlation. We also looked at the correlation between ranked data, which is called the Spearman rank correlation, and later at the point biserial correlation and phi, which are Pearson correlations based on cases in which one or both variables are dichotomies.

We saw that several things can affect the magnitude of the correlation aside from the true underlying relationship between the two variables. One of these is the restriction of the range of one or both variables, another is the use of a sample that combines two heterogeneous samples, and a third is the inclusion of outliers. There was also an important discussion of correlation and causation, and it would be well to go back and review Utts' list of explanations for relationships.

Finally, we examined a test of whether a sample correlation is large enough to imply a true relationship in the population. For this, you can either use tables that are present in the back of the book or take a probability value from the computer printout. We will later see another way of testing this relationship using what is called the t distribution. That is simply what the computer is doing when it gives you a probability.

Key Terms

Correlation, *184*

Correlation coefficient, *184*

Pearson product-moment correlation coefficient (r), *184*

Scatterplot (scatter diagram, scattergram), *184*

Predictor variable, *185*

Criterion variable, *185*

Regression lines, *186*

Negative relationship, *187*

Linear relationship, *191*

Curvilinear relationship, *191*

Covariance, *191*

Pearson product-moment correlation coefficient (r), *192*

Spearman's correlation coefficient for ranked data (r_S), *195*

Monotonic relationship, *196*

Range restrictions, *196*

Heterogeneous subsamples, *198*

Population correlation coefficient rho (ρ), *204*

Intercorrelation matrix, *208*

Point biserial correlation (r_{pb}), *211*

Dichotomous variables, *211*

Phi (ϕ), *211*

9.19 A Quick Review

A. In a scatterplot, which variable is plotted on the abscissa (X axis)?
Ans: If there is an obvious independent variable, that goes there. If not, the choice is pretty much arbitrary.

B. What does $\hat{Y}$ represent?
Ans: The predicted value of Y.

C. The regression line should be interpreted as
Ans: the line that gives the best prediction of Y for a given value of X.

D. A correlation of $-.81$ is significantly lower than a correlation of $+.81$. (T or F)
Ans: False. The sign only tells us the direction of the relationship.

E. Creating scatterplots with the points representing means rather than individual observations is very likely to give you a plot where the line _____.
Ans: is a better fit to the points

F. The covariance, by itself, is not a satisfactory statistic for presenting the degree of relationship between variables because _____.
Ans: it varies with the variance of the underlying variables, as well as with the degree of relationship

G. Spearman's correlation coefficient is simply _____ applied to ranks.
Ans: a Pearson correlation coefficient

H. List three things that can affect the relationship between two variables.
Ans: Range restrictions, heterogeneous subsamples, and nonlinear relationships.

I. Give three explanations why A might be related to B even though the relationship is not causal.

Ans: Both A and B change with time. A and B are both caused by a third, common variable. We may be looking at the relationship backward.

J. We would use a two-tailed test of r if _____.

Ans: we wanted to reject the null if the sample correlation was too large or too negative

K. A point biserial correlation applies to data where _____.

Ans: one variable is a dichotomy and the other is continuous

9.20 Exercises

9.1 In Sub-Saharan Africa, more than half of mothers lose at least one child before the child's first birthday. Below are data on 36 countries in the region, giving country, infant mortality, per capita income (in U.S. dollars), percentage of births to mothers under 20, percentage of births to mothers over 40, percentage of births less than two years apart, percentage of married women using contraception, and percentage of women with unmet family planning need. (http://www.guttmacher.org/pubs/ib_2-02.html) Available at the book's website as SubSaharanInfMort.dat. (Notice the effect of outliers.)

Country	InfMort	Income	% mom < 20	% mom > 40	<2 yrs apart	Using contraception	Need family planning
Benin Rep	104	933	16	5	17	3	26
Burkina Faso	109	965	17	5	17	5	26
Cameroon	80	1,573	21	4	25	7	20
Central African Rep	102	1,166	22	5	26	3	16
Chad Rep	110	850	21	3	24	1	missing
Côte d'Ivoire	91	1,654	21	6	16	4	28
Eritrea	76	880	15	7	26	4	28
Ethiopia	113	628	14	6	20	6	23
Gabon	61	6,024	22	4	22	12	28
Ghana	61	1,881	15	5	13	13	23
Guinea	107	1,934	22	5	17	4	24
Kenya	71	1,022	18	3	23	32	24
Madagascar	99	799	21	5	31	10	26
Malawi	113	586	21	6	17	26	30
Mali	134	753	21	4	26	5	26
Mozambique	147	861	24	6	19	5	7
Namibia	62	5,468	15	7	22	26	22
Niger	136	753	23	5	25	5	17
Nigeria	71	853	17	5	27	9	18
Rwanda	90	885	9	7	21	13	36
Senegal	69	1,419	14	7	18	8	35
Tanzania	108	501	19	5	17	17	22
Togo	80	1,410	13	6	14	7	32
Uganda	86	650	23	4	28	8	35
Zambia	108	756	30	4	19	14	27
Zimbabwe	60	2,876	32	4	12	50	13

a) Make a scatter diagram of InfMort and income.
b) Draw (by eye) the line that appears to best fit the data.
c) What effect do you suppose that the outliers have on income?

9.2 Calculate the correlations among all numeric variables in Exercise 9.1 using SPSS, or R. (In R read in the data as a data.frame (e.g., theData) and then use (cor(theData). You don't need to attach theData. You can also use plot(theData).)

9.3 Using one of the online calculators, how large a correlation would you need for the relationships shown in Exercise 9.2 to be significant? (This will involve a bit of trial and error.)

9.4 What are the strongest single predictors of infant mortality in Exercise 9.2?

9.5 What can we conclude from the data on infant mortality?

9.6 In Exercise 9.1 the percentage of mothers over 40 does not appear to be important, and yet it is a risk factor in other societies. Why do you think that this might be?

9.7 Two predictors of infant mortality seem to be significant. If you could find a way to use both of them as predictors simultaneously, what do you think you would find?

9.8 From the previous exercises, do you think that we are able to conclude that low income causes infant mortality?

9.9 Infant mortality is a very serious problem to society. Why would psychologists be interested in this problem any more than people in other professions?

9.10 Down syndrome is another problem that psychologists deal with. It has been proposed that mothers who give birth at older ages are more likely to have a child with Down syndrome. Plot the data below relating age to incidence. The data were taken from Geyer (1991).

Age	17.5	18.5	19.5	20.5	21.5	22.5	23.5	24.5	25.5
Births	13555	13675	18752	22005	23796	24667	24807	23986	22860
Down	16	15	16	22	16	12	17	22	15

Age	26.5	27.5	28.5	29.5	30.5	31.5	32.5	33.5	34.5
Births	21450	19202	17450	15685	13954	11987	10983	9825	8483
Down	15	27	14	9	12	12	18	13	11

Age	35.5	36.5	37.5	38.5	39.5	40.5	41.5	42.5	43.5
Births	7448	6628	5780	4834	3961	2952	2276	1589	1018
Downs	23	13	17	15	30	31	33	20	16

Age	44.5	45.5	46.5
Births	596	327	249
Downs	22	11	7

Plot a scatter diagram for the percentage of Down[8] syndrome cases (Down / Births) as a function of age.

9.11 Use the code given earlier for R to make this plot. The command would be plot(percent ~ age)

9.12 Why would you not feel comfortable computing a Pearson correlation on the data in Exercise 9.10?

9.13 One way to get around the problem you see in Exercise 9.12 would be to convert the incidence of Down syndrome to ranked data. Replot the data using ranked incidence and calculate the correlation. Is this a Spearman's correlation?

---

[8]This is the preferred U.S. spelling. Most of the world gives John Down credit by making it possessive.

9.14 Do Exercise 9.13 using *R*. You can rank the data with **ranked.data = rank(percent)**.

9.15 In the study by Katz, et al., referred to previously, in which subjects answered questions about passages they had not read, the question arises as to whether there is a relationship between how the students performed on this test and how they had performed on the SAT-Verbal when they applied to college. Why is this a relevant question?

9.16 The data relevant to Exercise 9.15 are the test scores and SAT-V scores for the 28 people in the group that did not read the passage. These data are

Score	58	48	48	41	34	43	38	53	41	60	55	44	43	49
SAT-V	590	590	580	490	550	580	550	700	560	690	800	600	650	580
Score	47	33	47	40	46	53	40	45	39	47	50	53	46	53
SAT-V	660	590	600	540	610	580	620	600	560	560	570	630	510	620

Make a scatterplot of these data and draw by eye the best-fitting straight line through the points.

9.17 Compute the correlation coefficient for the data in Exercise 9.16. Is this correlation significant, and what does it mean to say that it is (or is not) significant?

9.18 Interpret the results from Exercises 9.12–9.15.

9.19 The correlation in the Katz et al. study between Score and SAT-V for the 17 subjects in the group that did read the passage was .68. This correlation is not significantly different from the correlation you computed in Exercise 9.15, although it is significantly different from 0.00. What does it mean to say that the two correlations are not significantly different from each other?

9.20 Expand on Exercise 9.19 to interpret the conclusion that the correlations were not significantly different.

9.21 Do the results of the Katz et al. study fit with your expectations, and why?

9.22 Plot and calculate the correlation for the relationship between ADDSC and GPA for the data in Appendix D. Is this relationship significant? You can use both *R* and SPSS to do this.

9.23 Assume that a set of data contains a curvilinear relationship between *X* and *Y* (the best-fitting line is slightly curved). Would it ever be appropriate to calculate *r* on these data?

9.24 Several times in this chapter I referred to the fact that a correlation based on a small sample might not be reliable.

a) What does "reliable" mean in this context?
b) Why might a correlation based on a small sample not be reliable?

9.25 What reasons might explain the finding that the amount of money that a country spends on health care is not correlated with life expectancy?

9.26 Considering the data relating height to weight in Figure 9.8, what effect would systematic reporting biases from males and females have on our conclusions?

9.27 Draw a figure using a small number of data points to illustrate the argument that you could have a negative relationship between weight and height within each gender and yet still have a positive relationship for the combined data.

9.28 Sketch a rough diagram to illustrate the point made in the section on heterogeneous subsamples about the relationship between cholesterol consumption and cardiovascular disease for males and females.

9.29 The chapter referred to a study by Wong that showed that the incidence of heart disease varied as a function of solar radiation. What does this have to say about any causal relationship we might infer between the consumption of red wine and a lower incidence of heart disease?

9.30 David Lane at Rice University has an interesting example of a study involving correlation. This can be found at

 http://www.ruf.rice.edu/~lane/case_studies/physical_strength/index.html

Work through his example and draw your own conclusions from the data. (For now, ignore the material on regression.)

9.31 One of the examples in this chapter dealt with the relationship between vitamin D and cancer. Do a simple Internet search to find additional data on that question.

9.32 Use *R*, SPSS, or another program to reproduce the results shown in Figure 9.5. You can modify the *R* code given in Section 9.4.

9.33 Use one of the sources given in the text (*R* or http://vassarstats.net/rho.html) to calculate a confidence interval on the correlation between Expenditures for education and SATcombined from Figure 9.10. Interpret this interval.

9.34 Modify the code in the chapter's Web page by making y <− rnorm(50, 0, 1) + .3*x and plotting the result. The mean correlation should be about 28. Now change the sample size to N = 10 and repeat the plot. What does that suggest to you about the faith you can put in correlations from very small samples?

## CHAPTER 10

Regression

Correlation and regression go together so closely that they are often mentioned in the same breath. In this chapter we will look at how they differ and at what regression has to tell us that correlation does not. We will see how to obtain the equation for a regression line, which is the line that best fits a scatterplot of the data, and we will learn how to ask how well that line fits. We will then take up hypothesis testing with regression and look at the hypotheses that we are testing. We generally speak of regression as a way to predict what someone's score on a dependent variable will be. However, taken literally, "prediction" generally is not our purpose. Our purpose is most often one of understanding the relationship between variables that go into that prediction. Finally, we will use SPSS and R to produce a complete analysis of our data.

If you think of all the people you know, you are aware that there are individual differences in people's mental health. Some are cheerful and outgoing, some are depressed and withdrawn, some are aggressive and even unpleasant, and some have trouble sleeping and spend their nights worrying about things over which they have no control. How do we predict what any specific individual will be like?

This question is really too big and too general, so let's narrow it down. Suppose we take a standard checklist and ask a large number of students to indicate whether they have experienced a variety of psychological symptoms in the past month. Each person's score will be a weighted sum of the reported symptoms. The higher the score, the more problems he or she has experienced; conversely, the lower the score, the better that person's state of mental health. But again, how do we predict a person's score?

CONCEPTS THAT YOU WILL NEED TO REMEMBER FROM PREVIOUS CHAPTERS

Independent variable:	The variable you manipulate or are studying
Dependent variable:	The variable that you are measuring—the data
Scatterplot:	A graphic in which the paired data points are plotted in two-dimensional space
Correlation coefficient:	A measure of the relationship between variables
Regression line:	The straight line that best fits the points in a scatterplot
Standard error:	The standard deviation of the sampling distribution of a statistic
Standardization:	Converting raw scores to z scores, which have a mean ($\overline{X}$) of 0 and a standard deviation (s) of 1

If all that we have is a set of symptom scores, the best prediction we can make for any one individual is the group's mean. Since I have never met you and don't know anything about you, I will be less in error, *on average,* if I predict the sample mean ($\overline{X}$) than if I predict any other value. Obviously I won't always be right, but it's the best I can do.

But let's be a little more specific and assume that I know whether you are male or female. Here I have another variable I can use in making my prediction. In other words, I can use one variable to help me predict another. In this case, what prediction do you think I should make? I hope you will say that I should use the mean of males ($\overline{X}_M$) to make a prediction about a male and the mean of females ($\overline{X}_F$) to make a prediction about a female. On the average, I will do better than if I just use the overall mean. Notice that my prediction is *conditional* on gender. My prediction would be of the form, "Given that you are female, I would predict that ..." Notice that this is the same word "conditional" that we used when discussing conditional probabilities.

Now let's go one more step and instead of using a dichotomous variable, gender, we will use a continuous variable, stress. We know that psychological health varies with stress, in that people who experience a great deal of stress tend to have more symptoms than those who do not. Therefore, we can use people's stress levels to refine our prediction of symptoms. The process is more complicated and sophisticated than using a dichotomous variable such as gender, but the underlying idea is similar. We want to write an equation that explains how differences in one variable relate to differences in another and that allows us to predict a person's score on one variable from knowledge of that person's score on another variable. When we are interested in deriving an equation for predicting one variable from another, we are dealing with **regression**, the topic of this chapter. As I indicated above, I would probably not be very interested in predicting your actual symptom score. Instead, what really interests me is to see how stress relates to symptoms. Is the relationship strong? Is it linear? Is it the same for men and women?

Just as we did in our discussion of correlation, we will restrict our coverage of regression to those cases in which the best-fitting line through the scatter diagram is a straight line, or nearly so. This means that we will deal only with linear regression. This restriction is not as serious as you might expect because a surprisingly high percentage of sets of data turn out to be basically linear. Even in those cases in which the relationship is curvilinear (i.e., where the best-fitting line is a curve), a straight line often will provide a very good approximation, especially if we eliminate the extremes of the distribution of one or both of the variables.

10.1 The Relationship Between Stress and Health

Wagner, Compas, and Howell (1988) investigated the relationship between stress and mental health in first-year college students. Using a scale developed to measure the frequency, perceived importance, and desirability of recent life events, they created a measure of negative life events weighted by the reported frequency of each event and the respondent's subjective estimate of its impact. In other words, more weight was given to those events that occurred frequently and/or that the student felt had an important impact. This served as the measure of the subject's perceived social and environmental stress. The researchers also asked students to complete the Hopkins Symptom Checklist, assessing the presence or absence of 57 psychological symptoms. The stem-and-leaf displays and boxplots for the measures of stress and symptoms are shown in Table 10.1.

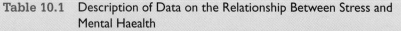

Table 10.1 Description of Data on the Relationship Between Stress and Mental Haealth

Stem-and-Leaf for Stress		Stem-and-Leaf for Symptoms	
0*	| 1123334	5.	| 8
0.	| 5567788899999	6*	| 112234
1*	| 011222233333444	6.	| 55668
1.	| 555555566667778889	7*	| 00012334444
2*	| 00000112222233333444	7.	| 57788899
2.	| 56777899	8*	| 00011122233344
3*	| 0013334444	8.	| 5666677888899
3.	| 66778889	9*	| 0111223344
4*	| 334	9.	| 556679999
4.	| 5555	10*	| 0001112224
		10.	| 567799
HI	| 58, 74	11*	| 112
		11.	| 78
Code: 2.| 5 = 25		12*	| 11
		12.	| 57
		13*	| 1
		HI	| 135, 135, 147, 186

Code: 5.\| 8 = 58

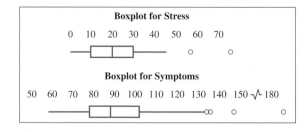

Before we consider the relationship between these variables, we need to examine the variables individually. The stem-and-leaf displays for both variables show that the distributions are unimodal but slightly positively skewed. Except for a few extreme values, there is nothing about either variable that should disturb us, such as extreme skewness or bimodality. Note that there is a fair amount of variability in each variable. This variability is important, because if we want to show that different stress scores are associated with differences in symptoms, we need to have differences to explain in the first place.

The boxplots in Table 10.1 reveal the presence of outliers on both variables. (The double circles indicate the presence of two overlapping data points.) The existence of outliers should alert us to *potential* problems that these scores may cause. The first thing we could do is to check the data to see whether these few subjects were responding in unreasonable ways; for example, do they report the occurrence of all sorts of unlikely events or symptoms, making us question the legitimacy of their responses? (Difficult as it may be to believe, some subjects have been known to treat psychological experiments with something less than the respect and reverence that psychologists think that they deserve.) The second thing to check is whether the same subject produced outlying data points on both variables. That would suggest that the subject's data, although legitimate, might have a disproportionate influence on the resulting correlations. (We saw this with the data on Northern Ireland in the last chapter.) The third thing to do is to make a scatterplot of the data, again looking for the undue influence of particular extreme data points. (Such a scatterplot will appear shortly in Figure 10.1.) Finally, we can run our analyses including and excluding extreme points to see what differences appear in the results. If you carry out each of these four steps on the data, you will find nothing to suggest that the outliers we have identified here influenced the resulting correlation or regression equation in any important way. These steps are important precursors to any good analysis, if only because they give us greater faith in our final results.

Preliminary steps
1. Use stem-and-leaf displays and boxplot to examine the data for unusual features.
2. Check to see that individual participants do not produce extreme scores on both variables in a way that will unduly influence the outcome.
3. Produce a scatterplot of the data.
4. Run the analyses below with, and without, questionable data to see if there is a difference in the outcomes.

10.2 The Basic Data

The data are shown in Table 10.2. The full data set is available for downloading at

 https://www.uvm.edu/~dhowell/fundamentals9/DataFiles/Tab10-2.dat

From these data you can calculate the correlation coefficient (covered in Chapter 9):

$$r = \frac{cov_{xy}}{s_x s_y}$$

For our data the result would be

$$r = \frac{134.301}{(13.096)(20.266)} = .506$$

This correlation is quite substantial for real data on psychological variables such as these. Using the calculator at vassarstats.net (select Correlation and Regression and then scroll down to The Significance of an Observed Value of r), the probability of a correlation of .506 with 105 df is .000 to three decimal places. (Actually it is .00000003, which is tiny.) We can therefore reject $H_0: \rho = 0$ and conclude that there is a significant relationship between stress and symptoms. As we saw in the previous chapter, it does not tell us that stress *causes* symptoms, although that is a possibility.

Table 10.2 Data from Wagner et al. (1988)

ID	Stress	Symptoms	ID	Stress	Symptoms	ID	Stress	Symptoms
1	30	99	37	15	66			
2	27	94	38	22	85	73	37	86
3	9	80	39	14	92	74	13	83
4	20	70	40	13	74	75	12	111
5	3	100	41	37	88	76	9	72
6	15	109	42	23	62	77	20	86
7	5	62	43	22	91	78	29	101
8	10	81	44	15	99	79	13	80
9	23	74	45	43	121	80	36	111
10	34	121	46	27	96	81	33	77
11	20	100	47	21	95	82	23	84
12	17	73	48	36	101	83	22	83
13	26	88	49	38	87	84	1	65
14	16	87	50	12	79	85	3	100
15	17	73	51	1	68	86	15	92
16	15	65	52	25	102	87	13	106
17	38	89	53	20	95	88	44	70
18	16	86	54	11	78	89	11	90
19	38	186	55	74	117	90	20	91
20	15	107	56	39	96	91	28	99
21	5	58	57	24	93	92	14	118
22	18	89	58	2	61	93	7	66
23	8	74	59	3	61	94	8	77
24	33	147	60	16	80	95	9	84
25	12	82	61	45	81	96	33	101
26	22	91	62	24	79	97	4	64
27	23	93	63	12	82	98	22	88
28	45	131	64	34	112	99	7	83
29	8	88	65	43	102	100	14	105
30	45	107	66	18	94	101	24	127
31	9	63	67	18	99	102	13	78
32	45	135	68	34	75	103	30	70
33	21	74	69	29	135	104	19	109
34	16	82	70	15	81	105	34	104
35	17	71	71	6	78	106	9	86
36	31	125	72	58	102	107	27	97

Descriptive Statistics		
	Stress	Symptoms
Mean	21.467	90.701
St. dev.	13.096	20.266
Covariance	134.301	
N	107	

You should recall that when we write "$\alpha = .05$, two-tailed," we are speaking of a two-tailed significance test that places 5% of the sampling distribution of r, when the null hypothesis is true, in the rejection region. We have 105 degrees of freedom because the degrees of freedom for correlation are equal to $N - 2$, where N is the number of *pairs* of observations. In rejecting the null hypothesis we are concluding that the obtained correlation is too extreme for us to think that it came from a population of pairs of scores where the population correlation (ρ) is 0.

10.3 | The Regression Line

We have just seen that there is a significant relationship between stress and psychological symptoms. We can obtain a better idea of what this relationship is like by looking at a scatterplot of the two variables and the regression line for predicting Symptoms (Y) on the basis of Stress (X). The scatterplot is shown in Figure 10.1, where the best-fitting line for predicting Y on the basis of X has been superimposed. You will see shortly where this line came from, but notice first the way in which the predicted Symptom scores increase linearly with increases in Stress scores. Our correlation coefficient told us that such a relationship existed, but it is easier to appreciate just what it means when you see it presented graphically. Notice also that the degree of scatter of points about the regression line remains about the same as you move from low values of stress to high values, although with a correlation of approximately .50 the scatter is fairly wide. We will discuss scatter again in more detail when we consider

Figure 10.1 Scatterplot of symptoms as a function of stress

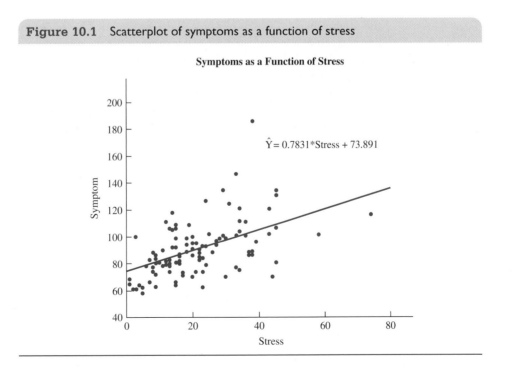

Symptoms as a Function of Stress

$\hat{Y} = 0.7831 * \text{Stress} + 73.891$

```
stress.data <- read.table("https://www.uvm.edu/~dhowell/fundamentals9/
DataFiles/Tab10-1.dat", header = TRUE)
attach(stress.data)
head(stress.data)
model1 <- lm(Symptoms ~ Stress) # "lm" represents "linear model."
summary(model1) print out the results
plot(Symptoms ~ Stress, main = "Symptoms as a Function of Stress", xlab =
   "Stress", ylab = "Symptoms")
abline(model1, col = "red")
legend(35,160, expression(hat(Y) == 0.7831*Stress + 73.891), bty = "n")
regress <- lm(Symptoms ~ Stress) # To be discussed later
summary(regress)
```

```
Call:
lm(formula = Symptoms ~ Stress)

Residuals:
   Min     1Q   Median    3Q     Max
-38.347 -13.197 -1.070 6.755 82.352

Coefficients:
            Estimate Std. Error t value  Pr(>|t|)
(Intercept) 73.8896    3.2714   22.587  < 2e-16 ***
Stress       0.7831    0.1303    6.012  2.69e-08 ***
---
Signif. codes: 0 '***' 0.001 '**' 0.01 '*' 0.05 '.' 0.1 ' ' 1

Residual standard error: 17.56 on 105 degrees of freedom
Multiple R-squared: 0.2561,   Adjusted R-squared: 0.249[1]
F-statistic: 36.14 on 1 and 105 DF, p-value: 2.692e-08
```

the assumptions on which our procedures are based. The equation for that regression line is given as a legend, and we will soon see how to compute it. The R code for this figure is shown below, although it contains material that you have not yet seen.

If you want to calculate this regression using SPSS, first load your data and then select **Analyze/Regression/Linear**. Then select your variables and click run. (It is always a good idea to click on the **Statistics** tab and request confidence intervals.) To plot the data, choose **Graphs/Legacy/Scatter/Simple**. Set the Y axis to NPI and the X axis to Year. You can pretty it up with **Titles** if you choose. However, it requires some effort to superimpose the line.

As you may remember from high school, the equation for a straight line is of the form $Y = bX + a$. (You may have used other letters in place of a and b, but these are the ones used by most statisticians.) For our purposes we will write the equation as

$$\hat{Y} = bX + a$$

---

[1]You may notice that R, and other software, includes the "Adjusted R-squared." I am not going to discuss this, and virtually no one ever makes reference to it in their publications. The adjustment is minor anyway, and is controversial.

where

$\hat{Y}$ = the *predicted* value of Y—pronounced "y-hat"

b = the **slope** of the regression line (the amount of difference in Y associated with a one-unit difference in X)

a = the **intercept** (the predicted value of Y when X = 0)

X is simply the value of the predictor variable, in this case, Stress. Our task will be to solve for those values of a and b that will produce the best-fitting linear function. In other words, we want to use our existing data to solve for the values of a and b such that the line (the values of $\hat{Y}$ for different values of X) will come as close as possible to the actual obtained values of Y.

Why, you may ask, did I use the symbol $\hat{Y}$, rather than Y, in my equation when I defined the equation for a straight line in terms of Y? The reason for using $\hat{Y}$ is to indicate that the values we are searching for are *predicted* values. The symbol Y represents, in this case, the actual *obtained* values for Symptoms. These are the symptom scores that our 107 different subjects reported. What we are looking for are predicted values ($\hat{Y}$) that come as close as possible to the Y values actually obtained, hence the different symbol.

Having said that we are looking for the best-fitting line, we have to define what we mean by "best." A logical way would be in terms of **errors of prediction**, that is, in terms of the $(Y - \hat{Y})$ deviations. Since $\hat{Y}$ is the value of the symptom variable that our equation would predict for a given level of stress, and Y is a value that we actually obtained, $(Y - \hat{Y})$ is an error of prediction, usually called the **residual**. We want to find the line (the set of $\hat{Y}$s) that minimizes such errors. We cannot just minimize the *sum* of the errors, however, because for any line that goes through the point $(\overline{X}, \overline{Y})$ that sum will be zero. Instead, we will look for the line that minimizes the sum of the *squared* errors, that is, that minimizes $\Sigma(Y - \hat{Y})^2$. (I said much the same thing in Chapter 5 when I discussed the variance. There I was discussing deviations from the mean, and here I am discussing deviations from the regression line—sort of a floating or changing mean. These two concepts—errors of prediction and variance—have much in common.) The fact that we are minimizing the squares of the residual gives our approach its name—"**least squares regression**."

It is not difficult to derive the equations for the optimal values for a and b, but I will not do so here. As long as you keep in mind that they are derived in such a way as to minimize squared errors in predicting Y, it is sufficient to state simply

$$b = \frac{cov_{xy}}{s_x^2}$$

and

$$a = \overline{Y} - b\overline{X} = \frac{\Sigma Y - b\Sigma X}{N}$$

You should note that the equation for *a* includes the value of *b*, so you need to solve for *b* first.

If we apply these equations (using the covariance and the variance) from Table 10.2, we obtain

$$b = \frac{cov_{xy}}{s_x^2} = \frac{134.301}{13.096^2} = \frac{134.301}{171.505} = 0.7831$$

and

$$a = \hat{Y} - b\overline{X} = 90.701 - (0.7831)(21.467) = 73.891$$

We can now write

$$\hat{Y} = 0.7831X + 73.891$$

This equation is our **regression equation**, and the values of *a* and *b* are called the **regression coefficients**. The interpretation of this equation is straightforward. Consider the intercept (*a*) first. If $X = 0$ (i.e., if the participant reports no stressful events in the past month), the predicted value of Y (Symptoms) is 73.891, quite a low score on the Hopkins Symptom Checklist. In other words, the intercept is the predicted level of symptoms when the predictor (Stress) is 0.0. Next, consider the slope (*b*). You may know that a slope is often referred to as the *rate of change*. In this example, $b = 0.7831$. This means that for every 1-point difference in Stress, we predict a 0.7831 point difference in Symptoms. This is the rate at which predicted Symptom scores change with changes in Stress scores. Most people think of the slope as just a numerical constant in a mathematical equation, but it really makes more sense to think of it as how much different you expect Y to be for a one-unit difference in X.

I have just covered a great deal of information. That is a lot to take in, so let's look at another example before we move on. We will take data from an interesting study by Trzesniewski, Donnellan, and Robins (2008). (See also Trzesniewski and Donnellan (2009).) They were testing an argument put forth by Twenge (2006), who "characterized Americans born in the 1970s, 1980s, and 1990s as 'Generation Me,' a label selected to capture their purported tendency to be more egotistical, entitled, and overconfident than previous generations." (If you were born during those decades, I'll bet you are thrilled with that characterization!) Trzesniewski et al. obtained data on the Narcissistic Personality Index (NPI) from eight different years. (A high score represents a more narcissistic individual.) These are mean scores of very large samples for each year. The data follow:

Year	1982	1996	2002	2003	2004	2005	2006	2007
NPI	0.39	.038	0.37	0.38	0.38	0.38	0.38	0.39

A scatterplot of these results is shown on the next page, and it certainly does not look as if narcissism is increasing, as Twenge believed.

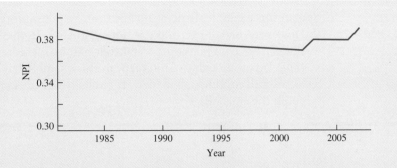

We need several sample statistics for our calculations, and they are shown in the following table, where year is represented as X and narcissism is represented as Y.

$\overline{X}$	s_x	$\overline{Y}$	s_x	cov_{XY}	N
1999.375	9.680	0.381	0.006	−0.018	8

The correlation is the covariance of X and Y divided by the standard deviations of the two variables.

$$r = \frac{cov_{XY}}{s_X s_Y} = \frac{-0.018}{(9.680)(0.006)} = \frac{-0.018}{0.058} = -.29$$

We have $N - 2 = 6$ degrees of freedom, and from Appendix D.2 or the vassarstats.net website, we find that we would need a correlation greater than ±.707 to be significant at the .05 level (i.e., at $\alpha = .05$). So we cannot reject the null hypothesis that the correlation in the population (β) is 0.00. (Keep in mind, however, that we had a very small sample.)

For the regression line we have

$$b = \frac{cov_{xy}}{s_x^2} = \frac{-0.018}{9.680^2} = \frac{-0.018}{93.702} = -0.00019$$

$$a = \overline{Y} - b\overline{X} = 0.381 - (-.00019)(1999.375) = 0.758$$

Therefore the regression line would be

$$\hat{Y} = -0.00019X + 0.758.$$

If the correlation is not significant, then the slope of the regression line will also be nonsignificant, meaning that there is no significant change in predicted Narcissism as a function of the year in which it was measured. Kids aren't getting more narcissistic, regardless of what society says! (If the relationship had been statistically significant we would be led to conclude that Narcissism scores actually decline by 0.00019 units for every one unit increase in Year of testing. This implies that at the time of the birth of Christ (the year 0) the mean NPI score would have been 0.758. I am being facetious here, but for a reason. An X value of 0 is often something that cannot be expected to occur in a reasonable setting. When X = 0 is very far from the rest of the X values, as it is in this example, little or no faith can be put on interpreting the intercept.) However, the relationship was not significant, so the best that we can say is that we have no reason to doubt that narcissism scores are not changing with time. (Even though the intercept in this example has no practical meaning for us, we still need to calculate it. It basically controls how high, or low, on the graph the line falls.)

What if we standardized the data?

Now we will return to the data on Symptoms and Stress. I hope you recall from Chapter 6 that if we convert each variable separately to a standard score (called a z score) we will have *standardized* data with a mean of 0 and a standard deviation of 1. Except for the change in mean and standard deviation, the data will be unaffected. Although we rarely work with standardized data, it is worth considering what b would represent if the data for each variable were standardized separately. In that case a difference of one unit in X or Y would represent a difference of one standard deviation in that variable. Thus if the slope were 0.75 for *standardized* data, we would be able to say that an increase of one standard deviation in X will be reflected in an increase of three-quarters of a standard deviation in Y. When speaking of the slope coefficient for standardized data, we often refer to the **standardized regression coefficient** as β (beta) to differentiate it from the coefficient for nonstandardized data (b). Fortunately we do not have to do any additional calculations, such as converting each data point to a z score, because we have other ways of knowing what would happen if we did standardize.

The interesting thing about the standardized slope (β) is that *when we have one predictor variable* it is equivalent to r, the correlation coefficient. (This will not be true when we come to multiple predictors in the next chapter.) Therefore we can say that if $r = .506$, β would also equal 0.506. Here a difference of one standard deviation between two students in terms of their Stress scores would be associated with a predicted difference of about one-half a standard deviation unit in terms of Symptoms. That gives us some idea of what kind of a relationship we are speaking about. When we come to multiple regression in the next chapter, we will find other uses for β. It is important to consider the fact that β is itself a measure of the size of an effect. If β had been only 0.04, we would know that changing stress level by a full standard deviation would only change the predicted symptom level by .04 standard deviation. That certainly would not be impressive evidence for the importance of stress in relation to symptoms. However with $\beta = .506$, that same difference of one standard deviation would be associated with half a standard deviation difference in symptoms, and that strikes me as meaningful.

A word is in order here about actually plotting the regression line. To plot the line, you can simply take any two values of X (preferably at opposite ends of the scale), calculate $\hat{Y}$ for each, mark the coordinates on the figure, and connect them with a straight line. I generally use three points, just as a check for accuracy. For the data on stress and symptoms, we have

$$\hat{Y} = 0.7831X + 73.891$$

When $X = 0$,

$$\hat{Y} = 0.7831 \times 0 + 73.891 = 73.891$$

When $X = 50$,

$$\hat{Y} = 0.7831 \times 50 + 73.891 = 113.046$$

The line then passes through the points ($X = 0$, $Y = 73.891$) and ($X = 50$, $Y = 113.046$), as shown in Figure 10.1.

It is important to point out that we have constructed a line to predict symptoms from stress, not the other way around. Our line minimizes the sum of the squared deviations of predicted symptoms from actual symptoms. If we wanted to turn things around and predict stress ratings from symptoms, we could not use this line—it wasn't derived for that purpose. Instead we would have to find the line that minimizes the squared deviations of predicted stress from actual stress. The simplest way to do this is just to go back to the equations for a and b, reverse which variable is labeled X and which is labeled Y, and solve for the new values of a and b. You then can use the same formulae that we have already used.

Regression to the mean

Sir Francis Galton, in the middle of 19th century, observed an interesting phenomenon. He noted that tall parents tended to have offspring who were shorter than they were, and short parents tended to have taller offspring. (He also noted a similar pattern with many other variables.) He worked on the problem for years, but his focus was generally on inheritance of traits. He first labeled the phenomenon "reversion," and then moved to "regression," which is where the name of this chapter came from and why the symbol for a correlation coefficient is r. At the time he referred to "regression to mediocrity," but the process then became known as "**regression to the mean**," which sounds a lot nicer.

From Galton's perspective the problem, and its explanation, does not require much in the way of statistics. Suppose that you take a test on English grammar. Your score is going to consist of two components. One is going to be your true knowledge of grammar, and the other is going to be an element of luck (good or bad). Suppose that you earned a 98, which was the highest grade in the class. If you take a similar test next week, we will probably find that you will do worse. You still have the same component of true knowledge, but luck is more likely to work against you than that it will work for you. (You reached into the pile of luck and pulled out an extreme piece of luck on the first test. From what you know about probability you should be aware that you are not likely to draw very high luck components on both tests.) This is analogous to Galton's observation with heights, and he spent considerable time working out what about the components of heredity are analogous to "luck." To Galton this was not a problem concerning least squares regression; it was simply a question about heredity and fitting theory to observation.

Let's look at it another way, which does involve statistics. If you standardize the class test scores for each test session separately, you will have absolutely no effect on the correlation coefficient between them. But we know from the earlier discussion that with standardized data the slope will be equal to the correlation. However, for all but the most trivial examples, the correlation coefficient is going to be less than 1. Suppose that the correlation between two tests in .80, and your score of 98 corresponds to a z score of 2.3. Then the standardized regression coefficient is also going to be .80, and the regression line for the standardized data will be

$$\hat{Y} = .80*2.3 + 0$$

(The intercept will always be 0 for standardized data). So if you were 2.3 standard deviations above the mean on the first test, my best *prediction* for the second test is .80*2.3 = 1.84 standard deviations above the mean. But there is someone else in the class who received a very low grade, and the same kind of reasoning works for him or her in reverse—his or her score will likely be higher on the second test. This is what is meant by "regression to the mean." *Predicted* scores on the second test will be closer to the mean than on the first test. Notice now that we are not working with actual scores, but with predictions of scores. In a sense, this is the statistical side of regression to the mean.

In sports, we commonly see examples of regression to the mean. The player who wins the "Rookie of the Year" award this year, and of whom everyone has great expectations for next year, is likely to be a disappointment in year two. This is called the "sophomore slump," and it has nothing to do with the fact that the player doesn't try as hard next year or has become rusty. It is what we would reasonably expect to happen.

There is a very common tendency to think that this means that over time there will be a general trend for all variables to regress toward a common mean. Thus if my generation is expected to be shorter than our tall parents and taller than our short parents, then my children's generation is likely to be shorter than the tall people in my generation and taller than the short parents in my generation, and so on. If that were true, we would expect that in 150 years everyone will be 58 inches tall, and of course we know that such a thing won't happen. *Regression to the mean is a phenomenon of individual data points, not a phenomenon of group characteristics.* Although we have lower expectations for higher scorers, there will still be variation and the performance of many in that high-scoring group will be above their expectations. Even though you probably won't score as well on your grammar test next time, you know from experience that test grades (taken as a whole) will look pretty much like what they did this time. (Regression to the mean also works backward in time. Predict parents' heights from children's heights and you will have the same phenomenon.)

An interesting study that relates very directly to regression to the mean was conducted by Grambsch (2008). She looked at regression to the mean as explaining some of the data on gun registration and murder rates and discovered that when you control for regression to the mean the data "give no support to the hypothesis that 'shall-issue laws' have beneficial effects in reducing murder rates." "Shall-issue" laws allow more people to carry guns and have been claimed to reduce crime.

Finally, all of this relates in an important way to the concept of random assignment. Suppose that you want to become famous by improving the level of mathematical knowledge in college students. You go out and administer a test, *pull out the worst students for special tutoring*, place them back in the class and then test all the students again. You are almost certain to be able to claim improved performance from those earlier "poor" students. It may not be that students' underlying knowledge improved at all. If those people were at the bottom of the heap in part because they just happened to have really bad luck on Day 1, the random luck component will likely not be as bad for the retest, and scores will improve even if tutoring was absolutely useless. This is a very important reason why we insist on random assignment of participants to groups when possible.

10.4 | **The Accuracy of Prediction**

The fact that we can fit a regression line to a set of data does not mean that our problems are solved. On the contrary, they have just begun. The important point is not whether a straight line can be drawn through the data (you can always do that), but whether that line represents a reasonable fit to the data—in other words, whether our effort was worthwhile.

Before we discuss errors of prediction, however, it is instructive to go back to the situation in which we want to predict Y without *any* knowledge of the value of X, which we considered at the very beginning of this chapter.

The Standard Deviation as a Measure of Error

You have the data set in Table 10.2. Suppose that I asked you to predict a particular individual's level of symptoms (Y) without being told what he or she reported in terms of stress for the past month. Your best prediction in that case would be the mean Symptom score ($\overline{Y}$). You predict the mean because it is closer, on average, to all the other scores than any other prediction would be. Think how badly you would generally do if your prediction were the smallest score or the largest one. Once in a while you would be exactly right, but most of the time you would be absurdly off. With the mean you will probably be exactly right more often (because more people actually fall in the center of the distribution), and when you are wrong you likely won't be off by as much as if you had made an extreme prediction. The error associated with your prediction will be the sample standard deviation of Y (s_Y). This is true because your prediction is the mean, and s_Y deals with deviations around the mean. Examining s_Y, we know that it is defined as

$$s_Y = \sqrt{\frac{\Sigma(Y - \overline{Y})^2}{N - 1}}$$

and the variance is defined as

$$s_{\hat{Y}}^2 = \frac{\Sigma(Y - \overline{Y})^2}{N - 1}$$

The numerator is the sum of squared deviations from $\overline{Y}$ (the point you would have predicted in this particular example).

The Standard Error of Estimate

Now suppose we want to make a prediction about the level of psychological distress (as measured by symptoms) that a person is likely to experience given that we know his or her reported level of stress. Suppose that the person's X value (Stress) is 15. In this situation we know both the relevant value of X and the regression equation, and our best prediction would be $\hat{Y}$. In this case $X = 15$, and $\hat{Y} = 0.7831 \times 15 + 73.891 = 85.64$. In line with our previous measure of error (the standard deviation), the error associated with this prediction will again be a function of the deviations of Y about the predicted point; however, in this case the predicted point is $\hat{Y}$ rather than $\overline{Y}$. Specifically, a measure of error can now be defined as

$$s_{Y-\hat{Y}} = \sqrt{\frac{\Sigma(Y - \hat{Y})^2}{N - 2}}$$

and again the sum is of squared deviations about the prediction ($\hat{Y}$) divided by $N - 2$, where N is the number of pairs. The statistic $s_{Y-\hat{y}}$ is called the **standard error of estimate** and is sometimes written $s_{Y.X}$ to indicate that it is the standard deviation of Y *predicted from* X. It is the most common (though not always the best) measure of the error of prediction. Its square, $s_{Y-\hat{y}}$, is called the **residual variance**, or **error variance**.

Table 10.3 shows how to calculate the standard error of estimate directly. The raw data for the first 10 cases are given in columns 2 and 3, and the predicted values of Y (obtained from $\hat{Y} = 0.7831X + 73.891$) are given in column 4. Column 5 contains the values of $Y - \hat{Y}$ for each observation. Note that the sum of that column ($\Sigma(Y - \hat{Y})$) is 0, because the sum of the deviations about the prediction is always 0—some over-estimate and some under-estimate Y. If we square and sum the deviations we obtain $\Sigma(Y - \hat{Y})^2 = 32,386.048$. From this sum we can calculate

$$s_{Y-\hat{Y}} = \sqrt{\frac{\Sigma(Y - \hat{Y})^2}{N - 2}} = \sqrt{\frac{32,386.048}{105}} = \sqrt{308.439} = 17.562$$

Finding the standard error this way is hardly a lot of fun, and I don't recommend that you do so. I present it because it makes clear what the term represents. Fortunately, a much simpler procedure exists that not only represents a way of calculating the standard error of estimate but also leads directly to even more important matters. But don't forget the formula we just used, because it best defines what it is we are measuring.

Table 10.3 First 10 Cases from Data of Wagner et al. (1988), Including $\hat{Y}$ and Residuals

Subject	Stress(X)	Symptoms (Y)	$\hat{Y}$	$(Y-\hat{Y})$
1	30	99	97.383	1.617
2	27	94	95.034	−1.034
3	9	80	80.938	−0.938
4	20	70	89.552	−19.552
5	3	100	76.239	23.761
6	15	109	85.636	23.364
7	5	62	77.806	−15.806
8	10	81	81.721	−0.721
9	24	74	91.901	−17.901
10	34	121	100.515	20.485
		Descriptive Statistics from Complete Data Set		
Mean	21.467	90.701	$\Sigma(Y - \hat{Y}) = 0.000$	
St. dev.	13.096	20.266	$\Sigma(Y - \hat{Y})2 = 32{,}386.048$	
Covariance	134.301			

r^2 and the Standard Error of Estimate

We have defined the standard error of estimate as

$$s_{Y-\hat{Y}} = \sqrt{\frac{\Sigma(Y - \hat{Y})^2}{N - 2}}$$

From here a small amount of algebraic substitution and manipulation, which I am omitting, will bring us to

$$s_{Y-\hat{Y}} = s_Y\sqrt{(1 - r^2)\left(\frac{N - 1}{N - 2}\right)}$$

From our data we now can calculate $s_{Y-\hat{Y}}$ in two different ways, and these give the same answer

1. $s_{Y-\hat{Y}} = \sqrt{\dfrac{\Sigma(Y - \hat{Y})^2}{N - 2}} = \sqrt{\dfrac{32{,}386.048}{105}} = 17.562$

2. $s_{Y-\hat{Y}} = s_Y\sqrt{(1 - r^2)\left(\dfrac{N - 1}{N - 2}\right)} = 20.266\sqrt{(1 - .506^2)\left(\dfrac{106}{105}\right)} = 17.562$

(The standard error was given in the R printout on page 232 as "Residual standard error.") Now that we have computed the standard error of estimate, we can interpret it as a form of standard deviation. Thus it is reasonable to say that the standard deviation of points *about the regression line* is 17.562. Another way of saying this is to say that $s_{Y-\hat{Y}}$ is the standard deviation of the errors that we make when using our regression equation. We would like that result to be as small as possible.

r^2 as a Measure of Predictable Variability

The squared correlation coefficient (r^2) is a very important statistic to explain the strength of the relationship we have between two variables. In what follows I am being a bit casual with my terminology. To explain things the perfectly correct way would require me to present several formulae and concepts that you don't really need to know. It is tempting to refer to several of the terms by using the word "variance," but they aren't truly variances. So I am going to use the wishy-washy terms "variation" and "variability," which stand for the variability of whatever we are talking about, however we choose to measure it.

When you start out with two variables (X and Y), there is probably a great deal of variability in Y, your dependent, or criterion, variable. Some of that variability is directly related to the predictor variable (X), and some is just plain noise, or what we call error. If X is a good predictor of Y, as it was in the example of Stress predicting Symptoms, then a big chunk of the variability in Stress is associated with variability in Symptoms, and this variability is measured by variation in $\hat{Y}$. By that I mean that much, though not all, of the reason that you and I differ in our levels of Symptoms is because we differ in our levels of Stress. If we had the same level of Stress we would have the same *predicted* level of Symptoms. If we have different levels of Stress then we have different *predicted* levels of Symptoms.

So now assume that I write a rather vague equation of the form

$$r^2 = \frac{\text{Variation in Symptoms explained by Stress}}{\text{Total Variation in Symptoms}}$$

If we do the arithmetic here the result will be a percentage. In other words, r^2 will equal the percentage of the variability in Symptoms that Stress is able to predict or explain. In our case we found an r of .506, so we can say that differences in Stress predict about 25% of the differences in Symptoms[2]. To put this another way, if we take a group of people and measure their Symptom levels, there will be a lot of differences between people. Some are very laid back and some are just plain "off the wall." But we now know that 25% of these differences among people are related to the fact that they experience different levels of Stress. And in the behavioral sciences, being able to explain 25% of the variability of some variable is impressive.

---

[2]The concept of r^2 is not all that intuitive. Suppose that I remarked that there seemed to be large differences in crime rates on different campuses. You might suggest that a chunk of that is due to different reporting standards. The statistic r^2 is simply putting a numeric value (a percentage) on what you have called "a chunk." Notice that we are focusing on *differences* in crime rates, not the rates themselves.

Now let's go to our example of narcissism. If the statement is true that people are becoming more narcissistic over time, then time should explain a large amount of changes in mean narcissism levels. But our correlation was $-.29$, which, when squared, says that we can only explain about 9% of differences in narcissism. Moreover, the correlation (and the regression coefficient (b)) are negative, which means that if anything, narcissism is generally *decreasing*, although the correlation is not significant. On top of that, we know that the correlation is far from significant.

This concept is important enough that it deserves a different way of explaining it. Suppose we are interested in studying the relationship between cigarette smoking (X) and age at death (Y). As we watch people die off over time, we notice several things. First we see that not all die at precisely the same age—there is variability in age at death regardless of (i.e., ignoring) smoking behavior. We also notice the obvious fact that some people smoke more than others. This is variability in smoking behavior regardless of age at death. We further find that cigarette smokers tend to die earlier than nonsmokers, and heavy smokers earlier than light smokers. Thus we write a regression equation to predict Y (Age at death) from X (Smoking). Because people differ in their smoking behavior, they will also differ in their *predicted* life expectancy ($\hat{Y}$), and this is the variability in $\hat{Y}$—that is, $\hat{Y}$ does not vary unless X varies.

We have one last source of variability: the variability in the life expectancy of those people who smoke exactly the same amount. It is error variability, that is, variability in Y that cannot be attributed to variability in X because these people did not differ in the amount they smoked. These several sources of variability (i.e., sums of squares) can be neatly summarized.

Sources of Variance in Regression

- Variability in amount smoked

- Variability in life expectancy

- Variability in life expectancy directly attributable to variability in smoking behavior

- Variability in life expectancy that cannot be attributable to variability in smoking behavior

If we consider the absurd extreme in which all nonsmokers die at exactly age 72 and all smokers smoke precisely the same amount and die at exactly age 68, then all the variability in life expectancy is directly predictable from variability in smoking behavior. If you smoke you will die at 68, and if you don't smoke you will die at 72. Here the correlation will be 1.00 and smoking would be predicting 100% of the variability in age at death.

In a more realistic example, smokers might tend to die earlier than nonsmokers, but within each group there would be a certain amount of variability in life expectancy. In this situation some of the variability in age at death is attributable to smoking and some is not. We want to be able to specify the *percentage* of the overall variability in life expectancy attributable to variability in smoking behavior. In other words, we want a measure that represents

$$\frac{\text{Predicted variability}}{\text{Total variability}}$$

As we have seen, that measure is r^2.

This interpretation of r^2 is extremely useful. If, for example, the correlation between amount smoked and life expectancy were an unrealistically high .80, we could say that $.80^2 = 64\%$ of the variability in life expectancy is directly predictable from the variability in smoking behavior. Obviously, this is a substantial exaggeration of the real world. If the correlation were a more likely $r = .20$, we could say that $.20^2 = 4\%$ of the variability in life expectancy is related to smoking behavior, whereas the other 96% is related to other factors. (While 4% may seem to you to be an awfully small amount, when we are talking about how long people will live, it is far from trivial, especially for those people affected.)

One problem associated with focusing on the squared correlation coefficient is maintaining an appropriate sense of perspective. If it is true that smoking accounts for 4% of the variability in life expectancy, it might be tempting to dismiss smoking as a minor contributor to life expectancy. You have to keep in mind, however, that an enormous number of variables contribute to life expectancy, including such things as automobile accidents, homicide, cancer, heart disease, and stroke. Some of those are related to smoking and some are not, and one that accounts for 4% or even 1% of the variability is a fairly powerful predictor. A variable that accounts for 4% of variability in course grades in a course is probably minor. But something that accounts for 4% of the variability in life expectancy is not to be dismissed so easily.

Rosenthal, Rosnow, & Rubin (2000) have suggested that it would be better to set aside the squared statistic (r^2) and simply use the unsquared version, r. Their main concern is that squaring a correlation produces a smaller value than the one you started with, which, as mentioned in the preceding paragraph, can lead us to think of an effect being smaller than it really is. Yes, it is nice to tie our measure to a logical referent, the percentage of variation associated with a particular variable, but an argument can be made for r as well. Earlier in this chapter we saw that when we think in terms of standardized measures, r is equal to β. That means that r can be taken as a measure of the degree to which one variable varies with another. Thus if $r = .75$, then two cases that differ on the predictor by one standard deviation would be predicted to differ on the dependent variable by three quarters of a standard deviation. That strikes me as a meaningful statistic.

It seems unfair in the text at this level to say, "You can do things this way; or you can do them another way" without giving much guidance as to which is better. But that is the nature of the beast. Fifteen years ago the routine advice would be to go with the squared correlation as a measure of effect size. Over the years there has come to be a slow movement away from that position and toward the use of the unsquared r. That is the position that I think is the better one, but, as you will see when we come to the analysis of variance, I am not always consistent myself. For a more extensive discussion of this issue, see Grissom & Kim (2012), p. 140.

It is important to note that phrases such as "accountable for," "attributable to," "predictable from," and "associated with" are not to be interpreted as statements of cause and effect. You could say that pains in your shoulder account for 10% of the variability in the weather without meaning to imply that sore shoulders cause rain, or even that rain itself causes sore shoulders. For example, your shoulder might hurt when it rains because carrying an umbrella aggravates your bursitis.

10.5 The Influence of Extreme Values

In Table 9.3 we saw a set of real data on the relationship between expenditures on alcohol and tobacco in 11 regions in Great Britain. We also saw that the inclusion of an unusual data point from Northern Ireland drastically altered the correlation from what it would have been without that observation. (Inclusion of that observation caused the correlation to drop from .784 to .224.) Let's see what effect that point has on the regression equation.

Table 10.4 contains the output for two solutions—the first with the aberrant observation, and the second without it. The regression lines are shown in parts (a) and (b) of Figure 10.2.

Notice the drastic change in the regression line. The slope went from .302 to 1.006, and the p value associated with those slopes exactly mirrored the p values for the corresponding correlations. This is an illustration that one unusual value can have a significant effect in pulling the regression line toward itself. This is a particularly good example because the observation in question is not particularly unusual when we look at one variable at a time. Moreover, it is a real data point, and not just an error on the part of someone who was collecting the data.

Table 10.4 SPSS Regression Solutions with and Without the Observation from Northern Ireland

(a) With Northern Ireland

| | Coefficients[a] | | | | |
| | Unstandardized Coefficients | | Standardized Coefficients | | |
Model	B	Std. Error	Beta	t	Sig.
1 (Constant)	4.351	1.607		2.708	.024
TOBACCO	.302	.439	.224	.688	.509

[a] Dependent Variable: ALCOHOL

(b) Without Northern Ireland

| | Coefficients[a] | | | | |
| | Unstandardized Coefficients | | Standardized Coefficients | | |
Model	B	Std. Error	Beta	t	Sig.
1 (Constant)	2.041	1.001		2.038	.076
TOBACCO	1.006	.281	.784	3.576	.007

[a] Dependent Variable: ALCOHOL

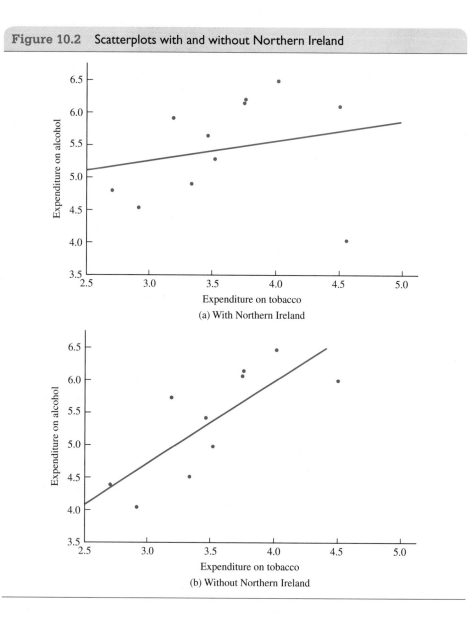

Figure 10.2 Scatterplots with and without Northern Ireland

(a) With Northern Ireland

(b) Without Northern Ireland

10.6 Hypothesis Testing in Regression

In the previous chapter we saw how to test a correlation coefficient for significance. We tested $H_0: \rho = 0$ because if $\rho = 0$, the variables are linearly independent, and if $\rho \neq 0$, the variables are related. When we come to regression problems, we have both a correlation coefficient and a slope, and it makes sense to ask if either is different from zero.[3] You know how to deal with r, but what about b?

The simplest approach to testing the slope is just to say that when you have only one predictor you don't need a separate test on b. If the *correlation* between Stress and Symptoms, for example, is significant, it means that Symptoms are related to Stress.

---

[3] You could also test the intercept, but such a test is usually not very interesting.

If the *slope* is significant it means that the predicted number of symptoms increases (or decreases) with the amount of stress. But that's saying the same thing! As you will see in a moment, the test for the slope is numerically equal to the test for the correlation coefficient. The easy answer, then, is to test the correlation. If that test is significant, then both the correlation in the population and the slope in the population are nonzero. But keep in mind that this is true only when we have one predictor. When we come to multiple predictors in the next chapter, that will no longer be the case.

An alternative approach is to use a test statistic we have not yet covered. I suggest that you just skim these two paragraphs and come back to them after you have read about *t* tests in Chapter 12. What we are going to do is calculate a statistic called *t* (using the slope, *b*) and look up *t* in a table or on our calculator. If the *t* we calculate is larger than the tabled *t*, we will reject H_0. Notice that this is the same kind of procedure we went through when we tested *r*. Our formula for *t* is

$$t = \frac{b}{\frac{s_{Y-\hat{Y}}}{s_X\sqrt{N-1}}} = \frac{b(s_X)\sqrt{N-1}}{s_Y\sqrt{(1-r^2)\frac{N-1}{N-2}}}$$

Then

$$t = \frac{b(s_X)\sqrt{N-1}}{s_Y\sqrt{(1-r^2)\frac{N-1}{N-2}}} = \frac{(0.7831)(13.096)\sqrt{106}}{20.266\sqrt{(1-.506)\frac{106}{105}}} = \frac{105.587}{17.563} = 6.01$$

I mention the *t* test here, without elaborating on it, because you are about to see that same *t* appear in the computer printout in the next section. (It was also in the R printout earlier.) To jump ahead, if you look at Figure 10.3, the last few lines show the values for the slope (labeled "Stress") and the intercept (labeled "Constant"). To the right is a column labeled "t" and another labeled "Sig" The entries under "t" are the *t* tests just referred to. (The test on the intercept is somewhat different, but it is still a *t* test.) The entries under "Sig" are the probabilities associated with those *t*s under H_0. In this example the associated probability is given by SPSS as .000. (The exact probability does not have a digit other than "0" until the 8th decimal place.) If the probability is less than .05, we can reject H_0. Here we will reject H_0 and conclude that the slope relating symptoms to stress is not zero. People with higher stress scores are predicted to have more symptoms. (Using the probability calculator at http://www.statpages.org/pdfs.html, we can simply enter *t* = 6.01, *df* = 105, and compute *p* = .0000. Using the calculator at www.danielsoper.com/statcalc3/, enter *r* = .506, sample size = 107, and compute the two-tailed probability as *p* = .00000003.)

10.7 | Computer Solution Using SPSS

I outlined the steps for using SPSS to find out regression equation earlier. Here I will go back to that because I want to show the actual printout. Figure 10.3 contains the printout from an SPSS analysis of the Symptoms and Stress data. An introduction

Figure 10.3   Regression analysis of relationship between symptoms and stress

Correlations

		SYMPTOMS	STRESS
Pearson Correlation	SYMPTOMS	1.000	.506
	STRESS	.506	1.000
Sig. (one-tailed)	SYMPTOMS	.	.000
	STRESS	.000	.
N	SYMPTOMS	107	107
	STRESS	107	107

Model Summary

Model	R	R Square	Adjusted R Square	Std. Error of the Estimate
1	.506[a]	.256	.249	17.56242

[a]Predictors: (Constant), STRESS

ANOVA[b]

Model		Sum of Squares	df	Mean Square	F	Sig.
1	Regression	11,148.382	1	11,148.382	36.145	.000[a]
	Residual	32,386.048	105	308.439		
	Total	43,534.430	106			

[a]Predictors: (Constant), STRESS
[b]Dependent Variable: SYMPTOMS

Coefficients[a]

Model		Unstandardized Coefficients		Standardized Coefficients	t	Sig.
		B	Std. Error	Beta		
1	(Constant)	73.890	3.271		22.587	.000
	STRESS	.783	.130	.506	6.012	.000

[a]Dependent Variable: SYMPTOMS

to how we request this analysis is briefly presented in the *Short Manual* section at this book's website. It is found in Chapter 6 of that manual. The basic links are **Analyze/Regression/ Linear**. Select Stress as the independent variable and Symptoms as the dependent variable. I suggest asking for confidence intervals under the Statistics button, and requesting the appropriate plots. The output starts by presenting the mean, the standard deviation, and the sample size of all cases, followed by the correlation coefficient matrix. Here you can see that the correlation of .506 agrees with our own calculation. For some reason SPSS chooses to report one-tailed significance probabilities, rather than the more traditional two-tailed values that it reports in other procedures. You can simply double the *p* value to have a two-tailed test. The next section presents the correlation coefficient again. This section also gives you the squared correlation (.256), the adjusted r squared, which we will skip, and the standard error of estimate ($s_{Y-\hat{Y}}$). These values agree with those that we have calculated. The section headed "ANOVA" (Analysis of Variance) is simply a test on the significance of the correlation coefficient. The entry "Sig." is the probability, under H_0, of a correlation as large as .506. Because the probability is given as .000, we will reject H_0 and conclude that there is a significant relationship between Symptoms and Stress. Finally, in the section headed "Coefficients" we see the slope (in column B, next to the word Stress) and the intercept directly above the slope. Skipping the next two columns we come to the t tests on these coefficients and the probability of those t values. I have already discussed the t on the slope. This is the same value we calculated using the formula given in Section 10.6. The t test on the intercept is simply a test that the true intercept is zero. We rarely would expect it to be, so this test is not particularly useful for most purposes.

Writing up the results

There are some pieces of information that would go into the write-up of a regression analysis that we have not yet covered. I am including them anyway to be thorough, but do not get too concerned with what they represent. We might write up these results this way:

> Wagner, Compas, and Howell (1988) conducted a study examining the relationship between stress and mental health in college students. They asked 107 college students to complete a checklist assessing the number and severity of negative life events that they had recently experienced. They also asked these same students to complete a checklist of psychological symptoms that they experienced in the past month. The relationship between these two variables addresses the issue of stress and mental health, and the literature would suggest that an increase in stressful events would be associated with an increase in the number of symptoms reported by the students.
>
> The analyses of these data confirmed the prediction and produced a correlation of .506 between the two variables ($r^2 = .256$), which is significant at $\alpha = .05$ ($F (1, 105) = 36.14$, $p = .000$). The regression equation has a slope $= 0.78$ ($t (105) = 6.012$, $p = .000$). Higher levels of stress are associated with higher levels of psychological symptoms, and stress accounts for approximately 25% of the variation in Symptoms. (I would not report the intercept here because it has no substantive meaning.)

10.8 Seeing Statistics

The applets contained on the website provide an excellent way for you to review what you have learned. They will also make it easier for you to recall that material on an exam, because you will have actively worked with it. In addition, the applets related to the t test will give you a head start on Chapters 12–14.

One of the important concepts to understand about a scatterplot with a regression line is just how the regression line helps us to predict Y. The applet entitled Predicting Y, shown below, illustrates this simple principle. As you move the slider on the X axis, you vary the value of X, and can read the corresponding value of $\hat{Y}$. For this particular example, when X = 2, Ŷ = 2.2. Additionally, by moving the sliders on the left and right, you can vary the intercept and the slope, respectively, and observe how the predictions change.

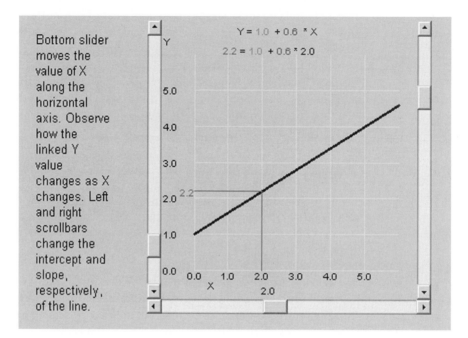

Calculate values of Ŷ for X = 2, 3, and 4. Then make the slope steeper, by moving the slider on the right up, and again calculate Ŷ for X = 2, 3, and 4. What has changed?

Now do the same thing, except this time change the intercept. Now how do the values of Ŷ change as we vary X?

I have said that the regression line is the "best-fitting" line through the data points. The following applet, named "Finding the best-fitting line," allows you to move the regression line vertically (i.e., changing its intercept) and to rotate it (i.e., changing its slope). The data in the following figure are taken from McClelland's original applet, and show the scores on a Statistical Knowledge Quiz (SKQ) before and after students have taken his statistics course. I have commented in several places that we often don't really care about the intercept. Well, if we don't care about it, why do we bother to calculate it? This applet helps to illustrate the answer to that question. If you use this applet to come up with a reasonable slope for the data, you can then use the small square to move the line up or down. As you move it too high or too low, the fit becomes terrible. This is the effect of the intercept. The intercept really tells you how high or low is optimal, and the slope then gives your prediction. Although we may not care about the actual value of the intercept, it is critical to identifying the line of best fit.

Adjust the line until you think that it is a "best fit." I happen to know that the best-fitting line has an intercept of 10.9, and a slope of 0.42. How does the line you fit compare to that?

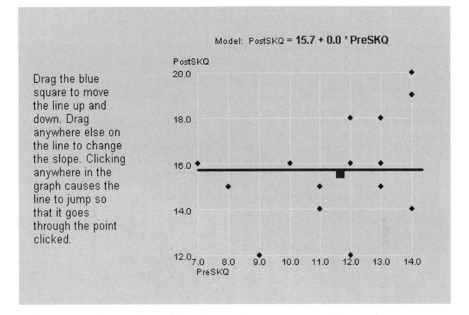

Model: PostSKQ = **15.7 + 0.0 * PreSKQ**

Drag the blue square to move the line up and down. Drag anywhere else on the line to change the slope. Clicking anywhere in the graph causes the line to jump so that it goes through the point clicked.

One of the applets in Chapter 9 allowed you to remove individual data points and observe the effect on the correlation between two variables. We will return to that applet here, though this time we will concentrate on the influence of extreme points on the regression line. The applet shown below is taken from the data in Figure 9.3.

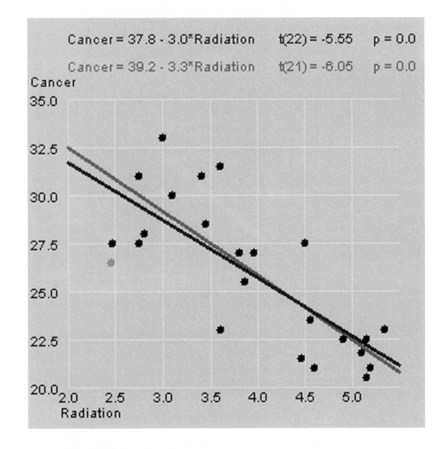

Cancer = 37.8 - 3.0*Radiation   t(22) = -5.55   p = 0.0

Cancer = 39.2 - 3.3*Radiation   t(21) = -6.05   p = 0.0

By clicking on the point at approximately (2.5, 26.5) I have changed the slope of the regression line from −3.0 to −3.3. The less steep line in this figure is the line for all 24 observations, whereas the steeper line fits the data, omitting the point on which I clicked.

You can click on each data point and see the effect on the slope and intercept.

One of the points in this chapter concerned the use of Student's t test to test the null hypothesis that the true slope in the population is 0.00 (i.e., the hypothesis that there is no linear relationship between X and Y.) The applet named SlopeTest illustrates the meaning of this test with population data that support the null hypothesis. A sample screen is illustrated here.

In this applet I have drawn 100 samples of five pairs of scores. I drew from a population where the true slope, and therefore the true correlation, is 0.00, so I know that the variables are not linearly related. For each of the 100 slopes that I obtained, the applet calculated a t test using the formula for t given in Section 10.6. The last 10 t values are given near the top of the display, and they range from −2.098 to 5.683. The distribution of all 100 values is given at the right, and the plot of the five observations for my 100th set is given at the left. (The green line on the left always has a slope of 0 and represents what the line would be with a huge sample with the null hypothesis being true.) Each time I click the "10 sets" button, I will draw 10 new sets of observations, calculate their slopes and associated t values, and add those to the plot on the right. If I click the "100 Sets" button, I will accumulate 100 t values at a time.

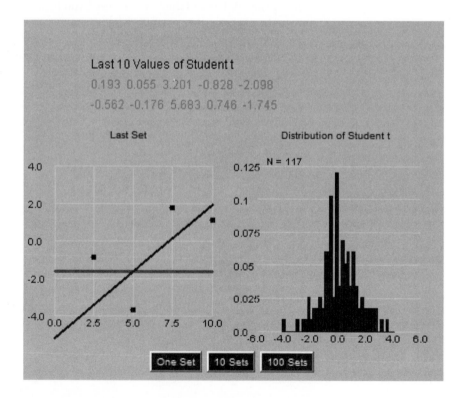

Run this applet. First generate one set at a time and note the resulting variation in t and how the regression line changes with every sample. Then accumulate 100 sets at a time and notice how the distribution of t smoothes out. Notice that our t values only rarely exceed ±3.00. (In fact, the critical value of t on 3 df is ±3.18.)

Now move to the lower applet on that page, which will sample 15 pairs per sample. Note how the *t* distribution narrows slightly with larger sample sizes.

We will use one final applet to illustrate the use of the *t* test for the slope. Several times in Chapters 9 and 10 I have focused on the data set showing the relationship between alcohol and tobacco use in Great Britain, and the influence of extreme data points. In Figure 10.3 I presented an SPSS printout showing the slope (unstandardized) and its standard error. Along with the sample size (*N*), that is all we need for calculating *t*.

The applet CalcT is shown next for the statistics from the complete data set (including Northern Ireland). I entered 0.302 as the slope, 0.0 as the null hypothesis to be tested (the hypothesis that the true slope is 0), and 0.439 as the standard error. I also entered the degrees of freedom as $N - 2 = 9$. Each time that I entered a number, I pressed the Enter key—*don't just move your mouse to another box without pressing Enter.* You can see that the resulting value of *t* is 0.688, and the figure at the bottom shows that the two-tailed probability is .509.

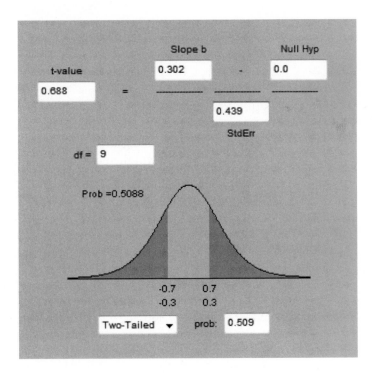

We see that the slope here is not significantly different from 0. Now enter the statistics from part (b) of Table 10.4, testing whether the relationship is significant once we remove the outlier.

10.9 A Final Example for Review

In Chapter 9 we obtained the correlation coefficient for the relationship between the rated quality of a course and the outcome of that course (as reflected by the average expected grade for students taking the course). The data are repeated in Table 10.5,

Table 10.5 A Worked Example of Predicting Course Quality from Grades

Expected Grade (X)	Overall Quality (Y)	Expected Grade (X)	Overall Quality (Y)
3.5	3.4	3.0	3.8
3.2	2.9	3.1	3.4
2.8	2.6	3.0	2.8
3.3	3.8	3.3	2.9
3.2	3.0	3.2	4.1
3.2	2.5	3.4	2.7
3.6	3.9	3.7	3.9
4.0	4.3		

Results Based on All 50 Cases

$$\Sigma X = 174.3$$
$$\Sigma X^2 = 613.65$$
$$\Sigma Y = 177.5$$
$$\Sigma Y^2 = 648.57$$
$$\Sigma XY = 621.94$$

which shows only the first 15 cases to conserve space, but the calculations are based on all 50 cases in my sample. As a stepwise review of regression calculations we will solve for the regression equation for predicting rated Overall Quality (Y) from Expected Grade (X). We will then consider the interpretation of the coefficients in that equation.

1. Our first step is to calculate the mean and the standard deviation of each variable, as follows:

$$\overline{Y} = 177.7/50 = 3.550$$

$$s_Y = \sqrt{\frac{648.57 - 177.5^2/50}{49}} = 0.6135$$

$$\overline{X} = 174.3/50 = 3.486$$

$$s_X = \sqrt{\frac{613.65 - 174.3^2/50}{49}} = 0.3511$$

2. The covariance is given as

$$cov_{XY} = \frac{\Sigma XY - \dfrac{\Sigma X \Sigma Y}{N}}{N-1} = \frac{621.94 - \dfrac{(174.3)(177.5)}{50}}{49} = .0648$$

3. To calculate the slope, we have

$$b = \frac{cov_{XY}}{s_X^2} = \frac{0.0648}{0.3511^2} = 0.5257$$

4. We calculate the intercept as

$$a = \overline{Y} - b(\overline{X}) = 3.55 - 0.5257(3.486) = 1.7174$$

5. Our equation is then

$$\hat{Y} = 0.5257(X) + 1.7174$$

6. We can interpret the result as follows. If we had a course in which students expected a grade of 0, our best guess is that the expected course rating would be 1.7174. That is not a meaningful statistic as far as interpretation is concerned because it is difficult to imagine a course in which everyone would expect to fail. In this case the intercept merely serves to anchor the regression equation.

7. A slope of 0.5257 can be interpreted to mean that if two courses differ by one point in expected grades, their overall ratings would be expected to differ by a little over one-half a point. Such a difference, then, would be expected between a course in which students anticipate a grade of C (2.0) and a course in which students anticipate a grade of B (3.0). Keep in mind, however, the earlier remarks about the fact that we are not making a causal statement here. We have no particular reason to conclude that lower expected grades *cause* lower ratings, although they are *associated* with lower ratings. Poor teaching could easily lead to both.

    If you are using SPSS, you can reproduce these results by selecting **Analyze/regression/linear**, identifying the dependent and independent variables, and then clicking on the **Statistics** button and selecting (**Estimates, Confidence Intervals, Model Fit, Descriptives**). The results follow.

Descriptive Statistics

	Mean	Std.Deviation	N
Overall	3.550	.6135	50
Grade	3.486	.3511	50

Correlations

		Overall	Grade
Pearson Correlation	Overall	1.000	.301
	Grade	.301	1.000
Sig. (1-tailed)	Overall	.	.017
	Grade	.017	.
N	Overall	50	50
	Grade	50	50

Variables Entered/Removed[a]

Model	Variables Entered	Variables Removed	Method
1	Grade[b]	.	Enter

[a]Dependent Variable: Overall
[b]All requested variables entered.

Model Summary

Model	R	R Square	Adjusted R Square	Std. Error of the Estimate
1	.301[a]	.090	.072	.5912

[a]Predictors: (Constant), Grade

ANOVA[a]

Model		Sum of Squares	df	Mean Square	F	Sig.
1	Regression	1.669	1	1.669	4.775	.034[b]
	Residual	16.776	48	.350		
	Total	18.445	49			

[a]Dependent Variable: Overall
[b]Predictors: (Constant), Grade

Coefficients[a]

Model		Unstandardized Coefficients		Standardized Coefficients			95.0% Confidence Interval for B	
		B	Std. Error	Beta	t	Sig.	Lower Bound	Upper Bound
1	(Constant)	1.718	.843		2.038	.047	.023	3.412
	Grade	.526	.241	.301	2.185	.034	.042	1.009

[a]Dependent Variable: Overall

Table 10.6 SPSS results for data in Table 10.5
Using R, the following code will give you what you want.

```
read.table("https://www.uvm.edu/~dhowell/fundamentals9/DataFiles/
  albatros.dat",
header = TRUE)
attach(rating.data)
print(cor(Overall, Grade))
regress <- lm(Overall ~ Grade)
summary(regress)
********************************
>print(cor(Overall, Grade))
[1] 0.3008006

> regress <- lm(Overall ~ Grade)
> summary(regress)

Call:
lm(formula = Overall ~ Grade)
```

```
Residuals:
    Min      1Q   Median      3Q      Max
-1.27787  -0.49838  0.04008  0.48367  1.15803

Coefficients:
            Estimate Std. Error t value Pr(>|t|)
(Intercept)  1.7176     0.8427   2.038   0.0471 *
Grade        0.5256     0.2405   2.185   0.0338 *
---
Signif. codes:  0 '***' 0.001 '**' 0.01 '*' 0.05 '.' 0.1 ' ' 1

Residual standard error: 0.5912 on 48 degrees of freedom
Multiple R-squared: 0.09048,    Adjusted R-squared: 0.07153
F-statistic: 4.775 on 1 and 48 DF,  p-value: 0.03379
```

10.10 Regression Versus Correlation

We spent Chapter 9 discussing correlation and then turned around in this chapter and said some of the same things about regression. You might be forgiven for asking why we need both. There are at least two answers to that question. When we have only one predictor variable, as we have had in these two chapters, the two approaches tell you many of the same things. The advantage of a correlation coefficient is that it is a single number that allows you to characterize quickly the *degree* to which two variables are related. When you can say that a specific test of manual skills is correlated .85 with performance on the job, you are saying something important. In that example I imagine that I would be saying something much less useful if I said that an increase of 10 points on the test is associated with a five-point difference in job performance. On the other hand, when you are interested in speaking about the magnitude of change, a regression coefficient is useful. If I could tell you that making birth control information available to an additional 10% of a population of women at high risk of producing a child who will not live for a year will decrease infant mortality by 9.7 percentage points, I am telling you something that is probably far more useful than telling you that the correlation between contraception and infant mortality in Sub-Saharan Africa is .44. Both statistics have their uses, and you can choose the one that best serves your needs.

When we come to the next chapter on multiple regression we will find that correlation and regression do not overlap so nicely. We might have a very high correlation between two predictors, taken together, and an outcome variable, but that might be due to one or the other, or both, of those predictors. The usual way of seeing which variables are important is to look at the regression coefficient. In fact, it is often the case that we will apply multiple regression in a setting where we know that the overall multiple correlation is almost certain to be significant, but we want to tease out the separate roles of the predictors.

10.11 Summary

I began this chapter by defining regression as the prediction of one variable from knowledge of one or more other variables, and I said that the regression line is the straight line that best represents the relationship between two variables. A regression line is a straight line of the form $\hat{Y} = bX + a$, where $\hat{Y}$ is the value of Y predicted from the value of X. The coefficient b is the slope of the regression line and a is the intercept. The slope is the rate at which the predicted value of Y changes for every one unit change in X. The intercept is the predicted value of Y when X is zero. The intercept anchors the line (it determines the height of the line, but not its slope), but frequently has little substantive meaning because $X = 0$ is often an unreasonable value in the data.

I next discussed the concept of regression to the mean. This refers to the fact that someone who scores high on one test will probably score lower on the next test, and the reverse is true for a person with unusually low scores. It also refers to the fact that our regression equation predicts the same phenomenon. It is important to keep in mind that this concept refers to individual observations and does not lead to groups of scores showing reduced variability over time.

I also discussed errors of prediction, which are the deviations between the Y value that was obtained and the $\hat{Y}$ value that was predicted. These errors are commonly called "residuals," because they are the differences left over after X has done its best at predicting Y. Our regression line is drawn to minimize the squares of these deviations, which is why we call the technique "least squares regression."

Finally, I briefly discussed the standard error of estimate, which is basically the standard deviation of the residuals, or deviations between Y and $\hat{Y}$. If you have large errors of prediction the standard error of estimate will be large. I drew the comparison between the standard error of estimate, which is a standard deviation about a regression line, and the normal standard deviation, which represents deviations about the mean. From there I went to the square of r (r^2) and said that it can be interpreted as the percentage of the variability in Y that can be predicted from the relationship between Y and X. I suggested that this is not always an easy measure to interpret because we don't have a good way of knowing what a high or low value of r^2 is in any given situation. Some authors suggest using r instead as our measure of effect size.

In the case of two variables, a significance test on r is equivalent to a significance test on b. However, I also gave a t test for b, which will produce the same result as a test on r, and this t test is printed in all computer printouts.

In this chapter I only looked at the case where we have one predictor. In the next chapter I will move to the situation in which we have several predictors to predict one criterion variable. That is known as multiple regression, while the case of one predictor is often called "simple regression."

Key Terms

Slope, *233*	Regression equation, *234*
Intercept, *233*	Standardized regression coefficient, β(beta), *236*
Residual, *233*	
Errors of prediction, *233*	Regression to the mean, *237*
Least squares regression, *233*	Standard error of estimate, *240*
Regression coefficients, *234*	Residual variance (error variance), *240*

10.12 A Quick Review

A. Regression refers to
Ans: computing the linear relationship between one (or more) variables and another.

B. A linear regression is one in which _____.
Ans: the best fitting line is a straight line.

C. In linear regression the symbol b is used to refer to the intercept. (T or F)
Ans: F. It refers to the slope.

D. Express "error of prediction" algebraically.
Ans: $(Y - \overline{Y})$

E. We often use the phrase "least squares regression" because _____
Ans: we are minimizing the squared errors of prediction.

F. We always need to compute a value for the intercept because that anchors our line, but do we always need to pay attention to it?
Ans: No, because sometimes it is so extreme that we would have little or no faith in the associated predicted score.

G. If we standardized our data and computed a slope (here called beta), what would beta tell us?
Ans: It would tell us the change (in standard deviation units) in the predicted value of Y for a change of one standard deviation in X.

H. The measure of error that we use with regression is called _____.
Ans: the standard error of estimate and can be thought of as the standard deviation around the regression line

I. Two important measures of the size of an effect in regression are _____ and _____.
Ans: r^2 and r

10.13 Exercises

I am assuming that you will use R, or SPSS, or any other available program to answer many of the questions in this chapter, However, it is not very difficult to obtain the results by hand calculation.

10.1   The following data are from 10 health-planning districts in Vermont. Y is the percentage of live births ≤ 2500 grams. X_1 is the fertility rate for women ≤ 17 or ≥ 35 years of age (X_1 is known as the "high-risk fertility rate."). X_2 is the percentage of births to unmarried women. Compute the regression equation for predicting the percentage of births of infants weighing less than 2500 grams (Y) on the basis of the high-risk fertility rate (X_1).

Use R, or SPSS, or any other available program to accomplish this (and the next several questions).

District	Y	X_1	X_2
1	6.1	43.0	9.2
2	7.1	55.3	12.0
3	7.4	48.5	10.4
4	6.3	38.8	9.8
5	6.5	46.2	9.8
6	5.7	39.9	7.7
7	6.6	43.1	10.9
8	8.1	48.5	9.5
9	6.3	40.0	11.6
10	6.9	56.7	11.6

10.2 Calculate the standard error of estimate for the regression equation in Exercise 10.1.

10.3 If, as a result of ongoing changes in the role of women in society, we saw a change in the age of childbearing such that the high-risk fertility rate jumped to 70 in Exercise 10.1, what would we predict for the incidence of birthweight < 2500 grams?

10.4 Why should you feel uncomfortable making a prediction in Exercise 10.3 for a rate of 70?

10.5 In Exercise 9.1 in Chapter 9 we saw data on infant mortality and risk factors. Why might you feel more comfortable making a prediction based on Income for Senegal than for Ethiopia or Namibia?

10.6 Again referring to Exercise 9.1 in Chapter 9, how does what you know about regression contribute to your understanding of infant health in developing countries?

10.7 Using the data in Table 10.2, predict the Symptom score for a Stress level of 45.

10.8 The mean Stress score in Table 10.2 was 21.467. What would your prediction be for a Stress score of 21.467? How does this compare to the mean Symptom score?

10.9 Suppose that we know that the correlation between two variables named X and Y is .56. What would you expect would happen to the *correlation* if we subtracted 10 points from every X score?

10.10 With regard to Exercise 10.9, suppose that the mean of X was 15.6 and the mean of Y was 23.8. What would happen to the *slope* and *intercept* if we subtracted 10 points from every Y?

10.11 Draw a diagram (or diagrams) to illustrate Exercise 10.10.

10.12 Make up a set of five data points (pairs of scores) that have an intercept of 0 and a slope of 1. (There are several ways to solve this problem, so think about it a bit.)

10.13 Take the data that you just created in Exercise 10.12 and add 2.5 to each Y value. Plot the original data and the new data. On the same graph, superimpose the regression lines.

a) What has happened to the slope and intercept?
b) What would happen to the correlation?

10.14 Generate $\hat{Y}$ and $(Y - \hat{Y})$ for the first five cases of the data in Table 10.2.

10.15 Using the data in Appendix D, compute the regression equation for predicting GPA from ADDSC. These data can be found at https://www.uvm.edu/~dhowell/fundamtnals9/DataFiles/Add.dat.

10.16 In the chapter we saw a study by Trzesniewski et al. (2008) on trends in narcissism scores over time. They also reported data on self-enhancement, which is the tendency to hold unrealistically positive views of oneself. The measure of self-enhancement (SelfEn) was obtained by asking students to respond on a 1–10 scale rating their intelligence relative to others. The researchers then calculated the difference between the rating predicted from SAT scores and the rating the student gave. The data are presented below. Positive scores represent self-enhancement.

Year	1976	1977	1978	1979	1980	1981	1982	1983	1984	1985	1986	1987	1988	1989	1990	1991
SelfEn	−.06	−.03	.00	−.01	.07	.06	.04	.03	.03	.03	.03	.07	.06	.03	.03	.04

Year	1992	1993	1994	1995	1996	1997	1998	1999	2000	2001	2002	2003	2004	2005	2006
SelfEn	.01	−.01	−.02	.02	.05	.00	.01	−.01	−.02	−.06	−.08	−.10	−.11	−.08	−.08

a) From these data can we say something about what changes have taken place in self-enhancement scores of college students over the years?
b) With several hundred thousand students in the combined sample, the authors of the original study actually based their analyses on individual scores rather than yearly means

to make the same computation. They found a correlation of $-.03$, which differs considerably from your result. Why is this not surprising?

c)   Which is the correct correlation for this question (yours or the authors'), or are they both correct?

10.17   Using the data on self-enhancement given in Exercise 10.16, add two scores to each year, keeping the year mean unchanged. (For example, if the 1982 mean SelfEn score was 0.40, you could make two other scores for that year by adding and subtracting .03 from 0.40.) This will give you $31 \times 3 = 93$ pairs of scores. Now compute the correlation and regression of SelfEn predicted from Year. Why does the correlation differ from the $r = .57$ computed in Exercise 10.16? What has happened to the slope, and why?

10.18   Why would we ever care if a slope is significantly different from 0?

10.19   The following data represent the actual heights and weights referred to in Chapter 9 for male college students.

a)   Make a scatterplot of the data.

Height	Weight	Height	Weight
70	150	73	170
67	140	74	180
72	180	66	135
75	190	71	170
68	145	70	157
69	150	70	130
71.5	164	75	185
71	140	74	190
72	142	71	155
69	136	69	170
67	123	70	155
68	155	72	215
66	140	67	150
72	145	69	145
73.5	160	73	155
73	190	73	155
69	155	71	150
73	165	68	155
72	150	69.5	150
74	190	73	180
72	195	75	160
71	138	66	135
74	160	69	160
72	155	66	130
70	153	73	155
67	145	68	150
71	170	74	148
72	175	73.5	155
69	175		

b) Calculate the regression equation of weight predicted from height for these data. Interpret the slope and the intercept.

c) What is the correlation coefficient for these data?

d) Are the correlation coefficient and the slope significantly different from zero?

10.20   The following data are the actual heights and weights referred to in Chapter 9 of female college students:

Height	Weight	Height	Weight
61	140	65	135
66	120	66	125
68	130	65	118
68	138	65	122
63	121	65	115
70	125	64	102
68	116	67	115
69	145	69	150
69	150	68	110
67	150	63	116
68	125	62	108
66	130	63	95
65.5	120	64	125
66	130	68	133
62	131	62	110
62	120	61.75	108
63	118	62.75	112
67	125		

a) Make a scatterplot of the data.

b) Calculate the regression coefficients for these data. Interpret the slope and the intercept.

c) What is the correlation coefficient for these data?

d) Are the correlation and the slope significantly different from zero?

10.21   Using your own height and the appropriate regression equation from Exercise 10.19 or 10.20, predict your own weight. (If you are uncomfortable reporting your own weight, predict mine—I am 5′8″ and weigh 156 pounds—well, at least I would like to think so.)

a) How much is your actual weight greater than or less than your predicted weight? (You have just calculated a residual.)

b) What effect will biased reporting on the part of the students who produced the data play in your prediction of your own weight?

10.22   Use your scatterplot of the data for students of your own gender and observe the size of the residuals. (*Hint:* You can see the residuals in the vertical distance of points from the line.) What is the largest residual for your scatterplot? Hint: You can print out the residuals in R by typing print(regress$residuals). You can do the same in SPSS by selecting Save from the main regression menu and checking "unstandardized residuals.")

10.23   Given a male and a female student who are both 5′6″, how much would they be expected to differ in weight? (*Hint:* Calculate a predicted weight for each of them using the regression equation specific to gender.)

10.24   The slope (*b*) used to predict the weights of males from their heights is greater than the slope for females. What does this tell us about male weights relative to female weights?

10.25 In Chapter 3 I presented data on the speed of deciding whether a briefly presented image was the same image as the one to its left or whether it was a reversed image. However, I worry that the trials are not independent, because I was the only subject and gave all of the responses. Use the data from the website (Ex10-25.dat) to see if response time was related to trial number. Was performance improving significantly over trials? Can we assume that there is no systematic linear trend over time? These data are also available for you to download from https:// www.uvm.edu/~dhowell/fundamentals9/DataFiles/Tab3-1.dat

10.26 Write a paragraph summarizing the results in Table 10.6 that is comparable to the paragraph in Chapter 9, Section 9.14 (Summary and Conclusions of Course Evaluation Study) describing the results of the correlational analysis.

10.27 Wainer (1997) presented data on the relationship between hours of TV watching and *mean* scores on the 1990 National Assessment of Educational Progress (NAEP) for eighth-grade mathematics assessment. The data follow, separated for boys and girls.

Hours TV Watched	0	1	2	3	4	5	6
Girls NAEP	258	269	267	261	259	253	239
Boys NAEP	276	273	292	269	266	259	249

a) Plot the relationship between Hours Watched and NAEP Mathematics scores separately for boys and girls (but put them on the same graph).

b) Find and interpret the slope and intercept for these data, again keeping boys and girls separate.

c) We know from other data that boys spend more time watching television than girls do. Could this be used as an explanation of performance differences between boys and girls? The R code for these plots is

10.28 You probably were startled to see the very neat relationships in Exercise 10.27. There was almost no variability about the regression line. I would, as a first approximation, guess that the relationship between television hours watched and standardized test performance would contain roughly as much scatter as the relationship between stress and symptoms, yet these data are far neater than the data in Figure 10.1. What might have caused this?

```
TV <- c(0,1,2,3,4,5,6)
GirlsNAEP <- c(258, 269, 267, 261, 259, 253, 239)
BoysNAEP <- c(276, 273, 292, 269, 266, 259, 249)
plot(GirlsNAEP ~ TV, type = "p", col = "red", ylim = c(240, 300), ylab =
"NAEP Score" ,xlab = "Hours Watching TV" )
regG <- lm(GirlsNAEP ~ TV)
abline(reg = regG, col = "red")
par(new = TRUE)
plot (BoysNAEP ~ TV, type = "p", col = "blue", ylim = c(240, 300), ylab =
"NAEP Score" ,xlab = "Hours Watching TV" )
regB <- lm(BoysNAEP ~ TV)
abline(reg = regB, col = "blue")
```

10.29 Draw a scatter diagram (of 10 points) on a sheet of paper that represents a moderately positive correlation between the variables. Now drop your pencil *at random* on this scatter diagram.

a) If you think of your pencil as a regression line, what aspect of the regression line are you changing as you move the pencil vertically on the paper?

b) What aspect of the regression line are you changing as you twist, or rotate, your pencil?

c) If you didn't remember any of the equations for the slope and intercept, how could you tell if your pencil was forming the optimal regression line?

10.30 There is some really excellent material on regression at the University of Newcastle in Australia. The address is

 https://surfstat.anu.edu.au/surfstat-home/surfstat-main.html

Go to this site and check both the links for "Statistical Inference" and for "Hotlist for Java Applets."

The Java applets are particularly nice because they allow you to manipulate data on the screen and see what difference it makes. Write a short description of the material you found there.

10.31 The data file named Galton.dat on this book's website contains Galton's data on heights of parents and children discussed in the section on regression to the mean. In these data, Galton multiplied mothers' and daughters' heights by 1.08 to give them the same mean as male heights, and then averaged the heights of both parents to produce the mid-parent height. The data are taken from Stigler (1999).

a) Regress child height against parent height.

b) Calculate the predicted height for children on the basis of parental height.

c) The data file contains a variable called Quartile ranging from 1 to 4, with 1 being the lowest quartile. In SPSS use **Analyze/Compare Means/One-way ANOVA** to give child means corresponding to each quartile. (Make Child the dependent variable and Quartile the independent variable.) Do the same for parent means.

d) Do the children of parents in the highest quartile have a lower mean than their parents, and vice versa for the children of parents in the lowest quartile?

e) Draw a scatterplot with parent quartile means on the X axis and child quartile means on the Y axis and also draw a 45-degree line that would represent parents having children with the same mean height.

## CHAPTER 11

Multiple Regression

This chapter will consider regression in which we use more than one predictor at a time and will look at what a second or third predictor can explain that was not predicted by the first, or first and second, predictor. We will also focus more than we have in the past on variability that we have not been able to explain. We will then look at tests of significance, which are largely an extension of what we saw in Chapter 10. Several different examples are used because they reinforce the material that we cover and offer additional insights into multiple regression.

In Chapters 9 and 10 we were looking at the relationship between one variable and another. We wanted either to determine the degree to which the two variables were correlated or to predict one criterion (dependent) variable from one predictor (independent) variable. In that situation we have a correlation coefficient (r) and regression equation of the form

$$\hat{Y} = bX + a.$$

But there is no good reason why we must limit ourselves to having only one predictor. It is perfectly appropriate to ask how well some linear combination of two, three, four, or more predictors will predict the criterion. To take a greatly oversimplified example, we could ask how well I could do if I just added together the number of stressful events you report experiencing over the last month, the number of close friends you have, and your score on a measure assessing how much control you feel you have over events in your life, and then used that total

CONCEPTS THAT YOU WILL NEED TO REMEMBER FROM PREVIOUS CHAPTERS

Correlation coefficient:	A measure of the relationship between variables
Slope (b):	Change in the predicted value for a one-unit change in a predictor
Intercept (a):	Predicted value when the predictors are all equal to zero
Regression line:	The straight line that best fits the points in a scatterplot, often written as $\hat{Y} = bX + a$
Standard error:	The standard deviation of the sampling distribution of a statistic
Standardized Regression Coefficient:	The slope when the variables have been standardized—i.e., converted to **z** scores
Residual variance:	The square of the average of squared deviations about the regression line

or composite score to predict your level of psychological symptoms. Of course, you could fairly argue that it makes no sense to add together three stressful events, five friends, and a score of 50, get an answer of 58, and think that the 58 means anything sensible. The variables are measured on completely different scales.

But I can work around the objection of measuring on different scales if I give different weight to each variable. There is no reason why I should have to give equal weight to a test score and the number of close friends you have. It might make much more sense to pay more attention to some variables than to others. Perhaps your sense of personal control over events is twice as important in predicting psychological distress as is the number of stressful events, and perhaps both of those are more important than the number of your friends. Moreover, we will have to add or subtract some constant to make the mean prediction come out to equal the mean Symptom score.

If we let the letters S, F, and C represent "Stress," "Friends," and "Control," we could have a regression equation that looks like

$$\hat{Y} = 2 \times S + 1 \times F + 4 \times C + 12$$

The general form of this equation would be written as

$$\hat{Y} = b_1 S + b_2 F + b_3 C + b_0$$

where b_1, b_2, and b_3 are the weights for predictors S, F, and C. In other words, they are slopes, or **regression coefficients**. The coefficient b_0 is simply the intercept, with the same meaning that it has had throughout our discussion of regression (although in simple regression we often denoted it as a).

Multiple regression solutions are very cumbersome to compute by hand, especially with more than two predictors, but they can be readily computed with any of the widely available statistical programs. In this chapter we will focus exclusively on solutions generated by computer software.

11.1 Overview

It will be helpful to begin with an example that represents an overview of various aspects of multiple regression. Then we can go back and look specifically at each of them with some actual data at hand. I will cover a lot of ground quite quickly, but my major purpose is to give you a general understanding of where we are going, rather than to impart a lot of technical information. You will see most of this again.

How do professors decide who will be offered admission to graduate school? Many years ago I collected data on admission to one graduate program. All faculty in that department rated several hundred graduate applications on a scale from 1 to 7, where 1 represented "reject immediately" and 7 represented "accept immediately." For a random sample of 100 applications I attempted to predict the mean rating (Rating) for each application (averaged over judgments based on all available information) on the basis of Graduate Record Exam Verbal score (GREV), a numerical rating of the combined letters of recommendation (Letters), and a numerical rating of the statements of purpose (Purpose). (My intent was to look at how people made decisions, not to predict who would be admitted.) The obtained regression equation was

$$\hat{Y} = 0.009 \times \text{GREV} + 0.51 \times \text{Letters} + 0.43 \times \text{Purpose} - 1.87$$

In addition, the correlation between Rating and the three predictors considered simultaneously (the **multiple correlation coefficient, R**) was .775.[1]

Squared Multiple Correlation

We can square the multiple correlation coefficient, just as we did in the one-predictor case, with a similar interpretation. The **squared correlation coefficient (R^2)** is .60. The interpretation of R^2 is the same as for the case of r^2 with one predictor. In other words, 60% of the variability in ratings can be accounted for by variability in the three predictors *considered together*. Put slightly differently, using GREV, Letters, and Purpose *simultaneously* as predictors, we can account for 60% of the variability in ratings of admissibility. Suppose that a couple of faculty members had a strange aversion to admitting students who were over the age of 40. (Probably in defiance of laws related to age discrimination.) That would affect their ratings, but that is not one of the measures I took. So variability related to age discrimination cannot be predicted by my formula, and thus goes into the 40% of the variability that I cannot predict. It is part of the error variance.

Interpretation

The regression equation in multiple regression is interpreted in much the same way it was interpreted in simple regression, wherein we had only one predictor. To make a prediction, we multiply the student's GREV score by 0.009. In addition, we multiply the rating of that student's letters of recommendation by 0.51 and the rating of the statement of purpose by 0.43. We then sum those results and subtract 1.87 (the intercept). For every one-unit change in GREV the predicted rating will increase by 0.009 unit, *assuming that Letters and Purpose remain unchanged*. Similarly, for every one-unit change in the rating of the letters of recommendation there will be a 0.51-unit change in the ratings, again assuming that the other two predictors are held constant. The most important words in that last sentence were "assuming that the other two predictors are held constant." We are back to that word "conditional" that we have seen several times before. We are dealing with one variable conditional on fixed values of the other variable(s). We will consider this in more depth shortly, but for now keep in mind that we are looking at one variable controlling for the effects of the other variables.

Standardized Regression Coefficients

In Chapter 10 I mentioned the standardized regression coefficient (β) and said that it represents the regression coefficient we would obtain if we standardized the variables, that is, converted the variables (separately) to z scores. Here is a good place to say something meaningful about β. In the equation given for predicting ratings from GREV, Letters, and Purpose, you might at first be inclined to suggest that GREV

---

[1]Note that I was predicting the rating that faculty would give, not the individual's actual success in graduate school. It is not very surprising that ratings would be related to GRE scores and what reviewers said about the candidate, though I would find it very surprising if the composite score correlated that highly with subsequent performance once admitted.

must not be very important as a predictor because it has such a small (unstandardized) regression coefficient (0.009). On the other hand, the regression coefficient for Letters is 0.51, which is more than 5,000 times greater. As we just saw, this regression equation tells us that a one-point difference in GREV would make (only) a 0.009 difference in our prediction, whereas a one-point difference in the rating of Letters would make a difference of about half a point in our prediction. But keep in mind that the variability of GREV is considerably greater than the variability of ratings of Letters. It is trivial to do one point better or worse on GREV (does anyone really care if your Verbal score was 552 instead of a 553—even ignoring the fact that the way the test is scored, values are rounded to the nearest 10s digit)? But Letters were rated on a seven-point scale, where a one-point difference is a big deal. This difference between the variances of our two measures is one major reason why we can't meaningfully compare regular (unstandardized) regression coefficients.

If I now told you that the *standardized* regression coefficient (β) for GREV was 0.72, while the β for Letters was 0.61, you would see that, *after we take the difference in the standard deviations of the variables into account*, the weights for these variables are approximately equal. (Another way of saying that is, "after we put both variables on an equal footing by standardizing them, their contributions are approximately equal.") A one standard deviation difference in GREV will make a 0.72 standard deviation difference in the prediction, while a one standard deviation difference in Letters will make a 0.61 standard deviation difference in the prediction. In this sense the two variables contribute about evenly to the prediction. But be careful of over interpreting what I have said. Using standardized weights (β) does make it easier to keep the contributions of the variables in perspective. However, this scheme is not foolproof. For reasons dealing with the intercorrelations of the predictor variables, β weights are not perfectly related to the importance of the contribution that each variable makes to the prediction. They are a good rough guide, but don't conclude that just because the value of 0.72 is greater than 0.61, GREV is more important than Letters. In the first place, it is not clear just what "more important than" means here. Additionally, some other measure of the contribution of each variable might favor Letters over GREV. The task of deciding on the relative importance of predictors is a difficult one (for predictors that are themselves highly correlated, maybe even a meaningless one). A much more extensive discussion of this problem is found in Howell (2012).

Redundancy among Predictors

The issue of correlation among predictors in multiple regression is an important one, and deserves discussion. Imagine an artificial situation wherein we have two predictor variables that are each correlated with the criterion, or dependent, variable, but are uncorrelated with each other. In this case the predictors have nothing in common, and the squared multiple correlation coefficient (R^2) will be equal to the sum of the squared correlations of each predictor with the dependent variable. Each predictor is bringing something new, and unique, to the prediction. That is the ideal case, but we very rarely work in a world where the predictors are not correlated with each other.

Consider the example of predicting ratings for admission to graduate school. It seems perfectly reasonable that you would likely have a better rating if you had a better GREV score. Similarly, it seems reasonable that you would have a better rating if you had stronger letters of recommendation. But GREV scores and Letters are themselves likely to be highly correlated. If you do well in your courses, you will probably do well on the GRE. In fact, I may even refer to your performance on the GRE when I write your letter of recommendation. If the reader on the other end looks at your GRE scores and then reads my letter, my letter is telling her some of what she already knew—this student knows a lot. Similarly, if the reader reads my letter and finds that you are a terrific student, she is not going to be very surprised when she turns to the GRE scores and sees that they are high. In other words, the two variables are to some extent redundant. Put another way, the total information in those two predictors is not the sum of the parts—it is something less than the sum of the parts. For a more prosaic example, suppose that I ask your mother to tell me all about you. (You would probably be surprised by how much she knew.) Then I find your father and ask him the same question. Do you think that Dad is going to add a lot to what I already know? I doubt it. What he has to say will largely overlap what your mother already told me. It is important to keep this redundancy in mind when thinking about multiple regression.

When the predictors are *highly* correlated with each other (a condition known as **multicollinearity**), the regression equation is very unstable from one sample of data to another. In other words, two random samples from the same population might produce regression equations that appear to be totally different from one another and yet would lead to nearly equally good prediction on average. I would strongly advise you to avoid using highly correlated predictors and even to avoid moderate intercorrelations when possible, though it isn't always possible.

11.2 Funding Our Schools

There has been an ongoing debate in this country about what we can do to improve the quality of primary and secondary education. It is generally assumed that spending more money on education will lead to better prepared students, but that is just an assumption. Guber (1999) addressed that question by collecting data for each of the 50 U.S. states, She recorded the amount spent on education (Expend), the pupil/teacher ratio (PTratio), average teacher's salary (Salary), the percentage of students in that state taking the SAT exams (PctSAT), the SAT verbal score (Verbal), the SAT math score (Math), and the combined SAT score (Combined)[2]. The data are shown in Table 11.1 and are available on the website for this book.[3] We will use only three of the variables, but you might work with some of the others on your own.

I have chosen to work with this particular data set because it illustrates several things. In the first place, it is a real data set that pertains to a topic of current interest. In addition, it illustrates what is, at first, a very puzzling result, and then allows us to explore that result and make sense of it. The difference between what we see with one predictor and what we see with two predictors is quite dramatic and illustrates some of the utility of multiple regression. Finally, these data illustrate well the need to think carefully about your measures and to not simply assume that they measure what you think they measure.

---

[2]It is important to note that the Educational Testing Service makes it very clear that it does not recommend using SAT scores as a way to rate education in different states. By the time that we have finished with this example I hope that you understand some of its reasoning.

[3]An abstract and a complete copy of this paper are available at https://www.amstat.org/publications/jse/v7n2_abstracts.html.

Table 11.1 Data on Performance Versus Expenditures on Education

State	Expend	PTratio	Salary	PctSAT	Verbal	Math	Combined
Alabama	4.405	17.2	31.144	8	491	538	1029
Alaska	8.963	17.6	47.951	47	445	489	934
Arizona	4.778	19.3	32.175	27	448	496	944
Arkansas	4.459	7.1	28.934	6	482	523	1005
California	4.992	24.0	41.078	45	417	485	902
Colorado	5.443	18.4	34.571	29	462	518	980
Connecticut	8.817	14.4	50.045	81	431	477	908
Delaware	7.030	16.6	39.076	68	429	468	897
Florida	5.718	19.1	32.588	48	420	469	889
Georgia	5.193	16.3	32.291	65	406	448	854
Hawaii	6.078	17.9	38.518	57	407	482	889
Idaho	4.210	19.1	29.783	15	468	511	979
Illinois	6.136	17.3	39.431	13	488	560	1048
Indiana	5.826	17.5	36.785	58	415	467	882
Iowa	5.483	15.8	31.511	5	516	583	1099
Kansas	5.817	15.1	34.652	9	503	557	1060
Kentucky	5.217	17.0	32.257	11	477	522	999
Louisiana	4.761	16.8	26.461	9	486	535	1021
Maine	6.428	13.8	31.972	68	427	469	896
Maryland	7.245	17.0	40.661	64	430	479	909
Massachusetts	7.287	14.8	40.795	80	430	477	907
Michigan	6.994	20.1	41.895	11	484	549	1033
Minnesota	6.000	17.5	35.948	9	506	579	1085
Mississippi	4.080	17.5	26.818	4	496	540	1036
Missouri	5.383	15.5	31.189	9	495	550	1045
Montana	5.692	16.3	28.785	21	473	536	1009
Nebraska	5.935	14.5	30.922	9	494	556	1050
Nevada	5.160	18.7	34.836	30	434	483	917
New Hampshire	5.859	15.6	34.720	70	444	491	935
New Jersey	9.774	13.8	46.087	70	420	478	898
New Mexico	4.586	17.2	28.493	11	485	530	1015
New York	9.623	15.2	47.612	74	419	473	892
North Carolina	5.077	16.2	30.793	60	411	454	865
North Dakota	4.775	15.3	26.327	5	515	592	1107
Ohio	6.162	16.6	36.802	23	460	515	975
Oklahoma	4.845	15.5	28.172	9	491	536	1027
Oregon	6.436	19.9	38.555	51	448	499	947
Pennsylvania	7.109	17.1	44.510	70	419	461	880
Rhode Island	7.469	14.7	40.729	70	425	463	888
South Carolina	4.797	16.4	30.279	58	401	443	844
South Dakota	4.775	14.4	25.994	5	505	563	1068
Tennessee	4.388	18.6	32.477	12	497	543	1040
Texas	5.222	15.7	31.223	47	419	474	893
Utah	3.656	24.3	29.082	4	513	563	1076
Vermont	6.750	13.8	35.406	68	429	472	901
Virginia	5.327	14.6	33.987	65	428	468	896
Washington	5.906	20.2	36.151	48	443	494	937
West Virginia	6.107	14.8	31.944	17	448	484	932
Wisconsin	6.930	15.9	37.746	9	501	572	1073
Wyoming	6.160	14.9	31.285	10	476	525	1001

Table 11.2 Stem-and-Leaf Display for Import Variables for the Data in Table 11.1

Expenditures	Combined SAT	Percentage Taking SAT
The decimal point is at the		The decimal point is two digit(s) to the right of the		The decimal point is one digit(s) to the right of the	
3 | 7	8 | 4	0 | 44555689999999
4 | 124456888888	8 | 578899999	1 | 01112357
5 | 01222234457788999	9 | 000000111233444	2 | 1379
6 | 0111224489	9 | 5888	3 | 0
7 | 001235	10 | 00112233344	4 | 57788
8 | 8	10 | 55567789	5 | 1788
8 | 068	11 | 01	6 | 0455888
		7 | 00004
		8 | 01

From the stem-and-leaf display in Table 11.2 you can see that the expenditure variable is slightly positively skewed, whereas the combined SAT score is roughly normal. The percentage of students taking the SAT is almost a bimodal variable, and we will discuss this shortly.

Two Variable Relationships

The most obvious thing to do with these data is to ask about the relationship between expenditure and outcome. We would presumably like to see that the more money we spend on education, the better our students do. Table 11.3 shows the Pearson correlations between some of our variables. You can easily reproduce Table 11.3, and then a scatterplot showing the relationships between these same variables, as shown in Figure 11.1.

Table 11.3 Correlations Between Selected Variables

	Correlations				
		Expend	Salary	PctSAT	Combined
Expend	Pearson Correlation	1	.870**	.593**	−.381**
	Sig. (2-tailed)	.	.000	.000	.006
	N	50	50	50	50
Salary	Pearson Correlation	.870**	1	.617**	−.440**
	Sig. (2-tailed)	.000	.	.000	.001
	N	50	50	50	50
PctSAT	Pearson Correlation	.593**	.617**	1	−.887**
	sig. (2-tailed)	.000	.000	.	.000
	N	50	50	50	50
Combined	Pearson Correlation	−.381**	−.440**	−.887**	1
	sig. (2-tailed)	.006	.001	.000	.
	N	50	50	50	50

**Correlation is significant at the 0.01 level (2-tailed).

Figure 11.1 Relationship between Expend and PctSAT

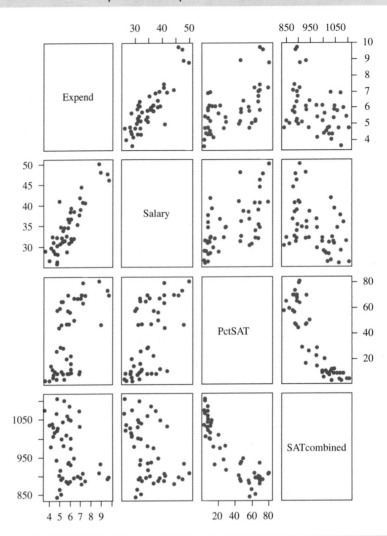

The R code is

```
schoolData <- read.table("http://www.uvm.edu/~dhowell/
fundamentals9/DataFiles/Tab11-1.dat", header = TRUE)
attach(schoolData)
schoolData <- schoolData[-2]    #Remove string variable "State" for future
                                analyses
smallData <- as.data.frame(cbind(Expend, Salary, PctSAT, SATcombined))
## Create a new data frame with only the variables of interest.
cor(smallData)                  #Produces Table 11.1
plot(smallData)                 #Produces Figure 11.3
```

For SPSS you can load the data and then use **Graphs/Legacy Dialogs/ Matrix Scatter** to produce the figure and use **Analyze/Correlate/ Bivariate** to produce the matrix of correlations.

Figure 11.1 gives us a general idea of the relationships among the variables, but if we want to look specifically at the relationship between the combined SAT score and expenditures, we are better off plotting just that relationship and superimposing the regression line. This can be seen in Figure 11.2. This figure is surprising because it would suggest that the more money we spend on educating our children the worse they do. The regression line is clearly decreasing and the correlation is −.38. Although that correlation is not terribly large, it is statistically significant and cannot just be ignored. Those students who come from wealthier schools tend to do worse. Why should this be?

An answer to our puzzle comes from knowing a bit about the SAT exam itself. Not all colleges and universities require that students take the SAT for admission[4], and there is a tendency for those that do require it to be the more prestigious universities in the northeastern U. S. and the far West, and they tend to take only the top students. In addition, the percentage of students taking the SAT varies drastically from state to state, with 81% of the students in Connecticut and only 4% of the students in Utah. The states with the lowest percentages tend to be in the West and Midwest, with the highest in the Northeast and far West. In states where a small percentage of the students is taking the exam, those are most likely to be the best students who have their eyes on Princeton, Harvard, U.C. Berkeley, and the like. (Including, of course, the University of Vermont.) These are students who are likely to do well. In Massachusetts and Connecticut, where most of the students take the SAT—the less able as well as the more able—the poorer students are going to pull

Figure 11.2   Combined SAT score as a function of expenditures on education

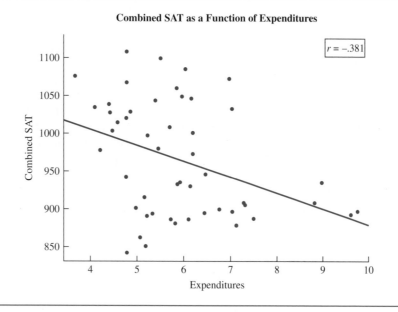

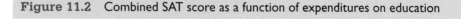

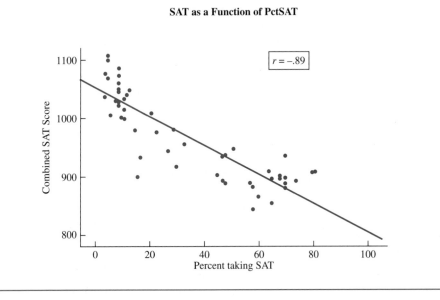

Figure 11.3 SAT scores as a function of percentage of students taking the exam

SAT as a Function of PctSAT

$r = -.89$

the state average toward the center. If this were true, we would expect to see a negative relationship between the percentage of students taking the exam (PctSAT) and the state's mean score. This is exactly what we find, as can be seen in Figure 11.3.

Notice the dramatic effect in Figure 11.3. The correlation coefficient is $-.89$, with the points clustering very close to the regression line. Notice also that you can see the effect of the bimodal distribution of PctSAT, with the bulk of the points clustering at one end or the other of the X axis.

Looking at One Predictor While Controlling for Another

The question that now arises is what would happen if we used both variables simultaneously as predictors of the combined score? What this really means, though it may not be immediately obvious, is that we will look at the relationship between Expend and Combined, *controlling for PctSAT*. When I say that we are controlling for PctSAT, I mean that we are looking at the relationship between Expend and Combined while holding PctSAT constant. Imagine that we had many thousands of states instead of only 50. Imagine also that we could pull out a collection of states that had exactly the same percentage of students taking the SAT—for example, 60%. Then we could look at only the students from those states and compute the correlation and regression coefficient for predicting Combined from Expend. These coefficients would be completely independent of PctSAT because all of those states have exactly the same score on that variable. Then we could draw another sample of states, perhaps those with 40% of their students taking the exam. Again we could correlate Expect and Combined for only those states and compute a regression coefficient. Notice that I have calculated two correlations and two regression coefficients here, each with PctSAT held constant at a specific value (40% or 60%). Because we are only imagining that we had thousands of states, we can go further and imagine that we repeated this process many times, with PctSAT held at a different specific value each time. For each of those analyses we would obtain a regression coefficient for the relationship between Expend and Combined, and an average of those many regression coefficients will be very close to the overall regression coefficient for Expend from the multiple regression that we will compute and which we will shortly examine. The same is true if we averaged the correlations.

Because in our imaginary exercise each correlation is based on a sample with a fixed value of PctSAT, each correlation is independent of PctSAT. In other words, if every state included in our correlation had 35% of its students taking the SAT, then PctSAT doesn't vary and it can't have an effect on the relationship between Expend and Combined. This means that, for these states, our correlation and regression coefficient between those two variables has *controlled for* PctSAT.

Obviously we don't have thousands of states—we only have 50 and that number is not likely to get much larger. However, that does not stop us from mathematically estimating what we would obtain if we could carry out the imaginary exercise that I just explained. And that is exactly what multiple regression is all about.

11.3 The Multiple Regression Equation

There are ways to think about multiple regression other than fixing the level of one or more variables, but before I discuss those I will show you a multiple regression on these data that I ran using a program called MYSTAT that you can find online at http://www.systat.com/Downloads.[5] The results are shown in Table 11.4. I have omitted some of the printout to save space. I chose to use MYSTAT so that you would see a slightly different way of printing out the results.

The first table presents the basic statistics for each of our variables. This is followed by a table giving the multiple correlation ($R = .905$), its square, and a statistic called the "adjusted squared multiple R." (The phrase "OLS Regression" stands for "Ordinary Least Squares Regression." We are trying to make the squared residuals "least.") In multiple regression, the correlation is always going to be positive, whereas the Pearson correlation can be positive or negative. There is a good reason for this, but I don't want to elaborate on that now. (If the correlations are always positive, how do we know when the relationship is negative? We look at the sign of the regression coefficient, and I'll come to that in a minute.) The squared correlation in multiple regression has the same meaning that it had in simple regression. Using Expend alone we were able to explain $(-.381)^2 = .145 = 14.5\%$ of the variation in Combined SAT scores (not shown in table). Using both Expend and PctSAT we can explain $.905^2 = .819 = 81.9\%$ of the variability in the Combined score. Below this value you will see an entry labeled Adj. R square. You can ignore that column. The adjusted R squared is actually a less biased estimate of the true squared correlation in the population, but we never report it. Simply use R and not the adjusted R.

You might recall that in Figure 11.3 we saw that the simple correlation between Combined and PctSAT was $-.89$, so perhaps we haven't gained all that much by moving to .905 by adding a second predictor. We will also look at this shortly.

---

[5]Use care here. Some of the sites that offer downloads try to sneak in all sorts of programs that you probably don't want. Check the link that shows up at the bottom of your screen, and read carefully before you click "Yes."

Table 11.4 Multiple Regression Predicting Combined from Expend and PctSAT

Descriptive Statistics			
	SATCOMBINED	EXPEND	PCTSAT
N of Cases	50	50	50
Minimum	844.000	3.656	4.000
Maximum	1,107.000	9.774	81.000
Arithmetic Mean	965.920	5.905	35.240
Standard Deviation	74.821	1.363	26.762
Variance	5,598.116	1.857	716.227

OLS Regression	
Dependent Variable	SATCOMBINED
H	50
Multiple R	0.905
Squared Multiple R	0.819
Adjusted Squared Multiple R	0.812
Standard Error of Estimate	32.459

Regression Coefficients B						
Effect	Coefficient	Standard Error	Std. Coefficient	Tolerance	t	p-value
CONSTANT	993.832	21.833	0.000		45.519	0.000
EXPEND	12.287	4.224	0.224	0.649	2.909	0.006
PCTSAT	−2.851	0.215	-1.020	0.649	-13.253	0.000

Analysis of Variance					
Source	SS	df	Mean Squares	F-ratio	p-value
Regression	224,787.621	2	112,393.810	106.674	0.000
Residual	49,520.059	47	1,053.618		

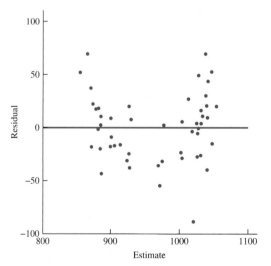

Plot of Residuals Versus Predicted Values

Skipping over the third subtable in Table 11.4 for the moment we come to a table labeled the "Analysis of Variance." We will spend quite a bit of time on the analysis of variance later in the book, and I am only going to point to two parts of this table here. Notice that there is a column labeled F and one labeled Sig. The F is a test of whether the multiple correlation coefficient in question is significantly different from 0. We saw a test on the significance of a correlation coefficient in Chapters 9 and 10. This is the same kind of test, though it uses a different statistic. When we had only one predictor (Expend) the correlation was $-.38$, as we saw in Table 11.3, and the probability of getting a correlation of that magnitude if the null hypothesis is true was .006. This is well less than .05, and we declared that correlation to be significantly different from 0. When we move to multiple regression and include the predictor PctSAT along with Expend, we have two questions to ask. The first is whether the multiple correlation using both predictors together is significantly different from 0.00, and the second is whether each of the predictor variables in the equation is contributing at greater than chance levels to that relationship. From the ANOVA table we see an $F = 106.674$, with an associated probability that rounds to .000. This tells us that using both predictors our correlation is significantly greater than 0. I will ask about the significance of the individual predictors in the next section.

To run this analysis in R we use the following code. I am not showing the output because it closely resembles what we just saw. The function that we will use, "lm," computes a "linear model," which is just what multiple regression is. To see the full printout we need to request "summary(model1)." Otherwise printing model1 just by itself ("print(model1)") doesn't give us much.

```
schoolData <- read.table("https://www.uvm.edu/~dhowell/
     fundamentals9/DataFiles/Tab11-1.dat", header = TRUE)
attach(schoolData)

model1 <- lm(SATcombined ~ Expend + PctSAT)
print(summary(model1))
plot(model1)      # The first plot is the residuals versus predicted

pred <- model1$fitted.values   # Extract predicted values
model2 <- lm(SATcombined~pred)   # Needed to draw line
plot(SATcombined~pred)   # Produces R's equivalent of Figure 11.3
abline(model2)
```

Returning to the earlier printout, we come to the most interesting part of the output. In the subtable labeled "Regression Coefficients" we see the full set of regression coefficients when using both predictors at the same time. From the second column we can see that our regression equation is

$$\hat{Y} = 993.832 + 12.287(Expend) - 2.851(PctSAT)$$

The value of 993.832 is the intercept, often denoted b_0 and here denoted simply as "constant." This is the predicted value of Combined if both Expend and PctSAT were 0.00, which they will never be. We need the intercept because it forces the average of our predictions to equal the average of the obtained values, but we rarely pay any real attention to it.

Just as a simple regression was of the form

$$\hat{Y} = bX + a,$$

a multiple regression, is written as

$$\hat{Y} = b_1X_1 + b_2X_2 + b_0$$

where X_1 and X_2 are the predictors and b_0 is the intercept. From the table we can see that the coefficient for Expend (call it b_1) is 12.287, and for PctSAT the coefficient (b_2) is -2.851. From the sign of these coefficients we can tell whether the relationship is positive or negative. The positive coefficient for Expend tell us that *now that we have controlled PctSAT* the relationship between expenditures and performance is positive—the more the state spends, the higher its (adjusted[6]) SAT score. That should make us feel much better. We can also see that when we control Expend, the relationship between PctSAT and Combined is negative, which makes sense. I explained earlier why increasing the percentage of a state's students taking the SAT would be expected to lower the overall mean for that state.

But you may have noticed that PctSAT itself had a correlation of $-.89$ with Combined, and perhaps Expend wasn't adding anything important to the relationship—after all, the correlation only increased to .905. If you look at the table of coefficients, you will see two columns on the right labeled t and p-value. These relate to significance tests on the regression coefficients. You saw similar t tests in Chapter 10. From the sig. column we can tell that all three coefficients are significant at $p < .05$. The intercept has no useful meaning, but the other two statistics are important. The coefficient for Expend is meaningful because it shows that increased spending does correlate with higher scores after we control for the percentage of students taking the exam. Similarly, after we control for expenditures, SAT scores are higher for those states who have few (presumably their best) students taking the test. So although adding Expend to PctSAT as predictors didn't raise the correlation very much, it was a statistically significant contributor. More importantly, adding PctSAT to the equation greatly changed what the data have to say. Instead of indicating that when we spend more money on education our students' performance decreases, we now see that expenditures increase their performance *after we adjust for the percentage of students in each state taking the exam.* That is quite a different story even if it does lead to only a very minor increase in R.

At the bottom of Table 11.4 I have included a kind of graphic that you have not seen before. This shows the relationship between the predicted value of performance and the residual (the differences$(Y_i - \hat{Y}_i)$). The latter is simply the difference between what the equation would predict and what the state's mean score actually was. The graphic doesn't look very interesting, and that is just the point. It is basically telling us that there is nothing systematically odd about our

---

[6]I say "adjusted" because it is the SAT score that has been adjusted for differences in PctSAT.

regression. If we did see an interesting pattern that would mean that there is something going on in the data that we have not taken into account. We want this plot to be boring.

I discussed earlier one of the ways of interpreting what a multiple regression was—for any predictor variable the slope is the relationship between that variable and the criterion variable if we could hold all other variables constant. And by "hold constant" we mean having a collection of participants who had all the same scores on each of the other variables. But there are two other ways of thinking about regression that are useful.

Another Interpretation of Multiple Regression

When we just correlate Expend with Combined and completely ignore PctSAT, there is a certain amount of variability in the Combined scores that is directly related to variability in PctSAT, and that was what was giving us that peculiar negative result. What we would really like to do is to examine the correlation between Expend and the Combined score when both are adjusted to be free from the influences of PctSAT. To put it another way, some of the differences in Combined are due to differences in Expend and some are due to differences in PctSAT. We want to eliminate those differences in both variables that can be attributed to PctSAT and then correlate the adjusted variables. That is actually a lot simpler than it sounds. I can't imagine anyone intentionally running a multiple regression the way that I am about to, but it illustrates what is going on.

We know that if we ran the simple regression predicting Combined from PctSAT, the resulting set of predicted scores would represent that part of Combined that is predictable from PctSAT. If we subtract the predicted scores from the actual scores, the resulting values(call them ResidCombined), will be that part of Combined that is *not* predictable from (is independent of) PctSAT. (These new scores are called "residuals," and we will have more to say about them shortly.) We can now do the same thing predicting Expend from PctSAT. We will get the predicted scores, subtract them from the obtained scores, and have a new set of scores(call them ResidExpend), that is also independent of PctSAT. So we now have two sets of residual scores—ResidCombined and ResidExpend—that are both independent of PctSAT. Therefore, PctSAT can play no role in their relationship.

If I now run the regression to predict the adjusted Combined score from the adjusted Expend score (i.e., ResidCombined with ResidExpend), I will have the following:

		Unstandardized Coefficients		Standardized Coefficients		
Model		B	Std. Error	Beta	t	Sig.
1	(Constant)	2.547E-14	4.542		.000	1.000
	Unstandardized Residual	12.287	4.180	.391	2.939	.005

Coefficients[a]

[a] Dependent Variable: Unstandardized Residual

Notice that the regression coefficient predicting the adjusted combined score from the adjusted expend score is 12.287, which is exactly what we had for Expend doing things the normal way. Notice also that the following table shows us that the correlation between these two corrected variables is .391, which is the correlation between Expend and Combined after we have removed any effects attributable to PctSAT.

Model Summary[b]				
Model	R	R Square	Adjusted R Square	Std. Error of the Esimate
1	.391[a]	.153	.135	32.11958743

[a] Predictors: (Constant), Unstandardized Residual
[b] Dependent Variable: Unstandardized Residual

I hope that no one thinks that they should actually do their regression this way. The reason I went through the exercise was to make the point that when we have multiple predictor variables we are adjusting each predictor for all other predictors in the equation. And the phrases "adjusted for," "controlling," and "holding constant" all are ways of saying the same thing.

A Final Way to Think of Multiple Regression

There is another way to think of multiple regression, and in some ways I find it the most useful. We know that in multiple regression we solve for an equation of the form

$$\hat{Y} = b_1 X_1 + b_2 X_2 + b_0$$

or, in terms of the variables we have been using

$$\widehat{Combined} = b_1 \, Expend + b_2 \, PctSAT + b_0$$

For each state I obtained the predicted scores from

$$\widehat{Combined} = 12.287 \times Expend - 2.851 \times PctSAT + 993.832$$

and stored the predicted scores as PredComb. (SPSS will do this for you if you use the Save button on the first dialog box under Regression. R will do it automatically, and the predicted scores can be obtained as model$fitted.values, where "model" is the name of the result.) Now if I correlate actual Combined with PredComb, the resulting correlation will be .905, which is our multiple correlation. (A scatterplot of this relationship is shown in Figure 11.4, which gives the squared multiple correlation as .8195, the square root of which is .905.)

The point of this last approach is to show that you can think of a multiple correlation coefficient as the simple Pearson correlation between the criterion (Combined) and the best linear combination of the predictors. When I say "best linear combination" I mean that there is no set of weights (regression coefficients) that will do a better job of predicting the state's combined score from those predictors. This is actually a very important point. There are a number of advanced techniques in statistics, which we are not going to cover in this book, that really come down to creating a new variable that is some optimal weighted sum of other variables, and then using that variable in the main part of the analysis. This approach also explains why multiple correlations are always positive, even if the relationship between two variables is negative. You would certainly expect the predicted values to be positively correlated with the criterion.

Figure 11.4 Scatterplot showing the relationship between the best linear combination of the predictors and combined

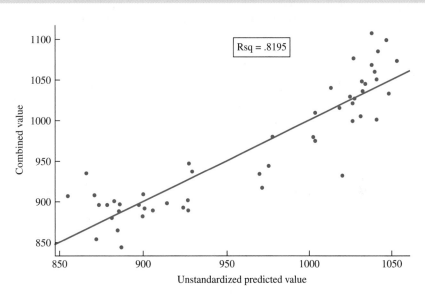

Review

We have covered a great deal of information, so I am going to go back and sum-marize the major points.

The basic form of a multiple regression equation is

$$\hat{Y} = b_1 X + b_2 Z + b_0$$

and the multiple correlation coefficient is represented as R. Just as with simple regression, the square of R, i.e., R^2, can be interpreted as the percentage of varia-tion in the dependent variable (Y) that is accounted for by the best linear com-bination of our predictors (X and Z). We also saw that standardized regression coefficients (βi) are useful for getting a sense of the importance of each variable because they put the variables on comparable footing.

I discussed the fact that if two of the predictors are themselves correlated, they explain overlapping proportions of the variability in Y, and so the resulting multiple regression is not equal to the sum of its parts. This is a particular problem when the predictors are highly correlated, because several quite different-looking regression equations could lead to very similar results.

We next looked at Guber's data on educational funding and saw expendi-ture has a very large negative relationship to performance, but that the relation-ship changes in both magnitude and sign when we control for the percentage of students from each state that take the SAT.

Finally, I discussed three different ways of looking at multiple regression:

- We can treat a regression coefficient as the coefficient we would get if we had a whole group of states that did not differ on any of the predictors except the one under consideration. In other words, all predictors but one are held constant, and we look at what varying that one predictor does.

■ We can think of a regression coefficient in multiple regression as the same as we would have in simple regression if we adjusted our two variables for any of the variables we want to control. In the above example it meant adjusting both Combined and Expend for PctSAT by computing the difference between the true score for that variable and the score predicted from the "nuisance variable" (or the "to be controlled variable"). The coefficient (slope) that we obtain is the same coefficient we find in the multiple regression solution.

■ We can think of the multiple correlation as the simple Pearson correlation between the criterion (call it Y) and another variable (call it $\hat{Y}$) that is the best linear combination of the predictor variables.

The Educational Testing Service, which produces the SAT, tries to have everyone put a disclaimer on results broken down by states that says that the SAT is not a fair way to compare the performance of different states. Having gone through this example you can see that one reason that ETS says this is that different states have different cohorts of students taking the exam, and this makes the test inappropriate as a way of judging a state's performance, regardless of whether or not it is a good way of judging the performance of individuals.

11.4 Residuals

When we make a prediction from a set of data, we don't expect to be right all the time. Sometimes our prediction will be a bit high, sometimes a bit low. And sometimes the actual data point will be far away from what we have predicted. It is worth looking briefly at these predictions and the errors of prediction, called **residuals**, because they tell us something more about multiple regression. Table 11.5 contains a sample of the data we saw earlier on expenditures for education. I have added two columns—one holding the predicted values and the other the residual values. In that table you can see that some of the predictions are quite accurate (the residual is small) and other predictions are poor (the residual is large). In Figure 11.3 we saw a scatterplot of the relationship between the SAT combined score and our best linear prediction of that score. Notice that there are two small numbers on that figure (34 and 48). These numbers refer to the states that produced those observations. State 34 is North Dakota and State 48 is West Virginia. Notice that both states had nearly the same predicted outcome (approximately 1050), but North Dakota well exceeded that prediction (1107) while West Virginia fell short by a similar amount (932).

These residuals, the difference between predicted and obtained, can either be random noise or they can be meaningful. With a difference of nearly 200 points, I would be inclined to take them seriously. I would ask what North Dakota knows about educating students that West Virginia does not. It isn't that the state spends significantly more on education or has significantly fewer students taking the SAT. We can rule out those possibilities because we are looking at the residuals after controlling for PctSAT and Expend. But a close examination of these states might lead to

Table 11.5 Predicted Values and Residuals for Selected States

State	Expend	PctSAT	Combined	Predict	Residual
Alabama	4.405	8	1029	1025.146	3.854
Alaska	8.963	47	934	969.962	−35.962
Arizona	4.778	27	944	975.562	−31.562
Arkansas	4.459	6	1005	1031.512	−26.512
California	4.992	45	902	926.874	−24.874
Colorado	5.443	29	980	978.030	1.970
Iowa	5.483	5	1099	1046.944	52.056
...	...	...	...	...	...
Mississippi	4.080	4	1036	032.557	3.443
Missouri	5.383	9	1045	034.311	10.688
Montana	5.692	21	1009	003.897	5.103
...	...	...	...	...	...
New Hampshire	5.859	70	935	866.253	68.747
New Jersey	9.774	70	898	914.355	−16.355
New Mexico	4.586	11	1015	1018.817	−3.817
New York	9.623	74	892	901.096	−9.096
North Carolina	5.077	60	865	885.156	−20.155
North Dakota	4.775	5	1107	1038.245	68.755
Ohio	6.162	23	975	1003.970	−28.970
...	...	...	...	...	...
Washington	5.906	48	937	929.551	7.4489
West Virginia	6.107	17	932	1020.400	−88.400
Wisconsin	6.930	9	1073	1053.319	19.681
Wyoming	6.160	10	1001	1041.007	−40.007

important hypotheses about what other things are important. We won't go into the specific analysis of residuals, but what we have seen suggests that identifying extreme residuals can be important.[7]

11.5 Hypothesis Testing

You saw in Chapter 10 that we can ask if the regression coefficient is significantly different from zero. In other words, we can ask if differences in one variable are related to differences in another. If the slope is not significantly different from zero, we have no reason to believe that the criterion is related to the predictor. That works very cleanly when we have only one predictor variable; in fact, I told you that a test on the correlation coefficient and a test on the regression coefficient are equivalent in the one-predictor case. But the situation is distinctly different when we have more than one predictor.

With more than one predictor we can ask if each of those coefficients, taken separately, is significantly different from 0. For states that are equal on PctSAT, does a difference in Expend lead to significant differences on Combined? And are states that are equivalent on Expend but different on PctSAT predicted to be significantly different on Combined? Put more directly, we want to test the null hypotheses

$$H_0 : \beta_1 = 0$$
$$H_0 : \beta_2 = 0$$

---

[7]See Howell (2012) for a discussion of how to evaluate the magnitude of the residuals.

against the alternative hypotheses

$$H_0 : \beta_1 \neq 0$$

$$H_0 : \beta_2 \neq 0$$

Tests on these hypotheses were given in the column labeled t in Table 11.4, along with the associated two-tailed probabilities in the next column. These tests are of the same kind we saw in the previous chapter, except that we are testing two individual slopes instead of one. Here you can see that the test for the slope for Expend is significantly different from zero because the probability value ($p = .006$) is less than .05. Similarly the slope of PctSAT is also significant ($t = -13.253, p < .000$), so even if you control for differences in the percentage of students in a state that are taking the SAT, expenditure on education makes a difference, and now it has a positive effect. In later chapters of this book we will look closely at t tests and F tests, which are commonly used to test hypotheses. For now all that you need to know is that there are standard significance tests and that decisions regarding significance can be made with reference to the probability value that follows the t of F.

One more major piece of information is given in Table 11.4 in the section "Analysis of Variance." This section is a test on the null hypothesis that there is no correlation between the set of predictors (Expend and PctSAT) *taken together* and the criterion. A significant effect here would mean that we reject the null hypothesis that the multiple correlation in the population is 0. In the table we see that $F = 106.674$ with an associated probability of .000. Since this probability is less than $\alpha = .05$, we will reject H_0 and conclude that Combined is predicted at better than chance levels by these two predictors taken together. In other words, we will conclude that the true correlation in the population is not zero.

These two kinds of significance tests (tests on slopes and the test on the multiple correlation) are presented in virtually all regression analyses. I have covered them in the order they were presented in the printout, but in general if the Analysis of Variance test on the relationship is not significant, it usually doesn't make much sense even to worry about the significance of individual predictors. Fortunately, for most of the regression problems we see, the overall relationship is significant and the real issue is the role of individual predictors.

11.6 Refining the Regression Equation

In Table 11.4 we saw that Expend and PctSAT were significant predictors of Combined. We also know from correlations in Table 11.3 that teacher's Salary is significantly related to Combined. Perhaps we should add Salary to our multiple regression. But before we do that, we need to think about the relationships we have among our variables. We know that Expend, PctSAT, and Salary are *each* significantly correlated with Combined. But they are also correlated among themselves, and those correlations are not trivial. (See Table 11.4.)

Because Salary is correlated with both of the other predictors, it may not have any *independent* contribution to make to the prediction of Combined. This is an empirical question, however, and is best answered by actually doing the regression. The results are shown in Table 11.6, where I have only included the table of coefficients. (The overall ANOVA on three predictors was significant.)

Table 11.6   Multiple Regression Predicting Combined from Expend, PctSAT, and Salary Using SPSS

Coefficients[a]

Model	Unstandardized Coefficients B	Std. Error	Standardized Coefficients Beta	t	Sig.
1 (Constant)	998.029	31.493		31.690	.000
Expend	13.333	7.042	.243	1.893	.065
PctSAT	−2.840	.225	−1.016	−12.635	.000
Salary	−.309	1.653	−.025	−.187	.853

[a] Dependent Variable: Combined

From Table 11.6 we see that PctSAT remains a significant predictor, but the probability value for Expend rises slightly above .05 and we can't reject the null hypothesis (H_0: slope in the population = 0) for that variable. We also see that Salary does not even come close to significance ($p = .853$). You might legitimately wonder why Salary does so poorly here when it was nicely correlated with Combined when treated alone. Related to this is the question of why Expend is no longer significant in the multiple regression. If you think about our variables you will realize that a great deal of the differences between states in terms of expenditures is directly related to teachers' salaries. So telling me that teachers in one state make more money than teachers in another state is nearly tantamount to telling me that the first state has a higher score on Expend. You haven't really added much new information. Therefore, I am not particularly surprised that Salary did not add anything—in fact it watered down the effect of Expend. (In a sense, it spread the effect of expenditures over two variables, neither of which was then significant.)

In this example, we have searched for a regression equation (a model of the data) that best predicts the criterion variable. But keep in mind that we had a slightly different purpose in mind—we wanted to know whether expenditures on education made a difference. In other words, we weren't just interested in any old equation that could predict Combined, but wanted to address specifically the role of Expend. We did this by starting with Expend and noticing that it was actually negatively related to outcome. We then added PctSAT because we knew that much of the variance in the outcome measure was related to how many people took the exam, which is a question that would be distinct from asking about Expend except that it is a variable that looks like it needs to be controlled because the PctSAT score varies between states. Finally, we thought about adding in Salary, and found that when we did so it had nothing to contribute—in fact it seemed to do harm. I explained this finding away by noting that Salary and Expend are intimately related, and that Salary has very little *extra* to offer. More often than not, the purpose of multiple regression is to offer an explanation of certain results rather than to come up with an actual prediction. There could be other variables in our data that could produce a higher correlation (though I doubt it), but the relationship we have tells us most about what motivated collecting the data in the first place.

There is substantial literature on the topic of choosing an optimum regression equation. Many of the techniques are known as **stepwise procedures**. An introduction to this literature and additional references can be found in Howell (2012). The only point to be made here is that automatic computational procedures for identifying regression models can be seductive. They often produce a nice-looking model, but they also capitalize on chance differences in the data. This produces a model that fits the current data well but that might not fit a new set of data nearly as well. Moreover, this might produce a model that fits nicely but really doesn't answer any question we might wish to ask. In trying to construct an optimal model, it is important to realize that what you know about the variables and the theoretical constructs in the field is far more important than the statistical vagaries of a set of data. You should treat stepwise regression with considerable caution; in fact, it is sometimes referred to in the statistical literature as "unwise regression."

11.7 Special Section: Using R to Solve a Multiple Regression Problem

Throughout the book I have used R to perform calculations and illustrate important points. But so far I haven't really discussed how to use R to solve a multiple regression problem. Although I like R and have used it for many of the calculations that I made for this chapter, I need to digress a bit and explain more about how to use R with multiple regression (and later with the analysis of variance.) This gives me an opportunity to explain something about the underlying structure of what R does.

The simplest R statement would be of the form

Model1 <- lm(SATcombined ~ Expend + PctSAT)

The letters "lm" stand for "linear model," and you should certainly be able to interpret the rest of that statement. But if I then asked it to print out "model," all that you would obtain is

```
Call:
lm(formula = SATcombined ~ Expend + PctSAT)

Coefficients:
(Intercept)       Expend       PctSAT
    993.832       12.287       -2.851
```

which looks a bit sparse. Where is all the other stuff, such as the correlation coefficient, the tests on the coefficients, etc.?

Well, if I had been writing the software I would have given it to you, but that isn't the R way. When our command given above runs, R creates an "object." That object contains just about everything that SPSS or any other program produces. But we have to get at them. The authors of R assumed that the most important result is the coefficients, and that is what they print out when you just print "model1." But, as you may have noticed in the short code sections, if you typed "summary(model1)" you would get a bit more, as follows.

```
Call:
lm(formula = SATcombined ~ Expend + PctSAT)
Residuals:
     Min      1Q  Median      3Q     Max
 -88.400 -22.884   1.968  19.142  68.755
Coefficients:
             Estimate Std. Error t value Pr(>|t|)
(Intercept) 993.8317    21.8332  45.519  < 2e-16 ***
Expend       12.2865     4.2243   2.909  0.00553 **
PctSAT       -2.8509     0.2151 -13.253  < 2e-16 ***
---
Signif. codes:  0 '***' 0.001 '**' 0.01 '*' 0.05 '.' 0.1 ' ' 1

Residual standard error: 32.46 on 47 degrees of freedom
Multiple R-squared:  0.8195,     Adjusted R-squared:  0.8118
F-statistic: 106.7 on 2 and 47 DF,  p-value: < 2.2e-16
```

Well, that's somewhat better, but it still leaves a lot out. Perhaps it is all you want for the moment. But, if you type "names(model1)", where "names" lists the pieces that have been attached to the model object, you will get

```
Names(model1)
[1] "coefficients"  "residuals"      "effects"
"rank"           "fitted.values"
 [6] "assign"        "qr"             "df.residual"
"xlevels"        "call"
[11] "terms"         "model"
```

This tells us that typing "model1$coefficients" will give us the regression coefficients, typing "model1$residuals" will give us the 50 residuals, and typing "model1$fitted.values" will give us the predicted values. You don't even want to ask what the "effects" are. Generally we can get by just by typing "summary(model1), but sometimes we need to dig deeper. For now, just be happy with summary(model1). If you want the matrix of intercorrelations, use the earlier command "cor(smallDatadf)." Getting the beta values takes a bit of work, but the relevant Web page for this book gives the commands. Above all, if you have any problems using *R* for multiple regression, don't forget Google. There are many good Web pages out there, and I recommend them highly.

11.8 A Second Example: What Makes a Confident Mother?

Leerkes and Crockenberg (1999) were interested in studying the relationship between how children were affected by their own mother's level of care and their later feelings of maternal self-confidence when they, in turn, became mothers. Their sample consisted of 92 mothers of five-month-old infants. Leerkes and Crockenberg expected to find that high levels of maternal care when the mother was a child translated to high levels of self-confidence when that child later became a mother. Furthermore, the researchers

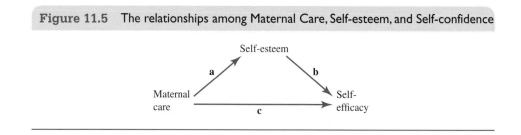

Figure 11.5   The relationships among Maternal Care, Self-esteem, and Self-confidence

postulated that self-esteem would also play a role. They argued that high levels of maternal care lead to high levels of self-esteem in the child, and that this high self-esteem later translates into high levels of self-efficacy as a mother (how effective you think you are as a mom). Similarly, low levels of maternal care were expected to lead to low levels of self-esteem, and thus to low levels of self-efficacy. This relationship is diagrammed above.

Leerkes and Crockenberg were interested in discussing the mediating role played by self-esteem (how self-esteem works to turn Maternal Care into self-efficacy), but we will ignore that issue for now and simply look at the prediction of Self-confidence from both Self-esteem and Maternal Care. The pattern of relationships is shown in Figure 11.5, and the intercorrelation matrix is given in Table 11.7. The data are on the website at Tab11.7.dat.

Here we can see that Maternal Care is correlated with both Self-esteem and Self-confidence, and Self-esteem is significantly correlated with Self-confidence. The next step is to use both Self-esteem and Maternal Care as predictors of Self-confidence. For purposes of illustration, I asked SPSS to first use Maternal Care as the only predictor and to then use both Maternal Care and Self-esteem as predictors. This is shown in the top part of the output in Table 11.8. In this table you will see both the results of correlating Self-confidence with Maternal Care (Model 1), and then the result of adding Self-esteem as a predictor (Model 2).

The first section of the printout shows that when Maternal Care is used alone as a predictor, the correlation (given in the column headed "zero-order") is .272. That is not a terribly high correlation, but we are talking about the effect

Table 11.7   Correlations among Maternal Care, self-Esteem, and Self-Confidence

	Correlations			
		MatCare	SelfEsteern	Confidence
MatCare	Pearson Correlation	1.000	.403**	.272**
	Sig. (2-tailed)		.000	.009
	N	92.000	92	92
SelfEsteern	Pearson Correlation	.403**	1.000	.380**
	Sig. (2-tailed)	.000		.000
	N	92	92.000	92
Confidence	Pearson Correlation	.272**	.380**	1.000
	Sig. (2-tailed)	.009	.000	
	N	92	92	92.000

** Correlation is significant at the 0.01 level (2-tailed).

of maternal behavior that might have occurred more than 20 years ago. When we add Self-esteem as a predictor, we see a somewhat different pattern. The multiple correlation coefficient increases from .272 with one predictor to .401 with both predictors.

The ANOVA table in the center shows that both the simple correlation and the multiple correlation with both predictors are significant. Finally, the bottom part of Table 11.8 gives the coefficients for the two solutions. When Maternal Care is taken by itself, β the standardized regression coefficient β is .272, telling us that a one standard deviation difference in Maternal Care is associated with about a quarter of a standard deviation increase in Self-confidence. The interesting thing is that when you add Self-esteem as a predictor along with Maternal Care, the standardized coefficient for Maternal Care drops to only .142 and is not significant as shown by the last two columns. However, Self-esteem is a significant predictor, with $\beta = .323$. The fact that Maternal Care is no longer a significant predictor when you add Self-esteem suggests that any effect of Maternal Care is through Self-esteem, rather than on its own. In other words, good Maternal Care leads to higher levels of Self-esteem, and that

Table 11.8   Multiple Regression Output Given by SPSS

Model Summary

Model	R	R Square	Adjusted R Square	Std. Error of the Estimate
1	.272[a]	.074	.063	.24023
2	.401[b]	.161	.142	.22992

a. Predictors: (Constant), MatCare
b. Predictors: (Constant), MatCare, SelfEsteem

ANOVA[c]

Model		Sum of Squares	df	Mean Square	F	Sig.
1	Regression	.414	1	.414	7.168	.009[a]
	Residual	5.194	90	.058		
	Total	5.607	91			
2	Regression	.903	2	.451	8.537	.000[b]
	Residual		4.705	89	.053	
	Total	5.607	91			

[a] Predictors: (Constant), MatCare
[b] Dependent (Constant), Matcare, SelfEsteem
[c] Dependent Variable: Confidence

Coefficients[a]

Model		Unstandardized Coefficients		Standardized Coefficients		
		B	Std. Error	Beta	t	Sig.
1	(Constant)	3.260	.141		23.199	.000
	MatCare	.112	.042	.272	2.677	.009
2	(Constant)	2.929	.173		16.918	.000
	MatCare	.058	.044	.142	1.334	.185
	SelfEsteem	.147	.048	.323	3.041	.003

[a] Dependent Variable: Confidence

enhanced Self-esteem leads to Self-confidence when the daughter becomes a mother many years later. This is the mediating effect that Leerkes and Crockenberg were actually looking for.

11.9 Third Example: Psychological Symptoms in Cancer Patients

There can be no doubt that a diagnosis of cancer is a disturbing event, and many, though not all, cancer patients show elevated levels of psychological symptoms in response to such a diagnosis. If we could understand the variables associated with psychological distress, perhaps we could implement intervention programs to prevent, or at least limit, that distress. That is the subject of this example.

Malcarne, Compas, Epping, and Howell (1995) examined 126 cancer patients soon after they were diagnosed with cancer and at a four-month follow-up. At the initial interviews (Time 1) they collected data on the patients' current levels of distress (Distress1), the degree to which they attributed the blame for the cancer to the type of person they are (BlamPer), and the degree to which they attributed the cancer to the kind of behaviors in which they had engaged, such as smoking or high-fat diets (BlamBeh). At the four-month follow-up (Time 2) the authors again collected data on the levels of psychological distress that the patients reported. (They also collected data on a number of other variables, which do not concern us here.)

A major purpose of this study was to test the hypothesis that psychological distress at follow-up (Distress2) was related to the degree to which the subjects blamed cancer on the type of person they are. It was hypothesized that those who blame themselves (rather than their actions) will show greater distress, in part because we do not easily change the kind of person we are, and therefore we have little control over the course, or the recurrence, of the disease. On the other hand, we do have control over our actions, and blaming our past behavior at least gives us some sense of control. (I blame my new knee on having run on pavement for 25 years, but at least I can say that that was my choice and one I am willing to pay for the opportunity to run all that time. But I am not going to start running again!)

If we want to predict distress at follow-up, one of the most important predictors is likely to be the level of distress at the initial interview. It makes sense to include this Time 1 distress measure (Distress1) in the prediction along with the initial level of personal blame (BlamPer), because we want to know if personal blame contributes to distress after we control for the initial level of distress. (Notice an important point here. I am *not* including Distress1 because I want to maximize the accuracy of my prediction, though it will probably do that. I am including Distress1 because I want to ask if BlamPer can contribute to explaining Distress2 even after we hold constant (or control for) Distress1. In other words, I am using multiple regression to develop or test a theory, not to make specific predictions about an individual outcome.) The dependent variable is distress at follow-up (Distress2). Because only 74 participants completed measures at follow-up, the resulting analysis is based on a sample size of 74. (You might ask yourself what might be wrong with drawing conclusions on only the 74 participants, out of an initial 126, who remained in the study after four months of treatment.) The results of this analysis are shown in Table 11.9.

The main part of the printout is given in the center of the table. Notice that we have a *t* test on all three coefficients and that all three *t* values are significantly

---

Table 11.9   Distress at Follow-Up as a Function of Distress and Self-Blame at Diagnosis

```
### Table 11.9 Analysis
distress.data <- read.table("http://www.uvm.edu/~dhowell/fundamentals9/DataFiles/
Tab11-9.dat", header = TRUE)
attach(distress.data)
model4 <- lm(DISTRES2 ~ DISTRES1 + BLAMPER)
summary(model4)


Call:
lm(formula = DISTRES2 ~ DISTRES1 + BLAMPER)

Residuals:
     Min       1Q   Median       3Q      Max
 -18.4965  -5.2708   0.6127   4.5273  17.5763


Coefficients:
Estimate Std. Error t value Pr(>|t|)
(Intercept)  14.2090      5.7161    2.486   0.01528 *
DISTRES1      0.6424      0.1024    6.275  2.43e-08 ***
BLAMPER       2.5980      0.8959    2.900   0.00496 **
---
Signif. codes:  0 '***' 0.001 '**' 0.01 '*' 0.05 '.' 0.1 ' ' 1

Residual standard error: 7.61 on 71 degrees of freedom
Multiple R-squared:  0.4343,   Adjusted R-squared:  0.4184
F-statistic: 27.25 on 2 and 71 DF,  p-value: 1.647e-09
```

different from 0.00. This tells us that higher distress at Time 2 is associated with higher distress at Time 1 and with a greater tendency for patients to blame the type of person they are for the cancer. The intercept is also significantly different from 0.00, but this is not of interest here.

In the next portion of the table we see that the squared multiple correlation is .434 (accounting for 43.4% of the variation in Distress2). We are going to ignore the adjusted R^2 value.

The F statistic from the analysis of variance table represents a test of the null hypothesis that the true multiple correlation coefficient in the population is 0. Because we have a large value of F and a very small value of p, we can reject that hypothesis in favor of the hypothesis that there is a true correlation between Distress2 and the combination of Distress1 and BlamPer.

You might be tempted to ask if perhaps additional predictors might improve our regression solution. For example, we also have data on the degree to which patients blame their cancer on their own behaviors (BlamBeh), and we might want to add that predictor to the ones we have already used. Although I strongly caution against throwing in additional variables just because you have them—your set of predictors should make some sort of logical sense on *a priori* grounds—I have added BlamBeh to the regression to illustrate what happens. Those results are presented in Table 11.10, where we can see that BlamBeh did not significantly improve our prediction.

I will not discuss this table in detail because it is essentially the same as the previous table. I will point out the magnitude of R^2 (.435) and the probability value associated

---

Table 11.10 Prediction of Distress2 as a Function of Distress1, BlamPer, and BlamBeh

Regression Analysis: Distress2 predicted from Distress1, BlamPer, and BlamBeh

```
Call:
lm(formula = DISTRES2 ~ DISTRES1 + BLAMPER + BLAMBEH)

Residuals:
    Min      1Q  Median      3Q     Max
-18.599  -5.265   0.669   4.413  17.482

Coefficients:
            Estimate Std. Error t value Pr(>|t|)
(Intercept)  14.0516     5.7822   2.430   0.0177 *
DISTRES1      0.6399     0.1035   6.184 3.69e-08 ***
BLAMPER       2.4511     1.0483   2.338   0.0222 *
BLAMBEH       0.2720     0.9900   0.275   0.7843
---
Signif. codes:  0 '***' 0.001 '**' 0.01 '*' 0.05 '.' 0.1 ' ' 1

Residual standard error: 7.66 on 70 degrees of freedom
Multiple R-squared:  0.4349,     Adjusted R-squared:  0.4107
F-statistic: 17.96 on 3 and 70 DF,  p-value: 9.547e-09
```

with the test on BlamBeh (.784). Notice that R^2 is virtually unchanged by the addition of BlamBeh, going from .434 to .435. This is an indication that BlamBeh is not contributing noticeably to the prediction of Distress2 *over and above the predictors that were already in the equation.* This does not mean that BlamBeh is not related to Distress2, but only that it has nothing to add beyond what we can tell from the other two predictors.

Notice also that the probability value associated with the BlamPer predictor (and the associated regression coefficient) has changed somewhat. This says nothing more than that the contribution of BlamPer is somewhat, though not much, reduced when a similar variable (BlamBeh) is added to the model. This is quite common and reflects the fact that BlamPer and BlamBeh are correlated ($r = .521$) and, to some extent, account for overlapping portions of the variability in Distress2.

Writing up the Breast Cancer Study

The following is a brief description of the study and a summary of the results. Notice the way in which the various statistics are reported.

Malcarne, Compas, Epping, and Howell (1995) collected data on 126 breast cancer patients shortly after they were diagnosed with cancer and at a four-month follow-up. The data included, among other variables, the level of distress at each interview and an estimate of the degree to which the patients blamed their cancer on "the type of person they are." At the time of the analysis, complete data were available on only 74 participants, and these 74 participants formed the basis for subsequent analyses.

At the four-month follow-up, the level of distress was regressed on both the level of distress shortly after diagnosis, and the personal blame variable. The overall regression was significant ($F(2,71) = 27.25$, and $R^2 = .434$. Both the level of distress at Time 1 ($b = 0.642$) and the degree of personal blame were significant predictors of distress at Time 2 ($b = 2.598$). ($t = 6.27; p = .000$ and $t = 2.90; p = .005$, respectively.)

When the degree to which subjects blamed their own behavior (rather than the type of person they are) was added to the equation, it did not contribute significantly to the prediction ($t = 0.27; p = .784$). We conclude that the degree to which participants blame themselves, rather than their behavior, for their cancer is an important predictor of future distress, and suggest that interventions focused on changing this self-perception might contribute toward lowering distress in breast cancer patients.

11.10 | Summary

I have already written a summary of the first half of the chapter in the section labeled "Review" on page 281. I suggest that you go back to that review and read it again carefully. Subsequent to the review, we looked at residuals, which are the differences between the value of $\hat{Y}$ that we would predict and the Y that we actually obtained. Large residuals are cause for caution, and we should examine them to see if those cases are in some special way unusual.

We then looked at hypothesis tests, and I made the point that these are "conditional" tests, although I did not specifically label them that way. To take the study of maternal behavior as an example, we say that when Maternal Care was taken as the only predictor it was significant, but when we added Self-esteem as a predictor, Maternal Care's significance dropped out. The point here is that in the first test Maternal Care was taken on its own, whereas in the second, Maternal Care was tested in the presence of variability in Self-esteem. If we were to hold Self-esteem constant, then Maternal Care would not be a significant predictor. Therefore, when we control for Self-esteem, we are also controlling for the correlation between Self-esteem and Maternal Care.

I presented material on refining a model, or a multiple regression solution. There are two important points here. First, some variables have priority in your analysis because they are the variables that you are most interested in studying. In that case, you should not just drop them from the analysis even if their regression coefficients are not significant. In addition, you do not want to throw in every variable you have just to see what happens. If you do, spurious relationships can, and do, appear. Stepwise regression, which is a method of adding more and more variables, is called "unwise regression" for a reason.

Key Terms

Multiple correlation coefficient (R), 267	Residuals, 282
Squared correlation coefficient (R^2), 267	Stepwise procedures, 286
Multicollinearity, 269	

11.11 A Quick Review

A. In simple regression the intercept is denoted as "a." How is it denoted in multiple regression?
Ans: b_0

B. Assume that the multiple correlation between a criterion measure and several predictors is .48. How would you interpret that?
Ans: $.48^2 = .23$. Twenty three percent of the variability in the dependent variable can be accounted for by variability in the predictors taken simultaneously.

C. How would you interpret a regression coefficient of 1.3?
Ans: For every one-point increase in the particular predictor the dependent variable is expected to increase by 1.3 points, *assuming that all other predictors are held constant.*

D. What do we mean by "multicollinearity?"
Ans: This refers to the fact that predictor variables are highly correlated with each other.

E. In standard computer printout, to what does the word "constant" refer?
Ans: the intercept

F. List two different ways to think of multiple regression.
Ans: a) The multiple correlation is the correlation between the best linear combination of variables and the dependent variable. b) A regression coefficient is the slope of the relationship between that variable and the dependent variable if we hold all other variables constant.

G. What is a residual?
Ans: It is the difference between the obtained value of Y and the predicted value of Y.

H. What do we mean by "stepwise regression" and why should you be wary of it?
Ans: Stepwise regression adds variables sequentially to the model, looking for the best possible prediction. It capitalizes on chance and can often leave out the variables that we care most about understanding.

I. What do we mean by a "mediated" relationship?
Ans: The relationship between two variables is mediated by a third in the sense that the first variable influences the third, which then in turn influences the second.

J. Why do we care about large residuals?
Ans: They show us where we are doing a poor job of prediction and may suggest oddities in the data.

11.12 Exercises

11.1 A psychologist studying perceived "quality of life" in a large number of cities ($N = 150$) came up with the following equation using mean temperature (Temp), median income in $1000 (Income), per capita expenditure on social services (SocSer), and population density (Popul) as predictors.

$$\hat{Y} = 5.37 - 0.01\text{Temp} + 0.05\text{Income} + 0.003\text{SocSer} - 0.01\text{Popul}$$

a) Interpret the above regression equation in terms of the coefficients.

b) Assume a city has a mean temperature of 55 degrees, has a median income of $12,000, spends $500 per capita on social services, and has a population density of 200 people per block. What is its predicted Quality of Life score?

c) What would we predict in a different city that is identical in every way except that it spends $100 per capita on social services?

11.2   Sethi and Seligman (1993) examined the relationship between optimism and religious conservatism by interviewing more than 600 subjects from a variety of religious organizations. We can regress Optimism on three variables dealing with religiosity. These are the influence of religion on their daily lives (Rel Inf), their involvement with religion (Rel Invol), and their degree of religious hope (belief in an after-life) (Rel Hope). The results are shown as SPSS printout.

Model Summary

Model	R	R Square	Adjusted R Square	Std. Error of the Estimate
1	.321[a]	.103	.099	3.0432

[a] Predictors: (Constant), relinvol, relinf, relhope

ANOVA[b]

Model		Sum of Squares	df	Mean Square	F	Sig.
1	Regression	634.240	3	211.413	22.828	.000[a]
	Residual	5519.754	596	9.261		
	Total	6153.993	599			

[a] Predictors: (Constant), relinvol, relinf, relhope
[b] Dependent Variable: optimism

Coefficients[a]

Model		Unstandardized Standardized		Coefficents Coefficients		
		B	Std. Error	Beta	t	Sig.
1	(Constant)	−1.895	.512		−3.702	.000
	relhope	.428	.102	.199	4.183	.000
	relinf	.490	.107	.204	4.571	.000
	relinvol	−.079	.116	2.033	−.682	.495

[a] Dependent Variable: optimism

Looking at the preceding printout,

a)   Are we looking at a reliable relationship? How can you tell?
b)   What is the degree of relationship between Optimism and the three predictors?
c)   What would most likely change in your answers to a) and b) if we had a much smaller number of subjects?

11.3   In Exercise 11.2, which variables make a significant contribution to the prediction of Optimism as judged by the test on their slopes?

11.4   In Exercise 11.2 the column headed "Tolerance" (which you have not seen before) gives you 1 minus the squared multiple correlation of that predictor with all other *predictors*. What can you now say about the relationships among the set of predictors?

11.5   On the basis of your answer to Exercise 11.4, speculate on one of the reasons why Religious Influence might be an important predictor of Optimism, while Religious Involvement is not.

11.6   Using the following (random) data, demonstrate what happens to the multiple correlation when you drop out cases from the data set (e.g., use 15 cases, then 10, 6, 5, 4).

Y	5	0	5	9	4	8	3	7	0	4	7	1	4	7	9
X_1	3	8	1	5	8	2	4	7	9	1	3	5	6	8	9
X_2	7	6	4	3	1	9	7	5	3	1	8	6	0	3	7
X_3	1	7	4	1	8	8	6	8	3	6	1	9	7	7	7
X_4	3	6	0	5	1	3	5	9	1	1	7	4	2	0	9

11.7 Calculate the adjusted R^2 for the 15 cases in Exercise 11.6. Twice in this chapter I said that we were going to ignore the adjusted R^2, even though it is a perfectly legitimate statistic. Can you tell what it is "adjusting" for?

11.8 The state of Vermont is divided into 10 health-planning districts, which correspond roughly to counties. The following data represent the percentage of live births of babies weighing less than 2500 grams (Y), the fertility rate for females 17 years of age or younger (X_1), total high-risk fertility rate for females younger than 17 or older than 35 years of age (X_2), percentage of mothers with fewer than 12 years of education (X_3), percentage of births to unmarried mothers (X_4), and percentage of mothers not seeking medical care until the third trimester (X_5). (There are too few observations for a meaningful analysis, so do not put faith in the results.)

Y	X_1	X_2	X_3	X_4	X_5
6.1	22.8	43.0	23.8	9.2	6
7.1	28.7	55.3	24.8	12.0	10
7.4	29.7	48.5	23.9	10.4	5
6.3	18.3	38.8	16.6	9.8	4
6.5	21.1	46.2	19.6	9.8	5
5.7	21.2	39.9	21.4	7.7	6
6.6	22.2	43.1	20.7	10.9	7
8.1	22.3	48.5	21.8	9.5	5
6.3	21.8	40.0	20.6	11.6	7
6.9	31.2	56.7	25.2	11.6	9

Use any regression program to compute the multiple regression predicting the percentage of births under 2500 grams.

11.9 Using the output from Exercise 11.8, interpret the results as if they were significant. (What is one of the reasons that this current analysis is not likely to be significant, even if those relationships are reliable in the populations?)

11.10 Mireault (1990) studied students whose parent had died during their childhood, students who came from divorced families, and students who came from intact families. Among other things, she collected data on their current perceived sense of vulnerability to future loss (PVLoss), their level of social support (SuppTotl), and the age at which they lost a parent during childhood (AgeAtLos). The can be found at

 http://www.uvm.edu/~dhowell/fundamentals9/DataFiles/Mireault.dat

Use the Mireault.dat data set and any available regression program to evaluate a model that says that depression (DepressT) is a function of these three variables. (Because only subjects in Group 1 lost a parent, you will need to restrict your analysis to those cases.)
If you name the complete data set "Gina."
In *R* you can create a data set for this specific group by

Gina.Loss<– subset(Gina, [Group == 1] .)

(Notice the double equal sign.)

11.11 Interpret the results of the analysis in Exercise 11.10.

11.12   The data set Harass.dat, included on this book's website, contains data on 343 cases created to replicate the results of a study of sexual harassment by Brooks and Perot (1991). The variables are, in order, Age, Marital Status (1 = married, 2 = not married), Feminist Ideology, Frequency of the Behavior, Offensiveness of the behavior, and the dependent variable, whether or not the subjects Reported incidents of sexual harassment (0 = no, 1 = yes). For each variable, higher numbers represent more of the property. Technically, this is a problem that might be better approached with what is called logistic regression, because the dependent variable is a dichotomy. However we can get a very close approximation to the optimal solution by using plain old linear multiple regression instead. Use multiple regression to predict whether or not sexual harassment will be reported, based on the variables you have here. Find a model that does not have many nonsignificant predictors.

11.13   In the previous question I was surprised that the frequency of behavior was not related to the likelihood of its being reported. Suggest why this might be.

11.14   In the text I have recommended against the use of stepwise procedures for multiple regression, whereby we systematically hunt among the variables to predict some sort of optimal equation.

a)   Explain why I would make such a recommendation.
b)   How, then, could I justify asking you to do just that in Exercise 11.12?

11.15   Use the table of random numbers (Table E.9 in the Appendix) to generate data for 10 cases on six variables, and label the first variable Y and the following variables X_1, X_2, X_3, X_4, and X_5. Now use any regression program to predict Y from all five predictors using the complete data set with 10 cases. Are you surprised at the magnitude of R?

11.16   Now restrict the data set in Exercise 11.15 to eight, then six, then five cases, and record the changing values of R. Remember that these are only random data.

11.17   The file at

https://www.uvm.edu/~dhowell/fundamentals9/DataFiles/Fig9-7.dat

contains Ryan's height and weight data discussed in connection with Table 9.1. Gender is coded 1 = male and 2 = female. Compare the simple regression of Weight predicted from Height with the multiple correlation of weight predicted from both height and gender.

11.18   In Exercise 11.17 we ran a multiple regression with Gender as a predictor. Now run separate regressions for males and females.

11.19   Compute a weighted average of the slopes of Weight predicted from Height for each gender in Exercise 11.18. Reasonable weighting coefficients would be the two sample sizes. (A weighted average is simply $(N_M \times b_M + N_F \times b_F)/(N_M + N_F)$.) How does that average compare to the slope for Height that you found in Exercise 11.17?

11.20   A great source of data and an explanation to go with them is an Internet site called the Data and Story Library (DASL) maintained by Carnegie Mellon University. Go to that site and examine the example on the relationship between brain size and intelligence. Use multiple regression to predict full-scale IQ from brain size (MRI-count) and Gender. The address is

https://lib.stat.cmu.edu/DASL/Datafiles/Brainsize.html

(I have replaced three missing pieces of data and converted "Female" to 2 and "Male" to 1. The revised data are available at the following URL. Use those data. https://www.uvm.edu/~dhowell/fundamentals9/DataFiles/BrainSize.dat)

11.21   Why would you think that it would be wise to include Gender in that regression?

11.22   Since you have the DASL data on brain size, note that it also includes the variables of height and weight. Predict weight from height and sex and compare with the answer for Exercise 11.17.

11.23 In examples like the Guber study on the funding of education, we frequently speak of variables like PctSAT as "nuisance variables." In what sense is that usage reasonable here, and in what sense is it somewhat misleading?

11.24 In several places in the chapter I have shoved aside the intercept by saying that we really don't care about it. If we don't care about it, why do we include it?

11.25 Using the data from Section 11.7 on the relationship between symptoms and distress in cancer patients, compute the predicted values of Distress2 using Distress1 and BlamPer. Correlate those values with the obtained values of Distress2 and show that this is equal to the multiple correlation coefficient.

11.26 In Exercise 9.1 we saw data on infant mortality and a number of other variables. There you predicted infant mortality from income. There is reason to believe that infants of young mothers are at increased risk, and there is considerable evidence that infant mortality can be reduced by the use of contraception. Does the multiple regression using all three of those predictor variables bear out these hypotheses?

Hypothesis Tests Applied to Means: One Sample

CONCEPTS THAT YOU WILL NEED TO REMEMBER FROM PREVIOUS CHAPTERS

Sampling distribution:	The distribution of a statistic over repeated sampling
Standard error:	The standard deviation of the sampling distribution of a statistic
Degrees of freedom:	An adjusted value of the sample size, often $N - 1$ or $N - 2$
Null hypothesis:	The hypothesis to be tested by a statistical test, denoted H_0
Research hypothesis:	The hypothesis that the study is designed to test, denoted H_1
$\mu, \sigma, \overline{X}, s$:	Mean and standard deviation of a population or a sample, respectively

In this chapter we will begin to discuss t tests, in this case the t test for one sample. We will start by looking at what we can expect sample means to look like if we draw many samples from one population. We will then go on to consider briefly the case where we want to know how to test a null hypothesis about a mean if we know the variance of the population from which it presumably came. Because we rarely know the population variance, we use this example mostly because it leads neatly to t tests, which apply to the case where the population variance is unknown. We will see what to do in that case and cover what governs our resulting values of t. Next, we will look at confidence intervals, which give us an idea of reasonable possible values of the true population mean. We will consider effect size measures to give us some handle on the meaningfulness of our result. Finally we will look at an example of a single sample where the emphasis is certainly not on a test of statistical significance. That is a case where confidence intervals tell us far more than a standard t test would.

In Chapter 8 we considered the general logic of hypothesis testing and ignored the specific calculations involved. In Chapters 9, 10, and 11 we looked at measures of the relationship between variables and considered hypothesis testing as a way of asking whether there is a reliable nonzero correlation between variables in the population (not just in our sample) and whether the regression coefficients (slope and intercept) are reliably different from zero. In this chapter we will begin concentrating mostly on hypothesis tests about means. In particular, we will focus on testing a null hypothesis about the value of a population mean.

We will start with an example based on an honors thesis by Williamson (2008), who was examining coping behavior in children of depressed parents. His study went much further than we will go, but it provides an illustration of a situation in which it makes sense to test a null hypothesis using the mean of a single sample.

Because there is evidence in the psychological literature that stress in a child's life may lead to subsequent behavior problems, Williamson expected that a sample of children of depressed parents would show an unusually high level of behavior problems. This suggests that if we use a behavioral checklist, such as the anxious/depressed subscale of Achenbach's Youth Self-Report Inventory (YSR), we would expect elevated scores from a sample of children whose parents suffer from depression. (The YSR is very widely used and has a known mean of 50. We will take 50 as the true population mean (μ).) It does not seem likely that these children would show reduced levels of depression, but to guard against that possibility we will test a two-tailed **experimental hypothesis** that the anxious/depressive scores among these children are *different from* similar scores from a normal sample. We can't test the experimental hypothesis directly, however. Instead we will test the null hypothesis (H_0) that the scores of stressed children came from a population of scores with the *same* mean as the population of scores of normal children, rejection of which would support the experimental hypothesis. More specifically, we want to decide between

$$H_0: \mu = 50$$

and

$$H_1: \mu \neq 50$$

I have chosen the two-tailed alternative form of H_1 because I want to reject H_0 if $\mu > 50$ *or if* $\mu < 50$.

Williamson had a sample of 166 children, each of whom came from a family in which one parent is depressed. But for simplicity let's start by assuming that there were only five children, though I will come back to the actual data shortly. Suppose that I asked the children to complete the Youth Self Report form and obtained the following scores:

48 62 53 66 51

This sample of five observations has a mean of 56.0 and a standard deviation of 7.65. Thus the five children have an average score six points above the mean of the population of normal children. But because this result is based on a sample of only five children, it is quite conceivable that the deviation from 50 could be due to chance (or, phrased differently, that the deviation may be due to sampling error). Even if $H_0: \mu = 50$ were true, we certainly would not expect our sample mean to be exactly 50.000. We probably wouldn't be particularly surprised to find a mean of 49 or 51. But what about 56? Is that surprisingly large? If so, perhaps we should not be willing to continue to entertain the idea that $\mu = 50$ and that these children look like a random sample from a normal population. Before we can draw any conclusions, however, we will have to know what values we reasonably could expect sample means to have if we really sampled from a population of normal children.

12.1 Sampling Distribution of the Mean

As you should recall from Chapter 8, the sampling distribution of any statistic is the distribution of values we would expect to obtain for that statistic if we drew an infinite number of samples from the population in question and calculated the statistic on each sample. Because we are concerned here with sample *means*, we need to know something about the sampling distribution of the mean. Fortunately all the important information about the sampling distribution of the mean can be summed up in one very important theorem: the **Central Limit Theorem**. The Central Limit Theorem is a factual statement about the distribution of means. It contains several concepts:

Given a population with mean μ and variance σ^2, the sampling distribution of the mean (the distribution of sample means) will have a mean equal to μ (i.e., $\mu_{\overline{X}} = \mu$) and a variance $\sigma_{\overline{X}}^2$ equal to σ^2/N (and standard deviation, $\sigma_{\overline{X}} = \sigma/\sqrt{N}$). The distribution will approach the normal distribution as N, the *sample size*, increases.

The Central Limit Theorem is one of the most important theorems in statistics because it not only tells us what the mean and the variance of the sampling distribution of the sample mean must be for any given sample size but also states that as N increases, the shape of this sampling distribution approaches normal, *whatever* the shape of the parent population. The importance of these facts will become clear shortly.

The rate at which the sampling distribution of the mean approaches normal is a function of the shape of the parent population. If the population itself is normal, the sampling distribution of the mean will be exactly normal regardless of N. If the population is symmetric but nonnormal, the sampling distribution of the mean will be nearly normal even for quite small sample sizes, especially if the population is unimodal. If the population is markedly skewed, we may require sample sizes of 30 or more before the means closely approximate a normal distribution.

We can illustrate the Central Limit Theorem with our sample of five children. Suppose that we take an infinitely large population of random numbers from a normal distribution with a population mean of 50 and a population standard deviation of 7.65. (Notice that I have set the population mean equal to the mean under the null hypothesis, and the population standard deviation equal to the sample standard deviation.) That population is diagrammed in Figure 12.1.

Now suppose we draw with replacement 10,000 samples of size 5 (i.e., $N = 5$) from the population shown in Figure 12.1 and plot the 10,000 resulting sample means. [Note that N refers to the size of each sample, not to the number of samples, which is very large (here, 10,000)]. Such sampling can be easily accomplished very quickly even on a laptop computer—the results of just such a procedure are presented in Figure 12.2(a). From Figure 12.2(a) it is apparent that the distribution of means is very nearly normal, as shown by the fit to the smoothed curve superimposed on the figure. If you were to go to the effort of calculating the mean and the standard

Figure 12.1 Normal distribution with $\mu = 50$ and $\sigma = 7.65$

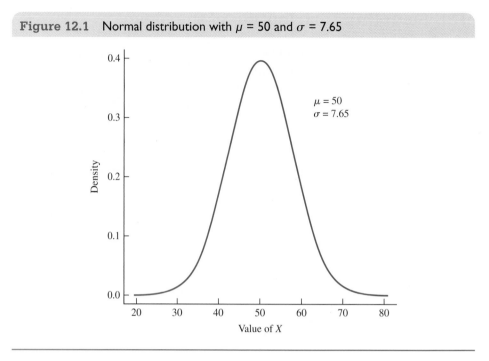

Figure 12.2a Computer-generated sampling distribution of the mean, $N = 5$

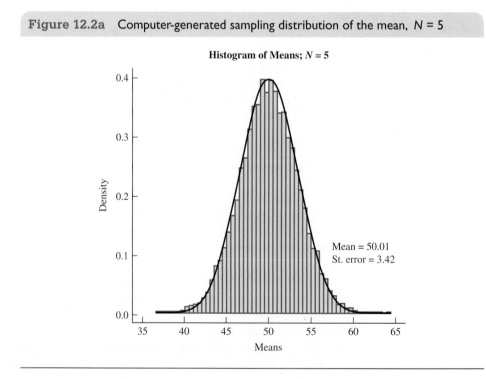

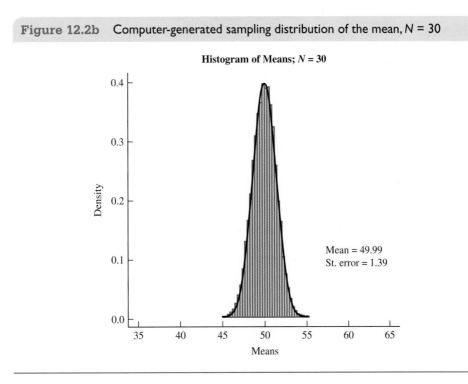

Figure 12.2b   Computer-generated sampling distribution of the mean, N = 30

Histogram of Means; $N = 30$

Mean = 49.99
St. error = 1.39

deviation of this distribution, you would find that they are extremely close to $\mu = 50$ and $\sigma_{\bar{X}} = \sigma/\sqrt{N} = 7.65/\sqrt{5} = 3.42$. (Remember that μ and $\sigma_{\bar{X}}$ refer to the mean and the standard deviation of the distribution of means.)

Suppose we repeat the entire procedure, only this time we draw 10,000 samples each with $N = 30$ observations. The results are plotted in Figure 12.2(b). There you can see that, just as the Central Limit Theorem predicted, the distribution is approximately normal, the mean (μ) is again very close to 50, and the standard deviation has been reduced to very nearly $28.87/\sqrt{30} = 1.42$. (The first time I ran a similar example many years ago it took approximately five minutes to draw such samples. Today it took me 1.5 *seconds*. Computer simulation is no longer a big deal, which is what is going to make randomization tests (see Chapter 20) the tests of the future.)

12.2 Testing Hypotheses about Means when σ Is Known

From the Central Limit Theorem we know all the important characteristics of the sampling distribution of the mean (its shape, its mean, and its standard deviation) even without drawing a single one of those samples. On the basis of this information we are in a position to begin testing hypotheses about means. For the sake of continuity it might be well to go back to something we considered with respect to the normal distribution. In Chapter 8 we saw that we could test a hypothesis about the population from which a single score (in that case a finger-tapping score) was drawn by calculating

$$z = \frac{X - \mu}{\sigma}$$

and then obtaining the probability of a value of z as low as or lower than the one obtained by using the tables, or online calculators, of the standard normal distribution. Thus we ran a one-tailed test on the hypothesis that the tapping rate (45) of a single individual was drawn at random from a normally distributed population of healthy tapping rates with a mean of 59 and a standard deviation of 7. We did this by calculating

$$z = \frac{X - \mu}{\sigma} = \frac{45 - 59}{7} = \frac{-14}{7} = -2.00$$

and then using online software, to find the area below $z = -2.00$. This value is .0228. Thus, approximately 2% of the time we would expect a score this low *or lower* if we were sampling from a healthy population. Because this probability was less than our selected significance level of $\alpha = .05$, we would reject the null hypothesis. We would conclude that we have sufficient evidence to diagnose the person's response rate as abnormal. The tapping rate for the person we examined was an unusual rate for healthy subjects. (But what would we have concluded had the probability been calculated as .064?) Although in this example we were testing a hypothesis about a single *observation*, exactly the same logic applies to testing hypotheses about sample *means*.

In most situations in which we test a hypothesis about a population mean we don't have any knowledge about the variance of that population. (This is the primary reason that we have *t* tests, which are the main focus of this chapter.) In a limited number of situations, however, we do know σ for some reason, and a discussion of testing a hypothesis when σ is known provides a good transition from what we already know about the normal distribution to what we want to know about *t* tests. The example of the anxious/depression subscale of the YSR (Achenbach's Youth Self-Report Inventory) is useful for this purpose because we know both the mean and the standard deviation for the population of that scale on Achenbach's YSR ($\mu = 50$ and $\sigma = 10$). We also know that our random sample of five children who were under stress had a mean score of 56.0, and we want to test the null hypothesis that these five children are a random sample from a population of normal children (i.e., normal with respect to their general level of behavior problems). In other words, we want to test H_0: $\mu = 50$ against the alternative H_1: $\mu \neq 50$, where μ represents the mean of the population from which these children were actually drawn.

Because we know the mean and standard deviation of the population of general behavior problem scores, we can use the Central Limit Theorem to obtain the sampling distribution of the mean when the null hypothesis is true without having to do all sorts of computer sampling. The Central Limit Theorem states that if we obtain the sampling distribution of the mean from this population, it will have a mean of 50, a variance of $\sigma^2/N = 10^2/5 = 100/5 = 20$, and a standard deviation of means (usually referred to as the standard error of the mean) of $\sigma/\sqrt{N} = 4.47$. This distribution is diagrammed in Figure 12.3. The arrow in the figure points to the location of our sample mean.

A short digression about the standard error is in order here, because this is a concept that runs throughout statistics. *The standard deviation of any sampling distribution is*

Figure 12.3   Sampling distribution of the mean for samples of $N = 5$ drawn from a population with $\mu = 50$ and $\sigma = 10$.

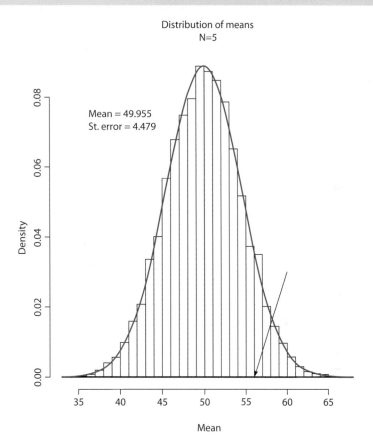

normally referred to as the standard error of that distribution. Thus the standard deviation of means is called the standard error of the mean (symbolized by $\sigma_{\overline{X}}$), whereas the standard deviation of differences between means, which will be discussed in Chapter 14, is called the standard error of differences between means and is symbolized $\sigma_{\overline{X}_1 - \overline{X}_2}$. Standard errors are critically important because they tell us how much statistics, such as the mean, vary from one sample to another. If the standard error is large, that tells you that whatever sample mean you happened to find, someone else doing the same study may find quite a different one. On the other hand, if the standard error is small, another person is likely to find a value fairly similar to yours. Notice the difference in the size of the standard errors in Figures 12.2a and 12.2b. This difference resulted from the much larger sample size in the latter case.

Because we know that the sampling distribution of the mean for 5 scores on the YSR is normally distributed with a mean of 50 and a standard error ($\sigma/\sqrt{N}$) of 4.47, we can find areas under the distribution by referring to tables of the standard normal distribution. For example, because two standard errors is $2(4.47) = 8.94$, the area to the right of $\overline{X} = 58.94$ is simply the area under the normal distribution greater than two standard deviations above the mean.

For our particular situation, we first need to know the probability of a sample mean greater than or equal to 56; thus we need to find the area above $\overline{X} = 56$. We can calculate this in the same way we did with individual observations, with only a minor change in the formula for z.

$$z = \frac{X - \mu}{\sigma}$$

becomes

$$z = \frac{\overline{X} - \mu}{\sigma_{\overline{X}}}$$

which can also be written as

$$z = \frac{\overline{X} - \mu}{\dfrac{\sigma}{\sqrt{N}}}$$

For our data this becomes

$$z = \frac{\overline{X} - \mu}{\dfrac{\sigma}{\sqrt{N}}} = \frac{56 - 50}{\dfrac{10}{\sqrt{5}}} = \frac{56 - 50}{4.47} = \frac{6}{4.47} = 1.34$$

Note that the equation for z used here has the same form as our earlier formula for z. The only differences are that X has been replaced by the sample mean ($(\overline{X}$) and σ has been replaced by the standard error of the mean ($\sigma_{\overline{X}}$)). These differences occur because we now are dealing with a distribution of means rather than with single observations; thus the data points are now means, and the standard deviation in question is now the standard error of the mean (the standard deviation of means). The formula for z continues to represent (1) a point on a distribution, minus (2) the mean of that distribution, all divided by (3) the standard deviation of the distribution. Rather than being concerned specifically with the distribution of $\overline{X}$, we now have re-expressed the sample mean in terms of a z score and can now answer the question with regard to the standard normal distribution.

From Table E.10 in the Appendices we find that the probability of a z as large as 1.34 is .0901. Because we want a two-tailed test of H_0, we need to double the probability to obtain the probability of a deviation as large as 1.34 standard errors in *either direction* from the mean. This is 2(.0901) = .1802. Thus with a two-tailed test (that stressed children have a mean behavior problem score that is different in *either direction* from that of normal children) at the .05 level of significance we would not reject H_0 because the obtained probability of such a value occurring when the null hypothesis is true is greater than .05. We would conclude that we have insufficient evidence in our small sample of five children to conclude that stressed children show more or fewer behavior problems than other children. Keep in mind that it is very possible that stressed children do indeed show more behavior problems, but our data are not sufficiently convincing on that score, primarily because we have too little data. (Remember the time your mother was sure that you had broken an ornament while using the living room as a gym, and you had, but she didn't have enough evidence to prove it? Your mother was forced to make a Type II error—she failed to reject the null hypothesis (your innocence) when it was actually false. In our example, even if the true population mean for stressed children is above 50, we don't have enough evidence to build a convincing case.)

To go back to the study referred to earlier, Williamson (2008) included 166 children from homes in which at least one parent had a history of depression. These children all completed the Youth Self Report, and the sample mean was 55.71 with a standard deviation of 7.35. We want to test the null hypothesis that these children come from a normal population with a mean of 50 and a standard deviation of 10. Then

$$z = \frac{\overline{X} - \mu}{\dfrac{\sigma}{\sqrt{N}}} = \frac{55.71 - 50}{\dfrac{10}{\sqrt{166}}} = \frac{5.71}{0.776} = 7.36$$

We cannot use the table of the normal distribution, simply because it does not go that high. (The largest value of z in the table is 4.00. However, even if our result had only been 4.00, it would have been significant with a probability less than .000 to three decimal places, so we can reject the null hypothesis in any event. The exact probability for a two-tailed test would be .00000000000018, which is obviously a significant result.) Therefore, Williamson has every reason to believe that the children in his study do not represent a random sample of scores from the anxious/depressed subscale of the YSR. They come from a population with a mean higher (more problematic) than normal.

The test of one sample mean against a known population mean, which we have just performed, is based on the assumption that the sample means are normally distributed, or at least that the distribution is sufficiently normal that we will be only negligibly in error when we refer to the tables of the standard normal distribution. Many textbooks state that we assume we are sampling from a normal population (i.e., behavior problem scores themselves are normally distributed), but this is not strictly necessary in practical terms. What is most important is to be able to assume that the sampling distribution *of the mean* (Figure 12.3) is nearly normal. This assumption can be satisfied in two ways: if either (1) the population from which we sample is normal or (2) the sample size is sufficiently large to produce at least approximate normality by way of the Central Limit Theorem. This is one of the great benefits of the Central Limit Theorem: It allows us to test hypotheses even if the parent population is not normal, provided only that N is sufficiently large. But Williamson also had the standard deviation of his sample. Why didn't we use that?

The simple answer to this question is that we have something better. We have the population standard deviation. The YSR and its scoring system have been meticulously developed over the years, and we can have complete confidence that the standard deviation of scores of a whole population of normal children will be 10, or vanishingly close to 10. And we want to test that our sample came from a population of normal children. We will see in a moment that we often do not have the population standard deviation and have to estimate it from the sample standard deviation, but when we do have it we should use it. For one thing, if these children really do score higher, I would expect that their sample standard deviation would underestimate σ. That is because the standard deviation of people who are biased toward one end of the distribution is very likely to be smaller than the standard deviation of scores that are more centrally placed.

12.3 | Testing a Sample Mean when σ Is Unknown (The One-Sample t Test)

The previous example was chosen deliberately from among a fairly limited number of situations in which the population standard deviation (σ) is known. In the general case, we rarely know the value of σ and usually will have to estimate it by way of the *sample* standard deviation (s). When we replace σ with s in the formula, however, the nature of the test changes. We can no longer declare the answer to be a z score and evaluate it with reference to tables of z. Instead we denote the answer as t and evaluate it with respect to tables of t, which are somewhat different. The reasoning behind the switch from z to t is not particularly complicated. The basic problem that requires this change to t is related to the sampling distribution of the sample variance. It's time to grit your teeth and look at a tiny amount of theory because (1) it will help you understand what you are doing and (2) it's good for your soul.

The Sampling Distribution of s^2

Because the t test uses s^2 as an estimate of σ^2, it is important that we first look at the sampling distribution of s^2. We want to get some idea of what kinds of sample variances we can expect when we draw a sample, especially with a small sample size. This sampling distribution gives us some insight into the problems we are going to encounter. You saw in Chapter 5 that s^2 is an *unbiased* estimate of σ^2, meaning that with repeated sampling the average value of s^2 will equal σ^2. Although an unbiased estimator is nice, it is not everything. The problem is that the shape of the sampling distribution of s^2 is quite positively skewed, especially for small sample sizes. An example of a computer-generated sampling distribution of s^2 (where $\sigma^2 = 138.89$) is shown in Figure 12.4. Because of the skewness of this distribution, an individual value of s^2 is more likely to underestimate σ^2 than to overestimate it, especially for small samples. (s^2 remains unbiased because when it overestimates σ^2 it does so to such an extent as to balance off the more numerous but less drastic underestimates.) Can you see what the problem is going to be if we just take our sample estimate (s^2) and substitute it for the unknown σ^2 and pretend that nothing has changed? As a result of the skewness of the sampling distribution of the variance, the resulting value of t is likely to be larger than the value of z we would have obtained had σ^2 been known, because any one sample variance (s^2) has a better than 50:50 chance of underestimating the population variance (σ^2).

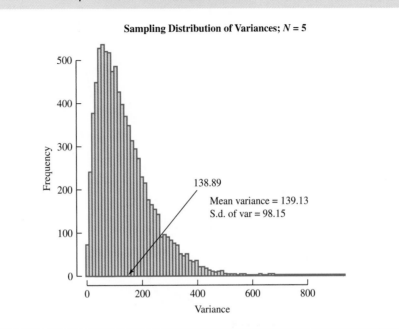

Figure 12.4 Sampling distribution of s^2 from a normally distributed population with $\mu = 50, \sigma^2 = 138.89$, and $N = 5$

Sampling Distribution of Variances; $N = 5$

138.89

Mean variance = 139.13
S.d. of var = 98.15

Variance

Frequency

The t Statistic

The t statistic is what will save us in this situation, because it is designed to account for the fact that we are using a sample estimate of s^2 rather than the population value of σ^2. We will take the formula that we just developed for z,

$$z = \frac{\overline{X} - \mu}{\sigma_{\overline{X}}} = \frac{\overline{X} - \mu}{\dfrac{\sigma}{\sqrt{N}}} = \frac{\overline{X} - \mu}{\sqrt{\dfrac{\sigma^2}{N}}}$$

and substitute s to give

$$t = \frac{\overline{X} - \mu}{s_{\overline{X}}} = \frac{\overline{X} - \mu}{\dfrac{s}{\sqrt{N}}} = \frac{\overline{X} - \mu}{\sqrt{\dfrac{s^2}{N}}}$$

Because we know that for any particular sample s^2 is more likely than not to be smaller than the appropriate value of σ^2, then the denominator is more likely than not to be too small, and the t formula is more likely than not to produce a larger answer than we would have obtained if we had solved for z using σ^2 itself. As a result it would not really be fair to treat the answer as a z score and use the table of z. To do so would give us too many "significant" results; that is, we would make more than 5% Type I errors when testing the null hypothesis at significance level $\sigma = .05$. (For example, when we were calculating z, we rejected H_0 at the .05 level of significance whenever z fell

Figure 12.5 *t* distribution for 1, 30, and ∞ degrees of freedom

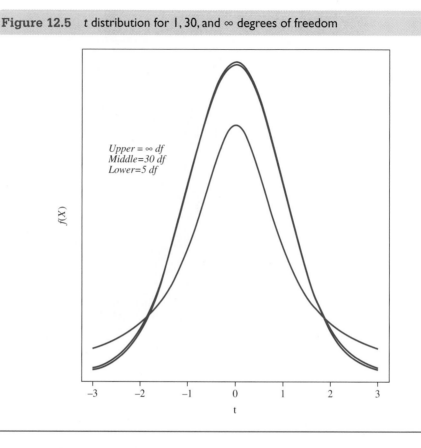

outside the limits of ±1.96. If we create a situation in which H_0 is true, repeatedly draw samples of $N = 5$, use s^2 in place of σ^2, and calculate t, we will obtain a value of ±1.96 or greater more than about 10% of the time. The cutoff point should really be 2.776, which is quite a bit larger than 1.96.)

William Gosset supplied the solution to this problem. Gosset showed that using s^2 in place of σ^2 would lead to a particular sampling distribution, now generally known as **Student's t distribution**.[1] As a result of Gosset's work, all we have to do is substitute s^2, which we know, for σ^2, which we don't know, denote the answer as t, and evaluate t with respect to its own distribution, much as we evaluated z with respect to the normal distribution. The t distribution is shown in Table E.6, and examples of the actual distribution of t for various sample sizes are shown graphically in Figure 12.5.

As you can see from Figure 12.5, the distribution of t varies as a function of the **degrees of freedom (*df*)**, which for the moment we will define as one less than the number of observations in the sample. Because the skewness of the sampling

---

[1]It is called "Student's t" because Gosset worked for the Guinness Brewing Company, which would not let him publish his results under his own name. He published under the pseudonym of "Student," hence our present-day reference to Student's t. I would think that someone as important as William Sealy Gosset would at least get his name spelled correctly. But almost half of the books that I checked, including earlier editions of my own books, spelled it "Gossett."

distribution of s^2 disappears as the number of degrees of freedom increases, the tendency for s to underestimate σ will also disappear. Thus for an infinitely large number of degrees of freedom t will become normally distributed and equivalent to z.

Degrees of Freedom

I have mentioned that the t distribution is dependent on its degrees of freedom, which are a function of the sample size (N). For the one-sample case, $df = N - 1$; the one degree of freedom is lost because we use the sample mean in calculating s^2. To be more precise, we obtain the sample variance (s^2) by calculating the deviations of the observations from their own mean ($X - \overline{X}$), rather than from the population mean ($X - \mu$). Because the sum of the deviations about the mean, $\Sigma(X - \overline{X})$, always equals 0, only N − 1 of the deviations are free to vary (the Nth is determined if the sum of the deviations is to be zero). For an illustration of this point consider the case of five scores whose mean is 10. Four of these scores can be anything you want (e.g., 18, 18, 16, 2), but the fifth score cannot be chosen freely. Here it must be −4 if the mean is going to be 10. In other words, there are only four *free* numbers in that set of five scores once the mean has been determined; therefore, we have four degrees of freedom. This is the reason the formula for s^2 (defined in Chapter 5) used N − 1 in the denominator. Because s^2 is based on N − 1 *df*, we have N − 1 degrees of freedom for t.

From now until the end of the book you will continually see references to the degrees of freedom. In many cases they will be $N - 1$ or $N - 2$, but sometimes they will be the number of groups minus 1, the number of categories minus 1, or something like that. In each case we lose one or more degrees of freedom because we have estimated one or more parameters using sample statistics.

Example of the Use of t: Do Children Always Say What They Feel?

On several occasions throughout this book I have referred to studies of children and adults under stressful situations. Often we find that stress produces negative reactions in the form of depression, anxiety, behavior problems, and so on. But in a study of the families of cancer patients, Compas and others (1994) observed that young children do not report an unusual number of symptoms of depression or anxiety. If fact they even look slightly better than average. Is it really true that young children somehow escape the negative consequences of this kind of family stressor? Can you think of an alternative hypothesis that might explain these results?

One of the commonly used measures of anxiety in children is called the Children's Manifest Anxiety Scale (CMAS) (Reynolds & Richmond, 1978). Nine items on this scale form what is often called the "Lie Scale." These items are intended to identify children who seem to be giving socially desirable responses rather than answering honestly. (Calling it a "lie" scale is not really being fair to the children; they are just trying to tell you what they think you want to hear.) Could it be that young children under stress score low on anxiety scores not because they have very little anxiety, but because the anxiety is masked by an attempt to give socially appropriate answers? One way of addressing this question is to ask if these children have unusually high scores on the Lie Scale. If so, it would be easier to defend the argument that children are just not telling us about their anxiety, not that they don't have any.

Compas et al. (1994) collected data on 36 children from families in which one parent had recently been diagnosed with cancer. Each child completed the CMAS, and their Lie Scale scores, among others, were computed. For this group of children the mean Lie Scale score was 4.39, with a standard deviation of 2.61. Reynolds and Richmond report a population mean for elementary school children of 3.87, but from their data it is not possible to determine the population standard deviation for only this age range of children. Therefore we are required to estimate the standard deviation (or variance) from the sample standard deviation (or variance) and use the t test.

We want to test the null hypothesis that the Lie Scale scores are a random sample from a population with a mean (μ) of 3.87, the population mean reported by Reynolds and Richmond. Therefore,

$$H_0: \mu = 3.87$$

$$H_1: \mu \neq 3.87$$

We will use a two-tailed test and work at the 5% level of significance.

From the previous discussion we have

$$t = \frac{\overline{X} - \mu}{s_{\overline{X}}} = \frac{\overline{X} - \mu}{\dfrac{s}{\sqrt{N}}}$$

The numerator of the formula for t represents the distance between the sample mean and the population mean given by H_0. The denominator represents an estimate of the standard deviation of the distribution of sample means—the standard error. This is the same thing that we had with z, except that the sample variance (or standard deviation) has been substituted for the population variance (or standard deviation). For our data we have

$$t = \frac{\overline{X} - \mu}{s_{\overline{X}}} = \frac{4.39 - 3.87}{\dfrac{2.61}{\sqrt{36}}} = \frac{0.52}{0.435} = 1.20$$

A t value of 1.20 in and of itself is not particularly meaningful unless we can evaluate it against the sampling distribution of t to determine whether it is a commonly expected value of t when H_0 is true. For this purpose, the critical values of t are presented in Table E.6, a portion of which is shown in Table 12.1. This table differs in form from the table of the normal distribution (z) because, instead of giving the area above and below each specific value of t, which would require too

Table 12.1 Abbreviated Version of Table E.6, Percentage Points of the t Distribution

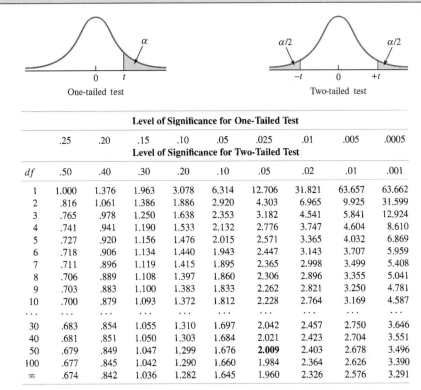

	Level of Significance for One-Tailed Test								
	.25	.20	.15	.10	.05	.025	.01	.005	.0005
	Level of Significance for Two-Tailed Test								
df	.50	.40	.30	.20	.10	.05	.02	.01	.001
1	1.000	1.376	1.963	3.078	6.314	12.706	31.821	63.657	63.662
2	.816	1.061	1.386	1.886	2.920	4.303	6.965	9.925	31.599
3	.765	.978	1.250	1.638	2.353	3.182	4.541	5.841	12.924
4	.741	.941	1.190	1.533	2.132	2.776	3.747	4.604	8.610
5	.727	.920	1.156	1.476	2.015	2.571	3.365	4.032	6.869
6	.718	.906	1.134	1.440	1.943	2.447	3.143	3.707	5.959
7	.711	.896	1.119	1.415	1.895	2.365	2.998	3.499	5.408
8	.706	.889	1.108	1.397	1.860	2.306	2.896	3.355	5.041
9	.703	.883	1.100	1.383	1.833	2.262	2.821	3.250	4.781
10	.700	.879	1.093	1.372	1.812	2.228	2.764	3.169	4.587
...	...	...	...	...	...	...	...	...	...
30	.683	.854	1.055	1.310	1.697	2.042	2.457	2.750	3.646
40	.681	.851	1.050	1.303	1.684	2.021	2.423	2.704	3.551
50	.679	.849	1.047	1.299	1.676	**2.009**	2.403	2.678	3.496
100	.677	.845	1.042	1.290	1.660	1.984	2.364	2.626	3.390
∞	.674	.842	1.036	1.282	1.645	1.960	2.326	2.576	3.291

Source: The entries in this table were computed by the author.

much space, the table gives those values of t that cut off particular critical areas, for example, the .05, .025, and .01 levels of significance. Also, in contrast to z, a different t distribution is defined for each possible number of degrees of freedom. We want to work at the two-tailed .05 level. The critical value generally is denoted t or, in this case, $t_{.05}$.[2]

To use the t tables, we must enter the table with the appropriate degrees of freedom. We have 36 observations in our data, so we have $N - 1 = 36 - 1 = 35$ df for this example. Table E.6 (or Table 12.1) tells us that the critical value for $t_{.05}(35)$ is ± 2.03. (I obtained that value by taking the average of the critical values for 30 and 40 df, because the table does not contain an entry for exactly 35 df.)

---

[2]This is a point that can be confusing. Some texts, such as this one, will use t_α to refer to critical value for a two-tailed test, assuming that you know that half of α is located in each tail. Other texts use the notation $t_{\frac{\alpha}{2}}$ to make it very clear that we know that half of α is in each tail. In our example, the critical value is $+2.03$. So, the notational scheme used here will be $t_\alpha = t_{.05} = \pm 2.03$, whereas other authors could equally validly write $t_{\frac{\alpha}{2}} = t_{.025} = 2.03$. Just be aware that throughout this book I always run tests at the two-tailed .05 level. (My use of $\pm$ (plus and minus) reveals that I am using a two-tailed test.)

The number in parentheses after $t_{.05}$, as in $t_{.05}$ (35), is the degrees of freedom. Our result tells us that if H_0 is true only 5% of the time would a t computed on a sample of 36 cases lie outside ± 2.03. Because the value we computed (1.20) was less than 2.03, we will not reject H_0. (The probability of $t < +1.20$ is given by the StatMate App on my cell phone as .238.) We do not have sufficient evidence to conclude that young children under stress perform any differently on the Lie Scale from a random sample of normal children. We will have to look elsewhere for an explanation of the low anxiety scores of these children. (To see if these children's *anxiety* scores really are below the population average, see Exercise 12.17.) Rather than going to the tables in the back of the book, you could go to http://www .statpages.org/pdfs.html, enter the degrees of freedom (35) and t (1.20), and find that the two-tailed probability is .2382. You would obtain a similar answer using *R* with the following code.

```
#Two-tailed t probability for t = 1.20 on 35 df.
2*(1-pt(1.20, 35))
[1] 0.2381992
```

I subtracted the probability of $t < 1.20$ from 1.00 to get the appropriate tail probability, and then I multiplied by 2 to produce a two-tailed probability. See the chapter's Web page for graphical code and illustration. I have plotted the t distribution with the one-tailed and two-tailed area in Figure 12.6.

Figure 12.6 Areas of the one- and two-tailed t distribution

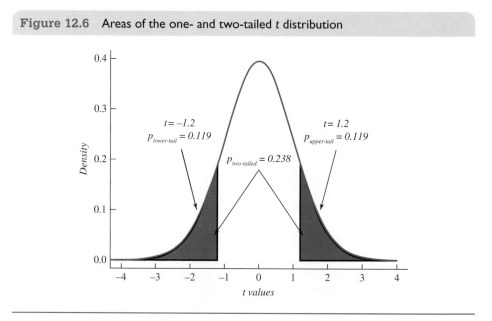

12.4 | Factors That Affect the Magnitude of t and the Decision about H_0

Several factors affect the magnitude of the t statistic and/or the likelihood of rejecting H_0:

1. the actual obtained difference $(\overline{X} - \mu)$
2. the magnitude of the sample variance (s^2)
3. the sample size (N)
4. the significance level (α)
5. whether the test is a one- or a two-tailed test

It should be obvious that the obtained difference between $\overline{X}$ and the mean (μ) given by H_0 is important. This follows directly from the fact that the larger the numerator, the larger the t value. But it is also important to keep in mind that the value of $\overline{X}$ is in large part a function of the mean of the population from which the sample was actually drawn. If this mean is denoted μ_1 and the mean given by the null hypothesis is denoted μ_0, then the likelihood of obtaining a significant result will increase as $\mu_1 - \mu_0$ increases.

When you look at the formula for t, it should be apparent that as s^2 decreases or N increases, the denominator $(s/\sqrt{N})$ itself will decrease and the resulting value of t will increase. Because variability introduced by the experimental setting itself (caused by ambiguous instructions, poorly recorded data, distracting testing conditions, and so on) is superimposed on whatever variability there is among participants, we try to reduce s by controlling as many sources of variability as possible. By obtaining as many participants as possible, we also make use of the fact that increasing N decreases $s_{\overline{X}}$.

Finally, it should be evident that the likelihood of rejecting H_0 will depend on the size of the rejection region, which in turn depends on α and the location of that region (whether a one-tailed or two-tailed test is used).

12.5 | A Second Example: The Moon Illusion

It will be useful to consider a second example, this one taken from a classic paper by Kaufman and Rock (1962) on the moon illusion. (We have already discussed a part of this paper in Chapter 5.) As you know, the moon, when seen coming just over the horizon, looks huge compared to the moon seen alone high in the sky near its zenith, or highest point. But why should that be, when the moon obviously doesn't expand and contract? Kaufman and Rock concluded that the moon illusion could be explained on the basis of the greater *apparent* distance of the moon when it is at the horizon. As part of a very complete series of experiments the authors initially sought to estimate the moon illusion by asking subjects to adjust a variable "moon" appearing to be on the horizon to match the size of a standard "moon" appearing at its zenith, or vice versa. (In these measurements they did not use the actual moon, but an artificial one created with a special apparatus.) One of the first questions we might ask is whether there really is a moon illusion using their apparatus, that is, whether a larger setting is required to match a horizon moon than to match a zenith moon. (If they can't produce an illusion, they need a different apparatus for carrying out their study.) The following data for 10 subjects are taken from Kaufman and Rock's paper and represent the ratio of the diameter of the variable moon and the standard moon. A ratio of 1.00 would indicate no illusion; a ratio other than 1.00 would represent an illusion. For example, a ratio of 1.5 would mean that the horizon moon appeared to have a diameter 1.5 times the diameter of the zenith moon. Evidence in support of an illusion would require that we reject $H_0: \mu = 1.00$ in favor of $H_1: \mu \neq 1.00$.

Obtained Ratio: 1.73 1.06 2.03 1.40 0.95 1.13 1.41 1.73 1.63 1.56

For these data $N = 10$, $\overline{X} = 1.463$, and $s = 0.341$. A t test on $H_0: \mu = 1.00$ is given by

$$t = \frac{\overline{X} - \mu}{s_{\overline{X}}} = \frac{\overline{X} - \mu}{\dfrac{s}{\sqrt{N}}} = \frac{1.463 - 1.000}{\dfrac{0.341}{\sqrt{10}}} = \frac{0.463}{0.108} = 4.29$$

From Table E.6 in the Appendices we see that with $10 - 1 = 9$ df for a two-tailed test at $\alpha = .05$ the critical value of $t_{.05}(9) = \pm 2.262$. The obtained value of t (often denoted t_{obt}) is 4.29. Because $4.29 > 2.262$, we can reject H_0 at $\alpha = .05$ and conclude that the true mean ratio under these conditions is not equal to 1.00. In fact, it is greater than 1.00, which is what we would expect on the basis of our experience. (It is always comforting to see science confirm what we have all known since childhood, but the results also mean that Kaufman and Rock's experimental apparatus performs as it should.) The exact two-tailed probability for $t = 4.29$ on 9 df using http://www.danielsoper.com/statcalc3/ (if you can stand the ads) is .002. What would we have concluded if t had been equal to -4.29?

12.6 How Large Is Our Effect?

For years, psychologists and others who use statistical techniques to analyze their data have been content to declare that they found a significant difference, and then consider their work done. People have suggested that this was not adequate, but their complaints largely went unheeded until not very many years ago. Those who did complain were arguing for some kind of statement by the experimenter that gave an indication not only that the difference was significant, but whether it was meaningful. If we use enough observations, we can almost always find even a meaningless difference to be significant.

One of those who was most involved in this debate was Jacob Cohen, whose name will appear frequently in this book. Cohen insisted that we should report what he termed a measure of **effect size**. By this he meant that he wanted to see a statistic that gave a meaningful indication of how large a mean was, or how different two means were. With very large samples, even a very small difference, which no one would care about, can be statistically significant. Significance isn't everything.

There are several different ways in which we could present information on the size of a difference. I will develop the concept of confidence intervals in the next section. I will also amplify on the concept of an effect size at greater length in the next several chapters, but at this point I want to focus only on the general idea—and the moon illusion data are ideal for this purpose. We know that we have a significant difference, but when we report this difference, we want to be able to convince the reader that he or she should care about the effect. If the moon looks just a tiny bit larger at the horizon, that may not be worth much comment.

Recall the nature of our dependent variable. Participants looked at the moon high in the sky and adjusted a "pseudo-moon" off to one side to appear to be the same size as the real moon. Then they looked at the moon just above the horizon, and made a similar adjustment. If the equipment did not perform as expected, and there were no moon illusion, the two settings would be about the same, and their ratio would be about 1.00. But in actual fact, the settings for the horizon moon were much larger than the settings for the zenith moon, and the average ratio of these two settings was 1.463. This means that, on average, the moon on the horizon appeared to be 1.463 times larger (or 46.3% larger) than the moon at its zenith. This is a huge difference—at least it appears so to me. (Notice that I am not referring to the measurement of the setting the participant made, but to the ratio of the sizes under the two conditions. This is important, because in psychology the actual measurement we make often depends on the particular way we measure it and is not necessarily meaningful in its own right. But here the ratio of measurements is, in fact, meaningful.)

This experiment illustrates a case wherein we can convey to the reader something meaningful about the size of our effect just by reporting the mean. We don't have to get fancy. When you tell your readers that the moon at the horizon appears nearly half again as large as the moon at its zenith, you are telling them something more than simply that the horizon moon appears significantly larger. You are certainly telling them much more than saying that the average setting for the horizon moon was 5.23 centimeters.

In this example we have a situation where the ratios that we collect are such that we can express important information simply by telling the reader what the mean ratio was. In the next few chapters you will see examples in which the magnitude of the mean is not particularly helpful, (e.g., participants improved 2.63 points in their self-esteem scores), and we will we need to develop better measures.

12.7 Confidence Limits on the Mean

The moon illusion is also an excellent example of a case in which we are particularly interested in estimating the true value of μ, the population mean, in this case the true ratio of the perceived size of the horizon moon to the perceived size of the zenith moon. As we have just seen, it makes sense here to say that "people perceive a moon on the horizon to be nearly 1.5 times as large as the apparent size of the moon at its zenith." The sample mean ($\overline{X}$), as you already know, is an unbiased estimate of μ. When we have one specific estimate of a parameter, we call it a **point estimate**, which is what the mean is here. There are also **interval estimates**, which set limits by a procedure that has a high probability of including the true (population) value of the mean (the mean, μ, of a whole population of observations). What we want, then, are **confidence limits** on μ. These limits enclose what is called a **confidence interval**.

In Chapter 6 we saw how to set what were called "probable limits" on an *observation*. In Chapter 9 we discussed setting confidence limits on a correlation coefficient. A similar line of reasoning will apply here.

If we want to set limits on μ, given the data at hand, what we really want to do is to ask how large or small μ could be without causing us to reject H_0 if we ran a t test on the obtained sample mean. In other words, if μ (the true size of the illusion) is actually quite small, we would have been unlikely to obtain the sample data. The same would be true if μ is quite large. At the other extreme, our ratio of 1.46 is probably a reasonable number to expect if the true mean ratio were 1.45 or 1.50. Actually, there is a whole range of values for μ for which data such as those we obtained would not be particularly unusual. We want to calculate those values of μ. In other words, we want to find those values of μ that would give us values of t that are just barely significant in each tail of the distribution.

Before we go further, let me clarify what we are trying to do—and more importantly what we are not trying to do. As I said in an earlier chapter, the logic of confidence limits looks a bit quirky to most people. You would probably like me to do a bit of calculation and tell you that μ must be between 1.22 and 1.71, for example. But I can't do that. But what I can do is to say that if μ were any smaller than 1.22, Kaufman and Rock would not have been likely to get the result that they obtained. I can also say that if μ were any larger than 1.71 they would not be very likely to obtain this result. So this result is consistent with the idea that μ is somewhere between 1.22 and 1.71.

An easy way to see what we are doing is to start with the formula for t and apply some simple algebra that you learned early in high school.

$$t = \frac{\overline{X} - \mu}{s_{\overline{X}}} = \frac{\overline{X} - \mu}{\dfrac{s}{\sqrt{N}}}$$

Because we have collected the data, we already know $\overline{X}$, s, and $\sqrt{N}$. We also know that the critical two-tailed value for t at $\alpha = .05$ is $t_{.05}(9) = \pm 2.262$. We will substitute these values into the formula for t and solve for μ, whereas we usually solve for t.

$$t = \frac{\overline{X} - \mu}{s_{\overline{X}}} = \frac{\overline{X} - \mu}{\dfrac{s}{\sqrt{N}}}$$

$$\pm 2.262 = \frac{1.463 - \mu}{\dfrac{0.341}{\sqrt{10}}} = \frac{1.463 - \mu}{0.108}$$

Rearranging to solve for μ, we have

$$\mu = \pm 2.262(0.108) + 1.463 = \pm 0.244 + 1.462$$

Using the $+0.244$ and -0.244 separately to obtain the upper and lower limits for μ, we have

$$\mu_{\text{upper}} = +0.244 + 1.463 = 1.707$$

$$\mu_{\text{lower}} = -0.244 + 1.463 = 1.219$$

Thus we can write the 95% confidence limits as 1.219 and 1.707 and the confidence interval as

$$CI_{.95} = 1.219 \leq \mu \leq 1.707$$

or, to write a general expression,

$$\boxed{CI_{.95} = \overline{X} \pm t_{.05}s_{\overline{X}} = \overline{X} \pm t_{.05}s/\sqrt{N}}$$

But where did that 95% figure come from? We have a 95% confidence interval because we used the two-tailed critical value of t at $\alpha = .05$, cutting off 2.5% in each tail. We are saying that the obtained value would fall within those limits 95% of the time. For the 99% limits we would take $t_{.01} = \pm 3.250$. Then the 99% confidence interval would be

$$CI_{.99} = \overline{X} \pm t_{.01}s_{\overline{X}} = 1.463 \pm 3.250(0.108) = 1.112 \leq \mu \leq 1.814$$

We now can say that the probability is .95 that an interval such as 1.219–1.707 includes the true mean ratio for the moon illusion, while the probability is .99 that an interval such as 1.112–1.814 includes μ. Note that neither interval includes the value 1.00, which represents no illusion. We already knew this for the 95% confidence interval because we had rejected that null hypothesis at $\alpha = .05$ when we ran the t test.

What we have here is something like what you see in the newspaper when you read that the public support for the president is 59% with a margin of error of 3%. A "margin of error" is basically just a confidence limit, and unless you were told otherwise, it is most likely a 95% confidence interval. Essentially the pollster is telling you that, given the size of the sample and the level of support, whatever number they found is most likely to be within three percentage points of the correct value.

Confidence intervals are demonstrated in Figure 12.7. To generate this figure, I drew 25 samples of $N = 4$ from a population with a mean (μ) of 5 and $\alpha = 1$. For every sample a 95% confidence interval on μ was calculated and plotted. For example, the limits produced from the first sample were approximately 3.16 and 6.88, whereas for the last sample the limits were 4.26 and 5.74. Because in this case we know that the true value of μ equals 5, I have drawn a vertical line at that point. Notice that the limits for samples 9 and 12 do not include $\mu = 5$. We would expect that the 95% confidence limits would encompass μ 95 times out of 100. Therefore, two misses out of 25 seems reasonable. Notice also that the confidence intervals vary in width. This variability can be explained by the fact that the width of an interval is a function of the standard deviation of the sample, and some samples have larger standard deviations than others.

I should repeat a point I made earlier about the interpretation of confidence limits. Statements of the form $p(1.219 \leq \mu \leq 1.707) = .95$ are not to be interpreted in the usual way. The parameter μ is not a variable. It does not jump around from experiment to experiment. Rather, μ is a constant, and the *interval* is what varies from

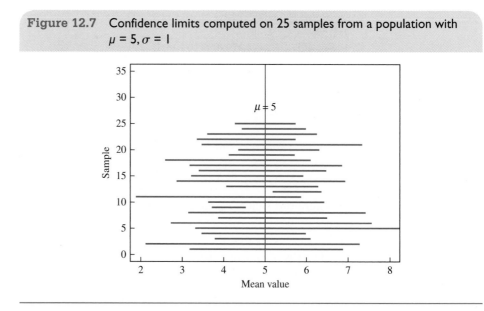

Figure 12.7 Confidence limits computed on 25 samples from a population with $\mu = 5, \sigma = 1$

experiment to experiment. Think of the parameter as a stake and the experimenter, in computing confidence limits, as tossing rings at that stake (parameter). Ninety-five percent of the time a ring of specified width will encircle the stake, and 5% of the time it will miss. A confidence statement is a statement of the probability that the ring has landed on the stake (i.e., the interval includes the parameter) and *not* a statement of the probability that the stake (parameter) landed inside the ring (interval). On the other hand, while that last statement is true, I would not fail a student in my course for saying that the probability is .95 that the true value of μ lies between 1.219 and 1.707.

12.8 Using SPSS and R to Run One-Sample t Tests

Figure 12.7 is an illustration of the use of SPSS to obtain a one-sample t test and confidence limits for the moon illusion data. You can see how to set up this analysis in SPSS by going to Chapter 7 of the *Shorter SPSS Manual* on this book's website. Notice that the results agree, within rounding error, with those we obtained by hand. Notice also that SPSS computes the exact probability of a Type I error (the **p value**) rather than comparing t to a tabled value. Although we concluded that the probability of a Type I error was less than .05, SPSS reveals that the actual two-tailed probability is .002. Most, if not all, computer programs operate in this way.

From the output in Figure 12.8 we could conclude that the mean ratio settings for the moon illusion, based on 10 subjects, was significantly greater than 1.00, which would be the expected setting if there were, in fact, no moon illusion. This could be written as $t(9) = 4.30, p = .002$.

The code for this analysis in R is quite straightforward. That code follows, although I have not presented the printout because it is basically the same as that of SPSS. If you run it, however, note that even though I asked for five breaks, to

> **Figure 12.8**   SPSS analysis for one-sample t tests and confidence limits

▶ *t* Test

One-Sample Statistics

	N	Mean	Std. Deviation	Std. Error Mean
RATIO	10	1.4630	.34069	.10773

One-Sample Test

	Test Value = 1					
					95% Confidence Interval of the Difference	
	t	*df*	Sig. (two-tailed)	Mean Difference	Lower	Upper
RATIO	4.298	9	.002	.4630	.2193	.7067

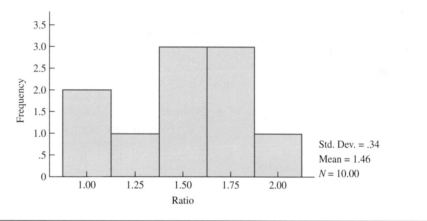

Ratio of Horizon/Zenith Moon

Std. Dev. = .34
Mean = 1.46
N = 10.00

repeat the histogram from SPSS, *R* had its own idea of what was right. Note also that I specified that I was testing against a null hypothesis of $\mu = 1$, because a ratio of 1.00 would represent no illusion.

```
# Moon illusion analysis
ratio < - c(1.73, 1.06, 2.03, 1.40, 0.95, 1.13, 1.41, 1.73, 1.63, 1.56)
cat( "The mean of the ratio scores is," mean(ratio),"\n")
cat("The standard deviation of ratio scores is," sd(ratio), "\n")
t.test(ratio, conf.int = .95, mu = 1)
hist(ratio, col = "red," breaks = 5, main = "Histogram of Ratio of Horizon to
Zenith," xlab = "Ratio")
```

12.9 A Good Guess Is Better than Leaving It Blank

We now will continue with the t test on means and work through another example of a t test on a null hypothesis about a single population mean (μ). In several places throughout this book we have worked with the study by Katz and his colleagues (1990) on the performance on an SAT-like exam when a group of students had not seen the passage on which the questions were based. The data from the 28 students in the group that had not seen the passage follow.

ID	1	2	3	4	5	6	7	8	9	10	11	12	13	14
Score	58	48	48	41	34	43	38	53	41	60	55	44	43	49

ID	15	16	17	18	19	20	21	22	23	24	25	26	27	28
Score	47	33	47	40	46	53	40	45	39	47	50	53	46	53

If the students had really guessed blindly, without even looking at the possible answers, we would expect that they would get 20 items correct by chance, because there were 100 items with five choices per item. On the other hand, if they can guess intelligently just by looking at the choices they are given, then they should do better than chance. So we want to test $H_0: \mu = 20$ against $H_0: \mu \neq 20$.

To solve for t we need to know the mean, the standard deviation, and the size of our sample.

$$\overline{X} = 46.2143, \, s = 6.7295, \, N = 28$$

Because we know $\overline{X}$, s_X, and N, and we know that we want to test the null hypothesis that $\mu = 20$, then we can set up a simple t test.

$$t = \frac{\overline{X} - \mu}{\dfrac{s}{\sqrt{N}}} = \frac{46.21 - 20}{\dfrac{6.73}{\sqrt{28}}}$$

$$= \frac{26.21}{1.27} = 20.61$$

With a t as large as 20.61, we don't even need to look up its probability. If we did, we would find a two-tailed critical value of t, on 27 df for $\alpha = .05$, of 2.052. Obviously we can reject the null hypothesis and conclude that the students were performing at better than chance levels.

We can calculate a 95% confidence interval based on our sample data.

$$CI_{.95} = \overline{X} \pm t_{.05}(s_X)$$

$$= 46.21 \pm 2.052(1.27)$$

$$= 46.21 \pm 2.61$$

$$43.6 \leq \mu \leq 48.82$$

Thus our confidence limits for the number correct in the population are 43.60 and 48.82.

Here is a situation in which I really have to ask what those confidence limits have told me. It is useful to know that students can guess at better than chance rates, although that has never been a closely held secret. But to know the confidence limits on such behavior probably has not advanced the cause of science very much. Sometimes confidence limits are very helpful—they may clarify the meaning of a result. Other times confidence limits look more like window dressing.

To carry this discussion further, let us look at effect sizes for a minute. I will write more about effect size calculations with one sample in the next chapter, but I want to anticipate that discussion here because it offers a nice contrast to what we said with the moon illusion example. When we were looking at the moon illusion, our dependent variable was the ratio of the horizon moon to the zenith moon, and that ratio has a clear interpretation. We saw that the horizon moon appeared to be nearly half again as large as the same moon seen overhead at its zenith. In the current example of the study by Katz et al., we don't have such a meaningful dependent variable. It probably will not satisfy you to know that participants correctly answered 46.21 questions correctly, or even to learn that they correctly answered 26.21 more questions than would be expected by chance. Is 26.21 a large number? Well, it depends on your point of reference.

To anticipate what I will say in Chapter 13, I am going to represent the mean performance in terms of the number of standard deviations it is above or below some point. In this particular case the size of a standard deviation was 6.73. It makes sense for me to ask how many standard deviations our mean was above the mean that would be expected by chance. So in this case I will divide 26.21 (the degree to which the participants' mean exceeded chance) by 6.73 and call this statistic $\hat{d}$. This measure was first advocated by Jacob Cohen, and is often referred to as Cohen's $\hat{d}$. Then

$$\hat{d} = \frac{\overline{X} - \mu}{5} = \frac{46.21 - 20}{6.73} = 3.89$$

On the basis of this result we can conclude that our participants scored nearly four standard deviations higher than we would have expected by chance. Four standard deviations is a lot, and I would conclude that they are doing very much better than chance responding would have predicted. If the effect size had been small (e.g., $\hat{d}= .15$), it is probably not worth a lot to guess. But when we see that we had an effect size of nearly 4, I hope that you come away with the idea that "if you don't know, guess!" That may be true even in those cases where the test scorer incorporates a correction for guessing.

I need to stress one complicating factor in calculating $\hat{d}$. As the formula shows, $\hat{d}$ is a ratio of the size of some effect (a mean or a difference in means) and a standard deviation. But before you jump in and use just any old standard deviation, you need to think about whether that standard deviation gives us a meaningful metric. In other words, does it make sense to convey the difference in standard deviation terms? I think that most people would agree that if we are talking about the moon illusion the mean setting itself is often sufficient—"the horizon moon appears to be nearly half again as large as the zenith moon." There we have just used the mean and did not involve the standard deviation at all. In the most recent example it would not be very useful to report simply how many items were correct, but it does seem meaningful to say that we are nearly four standard deviations above where we would be by chance. Just imagine a normal distribution plotted with a mean at 20 (the chance level) and imagine being four standard deviations above there. That's a big difference! However, there are other situations, another of which will appear in the next chapter, where there doesn't seem to be anything particularly meaningful in scaling a difference in standard deviation units. The task is to report some statistic that will give the reader a sense of what you have found, even if that is not statistically elegant.

Writing up the results of a one-sample t test

The following is an abbreviated version of what I would do if I were to write up this study.

> Katz et al. (1990) presented students with exam questions similar to those on the SAT, that required them to answer 100 five-choice multiple-choice questions about a passage that they had presumably read. One of the groups ($N = 28$) was given the questions without being presented with the passage, but members were asked to answer them anyway. A second group was allowed to read the passage, but it is not of interest to us here.
>
> If participants perform purely at random, those in the NoPassage condition would be expected to get 20 items correct just by chance. On the other hand, if participants read the test items carefully, they might be able to reject certain answers as unlikely regardless of what the passage said. A t test on H_0: $\mu = 20$ produced $t(27) = 20.61$, which has an associated probability under the null hypothesis that is far less than .05, leading us to reject H_0 and conclude that even without having seen the passage, students can perform at better than chance levels. Furthermore, the measure of effect size ($\hat{d} = 3.89$) shows that these students were performing at nearly four standard deviations better than we would have expected by chance, and that therefore their test-taking skills made an important contribution to their performance on this task.

12.10 Seeing Statistics

In this chapter we have used Student's t test to test the hypothesis that a sample came from a population with a specific mean, and we did this within the context of a situation in which we do not know the population standard deviation. We were required to use t specifically because we did not know that population standard deviation. McClelland's applets on this book's website are excellent for illustrating exactly what is happening here, and why the t distribution is more appropriate than the normal (z) distribution for answering our question.

Sampling Distribution of t

The first applet for Chapter 12 is named "Sampling Distribution of t." This applet is designed to allow you to draw samples from a particular population with a known mean ($\mu = 0$); calculate the mean, standard deviation, and t for each sample; and plot the result. For each sample we are testing the null hypothesis that the population mean is 0, and, because we know that it is true, we will have the sampling distribution of *t* when the null is true. (This distribution is often called the **central *t* distribution**.)

The opening screen, before you have done any sampling, looks like the following:

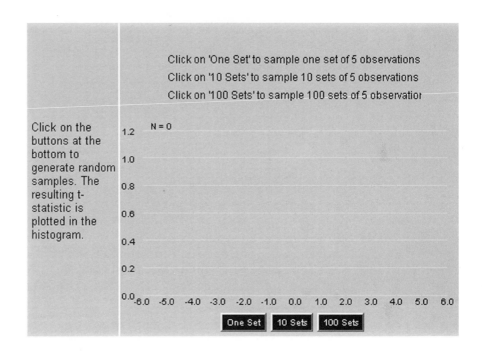

Notice that you can draw 1, 10, or 100 samples at a time, and each time you click one of the buttons you add those samples to the ones you have drawn already.

Start by drawing a number of individual samples, and note how the resulting *t* values vary from one sample to another. After you have drawn a number of individual samples, click on the button labeled "100 sets." Notice that some of the resulting *t* values are probably surprisingly large and/or small. (My first try gave me a *t* of about 4.5, and another of –4.0.) These extreme values would likely represent cases that would lead to rejection of the null hypothesis. Next, click on the "100 sets" button repeatedly until you have drawn 1,000 samples. Notice that the distribution is beginning to smooth out. Keep going until you have drawn 10,000 samples, and notice how smooth the distribution has become.

Comparing *z* and *t*

You might be inclined to view the distribution of *t* that you have just drawn as a *normal* distribution. It looks a lot like the normal distributions we have seen. But actually, it is a bit too wide. Under a normal distribution we would expect 5% of the values to exceed +1.96, but in our case, with only 4 *df*, 12.15% of the results would exceed +1.96. Thus if you were to use +1.96 as your cutoff, you would reject the null hypothesis far too often. The actual 5% cutoff (two-tailed) would be +2.776.

Let's explore this last idea a bit further. (We are more or less reproducing Figure 12.5.) If you go back to your browser and open the applet named "*t* versus *z*," you will see something that looks approximately like the following.

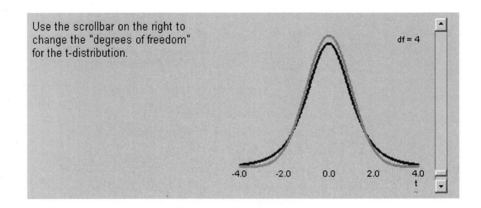

The red line (which is gray here, but red on your screen) represents the distribution of *z* (the normal distribution). The black line represents the *t* distribution. Notice how the tails of the *t* distribution are higher than those of the normal distribution. That means that we have to go farther out into each tail to find the 2.5% cutoff.

On the right side of this figure you will see a slider. Moving the slider up and down varies the degrees of freedom for *t* and allows you to see how the *t* distribution approaches the normal distribution as *df* increase. At what point would you be willing to conclude that the two distributions are "close enough?"

Confidence Intervals

While we are looking at McClelland's applets, we will take a look at an applet that he wrote illustrating confidence limits. In Figure 12.6 I showed you the results when I drew 25 samples, with their confidence limits, computed when the null hypothesis ($\mu = 5.0$) was true. In that case there were two confidence intervals that did not enclose $\mu = 5.0$, but the rest did. What might we expect to see if the null hypothesis is actually false?

The applet entitled "Confidence Limits" illustrates this situation. It hypothesizes a population mean of 100, but actually draws samples from a population wherein $\mu = 110$. For each sample the applet calculates, and draws, a 95% confidence limit. As you might hope and expect, many of these intervals, the red or light gray ones, do not include $\mu = 100$, though a number of them, the black ones, do. (Remember that μ is actually 110.) I have shown one result below, where I have drawn one sample.

The vertical dashed line represents the null hypothesis $\mu = 100$. The solid line represents the true mean of 110. Notice that for the first sample the limits are 101.0–120.0, which do not include 100, the hypothesized mean. Your one sample example will probably be different.

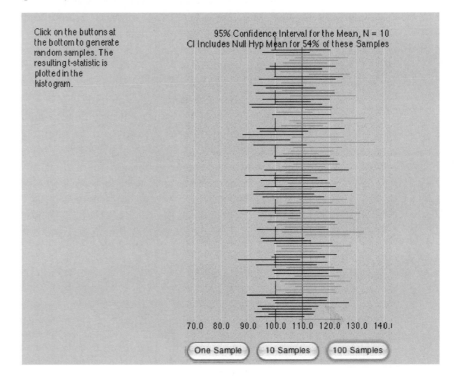

Click on the buttons at the bottom to generate random samples. The resulting t-statistic is plotted in the histogram.

95% Confidence Interval for the Mean, N = 10

Data:
101 97 118 109 106 121 100 102 140 114

120.0
101.0

Mean = 110.8
StDev= 13.0
S.E.M.=4.12
N   =10
t(9) =2.62   p = 0.0277
tCrit =2.26 for two-tailed at p = 0.05
Reject Null Hyp that mean = 100.0
lowerCl = 110.8 - 2.263(4.12) = 101.0
upperCl = 110.8 + 2.263(4.12) = 120.0

70.0 80.0 90.0 100.0 110.0 120.0 130.0 140.

One Sample   10 Samples   100 Samples

First start the applet and draw one sample. Do this repeatedly, and notice how the intervals vary. Then click on the button to draw 10 samples. Here it will be clear that some intervals include 110, the true mean, while others do not. Finally, draw 100 samples. My results follow.

Click on the buttons at the bottom to generate random samples. The resulting t-statistic is plotted in the histogram.

95% Confidence Interval for the Mean, N = 10
CI Includes Null Hyp Mean for 54% of these Samples

70.0 80.0 90.0 100.0 110.0 120.0 130.0 140.

One Sample   10 Samples   100 Samples

Now the second line of the heading above the graph will tell you what percentage of the intervals include the null hypothesis. (In this case it is 54%.) Repeat this several times and note how the answer varies. What we are beginning to discuss here is "power." Power is the probability of correctly rejecting a false null hypothesis. In this case, if the confidence intervals include 100 54% of the time, we will fail to reject the null 54% of the time. That means that $1 - .54 = 46\%$ of the time we will correctly reject the null, so for us power $= .46$. We will have much more to say about this later in the book.

12.11 Confidence Intervals Can Be Far More Important than a Null Hypothesis Test

Before I go on to discuss other forms of the *t* test, I want to bring up a related example where we can run a null hypothesis test, but where a confidence interval is far more useful.

Hart et al. (2013) were interested in studying orienting behavior in dogs. We know that many birds orient their migration by use of the earth's magnetic field, and there is evidence that some mammals can respond to magnetic fields as well. Hart et al. wondered if dogs were also sensitive to such fields. (Dogs are descended from wolves, who successfully navigate over a huge territory.)

Each morning I take my dog Toby for his walk, and while he sniffs around for exactly the perfect spot, I stand there with my little plastic bag, ready to do my part in this project. Hart and his colleagues wondered if the orientation that the dog finally chooses bears any relation to the earth's magnetic field. So they carefully recorded each dog's orientation for each operation. (They used 70 different dogs of 37 different breeds, for 1,893 observations over a two-year period.) Although there is a legitimate test of the null hypothesis that orientation is random (the Rayleigh test), that does not seem like an appropriate solution. We don't want to know just whether the orientation is random, but what that orientation is and what the confidence interval on that mean orientation is. I chose this example in part because it points to the case where a null hypothesis test is not particularly informative, as well as the case where a confidence interval is particularly helpful.

It turns out that the issue is slightly more complex, which actually gives added credibility to the test of the hypothesis that dogs prefer a particular orientation. The earth's magnetic field changes over time, being very stable on some occasions and unstable on others. Hart et al. broke the data down by three categories of field stability (stable, moderate, and unstable). They found clear evidence of a nearly North/South orientation (with a narrow confidence interval) when the field was stable, and much broader confidence intervals when the field was not. (In fact, they had almost no confidence that the interval for the most unstable category was even appropriate.) The results for the stable category are shown in Figure 7.8. For that case, the mean orientation was nearly North/South (173°/353°)[3]. The standard deviation was 29°, based on 43 cases. This gives us a confidence interval width, to the north, of

---

[3]Remember, we are speaking of compass directions, so 173° to the south is equivalent to 353° to the north, and we start recounting at 0 when we pass 360°. (The mean of 1° and 359° is obviously not (1 + 359)/2 = 180°.) Our statistics are actually called "circular statistics," the formulae for which can be found on Google, and with an *R* package called CircStats. This is the last time you will see circular statistics in this book.

$$CI = \mu \pm t_{.025}(se_{mean}) = \mu \pm 2.02\left(\frac{s}{\sqrt{N}}\right)$$

$$= \mu \pm 2.02\left(\frac{29}{\sqrt{43}}\right) = \mu \pm 2.02(4.42)$$

$$= 173° \pm 8.93 = 164° \, and \, 182°$$

and

$$= 353° \pm 8.93 = 344° \, and \, 2°$$

Thus we have a very narrow confidence interval width of only 18°. With a moderately unstable field, the mean orientation had a 95% confidence interval width of 46°, and with an unstable field the data were so erratic that they could not compute a reasonable confidence interval. For those particular data in the unstable condition the angle is roughly East-West, but that was not statistically different from random ($p = .233$). (After all, the mean had to come out to be some number, and if responses are random, East-West is as good as any.)

The point of using this example is that it illustrates a situation where the confidence interval is by far the most appropriate measure, outweighing any statistical test. Anyone looking at Figure 12.8 would have to agree that dogs behave very consistently with respect to North/South orientation. That figure says it all without any statistical test. We know far more about the behavior of dogs than we would if I simply stated that there was evidence that dogs do not orient at random. It is nice to know that with stable magnetic fields the orientation is very close to North/South, but I am far more impressed by noting how consistent the data are as given by the confidence interval.

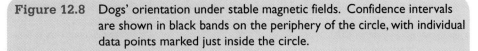

Figure 12.8   Dogs' orientation under stable magnetic fields. Confidence intervals are shown in black bands on the periphery of the circle, with individual data points marked just inside the circle.

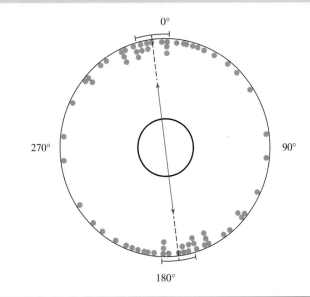

12.12 Summary

We began this chapter by considering the sampling distribution of the mean and how the information it gives is useful in testing hypotheses. The sampling distribution of the mean is simply the distribution of means over repeated sampling. The Central Limit Theorem, which is one of the most important theorems in statistics, tells us that the sampling distribution will have a mean equal to the population mean, a standard deviation equal to the population standard deviation divided by the square root of N, and will approach normal as the sample size increases. This theorem allows us to know what the results of repeated sampling would be without having to do that sampling.

We then covered testing the null hypothesis about a single mean when we know the population standard deviation, and this simply involved computing a z score by subtracting the hypothesized population mean from the sample mean and dividing by the standard error of the mean as given by the Central Limit Theorem. When we do not know the population standard deviation (and we generally don't), we simply substitute the sample standard deviation for the population standard deviation and call the result Student's t. But with t we need to take into account the degrees of freedom, which in the one-sample case will be one less than the sample size. When we calculate t we need to compare that against the t distribution because the answers are likely to be larger than they would be if we had known σ.

Several factors affect the size of t, and these include the actual difference between the sample mean and the mean under the null hypothesis, the size of the sample variance, and the sample size (N). The choice of a one- or two-tailed test will not affect the magnitude of t, but it will determine the critical value and thus can affect the probability of rejecting the null hypothesis.

We looked briefly at estimating effect size, and will look more closely at that in subsequent chapters. By "effect size" I mean some measure of how large our difference is. In the case of the moon illusion I argued that the mean adjustment is all that we need to understand how large an effect we have. In other situations we will want to scale our answer in terms of the size of a standard deviation, so as to be able to say something like "This mean was 1.5 standard deviations larger than the hypothesized population mean."

Finally, I discussed confidence limits, which represent our best guess about limits on the true population mean. We want to be able to say that 95% of the time when we carry out these computations we will have limits that bracket the true population mean. We will have more to say about confidence limits in subsequent chapters. At the very end, I superficially brought up the concept of power, and, that again, we will discuss in subsequent chapters.

Key Terms

Experimental hypothesis, 300	Degrees of freedom (*df*), 310
Central Limit Theorem, 301	Effect size, 316
Student's *t* distribution, 310	Point estimate, 317

Interval estimate, 317

Confidence limits, 317

Confidence interval, 317

p value., 320

Central *t* distribution, 325

12.13 A Quick Review

A. List three things that the central limit theorem tells us.
Ans: The mean equals the population mean; the standard deviation (standard error) equals the population standard deviation divide by the square root of N; and the distribution approaches normal as N increases.

B. Why do we care about the standard error of a statistic?
Ans: It tells us how variable that statistic is over repeated sampling.

C. How does the formula for *t* differ from the standard formula for *z*?
Ans: We replace X with $\overline{X}$; we replace μ with the mean under the null hypothesis, and we replace σ with our sample estimate of the standard error of the mean.

D. Why is the sampling distribution of the variance relevant to the use of *t* tests?
Ans: The sampling distribution is positively skewed, especially for small samples, so any particular sample standard deviation is more likely to underestimate σ than to overestimate it.

E. When we are dealing with one set of scores, the degrees of freedom for *t* will be _____.
Ans: N – 1

F. Name three things that affect the size of the *t* we calculate.
Ans: The size of the difference, the size of the variance, and the sample size.

G. What do we mean when we speak of an "effect size measure?"
Ans: We refer to some measure that tells about how large a difference is, in a meaningful metric, rather than whether or not it is statistically significant.

H. What do we mean by a confidence interval?
Ans: We are speaking about an interval that is calculated in such a way that it has a particular probability (often .95) of including the true population value of a parameter (often the population mean).

I. *In general*, what do we mean by Cohen's effect size measure *d*?
Ans: It is a measure of how far a sample mean differs from a population mean when expressed in terms of standard deviations.

J. What is the sampling distribution of *t*?
Ans: This is the distribution that the *t* statistic would take on over repeated sample *if the null hypothesis is true.*

12.14 Exercises

12.1 The following numbers represent 100 random numbers drawn from a rectangular population with a mean of 4.5 and a standard deviation of 2.6. Plot the distribution of these digits.

(They are available as a text file in the data files on the Web.)

```
6 4 1 5 8 7 0 8 2 1 5 7 4 0 2 6 9 0 9 6
4 9 0 4 9 3 4 9 8 2 0 4 1 4 9 4 1 7 5 2
3 1 5 2 1 7 9 7 3 5 4 7 3 1 5 1 1 0 5 2
7 6 2 1 0 6 2 3 3 6 5 4 1 5 9 1 0 2 6 0
8 3 9 3 3 8 5 5 7 0 8 4 2 0 6 3 7 3 5 1
```

12.2 I drew 50 samples of five scores each from the same population that the data in Exercise 12.1 came from, and calculated the mean of each sample. The means are shown below. Plot the distribution of these means.

```
2.8  6.2  4.4  5.0  1.0  4.6  3.8  2.6  4.0  4.8
6.6  4.6  6.2  4.6  5.6  6.4  3.4  5.4  5.2  7.2
5.4  2.6  4.4  4.2  4.4  5.2  4.0  2.6  5.2  4.0
3.6  4.6  4.4  5.0  5.6  3.4  3.2  4.4  4.8  3.8
4.4  2.8  3.8  4.6  5.4  4.6  2.4  5.8  4.6  4.8
```

12.3 Compare the means and the standard deviations for the distribution of digits in Exercise 12.1 and the sampling distribution of the mean in Exercise 12.2.

a) What would the Central Limit Theorem lead you to expect in this situation?
b) Do the data correspond to what you would predict?

12.4 Use R to repeat Exercises 12.1 and 12.2. (The code for this exercise can be found on the chapter's Web page along with other pieces of code. This code will generate its own set of 100 random observations and its own set of means of 5 observations.)

12.5 In what way would the result in Exercise 12.2 differ if you had drawn 50 samples of size 15? (If you answered Exercise 12.4, you can easily modify it to answer this question.)

12.6 In Table 11.1 in Chapter 11 we saw data on the state means of students who took the SAT exam. The mean Verbal SAT for North Dakota was 515. The standard deviation was not reported. Assume that 238 students took that exam.

a) Is this result consistent with the idea that North Dakota's students are a random sample from a population of students having a mean of 500 and a standard deviation of 100?
b) From what we learned in Chapter 11 about SAT scores and how, and why, they vary by state, would you feel comfortable concluding that people in North Dakota are smarter than people elsewhere?

12.7 Why do the data in Exercise 12.6 not really speak to the issue of whether education in North Dakota is generally in good shape?

12.8 Using the data from Table 11.1, compute the 95% confidence limits on the Pupil/Teacher ratio across the 50 states.

12.9 You would probably be nervous about inferring a population estimate and a confidence interval for the mean U.S. SAT Combined score from the data in Table 11.1, but you are probably much less worried about your confidence limits on Pupil/Teacher ratio in Exercise 12.8. Why would this be?

12.10 In Exercise 5.21 we saw, among other things, the weight gain of each of 29 anorexic girls who received cognitive behavioral therapy. What null hypothesis would likely be testing in this situation?

12.11 The data referred to in Exercise 12.10 (in pounds gained) follow. Run the appropriate t test and draw the appropriate conclusions.

ID	1	2	3	4	5	6	7	8	9	10
Gain	1.7	0.7	−0.1	−0.7	−3.5	14.9	3.5	17.1	−7.6	1.6
ID	11	12	13	14	15	16	17	18	19	20
Gain	11.7	6.1	1.1	−4.0	20.9	−9.1	2.1	−1.4	1.4	−0.3
ID	21	22	23	24	25	26	27	28	29	
Gain	−3.7	−0.8	2.4	12.6	1.9	3.9	0.1	15.4	−0.7	

12.12 Compute 95% confidence limits on μ for the data in Exercise 12.11.

12.13 As I entered the data into an R file for Exercise 12.11 I became a bit concerned about what they meant. Can you suggest a reason for my concern?

12.14 Use one of the free statistics programs that we have been using and reproduce the results for Exercises 12.11 and 12.12. This is an example where it is probably easier to enter the data by hand. (http://vassarstats.net/ is a good program to use. Select "t=Tests & Procedures", and then read their instructions carefully. Don't press a return after entering the hypothetical population mean.)

12.15 Compute a measure of effect size for the data in Exercise 12.11.

12.16 For the IQ data on females in data set Add.dat on the website, test the null hypothesis that $\mu_{female} = 100$. You can use SPSS or R, or any other program you have.

12.17 In Exercise 12.16 you probably solved for t instead of z. Why was that necessary?

12.18 Describe the procedures that you would go through to reproduce the results in Figure 12.4.

12.19 In Section 12.3 we ran a t test to test the hypothesis that young children under stress give what they perceive to be more socially desirable answers on an anxiety measure than normal children do. We never really tested the hypothesis that they report lower levels of anxiety. For the data on these 36 children the mean anxiety score was 11.00, with a standard deviation of 6.085. The population mean anxiety score for elementary school-aged children on this measure is reported as 14.55. Do our children show significantly lower levels of anxiety than children in the general population?

12.20 Compute the 95% confidence limits on mean anxiety for the data in Exercise 12.19.

12.21 Are the confidence limits that you calculated in Exercise 12.20 consistent with the results of the t test in Exercise 12.19?

12.22 Write a brief paragraph describing the research project in Exercise 12.19 and its results.

## CHAPTER 13

Hypothesis Tests Applied to Means: Two Related Samples

T his chapter will move from the one-sample case to the two-sample case, but here we will assume that the two samples of data were provided by the same participants. At first glance it looks as if this situation creates problems, but it turns out that it is very easy to get around the issues that arise. We will also consider the question of when we would, and would not, want to use related samples.

In Chapter 12 we considered the situation in which we had one sample mean $(\overline{X})$. We wanted to test to see if it was reasonable to believe that we would obtain such a mean if we had been sampling from a population with some specified population mean (which we denote μ_0). Another way of phrasing this is to say that we were testing to determine if the mean of the population from which we sampled (call it μ_1) could reasonably be considered to be equal to some particular value given by the null hypothesis (μ_0).

In this chapter we will move away from the case in which we perform a test on the mean of a single sample of data. Instead we will consider the case in which we have two **related samples** and we wish to perform a test on the

CONCEPTS THAT YOU WILL NEED TO REMEMBER FROM PREVIOUS CHAPTERS

t distribution:	Sampling distribution of the *t* statistic when the null hypothesis is true. Often called the "central *t* distribution"
Standard error:	The standard deviation of the sampling distribution of a statistic
Degrees of freedom:	An adjusted value of the sample size, often $N - 1$ or $N - 2$
Null hypothesis:	The hypothesis to be tested by a statistical test: H_0
Research hypothesis:	The hypothesis that the study is designed to test: H_1
$\mu, \sigma, \overline{X}, s$:	Mean and standard deviation of a population or a sample, respectively

difference between their two means. (The same analyses apply to what are variously called **repeated measures**, **matched samples**, paired samples, correlated samples, dependent samples, randomized blocks, or split plots, depending in part on the speaker's background.) As you will see, this test is similar to the test discussed in the previous chapter.

13.1 Related Samples

In many (but certainly not all) situations in which we will use the form of the t test discussed in this chapter, we will have two sets of data from the same participants. For example, we might ask 20 people to rate their level of anxiety before and after donating blood. Or we might record ratings of level of disability made using two different rating systems for each of 20 disabled individuals in an attempt to see whether one rating system leads to generally lower assessments than the other. In both examples we would have 20 sets of numbers, two numbers for each person, and we would expect these two sets of numbers (variables) to be correlated. We need to take this correlation into account in planning our t test. In the example of anxiety about donating blood, people differ widely in level of anxiety. Some seem to be anxious all the time no matter what happens, and others just take things as they come and don't worry about anything. Thus, there should be a relationship between an individual's anxiety level before donating blood and the anxiety level after donating blood. In other words, if we know that a person was one of the more anxious people before donation, we can make a reasonable guess that the same person was one of the more anxious people after donation. Similarly, some people are severely disabled, whereas others are only mildly so. If we know that a particular person received a high assessment using one system, it is likely that person also received a relatively high assessment using another system. The relationship between data sets doesn't have to be perfect—in fact, it probably never will be. The fact that we can make better than chance predictions is sufficient to classify two sets of data as related or matched. (To put this another way, we have related or matched samples whenever the two variables, such as the two sets of anxiety scores, are significantly correlated, and for all practical purposes that correlation will be positive.)

In the two preceding examples I have chosen situations in which each person in the study contributed two scores. Although this is the most common way of obtaining related samples, it is not the only way. For example, a study of marital relationships might involve asking husbands and wives to rate their satisfaction with their marriage, with the goal of testing to see whether wives are, on average, more or less satisfied than husbands. Here each individual would contribute only one score, but the couple as a unit would contribute a pair of scores. It is very probable that if the wife is very dissatisfied with the marriage, her husband isn't likely to be too happy either, and vice versa. This is a classic example of *matching* or *matched pairs*.

The many examples of experimental designs involving related samples all have one thing in common, and that is the fact that knowing one member of a pair of scores tells you something—maybe not much, but something—about the other member. Whenever this is the case, we say that the samples are related. This chapter deals with t tests on the difference between the means of two related samples. The important point about matched samples is illustrated in the previous examples. We know from the last chapter that to calculate a t we divide a difference by a function of the variance (specifically, the standard error). The larger the variance, the smaller the t, and the less likely it is that the difference will be significant. In our example of donating blood, there is a lot of variance in those data that have nothing to do with the kinds of differences we see from one measurement time to another. If we can get rid of that extra variance (between subjects variance), we will be more likely to reject the null. Having matched or paired samples allows us to do just that—get rid of extraneous error variance.

13.2 Student's t Applied to Difference Scores

Everitt, in Hand, et al., 1994, reported on family therapy as a treatment for anorexia. There were 17 girls in this experiment, and they were weighed before and after treatment. The weights of the girls, in pounds,[1] are given in Table 13.1. The row of difference scores was obtained by subtracting the Before score from the After score, so that a negative difference represents weight *loss*, and a positive difference represents a *gain*.

One of the first things we should probably do, although it takes us away from t tests for a moment, is to plot the relationship between Before Treatment and After Treatment weights, looking to see if there is, in fact, a relationship, and how linear that relationship is. Such a plot is given in Figure 13.1. Notice that the relationship is basically linear, with a slope quite near 1.0. A slope of 1.00 would tell us that how much the girl gained or lost by the end of therapy was not a function of how much she weighed at the beginning of therapy. In other words, heavy and light girls each *gain* approximately the same amount.

The primary question we wish to ask is whether subjects gained weight as a function of the therapy sessions, or, put differently, whether family therapy is an effective treatment for anorexia. We have an experimental problem here, because it is possible that weight gain resulted merely from the passage of time, and that therapy had nothing to do with it. However, Everitt also had a **control group**, which we will ignore for now, that did not receive therapy, and those members did not gain weight over the

Table 13.1 Data from Everitt on Weight Gain

ID	1	2	3	4	5	6	7	8	9	10
Before	83.8	83.3	86.0	82.5	86.7	79.6	76.9	94.2	73.4	80.5
After	95.2	94.3	91.5	91.9	100.3	76.7	76.8	101.6	94.9	75.2
Diff	11.4	11.0	5.5	9.4	13.6	−2.9	−.1	7.4	21.5	−5.3

ID	11	12	13	14	15	16	17	Mean	St. Dev.
Before	81.6	82.1	77.6	83.5	89.9	86.0	87.3	83.23	5.02
After	77.8	95.5	90.7	92.5	93.8	91.7	98.0	90.49	8.48
Diff	−3.8	13.4	13.1	9.0	3.9	5.7	10.7	7.26	7.16

---

[1]Everitt reported that these weights were in kilograms, but if so he has a collection of anorexic young girls whose mean weight is about 185 pounds, and that just doesn't sound reasonable. However, the example is completely unaffected by the units in which we record weight.

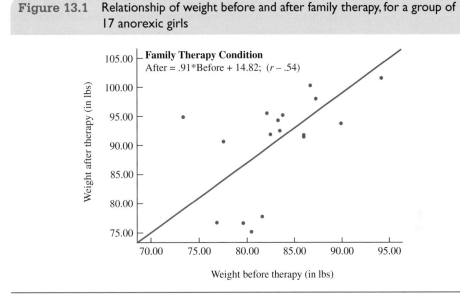

same period of time. This strongly suggests that the simple passage of time was not an important variable. (We will consider this group in Chapter 14.) If you were to calculate the weight of these girls before and after therapy, the means would be 83.23 and 90.49 lbs, respectively, which translates to a gain of a little more than seven pounds. However, we still need to test to see whether this difference is likely to represent a true difference in population means, or a chance difference. By this I mean that we need to test the null hypothesis that the mean in a *population* of Before scores is equal to the mean in a *population* of After scores. In other words, we are testing H_0: $\mu_A = \mu_B$.

As I suggested earlier, a problem arises when our Before and After scores are not independent, and we have such a relationship here, as you can see from Figure 13.1. That figure reports the correlation between the two measurements as .54. How much a girl weighs after therapy is clearly related to how much she weighed before therapy, which certainly sounds reasonable. This lack of independence would distort our *t* test if we couldn't find a way around it, but fortunately we do have a way around it, and so can proceed.

Difference Scores

Although it would seem obvious to view the data as representing two samples of scores, one set obtained before the therapy program and one after, it is also possible, and very profitable, to transform the data into one set of scores—the set of differences between X_1 and X_2 for each girl. These differences are called **difference scores**, or **gain scores**, and are shown in the third row of Table 13.1. They represent the degree of weight gain between one measurement session and the next—presumably as a result of our intervention. If the therapy program actually had *no* effect (i.e., if H_0 is true), the average weight would not change from session to session. By chance some girls would happen to have a higher weight After than Before, and some would have a lower weight, but *on the average* there would be no difference—the mean difference would be zero.

If we now think of our data as being the set of difference scores, the null hypothesis becomes the hypothesis that the mean of a population of difference scores (denoted μ_D) equals 0. Because it can be shown that $\mu_D = \mu_A - \mu_B$, we can write $H_0: \mu_D = \mu_A - \mu_B = 0$. But now we can see that we are testing a hypothesis using *one* sample of data (the sample of difference scores), and we already know how to do that from Chapter 12. Those of you who worked Exercise 12.11 in that chapter will probably suspect that you have done all this before, though with a different treatment condition. Yes, you have. In Chapter 12 we looked at data as if they consisted solely of gain scores, whereas in this chapter we start with before-and-after data and then move to gain scores. These are just two approaches with the same end. The only difference is that in Chapter 12 we were speaking of a test that applies to one set of data regardless of whether those data are differences between two scores for each person or, as in the case of the moon illusion example, simply one set of data.

The t Statistic

We are now at precisely the same place we were in the previous chapter when we had a sample of data and a null hypothesis ($\mu = 0$). The only difference is that in this case the data are difference scores, and the mean and the standard deviation are based on the differences. Recall that t was defined as the difference between a sample mean and a population mean, divided by the standard error of the mean. It is common practice to let the symbol $\overline{D}$ represent the sample of difference scores. Then we have

$$t = \frac{\overline{D} - 0}{s_{\overline{D}}} = \frac{\overline{D} - 0}{\dfrac{s_D}{\sqrt{N}}}$$

where $\overline{D}$ and s_D are the mean and the standard deviation of the difference scores and N is the number of difference scores (i.e., the number of *pairs*, not the number of raw scores). From Table 13.1 we see that the mean difference score was 7.26, and the standard deviation of the differences was 7.16. For our data

$$t = \frac{\overline{D} - 0}{s_{\overline{D}}} = \frac{\overline{D} - 0}{\dfrac{s_D}{\sqrt{N}}} = \frac{7.26 - 0}{\dfrac{7.16}{\sqrt{17}}} = \frac{7.26}{1.74} = 4.18$$

Degrees of Freedom

The degrees of freedom for the matched-sample case are exactly the same as they were for the one-sample case. Because we are working with the difference scores, N will be equal to the number of differences (or the number of *pairs* of observations, or the number of *independent* observations—all of which amount to the same thing). Because the variance of these difference scores (s^2_D) is used as an estimate of the variance of a population of difference scores (σ^2_D) and because this sample variance is obtained using the sample mean ($\overline{D}$), we will lose one *df* to the mean and have $N - 1$ *df*. In other words, df = number of *pairs* minus 1.

We have 17 difference scores in this example, so we will have 16 degrees of freedom. From Table E.6 in the Appendices, we find that for a two-tailed test at the .05 level of significance, $t_{.05}(16) = \pm2.12$. Our obtained value of t (4.18) exceeds

2.12, so we will reject H_0 and conclude that the difference scores were not sampled from a population of difference scores where $\mu_D = 0$. The actual p value, computed using www.statpages.org/pdfs.html, equals .001 to three decimal places. In practical terms this means that the subjects weighed significantly more after the intervention program than before it. Although we would like to think that this means that the program was successful, keep in mind the possibility that this could just be normal growth. The fact remains, however, that for whatever reason, the weights were sufficiently higher on the second occasion to allow us to reject H_0: $\mu_D = \mu_A - \mu_B = 0$.

To run this analysis using SPSS, simply use **Analyze/Compare Means/ One-Sample _t_ Test**. The 95% confidence intervals will be printed automatically, although you can click on the Options button to change that to 99% or whatever you wish. If you are using R, the only change that is required is to specify that GAIN is your dependent variable. Alternatively you can use the original before and after scores, so long as you tell R that these are paired measurements. That command would be **t.test(Before, After, paired = TRUE)**. That command would produce

```
t.test(Before, After, paired = TRUE)


     Paired t-test

data:  Before and After
t = -4.1849, df = 16, p-value = 0.0007003
alternative hypothesis: true difference in means is not equal to 0
95 percent confidence interval:
 -10.94471  -3.58470
sample estimates:
mean of the differences
          -7.264706

### You would have the same result if you typed t.test(Gain)
```

13.3 The Crowd Within Is Like the Crowd Without

The unusual title of this section comes from a study by Vul and Pashler (2008). The authors noted that judgments from groups are often better than judgments from individuals. For example, they asked participants to answer the question, "What percentage of the world's airports is located in the United States?" The correct answer is about 30%. I doubt that you knew that exactly, but you could probably make a reasonable guess—at least the answer would be more than 10% and less than 50%. Suppose that you guessed 25% and I guessed 37%. You are off by 5% and I am off by 7%, so on average you and I are off by 6%. (Remember, the size of an error is an absolute number—we drop the sign.) But if you take your guess and mine, our average is $(25 + 37)/2 = 31$, so our average guess is only off by 1. This won't work in favor of our average guess all the time, but frequently it will.[2]

---

[2]This question can be traced back at least as far as Galton in 1907. He observed a crowd of nearly 800 villagers guessing the weight of a bull. No one guessed correctly, but the mean of their guesses was 1197 lbs. The bull actually weighed 1198 lbs.

Vul and Pashler asked an interesting question. If it is true that multiple guesses from a group are usually a better estimate than guesses by individuals, what about multiple guesses from the same individual? In other words, if I record your guess of 25% and then come back sometime later and ask again, perhaps the average of your two guesses will be better than either guess alone. In fact, that should be true whenever there is a positive correlation between guesses that is not perfect.

The following data are not the same as those produced by Vul and Pashler, but the results accurately reflect their results. Suppose that we ran an experiment like the one by Vul and Pashler, and for our convenience let the correct answer always be 100, or else rescale the data so that is true. We use 15 participants, each of whom answers our questions on two occasions three weeks apart. Assume that we have the data shown in Table 13.2. The 5th column shows how far off the participants were when we averaged their two guesses and compared those to the true value of 100. The next two columns show each individual's errors on their first guess and on their second guess, while the 8th column averages those two errors. According to Vul and Pashler the entries in column 5 (the error of the average guess) should generally be smaller than the entries in the 8th column (the average of their errors), and thus the means of those two columns should differ.

There are several null hypotheses that we could test, but we will focus on comparing the means of columns 5 and 8 (Error of Average Guess versus Average Error). We are asking if the average of the errors is less than the errors of the averages.

Table 13.2   The Guessing Behavior of 15 Participants Each Given Two Guesses

Correct Answer	First Guess	Second Guess	Average Guess	Error of Average Guess	Error First	Error Second	Average Error	Difference
100	95	110	102.5	2.5	5	10	7.5	−5
100	105	112	108.5	8.5	5	12	8.5	0
100	101	90	95.5	4.5	1	10	5.5	−1
100	92	99	95.5	4.5	8	1	4.5	0
100	115	108	111.5	11.5	15	8	11.5	0
100	103	112	107.5	7.5	7	12	9.5	−2
100	97	95	96	4	3	5	4	0
100	90	98	94	6	10	2	6	0
100	96	90	93	7	4	10	7	0
100	110	95	102.5	2.5	10	5	7.5	−5
100	106	109	107.5	7.5	6	9	7.5	0
100	93	87	90	10	7	13	10	0
100	102	97	99.5	0.5	2	3	2.5	−2
100	108	110	109	9	8	10	9	0
100	95	107	101	1	5	7	6	−5
			Means	5.767	6.4	7.8	7.1	
			Mean Diff					−1.33
			Std. Dev.					2.024

This comes down to a t test on the null hypothesis that the difference scores come from a population with mean (μ) = 0. We are using a paired t test because the scores from the same person would not be independent. In this case the two guesses have a correlation of .76.

$$t = \frac{\overline{D} - \mu_D}{s_{\overline{D}}} = \frac{\overline{D} - 0}{\dfrac{s_D}{\sqrt{N}}} = \frac{-1.40}{\dfrac{2.165}{\sqrt{15}}} = \frac{-1.40}{0.559} = 2.50$$

We have 15 pairs of guesses, so we have 15 – 1 = 14 degrees of freedom. From the Appendix we find that for a two-tailed test at α = .05, the critical value of 14 df = 2.145. Because our obtained t exceeds the critical value, and we can reject the null hypothesis. (The exact two-tailed p value = .023.) We can conclude that the mean of a person's two guesses is, on average, better than the typical error in his or her two guesses taken separately.

Vul and Pashler (2008) pursued this question further, and their paper is worth reading. In fact, soon after it was published, several commentaries showed up on an Internet search. The researchers also showed that, on average, a person's first guess is less in error than the second guess, though the average of the two is even better.

13.4 Advantages and Disadvantages of Using Related Samples

In the next chapter we will consider experimental designs in which we use two independent groups of subjects rather than testing the same subjects twice (or some other method of having related samples of data). In many cases independent samples are useful, but before considering that topic, it is important that we consider the strengths and weaknesses of related samples.

Probably the most important advantage of designing an experiment around related samples is that such a procedure allows us to avoid problems associated with variability from participant to participant. Return for a moment to the data on weights of anorexic girls in Table 13.1. Notice that some participants (e.g., participant 9) began the study weighing considerably less than others. On the other hand, participant 8 began the study weighing well more than others. The advantage of related-samples designs is that these variations between participants do not enter into the data we analyze—the difference scores. A change from 73 pounds to 75 pounds is treated exactly the same as a change from 93 to 95. In not allowing variability from participant to participant in initial weight to influence the data by producing a large sample variance, related-samples designs have a considerable advantage over independent samples in terms of the ability to reject a false null hypothesis (power).

A second advantage of related samples over two independent samples is the fact that related samples allow us to control for extraneous variables. Had we measured one group of participants before they received therapy and a different group after, there may have been any number of differences between the groups that had nothing to do with our intervention but that would influence the results. That was not a problem in our study because we used the same participants for both measurement sessions.

A third advantage of related-measures designs is that they require fewer participants than do independent-sample designs for the same degree of power. This is a substantial advantage, as anyone who has ever tried to recruit participants can attest. It is usually a much easier task to get 20 people to do something twice than to get 40 people to do it once.

The primary disadvantage of related-measures designs is that there may be either an **order effect** or a **carry-over effect** from one session to the next, or the first measurement may influence the treatment itself though processes such as sensitization. For example, if we plan to give a test of knowledge of current events, followed by a crash course in current events, and then follow that with a retest using the same test, it is reasonable to conclude that subjects will be more familiar with the items the second time around and may even have looked up answers during the interval between the two test administrations. Similarly, in drug studies the effects of the first drug may not have worn off by the next test session. A common problem with related-measures designs arises when a pretest "tips off" subjects as to the purpose of the intervention. For example, a pretest on attitudes toward breast feeding might make you a wee bit suspicious when a stranger sits down beside you the next day and just happens to launch into a speech on the virtues of breast feeding. Whenever you have concerns that carry-over effects could contaminate your study or that treatment effects might be influenced by pretreatment measures, a related-measures design is *not* recommended. There are techniques for controlling, though not eliminating, order and carry-over effects, but we will not discuss them here. Would you anticipate that either of these effects might influence the data on the moon illusion or the anorexia data? If so, how might we control for such effects?

13.5 How Large an Effect Have We Found?—Effect Size

In Chapter 12 and earlier chapters, I discussed the fact that there has been an important trend within psychology and other disciplines to ask for some kind of statement from the experimenter indicating not only that the difference was significant, but also whether it is meaningful. As I indicated, if we use enough subjects, we can almost always find even a meaningless difference to be significant. I introduced Jacob Cohen's concept of effect size, by which he meant a statistic that gave a meaningful indication of how large a mean was, or how different two means were. If you looked at the answer that I gave on this book's website to Exercise 12.15 you will have seen that I stated that using the standard deviation of gain scores did not result in a very meaningful measure, although it is a good way to scale other kinds of outcome variables. The example we have in front of us is very similar to the study in Exercise 12.15 except that we have the pre- and post-scores as well as the gains. The presence of the pretreatment scores offers us a chance to come up with more than one useful measure.

The data on treatment of anorexia offer a good example of a situation in which there are multiple ways to report on the difference in terms that people will understand. All of us step onto a scale occasionally, and we have some general idea what it means to gain or lose five or 10 pounds. So for Everitt's data, we might simply report that the difference was significant ($t = 4.18$, $p = .001$) and that girls gained an average of 7.26 pounds. For girls who started out weighing, on average, 83 pounds, that is a substantial gain. In fact, it might make sense to convert pounds gained to a percentage, and say that the girls increased their weight by 7.26/83.23 = 9%. In this particular case, that may be the best approach.

An alternative measure would be to report the gain in standard deviation units. (Such a measure is often called a "standardized mean" or a "standardized mean difference.") As I said in the previous chapter, this idea goes back to Cohen,[3] who originally formulated the problem in terms of a parameter (d), where

$$d = \frac{\mu_1 - \mu_2}{\sigma}$$

In this equation, for the general case, the numerator is the difference between two population means, and the denominator is the standard deviation of either population. We can modify that slightly to let the numerator be the mean gain ($\mu_{\text{After}} - \mu_{\text{Before}}$), and the denominator is the population standard deviation of the pretreatment weights. To put this in terms of statistics, rather than parameters, we can substitute sample means and standard deviations instead of population values. This leaves us with

$$\hat{d} = \frac{\overline{X}_1 - \overline{X}_2}{s_{X_1}} = \frac{90.49 - 83.23}{5.02} = \frac{7.26}{5.02} = 1.45$$

I have put a "hat" over the d to indicate that we are calculating an estimate of d, and I have put the standard deviation of the pretreatment scores in the denominator. Our estimate tells us that, on average, the girls involved in family therapy gained nearly one and a half standard deviations of pretreatment weights over the course of therapy. The standard deviation of the pretest scores is meaningful because it is in the units of our original measurements. (Often the standard deviation of the *difference scores* is not very useful because it doesn't carry much meaning.) We can imagine the distribution of pretest scores (which had a mean at 83.23) and then mentally mark off 1.45 standard deviations above the mean. That is where the mean ended up for the posttest scores, and that is quite a difference. This situation is shown in the Figure 13.2. While simply reporting the gain in pounds may be appropriate for this example, for most examples the raw score units don't carry much meaning and expressing the difference in standard deviation units, which is what d does, is a much better approach.

In this particular example it might be easier to deal with the mean weight gain, rather than d, simply because people know something meaningful about weight. However, if this experiment had measured the girls' self-esteem, rather than weight, I would not know what to think if you said that they gained 7.26 self-esteem points. That scale means nothing to me. I would be impressed, however, if you said that they gained nearly one and a half standard deviations in self-esteem.

The preceding paragraph will probably leave you somewhat unsatisfied, because it is far more comfortable to be taught a simple rule that says "use this statistic is this situation." On the other hand, the argument put forth here is to "use whatever statistic your readers will find more meaningful." That degree of flexibility has its own kind

---

[3]To be fair, a number of people have worked on this problem, and they deserve credit. The most important were Hedges and Glass, and we often use their measure but give the credit to Cohen. With apologies to them, I will continue to refer to Cohen.

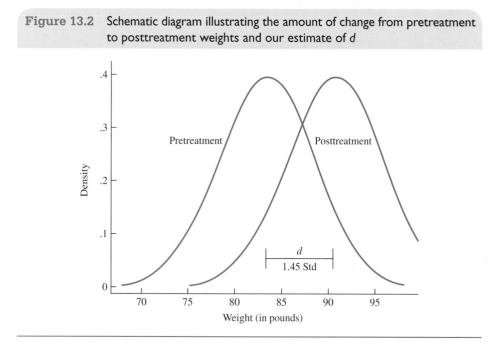

Figure 13.2 Schematic diagram illustrating the amount of change from pretreatment to posttreatment weights and our estimate of *d*

of comfort. As a general rule of thumb, if you have one set of scores that are not a set of differences, the standard deviation of those scores is an appropriate denominator. If, however, your set of scores are gain or difference scores, the standard deviation of the pretreatment data is likely to be a more meaningful denominator. But suppose that column 1 contains scores of women, and Column 2 contains scores of their husbands. Neither the standard deviation of wives nor of husbands would be an obvious choice for the denominator. In that case I would average the two variances, take the square root of that, and use that value in the denominator.

13.6 Confidence Limits on Change

Now I am probably going to confuse the situation even more by discussing the use of confidence limits when we have two related samples. As you should recall, a confidence interval for a single mean is generically written as

$$CI_{.95} = \overline{X} \pm t_{.05}(s_{\overline{X}}) = \overline{X} \pm t_{.05}(s/\sqrt{N})$$

The questions that arise concern the mean and the standard deviation that we insert in that equation to handle related samples. The general answer is that the mean is the difference between the two related means (often the difference between a pretest mean and a posttest mean). The standard deviation is the standard deviation of the *difference scores.* You are probably going to point out that this isn't what I used in estimating *d*, but I am not estimating *d* here, I am deriving a confidence interval, and that is quite a different thing. In the former case I was trying to give you an indication of how far the girls in this study had come in putting on weight. With confidence limits I am trying to establish an interval with a high probability of bracketing the true average weight gain.

For our anorexia example the mean weight gain was 7.26 pounds. The standard deviation of that set of gain scores was 7.16. Thus the confidence limits on mean gain in the population would be

$$CI_{.95} = \overline{X} \pm t_{.05}(s/\sqrt{N}) = 7.26 \pm 2.11(7.16/\sqrt{17}) = 7.26 \pm 3.66$$
$$3.6 \le \mu \le 10.92$$

The probability is .95 that an interval computed in this way includes the population mean gain. That result does not include zero, so is in line with the statistically significant *t* test we computed earlier.

13.7   Using SPSS and *R* for *t* Tests on Related Samples

Figure 13.3 is the printout of an SPSS computation of a *t* test on two related samples. The data in this example are those we have already seen on weight gain under family therapy. The data collected in the Before and After conditions are entered as two separate variables, and a paired *t* test is requested. The first part of the printout gives basic descriptive statistics. This is followed by the correlation between the two variables, and a *t* test on the significance of the correlation. Following this is a related-samples *t* test on the differences between the means. Notice that the *t* value (−4.185) agrees with the result computed by hand, except that SPSS subtracted After from Before and came up with a negative difference, and thus a negative *t*.

Figure 13.3   SPSS analysis of *t* test on related samples (the data were entered in two columns as pairs of scores)

Paired Samples Statistics

		Mean	N	Std. Deviation	Std. Error Mean
Pair 1	Before	83.2294	17	5.01669	1.21673
	After	90.4941	17	8.47507	2.05551

Paired Samples Correlations

		N	Correlation	Sig.
Pair 1	Before & After	17	.538	.026

Paired Samples Test

	Paired Differences							
				95% Confidence Interval of the Difference				
	Mean	Std. Deviation	Std. Error Mean	Lower	Upper	t	df	Sig. (2-tailed)
Pair 1 Before– After	−7.2647	7.15742	1.73593	−10.9447	−3.5847	−4.185	16	.001

The sign here is irrelevant, and depends merely on how you choose to calculate the difference scores.

As I showed earlier, the t test in R for paired differences could written as either

```
t.test(Before, After, paired = TRUE)
or
Gain <- After - Before
t.test(Gain)
```

13.8 Writing Up the Results

To write up the results of Everitt's study of family therapy for anorexia, we need to describe briefly the procedure to give a context. We should then mention the means before and after therapy and the resulting t test. We also need to include some measure of effect size (perhaps more than one) and draw some conclusions.

Everitt (in Hand, 1994) reported on a study of the effects of family therapy as a treatment for 17 anorexic girls. Girls were weighed before and after several weeks' involvement in family therapy. The mean pretreatment weight was 83.23 pounds and the mean posttreatment weight was 90.49 pounds, for a mean gain of 7.26 pounds. This difference was statistically significant ($t(16) = 4.18$, $p < .05$, or $p = .001$). Other data in this study suggest that the gain cannot simply be attributed to normal growth over time. The effect size estimate ($\hat{d}$) based on the pretreatment standard deviation was 1.45, indicating a gain of nearly one and a half standard deviations from pretreatment weight. In addition, the 95% confidence interval for weight gain was $3.6 \leq \mu \leq 10.92$, indicating that family therapy has the potential of leading to a noticeable change in weight.

13.9 Summary

This chapter was very much like the previous chapter in that we end up comparing the mean of a single column of data against a population mean (usually $\mu = 0$). Although we do start out with two sets of data, such as Guess1 and Guess2 in the Vul and Pashler example, the fact that the data are correlated because they come from the same set of individuals means that we need to take that correlation into account. The simplest way to do that is to create a column of difference scores and test if those scores are likely to have come from a population whose mean is zero.

We looked at two different examples using paired scores, both of which lead to significant results. Then we turned to the advantages of repeated measures. These include the fact that variability between one participant and another plays no role in the analysis. This means that we can have wide individual differences in performance and yet those differences do not influence our results. Another advantage is that using paired scores largely controls extraneous variables. The fact that the same person serves under both conditions means that the person brings largely the same thing to both measurements. Lastly, I noted that, all other things being equal, a repeated measures design is more powerful than a design with independent groups. The major problem with repeated measurements is that there may be carry-over effects from one trial to another or the presence of a first trial may influence how the person responds on a second trial.

We looked at several different measures of the size of an effect. In some cases simply reporting the difference in means is sufficient for your purposes. Often, however, especially when the variables do not have a lot of intuitive meaning, we need to fall back on a measure proposed by Cohen and modified slightly by others. In this case, we simply take the difference we are looking at and divide by the size of the standard deviation so as to give an answer in standard deviation units. I pointed out that most of the time when we do this we want to use the standard deviation of the first measure, and not the standard deviation of the differences.

Finally, we looked at confidence limits. These are simply an extension of what we have seen earlier. To calculate them we take the obtained mean and add and subtract from that the standard error of the mean difference times the critical value of t for the associated degrees of freedom. The purpose of confidence limits is to give us an indication of the possible range of values for the parameter in question.

Key Terms

Related samples, 334	Difference scores (gain scores), 337
Repeated measures, 335	Order effect, 342
Matched samples, 335	Carry-over effect, 342
Control group, 336	

13.10 A Quick Review

A. To what does the symbol μ_0 refer?
   Ans: The population mean under the null hypothesis.

B. What do we mean by "matched samples"?
   Ans: The observations come in pairs, such that the two items in the first row of data come from the same person or are related in some other way.

C. The major advantage of matched samples is that _____.
   Ans: they allow us to remove extraneous variance before calculating t

D. What is the usual null hypothesis with matched samples?
   Ans: The null hypothesis is that the population mean difference from one measurement to another, on the same person, is 0.

E. Give two advantages of a matched-samples study over a study with independent groups.
   Ans: Matched samples control for individual differences; they reduce the influence of extraneous variables.

F. What does a value of $\hat{d} = .95$ tell you?
   Ans: There was a difference of .95 standard deviation units between the two means.

G. In question "F," what would we use in the denominator to calculate $\hat{d}$?
   Ans: The standard deviation of a reference set of scores—very often the standard deviation of pretest scores.

H.   What is the difference in the standard deviation used to calculate $\hat{d}$ and the standard deviation used to calculate a confidence interval?
Ans: In the former we use the standard deviation of the pretest means, while in the latter we use the standard deviation of difference scores.

I.   What is a carry-over effect?
Ans: This refers to a situation in which something about the first measurement influences the second. For example, learning one task may interfere with the learning of a second task.

13.11 Exercises

13.1   Hout, Duncan, and Sobel (1987) reported on the relative sexual satisfaction of married couples. They asked each member of 91 married couples to rate the degree to which they agreed with "Sex is fun for me and my partner" on a four-point scale ranging from "never or occasionally" to "almost always." The data appear below (I know it's a lot of data, but it's an interesting question, and the data can always be downloaded from the book's website.):

Husband	1	1	1	1	1	1	1	1	1	1	1	1	1	1	1	
Wife	1	1	1	1	1	1	1	2	2	2	2	2	2	2	3	
Husband	1	1	1	1	2	2	2	2	2	2	2	2	2	2	2	
Wife	3	4	4	4	1	1	2	2	2	2	2	2	2	2	3	
Husband	2	2	2	2	2	2	2	2	2	3	3	3	3	3	3	
Wife	3	3	4	4	4	4	4	4	4	1	2	2	2	2	2	
Husband	3	3	3	3	3	3	3	3	3	3	3	3	3	4	4	
Wife	3	3	3	3	4	4	4	4	4	4	4	4	4	1	1	
Husband	4	4	4	4	4	4	4	4	4	4	4	4	4	4	4	
Wife	2	2	2	2	2	2	2	2	3	3	3	3	3	3	3	
Husband	4	4	4	4	4	4	4	4	4	4	4	4	4	4	4	4
Wife	3	3	4	4	4	4	4	4	4	4	4	4	4	4	4	4

Start out by running a matched-sample t test on these data. Why is a matched-sample test appropriate?

13.2   In the study referred to in Exercise 13.1, what, if anything, does your answer to that question tell us about whether couples are sexually compatible? What do we know from this analysis, and what don't we know?

13.3   For the data in Exercise 13.1, create a scatterplot and calculate the correlation between husband's and wife's sexual satisfaction. How does this amplify what we have learned from the analysis in Exercise 13.1? (For example, in R the commands would be **plot(wife ~ Husband)** and **cor(Wife, Husband.)**)

13.4   Use techniques developed in Chapter 12 and this chapter to construct 95% confidence limits on the true mean difference between the Sexual Satisfaction scores in Exercise 13.1.

13.5   Some would object that the data in Exercise 13.1 are clearly discrete, if not ordinal, as defined in Chapter 2, and that it is inappropriate to run a t test on them. Can you think what might be a counterargument? (This is not an easy question, and I really asked it mostly to make the point that there could be controversy here.)

13.6   Hoaglin, Mosteller, and Tukey (1983) present data on blood levels of beta-endorphin as a function of stress. They took beta-endorphin levels for 19 patients 12 hours before surgery and again 10 minutes before surgery. The data are presented on the next page, in fmol/ml:

Subject	12 Hours Before	10 Minutes Before
1	10.0	6.5
2	6.5	14.0
3	8.0	13.5
4	12.0	18.0
5	5.0	14.5
6	11.5	9.0
7	5.0	18.0
8	3.5	42.0
9	7.5	7.5
10	5.8	6.0
11	4.7	25.0
12	8.0	12.0
13	7.0	52.0
14	17.0	20.0
15	8.8	16.0
16	17.0	15.0
17	15.0	11.5
18	4.4	2.5
19	2.0	2.0

Based on these data, what effect does increased stress have on beta-endorphin levels?

13.7 Why would you use a paired t test in Exercise 13.6?

13.8 Create a scatterplot of the data in Exercise 13.6, and compute the correlation between the two sets of scores. What does this say that is relevant to the answer to Exercise 13.7?

13.9 We always need to look closely at our data. Sometimes we find things that are hard to explain. Look closely at the data in Exercise 13.6; what attracts your attention?

13.10 Compute a measure of effect size for the data in Exercise 13.6, and tell what this measure indicates.

13.11 Give an example of an experiment for which using related samples would be ill-advised because of carry-over effects.

13.12 Using the data in Table 13.2, ask whether people's first guess is usually better than their second guess. You can easily modify the code presented in the chapter to do this is R. (This parallels advice that you often receive about test taking to the effect that you should not go back and change a guessed answer unless you are sure that your new answer is correct. Vul and Pashler found a significant difference, but they had many more participants.)

13.13 Assume that the mean and the standard deviation of the difference scores in Exercise 13.6 would remain the same if we added more subjects. How many subjects would we need to obtain a t that is significant at $\alpha = .01$ (two-tailed)? (The difference was significant at $\alpha = .05$, but not at $\alpha = .01$.) (We will return to this general problem in Chapter 15.)

13.14 Modify the data in Exercise 13.6 by shifting the entries in the "12 hour" column so as to increase the relationship between the two variables. Run a t test on the modified data and notice the effect on t. (You could never do this with real data, because paired scores must be kept together, but doing so here reveals the important role played by the relationship between variables.)

13.15 Using your answer to Exercise 13.14 and your knowledge about correlation, how would you expect the degree of correlation between two variables (sets of data) to affect the magnitude of the t test between them?

13.16 In Section 13.4 I explained that by removing subject-to-subject variability from the data, related-samples designs prevent this variability from influencing the data on which the *t* test is run. This increases our ability to reject a false null hypothesis. Explain in your own words why this is so.

13.17 Whether or not you found a significant difference in Exercise 13.13, Vul and Pashler did. But are first guesses better than the average of the two?

13.18 If there were reason to believe that carry-over effects could influence the data on guessing behavior, how might we control such effects?

13.19 In the anorexia example in Section 13.2 I subtracted the After scores from the Before scores. What would have happened if I had done that the other way around?

13.20 What would happen if we took the data from the anorexia example in Table 13.1 and re-expressed the dependent variable in kilograms instead of pounds?

13.21 Many mothers experience a sense of depression shortly after the birth of a child, known as postpartum depression (PPD). Design a study to examine PPD and tell how you would estimate the mean increase in depression.

13.22 We have not discussed confidence limits on effect sizes, but Ken Kelly and Keke Lai, at Notre Dame, created an *R* library named MBESS to calculate such limits. Using the data in Table 13.1, compute confidence limits on the weight difference between Before and After scores. You can obtain that simply by looking at the result of **t.test(Before, After, paired = TRUE.)** Then calculate a confidence interval on the effect size (*d*). To do this you need to install, and then load, the MBESS library. Then you call for the function (ci.sm). The code is shown below.

```
data <- read.table("https://www.uvm.edu/~dhowell/fundamentals9/DataFiles/
Tab13-1.dat", header = TRUE)
attach(data)
library(MBESS)
t <- t.test(Before, After)
print(t)
cat("lower CI on mean = ", t$conf.int[1], "\nupper CI on mean = ", t$conf.int[2],"\n")
sm <- (mean(After) - mean(Before))/sd(Before)
cat("Standard mean difference (d) = ", sm,"\n")
ci.effectSize <- ci.sm(sm = 1.45, N = 17)
cat("Lower CI on effect size = ",
ci.effectSize$Lower.Conf.Limit.Standardized.Mean, "\n")
cat("Upper CI on effect size = ",
ci.effectSize$Upper.Conf.Limit.Standardized.Mean, "\n")
```

How would you interpret this result?

CHAPTER 14

Hypothesis Tests Applied to Means: Two Independent Samples

CONCEPTS THAT YOU WILL NEED TO REMEMBER FROM PREVIOUS CHAPTERS

Sampling distribution: The distribution of a statistic over repeated sampling

Standard error: The standard deviation of the sampling distribution of a statistic

t distribution: Sampling distribution of the t statistic when the null hypothesis is true. Often called the "central t distribution"

Degrees of freedom: An adjusted value of the sample size, often $N - 1$ or $N - 2$

Effect size ($\hat{d}$): A measure intended to express the size of a treatment effect in terms that are meaningful to the reader

Confidence Interval: An interval with a fixed (often 95%) probability of including the true population parameter (such as mean difference)

In moving to the case where samples are independent, we will first look at why having independent samples makes a difference. We will see that we are going to need to be making some assumptions that we did not make before, and that these assumptions are important to the t test. The difference between the t test that we used in the last two chapters and the one that we will use here will be discussed next, and we will then look at how we create confidence limits and, more importantly, effect sizes now that we have independent samples. Finally, we will see how to use SPSS and R to perform our calculations.

In Chapter 13 we considered a study in which we obtained a set of weights from anorexic girls before and after a family therapy intervention. In that example the *same* participants were observed both before and after the intervention. While that was a good way to evaluate the effects of this intervention program, in a great many experiments it is either impossible or undesirable to obtain data using repeated measurements of the same participants. For example, if we want to determine if

351

males are more socially inept than females, it clearly would be impossible to test the same people as males and then as females. Instead we would need a sample of males and a second, *independent*, sample of females.

Probably the most common use of the *t* test is to test the difference between the means of two independent groups. We might want to compare the mean number of trials needed to reach criterion in a simple visual discrimination task for two groups of rats—one raised under normal conditions and one raised under conditions of sensory deprivation. Or in a memory study we might want to compare levels of retention for a group of college students asked to recall active declarative sentences and a group asked to recall passive negative sentences. As a final example, we might place participants in a situation in which another person needed help. We could compare the mean latency of helping behavior when participants were tested alone and when they were tested in groups.

In conducting any experiment with two independent groups, we will almost always find that the two sample means differ by at least a small amount. The important question, however, is whether that difference is sufficiently large to justify the conclusion that the two samples were drawn from different populations—for example, using the case of helping behavior, is the mean of the population of latencies from singly tested participants different from the mean of the population of latencies from group-tested participants? Before we consider a specific example, we will need to examine the sampling distribution of differences between means and the *t* test that results from that sampling distribution. What we are doing here is analogous to what we did in Chapter 12 when speaking of the mean of one sample.

14.1 Distribution of Differences between Means

When we are interested in testing for a difference between the mean of one population (μ_1) and the mean of a second population (μ_2), we will be testing a null hypothesis of the form $H_0: \mu_1 - \mu_2 = 0$ or, equivalently, $\mu_1 = \mu_2$. Because the test of this null hypothesis involves the difference between independent sample means, it is important to digress for a moment and examine the **sampling distribution of differences between means**.

Suppose we have two populations labeled X_1 and X_2 with means μ_1 and μ_2 and variances σ_1^2 and σ_2^2. We now draw samples of size n_1 from population X_1 and of size n_2 from population X_2 and record the means and the differences between the means for each pair of samples. (I have gone from denoting sample sizes with capital Ns to lowercase ns because, when I have multiple samples, I will use N to refer to *the total number of scores in all samples* and n with a subscript to refer to the *number of observations in a particular group or sample*.) Because we are sampling independently from each population, the sample means will be independent. (Means are paired only in the trivial and irrelevant sense of being drawn at the same time.) Because we are only supposing, we might as well go all the way and suppose that we repeated this procedure an infinite number of times. The results are presented schematically in Figure 14.1. In the lower portion of this figure the first two columns represent the sampling distributions of $\overline{X}_1$ and $\overline{X}_2$, and the third column represents the sampling distribution of differences in means ($\overline{X}_1 - \overline{X}_2$). It is this third column in which we are most interested, because we are concerned with

Figure 14.1 Hypothetical set of means and differences between means when sampling from two populations

$$\sigma^2_{\overline{X}_1-\overline{X}_2} = \sigma^2_{\overline{X}_1} + \sigma^2_{\overline{X}_2} = \frac{\sigma^2_1}{n_1} + \frac{\sigma^2_2}{n_2}$$

	X_1	X_2	
	$\overline{X}_{11}$	$\overline{X}_{21}$	$\overline{X}_{11}-\overline{X}_{21}$
	$\overline{X}_{12}$	$\overline{X}_{22}$	$\overline{X}_{12}-\overline{X}_{22}$
	$\overline{X}_{13}$	$\overline{X}_{23}$	$\overline{X}_{13}-\overline{X}_{23}$
	...	...	...
	$\overline{X}_{1\infty}$	$\overline{X}_{2\infty}$	$\overline{X}_{1\infty}-\overline{X}_{2\infty}$
Mean	μ_1	μ_2	$\mu_1-\mu_2$
Variance	$\dfrac{\sigma^2_1}{n_1}$	$\dfrac{\sigma^2_2}{n_2}$	$\dfrac{\sigma^2_1}{n_1}+\dfrac{\sigma^2_2}{n_2}$
S.D.	$\dfrac{\sigma_1}{\sqrt{n_1}}$	$\dfrac{\sigma_2}{\sqrt{n_2}}$	$\sqrt{\dfrac{\sigma^2_1}{n_1}+\dfrac{\sigma^2_2}{n_2}}$

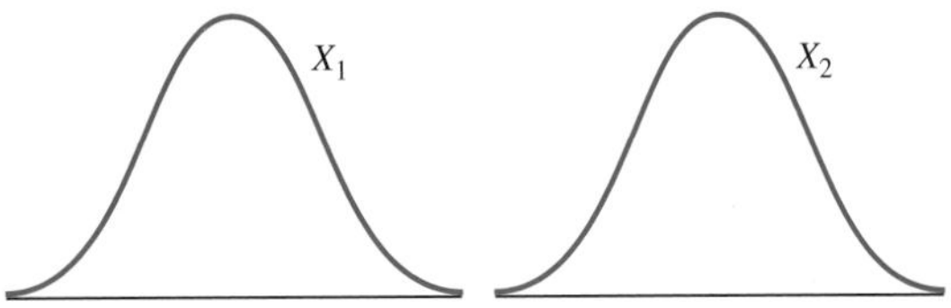

testing differences between means. The mean of this distribution can be shown to equal $\mu_1 - \mu_2$. The variance of this distribution is given by what is commonly called the **Variance Sum Law**, a limited form of which states

The variance of the sum or difference of two *independent* variables is equal to the sum of their variances.[1]

We know from the Central Limit Theorem that the variance of the distribution of $\overline{X}_1$ is σ^2_1/n_1 and the variance of the distribution of $\overline{X}_2$ is σ^2_2/n_2. Because the variables (sample means) are independent, the variance of the difference of these two variables is the sum of their variances. Thus

---

[1]The complete form of the law omits the restriction that the variables must be independent and states that the variance of their sum or difference is $\sigma^2_{X_1 \pm X_2} = \sigma^2_{X_1} + \sigma^2_{X_2} \pm 2\rho\sigma_{X_1}\sigma_{X_2}$ where ρ is the correlation coefficient in the population between X_1 and X_2. The minus signs apply when considering differences.

$$\sigma^2_{\overline{X}_1 \pm \overline{X}_2} = \sigma^2_{\overline{X}_1} + \sigma^2_{\overline{X}_2} = \frac{\sigma^2_1}{n_1} + \frac{\sigma^2_2}{n_2}$$

Having found the mean and the variance of a set of differences between means, we know most of what we need to know to test a hypothesis about such differences. The general form of the sampling distribution of mean differences is presented in Figure 14.2.

The final point to be made about this distribution concerns its shape. An important theorem in statistics states that the sum or difference of two independent normally distributed variables is itself normally distributed. Because Figure 14.2 represents the difference between two sampling distributions of means, and because we know the sampling distribution of means is at least approximately normal for reasonable sample sizes, then the distribution in Figure 14.2 must itself be at least approximately normal. (If you care to reproduce this figure just for fun, the R code can be found on the website. The labels are tricky, however, so you may want to take them as given.)

The *t* Statistic

Given the information we now have about the sampling distribution of differences between means, we can proceed to develop the appropriate test procedure. Assume *for the moment* that knowledge of the population variances (σ^2_1 and σ^2_2)

Figure 14.2 Sampling distribution of differences between means

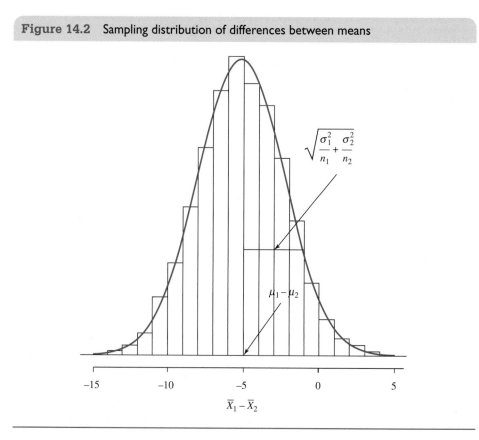

is not a problem. We have earlier defined z as *a* statistic (a point on the distribution) minus the mean of the distribution, divided by the standard error of the distribution. Our statistic in the present case is $(\overline{X}_1 - \overline{X}_2)$, the observed difference between the sample means. The mean of the sampling distribution is $(\mu_1 - \mu_2)$, and, as we saw, the **standard error of differences between means**, given the population variance (σ^2) is

$$\sigma_{\overline{X}_1 \pm \overline{X}_2} = \sqrt{\frac{\sigma_1^2}{n_1} + \frac{\sigma_2^2}{n_2}}$$

Remember, the standard error of any statistic (in this case the difference between two sample means) is the standard deviation of the sampling distribution of that statistic. As such it is a measure of how stable we expect that statistic to be.

Given what we know, we can write

$$z = \frac{(\overline{X}_1 - \overline{X}_2) - (\mu_1 - \mu_2)}{\sigma_{\overline{X}_1 - \overline{X}_2}}$$

$$= \frac{(\overline{X}_1 - \overline{X}_2) - (\mu_1 - \mu_2)}{\sqrt{\dfrac{\sigma_1^2}{n_1} + \dfrac{\sigma_2^2}{n_2}}}$$

The critical value for $\alpha = .05$ is $z = \pm 1.96$, as it was for the one-sample tests discussed in Chapter 12.

The preceding formula is not particularly useful except for the purpose of showing the origin of the appropriate t test, because we rarely know the necessary population variances. (Such knowledge is so rare that it isn't even worth imagining cases in which we would have it, although a few do exist.) However, just as we did in the one-sample case, we can circumvent this problem by using the sample variances as estimates of the population variances. For the same reasons discussed earlier for the one-sample t, this means that the result will be distributed as t rather than z.

$$t = \frac{(\overline{X}_1 - \overline{X}_2) - (\mu_1 - \mu_2)}{s_{\overline{X}_1 - \overline{X}_2}}$$

$$= \frac{(\overline{X}_1 - \overline{X}_2) - (\mu_1 - \mu_2)}{\sqrt{\dfrac{s_1^2}{n_1} + \dfrac{s_2^2}{n_2}}}$$

Because the null hypothesis is generally the hypothesis that $\mu_1 - \mu_2 = 0$, we usually drop that term from the equation and write

$$t = \frac{(\overline{X}_1 - \overline{X}_2)}{s_{\overline{X}_1 - \overline{X}_2}}$$

$$= \frac{(\overline{X}_1 - \overline{X}_2)}{\sqrt{\dfrac{s_1^2}{n_1} + \dfrac{s_2^2}{n_2}}}$$

Pooling Variances

We are almost there, but just a little more elaboration is needed. Although the equation for t that we just developed is quite appropriate when the sample sizes are equal, it can be improved with some modification for unequal sample sizes. This modification is designed to provide a better estimate of the population variance. One of the assumptions required for the use of t for two independent samples is that $\sigma_1^2 = \sigma_2^2$ (i.e., the samples come from populations with equal variances), regardless of the truth or falsity of H_0. Such an assumption is often a reasonable one and is called the assumption of **homogeneity of variance**. We often begin an experiment with two groups of participants who are equivalent and then do something to one (or both) group(s) that will raise or lower the participants' scores. (The example of Everitt's study to raise the weight of anorexic girls is a nice illustration.) In such a case it often makes sense to assume that the variances will remain unaffected. (You should recall that adding or subtracting a constant to a set of scores has no effect on its variance.) Because the population variances are assumed to be equal, this common variance can be represented by the symbol σ^2, without a subscript.

In our data we have two estimates of σ^2, namely s_1^2 and s_2^2. It seems appropriate to obtain some sort of an average of s_1^2 and s_2^2 on the grounds that this average should be a better estimate of σ^2 than either of the two separate estimates. We do not want to take the simple arithmetic mean, however, because doing so would give equal weight to the two estimates, even if one were based on considerably more observations. What we want is a **weighted average**, in which the sample variances are weighted by their degrees of freedom ($n_i - 1$). If we call this new estimate s_p^2 then

$$s_p^2 = \frac{(n_1 - 1)s_1^2 + (n_2 - 1)s_2^2}{n_1 + n_2 - 2}$$

The numerator represents the sum of the variances, each weighted by its degrees of freedom, and the denominator represents the sum of the weights or, equivalently, the degrees of freedom for s_p^2.

The weighted average of the two sample variances is usually referred to as a **pooled variance** estimate. Having defined our pooled estimate (s_p^2), we can now replace s_i^2 in the formula for t with s_p^2 to get

$$t = \frac{\overline{X}_1 - \overline{X}_2}{s_{\overline{X}_1 - \overline{X}_2}} = \frac{\overline{X}_1 - \overline{X}_2}{\sqrt{\dfrac{s_p^2}{n_1} + \dfrac{s_p^2}{n_2}}} = \frac{\overline{X}_1 - \overline{X}_2}{\sqrt{s_p^2 \left(\dfrac{1}{n_1} + \dfrac{1}{n_2} \right)}}$$

Notice that both this formula for t and the one we used in the previous section involve dividing the difference between the sample means by an estimate of the standard error of the difference between means. The only difference concerns the way in which this standard error is estimated. When sample sizes are equal, it makes absolutely no difference whether you pool variances; the resulting t will be the same. When the sample sizes are unequal, however, pooling can make an important difference.

Degrees of Freedom for t

You know that two sample variances (s_1^2 and s_2^2) have gone into calculating t. Each of these variances is based on squared deviations about their corresponding sample means; therefore, each sample variance has $n_i - 1$ df. Across the two samples, therefore, we will have $(n_1 - 1) + (n_2 - 1) = n_1 + n_2 - 2$ df. Thus the t for two independent samples will be based on $n_1 + n_2 - 2$ degrees of freedom.

Let's Stop to Review

We have just covered more formulae, with somewhat more emphasis on derivation, than you have seen previously in this book. It might be smart to stop and say something about what all of that is for. It isn't as cumbersome as it looks.

I started out by saying that if I want to know whether the means of two independent samples are significantly different, I need to know something about what differences between two means would look like. In other words, I need to know the sampling distribution of differences between means. Such a distribution would have a mean equal to the difference between the population means and would have a standard error equal to the square root of the sum of the population variances each divided by its corresponding sample size. Such a distribution would be at least approximately normal.

At this point I know the mean, the standard error, and the shape of the sampling distribution of differences between means. If I knew the population variances, I could now compute a z score as the difference in sample means, minus the difference in population means, divided by the standard error. This is the same kind of z score we have been seeing all along.

But we rarely know the population variances. So we do the same thing we did for earlier t tests—we substitute the sample variances for the population variances and call the result t. Just as we have done each time we substitute the sample variance for a population variance, we need to address the degrees of freedom. Because each sample variance is obtained by using the sample mean as an estimate of the corresponding population mean, we lose a degree of freedom, so our denominator will change from n to $n - 1$ *for each variance estimate.*

Finally, when you have two sample variances, you usually want to average them to get a better estimate of the population variance. We call this averaging "pooling." We use the pooled version whenever the sample variances are in general agreement with one another, especially when sample sizes are about equal.

You should stop at this point and go back through the last few pages to see how the review I just gave you fits with the formulae we've covered so far in this chapter.

Example: We Haven't Finished with Anorexia

To illustrate the use of *t* as a test of the difference between two independent means, let's undertake a different analysis of some of Everitt's data (Everitt in Hand et al., 1994) on the treatment of anorexia. In Chapter 13 I pointed out that the change in means doesn't necessarily imply that the difference is due to the family therapy intervention. Perhaps the girls just gained weight because they got older and taller. One way to control for this is to look at the amount of weight gained by the Family Therapy group in contrast with the amount gained by girls in a Control group, who received no therapy. If the only reason girls are gaining weight is because they are getting older and taller, that should affect both groups equally. If weight gain is due to therapy, only the therapy group would be expected to gain. Fortunately, Everitt provided us with data on the control group as well. The data are shown in Table 14.1, although I am presenting only the amount gained, not the amounts before and after treatment.

Table 14.1   Weight Gain in the Family Therapy and Control Groups

Control	Control	Family Therapy	Family Therapy
−0.5	3.3	11.4	9.0
−9.3	11.3	11.0	3.9
−5.4	0.0	5.5	5.7
12.3	−1.0	9.4	10.7
−2.0	−10.6	13.6	
−10.2	−4.6	−2.9	
−12.2	−6.7	−0.1	
11.6	2.8	7.4	
−7.1	0.3	21.5	
6.2	1.8	−5.3	
−0.2	3.7	−3.8	
−9.2	15.9	13.4	
8.3	−10.2	13.1	
Mean	−0.45		7.26
St. Dev.	7.99		7.16
Variance	63.82		51.23
n	26		17

Before we consider any statistical test—and ideally even before the data are collected—we must specify several features of the test. First, we must specify the null and alternative hypotheses. Using the subscripts "FT" and "C" for "family Therapy" and "Control" we have

$$H_0: \mu_{FT} = \mu_C$$

$$H_1: \mu_{FT} \neq \mu_C$$

The alternative hypothesis is bidirectional (we will reject H_0 if $\mu_{FT} < \mu_C$ or if $\mu_{FT} > \mu_C$; thus we are using a two-tailed test). For the sake of consistency with other examples in this book, we will let α, the probability of a Type I error equal .05. (It is important to keep in mind that there is nothing particularly sacred about these two decisions.[2]) Given the null hypothesis as stated, we can now calculate t:

$$t = \frac{\overline{X}_1 - \overline{X}_2}{s_{\overline{X}_1 - \overline{X}_2}} = \frac{\overline{X}_1 - \overline{X}_2}{\sqrt{\dfrac{s_1^2}{n_1} + \dfrac{s_2^2}{n_2}}}$$

Because we are testing $H_0: \mu_{FT} - \mu_C = 0$, the $\mu_{FT} - \mu_C$ term has been dropped from the equation. When we pool the variances, we obtain

$$s_p^2 = \frac{(n_1 - 1)s_1^2 + (n_2 - 1)s_2^2}{n_1 + n_2 - 2}$$

$$= \frac{25(63.82) + 16(51.23)}{26 + 17 - 2} = \frac{1595.50 + 819.68}{41} = \frac{2415.18}{41} = 58.907$$

Note that the pooled variance is somewhat closer in value to s_1^2 than s_2^2 because of the greater weight given s_1^2 in the formula due to the larger sample size. Then, substituting this common variance for the separate variances, we have

$$t = \frac{\overline{X}_1 - \overline{X}_2}{\sqrt{\dfrac{s_p^2}{n_1} + \dfrac{s_p^2}{n_2}}} = \frac{\overline{X}_1 - \overline{X}_2}{\sqrt{s_p^2\left(\dfrac{1}{n_1} + \dfrac{1}{n_2}\right)}} = \frac{-0.45 - 7.26}{\sqrt{58.907\left(\dfrac{1}{26} + \dfrac{1}{17}\right)}}$$

$$= \frac{-7.71}{\sqrt{5.731}} = \frac{-7.71}{2.394} = -3.22$$

For this example we have $(n_1 - 1) = 25$ df for Group C and $(n_2 - 1) = 16$ df for Group FT, making a total of $(n_1 - 1) + (n_2 - 1) = 41$ df. From the sampling distribution of t in Table E.6 in the Appendices, the critical value of $t_{.05}(41)$ is ± 2.021 (approximately). (The probability of t greater than ± 3.22 is .002.) Because the obtained value of t (i.e., t_{obt}) far exceeds t_a, we will reject H_0 (at $\alpha = .05$, two-tailed) and conclude that there is a difference between the means of the populations from which our observations were drawn. In other words, we will conclude (statistically) that $\mu_{FT} \neq \mu_C$ and (practically) that $\mu_{FT} > \mu_C$. In terms of the experimental variables, anorexic

---

[2]If we had a good reason for testing the hypothesis that μ_{FT} was five points higher than μ_C, for example, we could set $H_0: \mu_{FT} - \mu_C = 5$, although this type of situation is extremely rare. Similarly, we could set α at .01, .001, or even .10, although this last value is higher than most people would accept.

girls provided with family therapy gain significantly more than a control group provided with no therapy.[3]

If we ran this analysis using R, the results would be as follows. The code for this analysis can be found on the chapter's Web page. In this case I instructed R to pool the variances. For that reason the two analyses agree completely. The critical line of code simply reads

```
result1 <- t.test(Gain ~ Trtment, var.equal = TRUE)
```

Notice that the printout also gives the 95% confidence interval on the difference. Both of those limits are on the same side of 0.00, which is in confirmation of the significant t probability.

Two Sample t-test
data: Gain by Trtment
t = −3.2227, df = 41, p-value = 0.002491
alternative hypothesis: true difference in means is not equal to 0
95 percent confidence interval:
 −12.549248 −2.880164
sample estimates:
mean in group 1 mean in group 2
 −0.450000   7.264706

14.2 Heterogeneity of Variance

As we have seen, one of the assumptions behind the t test for two independent samples is the assumption of homogeneity of variance ($\sigma_1^2 = \sigma_2^2$). When this assumption does not hold (i.e., when $\sigma_1^2 \neq \sigma_2^2$), we have what is called **heterogeneity of variance**. Considerable work has been done examining the practical effect of heterogeneity of variance on the t test. As a result of this work we can come to some general conclusions about the kind of analysis that is appropriate with heterogeneous variances.

The first point to keep in mind is that our homogeneity assumption refers to population variances and not to sample variances—only rarely would we expect the sample variances to be exactly equal even if the population variances were equal. On the basis of sampling studies that have been conducted, the general rule of thumb is that if one sample variance is no more than four[4] times the other *and* if the sample sizes are equal or approximately equal, you may go ahead and compute and interpret t as you would

---

[3]Because the Family Therapy group presumably differed from the Control group only by the presence or absence of therapy, our conclusions can be made with respect to the effects of therapy. If the groups had also differed on some Because the Family Therapy group presumably differed from the Control Group only by the presence or absence of therapy, our only other dimension, e.g., the prior weight of the participants, then the results would be unclear, and therapy would be **confounded** with prior weight.

[4]The use of the number four here is probably conservative. Some people would argue for using the standard approach when variances are considerably more different than this as long as the sample sizes are roughly equal.

normally. Heterogeneity of variance is not likely to have a serious effect on your results under these conditions. On the other hand, if the variances are quite unequal and the sample sizes are also quite unequal, then an alternative procedure may be necessary.

When we have heterogeneity of variance, we do not pool the variances, but enter them into our formula separately. And in addition to not pooling the variance, we adjust the degrees of freedom to take account of the heterogeneity. The approach is commonly known as Welch's solution.

This procedure, however, is easy to apply. Simply compute t using the *separate* variance estimates (i.e., do not pool). Then adjust the degrees of freedom using the formula shown below. Finally, calculate the probability of the resulting t under the null hypothesis. The result of doing this is often reported by statistical software labeling it "Welch's two sample t test."

From the study by Everitt we have

$$\overline{X}_1 = -0.45 \quad \overline{X}_2 = 7.26$$
$$s_1^2 = 63.82 \quad s_2^2 = 51.23$$
$$n_1 = 26 \quad n_2 = 18$$

$$t = \frac{\overline{X}_1 - \overline{X}_2}{\sqrt{\dfrac{s_1^2}{n_1} + \dfrac{s_2^2}{n_2}}} = \frac{-0.45 - 7.26}{\sqrt{\dfrac{63.82}{26} + \dfrac{51.23}{17}}} = \frac{7.71}{2.338} = 3.297$$

Because the variances were very unequal (one was more than six times the other), we did not pool them. Next we need to calculate an adjusted df, designated as df''.

$$df'' = \frac{\left(\dfrac{s_1^2}{n_1} + \dfrac{s_2^2}{n_2}\right)^2}{\dfrac{\left(\dfrac{s_1^2}{n_1}\right)^2}{n_1 - 1} + \dfrac{\left(\dfrac{s_2^2}{n_2}\right)^2}{n_2 - 1}}$$

$$= \frac{\left(\dfrac{63.82}{26} + \dfrac{51.23}{17}\right)^2}{\dfrac{\left(\dfrac{63.82}{26}\right)^2}{25} + \dfrac{\left(\dfrac{51.23}{17}\right)^2}{16}}$$

$$= \frac{29.9003}{.2410 + .5676} = 36.978$$

That does look like a lot of work, but most software will do the work for you. For example, in R we can write

```
result1 <- t.test(GAIN ~ TRTMENT, var.equal = FALSE)
```

If you run that code you will see that the adjusted df" differs from ours by only .001, which is merely rounding error.

To run this analysis in SPSS you need, first, to have one column representing groups (usually coded 1 and 2) and a second column containing the dependent variable. Then select **Analyze/Compare Means/Independent Samples T Test**. Then assign the dependent variable as the Test Variable, the Group variable as the Grouping Variable, and define the coding (usually 1 and 2) of the Group variable. SPSS will produce both the normal solution and the Welch solution, the later indicated as "Equal variances not assumed."

(A more complete discussion of the problem of heterogeneity of variance can be found in Howell, 2012.)

What causes the variances to be heterogeneous?

What would we do if the variance in the Family Therapy group was very much larger than the variance in the Control group? (You should recall that it was not.) We *could* use an adjustment to the degrees of freedom and go our merry way. But we really should stop and ask "why?" What would cause the variance in that group to be so large? One very distinct possibility is that family therapy is particularly effective for some girls, but totally ineffective for others, whereas there would be no such effect in the control group. That would cause a substantial difference in the variances. Such a finding would be an important one and might lead us to shift our research interests. We might look more closely at family therapy and ask what about it is causing the differential effectiveness. In fact, that might be a much more important question than the one we started out asking. Heterogeneity of variance is not always just a nuisance. Sometimes it is telling us something important. Research is not just a study of means. Just as we should not focus entirely on statistical significance, but should also look at confidence limits and effect sizes, so too should we not forget about other ways in which groups might differ.

14.3 Nonnormality of Distributions

We saw earlier that another assumption required for the correct use of the *t* test is the assumption that the population(s) from which the data are sampled is (are) normally distributed—or at least that the sampling distribution of differences between means is normal. In general, as long as the distributions of sample data are roughly mound-shaped (high in the center and tapering off on either side), the test is likely to be valid. This is especially true for large samples (n_1 and n_2 greater than 30), because then the Central Limit Theorem almost guarantees near normality of the sampling distribution of differences between means.

14.4 A Second Example with Two Independent Samples

Adams, Wright, and Lohr (1996) were interested in some basic psychoanalytic theories that homophobia (an irrational fear of, or aversion to, homosexuality or homosexuals) may be unconsciously related to the anxiety of being or becoming homosexual[5]. They administered the Index of Homophobia to 64 heterosexual males and classed them as homophobic or nonhomophobic on the basis of their score. They then exposed homophobic and nonhomophobic heterosexual men to videotapes of sexually explicit erotic stimuli portraying heterosexual and homosexual behavior, and recorded their level of sexual arousal. Adams et al. reasoned that if homophobia was unconsciously related to anxiety about one's own sexuality, homophobic individuals would show greater arousal to the homosexual videos than would nonhomophobic individuals.

In this example we will examine only the data from the homosexual video. The data in Table 14.2 were created to have the same means and pooled variance as the data that Adams collected, so our conclusions will be the same as theirs.[6] The dependent variable is the degree of arousal at the end of the four-minute video, with larger values indicating greater arousal.

Before we consider any statistical test, and ideally even before the data are collected, we must specify several features of the test. First we must specify the null and alternative hypotheses:

$$H_0 : \mu_1 = \mu_2$$

$$H_1 : \mu_1 \neq \mu_2$$

The alternative hypothesis is bidirectional (we will reject H_0 if $\mu_1 < \mu_2$ or if $\mu_1 > \mu_2$), and thus we will use a two-tailed test, and we will choose to work at $\alpha = .05$. Given the null hypothesis as stated, we can now calculate t:

$$t = \frac{\overline{X}_1 - \overline{X}_2}{s_{\overline{X}_1 - \overline{X}_2}} = \frac{\overline{X}_1 - \overline{X}_2}{\sqrt{\dfrac{s_p^2}{n_1} + \dfrac{s_p^2}{n_2}}}$$

Table 14.2 Data from Adams et al. (1996) on Level of Sexual Arousal in Homophobic and Nonhomophobic Heterosexual Males

Homophobic						Nonhomophobic					
39.1	38.0	14.9	20.7	19.5	32.2	24.0	17.0	35.8	18.0	−1.7	11.1
11.0	20.7	26.4	35.7	26.4	28.8	10.1	16.1	−0.7	14.1	25.9	23.0
33.4	13.7	46.1	13.7	23.0	20.7	20.0	14.1	−1.7	19.0	20.0	30.9
19.5	11.4	24.1	17.2	38.0	10.3	30.9	22.0	6.2	27.9	14.1	33.8
35.7	41.5	18.4	36.8	54.1	11.4	26.9	5.2	13.1	19.0	−15.5	
8.7	23.0	14.3	5.3	6.3							
Mean	24.00					**Mean**	16.50				
Variance	148.87					**Variance**	139.16				
n	35					***n***	29				

---

[5]For a supporting view see Weinstein, Ryan, DeHaan et al. (2012), and for an alternative view of this issue, see Meier, Robinson, Gaither, & Heinert (2006).

[6]I actually added 12 points to each mean, largely to avoid many negative scores, but it doesn't change the results or the calculations in the slightest.

Because we are testing $H_0: \mu_1 - \mu_2 = 0$, the $\mu_1 - \mu_2$ term has been dropped from the equation. We should pool our sample variances because they are so similar that we do not have to worry about homogeneity of variance. Doing so we obtain

$$s_p^2 = \frac{(n_1 - 1)s_1^2 + (n_2 - 1)s_2^2}{n_1 + n_2 - 2}$$

$$= \frac{34(148.87) + 28(139.16)}{35 + 29 - 2} = 144.48$$

Notice that the pooled variance is slightly closer in value to s_1^2 than to s_2^2 because of the greater weight given s_1^2 due to its larger sample size. Then

$$t = \frac{\overline{X}_1 - \overline{X}_2}{\sqrt{\dfrac{s_p^2}{n_1} + \dfrac{s_p^2}{n_2}}} = \frac{24.00 - 16.50}{\sqrt{\dfrac{144.48}{35} + \dfrac{144.48}{29}}} = \frac{7.50}{\sqrt{9.11}} = 2.48$$

For this example we have $n_1 - 1 = 34$ df for the homophobic group and $n_2 - 1 = 28$ df for the nonhomophobic group, making a total of $n_1 - 1 + n_2 - 1 = 62$ df. From the sampling distribution of t in Appendix E.6, $t_{.025}(62) = \pm 2.003$ (with linear interpolation). Since the obtained value of t far exceeds t_α, we will reject H_0 (at $\alpha = .05$) and conclude that there is a difference between the means of the populations from which our observations were drawn. In other words, we will conclude (statistically) that $\mu_1 \neq \mu_2$ and (practically) that $\mu_1 > \mu_2$. In terms of the experimental variables, homophobic participants show greater arousal to a homosexual video than do nonhomophobic participants.[7] (The exact probability can be found at http://www.danielsoper.com/statcalc3/calc.aspx?id=8 or at http://statpages.org/pdfs.html as $p = .0159$. A screen-shot of the latter printout is shown in Figure 14.3 below.)

Figure 14.3   Probability calculator at http://www.statpages.org/pdfs.html

Student t

t	d.f.	p
2.48	62	0.0159
Calc t		Calc p

Note: p is the area in the two tails of the distribution

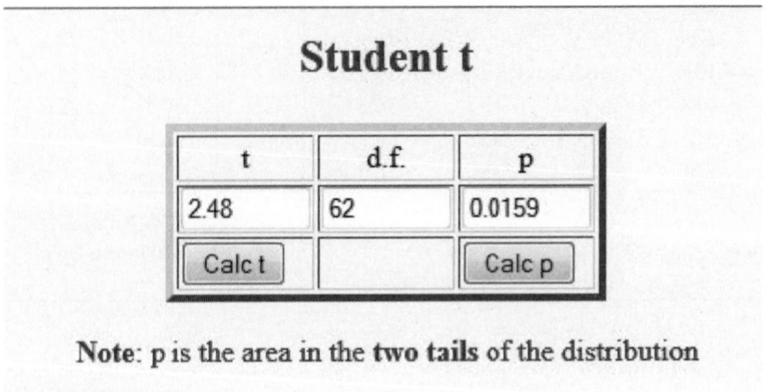

Source: John C. Pezzullo

---

[7]This is not an isolated result. Other experimenters have obtained similar results. A very interesting example on a closely related subject is a study by Willer, Rogalin, Conlon, & Wojnowicz (2013)

SPSS and *R*

Both SPSS and *R* give very similar results. The SPSS printout is shown below, followed by the printout from *R*.

SPSS

T-Test

[DataSet1] C:\Users\Dave\Dropbox\Webs\fundamentals9\DataFiles\Tab14-2.sav

Group Statistics

	Homophobic	N	Mean	Std. Deviation	Std. Error Mean
Arousal	y	35	24.000	12.2013	2.0624
	n	29	16.503	11.7966	2.1906

Independent Samples Test

		Levene's Test for Equality of Variances		t-test for Equality of Means						
									95% Confidence Interval of the Difference	
		F	Sig.	t	df	Sig. (2-tailed)	Mean Difference	Std. Error Difference	Lower	Upper
Arousal	Equal variances assumed	.391	.534	2.484	62	.016	7.4966	3.0183	1.4630	13.5301
	Equal variances not assumed			2.492	60.495	.015	7.4966	3.0087	1.4794	13.5138

R

```
# Adams et al. data on homophobia
data <- read.table("http://www.uvm.edu/~dhowell/
fundamentals9/DataFiles/Tab14-2.dat", header = TRUE)names(data)
attach(data)
t.test(Arousal ~ Homophobic, var.equal = TRUE)

      Two Sample t-test

data:  Arousal by Homophobic
t = -2.4837, df = 62, p-value = 0.01572
alternative hypothesis: true difference in means is not equal to 0
95 percent confidence interval:
-13.53012  -1.46298
sample estimates:
mean in group n mean in group y
   16.50345     24.00000
```

14.5 **Effect Size Again**

Again we come to the issue of presenting information to our readers that conveys the magnitude of the difference between our groups in addition to the statement, which we can already make, that the difference is statistically significant. The example from Adams et al. is a good one for this purpose, because it is a situation in which the actual value of the difference between means is not useful. None of us has any idea whether a difference of 7.5 points in sexual arousal is a large difference or a small one. We need a better measure.

In Chapters 12 and 13 we have used a statistic ($\hat{d}$) that represents the size of the difference between means (in raw score units) scaled by the size of the standard deviation. In this case, however, our standard deviation will be the estimated standard deviation of either population. When we had one set of observations we used the standard deviation of those observations. When we had difference scores, we generally used the standard deviation of the pretest scores. Here we have two standard deviations to choose from (one for each group) and we have two choices: 1) If there is a situation where one standard deviation seems to be the obvious one to use, use it. For example, if we have a true control group, its standard deviation seems like a logical choice. 2) If we don't have an obvious control group, we will pool the variances of the two groups we have and take the square root of that (i.e., s_p). (If we had noticeably different variances, we would most likely use the standard deviation of one sample and note to the reader that this is what we have done.)

For our data on homophobia, the pooled variance was 144.48, so we simply need to take its square root. Now we have

$$\hat{d} = \frac{\overline{X}_1 - \overline{X}_2}{s_p} = \frac{24.00 - 16.50}{\sqrt{144.48}} = \frac{24.00 - 16.50}{12.02} = 0.62$$

This result expresses the difference between the two groups in standard deviation units and tells us that the mean arousal for homophobic participants was nearly 2/3 of a standard deviation higher than the arousal of nonhomophobic participants. That strikes me as a big difference.

A word of caution: In the example of homophobia, the units of measurement were largely arbitrary, and a 7.5 difference had no intrinsic meaning to us. Thus it made more sense to express it in terms of standard deviations because we have at least some understanding of what that means. However, there are many cases wherein the original units are meaningful, for example, weight gain, and in that case it may not make much sense to standardize the measure (i.e., report it in standard deviation units). We might prefer to specify the difference between means, or the ratio of means, or some similar statistic. The earlier example of the moon illusion is a case in point. There it is very meaningful to speak of the horizon moon appearing approximately half-again as large as the zenith moon, and I see no advantage, and some obfuscation, in converting to standardized units. The important goal is to give the reader an appreciation of the size of a difference, and you should choose that measure that best expresses this difference. In one case a standardized measure such as $\hat{d}$ is best, and in other cases other measures, such as the distance between the means, is better. There is nothing to prevent you from using both.

14.6 Confidence Limits on $\mu_1 - \mu_2$

In addition to testing a null hypothesis about population means (i.e., testing H_0: $\mu_1 - \mu_2 = 0$) and stating an effect size, we should examine confidence limits on the difference between μ_1 and μ_2. The logic for setting these confidence limits is exactly the same as it was for the one-sample case in Chapter 12. The calculations are also exactly the same except that we use the *difference* between the means and the standard error of *differences* between means in place of the mean and the standard error of the mean. Thus for the 95% confidence limits on $\mu_1 - \mu_2$ we have

$$\boxed{CI_{.95} = (\overline{X}_1 - \overline{X}_2) \pm t_{.05}s_{\overline{X}_1 - \overline{X}_2}}$$

For the homophobia study we have

$$CI_{.95} = (\overline{X}_1 - \overline{X}_2) \pm t_{.05}s_{\overline{X}_1 - \overline{X}_2} = (24.00 - 16.5) \pm 2.00\sqrt{\frac{144.48}{35} + \frac{144.48}{29}}$$

$$= 7.50 \pm 2.00(3.018) = 7.5 \pm 6.04$$

$$1.46 \le (\mu_1 - \mu_2) \le 13.54$$

(R and SPSS produce the same result except that R's answers are negative because they subtracted the mean of the homophobic group from the mean of the nonhomophobic group, whereas we and SPSS did the reverse.) The probability is .95 that an interval computed as we computed this interval (1.46, 13.54) encloses the difference in arousal to homosexual videos between homophobic and nonhomophobic participants. Although the interval is wide, it does not include 0. This is consistent with our rejection of the null hypothesis, and it allows us to state that homophobic individuals are, in fact, more sexually aroused by homosexual videos than are nonhomophobic individuals. On the other hand, such a large interval should alert us to the fact that although we have a statistically significant effect, and although there is a fairly large effect size (0.62), there is considerable doubt as to the size of the difference between means.

14.7 Confidence Limits on Effect Size

Not only is it important to obtain the confidence intervals on the difference in means and a measure of effect size, but we also want to know about confidence intervals on that effect size.

Our statistic for the effect size is $\hat{d}$, where the carat simply indicates that this is an estimate. The corresponding effect size in the population would be represented by the Greek letter delta (δ).

The corresponding confidence interval is awkward to calculate, but there is software available to do so. One very nice program is by Cumming and Finch (2001), and I present a discussion of its use in a supplementary document found at https://www.uvm.edu/~dhowell/methods8/Supplements/Confidence Intervals on Effect Size.pdf. But we can also calculate the confidence intervals quite easily using R and its "MBESS" library by Kelley and Lai. We have seen this package before.

The simplest approach is to take the calculated standardized effect size value (0.62) as the standardized mean difference (smd), and the two sample sizes (35 and 29). This gives us

```
library(MBESS)
ci.smd(smd = 0.62, n.1 = 35, n.2 = 29)
$Lower.Conf.Limit.smd
[1] -1.124518
$smd
[1] -0.6227427
$Upper.Conf.Limit.smd
[1] -0.1161817
```

If you replace smd = .62 with ncp = −2.48 (the obtained *t* value), you will have the same result except for rounding error. The nice thing about using ncp = *t* is that this will calculate the standardized mean difference along the way.

14.8 Plotting the Results

There are a number of ways to plot the results of the study of homophobia to make them easier to understand. Perhaps the most common is a standard bar graph. In a bar graph the height of the bar above the X axis represents the sample mean, and there is one bar for each group. In many published research articles you will also see what are called "**error bars**." The problem with error bars is that it is not always easy to tell what the bar represents. In Figure 14.4 the error bars, which look something like I beams, represent one standard error above and below the mean. In other words, they are $\overline{X} \pm s/\sqrt{n}$. However, some authors would draw them to two standard errors either side of the means, and others would use them to represent either confidence limits or standard deviations. You have to look carefully to see what the author has done, and surprisingly often that is not stated.

From the data given above, the pooled variance was 144.48, for a pooled standard deviation of $\sqrt{144.48} = 12.02$. With 35 participants in the Homophobic group and 29 in the Nonhomophobic group, the standard errors would be

$$se_H = \frac{s_H}{\sqrt{n_H}} = \frac{12.02}{\sqrt{35}} = 2.03$$

and

$$se_{NH} = \frac{s_{NH}}{\sqrt{n_{NH}}} = \frac{12.02}{\sqrt{29}} = 2.23$$

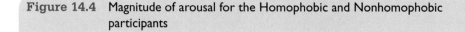

Figure 14.4 Magnitude of arousal for the Homophobic and Nonhomophobic participants

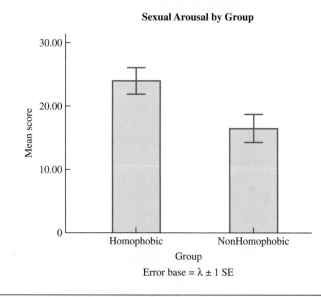

respectively. Then the ends of error bars will be $24.00 \pm 2.03 = 21.97$ and 24.03 for the Homophobic group and $16.50 \pm 2.23 = 14.27$ and 18.73 for the Nonhomophobic group. Notice that for this study the error bars are quite short. This tells us that if we were to repeat this study many times, the means for the Homophobic group would be likely to fall between approximately 22 and 24 about two-thirds of the time. Only very rarely would we expect to see a mean of the Homophobic group down in the area of the Nonhomophobic mean. This certainly looks like a robust effect.

14.9   Writing Up the Results

As we did in the previous chapter, we first need to outline what the reader needs to know. That means we have to describe the study in very brief terms, both its purpose and its procedures; report the means and standard deviations either in the text or as a table; report t, with its df and probability level, and our conclusion; and give some statement of the size of an effect. We then need a concluding sentence. A very brief version would look like:

> Adams, Wright, and Lohr (1996) investigated the relationship between homophobia and sexual arousal in homophobic and nonhomophobic participants. They theorized that homophobia might be related directly to anxiety about one's sexuality and that homophobic males would be more aroused by a homosexual video than nonhomophobic males.
>
> The authors tested 64 participants, 35 of whom scored high on a scale of homophobia and 29 of whom were not classed as homophobic. Each participant watched a sexually explicit video of homosexual behavior, and the participant's level of sexual arousal was assessed. Results showed that mean sexual arousal for the homophobic participants was 24.00 (SD = 12.20) while for the nonhomophobic group the mean level of arousal was 16.50 (SD = 11.80). A t test on the difference between means was statistically significant ($t(62) = 2.48$, $p = .016$). The 7.50 unit difference between conditions translates to $\hat{d} = 0.62$, indicating that the group means differed by nearly 2/3 of a standard deviation. The authors concluded that there was significant support for their theory that homophobia may result from a fear of one's own sexuality.

14.10   Do Lucky Charms Work?

Damisch, Stoberock, and Mussweiler (2010) conducted an interesting series of four studies examining whether superstition can actually improve behavior. All four studies gave consistent results, not only about the presence of an effect, but about possible reasons for that effect. We will focus on their study number three.

Damisch and her co-authors asked 41 university students to bring a lucky charm to an experiment. A random half of these students were asked to perform a memory task in the presence of their lucky charm. The other students left their lucky charm in another room while they performed the task in the absence of their lucky charm. The dependent variable was a combined measure of the time and the number of trials needed to complete the memory task satisfactorily. In this case a low score represents better performance. The data shown below in Table 14.3 have the same means and variances as the data Damisch et al. collected.

Table 14.3 Data from Damisch et al. (2010)

Lucky Charm Present					Lucky Charm Absent				
0.15	−1.07	−0.81	0.42	−1.06	0.47	1.48	−0.99	−0.22	−1.34
−0.42	−1.44	0.83	0.39	0.66	1.17	0.82	0.17	0.69	−0.13
0.76	−0.80	−0.84	−1.02	−0.03	1.62	0.51	−1.00	0.98	−2.02
0.03	−0.53	−0.71	0.11	−0.29	0.66	0.23	0.64	1.19	0.66
0.00									
		$\Sigma X_1 = -5.66$					$\Sigma X_2 = 5.59$		
		$\Sigma X_1^2 = 10.48$					$\Sigma X_2^2 = 19.47$		

This time I will lay out the problem as a series of steps because this will help to review the material we have covered in this chapter.

1. What are we testing? First we need to specify the null hypothesis, the significance level, and whether we will use a one- or a two-tailed test. We want to test the null hypothesis that our two groups will earn the same mean score on the task regardless of whether or not they are performing in the presence of their lucky charm, so we have H$_0$: $\mu_1 = \mu_2$. We will set alpha at $\alpha = .05$, in line with what we have been using throughout the book. Finally, we will choose to use a two-tailed test because it is conceivable that the presence of a lucky charm might be a distraction that leads to poorer performance.

2. Calculate the sample statistics: The means and the variances are

$$\overline{X}_1 = \frac{-5.66}{21} = -0.27 \qquad\qquad \overline{X}_2 = \frac{5.59}{20} = 0.28$$

$$s_1^2 = \frac{10.48 - \dfrac{-5.66^2}{21}}{20} = 0.448 \qquad s_2^2 = \frac{19.47 - \dfrac{5.59^2}{20}}{19} = 0.943$$

3. Pool the variances.

$$s_p^2 = \frac{(n_1 - 1)s_1^2 + (n_2 - 1)s_2^2}{n_1 + n_2 - 2}$$

$$= \frac{(20)0.448 + (19)0.943}{21 + 20 - 2} = 0.689$$

4. Calculate t.

$$t = \frac{\overline{X}_1 - \overline{X}_2}{\sqrt{\dfrac{s_p^2}{n_1} + \dfrac{s_p^2}{n_2}}} = \frac{-0.27 - 0.28}{\sqrt{\dfrac{0.689}{21} + \dfrac{0.689}{20}}} = \frac{-0.55}{0.259} = -2.12$$

5. Draw conclusions: For this example we have $n_1 + n_2 - 2 = 39$ degrees of freedom. From Table E.6 in the Appendices we find $t_{.05} = 2.021$. Because $2.021 < \pm 2.12$ we will reject the null hypothesis. (The actual probability under the t distribution is given by the StatsMate app on my iPhone as $p = .040$.) We will conclude that the presence of a lucky charm was associated with better mean performance on this task. (This result is consistent with the three other studies that Damisch et al. reported.)

6. Calculate an effect size measure. The effect size for this example is best calculated using Cohen's $\hat{d}$. In doing so we will use the square root of the pooled variance estimate as our standard deviation because there is no obvious reason to use the standard deviation of one of the groups. (You might argue that the group that performed in the absence of their lucky charm was a control group whose standard deviation would be appropriate, but I feel safer with a pooled estimate.)

$$\hat{d} = \frac{\overline{X}_1 - \overline{X}_2}{\sqrt{0.689}} = \frac{-0.27 - 0.28}{0.830} = \frac{-0.55}{0.830} = -0.66$$

This indicates that the group with the lucky charm present scored about 2/3 of a standard deviation lower than the group without their charm. Because lower scores represent better performance, it would appear that superstitious behaviors can lead to improved performance.

7. Calculate a confidence interval on $\hat{d}$. This is most easily done using the ci.smd function in R that we used before. The result is

```
Library(MBESS)
ci.smd (smd = -0.66, n.1 = 21, n.2 = 20)

$Lower.Conf.Limit.smd
[1] -1.285536
$smd
[1] -0.66
$Upper.Conf.Limit.smd
[1] -0.02646733
```

That confidence interval is very wide, but it does not include 0. We will see that the confidence interval on the mean difference is also very wide. But it is important to note that all four experiments that these authors conducted came to very similar conclusions.

8. Calculate confidence limits on the mean difference. The confidence limits are

$$CI_{.95} = (\overline{X}_1 - \overline{X}_2) \pm t_{(.05)}(s_{\overline{X}_1 - \overline{X}_2})$$

$$= (-0.27 - 0.28) \pm 2.021(0.259) = (-0.55) \pm 0.523$$

$$= -1.07 \le (\mu_1 - \mu_2) \le -.027$$

The problem with this confidence interval on the mean difference is that, *in this case*, it doesn't tell us very much. You and I are not familiar with the dependent variable that the authors created, so we don't have much of a sense of how big the values here really are. We are much better off with the effect size.

9. Write up the results:

> In an study designed to examine whether superstitious behavior can affect performance. Damisch et al. (2010) asked participants to perform a memory task in the presence or absence of a lucky charm that they brought to the experiment. The results showed that the group with their lucky charm present performed better ($\overline{X}$= –0.27, sd = .67) than those who did not have their lucky charm with them ($\overline{X}$= 0.28, sd = .97), $t(39)$ = 2.12, p= .04. Cohen's $\hat{d}$ = 0.66. Further experiments within this particular study showed that the lucky charm group reported a greater sense of self-efficacy, which the authors suggested as a reason to explain these results.

14.11 Seeing Statistics

We began this chapter by looking at the sampling distribution of the differences between means. A particularly good illustration of what that distribution looks like, and how it relates to the true difference between means, the sample size, and the population standard deviations, can be seen in an applet named Sampling Distribution of Mean Differences, contained on this book's website. An example of the opening screen follows.

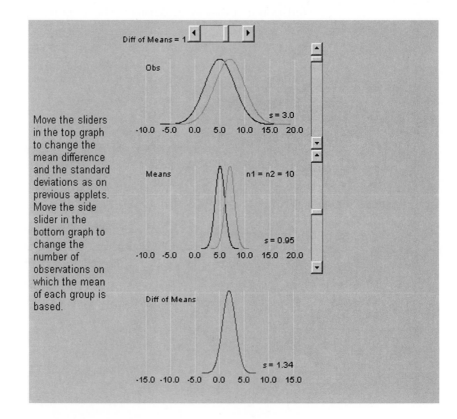

Move the sliders in the top graph to change the mean difference and the standard deviations as on previous applets. Move the side slider in the bottom graph to change the number of observations on which the mean of each group is based.

You see three sets of distributions. The pair at the top represents the populations from which we sample, while the one in the middle shows the distribution of means drawn from each population. The bottom distribution is the sampling distribution of mean differences. At the very top of the screen you see a slider that alters the difference between the population means. On the upper right is a slider that changes the standard deviations of the populations, and below that is a slider to change the sample sizes.

Move the top slider to see that as you increase the difference between population means, you also change the location of the sample distributions of means, and, more importantly for us, you change the mean of the sampling distribution of differences between means.

One additional applet (labeled t-test on differences between means) allows you to specify means, standard deviations, or sample sizes, and see what effect that has on both t and its associated probability. This applet calculates the t value and probability for a comparison of two means. The opening screen follows. Its use should be self-explanatory, but be sure to press the Enter or Return key after you enter each value.

	Mean	StDev	N
Group 1	7.157	2.585	7
Group 2	4.343	1.875	7

Change the numbers in any text box. Press "Enter" in a text box to update graph.

df	Mean Diff	StDev	t Statistic
$t(12) =$	2.814 /	1.207 =	2.33

Prob =0.038

-2.3   2.3
-2.8   2.8

Two-Tailed ▾   prob: 0.038

Take the data from the study of homophobia in Table 14.2, and enter the appropriate statistics. Does the answer agree with the one we obtained?

Using the same example, assume that we had only 10 participants in each group. Would the result still be significant? What does that tell you about the importance of sample size? (That will be discussed in the next chapter.)

14.12 Summary

Because this chapter focused on a comparison of the means of two samples, we began by looking at the standard error of mean differences, which is the standard deviation of a theoretical set of differences between means of two samples. With independent samples, this simply becomes the square root of the sum of each variance divided by its sample size.

We then invoked the Central Limit Theorem to show that the distribution of differences would be normally distributed under a broad range of conditions.

To calculate t we simply take the difference between our sample means and divide by our estimate of the standard error of the difference. In calculating this estimate we often pool the two separate variances, which means that we take a weighted average of the two variances and substitute that for each variance separately. The degrees of freedom for this t are the sum of the degrees of freedom for each sample, which comes down to $n_1 + n_2 - 2$.

We discussed heterogeneity of variance, which is the case where the two sample variances differ considerably. We saw that we can solve for t by using the individual variances in place of a pooled variance. We compensate for the heterogeneous variances by computing an adjusted degrees of freedom. This test is usually seen in computer output under the label of Welch's test.

We looked at effect size by using Cohen's $\hat{d}$. This is simply the difference in means divided by a standard deviation. The standard deviation you use could be the standard deviation of a control group, or the standard deviation of some logically selected group, or it could be the square root of the pooled variance. We also saw how to calculate two kinds of confidence limits for our example. One of these is the confidence limits on the difference between means. The other is a confidence interval on the effect size $\hat{d}$. The latter is much more easily calculated using available software, and two approaches to this were discussed. Ninety-five percent of the time when we calculate confidence limits in that way, they will encompass the difference in population means.

Finally, we looked at plotting the data with bar graphs. I included error bars on the graph that I produced, but pointed out that there is no universal agreement about the units of the error bars. Most often they are plus and minus a standard error, but they could also be plus or minus two standard errors or could be confidence limits. It is important that you make clear to the reader what the error bars represent.

Key Terms

Sampling distribution of differences between means, 352	Weighted average, 356
Variance Sum Law, 353	Pooled variance, 356
Standard error of differences between means, 355	Confounded, 360
Homogeneity of variance, 356	Heterogeneity of variance, 360

14.13 A Quick Review

A. Give two reasons why we would run an experiment with independent groups of scores.
Ans: Sometimes we cannot measure the same object under different conditions (e.g., males versus females) and sometimes the effect of the first treatment will too strongly influence the effect of the second treatment.

B. What is the difference between N and n?
Ans: The former refers to the total sample size while the latter refers to the sample size in an individual group.

C. What do we mean by "pooling variances"?
Ans: We take an average of the two variances, with the variance of each sample weighted by the size of the sample on which it was based.

D. What is meant by the assumption of "homogeneity of variance"?
Ans: The assumption that our two samples came from populations with the same variance, regardless of the values of the population means.

E. What do we mean when we say that two effects are "confounded"?
Ans: We mean that we cannot cleanly tell the difference between the two groups. For example, the groups may differ in ways other than the treatments that we are manipulating.

F. What do we mean by a "bidirectional" hypothesis?
Ans: This is really another way to say "two-tailed test." We will reject the null for large deviations *in either direction*.

G. How does the calculation of confidence limits on the difference between two means differ from the calculation when we have one mean?
Ans: The only difference is that for the former we use the difference between means and the standard error of mean differences.

H. What are error bars?
Ans: Error bars are lines drawn on a bar chart showing something about the variability means. They often represent one standard error above and below the mean, but sometimes other units (e.g., standard deviations) are used.

|14.14| **Exercises**

14.1 In Exercise 13.1 we had paired data because we had a response from both the husband and the wife within a married couple. Suppose that instead of using married couples we just took a large group of people and asked them to what extent they endorsed the statement "Sex is fun for me and my partner" on a four-point scales ranging from "never or occasionally" to "almost always." We then sorted the data on the basis of the gender of the respondent. We could conceivably get the data we had in Exercise 13.1, though without the pairing.

Analyze the data in Exercise 13.1 as if they had been collected from independent groups. What would you conclude?

14.2 The *t* value that you obtain in Exercise 14.1 will be somewhat smaller than the *t* value from Exercise 13.1. Why should we have anticipated this?

14.3 Why isn't the difference between the results of Exercises 13.1 and 14.1 greater than it is?

14.4 In the example in this chapter about the treatment of anorexia, what basic assumption would we have to make if we compared the final weights of the two groups (rather than comparing the amount of weight gain)?

14.5 What is the role of random assignment in the anorexia study?

14.6 What is the role of random sampling in the anorexia study?

14.7 Why can't we use random assignment in the study of homophobia, and what effect will that have on the conclusions we are allowed to draw?

14.8 The Thematic Apperception Test (TAT) presents participants with ambiguous pictures and asks them to tell a story about them. These stories can be scored in any number of ways. Werner, Stabenau, and Pollin (1970) asked mothers of 20 Normal and 20 Schizophrenic children to complete the TAT and then scored for the number of stories (out of 10) that exhibited a positive parent–child relationship. The data follow:

Normal	8	4	6	3	1	4	4	6	4	2
Schizophrenic	2	1	1	3	2	7	2	1	3	1

Normal	2	1	1	4	3	3	2	6	3	4
Schizophrenic	0	2	4	2	3	3	0	1	2	2

a) What would you assume to be the experimental hypothesis behind this study?
b) What would you conclude with respect to that hypothesis?

14.9 In Exercise 14.8 why might it be smart to look at the variances of the two groups?

14.10 In Exercise 14.8 a significant difference might lead someone to suggest that poor parent–child relationships are the cause of schizophrenia. Why might this be a troublesome conclusion?

14.11 Much has been made of the concept of *experimenter bias*, which refers to the fact that for even the most conscientious experimenters there seems to be a tendency for the data to come out in the desired direction. Suppose we use students as experimenters. All the experimenters are told that participants will be given caffeine before the experiment, but half the experimenters are told that we expect caffeine to lead to good performance, and half are told that we expect it to lead to poor performance. The dependent variable is the number of simple arithmetic problems the participant can solve in two minutes. The obtained data are as follows:

Expect good Performance	19	15	22	13	18	15	20	25	22
Expect Poor Performance	14	18	17	12	21	21	24	14	

What would you conclude from these results?

14.12 Calculate the 95% confidence limits on $\mu_1 - \mu_2$ for the data in Exercise 14.11.

14.13 Calculate a measure of effect size for the data in Exercise 14.11.

14.14 What would be the confidence limits on the results in Exercise 14.13?

14.15 Using the data in the file Add.dat on the Web, compare grade point averages for those having ADDSC scores of 65 or less with those having ADDSC scores of 66 or more.

14.16 Calculate Cohen's $\hat{d}$ for the data in Exercise 14.15.

14.17 What do the answers to Exercises 14.15 and 14.16 tell you about the predictive utility of the ADDSC score?

14.18 Brescoll and Uhlman(2008) investigated the hypothesis that when an observer views a video-tape of a male expressing anger as opposed to sadness, the male in the anger condition is accorded higher status than the male in the sadness condition. For 19 males the mean and standard deviation (in parentheses) of the anger condition were 6.47 (2.25). For the 29 men in the sad condition the mean and standard deviation were 4.05 (1.61). Is this difference significant?

14.19 Brescoll and Uhlman(2008), in the study described in Exercise 14.18, found the reverse effect for females. They thought that perhaps this latter result was related to the way anger is judged in females compared to males. When they compared judgments of a video of a group of 41 females who expressed anger without an attribution for the source of anger, women's perceived status had a mean and standard deviation of 3.40 (1.44). When the women on the video gave an external attribution for her anger (an employee stole something), their perceived status had a mean and standard deviation of 5.02 (1.66) with a standard deviation of 1.66.

a) Is this difference significant and what is the confidence interval on that difference?
b) What is the effect size and its confidence interval?

c) The corresponding means and standard deviations (in parentheses) for males were 5.42 (1.63) in the no-attribution condition and 4.14 (2.46) in the external attribution condition. Do we have evidence of a double standard for males and females?

14.20 Given the definition of a weighted average (see page 356), show what the pooled variance estimate (s_p^2) would be if the two sample sizes were equal. (*Hint:* Replace n_1 and n_2 with n.)

14.21 With respect to the previous exercise, what would happen if $s_1^2 = s_2^2$, regardless of n_i?

14.22 Demonstrate that, *because we have equal sample sizes*, I would have arrived at the same answer in Section 14.10 if I had not pooled the variances, although the degrees of freedom would probably differ.

14.23 Use *R* or other software to repeat the results for Exercise 14.8.

14.24 Use *R* or other software to repeat the results for Exercise 14.11.

## CHAPTER 15

Power

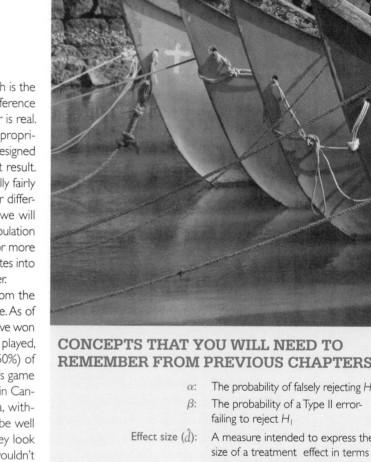

This chapter deals with **power**, which is the probability of finding a significant difference if the effect that you are looking for is real. We will see the importance of setting appropriate levels of power and why even a well-designed study will not always produce a significant result. Power is an important concept and is usually fairly simple to compute. To calculate power for differences in population means, for example, we will only need to estimate the differences in population means and the standard deviation of one or more populations. We can then take those estimates into account and calculate our estimate of power.

I have avoided taking my examples from the sports pages, but this is a great place for one. As of the time of writing, the New York Yankees have won 41 (62%) of the 66 games that they have played, while the Boston Red Sox have won 33 (50%) of their 66 games. If you had to bet on today's game between the two of them, and if you lived in Canterbury, England, or Melbourne, Australia, without any loyalty to either team, you would be well advised to bet on the Yankees because they look to be the better team. But you certainly wouldn't expect that they are a sure thing. The probabilities are in their favor, but you wouldn't stand there in astonishment if you heard they lost. The same thing is true for an experiment. Your treatment for dyslexia may be appreciably better than mine, but that doesn't mean that your clients are *always* going to come out doing better than my clients. Nor does it mean that, when compared to a control group, your treatment will always show a statistically significant difference. We have to keep in mind the fact that one team or one treatment is better than another doesn't always mean that it will win. It just means that they will win more often than they lose.

CONCEPTS THAT YOU WILL NEED TO REMEMBER FROM PREVIOUS CHAPTERS

α:	The probability of falsely rejecting H_0
β:	The probability of a Type II error- failing to reject H_1
Effect size ($\hat{d}$):	A measure intended to express the size of a treatment effect in terms that are meaningful to the reader
Pooled variance estimate:	The weighted average of two sample variances
Sampling distribution:	The distribution of a statistic, such as the mean, over repeated sampling

This is an important point that will come up again in Chapter 21 when we talk about meta-analysis. When we are trying to pull together a number of studies on a particular topic, we don't expect all of them to be significant. Moreover, the presence of a nonsignificant study, whose mean difference is in the right direction, can actually increase our confidence in a phenomenon.

We all seem to operate under a general belief that if we conduct an experiment to test a theory, that experiment will always come out in line with the theory: If the theory is true, the results will be statistically significant, and if the theory is wrong, they won't. But the world doesn't work that way, just as the Yankees don't always win. No one gives up on the Yankees if they lose a game, but we tend to give up on theories if the experiment doesn't come out the way the theory would predict. Maybe you just didn't look hard enough—that is, use enough observations. (Or maybe you did, and it was just not your day.)

Most applied statistical work is concerned primarily with minimizing (or at least controlling) the probability of a Type I error (α). We don't want to reject a true null hypothesis falsely any more often than necessary. When it comes to designing experiments, people generally tend to ignore that there is a probability (β) of another kind of error, the Type II error. Whereas Type I errors deal with the problem of *finding* a difference that is *not* there, Type II errors concern the serious problem of *not finding* a difference that *is* there. (In our baseball example, it is analogous to the probability of the Yankees not beating the Red Sox when they really are the better team.) When we consider the substantial cost in time and money that goes into a typical experiment, it is remarkably shortsighted of experimenters not to recognize that they may, from the start, have a very small chance of finding the effect for which they are looking, even if such an effect actually exists in the population and even if it is a nontrivial effect worth finding. And it is equally short-sighted of them to drop a line of research simply because the first study they ran was not statistically significant. That is why good experimenters often run a series of pilot studies to get the experimental design just right.

Investigators historically have tended to avoid concerning themselves with Type II errors. (Interestingly, people who play the horses wouldn't think of ignoring the fact that even the greatest horse sometimes loses, but we frequently ignore the fact that even the best experiments sometimes produce no significant difference.) Until recently, many textbooks ignored the problem altogether. Those books that did discuss the material discussed it in ways not easily understood by the book's intended audience. In the past 30 years, however, Jacob Cohen, a psychologist, has discussed the problem clearly and lucidly in several publications. He almost single-handedly forced psychologists to recognize that there is such a thing as statistical power and that it really is important. Cohen (1988) presents a thorough and rigorous treatment of the material. In Welkowitz, Cohen, and Ewen (2006), the material is treated in a slightly simpler way, through the use of an approximation technique, which is the approach adopted in this chapter. This approximation is based on the use of the normal distribution, and differences between the level of power computed with this method and with the more exact approach are generally negligible. (I will also present a more exact approach to power using free statistical software on your desktop or laptop.) Cohen (1992) has written an excellent five-page paper that is quite accessible, and I hand it out to anyone who asks me about statistical power. If you become interested in this topic or need to consider power in greater depth than we do in this chapter, you should have no difficulty with the sources just mentioned or with any of the many excellent papers Cohen published on a wide variety of topics. The fact that these papers were written some time ago, and I almost seem to refer to them as if they were recent, is an illustration of the fact that ideas change slowly—not only in statistical methods, but more generally.

JACOB COHEN

We have not had a biographical sketch for several chapters, but this chapter gives me the opportunity to write about a man that I consider the most responsible for bringing an appreciation of statistical issues to the psychological community. I have admired the man nearly all of my professional life, though I never had the opportunity to meet him.

Jacob Cohen was born in 1923 and entered City College of New York at the age of 15. Apparently he wasn't quite ready for college, because, as his wife and co-author Patricia Cohen wrote, "After two years of dismal performance (except in ping pong), he worked in war-related occupations . . ." (Cohen, 2005) and then entered the military (Cohen, 2005). After the Second World War he graduated from CCNY and earned his PhD at NYU. He then worked for the Veterans Administration, and during that time he developed Cohen's Kappa, a still widely used chance-corrected measure of agreement. In 1959 he moved to NYU, and stayed there until his retirement in 1993. He died in 1998, after having received during his lifetime about as many awards as the psychological community has to offer.

One of Cohen's most important publications was a paper in 1968 that combined linear regression and the analysis of variance (the subject of the next few chapters) in ways that psychologists had never really understood before then. (If I had only published one paper in my professional life, I wish this paper had been it.) He claimed that this paper was so successful because he was totally incapable of writing it at the level of statistical and mathematical sophistication that was generally expected. That is, he wrote a paper that people could actually understand! The material that he presented in that paper was highly influential and started an enormous series of papers by others.

In 1969 Cohen published his highly influential *Statistical Power Analysis for the Behavioral Sciences*. That book showed psychologists what power is, how to calculate it, how to design more powerful experiments, and how little power most of the experiments we run actually have. This caused many people to question the power of studies in psychology and eventually led, in various ways, to a questioning of the whole concept of statistical hypothesis testing. By the 1990s, Cohen was himself questioning our ideas of hypothesis testing, and an excellent summary of these ideas can be found in his 1990 paper titled "Things I have learned (so far)." Notice that last two words—Cohen never stopped learning, which is very fortunate for psychology.

Speaking in terms of Type II errors is a negative way of approaching the problem, since it focuses on our mistakes. The more positive approach is to speak in terms of power, which is defined as the probability of *correctly* rejecting a *false* H_0. Put another way, power equals $1 - \beta$. When we say that the power of a particular experimental design is .65, we mean that if the null hypothesis is false *to the degree we expect*, the probability is .65 that the results of the experiment will lead us to reject H_0. A more powerful experiment is one that has a greater probability of rejecting a false H_0 than does a less powerful experiment.

15.1 The Basic Concept of Power

Before I explain the calculation of power estimates, we can examine the underlying concept by looking at power directly using resampling. For this example we will take a study involving two independent groups testing the null hypothesis that $\mu_1 = \mu_2$. It is certainly an interesting study.

Joshua Aronson has done extensive work on what is known as "stereotype threat," which concerns the fact that "members of stereotyped groups often feel extra pressure in situations where their behavior can confirm the negative reputation that their group lacks a valued ability" (Aronson, Lustina, Good, Keough, Steele, & Brown, 1998). This feeling of stereotype threat is then hypothesized to affect performance, generally by lowering it from what it would have been had the individual not felt threatened. Considerable work has been done with ethnic groups who are stereotypically reputed to do poorly in some area, but Aronson et al. went a step further to ask if stereotype threat could actually lower the performance of White males—a group that is not normally associated with stereotype threat.

Aronson et al. (1998) used two independent groups of college students who were known to excel in mathematics, and for whom doing well in math was considered important. They randomly assigned 11 students to a Control group that was simply asked to complete a difficult mathematics exam. They assigned 12 students to a threat condition, in which they were told that Asian students typically did better than other students in math tests, and that the purpose of the exam was to help the experimenter to understand why this difference exists. Aronson reasoned that simply telling White students that Asians did better on math tests would arouse feelings of stereotype threat and diminish the students' performance.

The dependent variable in this study was the number of math problems solved correctly in the allotted time. The study found that for 11 students in the Control group, the mean and standard deviation were 9.64 and 3.17 respectively. For the 12 students in the Threat group the corresponding values were 6.58 and 3.03. A t test applied to these data produced a $t = 2.37$, which was significant at $p = .027$. This is an important finding, and it would not be unusual to try to replicate it. Suppose that we were planning to perform a replication, but wanted to use 20 students in each group—a control group and a threatened group. But before we spend the money and energy trying to replicate this study, we ought to have some idea of the probability of a successful replication. That is what power is all about.

To calculate power for our replication we need to have some idea of the mean and standard deviation of the populations of control and threatened respondents. Our best guess at those parameters would be the means and standard deviations that Aronson et al. found for their sample. They are not likely to be the exact parameters, but they are the best guess we have. So we will assume that the Control population would have a mean of 9.64 and a standard deviation of 3.17, and that the Threat population has a mean of 6.58 and a standard deviation of 3.03. We will also assume that the populations are normally distributed. As I said, we plan to use 20 participants in each group.

An easy way to model this situation is to draw 20 observations from a population of scores with mean and standard deviation equal to those of the Control condition. Similarly, we will draw 20 observations from a population with a mean and standard deviation equal to those of the experimental group. We will then calculate

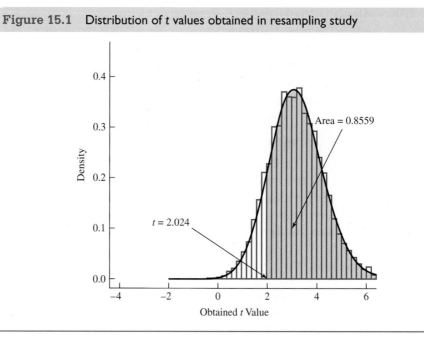

Figure 15.1 Distribution of *t* values obtained in resampling study

a *t* statistic for these data, store that *t* away, and then repeat the process 9,999 times. This will give us 10,000 *t* values. We also know that with 38 *df*, the critical value of $t_a(38) = \pm 2.024$, so we can ask how many of these 10,000 *t* values are statistically significant (i.e., are greater than or equal to ± 2.024).

The result of just such a sampling study is presented in Figure 15.1, with the appropriate *t* distribution superimposed. Notice that although 86% of the results were greater than $t = \pm 2.024$, 14% of them were less than the critical value. Therefore the power of this experiment, given the parameter estimates and sample size, is .86, the percentage of outcomes exceeding the critical value. This is actually a reasonable level of power for most practical work. It also happens to be almost the exact power level reported by online programs such as http://www.math.uiowa.edu/~rlenth/Power/. (You can download this particular program and run it directly from your desktop. See the information presented on the associated Web page. However, before trying this, look at the third paragraph in

http://www.uvm.edu/~dhowell/fundamentals9/SeeingStatisticsApplets/Applets.html

There is a problem running Java applets, and it is certainly not Lenth's fault.)

15.2 Factors Affecting the Power of a Test

Having looked at power from a heuristic perspective by actually drawing repeated samples, we will now look at it a bit more theoretically. As might be expected, power is a function of several variables. It is a function of (1) α, the probability of a Type I error, (2) the true alternative hypothesis (H_1), (3) the sample size, and (4) the particular test to be employed. With the exception of the relative power of independent versus matched samples, we will avoid this last relationship on the grounds that when the test assumptions are met, the majority of the procedures discussed in this book can be shown to be the uniformly most powerful tests of those available to answer the question at hand.

A Short Review

First we need a quick review of the material covered earlier in this book. Consider the two distributions in Figure 15.2. The distribution to the left (labeled H_0) represents the sampling distribution of the mean when the null hypothesis is true and $\mu = \mu_0$. The distribution on the right represents the sampling distribution of the mean that we would have if H_0 were false and the true population mean were equal to μ_1. The placement of this distribution depends entirely on what the value of μ_1 happens to be.

The heavily shaded right tail of the H_0 distribution represents α, the probability of a Type I error, assuming that we are using a one-tailed test (otherwise it represents $\alpha/2$). This area contains the sample means that would result in significant values of t. The second distribution (H_1) represents the sampling distribution of the mean when H_0 is false and the true mean is μ_1. It is readily apparent that even when H_0 is false, many of the sample means (and therefore the corresponding values of t) will nonetheless fall to the left of the critical value, causing us to fail to reject a false H_0, thus committing a Type II error. We saw this in the previous demonstration. The probability of this error is indicated by the lightly shaded area in Figure 15.2 and is labeled β. When H_0 is false and the test statistic falls to the right of the critical value, we will correctly reject a false H_0. The probability of doing this is what we mean by *power*, and it is shown in the unshaded area of the H_1 distribution.

Power as a Function of α

With the aid of Figure 15.2, it is easy to see why we say that power is a function of α. If we are willing to increase α, our cutoff point moves to the left, thus simultaneously

Figure 15.2 Sampling distribution of $\overline{X}$ under H_0 and H_1.

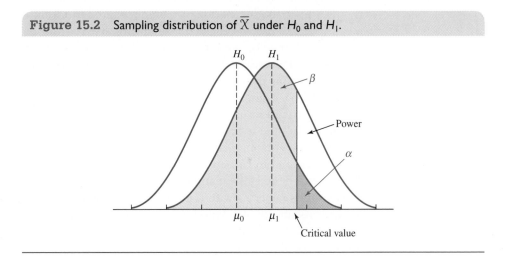

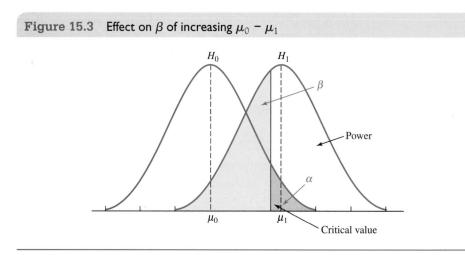

Figure 15.3 Effect on β of increasing $\mu_0 - \mu_1$

decreasing β and increasing power, although with a corresponding rise in the probability of a Type I error.

Power as a Function of H_1

The fact that power is a function of the true alternative hypothesis [more precisely $(\mu_0 - \mu_1)$, the difference between μ_0 (the mean under H_0) and μ_1 (the mean under H_1)] is illustrated by comparing Figures 15.2 and 15.3. In Figure 15.3 the distance between μ_0 and μ_1 has been increased, and this has resulted in a substantial increase in power, though there is still sizable probability of a Type II error. This is not particularly surprising, because all that we are saying is that the chances of finding a difference depend on how large the difference actually is.

Power as a Function of n and σ^2

The relationship between power and sample size (and between power and σ^2) is only a little subtler. Because we are interested in means or differences between means, we are interested in the sampling distribution of the mean. We know that the variance of the sampling distribution of the mean decreases as either n increases or σ^2 decreases, because $\sigma_{\bar{X}}^2 = \sigma^2/n$. Figure 15.4 illustrates what happens to the two sampling distributions (H_0 and H_1) as we increase n or decrease σ^2, relative to Figure 15.3. Figure 15.4 also shows that, as $\sigma_{\bar{X}}^2$ decreases, the overlap between the two distributions is reduced with a resulting increase in power. Notice that the two means (μ_0 and μ_1) remain unchanged from Figure 15.3.

If an experimenter is concerned with the power of a test, then he or she is most likely interested in those variables governing power that are easy to manipulate. Because n is more easily manipulated than is either σ^2 or the difference ($\mu_0 - \mu_1$), and because tampering with α produces undesirable side effects in terms of increasing the probability of a Type I error, discussions of power are generally concerned with the effects of varying sample size, although McClelland (1997) has pointed out that simple changes in experimental design can also increase the power of an experiment.

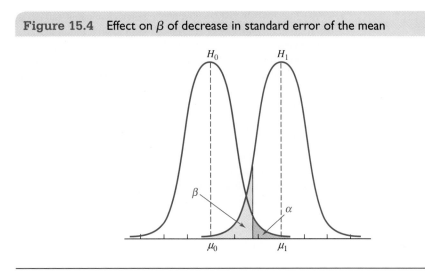

Figure 15.4   Effect on β of decrease in standard error of the mean

15.3 | Calculating Power the Traditional Way

As we saw in Figures 15.2 through 15.4, power depends on the degree of overlap between the sampling distributions under H_0 and H_1. Furthermore, this overlap is a function of both the distance between μ_0 and μ_1 and the standard error. One measure, then, of the degree to which H_0 is false would be the distance from μ_1 to μ_0 expressed in terms of the number of standard errors. The problem with this measure, however, is that it includes the sample size (in the computation of the standard error), when in fact we will usually wish to solve for the power associated with a given n or else for that value of n required for a given level of power. For this reason we will take as our distance measure, or **effect size (d)**

$$d = \frac{\mu_1 - \mu_0}{\sigma}$$

ignoring the sign of d, and incorporating n later. (This is basically the same d that I have elsewhere referred to as Cohen's d, although used for a slightly different purpose.) Thus, d is a measure of the degree to which μ_1 and μ_0 differ in terms of the standard deviation of the parent population. (For example if we pool the variances we have $d = (9.64 - 6.58)/3.10 = .987$, which simply says that the means under H_1 differ by near one standard deviation. I am using the pooled standard deviation here.) We see that d is estimated independently of n, simply by estimating μ_1, μ_0, and σ. In Chapter 14 we discussed effect size as the standardized difference between two means. We have the same measure here, though one of those means is the mean under the null hypothesis. I will point this out again when we come to comparing the means of two populations.

Estimating the Effect Size

The first task is to estimate d, because it will form the basis for future calculations. This can be done in three ways, ranging from most to least satisfactory:

1. *Prior research.* On the basis of past research, we can often get at least a rough approximation of d. Thus, we could look at sample means and variances from other studies and make an informed guess at the values we might expect for $\mu_1 - \mu_0$ and for σ. In practice, this task is not as difficult as it might seem, especially when you realize that a rough approximation is far better than no approximation at all.

2. *Personal assessment of how large a difference is important.* In many cases, an investigator is able to say something like, "I am interested in detecting a difference of at least 10 points between μ_1 and μ_0." The investigator is essentially saying that differences less than this have no important or useful meaning, whereas greater differences do. (This is particularly common in biomedical research, where we are interesting in decreasing cholesterol, for example, by a certain amount, and have no interest in smaller changes. A similar situation arises when we want to compare drugs and are not interested in the new one unless it is better than the old one by some predetermined amount.) Here we are given the value of $\mu_1 - \mu_0$ directly, without needing to know the particular values of μ_1 and μ_0. All that remains is to estimate σ from other data. As an example, the investigator might say that he or she is interested in finding a procedure that will raise scores on the Graduate Record Exam by 40 points above normal. We already know that the standard deviation for this test is approximately 100. Thus $d = 40/100 = .40$. If our hypothetical experimenter instead wants to raise scores by four-tenths of a standard deviation, he or she would be giving us d directly.

3. *Use of special conventions.* When we encounter a situation in which there is no way we can estimate the required parameters, we can fall back on a set of conventions proposed by Cohen (1988). Cohen more or less arbitrarily defined three levels of d:

Effect Size	d	Percentage of Overlap[1]
Small	.20	92
Medium	.50	80
Large	.80	69

Thus, *in a pinch*, the experimenter can simply decide whether he or she is after a small, medium, or large effect and set d accordingly. However, this solution should be chosen *only* when the other alternatives are not feasible. The right-hand column of the table is labeled Percentage of Overlap, and it records the degree to which the two distributions shown in Figure 15.2 overlap. Thus, for example, when $d = 0.50$, 80% of the two distributions overlap (Cohen, 1988). This is yet another way of thinking about how big a difference a treatment produces.

Cohen chose a medium effect to be one that would be apparent to an intelligent viewer, a small effect as one that is real but difficult to detect visually, and a large effect as one that is the same distance above a medium effect as "small" is below it. Cohen (1969) originally developed these guidelines only for those who had no other way of estimating the effect size. But as time went on and he became discouraged by the failure of many researchers to conduct power analyses, presumably because they think them to be too difficult, he made greater use of these conventions (see Cohen, 1992a). However, Bruce Thompson, of Texas A&M, made an excellent point in this regard. He was speaking of expressing obtained differences in terms of d, in place of

---

[1] I want to thank James Grice (Oklahoma State University) and Paul Barrett (University of Auckland) for providing the correct values for "Percentage of Overlap." There was an error in Cohen's original estimates.

focusing on the probability value of a resulting test statistic. He wrote, "Finally, it must be emphasized that if we mindlessly invoke Cohen's rules of thumb, *contrary to his strong admonitions*, in place of the equally mindless consultation of *p* value cutoffs such as .05 and .01, we are merely electing to be thoughtless in a new metric (emphasis added)" (Thompson, 2000). The point applies to any use of arbitrary conventions for *d*, regardless of whether it is for purposes of calculating power or for purposes of impressing your readers with how large your difference is. Lenth (2001) has argued convincingly that the use of conventions such as Cohen's are dangerous. We need to concentrate on both the value of the numerator and the value of the denominator in *d*, and not just on their ratio. Lenth's argument is really an attempt at making the investigator more responsible for his or her decisions, and I suspect that Cohen would have wholeheartedly agreed.

It may strike you as peculiar that the investigator is being asked to define the difference he or she is looking for before the experiment is conducted. Most people would respond by saying, "I don't know how the experiment will come out. I just wonder whether there will be a difference." Although many experimenters speak in this way (and I am no virtuous exception), you should question the validity of this statement. Do we really not know, at least vaguely, what will happen in our experiments; if not, why are we running them? Although there is occasionally a legitimate "I-wonder-what-would-happen-if experiment," in general, "I do not know" translates to "I have not thought that far ahead." Remember that most experiments are run to demonstrate to the rest of the world that a particular theory is correct, and that theory often tells us what kind of results to expect.

Recombining the Effect Size and *n*

We decided earlier to split the sample size from the effect size to make it easier to deal with *n* separately. We now need a method of combining the effect size with the sample size. We use the statistic δ **(delta)** $= d[f(n)]^2$ to represent this combination where the particular function of *n* [i.e., $f(n)$] will be defined differently for each individual test. The convenient thing about this system is that it will allow us to use the same table of δ for power calculations for all the statistical procedures to be considered.

15.4 Power Calculations for the One-Sample *t* Test

For our first example we will examine the calculation of power for the one-sample *t* test. In the previous section you saw that δ is based on *d* and some function of *n*. For the one-sample *t* test, that function will be $\sqrt{n}$, and δ will then be defined as

$$\delta = d\sqrt{n}$$

In this situation δ is called the **noncentrality parameter**. In Chapter 5 (Exercise 5.21) we saw data from a study of Everitt using cognitive behavior therapy as a treatment for

---

[2]About the only thing that will turn off a math-phobic student faster than reading "$f(n)$" is to have it followed in the next sentence with "$g(n)$." All it means is that δ depends on *n* in some as yet unspecified way.

anorexia. Now assume a clinical psychologist wants to replicate that study. Needing somewhere to start, he or she assumes that Everitt's data are a good representation of the population parameters in question. In other words, the psychologist is willing to assume that the population mean weight gain, with cognitive behavior therapy, is μ_1 = 3.00 lbs and the standard deviation (s) is 7.31. The null hypothesis would be that cognitive behavior therapy does not lead to weight gain, and therefore μ_0 = 0.00.

$$\hat{d} = \frac{3.00 - 0.00}{7.31} = 0.41$$

If he or she is going to run the same number of participants that Everitt did, then n = 29, and

$$\delta = \hat{d}\sqrt{n} = 0.41\sqrt{29} = 0.41(5.39) = 2.21$$

Although the experimenter expects the sample mean to be above the mean of the general population, he or she plans to use a two-tailed test at α = .05 to protect against unexpected events. Given δ, we can determine the power of the test immediately from Table E.5 in the Appendices. A portion of this table is reproduced in Table 15.1. To use either table, simply go down the left-hand margin until you come to the value of δ = 2.21 and then read across to the column headed .05; that entry will be the power of the test. Neither table has an entry for δ = 2.21, but they do have entries for δ = 2.20 and δ = 2.30. For α = .05 this means that power is between 0.60 and 0.63. By linear interpolation we will say that for δ = 2.21, power rounds to 0.60. This means that if H_0 is really false and μ_1 = 3 pounds, only 60% of the time will the clinician obtain data that will produce a significant value of t when testing the difference between her *sample* mean and that specified by H_0. This is a rather discouraging result because it means that if the true mean gain with cognitive behavior therapy is really 3.00 pounds, 100% − 60% = 40% of the time the study as designed will *not* obtain a significant result. The exact power for this experiment, as calculated at

 http://www.math.uiowa.edu/~rlenth/Power/

or using either R or a stand-alone program called G*Power is .568. You can see that the approximation is quite acceptable.

For R the code is

```
library(pwr)
pwr.t.test(n = 29, d = 0.41, sig.level = .05, type = "one.sample")
One-sample t test power calculation

          n = 29
          d = 0.41
  sig.level = 0.05
      power = 0.5682491[3]
alternative = two.sided
```

---

[3]Do we really believe the accuracy of this calculation to seven digits? I would say that 0.57 is close enough.

Table 15.1 Abbreviated Version of Table E.5, Power as a Function of δ and Significance Level

	Alpha for Two-Tailed Test			
δ	.10	.05	.02	.01
1.00	0.26	0.17	0.09	0.06
1.10	0.29	0.20	0.11	0.07
1.20	0.33	0.22	0.13	0.08
1.30	0.37	0.26	0.15	0.10
1.40	0.40	0.29	0.18	0.12
1.50	0.44	0.32	0.20	0.14
1.60	0.48	0.36	0.23	0.17
1.70	0.52	0.40	0.27	0.19
1.80	0.56	0.44	0.30	0.22
1.90	0.60	0.48	0.34	0.25
2.00	0.64	0.52	0.37	0.28
2.10	0.68	0.56	0.41	0.32
2.20	0.71	0.60	0.45	0.35
2.30	0.74	0.63	0.49	0.39
2.40	0.78	0.67	0.53	0.43
2.50	0.80	0.71	0.57	0.47
2.60	0.83	0.74	0.61	0.51
2.70	0.85	0.77	0.65	0.55
2.80	0.88	0.80	0.68	0.59
2.90	0.90	0.83	0.72	0.65
3.00	0.91	0.85	0.75	0.66

Because the experimenter was intelligent enough to examine the question of power before the experiment began, he or she still has the chance to make changes that will lead to an increase in power. The experimenter could, for example, set a at .10, thus increasing power to approximately 0.71, but this is probably unsatisfactory. (Journal reviewers, for example, generally hate to see a set at any value greater than .05.) Alternatively, the experimenter could make use of the fact that power increases as n increases.

Estimating Required Sample Sizes

It is fine to say that a thoughtful experimenter can increase power by increasing n, but how large an n is needed? The answer to that question depends simply on the level of power that is acceptable. Suppose you wanted to modify the previous example to have power equal to 0.80. The first thing you need to do is read Table E.5 backward to find what value for δ is associated with the specified degree of power. From the table we see that for power equal to 0.80, δ must equal 2.80. Thus we have δ and can solve for n simply by a minor algebraic manipulation:

$$\delta = d\sqrt{n}$$

$$n = \left(\frac{\delta}{d}\right)^2$$

$$= \left(\frac{2.80}{0.41}\right)^2 = 6.83^2 = 46.64$$

Because clients come in whole units, we will round off to 47. Thus if the experimenter wants to have an 80% chance of rejecting H_0 when $\hat{d} = 0.41$ (i.e., when $\mu_1 = 3.00$ or -3.00), he or she will have to provide therapy to 47 clients. Although the experimenter may feel that this is a large number of clients, there is no alternative other than to settle for a lower level of power and increase the chance of not finding anything.[4]

You might wonder why we selected power equal to 0.80 in the previous example. With this degree of power we still run a 20% chance of making a Type II error. It is a matter of practicality. Suppose, for example, that our experimenter had wanted power to equal 0.95. A few simple calculations will show that this would require a sample of $n = 77$; for power equal to 0.99 he or she would need approximately 105 participants. These may well be unreasonable sample sizes for a particular experimental situation or for the resources of the experimenter. While increases in power are generally bought by increases in n, at very high levels of power the cost can be very high. In addition, it is a case of diminishing returns because δ increases as a function of the square root of n. If you are taking data from files supplied by the U.S. Census Bureau, that is one thing. It is quite a different matter when you are studying identical twins reared apart. I should point out that Institutional Review Boards, who have to approve most research involving humans and animals, often balk at sample sizes that they consider excessive.

15.5 Power Calculations for Differences between Two Independent Means

When we wish to test the difference between two independent means, the treatment of power is very similar to our treatment of the case that we used for only one mean. In Section 15.4 we obtained d by taking the difference between μ under H_1 and μ under H_0 and dividing by σ. In testing the difference between two independent means, we will do basically the same thing, although this time we will work with mean differences. Thus, we want the difference between the two population means $(\mu_1 - \mu_0)$ under H_1 minus the difference $(\mu_1 - \mu_0)$ under H_0, divided by σ. (Recall that we assume $\sigma_1^2 = \sigma_2^2 = \sigma^2$.) In most usual applications, however, $(\mu_1 - \mu_0)$ under H_0 is zero, so we can drop that term from our formula. Thus,

---

[4]If you didn't have the table to look up $\delta = 2.80$, which is an approximation anyway, you could quickly rerun the R code that I gave to calculate power, varying the value of n until you find power $= .80$. Doing that, I would set n at 49.

$$d = \frac{(\mu_1 - \mu_2) - 0}{\sigma} = \frac{\mu_1 - \mu_2}{\sigma}$$

where the numerator refers to the difference to be expected under H_1 and the denominator represents the standard deviation of the populations. You should recognize that this is the same d that we saw in Chapter 14 where it was also labeled Cohen's d, or sometimes Hedges's g. The only difference is that here it is expressed in terms of population means rather than sample means.

In the case of two samples, we must distinguish between experiments involving equal ns and those involving unequal ns. We will treat these two cases separately.

Equal Sample Sizes

Assume we wish to test the difference between two treatments and expect that either the difference in population means will be approximately five points or else are interested only in finding a difference of at least five points. Further assume that from past data we think that σ is approximately 10. Then

$$d = \frac{\mu_1 - \mu_2}{\sigma} = \frac{5}{10} = 0.50$$

Thus, we are expecting a difference of one-half of a standard deviation between the two means, what Cohen (1988) would call a moderate effect.

First we will investigate the power of an experiment with 25 observations in each of two groups. We will define our noncentrality parameter, δ, in the two-sample case as

$$\delta = d\sqrt{\frac{n}{2}}$$

where n = the number of cases *in any one sample* (there are $2n$ cases in all). Thus,

$$\delta = (0.50)\sqrt{\frac{25}{2}} = 0.50\sqrt{12.5} = 0.50(3.54)$$

$$= 1.77$$

From Appendix Power, by interpolation for $\delta = 1.77$ with a two-tailed test at $\alpha = .05$, power $= .43$. Thus, if our investigator actually runs this experiment with 25 subjects, and if her estimate of δ is correct, then she has a probability of .43 of actually rejecting H_0 if it is false to the extent she expects, and a probability of .57 of making a Type II error. (The true value of power is .41 rather than .43, but the difference is just due to the fact that the tables are based on an approximation. Being off by .02 is no particular problem.)

We next turn the question around and ask how many subjects would be needed for power $= .80$. From Appendix Power, this would require $\delta = 2.80$.

$$\delta = d\sqrt{\frac{n}{2}}$$

$$\frac{\delta}{d} = \sqrt{\frac{n}{2}}$$

$$\left(\frac{\delta}{d}\right)^2 = \frac{n}{2}$$

$$n = 2\left(\frac{\delta}{d}\right)^2$$

$$= 2\left(\frac{2.80}{0.50}\right)^2 = 2(5.6)^2 = 62.72$$

n refers to the number of subjects per sample, so for power $= .80$, we need 63 subjects per sample for a total of 126 subjects.

Unequal Sample Sizes

We just dealt with the case in which $n_1 - n_2 - n$. However, experiments often have two samples of different sizes. This obviously presents difficulties when we try to solve for δ, because we need one value for n. What value can we use?

With reasonably large and nearly equal sample sizes, a conservative approximation can be obtained by letting n equal the smaller of n_1 and n_2. This is not satisfactory, however, if the sample sizes are small or if the two ns are quite different. For those cases we need a more exact solution.

One seemingly reasonable (but incorrect) procedure would be to set n equal to the arithmetic mean of n_1 and n_2. However, as we saw in Chapter 14, this method would weight the two samples equally when, in fact, we know that the variance of means is proportional not to n, but to $1/n$. The measure that takes this relationship into account is not the arithmetic mean but the **harmonic mean**, denoted as $\bar{n}_h$. For two samples with (n_1 and n_2) observations,

$$\bar{n}_h = \frac{2}{\dfrac{1}{n_1} + \dfrac{1}{n_2}} = \frac{2n_1n_2}{n_1 + n_2}$$

We can then use $\bar{n}_h$ in our calculation of δ.

We looked at the work on stereotype threat by Aronson et al. (1998) at the beginning of this chapter. Here we will go back to that work but focus on direct calculation. What Aronson actually found, which is trivially different from the sample data I generated in Chapter 14, were means of 9.58 and 6.55 for the Control and Threatened groups, respectively. Their pooled standard deviation was approximately 3.10. We will assume that Aronson's estimates of the population means and standard deviation are essentially correct. (They almost certainly suffer from some random error, but they are the best guesses that we have of those parameters.) This produces

$$d = \frac{\mu_1 - \mu_2}{\sigma} = \frac{9.58 - 6.55}{3.10} = \frac{3.03}{3.10} = 0.98$$

Perhaps I want to replicate this study in my research methods class, but I don't want to risk looking foolish and saying "Well, it should have worked when it actually flopped." My class has a lot of students, but only about 30 of them are males, and they are not evenly distributed across the lab sections. Because of the way that I have chosen to run the experiment, assume that I can expect that 18 males will be in the Control group and 12 in the Threat group. Then we will calculate the effective sample size (the sample size to be used in calculating δ) as

$$\bar{n}_h = \frac{2(18)(12)}{18 + 12} = \frac{432}{30} = 14.40$$

We see that the **effective sample size** is less than the arithmetic mean of the two individual sample sizes. In other words, this study has the same power as it would have had we run it with 14.4 subjects per group for a total of 28.8 subjects. Or, to state it differently, with unequal sample sizes it takes 30 subjects to have the same power 28.8 subjects would have in an experiment with equal sample sizes.
To continue,

$$\delta = d\sqrt{\frac{\bar{n}_h}{2}} = 0.98\sqrt{\frac{14.4}{2}} = 0.98\sqrt{7.2}$$
$$= 2.63$$

For $\delta = 2.63$, power = .75 at $\alpha = .05$ (two-tailed).

In this case the power is a bit too low to inspire confidence that the study will work out as a lab exercise is supposed to. I could take a chance and run the study, but it would be very awkward if the experiment failed.

An alternative would be to recruit some more students. I will use the 30 males in my course, but I can also find another 20 in another course who are willing to participate. At the risk of teaching very bad experimental design to my students by combining two different classes (at least it gives me an excuse to mention that this could be a problem), I will add in those students and expect to get sample sizes of 28 and 22. These sample sizes would yield $\bar{n}_h = 24.64$. Then

$$\delta = d\sqrt{\frac{\bar{n}_h}{2}} = 0.98\sqrt{\frac{24.64}{2}} = 0.98\sqrt{12.32}$$
$$= 3.44$$

From Appendix Power we find that power now equals approximately .93, which is sufficient for our purposes. (G*Power, which we will discuss shortly, gives an exact power estimate of .921, which is very close to what we have computed.)

My sample sizes were unequal, but not seriously so. When we have quite unequal sample sizes, and they are unavoidable, the smaller group should be as large as possible relative to the larger group. You should never throw away subjects to make sample sizes equal. This is just throwing away power.

15.6 Power Calculations for the *t* Test for Related Samples

When we move to the situation in which we want to test the difference between two matched samples, the problem becomes somewhat more difficult, and we must take into account the correlation between the two sets of observations. In earlier editions of this book I went into detail on how to calculate power in this situation, but on reflection I believe that there is little to be gained by putting you through that.

The basic idea is the same as for the two previous tests. We would define *d* as

$$d = \frac{\mu_1 - \mu_2}{\sigma_D} = \frac{\mu_D}{\sigma_D}$$

and substitute sample statistics for the parameters. If you had data from a previous study that gave you the necessary statistics, you could immediately solve for *d*. And because this really represents a test on one sample mean (the mean of the difference scores), we can calculate δ as

$$\delta = d\sqrt{N}$$

We then can refer to Table E.5 for the value of δ.

If you don't have good estimates of the necessary parameters, you *could* calculate power as if these were two separate (independent) groups of scores. That would give you an estimate of the lower bound of power. The true power would be somewhat higher, and perhaps considerably higher.

To use an actual example, we will go back to the data in Section 13.2 on the use of family therapy as a treatment for anorexia. There we had a set of weights at the beginning and end of therapy, and calculated a *t* on matched samples. Suppose that we would like to replicate this study to verify its conclusions, but we want to have a reasonable chance of finding a significant result. Because we know about the original study, we can make some reasonable guesses about what to expect. We know that Everitt's data found a difference of 7.26 pounds between the pre- and post-therapy weights. We also know that the standard deviation of the difference scores was 7.16, so we don't have to estimate it. With this information, and with Everitt's sample size of $N = 17$, we can calculate the power assuming that the statistics that he reported are equal to the actual population parameters.

$$d = \frac{\mu_1 - \mu_2}{\sigma_D} = \frac{7.26}{7.16} = 1.01$$

$$\delta = d\sqrt{n}$$
$$= 1.01\sqrt{17} = 4.162$$

From Appendix E we find that for a two-tailed test at $\alpha = .05$, power is approximately equal to .99. This strikes me as an unusually high degree of power, but keep in mind that Everitt reported an effect size of slightly over 1.00. That is certainly a very large effect, and I am frankly quite surprised that even the greatest therapy on earth would produce such an effect. (That is not to say that I don't believe Brian Everitt's data, but only that I am very surprised by them.) If the therapy works as well as Everitt's data would suggest, then we are almost certain to find a significant difference when we have 17 subjects in the replication study that we want to run.[5]

15.7 Power Considerations in Terms of Sample Size

Our discussion of power here illustrates that reasonably large sample sizes are generally a necessity if you are to run experiments that have a good chance of rejecting H_0 when it is, in fact, false, especially if the effect is small. A few minutes with a calculator will show you that if we want to have power equal to 0.80 and if we accept Cohen's definitions for small, medium, and large effects, our samples must be quite large. Table 15.3 presents the total sample sizes required (at power = .80, α = .05, two-tailed) for small, medium, and large effects for the tests we have been discussing. These figures indicate that power (at least a substantial amount of it) is a very expensive commodity, especially for small effects. While it could be argued that this is actually a good thing, since otherwise the literature would contain many more trivial results than it already does, that will come as little comfort to most experimenters. The general rule is to look for big effects, to use large samples, or to employ sensitive experimental designs such as those that involve the use of repeated measurements on the same subjects, reducing experimental error and thus making small differences translate into large effect sizes.

Table 15.2 Total Sample Sizes Required for Power = .80, α = .05, Two-Tailed

Effect Size	d	One-Sample t	Two-Sample t
Small	0.20	196	784
Medium	0.50	32	126
Large	0.80	13	49

15.8 You Don't Have to Do It by Hand

There are a great many sources of material on the Web for studying power. As I have already said, a simple Java program, written by Russ Lenth at the University of Iowa, that accepts keyboard input about sample sizes, effect sizes, and estimated standard deviations, is available at

 http://www.stat.uiowa.edu/~rlenth/Power/index.html

---

[5]I have come close to painting myself in a box here, and think I'm better off discussing it than hoping you won't notice. I have said that there are two kinds of effect sizes. There are measures that are designed to tell the reader how large an effect you found, and there are effect sizes measures, as used in this chapter, for calculating power. I have said that they are the same thing. They are, but you may notice that in the present example I obtained d using the standard error of the difference ($s_{\overline{X}_{post} - \overline{X}_{pre}}$), while in Chapter 13 I said that you should use the standard deviation of the pretreatment scores as your denominator. I am right in both cases, and the only good explanation is that we are using these statistics for different things. To calculate power you do need to estimate the standard error of the differences.

Table 15.3 Results from the Study by Aronson et al. (1998)

Treatment	Mean	St. Dev.	n
Control	9.64	3.17	11
Threat	6.58	3.03	12

From that page you can click on "download" and then download piface.jar. Running it will give you what you want. Be sure to read the section titled "If you're blocked by a security setting." He repeats a suggestion that I have given elsewhere when using Java applets.

We can illustrate the use of this program by considering the example of Aronson et al. (1998) that we used earlier in the chapter. In that example we assumed that we were going to replicate the study with 20 participants in each group. The statistics from that study are shown in Table 15.3, and we will use those as our estimates of the relevant population parameters.

When you run the software from the Web, or download and open "piface.jar", you will be asked to select the type of analysis. Select the two-sample t test from the first screen and click Run dialog. You will be presented with the display shown in Figure 15.5. When the screen first comes up you will see that each box contains a slider that allows you to change the values in the windows. But it is easier to type them in, and you can do that by clicking on the little button above what is now filled with the word "OK" for each entry. I have filled in the relevant entries. Because the variances were nearly equal, I pooled the variances and used the square root of that value for the individual estimates of σ. I also clicked the box labeled "Equal sigmas" so that the program would not compute a "corrected" number of degrees of freedom. Notice that it computes the total df as $n_1 + n_2 - 2 = 38$. The power is given as .8603, which agrees very well with the estimate of .8559 shown in Figure 15.1.

G*Power

My favorite piece of software among available programs that calculate power is called G*Power, which is available for PCs and Macs, and is free (Faul, Erdfelder, Lang, & Buchner, A. (2009)). It seems strange to complain that a program is too good, but G*Power has improved greatly over the years, with the complication that it is somewhat harder to use. I urge you to try it, though that may involve a bit of trial and error. If you are calculating power from a set of existing data, ask for "post-hoc power," though I have said elsewhere that I think that the name is unfortunate.

Going to
http://www.gpower.hhu.de/en.html

will allow you to download version 3 and the manual. Before using G*Power, I suggest reading the next section (Section 15.9), which will also allow you to understand the idea of post-hoc power.

Figure 15.5   Calculating power using Lenth's Piface program

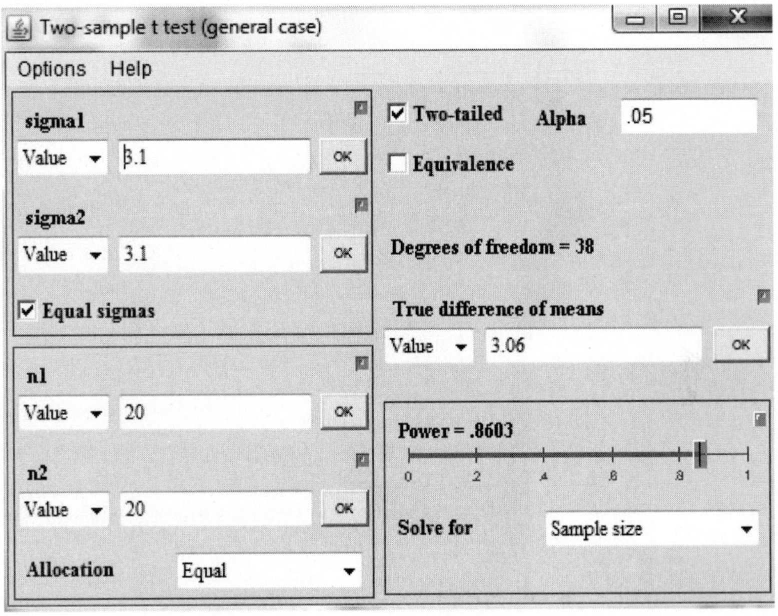

Figure 15.6 illustrates the result of using G*Power for the same example as the one in Figure 15.5. You can see that the resulting calculation gives the same value of power as that given by Lenth's program. It also shows how the two distributions would be expected to overlap. In addition, if you click on the button labeled "X-Y plot for a range of values," you will obtain a plot showing how power varies with sample size.

15.9 | Post-hoc (Retrospective) Power

Before leaving our discussion of power I need to talk about the concept of **post-hoc power**, also known as **retrospective power**. This has become somewhat of a touchy subject in behavioral science journals. There are two uses of the term. One of them, the one I call the *bad* one, involves running a study and then looking back to see what kind of power you had if you treat the means and variances that you found as real. A common suggestion in the literature claims that if the study was not significant, but had high retrospective power, then the results speak to the *acceptance* of the null hypothesis. It is like saying, "Well, I had a great chance to reject a true null, given the power I just calculated, and I didn't reject it, so it is probably true." (An alternative use would be to say, "Well my study didn't really have much power to start with, so don't hold it against me that I didn't reject the null. I'm sure it really is false even though I ran a poorly designed study that couldn't detect it.") This may sound pretty convincing, but as Hoenig and Heisey (2001) point out, there is a false premise here. It is not possible to fail to reject a null hypothesis and yet have high retrospective power. In fact, a result with p exactly at .05 will have a retrospective power of

Figure 15.6 Calculation of statistical power using G*Power

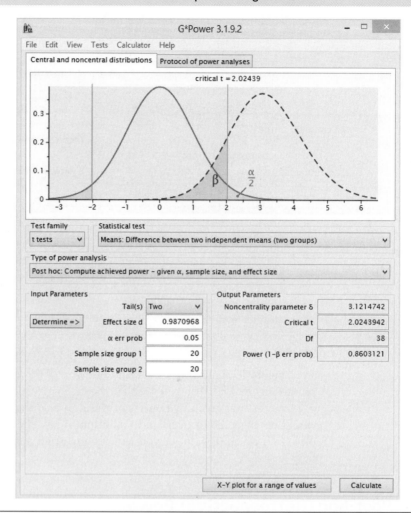

essentially .50,[6] and retrospective power will decrease for $p > .05$. It is impossible to even create an example of a study that just barely failed to reject the null hypothesis at $\alpha = .05$ but still has power of .80. Try it and you'll see that I'm right. If you play around with Lenth's Piface program you will see that he has a selection which will return "post hoc" power of 0.00 or 1.00 depending on whether your null was rejected in the experiment. He is just being cute and trying to make a point here—he doesn't like the concept of post-hoc power any more than I do.

But, I can't leave it at that. G*Power and some other programs also calculate what they refer to as post-hoc power, but they mean something more respectable. They refer to what we have done several times in this chapter, using results of a past experiment to calculate the power we might expect if we rerun that earlier study and use those parameter estimates as if they are the actual parameters. That is a perfectly good way to proceed. But don't try to use the concept to explain away the results you found in your current study.

---

[6]We saw this earlier where I calculated power for the replication of a modified version of the Aronson et al. study.

15.10 Summary

This chapter began by defining power as the probability of rejecting the null hypothesis when it is false. The discussion involved a review of Type I and Type II errors, which are the probability of falsely rejecting a true null hypothesis and the probability of failing to reject a false null hypothesis, respectively. The concept is most easily seen by overlaying graphs of the distribution of scores under H_0 and under some specified H_1. When you do this you can see the areas that are assigned to α, β, and power.

We discussed factors that affect the power of an experiment. The larger we set α, the more power we will have, but at a cost in Type I errors. The true difference between population means (for example $\mu_1 - \mu_0$ and $\mu_2 - \mu_2$), is perhaps that most important factor controlling power, which really means that big differences are easier to find than small ones. But the size of the population standard deviation and the size of the sample also play important roles. We combined these effects by defining Cohen's d as the difference in means divided by the sample standard deviation. We then went on to take the sample size into account, but only after defining d. When we include the sample size our result is called δ (delta) and is what we use when we go to power tables.

We examined one-sample tests, tests for two independent samples, and tests for related samples. The logic is basically the same for all three, and depends on the function that relates the sample size to d to produce δ.

With the two independent samples case we used two somewhat different approaches depending on whether or not we had equal sample sizes.

Perhaps the most important lesson to take away from this chapter is the fact that unless you are looking at quite large differences, a high level of power is going to require fairly large samples.

Key Terms

Power, *378*	Noncentrality parameter, *387*
Delta (δ), *387*	Harmonic mean, *392*

15.11 A Quick Review

    A. What do we mean by power?
       Ans: The probability of rejecting a false null hypothesis.

    B. List three things that affect the power of a test.
       Ans: The level of alpha, the size of the sample, and the size of the difference between means.

    C. Why does power depend upon sample size?
       Ans: As the sample size increases, with a fixed standard deviation, the standard error decreases and power therefore increases.

    D. As a rough estimate, a medium effect size would have $d =$ _____.
       Ans: 0.50

E.   What do we mean when we write "δ (delta) $= d[f(n)]$"?
Ans: We simply mean that delta is some function of n that we do not want to specify. The function will change under different experimental designs, but in the one-group case is.

$$\delta = \hat{d}\sqrt{n}$$

F.   Why do we have a special formula for calculating power in a two-group experiment with quite unequal sample sizes?
Ans: We want to give more weight to estimates based on larger samples.

G.   What name do we give to our adjusted sample size with unequal ns?
Ans: Effective sample size.

15.12 Exercises

15.1   Using G*Power or the Java program by Lenth (2011) referred to earlier, calculate power for the Adams et al. (1996) data in Table 14.2 on homophobia.

15.2   What is your subjective probability that the New York Yankees will win next year's World Series? What does that have to do with power?

15.3   In Section 12.3 we looked at a set of data on whether children who are stressed from their parents' divorce tend to tell us what they think we want to hear, rather than what they really feel. For those data the test on H_0 was not significant, even though the sample size was 36. Suppose that the experimenters had, in fact, actually estimated the mean and standard deviation of the population of stressed children exactly.

a)   What is the effect size in question?
b)   What is the value of δ for a sample size of 36?
c)   What is the power of the test?

15.4   Diagram the situation described in Exercise 15.3 along the lines of Figure 15.2.

15.5   In Exercise 15.3 what sample sizes would be needed to raise power to 0.70, 0.80, and 0.90?

15.6   Following on from Exercise 15.3, suppose that my colleagues were tired of having children tell them what they think we want to hear and gave them a heart-to-heart talk on the necessity of accurate reporting. Suppose that this reduced their population mean Lie score from 4.39 to 2.75, again with a standard deviation of 2.61. If we have 36 children for this analysis, what is the power of finding significantly fewer distortions in these children's reports than in the general population? The population of normal children still has a population mean of 3.87.

15.7   Diagram the situation described in Exercise 15.6 along the lines of Figure 15.2.

15.8   How many subjects would we need in Exercise 15.6 to have power = .80?

15.9   A neuroscience laboratory run by a friend of mine studied avoidance behavior in rabbits for many years and published numerous papers on the topic. It is clear from this research that, for animals that have not received any experimental treatment, the mean response latency on a particular task is 5.8 seconds with a standard deviation of two seconds (based on a very large number of rabbits). Now another investigator wants to create lesions in certain areas of the amygdala and demonstrate poorer avoidance conditioning in those animals. (The amygdala is associated with emotion, and if you reduce an emotional response you would be expected to reduce avoidance behavior.) She expects latencies to decrease by about one second (i.e., rabbits will repeat the punished response sooner), and she plans to run a one-sample t test (with H_0: $\mu_0 = 5.8$).

a)   How many subjects does she need in order to have at least a 50:50 chance of success?
b)   How many subjects does she need in order to have at least an 80:20 chance of success?

15.10   Suppose the investigator referred to in Exercise 15.9 decided that instead of running one group and comparing it against $\mu_0 = 5.8$, she would run two groups (one with and one without lesions). She would still expect the same degree of difference, however.

   a)   How many subjects does she now need (overall) if she is to have power equal 0.60?
   b)   How many subjects does she now need (overall) if she is to have power equal 0.90?

15.11   As it turns out, a research assistant has just finished running the experiment described in Exercise 15.10 without having carried out any power calculations. He tried to run 20 subjects in each group, but he accidentally tipped over a rack of cages and had to void five subjects in the experimental group. What is the power of this experiment?

15.12   Assume that I have just conducted a study comparing cognitive development of low birth weight (premature) and normal birth weight babies at one year of age. Using a score of my own devising, I found the sample means of the two groups to be 25 and 30, respectively, with a pooled standard deviation (s_p) of 8. There were 20 subjects in each group. If we assume that the true means and standard deviations have been estimated exactly, what was the *a priori* probability (the probability before the experiment was conducted) that this study would find a significant difference?

15.13   Let's modify Exercise 15.12 to have sample means of 25 and 28, with a pooled standard deviation of 8 and sample sizes of 20 and 20.

   a)   What is the *a priori* power of this experiment?
   b)   Run the *t* test on the data.
   c)   What, if anything, does the answer to (a) have to say about the answer to (b)?

15.14   Diagram the answer to Exercise 15.13.

15.15   Two graduate students have recently completed their dissertations. Each used a *t* test for two independent groups. One found a barely significant *t* using 10 subjects per group. The other found a barely significant *t* using 45 subjects per group. Which result impresses you more?

15.16   Make up a simple two-group example to demonstrate that for a total of 30 subjects, power increases as the sample sizes become more nearly equal.

15.17   A beleaguered PhD candidate has the impression that he must find significant results if he wants to defend his dissertation successfully. He wants to show a difference in social awareness, as measured by his own scale, between a normal group of students and a group of ex-delinquents. He has a problem, however. He has data to suggest that the normal group has a true mean equal to 38, and he has 50 of those subjects. For the other group he has access either to 100 college students who have been classed as delinquent in the past or to 25 high-school dropouts with a history of delinquency. He suspects that the scores of the college group come from a population with a mean of approximately 35, whereas the scores of the dropout group come from a population with a mean of approximately 30. He can use only one of these groups—which should it be?

15.18   Generate a table analogous to Table 15.2 for power equal to 0.80, with $\alpha = .01$, two-tailed.

15.19   Generate a table analogous to Table 15.2 for power equal to 0.60, with $\alpha = .05$, two-tailed.

15.20   Assume we want to test a null hypothesis about a single mean at $\alpha = .05$, one-tailed. Further assume that all necessary assumptions are met. Is there ever a case in which we are more likely to reject a true H_0 than we are to reject H_0 if it is false? (In other words, can power ever be less than α?)

15.21   If $\sigma = 15$, $n = 25$, and we are testing $H_0: \mu = 100$ versus $H_1: \mu > 100$, what value of the mean under H_1 would result in power being equal to the probability of a Type II error? (*Hint*: This is most easily solved by sketching the two distributions. Which areas are you trying to equate?)

15.22   Calculate the power of the anorexia experiment in Section 14.1, assuming that the parameters have been estimated correctly.

15.23 Use G*Power or Piface (Lenth's program) to calculate the power of the comparison of Thematic Apperception T scores from the parents of schizophrenic and normal subjects in Exercise 14.8.

15.24 Why would we ever want to calculate power after an experiment has been run, as we just did in Exercises 15.22 and 15.23?

15.25 The Web page for this chapter's R code includes code that will calculate power. Use that software to replicate the results you found in previous exercises.

## CHAPTER 16

One-Way Analysis of Variance

CONCEPTS THAT YOU WILL NEED TO REMEMBER FROM PREVIOUS CHAPTERS

Degrees of freedom *(df)*:	The number of independent pieces of information remaining after estimating one or more parameters
F statistic:	A test statistic, like *t*, that can be used to compare sample means
Effect size $(\hat{d})$:	A measure intended to express the size of a treatment effect in terms that are meaningful to the reader
Pooled variance estimate:	The weighted average of two sample variances
Sampling distribution:	The distribution of a statistic, such as the mean over repeated sampling
Heterogeneity of variance:	The situation when sample variance estimates are substantially unequal

We are about to begin three chapters related to the analysis of variance. We will start by asking what it is and what it does, and then we will look at why it would be called an analysis of *variance* when it actually compares means. The computations are quite simple, and after looking at the logic of the process we will briefly cover the calculations. We will move to the case of groups with different sample sizes and see how to incorporate unequal sized samples. This is a bit more complicated, but certainly not difficult. Once we have covered the basic analysis, we will move to procedures that will allow us to compare individual groups with one another. But even if differences are significant, they are not always important, so we will look at different measures of effect size. Finally, we will see how we can run the analysis using *R* and SPSS.

The **analysis of variance (ANOVA)** currently enjoys the status of being probably the most used statistical technique in psychological research, with multiple regression running a close second. The popularity and usefulness of this technique can be attributed to two facts. First, the analysis of variance, like *t*, deals with differences between sample means, but unlike *t*, it has no restriction on the number of means. Instead of asking merely whether two means differ, we can ask whether two, three, four, five, or *k* means differ. Second, the analysis of variance allows us to deal with two or more independent variables simultaneously, asking not only about the individual effects of each variable separately but also about the interacting effects of two or more variables.

403

This chapter will be concerned with the underlying logic of the analysis of variance and the procedures for the analysis of the results of experiments that employ only one independent variable. In addition, we will deal with a few related topics that are most easily understood in the context of a one-variable analysis (**one-way ANOVA**). Subsequent chapters will deal with the analysis of experiments that involve two or more independent variables and with designs in which repeated measurements are made on each participant.

16.1 The General Approach

Many features of the analysis of variance can be best illustrated by a simple example, so we will begin with a study by Giancola and Corman (2007). They were interested in studying the effects of a distracting task on aggressive behavior of subjects who had consumed a significant amount of alcohol. It is well known that alcohol often leads to aggressive behavior, but why should this be? Giancola and Corman began by assuming that alcohol facilitated aggression by focusing attention on more salient provocative cues rather than on less salient inhibitory ones. They reasoned that if they presented their subjects with a distracting task, attention would be focused on the task rather than on provocative cues, thus limiting aggression. However they also reasoned that if the task became too complex, its distracting effects would disappear and aggression would take over. (In fact, if the task is too complex that might generate confusion and frustration, which could in turn lead to aggression.)

Giancola and Corman asked their subjects to consume alcohol in an amount that raised their average blood alcohol level to about .10%. (That level would qualify drivers in most, if not all, states as driving while intoxicated.) Subjects then participated in a task that required them to remember the order in which squares in a 3 × 3 matrix were illuminated. The attentional demands of the task were varied by manipulating the number of squares that subjects had to keep in memory. Subjects played against a fictitious opponent who either delivered mild shocks to the subject or received mild shocks from the subject, dependent on supposed task performance. (In fact, there was no opponent, and the shocks that the subjects received had nothing to do with their performance.) The dependent variable (aggression) was based on the severity and duration of shocks that subjects delivered to opponents when they had the opportunity. (There was a control condition that did not consume alcohol, but we will ignore that condition for this example. There were no differences due to task difficulty in that condition.)

There were five groups in this study, varying in task difficulty. Subjects had to remember the pattern of either 0, 2, 4, 6, or 8 squares, and the groups were denoted as D0, D2, D4, D6, and D8. This notation refers to the number of squares in the distracting task the person had to remember. There were 12 subjects in each group, and the data, along with the means and standard deviations, are given in Table 16.1. (The data are based on the means and standard deviations reported in the original study.)

Table 16.1	Level of Shock Administered as a Function of Task Difficulty					
	D0	D2	D4	D6	D8	Total
	1.28	−1.18	−0.41	−0.85	2.01	
	1.35	0.15	−1.25	0.14	0.40	
	3.31	1.36	−1.33	−1.38	2.34	
	3.06	2.61	−0.47	1.28	−1.80	
	2.59	0.66	−0.60	1.85	5.00	
	3.25	1.32	−1.72	−0.59	2.27	
	2.98	0.73	−1.74	−1.30	6.47	
	1.53	−1.06	−0.77	0.38	2.94	
	−2.68	0.24	−0.41	−0.35	0.47	
	2.64	0.27	−1.20	2.29	3.22	
	1.26	0.72	−0.31	−0.25	0.01	
	1.06	2.28	−0.74	0.51	−0.66	
Mean	1.802	0.675	−0.912	0.544	1.889	0.800
Std. Dev.	1.656	1.140	0.515	1.180	2.370	1.800
Var.	2.741	1.299	0.265	1.394	5.616	3.168

The Null Hypothesis

As we know, Giancola and Corman were interested in testing the *research* hypothesis that the level of aggression varies with the level of distraction afforded by the recall task. Support for such a hypothesis would come from rejection of the standard *null* hypothesis

$$H_0: \mu_1 = \mu_2 = \mu_3 = \mu_4 = \mu_5$$

The null hypothesis could be false in a number of ways (e.g., all means could be different from each other, the first two could be equal to each other but different from the last three, and so on), but for now we are going to be concerned only with whether the null hypothesis is completely true or is false. This is frequently referred to as the omnibus null hypothesis. The alternative hypothesis will be the hypothesis that *at least* one mean is different from the others. The five hypothetical populations of aggression scores are illustrated in Figure 16.1. The placement of these populations from left to right is not intended to suggest that one population mean is necessarily larger than the population mean to its left. At this point I am saying nothing about the relative magnitude of the population means.

Figure 16.1 Graphical representation of populations of recall scores

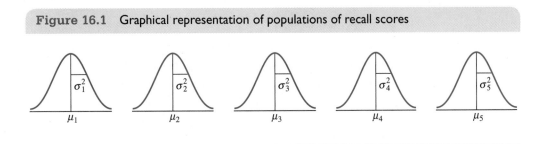

The analysis of variance is a technique for using differences between sample means to draw inferences about the presence or absence of differences between population means. Later in this chapter we will deal with the problem of whether only some of the means are equal. At this point I suspect that many of you would be convinced that the complete, or omnibus, null hypothesis cannot reasonably be true. (Do you really expect that people who have very minimal distraction will perform like people with a moderate degree of distraction?) But we start with the null hypothesis and then move on.

The Population

One of the difficulties people frequently encounter in the study of statistics concerns the meaning of the word *population*. As mentioned in Chapter 1, a population is a collection of *numbers*, not a collection of rats or people or anything else. Strictly speaking, we are not trying to say that a population of people who learned a list under one condition is the same population as the population of people who learned under a different condition—obviously they are not. Rather, we want to be able to say that a population of *scores* obtained under one condition has a mean greater than or less than the mean of a population of scores obtained under another condition. This may appear to be a rather trivial point, but it isn't. If you were to compare recall scores of people of different ages, for example, the populations of people certainly would differ in a variety of ways. However, it is not obvious beforehand that the recall scores will be different between the populations.

The Assumption of Normality

For reasons dealing with our final test of significance, we will make the assumption that aggression scores in each population are normally distributed around the population mean (μ_j). This is no more than the assumption that the observations in Figure 16.1 are normally distributed. We made this same assumption for the independent groups t test, but in that case there were only two populations. As with t, the assumption of normality deals primarily with the normality of the sampling distribution of the mean rather than the distribution of individual observations. Moreover, even substantial departures from normality may, under certain conditions, have remarkably little influence on the final result.

The Assumption of Homogeneity of Variance

A second major assumption that we will make is that each population of scores has the same variance, specifically

$$\sigma_1^2 = \sigma_2^2 = \sigma_3^2 = \sigma_4^2 = \sigma_5^2 = \sigma_e^2$$

Here the notation σ_e^2 indicates the common value held by the five variances. The subscript e is an abbreviation for *error*, because this variance is error variance, that is, variance unrelated to any group differences.[1] As you will see later, under certain

---

[1] In terms of the discussion in Chapter 10, this is error variance in the sense that it is variability that cannot be predicted from group membership, because people in the same group (population) obviously don't differ on the grouping variable.

conditions this assumption also can be relaxed without doing too much damage to the final result. In other words, the analysis of variance is robust with respect to violations of the assumptions of normality and homogeneity of variance.

The Assumption of Independence of Observations

Our third important assumption is that the observations are all independent of one another. For any two observations in an experimental treatment, we assume that knowing how one observation stands relative to the treatment (or population) mean tells us nothing about the other observation. (This assumption would be violated if, for example, participants cheated and copied off their neighbors or overheard each other's answers.) This assumption is one of the important reasons why participants are usually randomly assigned to groups whenever possible. Violation of the independence assumption can have serious consequences for an analysis.

A review of assumptions

For the analysis of variance we have three assumptions. We assume that each of the populations from which we sample are normally distributed, no matter how else they may differ. We assume that those populations all have the same variance, even if their means are different, and we assume that the observations are independent. For example, the fact that you scored above the mean has nothing to say about whether I will score above or below the mean.

16.2 | **The Logic of the Analysis of Variance**

The logic underlying the analysis of variance is not complicated—once you understand it, the rest of the discussion will make considerably more sense. (I don't expect that every student will have the logic down pat after reading this section once, but you should get the general idea. I recommend coming back to this section once again after you have read the whole chapter, and then probably coming back to it again the next day.) In this section I will simplify the presentation slightly by assuming that all groups have the same number of observations, though that is not a requirement of the analysis of variance. Consider for a moment the effect of our three major assumptions: normality, homogeneity of variance, and the independence of observations. By making the first two of these assumptions, we have said that the five populations represented in Figure 16.1 have the same shape and the same dispersion. As a result the only way left for them to differ is in terms of their means.

We will begin by making no assumption about H_0—it may be true or false. For any one treatment, the variance of the 10 scores in that group would be an estimate of the variance of the population from which the scores were drawn. Because we have assumed that all populations have the same variance, it is also one estimate of the common population variance (σ_e^2). If you prefer, you can think of

$$\sigma_1^2 \doteq s_1^2 \qquad \sigma_2^2 \doteq s_2^2 \qquad \ldots \qquad \sigma_5^2 \doteq s_5^2$$

where $\doteq$ is read "is estimated by." Because of our homogeneity assumption, all of these are estimates of σ_e^2. For the sake of increased reliability, if $n_1 = n_2 = \ldots = n_5 = n$, we can pool the five estimates by taking their mean. Therefore

$$\hat{\sigma}_e^2 = \bar{s}_j^2 = \frac{s_1^2 + s_2^2 + s_3^2 + s_4^2 + s_5^2}{5}$$

This is our best estimate of σ_e^2. Pooling of variances is exactly equivalent to what we did when we pooled variances in the t test (although here we have more than two variances). This average value of the five sample variances (s_j^2) is one estimate of the population variance (σ_e^2) and is what we will later refer to as $\mathbf{MS}_{\text{within}}$ or $\mathbf{MS}_{\text{error}}$ (read "mean square within" or "mean square error"). It is important to note that this estimate does *not* depend on the truth or falsity of H_0, because s_j^2 is calculated on each sample separately. For the data from the Giancola and Corman study, our pooled estimate of σ_e^2 will be

$$s_j^2 = (3.33 + 4.54 + 6.22 + 20.27 + 14.00)/5 = 9.67$$

Now let us assume that H_0 *is true*. If that is the case, then the five samples of 10 cases can be thought of as five independent samples from the same population. So we can examine the variance of their *means* to obtain another estimate of σ_e^2. Remember from earlier discussions that means are not as variable as observations. (Why should this be?) In fact, the Central Limit Theorem states that the variance of *means* drawn from the same population equals the variance of the population divided by the sample size. If H_0 is true, the sample means have been drawn from the same population (or identical populations, which amounts to the same thing), and therefore

$$\frac{\sigma_e^2}{n} \doteq s_{\bar{X}}^2$$

where n is the size of each sample. Here all samples will have the same size. We can reverse the usual order of things and, instead of estimating the variance of means from the variance of the population, we can estimate the variance of the population(s) from the variance of the sample means $(s_{\bar{X}}^2)$. If we simply clear fractions in the previous formula, we have

$$\sigma_e^2 \doteq n s_{\bar{X}}^2$$

This term is commonly known as $\mathbf{MS}_{\text{between groups}}$ or more simply $\mathbf{MS}_{\text{groups}}$ or $\mathbf{MS}_{\text{treatment}}$. In the previous section we had the case of the common population variance being estimated by the individual sample variances. Now we have a case where the common population variance is estimated by the variance of means—so long as the null hypothesis is true. So we have two different ways of estimating the same thing, but only if the null hypothesis is true. If the null is false, the variance of the means will overestimate the common population variance.

These few steps can be illustrated easily for five equal-sized groups in Figure 16.2. This figure emphasizes that the average of the sample variances is MS_{error} and the variance of the sample means *multiplied by the sample size* is MS_{group}.

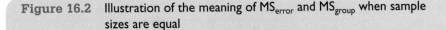

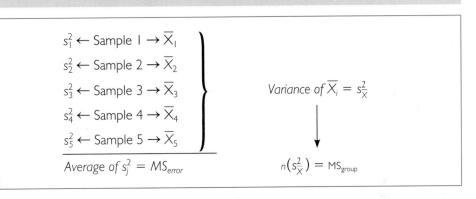

Figure 16.2   Illustration of the meaning of MS_{error} and MS_{group} when sample sizes are equal

We now have two estimates of the population variance (σ_e^2). One of these estimates, MS_{error}, is independent of the truth or falsity of H_0. It is *always* an estimate of the population variance. The other, MS_{group}, is an estimate of σ_e^2 *only as long as H_0 is true* (only as long as the conditions assumed by the Central Limit Theorem are met, namely that the samples are drawn from one population). Otherwise, MS_{group} would estimate the variability of different population means in addition to σ_e^2. If the two estimates (MS_{error} and MS_{group}) are roughly in agreement, we will have support for the truth of H_0; and if they disagree substantially, we will have support for the falsity of H_0. I can illustrate the logic just described by way of two very simple examples that have been deliberately constructed to represent more or less ideal results under the conditions H_0 true and H_0 false. Never in practice will data be as neat and tidy as in these examples.

EXAMPLE: The Case of a True H_0

Assume that we have an experiment involving three groups. As we saw earlier, when H_0 is true, $\mu_1 = \mu_2 = \mu_3$, and any samples drawn from these three populations can be thought of as coming from just one population. In the first example three samples of $n = 9$ have been chosen to resemble data that might be drawn from the same normally distributed population with a mean of 5 and a variance of 10. For example, these data might represent the number of information-seeking comments uttered by nine participants in each of three groups prior to the onset of a socialization-training experiment. Because the experiment has not yet begun, we hope not to find group differences. The data are presented in Table 16.2 for the $k = 3$ groups. From this table we can see that the average variance in each group is 9.250, a respectable estimate of $\sigma_e^2 = 10$. The variance of the group means is 1.000, and because we know H_0 to be true,

$$s_{\overline{X}}^2 \doteq \frac{\sigma_e^2}{n}$$

$$\sigma_e^2 \doteq ns_{\overline{X}}^2 = 9(1.000) = 9$$

This is our value for MS_{group}. This value is also reasonably in agreement with σ_e^2 and with our other estimate based on the variability within treatments. Because these two estimates agree, we would conclude that we have little reason to doubt the truth of H_0. Put another way, the three sample means do not vary more than we would expect if H_0 were true.

Table 16.2 Representative Data for the Case in Which H_0 Is True

Group 1	Group 2	Group 3
3	1	5
6	4	2
9	7	8
6	4	8
3	1	2
12	10	8
6	4	5
3	1	2
9	7	8
$\overline{X} = 6.3333$	4.3333	5.3333
$s_j^2 = 10.0000$	10.0000	7.7500

Grand mean $(\overline{X}_{gm}) = 5.3333$

$$s_{\overline{X}}^2 = \frac{\Sigma(\overline{X}_j - \overline{X}_{gm})^2}{k - 1} = 1.000$$

$$\bar{s}_j^2 = \frac{10.00 + 10.00 + 7.75}{3} = 9.250$$

$$MS_{error} = \bar{s}_j^2 = 9.25$$

$$MS_{group} = ns_{\overline{X}}^2 = 9(1.000) = 9$$

EXAMPLE: The Case of a False H_0

Next, consider an example in which I know H_0 to be false because I made it false. The data in Table 16.3 have been obtained by adding or subtracting constants to or from the data in Table 16.2. These data might represent the number of information-seeking comments uttered by people in three different groups at the *end* of our socialization-training sessions. We now have data that might have been produced by sampling from three different normally distributed populations, all with variance equal to 10. However, Group 1 scores might have come from a population with $\mu = 8$, whereas scores for Groups 2 and 3 might have come from a population, or populations, with $\mu = 4$. This represents a substantial departure from H_0, which stated that all population means were equal to each other.

In Table 16.3 you will note that the variance within each treatment remains unchanged, because adding or subtracting a constant has no effect on the variance within groups. This illustrates the earlier statement that the variance within groups (MS_{error}) is independent of the truth or falsity of the null hypothesis. The variance among the group means, however, has increased substantially, reflecting the differences among the population means. In this case the estimate of σ_e^2 based on sample means is $ns_{\overline{X}}^2 = 9(6.333) = 57$, a value that is way out of line with the estimate of 9.25 given by the variance within groups (MS_{error}). The most logical conclusion would be that $ns_{\overline{X}}^2$ is not estimating merely population variance (σ_e^2), but is estimating

Table 16.3	Representative Data for the Case in Which H_0 Is False	
Group 1	Group 2	Group 3
5	0	5
8	3	2
11	6	8
8	3	8
5	0	2
14	9	8
8	3	5
5	0	2
11	6	8
$\overline{X} = 8.3333$	3.3333	5.3333
$s_j^2 = 10.0000$	10.0000	7.7500

Grand mean $(\overline{X}_{gm}) = 5.6667$

$$s_{\overline{X}}^2 = \frac{\Sigma(\overline{X}_j - \overline{X}_{gm})^2}{k - 1} = 6.333$$

$$\overline{s}_j^2 = \frac{10.00 + 10.00 + 7.75}{3} = 9.250$$

$$MS_{error} = \overline{s}_j^2 = 9.25$$

$$MS_{group} = ns_{\overline{X}}^2 = 9(6.333) = 57$$

σ_e^2 *plus* the variance of the population means themselves. In other words, the scores differ not only because of random error but also because we have been successful in getting some of our participants to ask more information-seeking questions than others.

Summary of the Logic of the Analysis of Variance

From the preceding discussion we can state the logic of the analysis of variance concisely. To test H_0 we calculate two estimates of the population variance; one (MS_{error}) is independent of the truth or falsity of H_0, while the other (MS_{group}) is dependent on H_0. If the two are in approximate agreement, we have no reason to reject H_0. The means differ only to the extent that the sampling distribution of the mean leads us to expect when H_0 is true. If MS_{group} is much larger than MS_{error}, we conclude that underlying differences in treatment means must have contributed to the second estimate, inflating it and causing it to differ from the first. We therefore reject H_0. This illustrates how an analysis of *variance* allows us to draw inferences about *means*.

> **If we are testing means, why is it called the analysis of variance?**
>
> That is a very good question, and it often arises. But think about it for a moment. We are actually calculating two different variances, or, more precisely, variance estimates. The estimate based on variances within groups (MS_{within}) doesn't have anything to do with means. But the estimate based on the variance of means obviously does have something to do with sample means. If our two estimates are roughly equal, we conclude that the means don't differ. If our two estimates are quite unequal, we conclude that the means do differ. So although we are calculating estimates of variances, one of those estimates directly reflects differences among means, which is what we want to study.

16.3 | Calculations for the Analysis of Variance

Calculations in the analysis of variance are not difficult, but most people will solve problems using computer software. (Standard spreadsheet programs can usually be used for this purpose if you don't have something like R or SPSS.) So why should I present you with a set of formulae that you may never be called upon to use? I think that the answer lies in the fact that the calculations actually show you quite explicitly what you are doing. Each formula is expressed in terms of definitional, not computational, formulae, and each brings out the logic of what I have expressed above. I am omitting the more traditional computational formulae because I don't think that they would teach you much of anything.

Sums of Squares

In the analysis of variance most of our computations deal with the **sum of squares**, which, in this context, is merely the sum of squared deviations about the mean $\Sigma(X - \overline{X}_{gm})^2$ or some multiple of that. The advantage of sums of squares and the reason that we begin by calculating them is that they can be added and subtracted, whereas mean squares usually cannot. We will take the total sum of squares (SS_{total}) and partition or decompose it into that part that is due to variation between groups (SS_{group}) and that part that is due to variation within groups (SS_{error}). The additive nature of sums of squares makes this possible.

The Calculations

The data for Giancola and Corman's study have been reproduced in Table 16.4, with the resulting computations, which we will discuss in detail. I also show, in Figure 16.3, a plot of the data with standard error bars around each mean. (Notice that I specified that I have used the standard errors for the bars, rather than standard deviations or confidence limits. This is very important because writers often leave you wondering what the bars reflect.)

In part (a) of Table 16.4 you can see the data, the individual observations (X_{ij}), the individual group means $(\overline{X}_j)$, and the grand mean $(\overline{X}_{gm})$. We will use the notation $(\overline{X}_j)$ to represent the mean of the jth group throughout our discussion of the analysis of variance. In analyses in which there is more than one independent variable (factor), $\overline{X}_j$ can be extended to $\overline{X}_{row\,i}$ and $\overline{X}_{col\,j}$ without any loss of clarity. I use the notation X_{ij} to represent individual observations—the score of the ith person in group j.

Table 16.4   Level of Shock Administered as a Function of Task Difficulty

	D0	D2	D4	D6	D8	Total
	1.28	−1.18	−0.41	−0.45	2.01	
	1.35	0.15	−1.25	0.54	0.40	
	3.31	1.36	−1.33	−0.98	2.34	
	3.06	2.61	−0.47	1.68	−1.80	
	2.59	0.66	−0.60	2.25	5.00	
	3.25	1.32	−1.72	−0.19	2.27	
	2.98	0.73	−1.74	−0.90	6.47	
	1.53	−1.06	−0.77	0.78	2.94	
	−2.68	0.24	−0.41	0.05	0.47	
	2.64	0.27	−1.20	2.69	3.22	
	1.26	0.72	−0.31	0.15	0.01	
	1.06	2.28	−0.74	0.91	−0.66	
Mean	1.802	0.675	−0.912	0.544	1.889	0.800
Std. Dev.	1.656	1.140	0.515	1.180	2.370	1.800
Var.	2.741	1.299	0.265	1.394	5.616	3.168

Figure 16.3   Plot of Giancola and Corman's data on aggression as a function of level of distraction. Bars represent ±1 standard error.

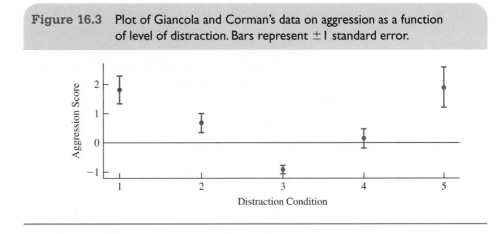

> **Table 16.5** Computations for Data in Table 16.4
>
> $SS_{total} = \Sigma(X_{ij} - \overline{X}_{gm})^2 = (1.28 - 0.80)^2 + (1.35 - 0.80)^2 + \cdots + (-0.66 - 0.80)^2$
>
> $\qquad = 186.918$
>
> $SS_{treat} = n\Sigma(\overline{X}_j - \overline{X}_{gm})^2 = 12((1.80 - 0.80)^2 + (0.675 - 0.80)^2 + \cdots + (1.889 - 0.80)^2)$
>
> $\qquad = 12(5.205) = 62.460$
>
> $SS_{error} = SS_{total} - SS_{treat} = 186.918 - 62.640 = 124.485$
>
> **Summary Table**
>
> | Source | df | SS | MS | F | p |
> |---|---|---|---|---|---|
> | Treatments | 4 | 62.460 | 15.615 | 6.90 | .000 |
> | Error | 55 | 124.458 | 2.263 | | |
> | Total | 59 | 186.918 | | | |

Table 16.5 shows the calculations required to perform a one-way analysis of variance. These calculations require some elaboration.

The means and the variances are exactly those found by Giancola and Corman, but because the data points are fictitious, there is little to be gained by examining the distribution of observations within individual groups—the data were actually drawn from normally distributed populations and then rounded to two decimal places. With real data it is important to examine these distributions first to make sure they are not seriously skewed, bimodal, or, even more important, skewed in different directions. Even for this example it is useful to examine the individual group variances as a check on the assumption of homogeneity of variance. Although the variances are not as similar as we might like (the variance for D8 is considerably larger than the variances of the other groups), they do not appear to be so drastically different as to cause concern. As you will see later, the analysis of variance is robust against violations of assumptions, especially when we have the same number of observations in each group.

SS_{TOTAL} The **SS$_{total}$** (read "total sum of squares") represents the sum of the squared deviations of all the observations from the grand mean, regardless of which treatment produced them.

$$SS_{total} = \Sigma(X_{ij} - \overline{X}_{gm})^2$$

SS_{GROUP} The **SS$_{group}$** term is a measure of differences due to groups (in effect, differences between group means) and is directly related to the variance of the group means. To calculate SSgroup, we simply square and then sum the deviations of the group means from the grand mean. This is then multiplied by the sample size to produce our second estimate of the population variance (σ_e^2) if H_0 is true:

$$SS_{group} = n\Sigma(\overline{X}_j - \overline{X}_{gm})^2$$

(Remember, in the analysis of variance we use lowercase n to stand for the number of observations in a group and uppercase N to stand for the total number of observations.)

SS_{ERROR} In practice SS_{error} is usually obtained by subtraction. Because it can be shown easily that

$$SS_{total} = SS_{group} + SS_{error}$$

then it must also be true that

$$\boxed{SS_{error} = SS_{total} - SS_{group}}$$

This calculation of SS_{error} is the procedure presented in Table 16.5.

The Summary Table

At the bottom of Table 16.5 is the summary table for the analysis of variance. It is called a summary table for the rather obvious reason that it summarizes a series of calculations, making it possible to tell at a glance what the data have to offer.

SOURCES OF VARIATION   The first column of the summary table, labeled "Source," contains the sources of variation—I use the word "variation" as being synonymous with the phrase "sum of squares." (I can't call it a variance because it is not. But it is a measure of variability, so I use the wishy-washy term "variation.") As you can see from the table, there are three sources of variation: the total variation, the variation due to groups (variation between group means), and the variation due to error (variation within groups). These sources reflect the fact that we have partitioned the total sum of squares into two portions, one portion representing variability between the several groups and the other representing variability within the individual groups.

DEGREES OF FREEDOM   The degrees of freedom column shows the allocation of the degrees of freedom between the two sources of variation. The calculation of df is probably the easiest part of our task. The total degrees of freedom (df_{total}) are always $N - 1$, where N is the total number of observations. The degrees of freedom between groups (df_{group}) always equal $k - 1$, where k is the number of groups. The degrees of freedom for error (df_{error}) are most easily thought of as what is left over, although they can be calculated more directly as the sum of the degrees of freedom within each treatment. In our example $df_{total} = 50 - 1 = 49$. Of these 49 df, four are associated with differences among the five groups, and the remaining 45 are associated with variability within groups.

A useful way to think of degrees of freedom is in terms of the number of deviations we have squared. SS_{total} is the sum of N squared deviations around one point—the grand mean. The fact that we have taken deviations around this one (estimated) point has cost us 1 df, leaving $N - 1$ df. SS_{group} is the sum of deviations of the k group means around one point (again the grand mean), and again we have lost 1 df in estimating this point, leaving us with $k - 1$ df. SS_{error} represents k sets of n deviations about one point (the relevant group mean), losing us 1 df for each group and leaving $k(n - 1) = N - k$ df.

SUMS OF SQUARES   There is little to be said about the column labeled SS. It simply contains the sums of squares obtained in part (b) of the table.

MEAN SQUARES   The column of mean squares contains the two estimates of σ_e^2. These values are obtained by dividing the sums of squares by their corresponding df. Thus $62.640/4 = 15.615$ and $124.458/55 = 2.263$. We typically do not calculate a MS_{total}, because we have no use for it. If we did, it would represent the variance of all N observations.

Although it is true that mean squares are variances, it is important to keep in mind what these terms are variances of. Thus MS_{error} is the (average) variance of the observations within each treatment. However, MS_{group} is not the variance of group means, but rather the variance of those means corrected by n to produce our second estimate of the population variance (σ_e^2); in other words it is an estimate of σ_e^2 based on the variance of group means.

THE F STATISTIC   The last column, headed F, is the most important one in terms of testing the null hypothesis. The **F statistic** is obtained by dividing MS_{group} by MS_{error}. As noted earlier, MS_{error} is an estimate of the population variance (σ_e^2). MS_{group} is also an estimate of population variance (σ_e^2) if H_0 is true, but not if H_0 is false. If H_0 is true, then both MS_{error} and MS_{group} are estimating the same thing, and as such they should be approximately equal. If that is the case, the ratio of one to the other will be approximately 1.00, give or take a fair amount for sampling error. All we have to do is compute the ratio and determine whether it is close enough to 1 to indicate support for the null hypothesis.

When we spoke about a t test, it was pretty clear what a one-tailed test meant. It meant that we would reject H_0 if the difference between the means was in the predicted direction. It also meant that we would reject H_0 if the value of t was of the correct sign, in both cases assuming that the difference (or t) was large enough. When we have multiple groups, however, the use of the label "one-tailed" is less clear. In one sense, we are running a one-tailed test because we will reject H_0 only if the computed value of F is significantly greater than 1.0. On the other hand, we could obtain a large value of F for a variety of reasons. In the analysis of variance we reject H_0 when the means are sufficiently far apart, without regard to which one(s) is (are) larger than others. Thus we have a one-tailed test of a non-directional H_0.

The question remains as to how much larger than 1.0 our value of F needs to be before we decide that there are differences among the population means and thus reject H_0.[2] The answer to this lies in the fact that if H_0 is true, the ratio

$$F = \frac{MS_{group}}{MS_{error}}$$

is distributed as the F distribution in Table E.3 in the Appendices. It will have df_{group} and df_{error} degrees of freedom. A portion of Table E.3 is reproduced as Table 16.5. Because the

---

[2]If H_0 is true, the expected value of F is not exactly 1.00, but it is so close that it doesn't make any difference to the point being made here. Also, there is usually no meaning to be assigned to an F very much less than 1.0, though we might be puzzled if our group means were much *closer* to each other than we would expect.

Table 16.5   Abbreviated Version of Table E.3, Critical Values of the F Distribution Where $\alpha = .05$

df denom.	Degrees of Freedom for Numerator									
	1	2	3	4	5	6	7	8	9	10
1	161.4	199.5	215.8	224.8	230.0	233.8	236.5	238.6	240.1	242.1
2	18.51	19.00	19.16	19.25	19.30	19.33	19.35	19.37	19.38	19.40
3	10.13	9.55	9.28	9.12	9.01	8.94	8.89	8.85	8.81	8.79
4	7.71	6.94	6.59	6.39	6.26	6.16	6.09	6.04	6.00	5.96
5	6.61	5.79	5.41	5.19	5.05	4.95	4.88	4.82	4.77	4.74
6	5.99	5.14	4.76	4.53	4.39	4.28	4.21	4.15	4.10	4.06
7	5.59	4.74	4.35	4.12	3.97	3.87	3.79	3.73	3.68	3.64
8	5.32	4.46	4.07	3.84	3.69	3.58	3.50	3.44	3.39	3.35
9	5.12	4.26	3.86	3.63	3.48	3.37	3.29	3.23	3.18	3.14
10	4.96	4.10	3.71	3.48	3.33	3.22	3.14	3.07	3.02	2.98
11	4.84	3.98	3.59	3.36	3.20	3.09	3.01	2.95	2.90	2.85
12	4.75	3.89	3.49	3.26	3.11	3.00	2.91	2.85	2.80	2.75
13	4.67	3.81	3.41	3.18	3.03	2.92	2.83	2.77	2.71	2.67
14	4.60	3.74	3.34	3.11	2.96	2.85	2.76	2.70	2.65	2.60
15	4.54	3.68	3.29	3.06	2.90	2.79	2.71	2.64	2.59	2.54
16	4.49	3.63	3.24	3.01	2.85	2.74	2.66	2.59	2.54	2.49
17	4.45	3.59	3.20	2.96	2.81	2.70	2.61	2.55	2.49	2.45
18	4.41	3.55	3.16	2.93	2.77	2.66	2.58	2.51	2.46	2.41
19	4.38	3.52	3.13	2.90	2.74	2.63	2.54	2.48	2.42	2.38
20	4.35	3.49	3.10	2.87	2.71	2.60	2.51	2.45	2.39	2.35
22	4.30	3.44	3.05	2.82	2.66	2.55	2.46	2.40	2.34	2.30
24	4.26	3.40	3.01	2.78	2.62	2.51	2.42	2.36	2.30	2.25
26	4.23	3.37	2.98	2.74	2.59	2.47	2.39	2.32	2.27	2.22
28	4.20	3.34	2.95	2.71	2.56	2.45	2.36	2.29	2.24	2.19
30	4.17	3.32	2.92	2.69	2.53	2.42	2.33	2.27	2.21	2.16
40	4.08	3.23	2.84	2.61	2.45	2.34	2.25	2.18	2.12	2.08
50	4.03	3.18	2.79	2.56	2.40	2.29	2.20	2.13	2.07	2.03
60	4.00	3.15	2.76	2.53	2.37	2.25	2.17	2.10	2.04	1.99
120	3.92	3.07	2.68	2.45	2.29	2.18	2.09	2.02	1.96	1.91
200	3.89	3.04	2.65	2.42	2.26	2.14	2.06	1.98	1.93	1.88
500	3.86	3.01	2.62	2.39	2.23	2.12	2.03	1.96	1.90	1.85
1000	3.85	3.01	2.61	2.38	2.22	2.11	2.02	1.95	1.89	1.84

shape of the F distribution, and thus areas under it, depend on the degrees of freedom for the two mean squares, this table looks somewhat different from other tables you have seen. In this case we select the column that corresponds to the degrees of freedom for the mean square in the numerator of F (i.e., $k - 1$) and the row that corresponds to the degrees of freedom for the mean square in the denominator (i.e., $k(n - 1)$). The intersection of the row and the column gives us the critical value of F at the level of α shown at the top of the table. (You can find a calculator for F probabilities online at

http://www.statpages.org/pdfs.html.)

At

http://www.danielsoper.com/statcalc3/

you can find a program that will calculate F for you from means, variances, and sample sizes, and another that will calculate the probability value. For R the code is simply **prob<-1 – pf(q = 6.90, df1 = 4, df2 = 55) = .00014.**

To use the table of the critical values of the F distribution, we first have to select the particular table corresponding to our level of α (in Table E.3 $\alpha = .05$, and in Table E.4 $\alpha = .01$). Then, because we have 4 df for the numerator (MS_{group}) and 55 df for the denominator (MS_{error}), we move down the fourth column to the row labeled 55. But there is no row that corresponds to exactly 55 df, so we will average the entries for the rows corresponding to 50 df and 60 df. The intersections of those rows and column 4 contain the entries 2.56 and 2.53, the average of which rounds to 2.54. This is the critical value of F. We would expect to exceed an F of 2.54 only 5% of the time if H_0 were true. Because our obtained $F = 6.90$ exceeds $F_{.05} = 2.54$, we will reject H_0 and conclude that the groups were sampled from populations with different means. The actual probability for F on 4 and 55 $df = .0001$. Had we chosen to work at $\alpha = .01$, Table E.4 in the Appendices shows that $F_{.01}(4,55) = 3.68$, and we would still reject H_0. (Notice the format for reporting the significance level and the degrees of freedom for F in the preceding sentence. That is the standard way of writing them.) Using R we can find the critical value at alpha = .05 by typing (**Fcrit<- qf(p = 0.95, df1 = 4, df2 = 55)**), though it makes more sense to enter F and request its probability, as shown in the earlier piece of R code. ($p = .00014$.)

Conclusions

On the basis of a significant value of F, we have rejected the null hypothesis that the treatment means in the population are equal. Strictly speaking, this conclusion indicates that at least one of the population means is different from at least one other mean, but we don't know exactly which means are different from which other means. We will pursue this question shortly with a different example. It is evident from the plot in Figure 16.3, however, that increasing the level of distraction, *up to a point*, decreases the level of aggressive behavior. But increasing distraction beyond that point is counterproductive. This tells at least something about the role of alcohol in aggressive behavior.

The minimalist approach to calculations

Every time I revise this book I move further and further away from calculations. I don't do that because I hate calculations (I actually like them), but because they often get in the way of understanding. So let's see just how far I can go with a minimum of formulae.

Early in the chapter I said that we take two variance estimates. One is the variance within each of the groups or conditions, and the other is the variance of the means, multiplied by the sample size.

1. From Table 16.4 I see that the variances of the five groups are 2.741, 1.299, 0.265, 1.394, and 5.616. The average is 2.263 and this is the MS_{error}. Each of those five variances had 11df, so we have a total of $5 \times 11 = 55df$ for MS_{error}.

2. We know that MS_{group} is the variance of the sample means multiplied by the size of each group. The means are 1.802, 0.675, −0.912, 0.544, 1.889, and the variance of those five means is 1.300. If we multiply that by 12 we have 15.61, which is MS_{group}. We computed the variance of five means, so we have $5 - 1 = 4 \, df$ for MS_{group}.

3. Now to get the F we divide MS_{group} by $MS_{error} = 15.61/2.263$, which is on 4 and 55 df.

Three or four calculations, depending on how you count.

Writing up the Results

Reporting results for an analysis of variance is somewhat more complicated than reporting the results of a t test. This is because we not only want to indicate whether the overall F is significant, but we probably also want to make statements about the differences between individual means. We won't discuss tests on individual means until later in the chapter, so this example will be incomplete. An abbreviated version of a statement about the results follows.

In a test of the hypothesis that alcohol tends to focus attention on more provocative, rather than less salient inhibitory cues, Giancola & Corman examined the effect of distracting stimuli on aggressive behavior. The groups differed in the level of distraction provided by the competing task. After consuming alcohol subjects were repeatedly presented with 0, 2, 4, 6, or 8 stimuli appearing in the cells of a 3×3 matrix, and were asked to report the order in which the stimuli appeared. They were told that if they responded faster than a fictitious opponent, they would then deliver shocks to that opponent. If they were slower, the opponent would deliver shocks to them. When participants were presented with no distracting stimuli, they administered shocks that were higher in intensity and longer in duration than if they experienced low levels of distraction. In addition, as the distraction task increased in complexity beyond a medium level, the decline in shock intensity and duration reversed itself. A one-way analysis of variance revealed that there were significant differences among the means of the five groups ($F(4,55) = 6.90$, $p = .000$). Visual inspection of the group means revealed that the level of administered shock decreased with increasing distraction but then increased again as the distraction task became more complex, as predicted by the theory. (Note: The behavior of a control condition that did not consume alcohol showed no significant differences with distraction level, although those data are not reported here.) (A good summary of results should go well beyond saying "the difference was significant." We will at least want to say something about the size of the effect, which we will come to shortly.)

The analysis of variance using R

You might expect that to run an analysis of variance we would use a function called "anova()," but except under special libraries the function is actually called "lm()," which stands for "linear model."

The code for *R* follows. (We will see the use of SPSS later in the chapter.) But let me first say a word about calculation. I have shown you how to calculate the analysis of variance by hand, and I think that those formulae are reasonably clear. You can see the logic of what you are doing. But computer software almost always makes the same calculations in a different way. If "Condition" is a factor—if it is a discrete variable with few levels—we can solve the problem by using multiple regression to predict the dependent variable from the Condition variable. In other words we use a standard multiple regression solution where the independent variable is a factor, or multiple factors when we come to the next chapter. I mention this because the code for *R* will look different from what you would expect. However it will give you exactly the same answer that you would obtain with the formulae that we have been using.

R code

```
data<- read.table("https://www.uvm.edu/~dhowell/fundamentals9/DataFiles/
  Tab16-1.dat", header = TRUE)
attach(data)
group<- factor(group)              # IMPORTANT! Specify that group is a factor
model1<- lm(dv ~ group)            # Calculate the linear model of dv predicted from group
anova(model1)
library(car)
Anova(model1)
_____

anova(model1)
- - - - - - -
Analysis of Variance Table


Response: dv
          Df      Sum Sq     Mean Sq     F value     Pr(>F)
group     4       62.46      15.6151     6.9005      0.0001415 ***
Residuals 55 124.46  2.2629


Signif. codes:  0 '***' 0.001 '**' 0.01 '*' 0.05 '.' 0.1 ' ' 1


library(car)
Anova(model1)
- - - - - - - - -
Response: dv
          Df      Sum Sq     Mean Sq     F value     Pr(>F)
group     4       62.46      15.6151     6.9005      0.0001415 ***
Residuals 55       24.46     2.2629

Signif. codes:  0 '***' 0.001 '**' 0.01 '*' 0.05 '.' 0.1 ' ' 1
```

From the code and output, you will see that I have solved the same problem twice, with identical answers. The first time I used the "anova" function in the base *R* package to obtain the output, whereas the second time I loaded the "car" library written by John Fox and then used the "Anova" command (note the uppercase "A"). For the one-way analysis of variance they will give the same answer. However when we come to factorial analyses in the next chapter, that will not always be true. I just wanted to introduce the use of the "car" library here. Notice that the answers are identical to those that we calculated by hand. Notice also that both solutions have a line called "Signif. Codes." These are used to indicate something about the significance level of the effect, where a single * means that the *F* was significant at $p < .05$, two stars means that it was significant at $p < .01$ and so on. Most software uses this approach, although many statisticians argue that it can sometimes be misleading and adds nothing to our understanding.

16.4 | Unequal Sample Sizes

Most experiments are designed originally with the idea of having the same number of observations in each treatment. Frequently, however, things do not work out that way. Participants in an experiment are often remarkably unreliable, and many fail to arrive for testing or are eliminated for failure to follow instructions. My favorite example is a report in the literature that I found as a graduate student. Sgro and Weinstock (1963) reported that an experimental animal was eliminated from the study for repeatedly biting the experimenter. Moreover, in studies conducted on intact groups, such as school classes, groups are nearly always unequal in size for reasons that, again, have nothing to do with the experiment.

If the sample sizes are not equal, the analysis discussed earlier is not appropriate without modification. For the case of one independent variable, however, this modification is relatively minor.

For the case of equal sample sizes we have defined

$$SS_{group} = n\Sigma(\overline{X}_j - \overline{X}_{gm})^2$$

where *n* is the number of observations in each group. We were able to multiply the sum of the squared deviations by *n* because *n* was common to all treatments. If the sample sizes differ, however, and we define n_j as the number of participants in the *j*th treatment ($\Sigma n_j = N$), we can rewrite the equation as

$$SS_{group} = \Sigma n_j(\overline{X}_j - \overline{X}_{gm})^2$$

which, when all n_j are equal, reduces to the original form. All we are doing here is multiplying each squared deviation by its own sample size as we go along.

AN ADDITIONAL
EXAMPLE:
Adaptation to
Maternal Roles

An additional example of a one-way analysis of variance will illustrate the treatment of unequal sample sizes. In a study of the development of low birth weight (LBW) infants (Nurcombe, Howell, Rauh, Teti, Ruoff, and Brennan, 1984), three groups of newborn infants differed in terms of birth weight and whether their mothers had participated in a training program about the special needs of low birth weight infants. The mothers were then interviewed when the infants were six months old.

There were three groups in the experiment—an LBW-Experimental group, an LBW-Control group, and a Full-Term-Control group. The two control groups received no special training, and so serve as reference points against which to compare the performance of the trained (experimental) group. The LBW-Experimental group received the intervention program, and we hoped to show that those mothers would adapt to their new role as well as mothers of full-term infants. On the other hand, we expected that mothers of low birth weight infants who did not receive the intervention program would have some trouble adapting. (Being a parent of a low birth weight baby is not an easy task, especially for the first few months. For rather

Table 16.6 Adaptation to Maternal Role in Three Groups of Mothers (Low Scores Are Associated with Better Adaptation)

(a) Data

Group 1 LBW-Experimental			Group 2 LBW-Control			Group 3 Full-Term		
24	10	16	21	17	13	12	12	12
13	11	15	19	18	25	25	17	20
29	13	12	10	18	16	14	18	14
12	19	16	24	13	18	16	18	14
14	11	12	17	21	11	13	18	12
11	11	12	25	27	16	10	15	20
12	27	22	16	29	11	13	13	12
13	13	16	26	14	21	11	15	17
13	13	17	19	17	13	20	13	15
13	14					23	13	11
						16	10	13
						20	12	11
						11		

n_j	29		27		37		$N = 93$
Mean$_j$	14.97		18.33		14.84		$\overline{X}_{gm} = 15.89$

(b) Calculations

$$SS_{total} = \Sigma(X_{ij} - \overline{X}_{gm})^2$$
$$= (24 - 15.89)^2 + (13 - 15.89)^2 + \cdots + (11 - 15.89)^2$$
$$= 2072.925$$
$$SS_{group} = \Sigma n_j(\overline{X}_j - \overline{X}_{gm})^2$$
$$= 29(14.97 - 15.89)^{22} + 27(18.33 - 15.89)^{22} + 37(14.84 - 15.89)^2$$
$$= 226.932$$
$$SS_{error} = SS_{total} - SS_{group} = 2072.925 - 226.932 = 1845.993$$

(c) Summary Table

Source	df	SS	MS	F	p
Group	2	226.932	113.466	5.53	.005
Error	90	1845.993	20.511		
Total	92	2072.925			

dramatic results from tracking these children for nine years, see Achenbach, Howell, C., Aoki, and Rauh, 1993.)

The actual data from this study are presented in part (a) of Table 16.6. Part (b) of the table shows the calculations for the analysis of variance, and part (c) contains the summary table. The dependent variable is the score on a maternal adaptation scale. Notice that the calculations are carried out just as they would be for the case of equal sample sizes except that for SS_{group} each value of $(\overline{X}_j - \overline{X}_{gm})^2$ is multiplied by the corresponding sample size as we progress.

From the summary table we can see that the obtained F value is 5.53 and that it is based on 2 and 90 degrees of freedom. From Table E.3 in the Appendices we have, through interpolation, $F_{.05}(2,90) = 3.11$. (Here 90 degrees of freedom is halfway between 60 and 120 df, so we won't be far off if we take as our critical value the value halfway between 3.15 and 3.07, which is 3.11.) Because $5.53 > 3.11$, we will reject H_0 and conclude that not all the scores were drawn from populations with equal means. (Using the software we have previously used, the exact probability is .005.) In fact, it looks as if the first and third groups are about equal, whereas the second (the LBW-Control group) has a higher mean (poorer adaptation). However, the F tells us only that we can reject $H_0: \mu_1 = \mu_2 = \mu_3$. It does *not* tell us which groups are different from which other groups. To draw those kinds of conclusions, we will need to use special techniques known as multiple comparison procedures.

16.5   Multiple Comparison Procedures

When we run an analysis of variance and obtain a significant F value, we have shown simply that the overall null hypothesis is false. We do not know which of a number of possible alternative hypotheses (e.g., $H_1: \mu_1 \neq \mu_2 \neq \mu_3 \neq \mu_4 \neq \mu_5$; $H_2: \mu_1 \neq \mu_2 = \mu_3 = \mu_4 = \mu_5$) is true. **Multiple comparison techniques** allow us to investigate hypotheses that involve means of individual groups or sets of groups. For example, we might be interested in whether Group 1 is different from Group 2 or whether the combination of Groups 1 and 2 is different from Group 3.

One of the major problems with making comparisons among groups is that unrestricted use of these comparisons can lead to an excessively high probability of a Type I error. For example, if we have 10 groups in which the *complete* null hypothesis is true ($H_0: \mu_1 = \mu_2 = \mu_3 = \dots = \mu_{10}$), t tests between all pairs of means will lead to making *at least* one Type I error 57.8% of the time. In other words, the experimenter who thinks she is working at the $\alpha = .05$ level of significance is actually working at $\alpha = .578$. Figure 16.4 shows how the probability of making at least one Type I error increases as we increase the number of *independent* t tests we make between pairs of means. While it is nice to find significant differences, it is not nice to find ones that are not really there. Psychologists have enough trouble explaining all the real differences that we find without having to worry about spurious differences as well. We need to find some way to make the comparisons we need but keep the probability of incorrect rejections of H_0 under control.

In an attempt to control the likelihood of Type I errors, statisticians have developed a large number of procedures for comparing individual means. (For a discussion of many of these techniques see Howell, 2012.) Fortunately, two relatively simple techniques provide reasonable control of the probability of Type I errors and are

Figure 16.4   Probability of a Type I error as a function of the number of pairwise comparisons where $\alpha = .05$ for any one comparison

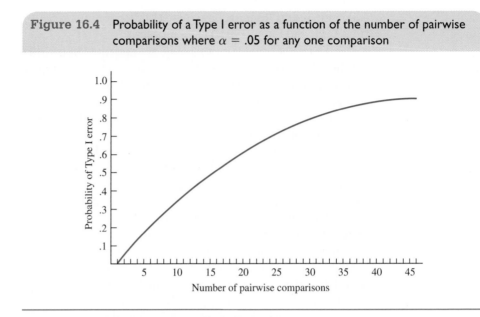

applicable to most multiple comparison problems you are likely to encounter. Aside from those techniques, there is a very useful rule of thumb. "Don't run a comparison unless it is actually meaningful for what you are doing. Never run a comparison just because you can."

Fisher's Least Significant Difference Test

The first procedure is often referred to as the **protected t** or **Fisher's least significant difference (LSD) test**. (If your instructor looks a little pale at the suggestion to use Fisher's least significant difference test, just wait a bit and I'll defend that suggestion. It is not as outrageous as people may think.) Fisher's procedure is one of the most liberal multiple comparison tests we have.

The procedures for using a protected t, or LSD test, are really very simple. *The first requirement for a protected t is that the F for the overall analysis of variance must be significant.* (This is the only multiple comparison test for which we impose that requirement.) If the F was not significant, no comparisons between pairs of means are allowed. You simply declare that there are no group differences and stop right there. On the other hand, if the overall F is significant, you can proceed to make any (or all) pairwise comparisons between individual means by the use of a modified t test. The modification is simply to run an appropriate t test but replace the pooled variance estimate (s_p^2) in the standard t formula with MS_{error} from the overall analysis of variance. (We generally do not make this replacement if the variances of the groups are very different from one another.) This replacement is a perfectly reasonable thing to do. Because MS_{error} is defined as the average of the variances within each group, if there were only two groups in the experiment, the MS_{error} from the analysis of variance would be the same as the s_p^2 from the two-sample t test on those group means. In comparing among several groups we use MS_{error} instead of s_p^2 because it is based on variability within *all* the groups rather than within just the two groups we are comparing at the moment. As such it is presumably a better estimate of σ_e^2. Along with the use of this error term comes the advantage that the resulting t will have df_{error} degrees of freedom rather than just the $n_1 + n_2 - 2$ degrees of freedom it would have had otherwise with a t test.

When we replace s_p^2 with MS_{error}, the formula for t becomes

$$t = \frac{\overline{X}_i - \overline{X}_j}{\sqrt{\dfrac{MS_{error}}{n_i} + \dfrac{MS_{error}}{n_j}}} = \frac{\overline{X}_i - \overline{X}_j}{\sqrt{MS_{error}\left(\dfrac{1}{n_i} + \dfrac{1}{n_j}\right)}}$$

To illustrate the use of the protected t, let's take the data on maternal adaptation from the previous example. In that case we did find a significant overall F, which will allow us to look further in our analysis. Given the nature of that study, we would be interested in asking two questions:

1. Are there differences between the mean of mothers in the LBW-Control group and the mean of mothers in the Full-Term group?

2. Are there differences between the mean of mothers in the LBW-Control group and the mean of mothers in the LBW-Experimental group?

The first question asks whether mothers of low birth weight infants have more difficulty adapting than do mothers of full-term infants. Neither group received intervention, so intervention is not a confounding variable. The second question asks whether the intervention program makes a difference in adaptation for mothers of low birth weight infants. Here both groups are composed of mothers of low birth weight infants, so birth weight is not a confounding variable. Note that it makes little sense to compare the LBW-Experimental group with the Full-Term group because if we did find a difference we could not tell whether it was due to intervention effects or to birth weight effects. In such a comparison, intervention and birth weight are confounded.

This last paragraph leads me to an important point that is often overlooked. Even with only three groups, there are several pairwise comparisons that you could make. One of them (LBW-Experimental versus Full-Term Control) does not make much sense, while the two that I am making do make sense. In choosing what to test, it is important that you make a sensible choice. Making silly comparisons is all too easy, and leads to a poor analysis. Think about what you are asking before you ask it.

The results on maternal adaptation are presented in Table 16.7, in which the obtained values of t are -2.77 and 3.04 for the two comparisons. We will use a two-tailed test at $\alpha = .05$, and we have 90 degrees of freedom for our error term. From Table E.3 we find that $t_{.05}(90) = \pm 1.99$ by interpolation. Thus for both comparisons we can reject the null hypothesis, because both values of the obtained t (t_{obt}) are more extreme (further from 0) than ± 1.99. We will therefore conclude that there is a difference in adaptation between mothers of low birth weight babies and those of full-term infants, with the full-term mothers showing better adaptation. We will also conclude that the intervention program is effective for mothers of low birth weight infants. The exact probabilities are .007 and .003, respectively.

Table 16.7 Fisher's Least Significant Difference Test Applied to Low Birth Weight and Full-Term Groups

	Group 1 LBW-Experimental	Group 2 LBW-Control	Group 3 Full-Term
$\overline{X}_j =$	14.97	18.33	14.84
$n_j =$	29	27	37
$MS_{error} =$	20.511		
$df_{error} =$	90		

(a) μ_1 versus μ_2

$$t = \frac{\overline{X}_1 - \overline{X}_2}{\sqrt{MS_{error}\left(\dfrac{1}{n_1} + \dfrac{1}{n_2}\right)}}$$

$$= \frac{14.97 - 18.33}{\sqrt{20.511\left(\dfrac{1}{29} + \dfrac{1}{27}\right)}}$$

$$= \frac{-3.36}{\sqrt{1.467}} = \frac{-3.36}{1.21} = -2.77$$

(b) μ_2 versus μ_3

$$t = \frac{\overline{X}_2 - \overline{X}_3}{\sqrt{MS_{error}\left(\dfrac{1}{n_2} + \dfrac{1}{n_3}\right)}}$$

$$= \frac{18.33 - 14.84}{\sqrt{20.511\left(\dfrac{1}{27} + \dfrac{1}{37}\right)}}$$

$$= \frac{3.49}{\sqrt{1.314}} = \frac{3.49}{1.15} = 3.04$$

You might ask why we call this particular multiple comparison procedure a "protected t." Or you may have heard somewhere that it is a bad idea to run all sorts of t tests between pairs of means, and it often is. This is a good place to address both of these concerns at the same time.

One of the primary considerations in running a set of multiple comparisons is to hold down the probability of making *at least* one Type I error. In other words, if we ran an analysis of variance and then three comparisons, we would want to ensure that the probability that we have made a Type I error *anywhere*, either in the original F or in any of the three comparisons, is low. The probability of making such an error is called the **familywise error rate** because it deals with the probability that the *family* of comparisons contains *at least one* Type I error. When we are talking about the familywise error rate, making 10 Type I errors is treated as no worse than making one. (Or perhaps I should phrase that in reverse—making one Type I error is as bad as making 10.) If we just ran t tests between all pairs of means, the familywise error rate would become unacceptably high if there were many means to compare. We need to impose some conditions to prevent that from happening, which is what a protected t test does, in part, by the simple expedient of requiring that no tests may be run unless the overall F from the analysis of variance is significant. To see why this simple step works, consider the following examples.

Suppose we have only two means and *the null hypothesis is true*. The probability of making a Type I error would be the probability that the original F was significant by chance, which is .05. If that F was significant, we have already made our Type I error, and even if we went on and ran a t test, which is actually testing the same null hypothesis, we couldn't make the situation worse. If the F was not significant, we cannot run the protected t (Fisher's LSD) and so do not increase the error rate. Thus with two means the familywise error rate is .05.

Now suppose we have three means. First, assume that the complete null hypothesis is true—that is, suppose that $\mu_1 = \mu_2 = \mu_3$. We obtain the overall F. The probability of finding a significant difference (which would be a Type I error because H_0 is true) is .05, and if we reported a significant difference, that represents our first Type I error out of the "at least one" that the familywise error rate protects against. If the F is not significant, we stop right there and have no further chances of making a Type I error. In other words, when the *complete* null hypothesis is true, the probability of making *at least one* Type I error is limited by our rule to .05, which is what we want. Next, suppose that the complete null hypothesis is false and that one mean is different from the other two (e.g., $\mu_1 = \mu_2 \neq \mu_3$). Then, because the complete null hypothesis is not true, it is impossible to make a Type I error with our overall F test. If we have a significant F, which we would hope to be the case, we can go on and test, for example, each pair of means—Group 1 versus Group 2, Group 1 versus Group 3, and Group 2 versus Group 3. But there is only one of those tests for which the null hypothesis is true ($\mu_1 = \mu_2$), and therefore there is only one chance of making a Type I error. Here again the probability of at least one Type I error is only .05. Finally, suppose that all means are different from each other. Here we have no possibility of making a Type I error, because there is no true null hypothesis to declare false erroneously. From examination of these possibilities we can conclude that *with three means the familywise error rate is also at most* .05.

So we have seen that with either two or three groups, Fisher's LSD test guarantees that the probability of making at least one Type I error will not exceed .05. That's great—it is just what we want. But suppose we had four or five groups. In that case it is possible that there is more than one true null hypothesis. For example, Groups 1 and 2 could be equal and Groups 3 and 4 could be equal. If $\mu_1 = \mu_2$ and $\mu_3 = \mu_4$, you have two chances of making a Type I error, and the true familywise error rate is nearly .10. But I would submit that this is not an outrageous error rate, given four means, and I would not cringe at using such a test, although it is not my favorite. Now if you want to talk about 10 means, that's a different story, and anyone who would use Fisher's test with 10 groups is asking for trouble. This is the complaint that is often raised against Fisher, but it's not really fair. If you look through the psychological literature (and I suspect it's true for all the behavioral sciences), you'll have a hard time finding experiments with even four groups. (Well, Giancola and Corman (2007) did have five groups, but that is unusual.) Ten-group experiments are almost unheard of, so why reject a test on the grounds that it doesn't work well for experiments that we have no intention of running anyway? Simply demanding a significant overall F before running multiple comparisons (which is where the protection comes from) is surprisingly effective in controlling familywise error rates when we have only a few groups. That is the reason I have stressed the protected t in this chapter. It does a good job of controlling the familywise error rate if you have a relatively small number of groups while at the same time being a test that you can easily apply and that has a reasonable degree of power.

The requirement of a significant overall F

Don't allow yourself to be carried away by the idea that the overall F should be significant before you proceed with individual tests. Fisher's LSD test is the only major test that carries that restriction. In the next test we will discuss, and in many others, there is absolutely no requirement that the overall F be significant before you proceed. In fact, imposing such a requirement would needlessly make those procedures less powerful.

The Bonferroni Correction

A second procedure that is simple to apply and that is popular is known as the **Bonferroni correction**, after a mathematician of that name who discovered the inequality on which the procedure is based. (It is frequently called the "Bonferroni test", but I prefer the term "correction" because it represents a corrected form of p value.) The basic idea behind this procedure is that if you run several tests (say c tests), each at a significance level represented by α', the probability of at least one Type I error can never exceed $c\alpha'$. Thus, for example, if you ran five tests, each at $\alpha' = .05$, the familywise error rate would be at most $5(.05) = .25$. But that is too high an error rate to make anyone happy. However suppose that you ran each of those five tests at the $\alpha' = .01$. Then the maximum familywise error rate would be $5(.01) = .05$, which is certainly acceptable. To put this in a way that is slightly more useful to us, if you want the overall familywise error rate to be no more than .05, and you want to run three tests, then run each of them at $\alpha' = .05/3 = .0167$. To run these tests, you do exactly what you did in Fisher's LSD test, though you omit any requirement about the overall F, and you reject only if the probability for any one test is less than .0167. The only difference is that you change the significance level for each individual test from α to α/c, where c is the number of comparisons.

The original difficulty with this approach was that we didn't have tables of significance at, for example, the .0167 level. However, most people today use standard computer software to run statistical analyses, and every package I have seen presents both the t or F value, and its associated probability level. For example, if I used SPSS on the low birth weight data, using the same comparisons I used with Fisher's test, I have two choices. With clearly unequal variances, we just run a t test between Group 1 and Group 2, and between Group 2 and Group 3. This is less than ideal because such a test will not pool the variances across all three groups, but if the variances are different it doesn't make a lot of sense to pool them. If I did it anyway, I would get the results shown in the Table 16.8.

The following is an abbreviated analysis of the maternal adaptation data using the LSD test. To set it up in SPSS, select **Analyze/General Linear Model/Univariate** then assign the appropriate variables, and click on **Post Hoc tests**. Then select **LSD** as your test. (Yes, LSD and not Bonferroni.) BUT, be sure that you only consider the comparison of Group 1 with Group 2 and Group 2 with Group 3. For a significant difference, the probability given must be less than $.05/2 = .025$.

Table 16.8   SPSS Analysis of Maternal Adaptation Data

Univariate Analysis of Variance

[DataSet2] c:\Users\Dave\Dropbox\Webs\fundamentals9\DataFiles\Tab16-6.sav

Between-Subjects Factors

		N
GROUP	1	29
	2	27
	3	37

Test of Between-Subject Effects

Dependent Variable: ADAPT

Source	Type III Sum of Squares	df	Mean Square	F	Sig.
Corrected Model	226.932[a]	2	113.466	5.532	.005
Intercept	23513.095	1	23513.095	1146.364	.000
GROUP	226.932	2	113.466	5.532	.005
Error	1845.993	90	20.511		
Total	25562.000	93			
Corrected Total	2072.925	92			

[a]R Squared = .109 (Adjusted R Squared = .090)

Post Hoc Tests
GROUP

Multiple Comparisons

Dependent Variable: ADAPT

LSD

					95% Confidence Interval	
(I) GROUP	(J) GROUP	Mean Difference (I-j)	Std. Error	Sig.	Lower Bound	Upper Bound
1	2	−3.37*	1.211	.007	−5.77	−.96
	3	.13	1.123	.910	−2.10	2.36
2	1	3.37*	1.211	.007	.96	5.77
	3	3.50*	1.146	.003	1.22	5.77
3	1	−.13	1.123	.910	−2.36	2.10
	2	−3.50*	1.146	.003	−5.77	−1.22

Based on observed means.
The error term is mean Square(Error) = 20.511.

We want to run these tests with an overall familywise error rate of .05, which, with two tests, means that each must have a probability lower than $\alpha = .05/2 = .025$ to be declared significant. Notice that both of these t tests met that criterion, with $p = .015$ and .002, respectively. We have no interest in looking at the comparison of Groups 1 and 3, so we don't care what that result is.

All Bonferroni tests can be carried out this way—using the LSD procedure and only looking at specific comparisons. We simply decide how many tests we intend to run, divide the desired familywise error rate (usually $\alpha = .05$) by that number, and reject whenever the probability of our test statistic is less than our computed value. However, be careful if you are using software to analyze your results. As I said above, most software programs, including SPSS, will have an option for the Bonferroni test, but that is probably not what you want. The program will assume that you want to test all possible pairs of means, and therefore adjusts the probability values accordingly. So you will be seeing what, for you, are the wrong probabilities. Because there are sometimes many means, that approach can be very conservative. Instead, use the LSD test and simply look at only those comparisons that you really care about. And let me stress the fact that you cannot just look at the means, pick the biggest differences, and decide to test them. You will get chance differences. You should decide on the tests to run on the basis of theory or logical procedures. Cheating is not allowed.

If we wanted to do the same thing using R, the following code will do that for us.

```
data<- read.table("https://www.uvm.edu/~dhowell/fundamentals9/DataFiles/
Tab16-6.dat", header = TRUE)
attach(data)
group<- factor(group) # Specify that group is a factor
model1<- lm(adapt ~ group)
anova(model1)
pairwise.t.test(adapt, group, p.adj = "none", pool.sd = true) # "none"
gives us the LSD test
Analysis of Variance Table
Response: adapt
              Df      Sum Sq    Mean Sq    F value    Pr(>F)
group          2      226.93    113.466    5.532      0.005421 **
Residuals     90     1845.99     20.511


       Pairwise comparisons using t tests with pooled SD


data:   adapt and group
        1          2
2     0.0066       -
3     0.9098     0.0030


P value adjustment method: none
```

Notice that these results are the same ones that we found with SPSS, though the display is set up differently.

Other Multiple Comparison *Procedures*

Many other procedures have been developed for sorting out differences among groups. The interesting thing is that they are all based roughly on the same kinds of considerations that we have seen in Fisher's LSD and the Bonferroni procedures. They attempt to hold the familywise error rate to some maximum (usually .05), and they do this by taking into account the number of groups (or, more often, the number of pairwise comparisons among groups). The best known of these is the **Tukey procedure**.[3] I won't go into it here, because it relies on a slightly different test statistic than we are used to. However, I should note that it compares every mean with every other mean, and does so in a way that keeps the maximum familywise error rate at .05 (or some other percentage if you prefer). Every piece of statistical software that I know will produce a Tukey test on demand.

An Additional Comment

It is important to keep in mind that we run multiple comparison tests to get at important features of our data. We should be asking important questions, not just running tests to see what happens. The one complaint that I have about tests like Tukey's is that they compare everything with everything else, adjusting the probability values accordingly, even though most of those comparisons are not of any great interest. My advice would be simply to run the comparisons that are useful to you and that answer research-based questions. If the familywise error rate then goes up to $\alpha = .10$, so be it. That is not the end of the world. This advice is in line with several of the changes that have taken place in behavioral statistics over the last 30 years. There is a greater emphasis on finding and reporting differences that are meaningful and in a way that people can understand that meaning. That is quite different from a field of statistics that is built on a set of rigid rules.

16.6 | Violations of Assumptions

As we have seen, the analysis of variance is based on the assumptions of normality and homogeneity of variance. In practice, however, the analysis of variance is a robust statistical procedure, and the assumptions can frequently be violated with relatively minor effects.

In general, if the populations can be assumed to be either symmetric or at least similar in shape (e.g., all negatively skewed) and if the largest variance is no more than four or five times the smallest, the analysis of variance is most likely to be valid. (Some argue that it would be valid for even greater differences between the variances.) It is important to note, however, that serious heterogeneity of variance and unequal sample sizes do not mix. If you have reason to anticipate noticeably unequal variances, make every effort to keep your sample sizes as nearly equal as possible. This

---

[3]This is the same John Tukey that we have seen several times in this book. He contributed to just about everything in statistics. This test is often referred to as "Tukey's test."

is particularly true when you plan to run a series of multiple comparisons. You should also keep in mind that if your groups have markedly different variances, perhaps that is the important finding of the study, rather than just differences in means.

For those situations in which the assumptions underlying the analysis of variance are seriously violated, there are alternative procedures for handling the analysis. Some of these procedures involve transforming the data (e.g., converting X to log[X]) and then performing standard statistical tests on the transformed data. Other procedures involve using quite different tests, some of which are discussed later in this book. (Also see the discussion of the Behrens-Fisher problem and the use of trimmed means and Winsorized variances in Howell, 2012.)

16.7 | The Size of the Effects

Simply because we obtain a significant difference among our treatment means does not mean that the differences are large or important. There are many real differences that are trivial. No statistical test can tell us whether a difference, no matter how large, is of any practical importance to the rest of the world. However, there are procedures that give us some help in this direction.

Rosenthal (1994) made a distinction between **d-family** measures and **r-family** measures. The former are based on differences between means, while the latter are based on some sort of correlation between the dependent variable and the levels of the independent variable. I have avoided speaking about *r*-family measures until now, because when we have only two groups I don't think they add to our understanding. On the other hand, *d*-family measures (such as Cohen's *d*) are hard to interpret when you have multiple groups unless you restrict the measure to differences between two groups or two sets of groups. I will start with the *r*-family measures.

r-family (Correlational) Measures

One of the simplest measures of the **magnitude of effect** is η^2 (**eta squared**). While η^2 is a biased measure (in the sense that it tends to overestimate the value we would obtain if we were able to measure whole populations of scores), its calculation is so simple and it is so useful as a first approximation that it is worth discussing. In this book I will restrict the discussion of η^2, and ω^2 which follows, to measuring the effect among several groups. In any analysis of variance, SS_{total} tells us how much overall variability there is in the data. Some of that variability is due to the fact that different groups of participants are treated differently and have different scores as a result, and some of it is just due to random error—differences among people who are treated alike. The differences we care about are the differences among scores that can be attributed to our treatment, or group, effects, and they are measured by SS_{group}. If we form the ratio

$$\eta^2 = \frac{SS_{group}}{SS_{total}}$$

we can determine what percentage of the variability among observations can be attributed to group effects. For our maternal adaptation data

$$\eta^2 = \frac{SS_{group}}{SS_{total}} = \frac{226.932}{2072.925} = .11$$

Thus we can estimate that 11% of the variability in adaptation scores can be attributed to group membership. Although that might appear at first to be a small percentage, if you stop and think about the high level of variability among mothers you have known, explaining even 11% of it is a noteworthy accomplishment.

Although η^2 is a quick and easy measure to calculate, one you can estimate in your head when reading research reports, it is a biased statistic. It will tend to overestimate the true value in the population. A much less biased estimate is afforded by another statistic, ω^2 (**omega squared**). For the analysis of variance discussed in this chapter we can define

$$\omega^2 = \frac{SS_{group} - (k-1)MS_{error}}{SS_{total} + MS_{error}}$$

where k stands for the number of groups. For our example

$$\omega^2 = \frac{SS_{group} - (k-1)MS_{error}}{SS_{total} + MS_{error}} = \frac{226.932 - (3-1)20.511}{2072.925 + 20.511} = 0.089$$

This value is somewhat lower than the value we obtained for η^2. However, it still suggests that we are accounting for approximately 9% of the variability.

d-family Measures (Effect Size)

An alternative measure of the size of our effect that is generally more meaningful is the measure of effect size based on Cohen's d. We saw such effect size measures in earlier chapters, and the one that will be most useful to us here is the measure that we used when we had two independent groups. With two groups, we defined an estimate of d as

$$\hat{d} = \frac{\overline{X}_1 - \overline{X}_2}{s}$$

where s is the square root of the pooled variance estimate (or sometimes the standard deviation of a control group).

Although it would be possible to algebraically extend this idea to more than two groups, to obtain a measure of the multiple differences between groups, it is difficult to know how to interpret such a result. For most situations, it makes much more sense to restrict ourselves to two-group comparisons and to speak about the difference between specific groups or sets of groups, rather than to make a global statement about differences among all groups simultaneously.

The data on maternal adaptation for mothers with low birth weight infants provides an excellent example of what I mean. The group means are reproduced in the following table.

	LBW-Exp	LBW-Control	Full-Term	Overall
Means	14.966	18.333	14.838	15.892
MS_{error}				20.511

In an earlier analysis we showed that this difference among groups is statistically significant ($F(2.90) = 5.53$, $p = .005$). However, we should also tell our readers something about the magnitude of the differences under discussion, and that statement should be phrased in terms that have meaning to the reader. Here it makes sense to fall back on specific comparisons, just as we did earlier when we compared the LBW-Control and Full-Term groups, and again when we compared the two low birth weight groups (LBW-Control versus LBW-Exp). You should recall that both of those differences are significant when we compare them using the Bonferroni correction.

If the raw score units had particular meaning, which they might have if our dependent variable was something such as weight, IQ, age, or some other commonly understood variable, then it would make sense simply to report the difference in original units of measurement, preferably providing an estimate of the standard deviation as a frame of reference. However, our dependent variable is the score on a measure of maternal adaptation, and it would not be very informative to simply report that the two low birth weight groups differed by 3.367 points. Neither you nor I have any real sense of whether that is a large or a small difference. However, we could express the effect size measure as $\hat{d}$, often known as Cohen's $\hat{d}$, which is a standardized measure of the difference.

Neither the LBW-Control nor the Full-Term groups received any special training, so a difference between them would reflect a difference due to birth weight. In this case

$$\hat{d} = \frac{\overline{X}_{LBW-C} - \overline{X}_{FT}}{s} = \frac{18.333 - 14.838}{\sqrt{20.511}} = \frac{3.495}{4.523} = 0.77$$

Here we see that the two groups differ by 0.77 standard deviation, which is a sizeable difference. There clearly is a noticeable effect due to birth weight. (The standard deviation used here is simply the square root of MS_{error}, and is the average standard deviation within groups.)

If we compare the two low birth weight groups, we find

$$\hat{d} = \frac{\overline{X}_{LBW-C} - \overline{X}_{LBW-E}}{s} = \frac{18.333 - 14.966}{4.523} = \frac{3.367}{4.523} = 0.74$$

This is another large effect. So we can conclude that the LBW-Control condition scores about three-quarters of a standard deviation higher (worse adaptation) than either the full-term group or the LBW group that receives the intervention. These measures tell us that there are important effects in the results of this experiment.

16.8 Writing Up the Results

When I described how we would write up the results of Giancola and Corman's study of performance under the influence of alcohol, I had not yet covered multiple comparisons and effect size measures, and so was not able to include that in the write-up. But with the study by Nurcombe et al. (1984) on maternal adaptation with low birth weight infants we do have those results. An abbreviated version of how these data might be written up follows.

Nurcombe et al. (1984) studied the effects of an intervention program for the mothers of low birth weight infants. A group of 37 mothers of full-term infants served as a control. A second group of 27 mothers of low birth weight infants was also assessed, and differences between these two groups address the question of the effects of low birth weight on maternal adaptation. Finally, a third group of 29 mothers of low birth weight infants received an intervention program designed to make them more aware of the often over-looked behavioral signals their infants produced.

The overall analysis of variance showed that the groups exhibited significant differences in maternal adaptation (F (2,90) = 5.53, p = .005). Using ω^2 as a correlation-based measure of effect showed that differences among the groups accounted for 8.9% of the overall variability in the dependent variable. Individual group comparisons showed that the two low birth weight groups differed significantly ($t(90) = -2.77$, with the group receiving the intervention ($\overline{X} = 14.97$) scoring better than the low birth weight control group ($\overline{X} = 18.33$) on the measure of maternal adaptation. Cohen's $\hat{d}$ applied to this difference was 0.74, indicating that the intervention group's mean was nearly three-quarters of a standard deviation below (better) than the nonintervention mean. A comparison of the low birth weight control condition with the full-term control condition produced a significant difference ($t(90) = 3.04$, $p < .05$). In this case $\hat{d} = 0.77$, showing that giving birth to a low birth weight infant can result in maternal adaptation scores that are three-quarters of a standard deviation above (worse than) for mothers of full-term infants.

16.9 A Final Worked Example

The following example illustrates a one-way analysis of variance with unequal sample sizes. It also illustrates the use of the Bonferroni procedure.

What does marijuana do, and how does it do it? Aside from its better known effects, marijuana increases, or in some cases decreases, locomotor (moving around) behavior. The nucleus accumbens is a forebrain structure that has been shown to be involved in locomotor activity in rats. (It is also thought to control feelings of pleasure.) Administration of low doses of tetrahydrocannabinol (THC, the major active ingredient in marijuana) is known to increase locomotor activity, whereas high doses are known to lead to a decrease in activity. In an attempt to examine whether THC is acting within the nucleus accumbens to produce its effects on activity, Conti and Musty (1984) bilaterally injected either a placebo or 0.1, 0.5, 1, or 2 micrograms (μg) of THC directly into the nucleus accumbens of rats. The investigators recorded the *change* in the activity level of the animals after injection. It was expected that activity would increase more with smaller injections than with larger ones. The data in Table 16.9 represent the amount of change (decrease) in each animal.[4]

The data are plotted in Figure 16.5.

---

[4]Although THC is expected to *increase* activity, the dependent variable is measured as a *decrease* in overall activity because the animals were becoming acclimated to a new situation and were thus exploring less. Thus, rather than an increase in activity, we actually are looking for less of a decrease. It's confusing!

Table 16.9 Data from the Study by Conti and Musty (1984)

Placebo	0.1μg	0.5μg	1μg	2μg	Total
30	60	71	33	36	
27	42	50	78	27	
52	48	38	71	60	
38	52	59	58	51	
20	28	65	35	29	
26	93	58	35	34	
8	32	74	46	24	
41	46	67	32	17	
49	63	61		50	
49	44			53	
Σ 340	508	543	388	381	2160
Mean 34.00	50.80	60.33	48.50	38.1	
n 10	10	9	8	10	47

Figure 16.5 Mean activity levels in the study by Conti and Musty (1984)

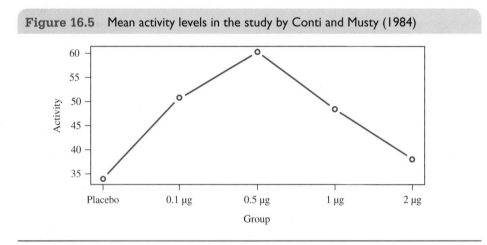

First we will set up the null hypothesis, which states that all of the samples were drawn from populations with the same mean. In other words, H_0: $\mu_1 = \mu_2 = \mu_3 = \mu_4 = \mu_5$. For consistency we will test this null hypothesis with a significance level of $\alpha = .05$.

Next we will run the overall analysis of variance, starting with the calculation of the sums of squares:

$$SS_{total} = \Sigma(X_{ij} - \overline{X}_{gm})^2 = (30 - 45.96)^2 + (27 - 45.96)^2 + \cdots + (53 - 45.96)^2$$

$$= 14{,}287.91$$

$$SS_{group} = \Sigma n_j(\overline{X}_j - \overline{X}_{gm})^2 = 10(34 - 45.96)^2 + \cdots + 10(38.10 - 45.96)^2$$

$$= 4193.41$$

$$SS_{error} = SS_{total} - SS_{group} = 14{,}287.91 - 4193.41 = 10{,}094.50$$

We can now put these terms into a summary table.

Source	df	SS	MS	F	p
Groups	4	4,193.41	1048.35	4.36	.005
Error	42	10,094.50	240.35		
Total	46	14,287.91			

We have 4 *df* for Groups and 42 *df* for Error. The probability of this result under the null hypothesis is $p = .005$, so we will reject the null hypothesis and conclude that there are differences in activity levels among the five drug groups, presumably reflecting differences due to the dosage of THC administered.

Comparisons of Individual Groups

The experimental hypothesis had predicted that the Placebo group would show smaller increases (or greater decreases) in activity than the medium dose group. Therefore, we might want to compare the Placebo group with the 0.5-μg group. It would also be interesting to compare the 2 μg group with the 0.5 μg group to show that a medium dose had a greater effect than a large dose. We will make both these comparisons using the Bonferroni correction. As already discussed, we will perform this analysis by first running *t* tests between the groups, just as we did with the protected *t*. However, this time I will not pool the variances as an illustration of that analysis.

Comparison of Groups 3 and 1 (0.5 μg versus Placebo):

$$t = \frac{\overline{X}_3 - \overline{X}_1}{\sqrt{MS_{error}\left(\dfrac{1}{n_3} + \dfrac{1}{n_1}\right)}}$$

$$= \frac{60.33 - 34.00}{\sqrt{240.35\left(\dfrac{1}{9} + \dfrac{1}{10}\right)}}$$

$$= \frac{26.33}{\sqrt{240.35(0.2111)}} = \frac{26.33}{\sqrt{50.74}} = \frac{26.33}{7.12} = 3.70$$

Comparison of Groups 3 and 5 (0.5 μg versus 2μg):

$$t = \frac{\overline{X}_3 - \overline{X}_5}{\sqrt{MS_{error}\left(\dfrac{1}{n_3} + \dfrac{1}{n_5}\right)}}$$

$$= \frac{60.33 - 38.10}{\sqrt{240.35\left(\dfrac{1}{9} + \dfrac{1}{10}\right)}}$$

$$= \frac{22.23}{\sqrt{240.35(0.211)}} = \frac{22.23}{\sqrt{50.74}} = \frac{22.23}{7.12} = 3.12$$

Because we ran only two tests, we can evaluate those t values against t at $\alpha = .05/2 = .025$. We could use a program such as the one at http://statpages.org/pdfs.html to calculate the actual probabilities. (They are .0018 and .0065, respectively). Both of these differences are clearly significant. The experimental hypothesis had predicted that a moderate dose of THC would produce greater increases (or smaller decreases) in activity than either no THC or a large dose of THC. These hypotheses are both supported by this experiment.

Magnitude of Effect and Effect Size Measures

As we did previously, we can assess the magnitude of effect of the treatment variable with either η^2 or ω^2, or we can calculate $\hat{d}$ for specific group comparisons.

$$\eta^2 = \frac{SS_{group}}{SS_{total}} = \frac{4{,}193.41}{14{,}287.91} = .29$$

$$\omega^2 = \frac{SS_{group} - (k-1)MS_{error}}{SS_{total} + MS_{error}} = \frac{4{,}193.41 - (5-1)240.35}{14{,}287.91 + 240.35} = .22$$

These two measures show that group effects account for about a quarter of the variation in this study.

Effect size measures of differences between specific groups are another way of examining the magnitude of the effect of THC. Conti and Musty (1984) had expected that medium doses of THC would lead to the highest level of activity, so it makes sense to report on the difference between the means of the Control group (which received no THC) and the 0.5-μg group (which received a moderate dose).

$$\hat{d} = \frac{\overline{X}_{.5\,\mu g} - \overline{X}_{Control}}{s} = \frac{60.33 - 34.00}{\sqrt{240.35}} = \frac{26.33}{15.503} = 1.70$$

This is a very substantial difference (nearly one and three-quarters standard deviations), reflecting the very important influence that THC has on activity in rats.[5]

16.10 Seeing Statistics

In Section 16.3 we discussed the F distribution, and saw that it depended on (1) the number of groups (df for groups), (2) the number of observations within groups (df for the error term), and (3) the magnitude of F (the larger the F, the smaller the associated probability). An applet to illustrate these characteristics is available on the website labeled F probabilities. An example of that applet is shown.

---

[5]Some people would suggest that, because the 0.0 μg is a true control group, its standard deviation might be better used to scale d. In this case it would not make a very great difference, and I have used the square root of the pooled variance.

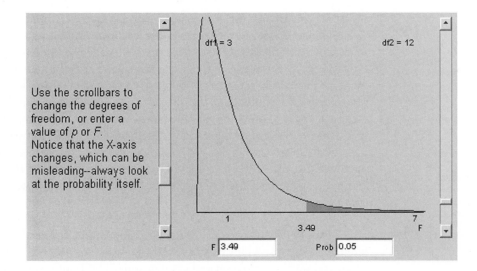

At the bottom of this applet you will see an *F* value and its associated probability. You can change either of those values and the other will change accordingly. For example, if you have 3 and 12 *df*, and enter .01 into the probability box, the *F* will change to 5.94, which is the critical value at $\alpha = .01$.

On the left and right of the display you will see sliders. If you move the one on the left, you will see the degrees of freedom for groups change. Similarly, moving the one on the right alters the degrees of freedom for error.

- What happens as you increase the *df* for error in terms of the size of the critical value of *F*? (You have to be careful to look at the critical value, and not just at the distribution itself, because part of the reason that the distribution appears to get wider is because the scale on the X axis has to change to accommodate the graphed values.)

- What happens if you increase the number of groups—and therefore the degrees of freedom for groups? (Again, notice that the scale on the X axis changes.)

- What is the critical value for *F* at $\alpha = .05$ for the Maternal Adaptation example in Table 16.6?

16.11 Summary

The analysis of variance is one of our most powerful statistical tools. In this chapter we restricted our discussion to what is called a one-way design, meaning that groups differ along only one dimension. We considered the null hypothesis that every population mean is equal to every other population mean, and the alternative hypothesis that *at least* one of the means is different from at least one other mean. We also considered the assumptions that are required for the analysis of variance, which are that the data are normally distributed, the populations have equal variances, and the observations are independent.

The logic of the analysis of variance boils down to the idea that if the null hypothesis is true, an estimate of the common population variance based on variability within groups, and an estimate based on the variability of the group means, should agree within reasonable limits. If there are true group differences, this would increase the variance estimate made on group means without changing the within-groups variance, leading to large differences between the two variance estimates. We judge the magnitude of these differences in variance by reference to the tables of the F distribution or to software that prints the exact probability value. The calculations inherent in running the analysis parallel the logic of creating two variance estimates.

After doing our calculations we enter the results in a standard summary table, consisting of the source of variability; the degrees of freedom; sums of squares and mean squares, which are our variance estimates; and the F statistic.

With a one-way analysis of variance we can easily handle unequal sample sizes just by taking the different values of n_i as we go along, rather than using a common value of n at the end of our calculations. This will not be true when we come to more complex designs.

We looked at multiple comparison procedures, which let us ask questions about differences between specific means. I recommended Fisher's Least Significant Difference (LSD) test when you have only a few means and the Bonferroni correction when you want to make several comparisons. The Bonferroni correction simply reduces the level of α for each comparison by dividing the desired familywise error rate by the number of comparisons. I further put in a plea to restrict the number of comparisons you run to only those that address important questions, rather than laying waste all around you looking at all possible comparisons.

Finally, we looked at two different kinds of measures of effect size. The measures based on the correlation coefficient (eta squared and omega squared) are useful because they allow us to work with multiple groups at once, but the measures based on Cohen's d, though restricted to pairwise comparisons of means, are generally more interpretable.

Key Terms

16.12 A Quick Review

A. What are two main assumptions behind the analysis of variance?
Ans: Normality; homogeneity of variance; independence of observations.

B. What does MS_{error} represent?
Ans: Error variance.

C. What does $MS_{between}$ represent?
Ans: The variability of group means.

D. Why is it called the analysis of variance if it is really a test on means?
Ans: The analysis of variance uses the variance within groups to estimate what the variance between groups would be if the null hypothesis is true. If the two estimates are way out of line with each other, we conclude that the variance between group means is due to something besides error variance.

E. What is the general rule for degrees of freedom?
Ans: The degrees of freedom for an effect are one less than the number of squared deviations that went into calculating that effect.

F. Is the analysis of variance a one-tailed test or a two-tailed test?
Ans: It is a one-tailed test of a nondirectional H_0.

G. What do we mean by "multiple comparison procedures"?
Ans: These are statistical tests that compare individual means or sets of means with each other.

H. Do we need a significant overall F before running multiple comparison tests?
Ans: No, except for Fisher's LSD test where a significant overall F is part of the logic of the test.

I. Why not just use plain old t tests instead of multiple comparison procedures?
Ans: If we don't control the familywise error rate it can get out of hand.

J. Name three multiple comparison tests.
Ans: Fisher's LSD, the Bonferroni correction, and Tukey's test.

K. What does it mean when we say that a statistical test is "robust"?
Ans: It means that it is relatively insensitive to violations of underlying assumptions.

L. The coefficient η^2 is an _____ measure of effect size and is basically just the percentage of _____.
Ans: r-family; total variability that can be attributed to variability between groups.

16.13 Exercises

16.1 An important study in the memory literature is an old study by Eysenck (1974) in which he compared the recall of older participants under one of five levels of processing of the material. He demonstrated that when asked to perform a higher level of processing of a list of words, participants showed better recall at a later time. Another aspect of Eysenck's study compared Younger and Older participants on their ability to recall material in the face of instructions simply telling that they should memorize the material for later recall. (Presumably this task required a high level of processing, which older participants might not do well.) The data on 10 participants in each group follow, where the dependent variable is the number of items recalled.

Younger	21	19	17	15	22	16	22	22	18	21
Older	10	19	14	5	10	11	14	15	11	11

a) Conduct the analysis of variance comparing the means of these two groups.
b) Conduct an independent groups *t* test on the data and compare the results to those you obtained in part (a). Your *t* should simply be the square root of *F*.

16.2 Another way to look at the Eysenck study mentioned in Exercise 16.1 is to compare four groups of participants. One group consisted of Younger participants who were presented the words to be recalled in a condition that elicited a Low level of processing. A second group consisted of Younger participants who were given a task requiring the Highest level of processing (as in Exercise 16.1). The two other groups were Older participants who were given tasks requiring either Low or High levels of processing. The data follow:

Younger/Low	8	6	4	6	7	6	5	7	9	7
Younger/Hi	21	19	17	15	22	16	22	22	18	21
Older/Low	9	8	6	8	10	4	6	5	7	7
Older/Hi	10	19	14	5	10	11	14	15	11	11

Conduct a one-way analysis of variance on these data.

16.3 Now we will expand on the analysis of Exercise 16.2.

a) Run a one-way analysis of variance on treatments 1 and 3 combined (*n* = 20) versus treatments 2 and 4 combined. What question are you answering?
b) Why might your answer to part (a) be difficult to interpret?
c) We will see a more appropriate analysis of variance for this design in the next chapter.

16.4 Refer to Exercise 16.1. Assume that we collected additional data and had two more participants in the Younger group with scores of 13 and 15.

a) Rerun the analysis of variance.
b) Run an independent groups *t* test without pooling the variances.
c) Run an independent groups *t* test after pooling the variances.
d) For (b) and (c), which of these values of *t* corresponds (after squaring) to the *F* in (a)?

16.5 Calculate η^2 and ω^2 for the data in Exercise 16.1 and write an interpretation.

16.6 Calculate η^2 and ω^2 for the data in Exercise 16.2 and write an interpretation.

16.7 Foa, Rothbaum, Riggs, and Murdock (1991) conducted a study evaluating four different types of therapy for rape victims. The Stress Inoculation Therapy (SIT) group received instructions on coping with stress. The Prolonged Exposure (PE) group went over the events in their minds repeatedly. Those in the Supportive Counseling (SC) group were taught a general problem-solving technique. Finally, the Waiting List (WL) control group received no therapy. Data with the same characteristics as theirs follow, where the dependent variable was the severity rating of a series of symptoms.

Group	*n*	Mean	S. D.
SIT	14	11.07	3.95
PE	10	15.40	11.12
SC	11	18.09	7.13
WL	10	19.50	7.11

a) Run the analysis of variance, ignoring any problems with heterogeneity of variance, and draw whatever conclusions are warranted. (Note that you have to be a little creative here, but it is not a difficult exercise.)
b) Draw a graph showing the means of the four groups.
c) What does rejection of the null hypothesis mean?

16.8 Calculate η^2 and ω^2 for the data in Exercise 16.7, and interpret their meaning.

16.9 Use the *R* code on this chapter's Web page to generate data that could lie behind exercise 16.7 and then run the analysis of variance.

16.10 How do the results of Exercise 16.9 compare with the results you obtained in Exercise 16.7? (They should agree, but not too closely.)

16.11 What would happen if the sample sizes in Exercise 16.7 were twice as large as they were?

16.12 Use protected *t* tests for the data in Exercise 16.7 or 16.9 to clarify the meaning of the significant *F*.

16.13 Use the *R* code in Section 16.3 to run the analysis of the data in Exercise 16.2.

16.14 Perform a Bonferroni correction for the analysis of section 16.10. What comparisons make sense to you?

16.15 Calculate $\hat{d}$ for the comparisons you made in Exercise 16.12 and interpret the meaning of each.

16.16 The data in Exercises 16.7 and 16.11 both produced a significant *F*. Do you have more or less faith in one of these effects? Why?

16.17 For the data in Appendix D, form three groups. (These data are available at www.uvm .edu/~dhowell/fundamentals9/DataFiles/Add.dat). Group 1 has ADDSC scores of 40 or below, Group 2 has ADDSC scores between 41 and 59, and Group 3 has ADDSC scores of 60 or above. Run an analysis of variance on the GPA scores for these three groups. You can use *R* for this analysis by using the commands:

```
add.dat<- read.table(http://www.uvm.edu/~dhowell/fundamentals9/DataFiles/
Add.dat", header = TRUE)
attach(add.dat)
N <- length(ADDSC)
grp<- numeric(N)
for (i in 1:N) {
if (ADDSC[i] < 41)
  {grp[i] <- 1}
else if (ADDSC[i] < 60)
  {grp[i] <- 2}
}
else
  {grp[i] <- 3}
}
grp<- factor(grp)
means<- tapply(ADDSC, grp, mean)
cat("The group means are = ",means)
model3<- lm(ADDSC ~ grp)
anova(model3)
```

16.18 Compute η^2 and ω^2 from the results in Exercise 16.17.

16.19 Darley and Latané (1968) recorded the speed with which participants summoned help for a person in trouble. Some participants thought that they were alone with the person (Group 1, $n = 13$), some thought that one other person was there (Group 2, $n = 26$), and others thought that four other people were there (Group 3, $n = 13$). The dependent variable was speed $(1/\text{time} \times 100)$ to call someone for help. The mean speed scores for the three groups were

0.87, 0.72, and 0.51, respectively. The MS_{error} was 0.053. Reconstruct the analysis of variance. What would you conclude?

16.20 Using the data in Exercise 16.2, calculate SS_{error} directly rather than by subtraction and show that this is the same answer you found in that exercise.

16.21 Use the Bonferroni correction for the data in Exercise 16.2 to compare the Younger/Low with the Older/Low group, and the Younger/High with the Older/High group.

16.22 Use the Bonferroni correction for the data in Exercise 16.7 to compare the WL group with each of the other three groups. What would you conclude? How does this compare to the answer for Exercise 16.10?

16.23 Calculate $\hat{d}$ for the comparison of WL with SIT in Exercise 16.22 using the standard deviation of the Control group to standardize the difference.

16.24 What effect does smoking have on performance? Spilich, June, and Renner (1992) asked non-smokers (NS), smokers who had delayed smoking for three hours (DS), and smokers who were actively smoking (AS) to perform a pattern recognition task in which they had to locate a target on a screen. The dependent variable was latency (in seconds). The data are presented below. Use any statistical program to plot the resulting means and run the analysis of variance. On the basis of these data is there support for the hypothesis that smoking has an effect on performance?

Nonsmokers	Delayed Smokers	Active Smokers
9	12	8
8	7	8
12	14	9
10	4	1
7	8	9
10	11	7
9	16	16
11	17	19
8	5	1
10	6	1
8	9	22
10	6	12
8	6	18
11	7	8
10	16	10

16.25 In the study referred to in Exercise 16.24, Spilich et al. (1992) also investigated performance on a cognitive task that required the participant to read a passage and then to recall it later. This task has much greater information processing demands than the pattern recognition task. The independent variable was the three smoking groups referred to in Exercise 16.24. The dependent variable was the number of propositions recalled from the passage. The data follow.

Nonsmokers	Delayed Smokers	Active Smokers
27	48	34
34	29	65
19	34	55
20	6	33

56	18	42
35	63	54
23	9	21
37	54	44
4	28	61
30	71	38
4	60	75
42	54	61
34	51	51
19	25	32
49	49	47

Run the analysis of variance on these data and draw the appropriate conclusions.

16.26 Use the Fisher LSD test to compare active smokers with nonsmokers and to compare the two groups of smokers on the data in Exercise 16.25 What do these data suggest about the advisability of smoking while you are studying for an exam and the advisability of smoking just before you take an exam?

16.27 Spilich et al. (1992) ran a third experiment in which the three groups of smokers participated in a driving simulation video game. The AS group smoked immediately before the game but not during it. The data follow, where the dependent variable is an adjusted score related to the number of collisions. Run the analysis of variance and draw the appropriate conclusions.

Nonsmokers	Delayed Smokers	Active Smokers
15	7	3
2	0	2
2	6	0
14	0	0
5	12	6
0	17	2
16	1	0
14	11	6
9	4	4
17	4	1
15	3	0
9	5	0
3	16	6
15	5	2
13	11	3

16.28 The three experiments by Spilich et al. (1992) on the effects of smoking on performance find conflicting results. Can you suggest why the results are different?

16.29 Langlois and Roggman (1990) took facial photographs of males and females. They then created five groups of composite photographs by computer-averaging the individual faces. For one group the computer averaged 32 randomly selected same-gender faces, producing a quite recognizable face with average width, height, eyes, nose length, and so on. For the other groups the composite faces were averaged over either 2, 4, 8, or 16 individual faces. Each group saw six separate photographs, all of which were computer-averaged over the appropriate number of individual photographs. Langlois and Roggman asked participants to rate the attractiveness of the faces on a 1–5 scale, where 5 represents "very attractive." The data have been constructed to have the same means and variances as those reported by Langlois and Roggman.

Data on rated attractiveness

	Group 1	Group 2	Group 3	Group 4	Group 5
	2.201	1.893	2.906	3.233	3.200
	2.411	3.102	2.118	3.505	3.253
	2.407	2.355	3.226	3.192	3.357
	2.403	3.644	2.811	3.209	3.169
	2.826	2.767	2.857	2.860	3.291
	3.380	2.109	3.422	3.111	3.290
Mean	2.6047	2.6450	2.8900	3.1850	3.2600

a) Specify a research hypothesis that could lie behind this study.
b) Run the appropriate analysis of variance.
c) What do these data tell us about how people judge attractiveness?

16.30 Using the data from Exercise 16.29

a) Calculate η^2 and ω^2.
b) Why do the two estimates of the magnitude of effect in part a) differ?
c) Calculate a measure of $\hat{d}$, using the most appropriate groups.

16.31 Use R or SPSS to reproduce the analysis in Exercise 16.27.

16.32 Use Lenth's Piface program or the one at

www.statpages.org/pdfs.html

to reproduce the probability values given in Exercise 16.31.

## CHAPTER 17

Factorial Analysis of Variance

This chapter will look at a slightly more complex analysis of variance and address the question of what we do when we have more than one independent variable at the same time. The analysis is not particularly difficult, but we will have to consider the difference between a main effect and a simple effect and look closely at interactions. We will then look at the case of unequal sample sizes, where we will find that the solution is not simple. Finally, we will examine the different kinds of effect sizes and how and when we would use each.

In Chapter 16 we dealt with a one-way analysis of variance, which is an experimental design having only one independent variable. In this chapter we will extend the analysis of variance to cover experimental designs involving two or more independent variables. For purposes of simplicity we will consider experiments involving only two independent variables, although the extension to more complex designs is not difficult (see Howell, 2012).

Why do older people often seem not to remember things as well as younger people? Do they not pay attention? Do they just not process the material as thoroughly? Do they know less? Or do they really do just as well, but are we more likely to notice when they forget than when younger people do? (I hope the last explanation is true, because I seem to be forgetting a lot of things.) In the exercises for Chapter 16 we considered a study by Eysenck (1974) in which he asked participants to recall lists of words to

CONCEPTS THAT YOU WILL NEED TO REMEMBER FROM PREVIOUS CHAPTERS

SS_{Total}, SS_{Group}, SS_{error}:	Sums of squares of all scores, of group means, and within groups
MS_{Group}, MS_{error}:	Mean squares for group means, and within groups
F statistic:	Ratio of MS_{group} over MS_{error}
Degrees of freedom:	The number of independent pieces of information remaining after estimating one or more parameters
Effect size ($\hat{d}$):	A measure intended to express the size of a treatment
Eta^2 (η^2), omega^2 (ω^2):	Correlation-based measures of effect size
Multiple comparisons:	Tests on differences between specific group means in terms that are meaningful to the reader

which they had been exposed under conditions that required different levels of processing. In that example we were interested in determining whether recall was related to the level at which material was processed initially. Eysenck's study was actually more complex. He was interested in whether level-of-processing notions using five different levels of processing could explain differences in recall between older and younger participants. If older participants do not process information as deeply, they might be expected to recall fewer items than would younger participants, especially in conditions that entail greater processing. This study has two independent variables (Age and recall Condition), which we will refer to as **factors**. The experiment is an instance of what is called a **two-way factorial design**.

To expand this experiment even further, we could classify participants additionally as male and female. We then would have what is called a *three-way factorial design*, with Age, Condition, and Gender as factors. I will not discuss three-way designs in this chapter, but they are really just an extension of two-way designs.

17.1 Factorial Designs

An experimental design in which every level of every factor is paired with every level of every other factor is called a factorial design. In other words, a **factorial design** is one in which we include all *combinations* of the levels of the independent variables. Table 17.1 illustrates the two-way design of Eysenck's study. In the factorial designs discussed in this chapter, we will consider only the case in which different participants serve under each of the treatment combinations. For instance, in our example one group of younger participants will serve in the Counting condition, a different group of younger participants in the Rhyming condition, and so on. Because we have 10 combinations of our two factors (5 recall Conditions × 2 Ages), we will have 10 different groups of participants. When a research plan calls for the *same* participant to be included under more than one treatment combination, we speak of repeated-measures designs. Repeated-measures designs will be discussed in Chapter 18.

Factorial designs have several important advantages over one-way designs. First, they allow greater generalizability of the results. Consider Eysenck's study for a moment. If we were to run a one-way analysis of variance using the five Conditions with only older participants, our results would apply only to older participants, which, I suspect, would be a serious limitation of our findings. When we use a factorial design with both older and younger participants, we are able to determine whether differences between Conditions apply to younger participants as well as older ones. We are also able to determine whether age differences in recall apply to all tasks, or whether younger (or older) participants excel on only certain kinds of tasks. Thus factorial designs allow for a much broader interpretation of the results and at the same time give us the ability to say something meaningful about the results for each of the independent variables.

Table 17.1   Diagrammatic Representation of Eysenck's Two-Way Factorial Study

	Counting	Rhyming	Adjective	Imagery	Intentional
Younger					
Older					

The second important feature of factorial designs is that they allow us to look at the **interaction** of variables. We can ask whether the effect of Condition is independent of Age or whether there is some interaction between Condition and Age. I suspect that Eysenck really was not particularly interested in knowing whether recall was better following more in-depth processing. He already knew that from other work. And he probably was not terribly surprised to see that younger participants did better than older ones. I'm sure you weren't surprised. But what Eysenck really cared about was whether the difference in recall between younger and older participants varied as a function of processing. If it did, he would have evidence that memory decline that we see in some older people relates to the degree of processing individuals do, and that is an important and interesting finding. Interaction effects such as these are often among the most interesting results we obtain.

A third advantage of a factorial design is its economy. Because we are going to average the effects of one variable across the levels of the other variable, a two-variable factorial will require fewer participants than would two one-way designs for the same degree of power. Essentially, we are getting something for nothing. Suppose we had no reason to expect an interaction of Age and Condition. Then, with 10 older participants and 10 younger participants in each Condition, we would have 20 scores for each of the five conditions. If we instead ran a one-way with younger participants and then another one-way with older participants, we would need twice as many participants overall for each of our experiments to have 20 participants per condition, and we would have two experiments.

As mentioned earlier, factorial designs are labeled by the number of factors involved. A factorial design with two independent variables, or factors, is called a two-way factorial, and one with three factors is called a three-way factorial. An alternative method of labeling designs is in terms of the number of levels of each factor. Eysenck's study had two levels of Age and five levels of Condition. As such, it is a **2 × 5 factorial**. A study with three factors, two of them having three levels and one having four levels, would be called a $3 \times 3 \times 4$ factorial. The use of such terms as "two-way" and "2 × 5" are common ways of designating designs, and both will be used in this book.

In much of what follows, we will concern ourselves primarily with the two-way analysis. Higher-order analyses follow relatively easily once you understand the two-way, and many of the related problems we will discuss are most simply explained in terms of two factors.

Notation

I will keep the notation as simple as possible to avoid unnecessary confusion. In the previous chapter on one-way designs it was easier to keep the notation clear. Here we will need to be a bit more specific. Names of factors generally are designated by the first letter (uppercase) of the factor name, and the individual levels of each factor are indicated by that uppercase letter with the appropriate subscript (in Condition, for instance, Counting would be designated as C_1, Rhyming as C_2, and Intentional as C_5). The number of levels of the factor will be denoted by a lowercase letter corresponding to that factor. Thus Condition (C) has $c = 5$ levels, whereas Age (A) has $a = 2$ levels. Any specific combination of one level of one factor and one level of another factor (e.g., Older participants in the Rhyming condition) is called a **cell**, and the number of observations per cell will be denoted by n. The total number of

Table 17.2 Factorial Design of Eysenck's Study

Age	Conditions					
	Counting	Rhyming	Adjective	Imagery	Intentional	Totals
Younger	$\overline{X}_{11}$	$\overline{X}_{12}$	$\overline{X}_{13}$	$\overline{X}_{14}$	$\overline{X}_{15}$	$\overline{X}_{A1}$
Older	$\overline{X}_{21}$	$\overline{X}_{22}$	$\overline{X}_{23}$	$\overline{X}_{24}$	$\overline{X}_{25}$	$\overline{X}_{A2}$
Totals	$\overline{X}_{C1}$	$\overline{X}_{C2}$	$\overline{X}_{C3}$	$\overline{X}_{C4}$	$\overline{X}_{C5}$	$\overline{X}_{gm}$

observations is N, and in our example, $N = acn = 2 \times 5 \times 10 = 100$ because there are $a \times c = 10$ cells, each with 10 participants. Table 17.2 shows the factorial design of Eysenck's study.

The subscripts i and j are used as general (nonspecific) notations for the level of rows and columns. Thus, cell_{ij} is the cell in the ith row and the jth column. For example, cell_{22} in Table 17.2 would be the Older participants (row 2) in the Rhyming Condition (column 2). The means for the individual levels of Age will be denoted as $\overline{X}_{Ai}$, and the means for the individual levels of Condition will be denoted as $\overline{X}_{Cj}$. The subscripts A and C refer to the variable names. Cell means are denoted as $\overline{X}_{ij}$, and the **grand mean** (the mean of all N scores) is shown as $\overline{X}_{gm}$.

The notation described here will be used throughout our discussion of the analysis of variance, and it is important that you thoroughly understand it before proceeding. The advantage of this system is that it easily generalizes to other examples. For example, if we had a Drug × Gender factorial, it should be clear that $\overline{X}_{D1}$ and $\overline{X}_{G2}$ refer to the means of the first level of the Drug variable and the second level of the Gender variable, respectively.

17.2 The Eysenck Study

As we have been discussing, Eysenck conducted a study varying Age as well as recall Condition. The study included 50 participants 18–30 years of age and 50 participants 55–65 years of age. The data in Table 17.3 have been created to have the same means and standard deviations as those reported by Eysenck. The table contains all the calculations for the standard analysis of variance, and we will discuss each of those in turn. Before we begin the analysis, it is important to note that the data themselves are approximately normally distributed with acceptably homogeneous variances. Boxplots are not given in the table because the individual data points are artificial, though not the means and variances. For real data it would be well worth your effort to compute them. You can tell from the cell and marginal means that recall appears to increase with greater processing, and younger participants seem to recall more items than do older participants. Notice also that the difference between younger and older participants seems to depend on the task, with greater differences for those tasks that involve deeper processing. If significant, this would be an interaction of Age with Condition. We will consider these results further after we consider the analysis itself.

It will avoid confusion later if I take the time here to define two important terms. We have two factors in this experiment—Age and Condition. If we look at the differences between older and younger participants, *ignoring the particular Conditions*, we are dealing with what is called the **main effect** of Age. Similarly, if we look

Table 17.3 Data and Calculations for Example from Eysenck (1974)

(a) Data

	Counting	Rhyming	Adjective	Imagery	Intentional	Mean$_i$
			Recall Conditions			
Old	9	7	11	12	10	
	8	9	13	11	19	
	6	6	8	16	14	
	8	6	6	11	5	
	10	6	14	9	10	
	4	11	11	23	11	
	6	6	13	12	14	
	5	3	13	10	15	
	7	8	10	19	11	
	7	7	11	11	11	
Mean$_{1j}$	7.0	6.9	11.0	13.4	12.0	10.06
Young	8	10	14	20	21	
	6	7	11	16	19	
	4	8	18	16	17	
	6	10	14	15	15	
	7	4	13	18	22	
	6	7	22	16	16	
	5	10	17	20	22	
	7	6	16	22	22	
	9	7	12	14	18	
	7	7	11	19	21	
Mean$_{2j}$	6.5	7.6	14.8	17.6	19.3	13.16
Mean$_j$	6.75	7.25	12.9	15.5	15.65	11.61

(b) Calculations

$$SS_{total} = \Sigma(X - \overline{X}_{gm})^2 = \Sigma X^2 - \frac{(\Sigma X)^2}{N}$$
$$= 16,147 - \frac{11.61^2}{100} = 16,147 - 13,479.21$$
$$= 2667.79$$

$$SS_A = nc\Sigma(\overline{X}_A - \overline{X}_{gm})^2$$
$$= 10 \times 5[(10.06 - 11.61)^2 + (13.16 - 11.61)^2]$$
$$= 240.25$$

$$SS_C = na\Sigma(\overline{X}_C - \overline{X}_{gm})^2$$
$$= 1514.94$$
$$= 10 \times 2[(6.75 - 11.61)^2 + (7.25 - 11.61)^2 + \cdots + (15.65 - 11.61)^2]$$
$$= 1514.94$$

$$SS_{cells} = n\Sigma(\overline{X}_{AC} - \overline{X}_{gm})^2$$
$$= 10[(7.0 - 11.61)^2 + (6.9 - 11.61)^2 + \cdots + (19.3 - 11.61)^2]$$
$$= 1945.49$$

(continued)

Table 17.3 Data and Calculations for Example from Eysenck (1974)

$SS_{AC} = SS_{cells} - SS_A - SS_C = 1945.49 - 240.25 - 1514.94 = 190.30$
$SS_{error} = SS_{total} - SS_{cells} = 2667.79 - 1945.49 = 722.30$

(c) Summary Table

Source	df	SS	MS	F	P
A (Age)	1	240.25	240.250	29.94**	.0000
C (Condition)	4	1514.94	378.735	47.19**	.0000
AC	4	190.30	47.575	5.93**	.0003
Error	90	722.30	8.026		
Total	99	2667.79			

* $p < .05$, ** $p < .01$

at differences among the five Conditions, *ignoring the Age of participants*, we are dealing with the main effect of Conditions.

An alternative method of looking at the data would be to compare the means of the five conditions for only the older participants. (This is what we did in Chapter 16.) Or we might compare older and younger participants for only the data from the Counting task, or we might compare older and younger participants on the Intentional task. In these three examples we are looking at the effect of one factor for the data at only *one* level of the other factor. When we do this, we are dealing with a **simple effect**—the effect of one factor at one level of the other factor. A main effect, on the other hand, is that of a factor *ignoring* (or averaging across) the other factor. If we say that tasks that involve more processing lead to better recall, we are speaking of a main effect. If we conclude that *for younger participants* tasks that involve more processing lead to better recall, we are speaking about a simple effect. We will have more to say about simple effects and their calculations shortly. For now it is important only that you understand the terminology.

Calculations

The calculations for the sums of squares appear in part (b) of Table 17.3. Many of these calculations should be familiar, since they resemble the procedures used with a one-way design. For example, SS_{total} can be computed the same way it was in Chapter 16, although here I used a computationally simpler approach. I summed all the squared observations and subtracted $(\Sigma X)^2/N$.

The sum of squares for the Age factor (SS_A) is nothing but the SS_{group} that we would obtain if this were a one-way analysis of variance without the Condition factor. In other words, we simply sum the squared deviations of the two Age means from the grand mean and multiply by the number of observations for each mean. We use nc as the multiplier here because each age has n participants at each of c levels. The same procedures are followed in the calculation of SS_C, except that here we ignore the presence of the Age variable.

You will notice that $\Sigma(\overline{X}_A - \overline{X}_{gm})^2$ is multiplied by nc and $\Sigma(\overline{X}_C - \overline{X}_{gm})^2$ is multiplied by na, where a and c represent the number of levels of Age and Condition, respectively. Please don't try to remember these multipliers as formulae; you will be wasting your time. They represent the number of scores per means and nothing more. They are exactly analogous to the multiplier (n) we used in the one-way analysis when we wanted to turn a variance of means into an estimate of the population variance (σ_e^2). The only difference is that in a one-way analysis, n represented the number of observations per treatment, and here it represents the number of observations per cell—because c cells are involved with each Age level, there must by nc observations for each Age mean ($\overline{X}_A$).

Having obtained SS_{total}, SS_A, and SS_C, we come to an unfamiliar term, **SS_{cells}**. This term represents the variability of the individual cell means and is, in fact, only a dummy term; it will not appear in the summary table. It is calculated just like any other sum of squares. We take the deviations of the 10 cell means from the grand mean, square and sum them, and multiply by n, the number of observations per mean. The usefulness of this term will become clear when we calculate a sum of squares for the interaction of Age and Condition. (It may be easier to understand the calculation of SS_{cells} if you think of it as what you would have if you viewed this as a study with 10 "groups" and calculated SS_{group}.)

SS_{cells} is a measure of how much the cell means differ. Two cell means may differ for any of three reasons, other than sampling error: (1) because they come from different levels of A (Age); (2) because they come from different levels of C (Condition); or (3) because of an interaction between A and C. We already have a measure of how much the cell means differ, since we know SS_{cells}. SS_A tells us how much of this difference can be attributed to differences in Age, and SS_C tells us how much can be attributed to differences in Condition. Whatever cannot be attributed to Age or Condition must be attributable to the interaction between Age and Condition (SS_{AC}). Thus SS_{cells} has been partitioned into its three constituent parts—SS_A, SS_C, and SS_{AC}. To obtain SS_{AC}, we simply subtract SS_A and SS_C from SS_{cells}. Whatever is left over is SS_{AC}. In our example

$$SS_{AC} = SS_{cells} - SS_A - SS_C$$
$$= 1945.49 - 240.25 - 1514.94 = 190.30$$

All that we have left to calculate is the sum of squares due to error. Just as in the one-way analysis, we will obtain this by subtraction. The total variation is represented by SS_{total}. Of this total, we know how much can be attributed to A, C, and AC. What is left over represents unaccountable variation or error. Thus

$$SS_{error} = SS_{total} - (SS_A + SS_C + SS_{AC})$$

This provides us with our sum of squares for error, and we now have all of the necessary sums of squares for our analysis.

Notice that with the exception of the interaction term, a two-way factorial is treated just like two one-way designs. We calculate Age effects as if there were no separate Conditions, and we calculate Condition effects as if there we no separate Ages. And the error term is just the variability of bunches of people in each cell.

Part (c) of Table 17.3 is the summary table for the analysis of variance. The source column and the sum of squares column are fairly obvious from what has already been said. The degrees of freedom column should also be familiar from what you know about the one-way. The total degrees of freedom (df_{total}) are always equal to $N-1$. The degrees of freedom for Age and Condition are the number of levels of the variable minus 1. Thus, $df_A = a - 1 = 1$ and $df_C = c - 1 = 4$. The number of degrees of freedom for any interaction is simply the product of the degrees of freedom for the components of that interaction. Thus, $df_{AC} = df_A \times df_C = (a - 1)(c - 1) =$

$1 \times 4 = 4$. Finally, the degrees of freedom for error can be obtained by subtraction. Thus $df_{error} = df_{total} - df_A - df_C - df_{AC}$. Alternatively, because MS_{error} is the average of the AC cell variances, and because each cell variance has $n - 1$ df, MS_{error} has $ac(n - 1)$ degrees of freedom. These rules for degrees of freedom apply to any factorial analysis of variance, no matter how complex.

Just as with the one-way analysis of variance, the mean squares are obtained by dividing the sums of squares by the corresponding degrees of freedom. This is the same procedure we will use in any analysis.

Finally, to calculate F, we divide each MS by MS_{error}. Thus, for Age, $F_A = MS_A/MS_{error}$; for Condition, $F_C = MS_C/MS_{error}$; and for AC, $F_{AC} = MS_{AC}/MS_{error}$. Each F is based on the number of degrees of freedom for the term in question and the df_{error}. Thus the F for Age is on $2 - 1 = 1$ and 90 df, and the F for Condition and the F for the Age $\times$ Condition interaction are based on 4 and 90 df ($5 - 1 = 4$ for Condition and $(5 - 1)$ $(2 - 1)$ for the interaction). From Table E.3 in the Appendices, we find that the critical values of F are $F_{.05}(1,90) = 3.96$ (by interpolation) and $F_{.05}(4,90) = 2.49$ (again by interpolation). Notice that by convention a single asterisk is used next to an F that is significant at $p < .05$, and a double asterisk is used next to an F that is significant at $p < .01$. In the next example I will replace the asterisks with the exact p value, which is a more modern way of reporting the results; however, here I have done it both ways.

Interpretation

From part (c) of Table 17.3, the summary table, you can see that there were significant effects for Age, Condition, and their interaction. In conjunction with the cell means, it is clear that younger participants recall more items overall than do older participants. It is also clear that those tasks that involve greater depth of processing lead to better recall overall than do tasks that involve less processing, which is in line with the differences we found in Chapter 16. The significant interaction tells us that the effect of one variable depends on the level of the other variable. For example, differences between older and younger participants on the easier tasks, such as Counting and Rhyming, are less than the differences between younger and older participants on those tasks that involve greater depths of processing, such as Imagery and Intentional. Another view is that differences among the five conditions are less extreme for the older participants than they are for the younger ones.

The results support Eysenck's hypothesis that older participants do not perform as well as younger participants on tasks that involve a greater depth of processing of information but do perform about equally with younger participants when the tasks do not involve much processing. These results do not mean that older participants are not *capable* of processing information as deeply. Older participants simply may not make the effort that younger participants do. Whatever the reason, they do not perform as well on those tasks.

17.3 Interactions

A major benefit of factorial designs is that they allow us to examine the interaction of variables. Indeed in many cases the interaction term may be of greater interest than are the main effects (the effects of factors taken individually). Consider, for example, the study by Eysenck. The means are plotted in Figure 17.1 for each age

Figure 17.1   Cell means for data in Table 17.3

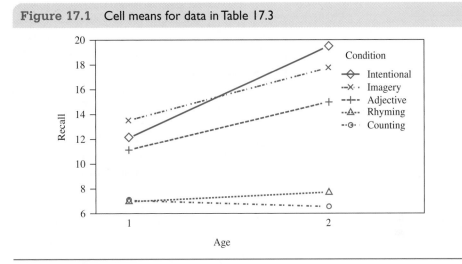

group separately. Such a plot is often called an "interaction plot," and the *R* code for this plot is given below the figure. In Figure 17.1 you can see clearly what I referred to in the interpretation of the results when I said that the differences due to Conditions were greater for younger participants than for older ones. The fact that the two lines are not parallel is what we mean when we speak of an interaction. If Condition differences were the same for the two Age groups, the lines would be parallel—whatever differences between Conditions existed for younger participants would be equally present for older participants. This would be true regardless of whether younger participants were generally superior to older participants or whether the two groups were comparable. Raising or lowering the entire line for younger participants would change the main effect of Age, but it would have no effect on the interaction.

R code for Figure 17.1

```
Eysenck.data <-
read.table("http://www.uvm.edu/~dhowell/fundamentals9/DataFiles/Tab17-3.dat", header = TRUE)
names(Eysenck.data)  # Prints out the names of the variables
attach(Eysenck.data)
Condition <-  factor(Condition); Age <- factor(Age)
levels(Condition) <-  c("Counting", "Rhyming", "Adjective","Imagery","Intentional")
interaction.plot(x.factor = Age, trace.factor = Condition, response = Recall, fun = mean,
type = "b", xlab = "Age", ylab = "Recall", col = "blue", pch = 1:5)
```

The situation may become clearer if you consider several plots of cell means that represent the presence or absence of an interaction. In Figure 17.2 the first three plots represent the case in which there is no interaction. In all three cases the lines are parallel, even when they are not straight. Another way of looking at this is to say

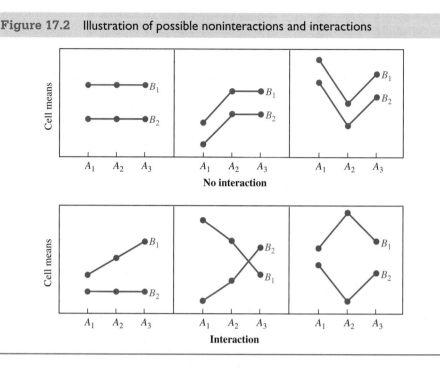

Figure 17.2 Illustration of possible noninteractions and interactions

that the difference between B_1 and B_2 (the effect of factor B) at A_1 is the same as it is at A_2 and at A_3. In the second set of three plots the lines clearly are not parallel. In the first plot one line is flat and the other rises. In the second plot the lines actually cross. In the third plot the lines do not cross, but they move in opposite directions. In every case the effect of B is *not* the same at the different levels of A. Whenever the lines are (significantly) nonparallel, we say that we have an interaction.

Many people will argue that if you find a significant interaction, the main effects should be ignored. I used to be in the opposing camp, but even I have come to realize that there is usually not much point in getting excited over a main effect if there is a significant interaction. It is not wrong to look at main effects in that case, but it probably isn't very productive. Yes, it is true that younger participants outperform older participants in almost every treatment condition, but that is not the important story that these data reveal, and it is not particularly productive to focus on that.

17.4 Simple Effects

I earlier defined a simple effect as the effect of one factor (independent variable) at one level of the other factor, for example, differences among Conditions for the younger participants. The analysis of simple effects can be an important technique for analyzing data that contain significant interactions. In a very real sense such analysis allows us to "tease apart" interactions. As I have just suggested, if you have an interaction you should probably ignore the main effect and jump right into simple effects. This is illustrated nicely in a second example that we will look at in a few pages.

I will use the Eysenck data to illustrate how to calculate and interpret simple effects. Table 17.4 reproduces the cell means and the summary table from Table 17.3 and contains the calculations involved in obtaining all the simple effects. As

Table 17.4   Calculation of Simple Effects for Data from Table 17.3

(a) Cell means ($n = 10$)

	Counting	Rhyming	Adjective	Imagery	Intentional	Mean
Older	7.0	6.9	11.0	13.4	12.0	10.06
Younger	6.5	7.6	14.8	17.6	19.3	13.16
Mean	6.75	7.25	12.90	15.50	15.65	11.61

(b) Calculations

Conditions at Each Age

$$SS_{C \text{ at Old}} = 10 \times [(7.0 - 10.06)^2 + (6.9 - 10.06)^2 + \cdots + (12 - 10.06)^2] = 351.52$$
$$SS_{C \text{ at Young}} = 10 \times [(6.5 - 13.16)^2 + (7.6 - 13.16)^2 + \cdots + (19.3 - 13.16)^2] = 1353.72$$

Age at Each Condition

$$SS_{A \text{ at Counting}} = 10 \times [(7.0 - 6.75)^2 + (6.5 - 6.75)^2] = 1.25$$
$$SS_{A \text{ at Rhyming}} = 10 \times [(6.9 - 7.25)^2 + (7.6 - 7.25)^2] = 2.45$$
$$SS_{A \text{ at Adjective}} = 10 \times [(11.0 - 12.9)^2 + (14.8 - 12.9)^2] = 72.20$$
$$SS_{A \text{ at Imagery}} = 10 \times [(13.4 - 15.5)^2 + (17.6 - 15.5)^2] = 88.20$$
$$SS_{A \text{ at Intentional}} = 10 \times [(12.0 - 15.65)^2 + (19.3 - 15.65)^2] = 266.45$$

(c) Summary Tables

Overall Analysis

Source	df	SS	MS	F
A (Age)	1	240.25	240.250	29.94**
C (Condition	4	1514.94	378.735	47.19**
AC	4	190.30	47.575	5.93**
Error	90	722.30	8.026	
Total	99	2667.79		

* $p < .05$, ** $p < .01$

Simple Effects

Source	df	SS	MS	F
Conditions				
C at Old	4	351.52	87.88	10.95**
C at Young	4	1353.72	338.43	42.17**
Age				
A at Counting	1	1.25	1.25	<1
A at Rhyming	1	2.45	2.45	<1
A at Adjective	1	72.20	72.20	9.00**
A at Imagery	1	88.20	88.20	10.99**
A at Intentional	1	266.45	266.45	33.20**
Error	90	722.30	8.026	

* $p < .05$, ** $p < .01$

a general rule, I do not recommend running *all* simple effects. Testing all possible effects drastically increases the probability of a Type I error. Run only those that are particularly relevant to your purposes. I have run them all here simply to illustrate the procedure.

The first summary table in part I of Table 17.4 reveals significant effects due to Age, Condition, and their interaction. We discussed these results earlier in conjunction with the original analysis. As I said there, the presence of an interaction means that there are different Condition effects for the two Ages and different Age effects for the five Conditions. It thus becomes important to ask whether our general Condition effect really applies for older as well as younger participants and whether there really are Age differences under all Conditions. The analysis of these simple effects is found in part (b) of Table 17.4 and in the second summary in part (c). Remember, I have shown all possible simple effects for the sake of completeness. In practice you should examine only those effects in which you are interested.

Calculation of Simple Effects

In part (b) of Table 17.4 you can see that $SS_{C \text{ at Old}}$ is calculated in the same way as any sum of squares. We simply calculate SS_C using only the data for the older participants. If we consider only those data, the five Condition means are 7.0, 6.9, 11.0, 13.4, and 12.0. Thus the sum of squares will be

$$SS_{C \text{ at Old}} = n\Sigma(\overline{X}_{C_{j \text{ at Old}}} - \overline{X}_{\text{old}})^2$$
$$= 10 \times [(7 - 10.06)^2 + (6.9 - 10.06)^2 + \cdots + (12 - 10.06)^2]$$
$$= 351.52$$

The other simple effects are calculated in the same way, by ignoring all data in which you are not interested at the moment.

The degrees of freedom for the numerator of simple effects are calculated in the same way as for the corresponding main effects. This makes sense because the number of means we are comparing remains the same—there are five Condition means. Whether we use all the participants or only part of them, we still are comparing five conditions and have $5 - 1 = 4$ *df* for Conditions.

An important question that arises in the computation of simple effects is the choice of the error term with which we calculate *F*. In the example above, I chose the error term from the overall analysis of variance, and divided each MS_{between} by that value(8.026). There is a good reason to do this. If you have homogeneity of variance in your design the average of the 10 cell variances is a better estimate of error than the average of 2 or 5 variances. In addition, the overall design has 90 *df* for error, giving us more power than using separate error terms on fewer *df*. This is the way that I would normally recommend calculating *F*.

This analysis in *R* and SPSS

But, a problem arises when you use SPSS or *R*. The easiest way to calculate simple effects using SPSS is to split the file into either Age groups or Condition groups using **Data/Split file** and then running the analysis specifying that the independent variable is either Age or Condition. This will give you all of the appropriate analyses, using an analysis-specific error term. In other words, the error term for each F is the one from just that set of data. You have to do a bit more work in R, but you essentially do the same thing. By splitting the data you lose power because you lose degrees of freedom for error, and you fail to pool the separate variance estimates. But **the Split file** approach will work in SPSS and the R code for this approach is shown below.

```
Eysenck.data <-
read.table("http://www.uvm.edu/~dhowell/fundamentals9/DataFiles/Tab17-3.dat", header = TRUE)
names(Eysenck.data)
attach(Eysenck.data)

levels(Condition) <- c("Counting", "Rhyming", "Adjective","Imagery","Intentional")
interaction.plot(x.factor = Age, trace.factor = Condition, response = Recall, fun = mean,
type = "b", xlab = "Age", ylab = "Recall", col = "blue", pch = 1:5)

model <- lm(Recall ~ Age* Condition)    # Main and Interaction Effects
anova(model)

data1 <- subset(Eysenck.data, Age == 1)
data2 <- subset(Eysenck.data, Age == 2)

modelAge1 <- lm(Recall ~ factor(Condition), data = data1)  # Simple effect Age = 1
modelAge2 <- lm(Recall ~ factor(Condition), data = data2)  # Simple effect Age = 2
anova(modelAge1)
anova(modelAge2)
```

You can use a pooled error term if you wish, but that means that you calculate the separate solutions and then go back and recalculate F by dividing by the pooled error term from the overall analysis. I do not use that approach in this book simply because it makes the discussion of simple effects more complex. However if you want to use computer software and still use a pooled error term, see the Web page that I have written at the book's website.

(https://www.uvm.edu/~dhowell/fundamentals9/Chapters/Chapter17/ SimpleEffects.html)

Interpretation

From the column labeled F in the simple effects summary table in Table 17.4, it is evident that differences due to Conditions occur for both ages, although the sum of squares for the older participants is only about one-quarter of what it is for the younger ones. With regard to the Age effects, however, no differences occur on the lower-level tasks of counting and rhyming, but differences do occur on the higher-level tasks. In other words, differences between age groups show up only for those tasks involving higher levels of processing. This result is basically what Eysenck set out to demonstrate.

17.5 Measures of Association and Effect Size

We can look at the magnitude of an effect in two different ways, just as we did with the one-way analysis. We can either calculate an r-family measure, such as $\hat{\eta}^2$ or $\hat{\omega}^2$, or we can calculate Cohen's $\hat{d}$, a very useful measure of effect size. Normally, when we are examining an omnibus F, we use an r-family measure. However, when we are looking at a difference between individual pairs of means, it is usually more meaningful to calculate an effect size estimate ($\hat{d}$).

r-family measures

As with the one-way design, it is both possible and often desirable to calculate the magnitude of effect associated with each independent variable. The most easily computed measure is again $\hat{\eta}^2$ (eta squared), although it is still a biased estimate of the value that we would get if we obtained observations on whole populations. For each effect (main effects and interactions) in the factorial design we compute $\hat{\eta}^2$ by dividing the sum of squares for that effect by SS_{total}. For our example

$$\hat{\eta}^2_A = \frac{SS_A}{SS_{total}} = \frac{240.25}{2667.79} = 0.09$$

$$\hat{\eta}^2_C = \frac{SS_C}{SS_{total}} = \frac{1514.94}{2667.79} = 0.57$$

$$\hat{\eta}^2_{AC} = \frac{SS_{AC}}{SS_{total}} = \frac{190.30}{2667.79} = 0.07$$

Thus within this experiment differences due to Age account for 9% of the overall variability, differences due to Condition account for 57% of the variability, and differences due to the Age × Condition interaction account for 7% of the variability. The remaining 27% of the variability in this experiment is assigned to error variance.

As with the one-way analysis, $\hat{\eta}^2$ is handy for making rough estimates of the contribution of variables, but a less biased estimate is given by $\hat{\omega}^2$ (omega squared). The calculations, though somewhat more cumbersome, are straightforward.

$$\hat{\omega}^2_A = \frac{SS_A - (a-1)MS_{error}}{SS_{total} + MS_{error}} = \frac{240.25 - (1)8.026}{2667.79 + 8.026} = 0.087$$

$$\hat{\omega}^2_C = \frac{SS_C - (c-1)MS_{error}}{SS_{total} + MS_{error}} = \frac{1514.94 - (4)8.026}{2667.79 + 8.026} = 0.554$$

$$\hat{\omega}^2_{AC} = \frac{SS_{AC} - (a-1)(c-1)MS_{error}}{SS_{total} + MS_{error}} = \frac{190.30 - (4)8.026}{2667.79 + 8.026} = 0.059$$

Notice that these values are slightly smaller than the values for $\hat{\eta}^2$, although their interpretation is basically the same.

When it comes to calculating $\hat{d}$, the procedure that we will use is essentially the same as it was for the one-way. Because we are most interested in an effect size for the comparison of two groups, or subsets of groups, we simply take the difference between the groups and divide that by our estimate of the standard deviation within groups, which is $\sqrt{MS_{error}}$. We can do this for either of the two main effects (Age and Condition) or for any of the simple effects, although this is more difficult when we have more than two groups. To use Age as an example,

$$\hat{d} = \frac{\overline{X}_{Younger} - \overline{X}_{Older}}{s} = \frac{13.16 - 10.06}{\sqrt{8.026}} = \frac{3.10}{2.833} = 1.09$$

The difference in recall between older and younger participants is a bit over one standard deviation, which is quite a big difference.

To look at Condition, we need to select a pair (or pairs) of means. For this example we will focus on the older participants, whom we expect to profit less from cognitive processing of information. (I chose this because I anticipate that an effect for younger participants would be even greater.) The Counting condition clearly represents the bare minimum of cognitive processing, while the Image condition is probably at the high end. For the older participants we have

$$\hat{d} = \frac{\overline{X}_{Imagery} - \overline{X}_{Count}}{s} = \frac{13.40 - 7.00}{\sqrt{8.026}} = \frac{6.40}{2.833} = 2.26$$

Here the two groups differ by about two and a quarter standard deviations—again, a very large effect. Clearly, the level of processing plays an important role in the amount of material people are able to recall. The methods for estimating the magnitude of effect for variables in a factorial design are simple extensions of the methods used with a one-way design. Again, we have the measures that are analogous to squared correlations ($\hat{\eta}^2$ and $\hat{\omega}^2$) and the effect size measure $\hat{d}$.

Several times I have referred to "means or sets of means," and perhaps it would be smart to look at a case where we would want to have an effect measure directed at sets of means. This example will be a bit strained because I do not have a nice clean reason for using the sets that I do, but you will have to give me a bit of leeway.

Two of Eysenck's conditions (Counting and Rhyming) really don't require much in the way of mental effort, whereas two of them (Adjective and Imagery) require the participant to think seriously about the words. Suppose that we wanted to compare those two sets, and we want to do so for the younger participants. The means for Counting and Rhyming are 6.5 and 7.6, for a combined mean of (6.5 + 7.6)/2 = 7.05. For Adjective and Imagery, the mean is (14.8 + 17.6)/2 = 16.2. Therefore

$$\hat{d} = \frac{\overline{X}_{C\&R} - \overline{X}_{A\&I}}{s} = \frac{7.05 - 16.2}{\sqrt{8.026}} = -3.23$$

We can therefore conclude that the difference in the means of the two sets of conditions is about three and a quarter standard deviations, which is a huge difference.

A complication

Throughout this book I have avoided the common practice of putting asterisks next to section headings that are more difficult and that might be skipped. However, this section is just such a section, and I am inserting it so that you have a flavor of what the issues are. I am not expecting everyone to clap their forehead and say, "Oh, of course!" Look to Howell (2012), Kline (2004), or Grissom & Kim (2012) for a more thorough discussion of these issues.

As was the case with t tests, the one-way analysis of variance, and the analyses we have done so far in this chapter, we will define our effect size as

$$\hat{d} = \frac{\overline{X}_1 - \overline{X}_2}{\hat{s}}$$

where the "hats" indicate that we are using estimates based on sample data. There is no real difficulty in estimating the numerator, because it is just the difference between two means (or the means of sets of means). On the other hand, our estimate of the appropriate standard deviation will depend on our variables. Some variables normally vary in the population (e.g., amount of caffeine a person drinks in a day, gender, intelligence) and are, at least potentially, what Glass, McGaw, and Smith (1981) call a "variable of theoretical interest." Age, extraversion, metabolic rate, and hours of sleep are other examples. On the other hand, many experimental variables, such as the number of presentations of a stimulus, area of cranial stimulation, size of a test stimulus, and presence or absence of a cue during recall do not normally vary in the population, and are of less theoretical interest (though they may be very important to that particular experiment). This distinction is a slippery one, and if a manipulated variable is not of theoretical interest, why are we manipulating it?

It might make more sense if we look at the problem slightly differently. Suppose that I ran a study to investigate differences among three kinds of psychotherapy. If I just ran that as a one-way design, my error term would include variability due to all sorts of things, one of which would be variability between men and women in how they respond to different kinds of therapy. Now suppose that I ran the same study but included gender as an independent variable. In effect, I am controlling for gender, and the regular MS_{error} term would not include gender differences because I have "pulled them out" in my analysis. So MS_{error} would be smaller here than in the one-way. That's a good thing in terms of power, but it may not be a good thing if I use the square root of MS_{error} in calculating the effect size. If I did, I would have a different-sized effect due to psychotherapy in the one-way experiment than I have in the factorial experiment. That doesn't seem right. The effect of therapy ought to be pretty much the same in the two cases. (Sex happens! So it should be involved in our measure.) So what I will do instead is to put that gender variability, and the interaction of gender with therapy, back into error when it comes to computing an effect size.

But suppose that I ran a slightly different (and slightly weird) study where I examined the same three different therapies, but also included, as a second independent variable, whether or not the patient sat in a cold tub of water during therapy. Now, patients don't normally sit in a cold tub of water, but it would certainly be likely to add variability to the results. That variability would not be there in the one-way design because we can't imagine some patients bringing in a tub of water and sitting in it. And it is variability that I wouldn't want to add back into the error term because it is in many ways artificial. The point is that I would like the effect size for types of therapy to be the same whether I used a one-way or a factorial design. To accomplish that, I would add effects due to Gender and the Gender × Therapy interaction back into the error term in the first study, and withhold the effects of Water and its interaction with Therapy in the second example.

As I said at the start, this is a slippery area and there is plenty of room for argument about when you should, and should not, adjust that error term. Different people might reasonably choose different approaches. Those are some of the fun issues in statistics, though I don't expect students to appreciate all the fun.

I am not going to show you exactly how we can manipulate our error term, because it is not something that I think that you are likely to want to do in the near future. But I can hint at the solution, and you can find an extended discussion in Howell (2012), and perhaps a better one in Kline (2004) or Grissom & Kim (2012, Chapter 7). If we want to add the effect of Gender and its interaction with Therapy back into the error term, all we need to do is to combine SS_{error}, SS_{Gender}, and $SS_{Interaction}$ into a new SS_{error} term, combine their degrees of freedom, and then divide one by the other. The square root of this *adjusted* standard deviation will serve as the denominator for $\hat{d}$. In the case of the cold bathtub, we don't want that variability added back in, so we just use the MS_{error} from our overall analysis as our denominator.

17.6 | Reporting the Results

We have carried out a number of calculations to make various points, and I would certainly not report all of them when writing up the results. What follows is the basic information that I think needs to be presented:

> In an investigation of the effects of different levels of information processing on the retention of verbal material, participants were instructed to process verbal material in one of four ways, ranging from the simple counting of letters in words to forming a visual image of each word. Participants in a fifth condition were not given any instructions about what to do with the items except to memorize them for later recall. A second dimension of the experiment compared Younger and Older participants on recall, thus forming a 2 × 5 factorial design.
>
> The dependent variable was the number of items recalled after three presentations. There was a significant Age effect ($F(1,90) = 29.94$, $p = .000$, $\hat{\omega}^2 = .087$), with younger participants recalling more items than did older participants. There was also a significant effect due to Condition ($F(4,90) = 47.19$, $p = .000$, $\hat{\omega}^2 = .554$), and visual inspection of the means shows that there was greater recall for conditions in which there was a greater degree of processing. Finally, the Age by Condition interaction was significant ($F(4,90) = 5.93$, $p = .017$, $\hat{\omega}^2 = .059$), with a stronger effect of Condition for the younger participants. (Notice that I have presented the exact F probabilities, instead of $p < .05$, as an example.)
>
> When we look at differences in recall between younger and older participants, $\hat{d}$ is equal to 1.09, indicating a difference of more than a standard deviation. (However, this difference is considerably greater for conditions involving greater processing, and is negligible for conditions involving minor processing.)

For older participants the difference between a condition with minimal processing and one with maximal processing had $\hat{d} = 2.26$. The effect size would be even greater if computed on younger participants.

This study has clearly shown that the common observation that older people do not recall information as well is tied to the level of processing. In tasks requiring little processing, there are no Age effects, whereas there are substantial Age effects for tasks involving greater processing.

17.7 | Unequal Sample Sizes

When we were dealing with a one-way analysis of variance, unequal sample sizes did not present a serious problem—we simply adjusted our formula accordingly. That is definitely *not* the case with factorial designs. Whenever we have a factorial design with unequal cell sizes, the calculations become considerably more difficult, and the interpretation can be very unclear. The best solution is not to have unequal *ns* in the first place. Unfortunately, the world is not always cooperative, and unequal *ns* are often the result. Standard statistical software usually provides the results that are most likely to be meaningful as the default. However, there are situations in which the standard solution is less than optimal. I will not cover the computational steps for unequal sample sizes because it is highly unlikely that you would ever run such an analysis by hand. I assume that you will use software such as SPSS or SAS, and their default solution is generally the one that you want (*R* requires special care—use the "car" library, set the contrast option as shown below, and use the Anova function asking for type 3 analyses.)[1] An extensive discussion of the problem of unequal sample sizes is contained in Howell (2012).

17.8 | Masculine Overcompensation Thesis: It's a Male Thing

We will look at one more example of a factorial design, again with equal sample sizes. Willer, Rogalin, Conlon, & Wojnowicz (2013) carried out a fascinating series of experiments looking at what is known as "masculine overcompensation" to explain behavioral choices. "The masculine overcompensation thesis asserts that men who feel insecure about their masculinity enact extreme masculine behaviors in an effort to achieve masculine status in their eyes and others" (Willer, Rogalin, Conlon, &Wojnowicz, 2013). The basic idea is that if you were a male and I could somehow make you feel less masculine, you would then be more likely to respond in more stereotypic masculine behavior. You might, for example, be more likely to buy a gun, go to a prize fight, denounce gay males, order a Hummer, or watch a violent movie. You may see parallels between this theory and the work by Adams et al. (1996) on homophobia that we covered earlier in the book.

Willer asked male and female participants to fill out a "gender identity survey" and then told them (randomly) that they scored in the male or female range on the scale. This was a 2×2 design with male and female participants crossed with male

---

[1] The code would be
library(car)
options(contrasts = c('contr.sum', 'contr.poly'))
model<– lm(Recall ~ Age * Condition)
Anova(model, type = 3)

and female feedback. (The feedback was independent of anything the participant had marked on the survey. Willer just made it up.) Following the feedback, participants filled out two survey packets. One dealt with support for an amendment banning same-sex marriage and with support for George W. Bush and the Iraq war. The other described four different cars (an SUV, a minivan, a coupe, and a sedan) and asked the participant to rate the quality of each car and how much he or she would be willing to pay for each car. The results were basically the same whether the participant was rating the war, gay marriage, or cars, but we will look at the data on homosexuality. Willer's hypothesis was that when a male was told that he scored nearer the female end of the sexuality scale, he would feel threatened and compensate by engaging in more masculine kinds of behavior, in this case raising his score on a scale of hostility toward homosexuality. Willer did not expect there would be similar differences in female participants in the two conditions.

The data in Table 17.5 were generated from populations with the same means and standard deviations that Willer found, though some minor changes were made to compensate for forcing the sample sizes to all equal 25. (I also suspect that Willer's data was positively skewed, but equally in each condition.) The labels "Confirmed" and "Threatened" relate to whether the feedback would be perceived as in line with an individual's own gender or the opposite gender.

From the means in Table 17.5b it would appear that there is some support for Willer's theory. When males were told that they scored toward the feminine end of

Table 17.5a   Data for Masculine Overcompensation Study

Condition	Opposition to Homosexuality									
Male Threat	2.62	5.26	3.86	4.98	2.81	3.95	4.49	5.35	6.66	6.04
	3.46	4.42	4.19	4.33	4.18	6.84	6.11	5.67	1.66	3.33
	1.92	4.13	3.74	3.25	3.40					
Male Confirm	3.97	0.19	3.27	1.56	1.30	6.75	5.93	1.84	0.72	4.26
	0.83	3.59	2.86	4.44	3.24	2.12	4.17	0.77	3.03	2.84
	2.93	1.52	0.37	2.28	0.57					
Female Threat	4.21	3.54	3.47	0.06	2.95	0.28	4.02	2.27	0.54	4.10
	1.06	1.79	5.06	3.02	2.05	4.26	3.26	3.40	3.65	0.12
	1.46	3.98	2.05	3.79	5.30					
Female Confirm	2.44	5.39	1.10	2.95	4.64	5.83	2.24	2.17	1.55	4.05
	0.52	1.47	2.99	5.12	2.63	2.94	1.78	5.67	1.49	0.22
	3.57	0.54	3.83	3.03	4.34					

Table 17.5b   Row, Column, and Cell Means

	Threat	Confirm	Row Mean
Male	4.266 (1.364)	2.614 (1.718)	**3.440**
Female	2.788 (1.538)	2.900 (1.648)	**2.844**
Col. Mean	**3.527**	**2.757**	**3.142**

> **Table 17.6** Analysis of Variance Summary Table for the Study of Masculine Overcompensation[2]
>
> $$SS_{Total} = \Sigma(X - \overline{X}_{gm})^2 = \Sigma X^2 - \frac{(\Sigma X)^2}{N} = 1267.712 - \frac{(314.19)^2}{100} = 280.558$$
>
> $$SS_G = nc\Sigma(\overline{X}_G - \overline{X}_{gm})^2 = (25)(2)[(3.440 - 3.142)^2 + (2.844 - 3.142)^2] = 8.886$$
>
> $$SS_T = ng\Sigma(\overline{X}_t - \overline{X}_{gm})^2 = (25)(2)[(3.527 - 3.142)^2 + (2.757 - 3.142)^2] = 14.815$$
>
> $$SS_{Cells} = n\Sigma(\overline{X}_{cg} - \overline{X}_{gm})^2 = 25\left[\begin{array}{l}(4.266 - 3.142)^2 + (2.614 - 3.142)^2 \\ + (2.788 - 3.142)^2 + (2.900 - 3.142)^2\end{array}\right]$$
>
> $$43.158$$
>
> $$SS_{TG} = SS_{cells} - SS_G - SS_C = 43.158 - 8.886 - 14.815 = 19.457$$
>
> $$SS_{error} = SS_{total} - SS_{cells} = 262.281 - 44.661 = 217.620$$
>
> Overall Analysis
>
> | Source | df | SS | MS | F | p |
> |---|---|---|---|---|---|
> | G (Gender) | 1 | 8.886 | 8.866 | 3.594 | .061 |
> | C (Threat) | 1 | 14.815 | 14.815 | 5.991 | .016 |
> | G*T | 1 | 19.457 | 19.457 | 7.868 | .006 |
> | Error | 96 | 237.400 | 2.473 | | |
> | Total | 99 | 280.558 | | | |

the scale they were scored as higher on opposition to homosexuality than males who were told that they scored in the male end of the scale.

The calculations are shown in Table 17.6.

From the summary table we can see that both the *F* for Gender and the *F* for Threat are significant. But those effects were not of particular interest to Willer. He was mainly interested in differences between Threat conditions at each level of gender. The interaction is also significant, and that is what is of most interest to us at this point. But the true focus is on simple effects. When we examine the means we see that there appears to be only a small difference due to the Threat condition for females, but a considerably larger difference for males. It is tending to look as if, when their sexual identity was threatened, males engaged in stereotypic masculine behavior.

Because the purpose of this study was primarily to look at how males respond when there is some threat to their masculinity, it makes the most sense to look at the simple effect of Threat condition on each Gender. (In fact, I think that a case could be made for starting with simple effects and not even looking for main effects, because they have little to do with the theory. That is pretty much what Willer did.) The simple effects summary tables will appear in the next section, so the calculations won't be repeated here. But it is important to note that the *F* for the comparison of the two conditions for males was 5.899 on 1 and 48 *df*. This is significant; *p* = .019. For females the *F* was 0.569, which is not significant.[3] Therefore, we can conclude that when males are told that they fall on the female side of a scale of sexuality (and presumably feel

---

[2]This table and one produced by SPSS will differ slightly due to rounding error.
[3]I should tell you that for SPSS if you want to run separate analyses for each gender, begin by going to **Data/Split file** and then tell it to split subsequent analyses on the basis of Gender.

threatened), they are more likely to display hostile attitudes toward homosexuals. The same is not true for females, whose simple effect test did not lead to rejection of the null hypothesis and moved in the opposite direction. (Willer found very similar results when he looked at support for violent military action, support for George W. Bush, and ratings of the desirability of SUVs.) In other words, this appears to be a robust finding.

If you wish to do this analysis using R, the code can be found at the Web page for this chapter under the name SimpleEffectsWiller.R. I used the "set.seed" command so that everyone will draw the same random sample in running the analysis.

Other ways of looking at these simple effects

In the next section using SPSS you will see the simple effects tested as two one-way analyses of variance, one for each Gender. There are two other ways that we could look at the simple effects. First, we could repeat the F tests but this time use the pooled error term from the overall analysis of variance. The other way to approach the simple effects is to note that with two conditions, we can use a t test for two independent samples our analysis. If you use t, the resulting values are $t = 3.766$ for males and -0.249 for females. We would reject the null hypothesis for males. If you square those t values you get 14.184 and 0.062, which are identical to the F values we originally calculated. That is true because an F test on two conditions is exactly equivalent to the square of the t testing those same means.

17.9   Using SPSS for Factorial Analysis of Variance

The printout from an SPSS analysis of the data in the previous example is shown in Figure 17.3. The first variable in the data set is coded 1 or 2, and indicates whether the participant was male (1) or female (2). The second variable indicates whether the participant was in the Threat (1) or the Confirm (2) group. The third

Figure 17.3   SPSS analysis of Willer's data

Univariate Analysis of Variance
gender = Male

Tests of Between-Subjects Effects[a]

Dependent Variable: score

Source	Type III Sum of Squares	df	Mean Square	F	Sig.	Partial Eta Squared
Corrected Model	34.114[b]	1	34.114	14.184	.000	.228
Intercept	591.680	1	591.680	246.010	.000	.837
threat	34.114	1	34.114	14.184	.000	.228
Error	115.445	48	2.405			
Total	741.239	50				
Corrected Total	149.559	49				

[a]gender = 1

[b]R Squared = .228 (Adjusted R Squared = .212)

(continued)

gender = Female

Tests of Between-Subjects Effects[a]

Dependent Variable: score

Source	Type III Sum of Squares	df	Mean Square	F	Sig.	Partial Eta Squared
Corrected Model	.158[b]	1	.158	.062	.804	.001
Intercept	404.360	1	404.360	159.151	.000	.768
threat	.158	1	.158	.062	.804	.001
Error	121.955	48	2.541			
Total	526.473	50				
Corrected Total	122.113	49				

[a]gender = 2

[b]R Squared = .001 (Adjusted R Squared = −.020)

column contains the dependent variable. After the overall analysis of variance are the tests on simple effects. You can produce these in SPSS by going to the drop-down menu labeled **Data** and asking it to split the file on the basis of gender. Then when you run the analysis you will obtain an analysis for males and separate analysis for females.

17.10 Seeing Statistics

On this book's website you will find an interesting applet that allows you to look at, and manipulate, main effects and interactions. An example of this display follows.

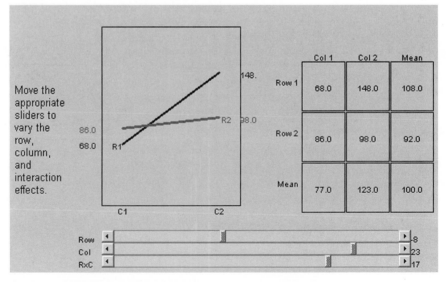

The best way to understand what this applet does is to play with it. At the bottom of the display you will see a slider for the row effect. If you move that left and right, you will alter the row effect that shows in your graph. Basically, you will move the two lines apart vertically. If you then use the slider labeled "Col," you will manipulate the column effect, which will have the result of rotating the lines by raising or lowering the right-hand ends of the lines. Finally, by manipulating the bottom slider you can increase or decrease the interaction, which has the effect of changing the degree to which the lines run nonparallel to each other.

- Use the data from Table 17.3 on recall as a function of Age and Condition, ignore the three middle conditions, and focus on the Counting and Intentional conditions. By using all three sliders, you should be able to build the appropriate main and interaction effects. You can't exactly replicate what the data show, but you can come reasonably close.

- Now increase or decrease either the row effect of the column effect. You should see what we mean when we say that those effects are independent. In other words, the column (and the interaction) effect do not change just because we have increased the size of the row effect.

- Now create a display that has a substantial Row effect, but absolutely no column or interaction effect.

17.11 Summary

In this chapter we extended the discussion of the analysis of variance to include designs involving two independent variables. In this analysis we assumed that there are still different participants in the different cells. We defined a factorial design as one in which we have two or more independent variables and in which every level of every independent variable is paired with every level of every other independent variable. We considered some of the advantages of factorial designs, especially that they allow us to look at the interaction effects of two variables. An interaction effect is the finding that whatever happens at one level of an independent variable, something else happens at another level. For example, in Willer's study of homosexuality, the difference between the Threatened and Confirmed conditions were quite different for males and females. Males who were told that they scored at the female end of the scale (Threatened) responded with more masculine behavior, whereas just the opposite happened for females (who responded with slightly more masculine behavior when their gender was Confirmed), though for females the effect was quite small and not significant.

We considered the difference between main effects, which is the effect of one variable collapsed across the levels of the other variable, and simple effects, which is the effect of one variable at *one* level of the other variable. Simple effects, like interactions, are often the most interesting part of an analysis of data.

We looked at the calculation of an analysis of variance for a factorial design and found that in many ways it is just an extension of what we covered in the previous chapter on one-way designs. For the main effects we simply ignore the presence of the other variable when we do our calculations. The calculation is different for the interaction, but essentially we just treat all of the cells as if they were a one-way to calculate SS_{cells} and then we subtract the two main effects from SS_{cells} to get the interaction term. We then get mean squares by dividing the sums of squares by their degrees of freedom, and then calculate our F by dividing each mean square by the error mean square. I mentioned that when we have unequal sample sizes the analysis is computed a bit differently, although you enter the same commands. I have not expanded on that topic here, but much of the software that you will use performs what most psychologists consider to be the appropriate analysis. (This is not the case in the anova function in the base package of R. You need the "car" library and the Anova function.)

Finally, we looked at ways of calculating measures of effect size. The r-family measures (η^2 and ω^2) are simple extensions of what we saw in Chapter 16. The calculation of d is similar to calculations in a one-way design, but the choice of the denominator (our estimate of error) is not always a clear one.

Key Terms

Factors, 448	Cell, 449
Two-way factorial design, 448	Grand mean, 450
Factorial design, 448	Main effect, 450
Interaction, 449	Simple effect, 452
2 × 5 factorial, 449	SS_{cells}, 453

17.12 A Quick Review

A. What is a factorial design?
   Ans: An experimental design in which every level of every factor is paired with every level of every other factor.

B. What is a 2 × 3 factorial design?
   Ans: It is a design with two independent variables, one with two levels and the other with three levels.

C. What is a simple effect?
   Ans: The effect of one independent variable at one level of the other independent variable.

D. What do we mean by a cell in a factorial design?
   Ans: It is the set of data for participants at one level of one variable and one level of the second variable.

E. How do we calculate the error sum of squares for a factorial design?
   Ans: It is the sum of squares left over after we subtract the main and interaction sums of squares from the total sum of squares. It is variability that does not belong to any of the effects in the design.

F. What should you say about main effects if there is a significant interaction?
   Ans: Usually we will ignore main effects in that case, although there is no rule that says we must. Usually simple effects would be more appropriate in this case.

G. When would you likely use a *d*-family measure of effect size in an analysis of variance?
Ans: They are generally used only when you are comparing two groups or sets of groups. Their meaning is fuzzy when applied to three or more groups at a time.

H. What would an *r*-family measure of effect size tell us for a factorial design?
Ans: It would represent the percentage of variation in that study that can be accounted for by differences in the effect under consideration.

I. What is often the most important feature of a factorial analysis of variance?
Ans: The ability to examine the interaction between variables.

17.13 Exercises

17.1   Thomas and Wang (1996) looked at the effects of memory on the learning of foreign vocabulary. Most of you have probably read that a good strategy for memorizing words in a foreign language is to think of mnemonic keywords. For example, in Tagalog (the official language of the Philippines), the word for eyeglasses is *salamin*. That word sounds much like our "salmon," so a possible strategy would be to imagine a picture of a salmon wearing glasses. This type of encoding strategy has been recommended for years, and people who try it generally report good immediate recall of foreign vocabulary. This fits nicely with dual-coding theories, in which the word is viewed as being stored both lexically and visually.

However, the studies that have looked at this phenomenon have generally asked the same participants to repeatedly recall items at several different times. Since each recall session means an additional practice session, practice and time effects are confounded. To get around this problem, Thomas and Wang used different participants at the two recall intervals. Data with very nearly the same means and variances as theirs are presented below.

Thomas and Wang ran a study in which they divided participants into one of three "Strategy" groups, and then tested them at one of two times (five minutes or two days). The strategies were

Keyword-Generated   Participants generated their own keywords to help them to remember 24 Tagalog words.

Keyword-Provided   The experimenters provided the keywords to help the participants to remember 24 Tagalog words.

Rote Learning   Participants were simply instructed to memorize the meaning of the Tagalog words.

The dependent variable was the number of English words recalled at either five minutes or two days.

Generated/5m	18	9	22	21	11	10	16	13	4	15	21	17	17
Provided/5m	24	19	19	23	21	23	19	22	20	21	18	18	20
Rote/5m	7	21	14	18	12	24	15	11	16	11	18	24	9
Generated/2d	7	8	7	2	6	4	4	4	5	2	2	1	0
Provided/2d	2	1	2	4	0	2	2	4	0	3	0	2	4
Rote/2d	15	23	9	18	13	7	7	3	5	12	26	15	13

a) How would you characterize this design?
b) What would be a reasonable *a priori* research hypothesis?
c) Calculate the cell means and standard deviations.

17.2 Plot the means for the data in Exercise 17.1 to show what the data have to say.

17.3 Run the analysis of variance using R or SPSS for the data in Exercise 17.1 and draw the appropriate conclusions.

17.4 The interaction in the analysis for Exercise 17.3 suggests that it would be profitable to examine simple effects. Compute the simple effects for the differences due to Strategy within each time interval and interpret the results. (I suggest that you split the file and run a separate analysis at each level of time.)

17.5 Use the Bonferroni test from Chapter 16 to elaborate on the results of Exercise 17.4.

17.6 The results in Exercises 17.1–17.4 are certainly extreme, and the statistics look unusual. What might trouble you about these data?

17.7 With respect to the previous five exercises, what have you learned about how you might study for your next Spanish exam?

17.8 In a study of mother–infant interaction, mothers are rated by trained observers on the quality of their interactions with their infants. Mothers were classified on the basis of whether this was their first child (primiparous versus multiparous) and whether the infant was low birth weight (LBW) or full-term (FT). (Full term generally means normal birth weight.) The data represent a score on a 12-point scale, on which a higher score represents better mother–infant interaction.

Primip/LBW	6	5	5	4	9	6	2	6	5	5
Primip/FT	8	7	7	6	7	2	5	8	7	7
Multip/LBW	7	8	8	9	8	2	1	9	9	8
Multip/FT	9	8	9	9	3	10	9	8	7	10

Run and interpret the appropriate analysis of variance.

17.9 Referring to Exercise 17.8, it seems obvious that the sample sizes do not reflect the relative frequency of these characteristics in the population. Would you expect the mean for all these primiparous mothers to be a good estimate of the population of primiparous mothers? Why or why not?

17.10 Use simple effect procedures to compare low birth weight and normal birth weight conditions for multiparous mothers. (Do this by recalculating the error term for multiparous mothers rather than using MS_{error} from the complete experiment.)

17.11 In Exercise 17.10 you used traditional simple and effect procedures.

a) What would happen if you simply ran a t test between LBW and FT means for multiparous mothers using MS_{error} as the pooled error term?
b) What would be different if you used the pooled variances of the two groups being compared?

17.12 In Chapter 16 we had three different examples from a study by Spilich et al. (1992) in which we compared three groups on the basis of smoking behavior. We can set this design up as a 3 × 3 factorial by using Task as one variable and Smoking group as the other. The dependent variable was the number of errors the participant made on that task. These data are repeated on the next page.

Pattern Recognition			Recall Task			Driving Simulation		
Non-Smoke	Delay Smoke	Active Smoke	Non-Smoke	Delay Smoke	Active Smoke	Non-Smoke	Delay Smoke	Active Smoke
9	12	8	27	48	34	15	7	3
8	7	8	34	29	65	2	0	2
12	14	9	19	34	55	2	6	0
10	4	1	20	6	33	14	0	0
7	8	9	56	18	42	5	12	6
10	11	7	35	63	54	0	17	2
9	16	16	23	9	21	16	1	0
11	17	19	37	54	44	14	11	6
8	5	1	4	28	61	9	4	4
10	6	1	30	71	38	17	4	1
8	9	22	4	60	75	15	3	0
10	6	12	42	54	61	9	5	0
8	6	18	34	51	51	3	16	6
11	7	8	19	25	32	15	5	2
10	16	10	49	49	47	13	11	3

Plot the cell means for this design.

17.13 Run the analysis of variance on the data in Exercise 17.12 and draw the relevant conclusions.

17.14 Even without picking up your pencil you can probably determine at least one conclusion about the data in Exercise 17.13. What is that conclusion, and why is it of no interest?

17.15 Compute the necessary simple effects to explain the results of Exercise 17.13. What do these results tell you about the effects of smoking?

17.16 For Exercise 17.15 use the protected t test to compare the Nonsmoking group to the other two groups in the Driving Simulation task.

17.17 If you go back to Exercise 16.2, you will see that it really forms a 2×2 factorial. Run the factorial analysis and interpret the results. (The data are reproduced here.)

Young/Low	8	6	4	6	7	6	5	7	9	7
Younger/Hi	21	19	17	15	22	16	22	22	18	21
Older/Low	9	8	6	8	10	4	6	5	7	7
Older/Hi	10	19	14	5	10	11	14	15	11	11

17.18 In Exercise 16.3 you ran a test between Groups 1 and 3 combined versus Groups 2 and 4 combined. How does that test compare to testing the main effect of Location in Exercise 17.16? Is there any difference?

17.19 Nurcombe, Howell, Rauh, Teti, Ruoff, and Brennan (1984) conducted an intervention program with mothers of low birth weight infants (LBW). (It is often difficult to recognize signals from low birth weight infants, and the program offered training in this domain.) One group of mothers received instruction on responding to subtle signals of LBW infants, while another group did not receive such instruction. A third group of mothers of normal birth weight infants served as a control group. In addition, mothers were divided by education level. Partial data from that study follow.

(a) Data

		Group		
Education	Group 1 LBW- Experimental	Group 2 LBW- Control	Group 3 Full Term	Age Means
High School	14	25	18	
Education or	20	19	14	
Less	22	21	18	
	13	20	20	
	13	20	12	
	18	14	14	
	13	25	17	
	14	18	17	
Mean	15.875	20.250	16.250	17.485
More Than	11	18	16	
High School	11	16	20	
Education	16	13	12	
	12	21	14	
	12	17	18	
	13	10	20	
	17	16	12	
	13	21	13	
Mean	13.125	16.500	15.625	15.083
Group Means	14.500	18.375	15.938	16.271

a) Run the appropriate analysis of variance on these results.
b) What would you conclude about the efficacy of the intervention program?

17.20 Calculate η^2 and ω^2 for the Maternal Adaptation data in Exercise 7.19.

17.21 Calculate $\hat{d}$ for the main effect of Group in the data in Exercise 17.17.

17.22 Calculate $\hat{d}$ for the difference due to education in Exercise 17.19. Next ignore the normal birth weight condition in Exercise 17.19 and calculate $\hat{d}$ for comparing the two low birth weight groups.

17.23 Make up a set of data for a 2×2 design that has no main effects but does have an interaction.

17.24 Describe a reasonable experiment in which the primary interest would be in the interaction effect.

17.25 Calculate η^2 and ω^2 for the data in Exercise 17.1.

17.26 Calculate $\hat{d}$ for the two main effects for the data in Exercise 17.1. (Choose two groups to compare that seem reasonable from what you understand about the design of the experiment.)

17.27 Calculate η^2 and ω^2 for the data in Exercise 17.13.

17.28 Calculate $\hat{d}$ for the two main effects for the data in Exercise 17.13, choosing suitable groups for comparison.

17.29 By comparing the formulae for η^2 and ω^2, tell when these two different statistics would be in close agreement and when they would disagree noticeably.

17.30 In the Eysenck (1974) study analyzed in Section 17.1, the real test of Eysenck's hypothesis about changes with age is found in the interaction. Why?

17.31 In the discussion of the results in Table 17.4, I stated that you should not routinely calculate every possible simple effect, but should look at only those in which you are interested. Explain why you think I said this, with reference to the discussion of familywise error rate in Chapter 16.

17.32 Becky Liddle at Auburn University published a study in 1997 on disclosing sexual orientation in class. She taught four sections of the same class, and at the week of the final lecture she disclosed her lesbian identity to two of the sections, and withheld it from the two others. She was concerned with the issue of whether disclosure would influence student evaluations of the course. The means and average variance for the two conditions, further broken down by gender of the students, are presented below. There were 15 students in each cell. Perform a two-way analysis of variance and draw the appropriate conclusions. (The means are the same that Liddle found, but because I could not control for difference in *midterm* evaluations, as she did, the effect of gender is different from the effect she found. The other effects lead to similar conclusions.)

Sexual Identification:

	Disclose	Not Disclose	Mean
Female	37.15	36.56	36.86
Male	33.00	33.00	33.00
Means	35.08	34.78	34.93

Average within-cell variance = 20.74

## CHAPTER 18

Repeated-Measures Analysis of Variance

In this chapter we will move to the case where we have multiple scores from the same person. We will examine why it is important to take into account that repeated measures are not independent, and we will see how to carry out the analysis. We will also look at making multiple comparisons among treatment means and consider the advantages and disadvantages of such designs.

In the previous two chapters we have been concerned with experimental designs in which there are different subjects in each group or cell. These designs are called **between-subjects designs** because they involve comparisons between different groups of subjects. However, many experimental designs involve having the same subject serve under more than one treatment condition. For example, we might take a baseline measurement of some behavior (i.e., a measurement before any treatment program begins), take another measurement at the end of a treatment program, and yet a third measurement at the end of a six-month follow-up period. Designs such as this one, in which participants are measured repeatedly, are called **repeated-measures designs** and are the subject of this chapter. Here comparisons are made of scores within the same subjects, and they are often called **within-subjects designs**. You may recognize that what will be a repeated-measures analysis of variance is very much like

CONCEPTS THAT YOU WILL NEED TO REMEMBER FROM PREVIOUS CHAPTERS

SS_{Total}, SS_{Group}, SS_{error}:	Sums of squares of all scores, of group means, and within groups
MS_{Group}, MS_{error}:	Mean squares for group means, and within groups
Interaction:	The situation where the effect of one variable depends, or is conditional on, another variable
Degrees of freedom:	The number of independent pieces of information remaining after estimating one or more parameters
Effect size ($\hat{d}$):	A measure intended to express the size of a treatment effect in terms that are meaningful to the reader
Eta^2 (η^2), omega^2 (ω^2):	Correlation-based measures of effect size
Multiple comparisons:	Tests on differences between specific group means

what I earlier called a *t* test for related samples, although we are not restricted to only two measurement conditions. In fact this is just the general case of that *t* test. In the same vein everything I said about the *t* test for related samples applies here. If two or more samples are related in any way—not just multiple measures on the same subjects—then this design applies. By far the most common use of this design is in cases in which the same set of participants are measured repeatedly on the same dependent variable, and that is the model followed in this chapter.

There are a wide variety of repeated-measures designs, depending on whether each subject[1] serves under all levels of all variables or whether some independent variables involve different groups of subjects while others involve the same subjects. In this chapter we will be concerned only with the simplest case, in which there is one independent variable and each subject serves under all levels of that variable. For analysis of more complex designs you can refer to Howell (2012) or Winer, Brown, and Michels (1991).

18.1   An Example: Depression as a Response to an Earthquake

Nolen-Hoeksema and Morrow (1991) had the good fortune to have administered a measure of depression to college students three weeks before the Loma Prieta earthquake in California in 1989. This was a major earthquake that would be expected to have measurable effects on students. Having collected these data, they went out and collected repeated data to track adjustment. The data that follow are modeled loosely on their findings. Our measurements are taken every three weeks, starting two weeks before the earthquake, and the data are shown in Table 18.1.

Look first at part (a) in Table 18.1. You will notice that there is a great deal of variability in the data, but much of that variability comes from the fact that some people exhibit more depression than others, which really has very little to do with the effects of the earthquake. The fact that you are more depressed in *general* than I am does not speak at all to the issue of whether the earthquake had the effect of increasing depression in those who experienced it. These are just individual differences in severity of depression. They lead to a correlation between the observations at one time and the observations at another time. Factoring this correlation out of the overall earthquake effect is what makes this design so powerful. What we are able to do with a repeated-measures design that we were not able to do with between-subjects designs is to remove this variability in people's *general* level of depression from SS_{total}. This has the effect of removing subject differences from the error term and producing a smaller MS_{error} than we would have otherwise. We do this by calculating a term called $SS_{subjects}$, which measures differences among people in terms of their reported depression. The $SS_{subjects}$ term is then subtracted from SS_{total}, along with SS_{weeks}, when we calculate SS_{error}. (In the previous design, in which every score represented a different subject, if we had calculated $SS_{subjects}$ it would have been the same thing as SS_{total}.)

---

[1]Standard APA format calls for identifying human subjects as "participants," or a similar term. However, the word "subject" is still used with statistical analyses, and it is used throughout this chapter because that is the standard way to refer to these experimental designs. You will see that SPSS refers to them in that way.

Table 18.1 Depression Scores Before and After an Earthquake. (Based on Nolan-Hoeksema and Morrow (1991).)

(a) Data

Subject	Week 0	Week 3	Week 6	Week 9	Week 12	Subject Mean
1	6	10	8	4	5	6.6
2	2	4	8	5	6	5.0
3	2	4	8	5	5	4.8
4	4	5	8	10	7	6.8
5	4	7	9	7	11	7.6
6	5	7	9	7	7	7.0
7	2	9	11	8	7	7.4
8	6	9	11	8	8	8.4
9	13	10	11	8	8	10.0
10	7	3	11	8	11	8.0
11	7	12	8	8	10	9.0
12	7	10	11	9	11	9.6
13	9	10	13	10	10	10.4
14	9	11	12	6	12	10.0
15	11	11	12	19	6	11.8
16	11	12	12	12	19	13.2
17	12	12	12	13	15	12.8
18	12	12	13	13	15	13.0
19	7	12	13	13	14	11.8
20	13	10	13	14	15	13.0
21	13	14	11	15	15	13.6
22	13	14	14	17	16	14.8
23	13	14	15	11	16	13.8
24	14	14	15	20	14	15.4
25	15	17	16	21	18	17.4
Weekly Mean	**8.68**	**10.12**	**11.36**	**10.84**	**11.24**	**10.448**

Grand mean = 10.448 ΣX = 1306.00 ΣX^2 = 15596.00
N = 125 w = # weeks = 5 n = # of subjects = 25

(b) Calculations

$$SS_{total} = \Sigma(X - \overline{X}_{gm})^2 = \Sigma X^2 - \frac{(\Sigma X)^2}{N} = 15{,}596.00 - \frac{1306^2}{125} = 1950.912$$

$$SS_{subjects} = w\Sigma(\overline{X}_{subjects} - \overline{X}_{gm})^2 = 5[(6.80 - 10.448)^2 + \cdots + (17.40 - 10.448)^2]$$

$$= 1375.712$$

$$SS_{weeks} = n\Sigma(\overline{X}_{week} - \overline{X}_{gm})^2 = 25[(8.68 - 10.448)^2 + \cdots + (11.24 - 10.448)^2]$$

$$= 121.152$$

$$SS_{error} = SS_{total} - SS_{subjects} - SS_{weeks} = 1950.912 - 1375.712 - 121.152 = 454.048$$

(c) Summary Table

Source	df	SS	MS	F	p
Subjects	24	1375.712			
Weeks	4	121.152	30.288	6.40	.0001
Error	96	454.048	4.730		
Total	124	1950.912			

From part (b) in Table 18.1 you can see that SS_{total} is calculated in the usual manner. Similarly $SS_{subjects}$ and SS_{weeks} are calculated just as main effects always are (square the deviations of the subject or group means from the grand mean, sum, and multiply by the number of observations per mean.) Finally, the error term is obtained by subtracting $SS_{subjects}$ and SS_{weeks} from SS_{total}.

The summary table, part (c) of Table 18.1, shows that I have computed an F for Weeks but not for Subjects. The reason is that MS_{error} is not an appropriate denominator for an F on subjects, nor do we have a term that would be. Therefore we cannot test the Subjects variable. This is not a great loss, however, because we rarely are concerned with determining whether subjects are different from one another. We computed $SS_{subjects}$ only to allow us to remove those differences from the error term and thus compute an appropriate error term to test Weeks.

You may have noticed that no Subjects × Weeks interaction is shown in the summary table. With only one score per cell, the interaction term *is* the error term; in fact some people prefer to write $S \times W$ instead of Error. No matter whether you think of it as Error or as the $S \times W$ interaction, this term is still the appropriate denominator for the F on Weeks.

The F value for Weeks is 6.40, based on 4 and 96 degrees of freedom. The critical value of F on 4 and 96 df is $F_{.05}(4,96) = 2.49$; $p = .0001$. We can therefore reject $H_0: \mu_1 = \mu_2 = \ldots = \mu_5$ and conclude that the earthquake was associated with a statistically significant increase in depression scores. It will be easier to see what has happened if we look at the means across weeks, plotted in Figure 18.1.

Notice that the calculations in Table 18.1 do not differ in any important way from the calculations in the two preceding chapters. We simply take deviations of a specific set of means (such as group or subject means) from the grand mean, square those deviations, and sum the results. We then multiply by an appropriate constant, which is just the number of observations on which each of those means is based. The degrees of freedom are just the number of mean deviations in question minus one.

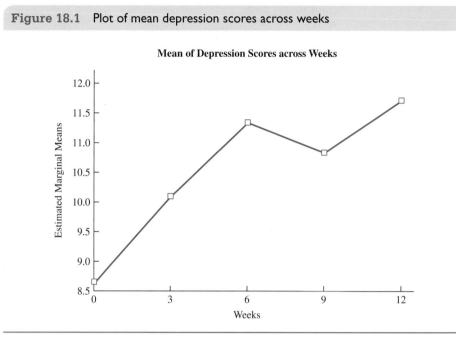

Figure 18.1 Plot of mean depression scores across weeks

From Figure 18.1 we can see that depression increased for the first two measurements following the earthquake and then began to level off. It had not, however, begun to fall even after 12weeks.

Using SPSS for a Repeated-Measures Design

I suspect that students and others are even less likely to calculate a repeated-measures design by hand than they would be to use hand calculation for the simpler designs. So I will jump into showing you how to use SPSS to make those calculations. I will then move to R, which is a bit more complex for reasons that will become apparent shortly.

Repeated-measures analyses can be a problem with some statistical software. SPSS will run the analysis fairly easily, although the printout is not what you might expect. I will present an abbreviated version of that printout in Figures 18.2 and 18.3. Note how the data need to be entered into a data file (one row per subject) and what choices to make in the various dialog boxes. I only show the data for the first 10 subjects, to save space.(Be sure that you load the complete data from Table 18.1 and not the partial data in Figure 18.2.)

Notice that each line represents the data for a single participant. We then use the SPSS **Analyze/General Linear Model/Repeated Measures** . . . command to specify the design of our analysis. Because the way you need to set up the analysis is unusual, I have shown the two important dialog boxes in Figure 18.3.

Figure 18.2   SPSS analysis of the earthquake data—the above are data for only the first 10 subjects.

	week0	week3	week6	week9	week12
1	6.0	10.0	8.0	4.0	5.0
2	2.0	4.0	8.0	5.0	6.0
3	2.0	4.0	8.0	5.0	5.0
4	4.0	5.0	8.0	10.0	7.0
5	4.0	7.0	9.0	7.0	11.0
6	5.0	7.0	9.0	7.0	7.0
7	2.0	9.0	11.0	8.0	7.0
8	6.0	9.0	11.0	8.0	8.0
9	13.0	10.0	11.0	8.0	8.0
10	7.0	3.0	11.0	8.0	11.0

Source: SPSS, an IBM Company

Figure 18.3   Dialog boxes showing how to specify the repeated measures analysis using SPSS

(a) Specify a name for the repeated measures, and the number of levels.

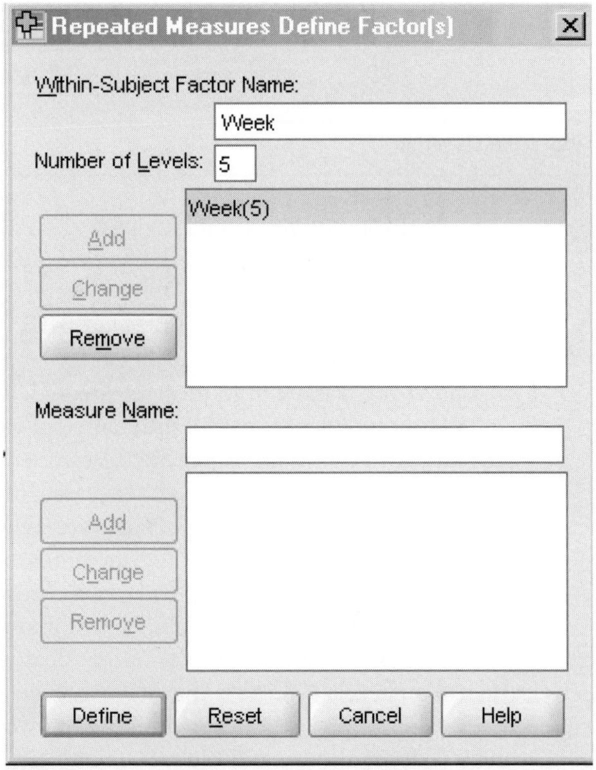

Source: SPSS, an IBM Company

> **Figure 18.3** Dialog boxes showing how to specify the repeated measures analysis using SPSS (*Continued*)

(b) Specify the design.

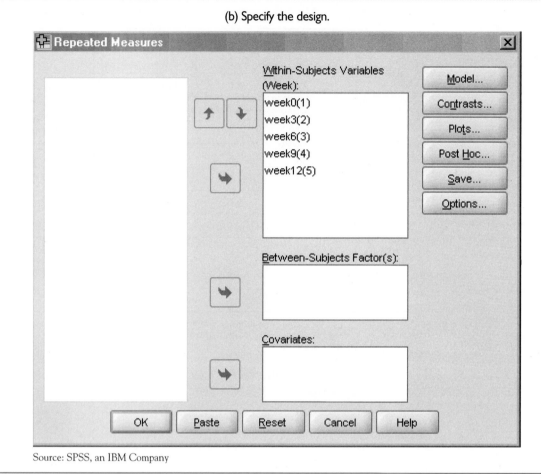

Source: SPSS, an IBM Company

At this point you would click on the **Add** button to move the information to the window, and then click on the **Define** button, which would bring you to the next dialog box.

In the dialog box shown in Figure 18.3 (b) I have specified that the scores for the five Weeks are the within-subject variables. I don't have any between-subjects variables (or covariates), so those boxes are left blank.

The most relevant part of the analysis of variance is shown in Figure 18.4. You can see that the results in this figure are the same as the results we obtained in Table 18.1.

Although many of the numerical values in Figure 18.4 can be found in Table 18.1, there are many that are new. This requires some explanation.

When SPSS runs a repeated-measures analysis of variance, it breaks the summary table into that part that deals with repeated measures (Within-subject effects) and that part that deals with measures that are not repeated across the same subjects (Between-subject effects). In the output dealing with Within-subject effects, you see the test on Weeks, which is the effect that we particularly care about. This F (6.404) is the same F that we obtained before. However, in that same table you see references to Greenhouse and Geisser, Huynh and Feldt, and Lower Bound. These are just corrections to the degrees of freedom that can be applied when we violate the

Figure 18.4 Selected output from SPSS

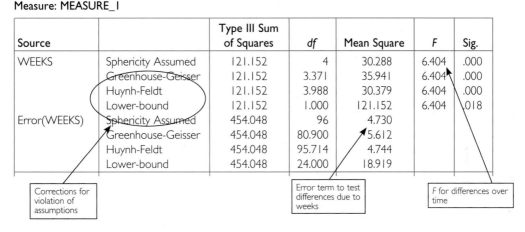

Tests of Within-Subjects Effects

Measure: MEASURE_1

Source		Type III Sum of Squares	df	Mean Square	F	Sig.
WEEKS	Sphericity Assumed	121.152	4	30.288	6.404	.000
	Greenhouse-Geisser	121.152	3.371	35.941	6.404	.000
	Huynh-Feldt	121.152	3.988	30.379	6.404	.000
	Lower-bound	121.152	1.000	121.152	6.404	.018
Error(WEEKS)	Sphericity Assumed	454.048	96	4.730		
	Greenhouse-Geisser	454.048	80.900	5.612		
	Huynh-Feldt	454.048	95.714	4.744		
	Lower-bound	454.048	24.000	18.919		

Corrections for violation of assumptions

Error term to test differences due to weeks

F for differences over time

Tests of Between-Subjects Effects

Measure: MEASURE_1

Transformed Variable: Average

Source	Type III Sum of Squares	df	Mean Square	F	Sig.
Intercept	13645.088	1	13645.088	238.046	.000
Error	1375.712	24	57.321		

$SS_{subjects}$

F on H_0: grand mean = 0

assumption that correlations between pairs of weeks are equal. See Howell (2012) for a more extensive discussion of this.

In the Between-Subjects part of the output you normally see tests related to differences between subjects. Here we don't have a between-subjects variable (as we would if we broke the data down by males and females, who obviously must be based on different subjects), and so the only test here is a test on the null hypothesis that the grand mean is 0. Such a test is only rarely of interest, and we usually ignore it.

18.2 Multiple Comparisons

If we wanted to carry the analysis further and make comparisons among means, we could use the protected t procedure discussed in Chapter 16. (Alternatively, we could use a Bonferroni test by dividing the selected significance level by the number of tests. The arithmetic for both tests would be the same.) The MS_{error} in this analysis would be the appropriate term to use in the protected t. For our data the results are clear-cut, and there is little or nothing to be gained by making multiple comparisons. However, I will illustrate the procedure by comparing the mean depression score before the earthquake with the mean of all of the depression scores after the earthquake. Because the overall F was significant, we can use the protected t to make this comparison.

The mean depression score before the earthquake can be read from Table 18.1 as 8.68. We can then average the post-earthquake means as

$$\overline{X}_{post} = \frac{10.12 + 11.36 + 10.84 + 11.24}{4} = 10.89$$

To compare depression pre- and post-earthquake we have

$$t = \frac{\overline{X}_i - \overline{X}_j}{\sqrt{MS_{error}\left(\dfrac{1}{n_i} + \dfrac{1}{n_j}\right)}} = \frac{\overline{X}_{pre} - \overline{X}_{post}}{\sqrt{MS_{error}\left(\dfrac{1}{n_{pre}} + \dfrac{1}{n_{post}}\right)}}$$

$$= \frac{8.68 - 10.89}{\sqrt{4.74\left(\dfrac{1}{25} + \dfrac{1}{100}\right)}} = \frac{-2.21}{\sqrt{0.237}} = -4.54$$

This t has df_{error} degrees of freedom because MS_{error} was used in place of the pooled variance. A t of -4.54 clearly is significant at $\alpha = .05$; ($p = .000$). Thus we can conclude that depression scores are significantly higher, on average, after the earthquake. Note that we were able to run the protected t test *as if* the means were from two independent samples because the error term has been adjusted accordingly.[2]

You might wonder how we can apply what *appears* to be a standard independent-groups t test when we know that the data are not independent. You will recall that in Chapter 13 we handled dependent observations by forming differences and then taking the standard deviation of the differences. From footnote 1 in Chapter 14 (p. 353) you could infer that the reason why we work with difference scores is because we could not calculate the variances of differences of non-independent samples directly from variables X_1 and X_2 unless we knew the correlations between X_1 and X_2. In other words, we do it to obtain a correct error term. However, for a repeated-measures analysis of variance, MS_{error} is, in fact, a correct estimate of the standard error of the differences, even though we don't use difference scores to calculate it. You can easily demonstrate this to yourself by running a repeated-measures analysis of variance and a t test for two related samples on the same set of data (e.g., use Week 0 and Week 3 from this study) and noting the similarities among the terms you calculate. (With one df in the numerator, $F = t^2$.)

I chose the comparison that I just tested for specific reasons, even though no particular comparison was required for us to see what was going on in the data. The first reason for choosing this comparison is that it represents a reasonable thing to test—are scores after the earthquake higher than those collected before the earthquake? The second reason for choosing this comparison is that it illustrates how we

---

[2] Some people would be tempted to test all of the differences, such as whether Week 5 is significantly different from Week 4. In most cases that is probably a bad idea. First of all, you probably don't care whether that difference happens to be statistically significant or not. It would not add appreciably to your knowledge if you did have that comparison. At the same time, increasing the number of tests increases the error rate. Do not run a test unless you really care about the answer.

can compare one mean with a combination of other means. All we have to do is to average the post-earthquake means and compare that result with the pre-earthquake means. Notice that I kept track of the number of scores going into each mean (25 and 100).

18.3 | **Effect Size**

The example involving depression offers a meaningful example of the use of effect size measures. First, we are dealing with a problem that affects many people, especially those living in earthquake zones. It is important not only to know that depression scores rise following an earthquake but also to have a measure on just how large a difference there is. Because depression scores do not have direct meaning to people, saying that depression increased by 2.2 points is not particularly informative. This example is an ideal case wherein we might wish to scale and report the difference in terms of standard deviation units.

For the pre-earthquake measurement the mean depression score was 8.68. After the earthquake, depression averaged out to 10.89. We could either scale this increase by the size of the standard deviation for the pre-earthquake scores or by the pooled overall standard deviation, which is the square root of MS_{error}. I will do it both ways to make a point.

We will again use $\hat{d}$ as our measure of effect size, and we will calculate $\hat{d}$ first using the pre-earthquake standard deviation (4.14). We subtract the pre-quake score from the post-quake score so as to have a positive value of $\hat{d}$ representing an increase in depression.

$$\hat{d} = \frac{\overline{X}_{post-quake} - \overline{X}_{pre-quake}}{s} = \frac{10.89 - 8.68}{4.14} = \frac{2.21}{4.14} = 0.53$$

This tells us that post-quake scores are about half a standard deviation higher than they were before the quake. That is a substantial difference.

If we use the square root of $MS_{error} = \sqrt{4.74} = 2.18$, we will have a measure of effect size that is

$$\hat{d} = \frac{\overline{X}_{post-quake} - \overline{X}_{pre-quake}}{s} = \frac{10.89 - 8.68}{2.18} = \frac{2.21}{2.18} = 1.01$$

and this result is nearly double the result we found using the pre-quake standard deviation. The reason that we find such a difference is that when using $\sqrt{MS_{error}}$ we are factoring out the correlation among scores, and therefore we are factoring out individual differences in depression. Since differences between people in terms of depression is a normal part of life, it seems reasonable to leave it in when we calculate an effect size measure. (See the discussion in Chapter 13, where I talk about this issue.) This would mean going with the figure of 0.53. This distinction is not an easy one to see, and it is not always easy to choose the correct approach. The general suggestion would be to use the standard deviation of a control condition (e.g., pre-test scores) if one is available. Here the pre-quake score is a logical control condition.

18.4 Assumptions Involved in Repeated-Measures Designs

As I have said, repeated-measures designs involve the same assumptions of normality and homogeneity of variance required for any analysis of variance. In addition, they require (for most practical purposes) the assumption that the correlations among pairs of levels of the repeated variable are constant.[3] In the case of our example this would mean that we assume that (in the population) the correlation between Week 0 and Week 3 is the same as the correlation between Weeks 3 and 4, and so on. For example, if the correlation between depression at Week 0 and depression at Week 3 is 0.50, then the correlation between depression scores for any other pairs of weeks should also be about 0.50. This is a rather stringent assumption and one that probably is violated at least as often as it is met. The test is not seriously affected unless this assumption is seriously violated. If it is seriously violated, there are two things you can do to ease the situation. The first thing you can do is to limit the levels of the independent variable to those that have a chance of meeting the assumption. For example, if you are running a learning study in which *everyone* starts out knowing nothing and ends up knowing everything, the correlation between early and late trials will be near zero, whereas the correlations between pairs of intermediate trials probably will be high. In that case do not include the earliest and latest trials in your analysis. (They wouldn't tell you much anyway.)

The second thing you can do is to use a procedure whose degrees of freedom have been adjusted appropriately, which we just saw. For our example we had $(w - 1)$ and $(w - 1) \times (n - 1)$ *df* for our *F*. It has been shown that if you took the same *F* but evaluated it on 1 and $(n - 1)$ *df*, you would have a very conservative test no matter how serious the violation. For our example this would mean evaluating our obtained *F* against $F(1,8) = 5.32$. We would still reject our null hypothesis ($p = .050$.) even using this conservative test. Greenhouse and Geisser (1959), and later Huynh and Feldt (1976), derived less conservative corrections to the degrees of freedom. Their tests are generally the appropriate ones. For a further discussion of these corrections, see Howell (2012).

Using *R* for Repeated-Measures

Running a repeated-measures analysis of variance in *R* is a bit more complicated. SPSS did something behind the scenes which you couldn't see. It transformed the data into what is often called the "long format." If you look at Table 18.1 you see that the data are spread out across the page, with one column for each variable. This is called the "wide format." What SPSS and *R* do is to run the data down the page. For example, you take the data for Week 3 and write it below the data for Week 0. Then you take the data for Week 6 and write it below those other two weeks, and so on. Now you have a column for Subjects and a column for the dependent variable. But we need one more column—labeled Weeks. It would have 25 1s, followed by 25 2s, and so on.

---

[3]The assumption isn't actually about the correlations, but about the pattern of covariances; it is much easier to comprehend, and not very far wrong, to think in terms of the correlations.

That sounds pretty easy if you are doing it by hand, but it is much messier if you are using *R* to do it. As I said, SPSS does it automatically, but unless you enter the data into a file in the long format, *R* can be a nuisance. But let's suppose that I create the file by hand in the long format. I will show how to have *R* make the adjustment from the wide format in a Web page for this chapter, but for now let's deal with one complication at a time.

I have a data file with three columns: one labeled Subjects, one labeled Week, and one labeled Depress. (You can find that on the Web in the DataFiles directory and named earthquakeLong.dat.) The code and the result follow.

R Code for Earthquake Data

```
   # Data were entered in the long format
dataLong <- read.table("earthquakeLong.dat", header = TRUE)
head(dataLong)
attach(dataLong)
Subject <- factor(Subject)
Week <- factor(Week)
cat("\nWeek Means","\n")
tapply(Depress, Week, mean)      #Print out the Week means
cat("\nSubject Means","\n")
tapply(Depress, Subject, mean)   #Print out the Subject means

  # Actual formula and calculation
earthquake.aov <- aov(Depress ~ Week + Error(Subject/Week))
  # This is really saying that the error term is MS(subjects within
weeks)
print(summary(earthquake.aov))
```

```
Error: Subject
             Df    Sum Sq    Mean Sq    F value    Pr(>F)
Residuals    24    1376      57.32

Error: Subject:Week
             Df    Sum Sq    Mean Sq    F value    Pr(>F)
Week         4     121.2     30.29      6.404      0.00013 ***
Residuals    96    454.0     4.73
---
Signif. codes:  0 '***' 0.001 '**' 0.01 '*' 0.05 '.' 0.1 ' ' 1
```

18.5   Advantages and Disadvantages of Repeated-Measures Designs

The major advantage of repeated-measures designs has already been discussed. Where there are large individual differences among subjects, these differences lead to large variability in the data. When subjects are measured only once, we cannot separate subject differences from random error, and everything goes into the error term. (That is what happened when we used the standard deviation of pre-quake scores to calculate $\hat{d}$.) When we measure subjects repeatedly, however, we can assess subject differences and separate them from error. This produces a more powerful experimental design and thus makes it easier to reject H_0.

The disadvantages of repeated-measures designs are similar to the disadvantages we discussed with respect to related-sample t tests (which are just special cases of repeated-measures designs). When subjects are used repeatedly, there is always the risk of carry-over effects from one trial to the next. For example, the drug you administer on Trial 1 may not have worn off by Trial 2. Similarly, subjects may learn something in early trials that will help them in later trials. In some situations this problem can be reduced by **counterbalancing** the order in which treatments are administered. Thus half the subjects might have Treatment A followed by Treatment B, and the other half might receive Treatment B followed by Treatment A. This counterbalancing will not make carry-over effects disappear, but it may make them affect both treatments equally. And obviously we cannot counterbalance Weeks in our example, because we cannot measure Week 3 before we measure Week 0. Although there are disadvantages associated with repeated-measures designs, in most situations the advantages outweigh the disadvantages, and such designs are popular and extremely useful in experimental work.

18.6 Writing Up the Results

If I were writing up the results of this study I would give a short introduction as to why the study was run, and I would most likely plot the means over time (here I have just indicated that the figure should be included in standard APA form). I would give both the F and p value from the overall analysis and the results of any subsequent tests that I ran, and an effect size for those subsequent tests. My write-up would look as follows.

Nolan-Hoeksema and Morrow (1991) collected data on depression from a large group of students as part of a different study. Because the Loma Prieta earthquake occurred shortly after their data collection, they tracked these same participants and collected depression scores every three weeks through Week 12. The weekly means are shown in Figure 1 below and show that depression scores increased for several weeks after the earthquake and then began to level off.

A repeated measures analysis of variance on these data produced a significant result ($F(4,96) = 6.404$, $p = .000$). A subsequent comparison of the pre-earthquake measure with the mean of the post-earthquake measures was statistically significant ($t(96) = -4.54$), indicating that depression scores increased significantly in the weeks after the earthquake. A measure of effect size, using the pre-earthquake standard deviation as the basis for standardization, yielded $\hat{d} = 0.53$, indicating an increase in depression scores of just more than half a standard deviation. As is apparent in Figure 1, by Week 12 the depression scores appear to be leveling off, but have not started to return to baseline levels.

18.7 | A Final Worked Example

As a final example I will adapt an example from Chapter 16 to illustrate the differences and similarities between the repeated-measures design and the more traditional between-subjects design. In Chapter 16 we used the data from Eysenck (1974) on recall as a function of depth of processing and examined the effect of recall Condition on older subjects. In Table 18.2 I use the same set of numbers for the sake of continuity. However, I have rearranged the data points to look like what we would expect if the data came from 10 subjects who served under all of the five recall conditions, rather than from 50 subjects who each served under only one condition.[4] I have merely shifted scores up and down in a column so that an individual who was one of the poor performers under one condition is also a poor performer under the other conditions, and similarly for the subjects showing good recall. The numbers in each Condition are still the same. I did this in such a way as to create correlations between the weeks. (If you moved these new data back into Chapter 16, you would obtain exactly the same results that we found there.) The data follow, with an additional column on the right for the subject means.

First we will calculate the SS_{total}:

$$SS_{total} = \Sigma(X - \overline{X}_{gm})^2 = \Sigma X^2 - \frac{(\Sigma X)^2}{N} = 4^2 + 5^2 + \ldots + 19^2 - \frac{503^2}{50}$$

$$= 5847 - 5060.18 = 786.82$$

We now have two main effects to calculate, one based on the Condition totals and one based on the Subject totals:

$$SS_{conditions} = n\Sigma(\overline{X}_C - \overline{X}_{gm})^2 = 10[(7.00 - 10.06)^2 + \ldots + (12.00 - 10.06)^2]$$

$$= 351.52$$

Table 18.2   Repeated-Measures Analysis Applied to the Eysenck Example

	Condition					
Subject	Count	Rhyming	Adjective	Imagery	Intentional	Subject Mean
1	4	3	6	9	5	5.40
2	5	6	8	12	10	8.20
3	6	6	10	11	15	9.60
4	6	8	11	11	11	9.40
5	7	6	14	11	11	9.80
6	7	7	11	10	11	9.20
7	8	7	13	19	14	12.20
8	8	6	13	16	14	11.40
9	9	9	13	12	10	10.60
10	10	11	11	23	19	14.80
Means	7.00	6.90	11.00	13.40	12.00	10.06

---

[4]We would *never* cavalierly rearrange real data like this. I did it here only to show the differences and similarities between the two experimental situations.

$$SS_{subjects} = c\Sigma(\overline{X}_S - \overline{X}_{gm})^2 = 5[(5.40 - 10.06)^2 + \ldots + (14.80 - 10.06)^2]$$
$$= 278.82$$

The error term can now be obtained by subtraction:

$$SS_{error} = SS_{total} - SS_{conditions} - SS_{subjects}$$
$$= 786.82 - 351.52 - 278.82 = 156.48$$

This error term is also equivalent to the Conditions $\times$ Subjects interaction, as described earlier.

We now set up the summary table:

Source	df	SS	MS	F	p
Subjects	9	278.82			
Conditions	4	351.52	87.88	20.22	.000
Error	36	156.48	4.35		
Total	49	786.82			

To test the F for the Conditions effect, we go to http://www.statpages.org/pdfs.html, and find $p = .000$, and we will reject the null hypothesis and conclude that recall of verbal material varies with the conditions under which that material is learned.

If you go back to Section 16.3, you will see that when I analyzed the same basic data set as a between-subjects design I obtained an F of 9.08 instead of 20.22. The difference is that in this analysis I have treated the data as if they were repeated measures and thus subtracted out differences due to subjects from the error term. Notice two things. In the earlier analysis the $SS_{Conditions}$ was 351.52, which is exactly what it is here. SS_{error} in the earlier analysis was 435.30. If you were to subtract from that the $SS_{subjects}$ (278.82) that we have here, you would get 156.48, which is the present SS_{error}. So you can see that we literally have subtracted out the sum of squares due to individual differences from our error term to make a more powerful test.

It is important to keep in mind that, for the sake of an example, I have moved the data around slightly to produce subjects who were consistently poor or consistently good. But this is nothing more than you would expect to find if you used the same subjects under all conditions. From a comparison of the F here and the one in Chapter 16, you can see that you generally increase the power of an experiment (on within-subject terms) and therefore the probability of finding a significant difference by using a repeated-measures design, if it is practical and appropriate.

18.8 Summary

In this chapter you saw how to handle data in which individual subjects served under all levels of one or more independent variables. When we have different participants in the different conditions we have what is called a between-subject design, whereas when the same participants serve in each condition we have a repeated-measures, or a within-subject, design.

We saw that the calculations for a repeated-measures design are very similar to those in the earlier designs we have discussed. You always calculate sums of squares in the same general way—sum the squares of deviations from the grand mean and then multiply by the appropriate constant. The difference here is that we are, in effect, subtracting the sum of squares for subjects from what would otherwise be our error term, giving us a more powerful test.

We saw that the testing of multiple comparisons is done in essentially the same way that we did it in the previous chapters. However, when the repeated measure is something like time, which is an ordered dimension, specific comparisons are often not necessary. If performance is increasing over time, it may not matter if the test on $Time_3$ versus $Time_4$ is significant—it is the overall trend that we care about. But I did show you that you could compare one time (pre-earthquake) with the average of several other times (post-earthquake) simply by obtaining the mean of the post-quake times and comparing that one mean with the pre-quake mean, taking the appropriate sample sizes into account.

As a measure of effect size we can use Cohen's $\hat{d}$, but we need to think about what standard deviation is appropriate for the denominator. Often a pre-test standard deviation makes more sense than a square root of MS_{error}.

Key Terms

Between-subjects designs, 476	Within-subjects designs, 476
Repeated-measures designs, 476	Counterbalancing, 488

18.9   A Quick Review

A. Why are some designs called "between-subjects" designs?
    Ans: These designs have different subjects in the different groups or cells, so comparison across groups is a comparison between the subjects in the different cells.

B. An important reason why repeated-measures designs are more powerful than between-subject designs is that we can factor out individual differences in the dependent variable. (T or F)
    Ans: True

C. Why is there no explicit interaction term in the design that we have been examining?
    Ans: The interaction and the error term would be the same thing.

D. What kind of multiple comparisons should you use for repeated-measures data?
    Ans: I recommend as few tests as possible on important questions. Either Fisher's protected-t or the Bonferroni correction will serve this purpose.

E. What is the effect size measure that is often used with repeated measures?
    Ans: We generally compare two measures or sets of measures using $\hat{d}$. The choice of the error term used in calculating $\hat{d}$ requires some thought.

F. What underlying assumption do we have with repeated-measures designs that is not necessary for between-subject designs?
    Ans: The correlation between any two sets of measures is approximately equal to the correlation between any other two sets of measures.

G. What is a disadvantage of within-subject designs, and is it always a disadvantage?
Ans: Such designs are subject to carry-over effects from one trial to another. However if you are studying something like learning, you hope to see carry-over effects.

H. For the same set of data, what is the difference between the error term in the between-subjects analysis and the error term in the repeated measures analysis?
Ans: In the repeated-measures design $SS_{Subjects}$ has been subtracted from the error term you would have in the between-subjects design.

18.10 Exercises

18.1 Migraine headaches are a problem for many people, and one way of treating them involves relaxation therapy. A study of the effectiveness of relaxation techniques in the treatment of migraines was conducted by Blanchard, Theobald, Williamson, Silver, and Brown (1978). The data that follow are in agreement with those found by Blanchard et al. (Their study was more complex than the one examined here.) I have calculated ΣX^2 to save you work.

	Baseline			Training		
Subject	Week 1	Week 2	Week 3	Week 4	Week 5	Subject Mean
1	21	22	8	6	6	12.6
2	20	19	10	4	9	12.4
3	7	5	5	4	5	5.2
4	25	30	13	12	4	16.8
5	30	33	10	8	6	17.4
6	19	27	8	7	4	13.0
7	26	16	5	2	5	10.8
8	13	4	8	1	5	6.2
9	26	24	14	8	17	17.8
Weekly Means	20.78	20.00	9.00	5.78	6.78	12.47

Grand Mean $= 12.47$ $\Sigma X = 561$ $\Sigma X^2 = 10.483$

Calculate and plot the appropriate column means.

18.2 Run a repeated-measures analysis of variance on the data in Exercise 18.1 and explain your results.

18.3 If you were designing the study referred to in Exercise 18.1, what else would you like to have collected to clarify the meaning of your results?

18.4 Using the data from Week 2 and Week 3 of Exercise 18.1, run a matched-sample t test to test the hypothesis that migraines decreased from before to after relaxation therapy.

18.5 Run a repeated-measures analysis of variance on the same data that you used in Exercise 18.4 and draw the appropriate conclusions.

18.6 For Exercise 18.5 compare the results you had in the two analyses.

18.7 Calculate $\hat{d}$ as an effect size estimate to elaborate on the results in Exercise 18.4.

18.8 Use the protected t tests with the data in Exercise 18.1 to help you interpret the results. However this time compare the mean of the two baseline measures with the mean of the three training measures. (*Hint:* As I pointed out, you can calculate the t test as if these were independent samples because MS_{error} has been adjusted accordingly by removing subject differences.)

18.9 Calculate an estimate of d for the comparison you made in Exercise 18.8.

18.10 St. Lawrence, Brasfield, Shirley, Jefferson, Alleyne, and O'Brannon (1995) investigated the effects of an eight-week Behavioral Skills Training (BST) program aimed at reducing the risk of HIV infection among African-American adolescents. The study followed males and females from a pretest to a 12-month follow-up, recording the frequency of condom-protected sex. (They also had a control condition, but I am going to look only at the males in the BST condition for this exercise.) The actual dependent variable is 1,000 times the natural logarithm of the frequency of protected sex. (I multiplied the log by 1,000 to eliminate decimal values.) The data for males follow.

Pretest	Posttest	Follow-up Six Months	Follow-up 12 Months
07	22	13	14
25	10	17	24
50	36	49	23
16	38	34	24
33	25	24	25
10	07	23	26
13	33	27	24
22	20	21	11
04	00	12	00
17	16	20	10

(a) Calculate and plot the means.
(b) Use the analysis of variance to draw the appropriate conclusions.

18.11 Rerun the analysis for the data in Exercise 18.10 using R or SPSS. (If you are using R you can either see the Web page referred to earlier or read your data from Ex18-10Long.dat.)

18.12 In the study discussed in Exercise 18.10, the authors also ran a control group under the same conditions, but without the BST intervention. Those data (for males) follow.

Pretest	Posttest	Follow-up Six Months	Follow-up 12 Months
00	00	00	00
69	56	14	36
05	00	00	05
04	24	00	00
35	08	00	00
07	00	09	37
51	53	08	26
25	00	00	15
59	45	11	16
40	02	33	16

(a) Calculate the means for these data and plot them on the same graph used in Exercise 18.9.
(b) Run the analysis of variance on these data.

18.13 What would you conclude from the comparison of the answers to Exercises 18.10 and 18.12? (You do not know how to run the appropriate analysis of variance with an extra between-subjects variable labeled "Group," though you might be able to figure it out if you have the appropriate software. However, the analysis itself is not the issue.)

18.14 The combined data for Exercises 18.10 and 18.12 are presented in the data file named Ex18.14. I have added another variable named Group and coded it 1 and 2. This is a between-subject variable. Go to the website for the chapter and load Between1Within1.r. Run that and interpret the results.

18.15 Use Bonferroni *t* tests with the data in Table 18.1 to compare performance at the following points:

a) Week 0 and Week 6
b) Week 0 and Week 12
c) Week 3 and Week 12

(*Hint:* See the hint in Exercise 18.8. I would not recommend all of those comparisons for an actual study unless you have a very good reason for doing so.)

18.16 Write a short paragraph describing the results of the analysis of the data in Exercise 18.1.

18.17 Use SPSS to reproduce the results that *R* gave you in Exercise 18.14.

## CHAPTER 19

Chi-Square

Now we are about to move from measurement data, which has been the topic of the previous chapters, to categorical data. We will see that the analysis of categorical data is quite different from what we have been doing. We will begin with data distributed across one dimension and then move to the more interesting situation where data are distributed across two dimensions. In the latter case we will see that we are interested in testing for the lack of independence of the two independent variables. We will then look at proportions and how they can be set up as contingency tables and analyzed that way. Effect size measures are calculated differently with categorical data, and we will spend a fair amount of time on risks, odds, and their ratios.

In Saint-Exupery's *The Little Prince* the narrator, remarking that he believes the prince came from an asteroid known as B-612, explains his attention to such a trivial detail as the precise number of the asteroid with the following comment:

> Grown-ups love figures. When you tell them you have made a new friend, they never ask you any questions about essential matters. They never say to you, "What does his voice sound like? What games does he love best? Does he collect butterflies?" Instead they demand: "How old is he? How many brothers has he? How much does he weigh? How much does his father make?" Only from these figures do they think they have learned anything about him.[1]

---

[1]Antoine de Saint-Exupery, *The Little Prince*, trans. Katherine Woods (New York: Harcourt Brace Jovanovich, Inc., 1943), pp. 15–16.

CONCEPTS THAT YOU WILL NEED TO REMEMBER FROM PREVIOUS CHAPTERS

Categorical variable:	A variable that represents counts of the number of observations falling into each of several categories
Interaction:	The situation where the effect of one variable depends on, or is conditional on, another variable
Degrees of freedom:	The number of independent pieces of information remaining after estimating one or more parameters
Effect size ($\hat{d}$):	A measure intended to express the size of a treatment effect in terms that are meaningful to the reader
Independent observations:	Observations in which the result for one measurement does not have any effect on the next measurement

In some ways the first chapters of this book have concentrated on dealing with the kinds of numbers Saint-Exupery's grown-ups like so much. This chapter will be devoted to the analysis of largely nonnumerical data.

In Chapter 11 I drew a distinction between measurement data (sometimes called quantitative data) and categorical data (sometimes called frequency data). When we deal with measurement data, each observation represents a score along some continuum, and the most common statistics are the mean and the standard deviation. When we deal with categorical data, on the other hand, the data consist of the frequencies of observations that fall into each of two or more categories ("Does your friend have a gravelly voice or a high-pitched voice?" or "Is he or she a collector of butterflies, coins, or baseball cards?").

As an example, we could ask 100 participants to classify a vaguely worded newspaper editorial as to whether it favored or opposed unrestricted dissemination of birth control information (no neutral or undecided response is allowed). The results might look as follows:

Editorial View Seen as

In Favor	Opposed	Total
58	42	100

Here the data are the numbers of observations that fall into each of the two categories. Given such data, we might be interested in asking whether significantly more people view the editorial as in favor of the issue than view it as opposed or whether the editorial is really neutral and the frequencies just represent a chance deviation from a 50:50 split. (Recall that participants were forced to choose between *in favor of* and *opposed.*)

A differently designed study might collect the same data on the newspaper editorial but try to relate those data to the individual's own views on the topic. Thus we might also classify respondents with respect to their views about the dissemination of birth control information. This study might arrive at the following data:

Respondent's View	Editorial View Seen as		
	In Favor	Opposed	Total
In Favor	46	24	70
Opposed	12	18	30
Total	58	42	100

Here we see that people's judgments of the editorial depend on their own point of view. The majority (46/70) of those in favor of the unrestricted dissemination of birth control information view the editorial as being on their side and the majority of those opposed generally see the editorial as siding with them (18/30). In other words, respondents' personal opinions and their judgments about the editorial are not independent of one another. (In the words of Chapter 17, they interact.)

Although these two examples appear somewhat different in terms of the way the data are arranged and in terms of the experimental questions being asked, the same statistical technique—**the chi-square test**—is applicable to both. However, because the research questions we are asking and the way that we apply the test are different in the two situations, we will deal with them separately.

19.1 # One Classification Variable: The Chi-Square Goodness-of-Fit Test

We will start with a simple but interesting example with only two categories and then move on to an example with more than two categories. Our first example comes from a paper that was published in the *Journal of the American Medical Association* on therapeutic touch (Rosa, Rosa, Sarner, & Barrett, 1996). One of the things that made this an interesting paper is that the second author, Emily Rosa, was only 11 years old at the time, and she was the principal experimenter.[2] To quote from the abstract, "Therapeutic Touch (TT) is a widely used nursing practice rooted in mysticism but alleged to have a scientific basis. Practitioners of TT claim to treat many medical conditions by using their hands to manipulate a 'human energy field' perceptible above the patient's skin." Emily recruited 21 practitioners of therapeutic touch, blindfolded them, and then placed her hand over one of their hands. If therapeutic touch is a real phenomenon, the principles behind it suggest that the participants should be able to identify which of their hands is below Emily's hand. Out of 280 trials, the participant was correct on 123 of them, which is an accuracy rate of 44%. By chance, we would expect the participants to be correct 50% of the time, or 140 times.

Although we can tell by inspection that participants performed even worse than chance would predict, I have chosen this example in part because it raises an interesting question of the statistical significance of a test. We will return to that issue shortly. The first question that we want to answer is whether the data's departure from chance expectation is significantly greater than chance. The data follow in Table 19.1.

Even if participants were operating at chance levels, one category of response is likely to come out more frequently than the other. What we want is a **goodness-of-fit test** to ask whether the deviations from what would be expected by chance are large enough to lead us to conclude that responses weren't random.

The most common and important formula for the chi-square statistic (χ^2) involves a comparison of observed and expected frequencies. The **observed frequencies**, as the name suggests, are the frequencies you actually observed in the data—the numbers in row two of Table 19.1. The **expected frequencies** are the frequencies you would expect *if the null hypothesis were true*. The expected frequencies are shown in

Table 19.1	Results of Experiment on Therapeutic Touch		
	Correct	Incorrect	Total
Observed	123	157	280
Expected	140	140	280

---

[2]The interesting feature of this paper is that Emily Rosa was an invited speaker at the "Ig Noble Prize" ceremony sponsored by the Annals of Improbable Research, located at MIT. This is a group of "whacky" scientists, to use a psychological term, who look for and recognize interesting research studies. Ig Nobel Prizes honor "achievements that cannot or should not be reproduced." Emily's invitation was meant as an honor, and true believers in therapeutic touch were less than kind to her. The society's Web page is located at http://www.improb.com/ and I recommend going to it when you need a break from this chapter.

row three of Table 19.1. We will make the very important, and I think reasonable, assumption that participants' responses are independent of each other. (In this use of "independence" I mean that what the *participant reports* on trial k does not depend on what he or she reported on trial $k - 1$, though it does not mean that the two different *categories* of choice are equally likely, which is what we are about to test.)

Because we have two possibilities over 280 trials, if the participant were choosing at random we would expect that there would be 140 correct and 140 incorrect choices. We will denote the observed number of choices with the letter "O" and the expected number of choices with the letter "E." Then our formula for chi-square is

$$\chi^2 = \Sigma \frac{(O - E)^2}{E}$$

where summation is taken over both categories of response.

This formula makes intuitive sense. Start with the numerator. If the null hypothesis is true, the observed and expected frequencies (O and E) would be reasonably close together and the numerator would be small, even after it is squared. Moreover, how large the difference between O and E is will depend to some extent on how large a number we expected. If we were talking about 140 correct, a difference of five choices would be a small difference. But if we had expected 10 correct choices, a difference of five would be substantial. To keep the squared size of the difference in perspective relative to the number of observations we expect, we divide the former by the latter ($[O - E]^2/E$). Finally, we sum over both possibilities to combine these relative differences. This test, in the form to be seen shortly, was initially proposed by Karl Pearson, and it is often referred to as the Pearson chi-square test. This is the same Pearson who gave us the Pearson product-moment correlation. In proposing the test, Pearson got the degrees of freedom wrong, and when Fisher proved that Pearson was wrong, things took another nasty turn. To quote Agresti (2002), Pearson did not like being corrected and wrote, "I hold that such a view [Fisher's] is erroneous and that the writer has done no service to the science of statistics by giving it broad-cast circulation . . . I trust my critic will pardon me for comparing him with Don Quixote tilting at the windmill; he must either destroy himself, or the whole theory of probable errors. . . ." Fisher did not "pardon" him. In fact, he made things worse by using data from Pearson's own son (Egon) to prove his case.

The χ^2 statistic for these data using the observed and expected frequencies given in Table 19.1 follows.

$$\chi^2 = \Sigma \frac{(O - E)^2}{E} = \frac{(123 - 140)^2}{140} + \frac{(157 - 140)^2}{140}$$

$$= \frac{-17^2}{140} + \frac{17^2}{140} = 2(2.064) = 4.129$$

The Chi-Square Distribution

Throughout this book, whenever we have calculated a statistic, such as t or F, we have evaluated it against a value in the appropriate Appendix or online computer programs such as the one at http://www.statpages.org/pdfs.html. The value in most tables tells us how large a value we might expect for the statistic if the null hypothesis were true; and if we exceed that value, we reject the null hypothesis. The same holds with the chi-square test. To test the null hypothesis that the probabilities of making

Table 19.2   Abbreviated Version of Table E.1, Upper Percentage Points of the χ^2 Distribution

df	.995	.990	.975	.950	.900	.750	.500	.250	.100	.050	.025	.010	.005
1	0.00	0.00	0.00	0.00	0.02	0.10	0.45	1.32	2.71	3.84	5.02	6.63	7.88
2	0.01	0.02	0.05	0.10	0.21	0.58	1.39	2.77	4.61	5.99	7.38	9.21	10.60
3	0.07	0.11	0.22	0.35	0.58	1.21	2.37	4.11	6.25	7.82	9.35	11.35	12.84
4	0.21	0.30	0.48	0.71	1.06	1.92	3.36	5.39	7.78	9.49	11.14	13.28	14.86
5	0.41	0.55	0.83	1.15	1.61	2.67	4.35	6.63	9.24	11.07	12.83	15.09	16.75
6	0.68	0.87	1.24	1.64	2.20	3.45	5.35	7.84	10.64	12.59	14.45	16.81	18.55
7	0.99	1.24	1.69	2.17	2.83	4.25	6.35	9.04	12.02	14.07	16.01	18.48	20.28
8	1.34	1.65	2.18	2.73	3.49	5.07	7.34	10.22	13.36	15.51	17.54	20.09	21.96
9	1.73	2.09	2.70	3.33	4.17	5.90	8.34	11.39	14.68	16.92	19.02	21.66	23.59
⋮	⋮	⋮	⋮	⋮	⋮	⋮	⋮	⋮	⋮	⋮	⋮	⋮	⋮

correct and incorrect choices are equal, we need to evaluate the obtained χ^2 against the sampling distribution of chi-square in Table E.1 in Appendix E. (A portion of that table is presented in Table 19.2.)

Using the calculator at http://www.statpages.org/pdfs.html, we see the following result.

Chi-Square

ChiSq	d.f.	p
4.129	1	0.0422
Calc ChiSq		Calc p

Note: *p* is a "one-tailed" area (from Chi-Sq to infinity)

We can also use *R* with the simple command

```
>1-pchisq(4.129, 1)
[1] 0.04215425
```

The chi-square distribution, like many other distributions we have seen, depends on the degrees of freedom. These are found running down the left side of Table 19.2. For the goodness-of-fit test the degrees of freedom are defined as $k - 1$, where k is the number of categories (in our example, 2). Examples of the chi-square distribution for four different degrees of freedom are shown in Figure 19.1, along with the critical values and shaded rejection regions for $\alpha = .05$. You can see that the critical value for a specified level of α (e.g., $\alpha = .05$) will be larger for larger degrees of freedom. For our example we have $k - 1 = 2 - 1 = 1$ df. From Table 19.2 you will see that, at $\alpha = .05$, $\chi^2_{.05}(1) = 3.84$. Thus when H_0 is true, only 5% of the time would we obtain a value of $\chi^2 \geqslant 3.84$. Because our obtained value is 4.129, we will reject H_0 and conclude that the therapeutic touch judge does not make correct and incorrect choices equally often. (The exact probability of that chi-square is .0422.) The practitioners that Emily Rosa tested would appear not to be guessing at random. In fact, their performance was statistically worse than random.

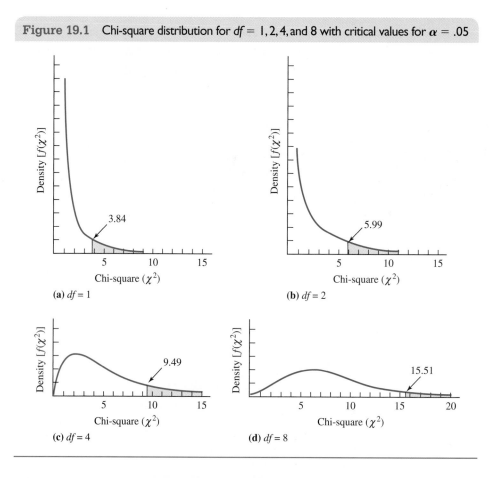

Figure 19.1 Chi-square distribution for $df = 1, 2, 4,$ and 8 with critical values for $\alpha = .05$

As I suggested earlier, this result could raise a question about how we interpret a null hypothesis test. Whether we take the traditional view of hypothesis testing or the view put forth by Jones and Tukey (2000) that the null is never true and should not influence our procedures, we can conclude that the difference is greater than chance. If the pattern of responses had come out favoring the effectiveness of therapeutic touch, we would come to the conclusion supporting therapeutic touch. But these results came out significant in the opposite direction, and it is difficult to argue that the effectiveness of touch has been supported because respondents were *wrong* more often than expected. Personally, I would conclude that we can dismiss the effectiveness of therapeutic touch. But there is an inconsistency here! If we had 157 correct responses I would say, "See, the difference is significant!" But when there are 157 *incorrect*, an equally improbable result, responses, I say, "Well, that's just bad luck and the difference really isn't significant." That makes me feel guilty because I am acting inconsistently. On the other hand, there is no credible theory that would predict participants being significantly wrong, so there is no real alternative explanation to support. People simply did not do as well as they should have if therapeutic touch works. (Sometimes life is like that!)

I should note that here, as in the analysis of variance, we are using a one-tailed test of a nondirectional null hypothesis. By that I mean that we reject only for large values of χ^2, not for small ones. In that sense the test is one-tailed. However, we will obtain large values of χ^2, in the two-category case, regardless of which category has the larger obtained frequency. In that sense the test is two-tailed. Multiple categories have a wide variety of patterns of differences that would lead to rejection, and the test could be thought of as multi-tailed or nondirectional.

Extension to the Multicategory Case

Many psychologists are particularly interested in how people make decisions, and they often present their subjects with simple games. A favorite example is called the Prisoner's Dilemma, and it consists of two prisoners (players) who are being interrogated separately.[3] The optimal strategy in this situation is for each player to remain silent rather than to plead guilty. However, people often depart from optimal behavior. Psychologists use such a game to see how human behavior compares with optimal behavior. Because I want an example with more than two categories, we are going to look at a different type of game, the universal children's game of "rock/paper/scissors," often abbreviated as "RPS." In case your childhood was a deprived one, I will describe how it works. In this game, each of two players "throws" a sign. A fist represents a rock, a flat hand represents paper, and two fingers represent scissors. Rocks break scissors, scissors cut paper, and paper covers rock. So if you throw scissors and I throw rock, I win because my rock will break your scissors. But if I had thrown paper when you threw scissors, you'd win because scissors cut paper. Children can keep this up for an awfully long time. (Some adults take this game very seriously, and you can get a flavor of what is involved by going to a fascinating article at http://www.danieldrezner.com/archives/002022.html. The topic is not as simple as you might think. There is even a World RPS Society with its own Web page.)

It seems obvious, at least to me, that in rock/paper/scissors the optimal strategy is to be completely unpredictable and to throw each symbol equally often. Moreover, each throw should be independent of others so that your opponent can't predict your next throw. There are, however, other strategies, each with its own advocates. Aside from adults who go to championship RPS competitions, the most common players are children on the playground. Suppose that we ask a group of children who is the most successful RPS player in their school and we then follow that player through a game with 75 throws, recording the number of throws of each symbol. The results of this hypothetical study are given in Table 19.3.

Although our player should throw each symbol equally often, our data suggest that she is throwing Rock more often than would be expected. However, this may just be a random deviation due to chance. Even if you are deliberately randomizing your

Table 19.3	Number of Throws of Each Symbol in a Playground Game of Rock/Paper/Scissors		
Symbol	Rock	Paper	Scissors
Observed	30	21	24
Expected	(25)	(25)	(25)

---

[3]See http://en.wikipedia.org/wiki/Prisoner's_dilemma for a more complete description of the Prisoner's Dilemma.

throws, one is likely to come out more frequently than others. (Moreover, people are notoriously poor at generating random sequences.) What we want is a goodness-of-fit test to ask whether the deviations from what would be expected by chance are large enough to lead us to conclude that this child's throws weren't random, but that she was really throwing Rock at greater than chance levels.

The χ^2 statistic for these data using the observed and expected frequencies given in Table 19.3 follows. Notice that it is a simple extension of what we did when we had two categories.

$$\chi^2 = \Sigma\frac{(O - E)^2}{E}$$

$$= \frac{(30 - 25)^2}{25} + \frac{(21 - 25)^2}{25} + \frac{(24 - 25)^2}{25} = \frac{5^2 + 4^2 + 1^2}{25}$$

$$= 1.68$$

In this example we have three categories and thus 2 df. The critical value of χ^2 on 2 df = 5.99, and we have no reason to doubt that our player was equally likely to throw each symbol ($p = .4317$).

19.2 Two Classification Variables: Analysis of Contingency Tables

In the two previous examples we considered the case in which data are categorized along only one dimension (classification variable). Often, however, data are categorized with respect to two (or more) independent variables, and we are interested in asking whether those variables are independent of one another. To put this in the reverse, we often are interested in asking whether the distribution of one variable is *contingent* or *conditional* on a second variable. In this situation we will construct a **contingency table** showing the distribution of one variable at each level of the other. We saw one example of this kind of question when we wondered if the choices people made about the orientation of a newspaper editorial on birth control information depended on (was contingent on) the individual's own personal beliefs. Another example is offered in a study by Walsh et al. (2006) on the use of an antidepressant in the treatment of anorexia.

It has long been hypothesized that depression is one reason that girls who have been successfully treated for anorexia nervosa tend to relapse after treatment. (Even after returning to normal weight, 30% to 50% of patients are back in the hospital within one year.) A very common approach is to prescribe Prozac, or a related drug, to newly recovered patients with the idea that the drug will reduce depression, which will in turn reduce relapse.

Walsh et al. sampled 93 patients who had been successfully restored to an acceptable body mass. Forty-nine of these patients were then prescribed Prozac for one year, while 44 of them were given a placebo. This was a **double-blind study** in which neither the patient nor the study coordinators knew whether the drug or the placebo was being administered. The dependent variable was the number of patients in each group who successfully maintained their weight over one year. The data follow in Table 19.4 in the form of a contingency table. (Expected frequencies are shown in parentheses.)

	Outcome		
Treatment	Success	Relapse	Total
Drug	13 (14.226)	36 (34.774)	49
Placebo	14 (12.774)	30 (31.226)	44
Total	27	66	93

Table 19.4   The Relationship between Prozac and Anorexia

This table is not encouraging. It shows that not only did the Drug group not outperform the Placebo group, they actually underperformed that group (26.5% versus 31.5%). We still want to know if the underperformance is statistically significant or is simply a chance result. (It is conceivable that Prozac actually decreases a girl's ability to maintain weight, in which case it would actually be harmful to prescribe it to this population.)

Expected Frequencies for Contingency Tables

For a contingency table the expected frequency for a given cell is obtained by multiplying together the totals for the row and column in which the cell is located and dividing by the total sample size (N). (These totals are known as **marginal totals** because they sit at the margins of the table.) If E_{ij} is the expected frequency for the cell in row i and column j, R_i and C_j are the corresponding row and column totals, and N is the total number of observations, we have the following formula[4]:

$$E_{ij} = \frac{R_i C_j}{N}$$

For our example

$$E_{11} = \frac{49 \times 27}{93} = 14.226$$

$$E_{12} = \frac{49 \times 66}{93} = 34.774$$

$$E_{21} = \frac{44 \times 27}{93} = 12.774$$

$$E_{22} = \frac{44 \times 66}{93} = 31.226$$

Calculation of Chi-Square

Now that we have the observed and expected frequencies in each cell, the calculation of χ^2 is straightforward. We simply use the same formula that we have been using all along, although we sum our calculations over all cells in the table.

---

[4]This formula for the expected values is derived directly from the formula for the probability of the joint occurrence of two *independent* events given in Chapter 7 on probability. For this reason the expected values that result are those that would be expected if H_0 were true and the variables were independent. A large discrepancy in the fit between expected and observed would reflect a large departure from independence, which is what we want to test.

$$\chi^2 = \Sigma \frac{(O - E)^2}{E}$$

$$= \frac{(13 - 14.226)^2}{14.226} + \frac{(36 - 34.774)^2}{34.774} + \frac{(14 - 12.774)^2}{12.774} + \frac{(30 - 31.226)^2}{31.226}$$

$$= .315$$

Degrees of Freedom

Before we can compare our value of χ^2 to the value in Table E.1, we must know the degrees of freedom. For the analysis of contingency tables, the degrees of freedom are given by

$$df = (R - 1)(C - 1)$$

where

R = the number of rows in the table

and

C = the number of columns in the table

For our example we have $R = 2$ and $C = 2$; therefore, we have $(2 - 1)(2 - 1) = 1$ df. It may seem strange to have only 1 df when we have four cells, but once you know the row and column totals, you need to know only one cell frequency to be able to determine the rest.[5]

Evaluation of χ^2

With 1 df the critical value of χ^2, as found in Table E.1, is 3.84. Because our value of 0.315 falls below the critical value, we will not reject the null hypothesis that the variables are independent of each other. ($p = .5746$.) In this case we will conclude that we have no evidence to suggest that whether a girl does or does not relapse is dependent on whether she was provided with Prozac or a placebo. Notice that I have not said that we have proven that the two variables are independent, but only that we have not shown that they are related. However, given the fact that the difference actually favored the placebo and that the probability under the null was so large (the probability of chi-square > 0.315 can be found using R as **print(1 − pchisq(0.315, 1))**. That probability is 0.575), we certainly would be justified in acting as if we have shown that Prozac did not have the desired effect. We have not proven the null hypothesis, but if I were the patient's doctor I would probably now be reluctant to think that I could solve things by administering Prozac.

Using SPSS

Using SPSS to calculate chi-square can be a bit tricky at first. There are two ways to enter the data. The long way would be to make two columns with 13 pairs of 1 and 1

---

[5]This is where Karl Pearson had gone wrong. He thought that the degrees of freedom would be $RC - 1$ instead of $(R - 1)(C - 1)$.

in each column, then add on 14 pairs of 1 and 2, then 30 pairs of 2 and 1, and finally 36 pairs of 2 and 2. The first column could be labeled Row and the second labeled Column. Then go to **Analyze/Descriptive Statistics/ Crosstabs** and specify Row and Column as the variables. But be sure to click on the Statistics button and tell it that you want a chi-square test. It won't give you that test otherwise. But that is the hard way of entering data. You have to enter two columns of 93 rows. If your data happen to come that way, that's fine, but if you just want to enter a contingency table, it can be done much more easily. Just enter the data as in the following table.

	Row	Column	Frequency
1	1.00	1.00	13.00
2	1.00	2.00	36.00
3	2.00	1.00	14.00
4	2.00	2.00	30.00
5			

But now you have to do one more thing. Go to **Data/Weight Cases** and tell it to weight the cases by Frequency. Now you can run the chi-square test just as I described when you entered the data the hard way.

Using R

Things are somewhat easier in R. The following code will give you what you want.

```
# Chi-square tests and probabilities
data <- matrix(c(13, 36, 14, 30), byrow = TRUE, ncol = 2)
result <- (chisq.test(data, correct = FALSE))    #Don't use Yates'
correction - see below
print(result)
print(1-pchisq(0.3146, df = 1))    #Not necessary as the result will
contain the probability.
```

In the Web page for this chapter I show how to enter the data as 93 pairs of 1 and 2, although I can't imagine why you would want to do that.

19.3 | Possible Improvements on Standard Chi-Square

The result of a chi-square test when the data contain few observations can be very discontinuous. For example, if we simply took the first row of Table 19.4 and changed the entries from 13 and 36 to 12 and 37, the resulting chi-square would change from .315 to .618, which is a huge change. When we try to evaluate our obtained chi-square against tables that assume an underlying continuous distribution of chi-square, the fit is poor.

Some books advocate that for 2×2 tables you apply what is called a correction for continuity (also known as Yates' correction, after Frank Yates, who derived it), which simply amounts to reducing each numerator by one-half unit before squaring. This correction was once quite common, but it has lost favor as we have learned more about the analysis of contingency tables. The ready availability of Fisher's exact test, to be discussed next, makes the correction superfluous. For more extensive coverage see Howell (2012), who generally doesn't recommend it either.

Fisher's Exact Test

Fisher introduced what is called **Fisher's Exact Test** in 1934 at a meeting of the Royal Statistical Society. Without going into details, Fisher's proposal was to take all possible 2×2 tables that could be formed from the fixed set of marginal totals (i.e., without changing the totals on the right and bottom margins of the contingency table.) For example, the following three tables all have the same marginal totals but different cell frequencies.

	Outcome			Outcome			Outcome		
	Success	Relapse	Total	Success	Relapse	Total	Success	Relapse	Total
Drug	13	36	49	12	37	49	11	36	49
Placebo	14	30	44	14	30	44	16	30	44
Total	27	66	93	27	66	93	27	66	93

Fisher could, for example, calculate a statistic such as chi-square for each table. (His statistic was not chi-square, but that is not important.) He could then determine the proportion of those tables whose results (chi-square values) are as extreme, or more so, than the table we obtained from our data. If this proportion is less than α, we reject the null hypothesis that the two variables are independent and conclude that there is a statistically significant relationship between the two variables that make up our contingency table. I am assuming that you will do the calculations using statistical software rather than by hand, and so will not elaborate on the necessary steps. For our example, SPSS automatically gives the exact two-sided probability as .650, which again leads us to retain the null hypothesis. To use R, the command is **fisher.test(data)**.

Randomization tests

This suggestion by Fisher is the first time that we have seen this approach to hypothesis testing. Throughout the book we have dealt with tests in which we can go to statistical tables or a probability calculator and obtain a theoretical probability under the null hypothesis. Fisher's test does not rely on such tables. He enumerates all possible outcomes, given the marginal totals, and asks what percentage of them is more extreme than the result we obtained. No theoretical distribution is involved. You will see that we come back to this kind of approach in the next chapter.

Fisher's Exact Test versus Pearson's Chi-Square

We now have at least two statistical tests for 2×2 contingency tables—which one should we use? Probably the most common solution is to go with Pearson's chi-square; perhaps because "that is what we have always done." In previous editions of this book I recommended against Fisher's Exact Test, primarily because of its reliance on fixed marginal totals. However, in recent years there has been an important growth of

Table 19.5 Eye Color as a Function of Gender

Gender	Eye Color				Total
	Blue	Brown	Green	Hazel	
Female	370	352	198	187	1,107
Male	359	290	110	160	919
Total	729	642	308	347	2,026

interest in permutation and randomization tests, of which Fisher's Exact Test is an example. I am extremely impressed with the logic and simplicity of such tests and have come to side with Fisher's Exact Test. In most cases, the conclusion you will draw will be the same for the two approaches, though this is not always the case. When we come to tables larger than 2×2, Fisher's approach does not apply, without modification, and there we almost always use the Pearson chi-square. (But see Howell & Gordon, 1976.)

19.4 | Chi-Square for Larger Contingency Tables

The previous example involved two variables (Drug and Outcome), each of which had two levels. This particular design is referred to as a 2×2 contingency analysis and is a special case of more general $R \times C$ designs (where R and C represent the number of rows and columns). For an example of the treatment of a larger contingency table we will analyze some data presented by Froelich and Stephenson (2013). The authors collected the data from an online survey of more than 2,000 cases, looking at the relationship between gender and eye color. I would have assumed that there would not be any reason for the eye color of females to differ from the eye color of males, but perhaps I am wrong. The data appear in Table 19.5.

We can plot these data with R. The code for doing so can be found on the R page for this chapter. The results are shown in Figure 19.2.

Figure 19.2 Eye color in relation to gender

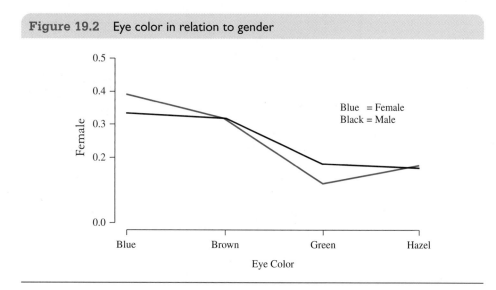

From simply looking at Figure 19.2 it is difficult to see whether there is a gender effect or not. The hand calculation of chi-square for these data would be the same as for the 2 × 2 tables, except that they are more entries. If we use *R* for our calculations we have the following very simple code.

R Code

```
# Amy G. Froelich
# W. Robert Stephenson
# Iowa State University
# Journal of Statistics Education
# Volume 21,
# Number2(2013),\www.amstat.org/publications/jse/v21n2/froelich_ds.pdf

counts <- matrix(c(370, 352, 198, 187, 359, 290, 110, 160), byrow =
TRUE, nrow= 2)
print(counts)
print(chisq.test(counts, correct = FALSE))
print(fisher.test(count))
```

```
        Pearson's Chi-squared test

[1] "Cell totals"
      [,1] [,2] [,3] [,4]
[1,]  370  352  198  187
[2,]  359  290  110  160


        Pearson's Chi-squared test

data:  counts
X-squared = 16.0906, df = 3, p-value = 0.001087



        Fisher's Exact Test for Count Data

data:  counts
p-value = 0.00101
alternative hypothesis: two.sided
```

You can see that I entered the data as a matrix with two rows and four columns. I included the command "correct = FALSE" to instruct the program not to apply Yates' correction. If we want to use Fisher's test instead, the last command will do that. Given the very large size of the sample, I would be extremely surprised if Fisher's test produced a result that is more than trivially different from that produced by chi-square.

The results of this analysis suggest that there is a significant effect due to gender. Women are somewhat less likely to have blue eyes and somewhat more likely to have green eyes. The other two colors are nearly equivalent for Males and Females. The main reason that I chose this example is because the data don't really look all that different for Females and Males, but the chi-square statistic is clearly significant. That results primarily from the fact that we have such a large sample size. We need to be careful in interpreting statistical tests with very large sample sizes, because differences that are relatively minor and unimportant can still be significant if we have enough cases. This would be a very good reason for you to ask about a measure of effect size. Unfortunately, we don't have a very good test. Agresti (2002) has pointed out that while odds ratios and risk ratios are helpful for 2 × 2 tables, and we will see these statistics shortly, there is not a good way to produce a similar statistic for larger tables. We can work with multiple odds ratios, but that is well beyond what we want here and really is not all that helpful.

19.5 The Problem of Small Expected Frequencies

Chi-square is an important and valid test for examining either goodness of fit or the independence of variables (contingency tables). However, the test is not as good as we would like when the *expected* frequencies are too small. The chi-square test is based in part on the assumption that if an experiment were repeated an infinite number of times with the same number of participants, the obtained frequencies in any given cell would be normally distributed around the expected frequency. But if the expected frequency is small (e.g., 1.0), there is no way that the observed frequencies *could* be normally distributed around it. (The frequencies must be integers and you can't have frequencies less than zero.) In cases in which the expected frequencies are too small, chi-square may not be a valid statistical test. The problem, however, is how we define "too small." There are almost as many definitions as there are statistics textbooks, and the issue still is being debated in the journals. Here I take the admittedly conservative position that for small contingency tables (nine or fewer cells) all expected frequencies should be at least 5. For larger tables this restriction can be relaxed somewhat. There are people who argue that the test is conservative and produces few Type I errors, even with much smaller expected frequencies, but even they are forced to admit that when the total sample size is very small—as is frequently the case when the expected frequencies are small—the test has remarkably little power to detect false null hypotheses.

Fisher's Exact Test does not depend on an assumption about an underlying distribution. This means that small expected frequencies do not pose the problem for Fisher's test that they do for the traditional chi-square test. When you have small expected frequencies you are likely to be better off using Fisher's test, but even there, with small expected frequencies you have relatively little power to reject a false null hypothesis. (Daniel Soper, at http://www.danielsoper.com/statcalc3/ offers an online calculator for Fisher's Exact Test for 2 × 3 and 3 × 3 tables.) As we have seen, R can produce an exact test for tables of any size.

19.6 The Use of Chi-Square as a Test on Proportions

The chi-square test can be used as a test on proportions or differences between two independent proportions. This is the same test we have been using all along. We simply change the way we conceive of our proportions (i.e., we change proportions to frequencies).

The most common question to ask with respect to proportions concerns whether one proportion is significantly higher or lower than another. A good example of this is found in a study of helping behavior by Latané and Dabbs (1975). In that study, experimenters were instructed to walk into elevators and, just after the elevator started, drop a handful of pencils or coins on the floor. The dependent variable was whether bystanders helped pick up the pencils. One of the independent variables was the gender of the bystanders. The study was conducted in three cities (Columbus, Seattle, and Atlanta), but we will concentrate on the data from Columbus, where gender differences were least. We will also ignore any effect of the gender of the experimenter. Basically Latané and Dabbs found that 23% of the female bystanders and 28% of the male bystanders helped pick up the dropped items. (It is interesting that about three-quarters of the bystanders just stood there staring at the ceiling as if nothing had happened. Latané's work has had a depressing effect on my belief in human goodness.) The question of interest is whether the difference between 23% and 28% is statistically significant. To answer this question, we must know the total sample sizes. In this case there were 1,303 female bystanders and 1,320 males. (Notice the large sample sizes that are easily obtained in this type of experiment.) Because we know the sample sizes, we can convert the cell proportions to cell frequencies easily.

Proportional Data

	Sex of Bystander	
	Female	Male
Help	23%	28%
No Help	77%	72%
Number	1,303	1,320

Frequency Data

	Sex of Bystander		
	Female	Male	Total
Help	300	370	670
	(332.83)	(337.17)	
No Help	1,003	950	1,953
	(970.17)	(982.83)	
Total	1,303	1,320	2,623

The entry of 300 in the upper left corner of the table was obtained by taking 23% of 1,303 females. The other entries were obtained in an analogous way. The values in parentheses are the expected frequencies, computed in the normal way. We calculate χ^2 as follows:

$$\chi^2 = \Sigma \frac{(O - E)^2}{E}$$

$$= \frac{(300 - 332.83)^2}{332.83} + \frac{(370 - 337.17)^2}{337.17} + \frac{(1,003 - 970.17)^2}{970.17}$$

$$+ \frac{(950 - 982.83)^2}{982.83} = 8.64$$

The critical value on 1 df at $\alpha = .05$ is 3.84, so I will reject H_0 and conclude that the proportions are significantly different. ($p = .0033$.) We can conclude that under the conditions of this study males are more willing to help than females. (This study was conducted more than 30 years ago. Do you think that we would obtain similar results today?)

A word of warning when using proportions: You will have noticed that we converted proportions to frequencies and then ran the chi-square test on the frequencies. This is the *only* correct way to do that. I sometimes see people form a contingency table with the proportions themselves, rather than frequencies, as cell entries and then go ahead and compute χ^2 as if nothing were wrong. But something is *very* wrong. They will not have a legitimate value of χ^2, and their test will be incorrect. Proportions, even if you throw away the decimal point and pretend that they are whole numbers, are not legitimate data for a chi-square test. You must use frequencies.

19.7 | Measures of Effect Size

The fact that a relationship is "statistically significant" doesn't tell us very much about whether it is of practical significance. The fact that two independent variables are not statistically independent does not mean that the lack of independence is important or worthy of our attention. In fact, if you allow the sample size to grow large enough, almost any two variables would likely show a statistically significant lack of independence. We saw that with the data on eye color.

What we need, then, are ways to go beyond a simple test of significance to present one or more statistics that reflect the size of the effect we are looking at. As we have seen elsewhere in this book, there are two different types of measures designed to represent the size of an effect. One type, the *d*-family by measures, is based on one or more measures of the *differences* between groups or levels of the independent variable. The other type of measure, the *r*-family measures, represents some sort of correlation coefficient between the two independent variables. I will not cover the *r*-family measures here because they rarely give us a good intuitively appealing measure. (Essentially you could simply score people as 1 or 2 depending on whether they received the drug or the placebo, again score them 1 or 2 depending on whether they relapsed, and then correlate those two variables.)

An Example

An important and classic study of the beneficial effects of small daily doses of aspirin on reducing heart attacks in men was reported in 1988. More than 22,000 physicians were administered aspirin or a placebo on a daily basis, and the incidence of later heart attacks was recorded. The data are shown in Table 19.6. Notice that this design is a **prospective study** because the treatments (aspirin versus no aspirin) were applied and then future outcome was determined. (A **retrospective study** would select people who had, or had not, experienced a heart attack and then look backward in time to see whether they had been in the habit of taking aspirin in the past. That may sound like a similar design, but it's not.)

Table 19.6	The Effect of Aspirin on the Incidence of Heart Attacks		
	Outcome		
	Heart Attack	No Heart Attack	
Aspirin	104	10,933	11,037
Placebo	189	10,845	11,034
	293	21,778	22,071

For these data, $\chi^2 = 25.014$ on one degree of freedom, which is statistically significant at $\alpha = .05$, ($p = .0000$) indicating that there is a relationship between whether or not one takes aspirin daily and whether one later has a heart attack.[6]

d-family: Risks and Odds

Two important concepts with categorical data, especially for 2×2 tables, are the concepts of risks and odds. These concepts are closely related, and often confused, but they are basically very simple. We looked at these measures in Chapter 7, but that was long ago and they are worth reviewing.

For the aspirin data, 0.94% (104/11,037) of people in the aspirin group and $1.71 \leqq$ (189/11,034) of those in the control group suffered a heart attack during the study. (Unless you are a middle-aged male worrying about your health, the numbers look rather small. But they are important.) These two statistics are commonly referred to as risk estimates because they describe the risk that someone with, or without, aspirin will suffer a heart attack. Risk measures offer a useful way of looking at the size of an effect.

The **risk difference** is simply the difference between the two proportions. In our example, the difference is 1.71% − 0.94% = .77%. Thus, there is about three-quarters of a percentage point difference between the two conditions. Put another way, the difference in risk between a male taking aspirin and one not taking aspirin is about three-quarters of 1%. This may not appear to be very large, but keep in mind that we are talking about heart attacks, which are serious events.

One problem with a risk difference is that its magnitude depends on the overall level of risk. Heart attacks are quite low-risk events, so we would not expect a huge difference between the two conditions. (In contrast, Pugh [1983] studied conviction for rape depending on whether the *victim* was portrayed as being at fault. The probability of being convicted in either event was quite high, so there was a lot of room for the two conditions to differ. He found a 30 percentage point difference in favor of conviction when the victim was not portrayed as at fault. Does that mean that Pugh's study found a much larger effect size than the aspirin study? Well, it depends—it certainly did with respect to risk difference.)

Another way to compare the risks is to form a **risk ratio**, also called **relative risk**, which is just the ratio of the two risks. For the heart attack data the risk ratio is

$$RR = Risk_{\text{no aspirin}}/Risk_{\text{aspirin}} = 1.71\%/0.94\% = 1.819$$

---

[6]It is important to note that, although taking aspirin daily is associated with a lower rate of heart attack, more recent data have shown that there are important negative side effects. Current literature suggests that other alternatives may be at least as effective with fewer side effects.

Thus the risk of having a heart attack if you do not take aspirin is 1.8 times higher than if you do take aspirin. That strikes me as quite a difference.

One problem with risk, that is also a problem with odds, which we will cover next, is that they are easy to misinterpret. A good example is a discussion by David Zimmerman that can be found at http://www.columbia.edu/cu/21stC/issue-1.3/metaheart.html. He noted a brief technical report of a meeting of the American Heart Association. Calcium-channel blockers are supposed to reduce the risk of heart attack, but a report at the meeting showed that under some conditions a certain class of channel-blocking drugs increased the risk from .01 to .016. The Associated Press promptly reported that six million patients taking a class of drugs that are designed to lower their risk may actually increase it by 60%. That is scary. But, first of all, there are not six million patients taking those particular drugs. Second, this confuses absolute and relative risk. If you are one of those patients, your relative risk did increase by only 60%, but your absolute risk only increased by six-tenths of one percent. We have to be very careful with measures of risk and odds so as not to draw inappropriate conclusions from them.

We must consider a third measure of effect size, and that is the **odds ratio**. At first glance, odds and odds ratios look like risk and risk ratios, and they are often confused, even by people who know better. (In a previous edition, although I knew better, I referred to odds, but described them as risks, much to my chagrin.) Recall that we defined the *risk* of a heart attack in the aspirin group as the number having a heart attack divided by the *total number of people in that group*. (e.g., 104/11,037 = 0.0094 = 0.94%.) The **odds** of having a heart attack for a member of the aspirin group is the number having a heart attack divided by the number *not having a heart attack*. (e.g., 104/10,933 = 0.0095.) The difference (though very slight when we are looking at rare events) comes in what we use as the denominator—risk uses the total sample size and is thus the proportion of people in that condition who experience a heart attack. Odds uses as a denominator the number *not* having a heart attack and is thus the ratio of the number having an attack versus the number not having an attack. Because the denominators are so much alike in this example, the results are almost indistinguishable. That is certainly not always the case. In Pugh's example, the *risk* of being convicted of rape in the low-fault condition is 153/177 = 0.864 (86% of the cases are convicted), whereas the *odds* of being convicted in the low-fault condition are 153/24 = 6.375 (the odds of being convicted are 6.4 times the odds of being found innocent).

Just as we can form a risk ratio by dividing the two risks, we can form an **odds ratio** by dividing the two odds. For the aspirin example the odds of heart attack given that you did not take aspirin were 189/10,845 = 0.017. The odds of a heart attack given that you did take aspirin were 104/10,933 = 0.010. The odds ratio is simply the ratio of these two odds and is

$$OR = \frac{Odds \mid No\ Aspirin}{Odds \mid Aspirin} = \frac{0.0174}{0.0095} = 1.83$$

Thus, the odds of a heart attack without aspirin are 1.83 times higher than the odds of a heart attack with aspirin.[7]

---

[7]In computing an odds ratio, there is no rule about which odds go in the numerator and which in the denominator. It depends on convenience. Where reasonable, I prefer to put the larger value in the numerator to make the ratio come out greater than 1.0, simply because I find it easier to talk about that way. If we reversed them in this example, we would find OR = 0.546, and conclude that your odds of having a heart attack in the aspirin condition are about half of what they are in the No Aspirin condition. That is simply the inverse of the original OR (0.546 = 1/1.83).

Why do we have both odds and risk?

Why do we have to complicate things by having both odds ratios and risk ratios? Why can't we just toss one out and use the other? That is a very good question, and it has some good answers. Risk is something that I think most of us understand. When we say the risk of having a heart attack in the No Aspirin condition is .0171, we are saying that 1.71% of the participants in that condition had a heart attack, and that is pretty straightforward. Many people prefer risk ratios for just that reason. In fact, Sackett, Deeks, and Altman (1996), in an article entitled *"Down with odds ratios!"*, argued strongly for the risk ratio on just those grounds—they feel that odds ratios, while accurate, are misleading. When we say that the odds of a heart attack in that condition are .0174, we are saying that the odds of having a heart attack are 1.74% of the odds of not having a heart attack. That may be a popular way of setting bets on race horses, but it leaves me dissatisfied.[8] So why have an odds ratio in the first place?

An important point is that an odds ratio can be calculated in situations in which a true risk ratio cannot be. In a retrospective study, where we find a group of people who had heart attacks and another group of people who did not have heart attacks and we look back to see if they took aspirin, we can't really calculate *risk*. Risk is future oriented. If we give 1,000 people aspirin and withhold it from 1,000 others, we can look at these people 10 years down the road and calculate the risk (and risk ratio) of heart attacks. But if we take 1,000 people with (and without) heart attacks and look backward, we can't really calculate risk because we have sampled heart attack patients at far greater than their normal rate in the population (50% of our sample has had a heart attack, but certainly 50% of the population does not suffer from heart attacks). But we can always calculate odds ratios. And, *when we are talking about low probability events*, such as having a heart attack, the odds ratio is usually a very good estimate of what the risk ratio would be if we could calculate it. The odds ratio is equally valid for prospective and retrospective sampling designs. That is important.

19.8 A Final Worked Example

We will take as our final example a study by Geller, Witmer, and Orebaugh (1976). These authors were studying littering behavior and were interested in, among other things, whether a message about not littering would be effective if placed on the fliers often given out in supermarkets advertising the daily specials. (This experiment was used in Chapter 7 to illustrate probability concepts.) To simplify a more complex study, two of Geller's conditions involved passing out handbills in a supermarket. Under one condition (Control) the handbills contained only a listing of the daily specials. In the other condition (Message), the handbills also included the notation, "Please don't litter. Please dispose of this properly." At the end of the day Geller and his students searched the store for handbills. They recorded the number found in trashcans; the number left in shopping carts, on the floor, and in various other

---

[8]An excellent website that makes this point better than I can is http://itre.cis.upenn.edu/~myl/languagelog/archives/004767.html. It makes clear how odds ratios can easily mislead.

Table 19.7 Data from Study by Geller, Witmer, and Orebaugh (1976)

	Trashcan	Litter	Removed	Total
Control	41	385	477	903
	(61.66)	(343.98)	(497.36)	
Message	80	290	499	869
	(59.34)	(331.02)	(478.64)	
Total	121	675	976	1,772

places where they didn't belong (denoted Litter); and the number that could not be found and were apparently removed from the premises. The data obtained under the two conditions are shown in Table 19.7 and are taken from a larger table reported by Geller et al. Would you expect that such a notice on a handbill would have much effect on what *you* did with that handbill when you were finished with it? (I don't read handbills like that, but my wife searches for bargains before she takes another step.)

We can analyze this contingency table appropriately by using the chi-square test because we have 1,772 independent observations falling into six mutually exclusive cells. We will test the null hypothesis that the location of the fliers at the end of the day is independent of the instructions on the flier, and we will set $\alpha = .05$.

We calculate the expected frequencies by the same procedure we have used before. Namely, for a contingency table the expected frequencies are given by $E = RT \times CT/GT$, where RT, CT, and GT stand for row, column, and grand totals, respectively. Therefore, if H_0 were true, the expected number of fliers from the Control group (the fliers without the message) found in the trashcan, would be $E_{11} = (903)(121)/1,772 = 61.66$. Similarly, the number of people who received the antilittering message and removed their fliers would be expected to be $E_{23} = (869)(976)/1,772 = 478.64$.

The calculation of χ^2 is based on the same formula we have been using all along:

$$\chi^2 = \Sigma \frac{(O - E)^2}{E}$$

$$= \frac{(41 - 61.66)^2}{61.66} + \frac{(385 - 343.98)^2}{343.98} + \cdots + \frac{(499 - 478.64)^2}{478.64}$$

$$= 25.79$$

There are 2 *df* for this analysis because $(R - 1)(C - 1) = (2 - 1)(3 - 1) = 2$. The critical value of $\chi^2_{.05}(2) = 5.99$, so we are led to reject H_0 at $p = .0000$ and to conclude that the location in which handbills were left depended on the instructions given. In other words, Instruction and Location are not independent. From the data it is evident that when subjects were asked not to litter, a higher percentage of handbills were thrown into the trashcan or taken out of the store, and fewer were left lying in the shopping carts or on the floors and shelves.

If you were writing up these results, you would probably want to say something like the following:

In an attempt to investigate whether people respond to antilittering messages on handbills, 1,772 shoppers at a local supermarket were given handbills advertising daily specials. Approximately half of these fliers contained a message asking people not to litter and to dispose of the handbill in an appropriate place, while the other half did not contain such a message. At the end of the day a count was made of the number of messages found in the trash, the number that were found as litter, and the number that were removed from the store. These were classified by the presence or absence of the message on the flier, and a chi-square test was applied to the results. For these data $\chi^2(2) = 25.79$, $p = .000$. Examination of the results indicated that a smaller percentage of the handbills containing the antilittering message was found as litter, and a higher percentage was placed in the trash or removed from the store.

19.9 A Second Example of Writing up Results

We will take as a second example of how to write up results using as our example the study of rape convictions (Pugh, 1983). It is a good example because the question is timely, even though it is an old study, and the statistics are straightforward. If you were writing up those results, you would probably want to say something like the following:

In examining the question of whether a defense lawyer's attempt to place blame on the victim of rape would influence a jury's decision in a rape case, jury participants were presented with a situation in which the victim was characterized by the defense as either partly responsible for the rape or not responsible. The jurors were then asked to make a judgment about whether the defendant was guilty or not guilty of the crime. When the victim was portrayed as low in fault, 86% of the time the defendant was judged to be guilty. When the victim was portrayed as high in fault, the defendant was judged guilty only 58% of the time. A chi-square test of the relationship between Fault and Guilt produced $\chi^2(1) = 35.93$, which is statistically significant at $p = .0000$. This is associated with an odds ratio of 4.61, indicating that the odds of being found guilty of rape are more than four and a half times higher in the condition in which the victim is portrayed as not bearing fault for the rape. The odds ratio would indicate that we are speaking of a meaningful difference between the two conditions.

19.10 Seeing Statistics

The applet entitled Mosaic Two-Way, which can be found on the website, illustrates the meaning of chi-square in a 2×2 contingency table. The display that follows was taken from data that McClelland originally produced, although the variable names have been changed. In this display the darker the rectangle, the greater the number of observations in that cell over what would be expected if the null hypothesis were true. On the other hand, the lighter the rectangle, the more the observations fall below expectation.

You can enter the data from the study by Walsh on depression and anorexia. Which cells are over- and underrepresented?

You can also enter the data from Latané and Dabbs in Section 19.6. Now which cells are overrepresented?

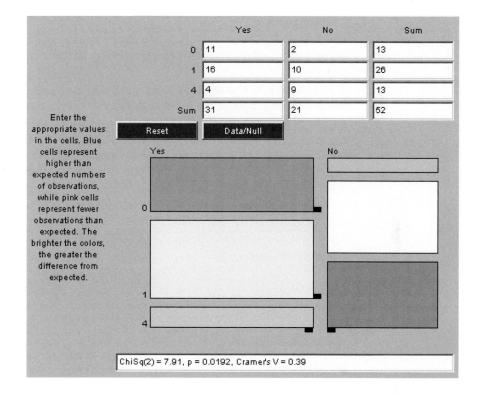

Finally, using the Latané and Dabbs example again, assume that you could add 10 observations to any one cell. Where should you add those observations to produce the greatest increase in chi-square?

19.11 Summary

This chapter discussed the use of the chi-square test for the analysis of frequency data. We first considered the test for goodness-of-fit for the situation in which there is only one variable of classification. In this situation the test is normally used to ask if the observations are equally distributed across the levels of the classification, though if a theory specifies a different kind of distribution, the test will also work for that.

We then looked at the chi-square test applied to contingency tables. A contingency table is a two-dimensional table in which each observation is classified on the basis of two variables simultaneously. Chi-square is used to test the null hypothesis that the two variables are independent. If they are independent, then the expected cell frequencies can be computed as the product of the row and column totals divided by the grand total. The test can then be applied just as it was in the one-dimensional case by squaring the differences between obtained and expected cell frequencies, dividing by the expected frequency, and then summing across all cells.

The degrees of freedom for the contingency table are the product of one less than the number of rows times one less than the number of columns.

We discussed Fisher's Exact Test as an alternative to calculating the traditional chi-square statistic. That test is often a better test when one or more of the expected frequencies is small, but it is a test that you would only compute using computer software.

We covered a test on the difference between two proportions and suggested that you need to convert the proportions to frequencies and then run the chi-square test on those frequencies. You cannot enter the proportions themselves into the chi-square formula.

With respect to a measure of effect size we looked at odds, risks, and their ratios. Risk is defined simply as the number of observations in that cell divided by the total number of observations. In that sense it is really a percentage. Odds, on the other hand, divide the number of observations in a cell by the number of observations not in that cell. Both odds and risks can be converted to ratios. The risk ratio is simply the ratio of two risks, and the odds ratio is the ratio of two odds. Risk ratios come closer to what people take them to be, the relative risk of two outcomes, but odds ratios are harder to understand. One strength of odds ratios is that if an event is of quite low probability, the odds ratio is a good approximation of what the risk ratio would be if we could calculate one, since we cannot calculate risk ratios directly in a retrospective study.

Key Terms

Chi-square test, 496	Fisher's Exact Test, 506
Goodness-of-fit test, 497	Prospective study, 511
Observed frequencies, 497	Retrospective study, 511
Expected frequencies, 497	Risk difference, 512
Contingency table, 502	Risk ratio (relative risk), 512
Double-blind study, 502	Odds, 513
Marginal totals, 503	Odds ratio, 513

19.12 A Quick Review

A. Why do you suppose it is called a "goodness-of-fit" test?
Ans: We are testing how "good" a fit we have between the data that we collected and the results we would expect by chance.

B. What is a contingency table?
Ans: It is a table that shows the frequency of occurrence of outcomes of one level of the independent variable across the levels of the other independent variable.

C. What is a double-blind study?
Ans: It is a study in which neither the participants (subjects) nor the people collecting the data know to which condition the participant was assigned.

D. What are "marginal totals"?
Ans: The totals of the rows and columns and the grand total.

E. Give one advantage of Fisher's Exact Test over the traditional chi-square test.
Ans: Fisher's test does not rely on any approximation to some theoretical distribution. (OK, I admit that this was not an easy question.)

F. How do you use the chi-square test to perform tests on proportions?
    Ans: You convert proportions to frequencies and work with the frequencies.

G. What is a prospective study?
    Ans: It is a study in which some treatment is applied and then, *later*, some measure is taken as the dependent measure. This is as opposed to a retrospective study where we get cancer or control patients and then look *back* to see whether or not they once smoked.

H. What is another name for "risk ratio"?
    Ans: Relative risk

I. What does it mean to say that a risk ratio for cancer among long-term smokers and nonsmokers is 24.2?
    Ans: It means that a long-term heavy smoker is 24.2 times as likely to get cancer than a nonsmoker.[9]

19.13 Exercises

19.1 The chair of a psychology department suspects that some of his faculty are more popular than others. There are three sections of Introductory Psychology (taught at 10:00 A.M., 11:00 A.M., and noon) by Professors Anderson, Klansky, and Kamm. The number of students who enroll for each section are given.

Professor Anderson	Professor Klansky	Professor Kamm
25	32	10

Run the appropriate chi-square test and interpret the results.

19.2 From the point of view of designing a valid experiment an important difference exists between Exercise 19.1 and a similar example used in this chapter. The data in Exercise 19.1 will not really answer the question that the chair wants answered. What is the problem, and how could the experiment be improved?

19.3 I have a theory that if you ask participants to sort one-sentence characteristics of people (e.g., "I eat too fast") into five piles ranging from *not at all like me* to *very much like me*, the percentage of items placed in each pile will be approximately 10%, 20%, 40%, 20%, and 10% for the five piles. I have one of my children sort 50 statements and obtain the following data:

8   10   20   8   4

Do these data support my hypothesis?

19.4 To what population does the answer to Exercise 19.3 generalize?

19.5 In an old, but very important and influential, study by Clark and Clark (1939), Black children were shown Black dolls and White dolls and were asked to select one to play with. Out of 252 children, 169 chose the White doll and 83 chose the Black doll. What can we conclude about the behavior of these children?

---

[9]For more data on this issue see http://www.wsiat.on.ca/english/mlo/smoking.htm. Retrieved 8/3/2012. That figure of 24.2 is not an exaggeration.

19.6 Following up the study referred to in Exercise 19.5, Hraba and Grant (1970) repeated the Clark and Clark study. The studies were not exactly equivalent, but they were close enough and the results are interesting. They found that out of 89 Black children, 28 chose the White doll and 61 chose the Black doll. Run the appropriate chi-square test on their data and interpret the results.

19.7 Combine the data from Exercises 19.5 and 19.6 into a two-way contingency table and run the appropriate test. How does the question that the two-way classification addresses differ from the questions addressed by Exercises 19.5 and 19.6?

19.8 We know that smoking has all sorts of ill effects on people, and among other things there is evidence that it affects fertility. Weinberg and Gladen (1986) examined the effects of smoking on the ease with which women become pregnant. They took 586 women who had planned pregnancies, and asked them how many menstrual cycles it had taken for them to become pregnant after discontinuing contraception. They also sorted the women into whether they were smokers or nonsmokers. The data follow.

	1 Cycle	2 Cycles	3+ Cycles	Total
Smokers	29	16	55	100
Nonsmokers	198	107	181	486
Total	227	123	236	586

Does smoking affect the ease with which women become pregnant? (I do not recommend smoking as a birth control device.)

19.9 How would you modify the analysis of the data in Exercise 19.8 if you also had the data on smoking behavior of the partners of these women?

19.10 Use the data in Exercise 19.8 to demonstrate how chi-square varies as a function of sample size.

a) Double each cell entry and recompute chi-square.
b) What does this have to say about the role of the sample size in hypothesis testing?

19.11 Howell and Huessy (1985) used a rating scale to classify children as to whether or not they showed Attention Deficit Disorder (ADD)–like behavior in the second grade. They then classified these same children again in the fourth and fifth grades. At the end of the ninth grade they examined school records and noted which children were enrolled in remedial English. In the following data all children who were ever classified as ADD have been combined into one group (labeled ADD):

Classification	Remedial English	Nonremedial English	Total
Normal	22	187	209
ADD	19	74	93
Total	41	261	302

Does ADD classification in elementary school predict enrollment in remedial and nonremedial English in high school? Modify the *R* code that we have used in the text to make your calculation.

19.12 In Exercise 19.11 children were classified as those who never showed ADD-like behavior and those who showed ADD behavior at least once in the second, fourth, or fifth grade. If we do not collapse across categories, we obtain the following data:

Exhibition of ADD-Like Behaviors	Remedial English	Nonremedial English
Never	22	187
Grade 2	2	17
Grade 4	1	11
Grades 2 & 4	3	16
Grade 5	2	9
Grades 2 & 5	4	7
Grades 4 & 5	3	8
Grade 2, 4, & 5	4	6

a) Run the chi-square test, again using R.

b) What would you conclude, ignoring the small expected frequencies?

c) How comfortable do you feel with these small expected frequencies? How might you handle the problem?

19.13 It would be possible to calculate a one-way chi-square test on the data in column 1 of Exercise 19.12. What hypothesis would you be testing if you did that? How would that hypothesis differ from the one you tested in Exercise 19.12?

19.14 In a study of eating disorders in female adolescents, Gross (1985) asked each of her participants whether they would prefer to gain weight, lose weight, or maintain their current weight. (*Note*: Only 12% of the girls in Gross's sample were actually more than 15% above what normative tables say they should weigh, a common cutoff for a label of "overweight.") When she broke down the data for girls by race (African-American versus White), she obtained the following results. (Other races have been omitted because of small sample sizes.)

	Reducers	Maintainers	Gainers	Total
White	352	152	31	535
African-American	47	28	24	99
Total	399	180	55	634

a) What conclusions can you draw from these data?

b) Ignoring race, what conclusions can you draw about adolescent girls' attitudes toward their own weight?

19.15 Stress has long been known to influence physical health. Visintainer, Volpicelli, and Seligman (1982) investigated the hypothesis that rats given 60 trials of inescapable shock would be less likely to later reject an implanted tumor than would rats who had received 60 trials of escapable shock or 60 no-shock trials. They obtained the following data:

	Inescapable Shock	Escapable Shock	No Shock	Total
Reject	8	19	18	45
No Reject	22	11	15	48
Total	30	30	33	93

Using the R code in this chapter, what would you conclude from these data?

19.16 Suppose that in the study by Latané and Dabbs (1975), referred to in Section 19.6, only 100 males and 100 females were involved. Compute χ^2.

19.17 What does the answer to Exercise 19.16 say about the effects of sample size on the power of an experiment?

19.18 Dabbs and Morris (1990) examined archival data from military records to study the relationship between high testosterone levels and antisocial behavior in males. Out of the 4,016 men in the normal testosterone group, 10.0% had a record of adult delinquency. Out of the 446 men in the high testosterone group, 22.6% had a record of adult delinquency.

a) Create a contingency table of *frequencies*, classifying men by High and Normal testosterone levels and by Delinquency and Nondelinquency.
b) Compute χ^2 for this table.
c) Plot the data in a way as to illustrate this relationship.
d) Draw the appropriate conclusions.

19.19 In the study described in Exercise 19.18, 11.5% of the Normal testosterone group and 17.9% of the High testosterone group had a history of childhood Delinquency.

a) Is there a significant relationship between these two variables?
b) Interpret this relationship.
c) How does this result expand on what we already know from Exercise 19.18?

19.20 Calculate the odds ratio of adult delinquency for the data in Exercise 19.18.

19.21 Calculate the odds ratio of childhood delinquency for the data in Exercise 19.19.

19.22 Let's see how students and faculty compare on a basic statistical question. Zuckerman, Hodgins, Zuckerman, and Rosenthal (1993) surveyed 550 people and asked a number of questions on statistical issues. In one question a reviewer warned a researcher that she had a high probability of a Type I error because she had a small sample size. The researcher disagreed. Participants were asked, "Was the researcher correct?" The proportions of respondents, partitioned among students, assistant professors, associate professors, and full professors, who sided with the researcher and the total number of respondents in each category were as follows:

	Students	Assistant Professors	Associate Professors	Full Professors
Proportion	.59	.34	.43	.51
Sample Size	17	175	134	182

(*Note*: These data mean that 59% of the 17 students who responded sided with the researcher. When you calculate the actual *obtained* frequencies, round to the nearest whole person.)

a) Who do you think was correct?
b) What do these data tell you about differences among groups of respondents? (*Note*: The *researcher* was correct. Our tests are specifically designed to hold the probability of a Type I error at α, regardless of the sample size. The researcher did, however, have little power.)

19.23 The Zuckerman et al. paper referred to in the previous question hypothesized that faculty were less accurate than students because they have a tendency to give negative responses to such questions. ("There must be a trick.") How would you test such a hypothesis?

19.24 Calculate the odds ratio for the 2 × 2 table from Exercise 19.7 that combines the data of Clark and Clark (1939) and Hraba and Grant (1970).

19.25 Combine the data in Exercise 19.14 by adding together the Maintainers and Gainers categories. Then compute an odds ratio to say something about racial differences in high-school girls' perceptions of weight.

19.26 Use an odds ratio and a risk ratio to clarify the results of the Dabbs and Morris study of testosterone in Exercise 19.18. Which of those two statistics would you prefer?

19.27   Peterson (2001) reports data on a study by Unah and Boger (2001) examining the death penalty in North Carolina from 1993 to 1997. The data in the table below show the outcome of sentencing for White and nonWhite (mostly Black and Hispanic) defendants when the victim was White. The expected frequencies are shown in parentheses.

Defendant's Race	Death Sentence		Total
	Yes	No	
NonWhite	33	251	284
	(22.72)	(261.28)	
White	33	508	541
	(43.28)	(497.72)	
	66	759	825

What can we conclude about the fairness of sentencing?

19.28   Hout, Duncan, and Sobel (1987) reported data on the relative sexual satisfaction of married couples. They asked each member of 91 married couples to rate the degree to which they agreed with "Sex is fun for me and my partner" on a four-point scale ranging from "never or occasionally" to "almost always." The data appear below:

Husband's Rating	Wife's Rating				TOTAL
	Never	Fairly Often	Very Often	Almost Always	
Never	7	7	2	3	19
Fairly Often	2	8	3	7	20
Very Often	1	5	4	9	19
Almost Always	2	8	9	14	33
TOTAL	12	28	18	33	91

a)   What hypothesis would you like to test with these data?
b)   Use Pearson's chi-square to test your hypothesis. What would you conclude?
c)   Finally, what if you combined the Never and Fairly Often categories and the Very Often and Almost Always categories? Would the results be clearer, and under what conditions might this make sense?

## CHAPTER 20

Nonparametric and Distribution-Free Statistical Tests

This chapter represents a change, not only in how we approach hypothesis testing, but also in relation to previous editions of this book. Most of the statistical procedures we have discussed in the preceding chapters have involved the estimation of one or more parameters of the distribution of scores in the population(s) from which the data were sampled as well as assumptions concerning the shape of that distribution. For example, the t test makes use of the sample variance (s^2) as an estimate of the population variance (σ^2) and also requires the assumption that the population from which we sampled is normal (or at least that the sampling distribution of the mean is normal). Tests, such as the t test, that involve assumptions either about specific parameters or about the distribution of the population are referred to as **parametric tests**. An important feature of parametric tests is that they allow us to easily set confidence intervals on the statistic in question.

For many years the alternative approach to hypothesis testing was referred to as **nonparametric tests**, and basically relied on first converting the data to ranks and then running an analysis on those ranks. When I first started

CONCEPTS THAT YOU WILL NEED TO REMEMBER FROM PREVIOUS CHAPTERS

SS_{total}, SS_{group}, SS_{error}:	Sums of squares of all scores, of group means, and within groups
MS_{group}, MS_{error}:	Mean squares for group means, and within groups:
F statistic:	Ratio of MS_{group} over MS_{error}
Degrees of freedom:	The number of independent pieces of information remaining after estimating one or more parameters
Effect size ($\hat{d}$):	A measure intended to express the size of a treatment
Eta^2 (η^2), omega^2 (ω^2):	Correlation-based measures of effect size
Multiple comparisons:	Tests on differences between specific group means in terms that are meaningful to the reader

teaching statistical methods I devoted a whole semester to nonparametric tests, but over the years I reduced that coverage in favor of parametric tests. But now the field is making a different type of change, moving from the traditional tests to what are called **randomization tests** or **permutation tests**. These tests are still nonparametric because they do not involve parameter estimates and can handle nonnormal data, but they are considerably less formal than the traditional nonparametric tests. At the rate that the field is changing, I suspect that in the next 10 years randomization tests will largely replace not only the traditional nonparametric tests, but also the standard parametric tests such as t and F. And I think that will be a good thing. If you look at software such as SPSS, more and more of the analyses offer you an option for Bootstrap or Exact or Monte Carlo. These all involve randomization of the data in some form.

When I use the term "randomization" test in this chapter, I am referring to the newer approach. The traditional nonparametric tests also rely on randomization of the data (in the form of ranks), but I am reserving the form for tests that randomize the raw data.

But as the emphasis moves from the traditional nonparametric tests toward the newer randomization tests, this chapter needs to change. I still need to cover the older tests because you will be expected to know about them. But I also need to give you an idea about randomization tests. Moreover I need to do both of these things in about the same amount of space as I devoted to nonparametric tests in previous editions. And this means I have to change the nature of the chapter.

What I have done is to focus my discussion of nonparametric procedures on one test, including its rationale and computation, and to then briefly cover the rest without going into the calculations needed. I do that for two reasons. Once you understand what one of these tests is all about, you will have a pretty good idea of how to extrapolate that understanding to other tests. In addition, I think that it is unlikely that you will involve yourself in hand calculation, so saying "Go to SPSS or R to run this test." is probably sufficient.

When it comes to the randomization tests, I follow pretty much the same approach. Again, if you understand the logic behind one randomization test, you should be able to extrapolate that knowledge easily to others. And no one would ever be likely to consider hand calculation of randomization tests, so coverage of computation reduces to showing where you can find these tests on the Internet or create them yourself. If you really want more complete coverage of either kind of test, I give you links to Web pages that I have created that provide just that kind of coverage.

20.1 | Traditional Nonparametric Tests

Almost all of the traditional nonparametric tests involve ranking the raw data (without regard to group differences in most cases), and then operating on the ranks. They are often called **rank-randomization tests**. In fact, Conover and Iman (1981) show that you will obtain nearly the same result as the usual Wilcoxon-Mann-Whitney analysis, for example, if you simply convert the data to ranks and then run a standard t test on those ranks. We are not going to take their approach, but it does show an important relation between parametric and nonparametric procedures.

Why did we use ranks for these tests?

You might reasonably ask why we would use ranks to run any of the tests in this chapter. There are three good reasons why these tests were designed around the substitution of ranks for raw data. In the first place, ranks can eliminate or reduce the effects of extreme values. The two highest ranks of 20 items will be the values 19 and 20. But the highest raw score values could be 77 and 78 or 77 and 130. It makes a difference with raw scores, but not with ranks.

A second advantage of ranks is that we know certain of their properties, such as that the sum of a set of ranks is $N \times (N+1)/2$. This greatly simplifies calculations. This was especially important in the days before high-speed computers.

The third advantage is that once Wilcoxon worked out the critical value of the test statistic when there are eight observations in one group and 13 in another, he never had to solve that problem again in making up statistical tables. This makes is possible to provide exact probability tables, so long as the total sample size is not too large. The next time you have eight scores in one group and 13 in another, converting to ranks will yield the same critical value. However, with raw scores you would have to set a cutoff for every conceivable collection of eight scores in one group and 13 in another.

The Wilcoxon-Mann-Whitney Rank-Sum Test

I will begin with the test that is often called the **Wilcoxon-Mann-Whitney Rank Sum test**. It was derived by Frank Wilcoxon, and by Mann and Whitney, but I will refer to it as the rank-sum test to distinguish it from another test by Wilcoxon (the matched-pairs signed-ranks test) that we will discuss next. It is designed to test the difference between two independent groups, much as the two-sample t test does. One difference between rank-sum test and t tests is that the former replaces the actual observations with ranks. If there are no differences between groups, some of the larger ranks and some of the lower ranks would fall in each group. That is what we are really testing. If all of the high ranks fall in one group and the low ranks fall in the other, we are pretty sure that something is going on concerning group differences.

The rank-sum test statistic, which I will call W_S here, involves converting the data to ranks and simply summing the ranks in each of the groups. We will set W_S equal to the sum of the ranks in the smaller group or, if the groups are of equal size, the smaller of the two sums. We then either refer W_S to tables that Wilcoxon and others have derived, or, if the sample sizes are large, to tables of z. For large sample sizes the approximation is excellent.

I am spending more time on this test because the other nonparametric tests are similar in the way they deal with ranks. If you understand this test, it is not too difficult to understand what the other tests are doing.

It is particularly useful to discuss the tables of critical values of W_S. If you think about two small samples, such as (12, 17, 14) and (13, 19, 20), we can rank those scores without regard to groups. The ranks are (1, 4, 3) and (2, 5, 6), their sums are 8 and 13, and W_S would be the smaller of 8 and 13, which is 8. Set that number aside. For such small samples we can come up with all possible combinations of ranks. For six observations, with three in each group, the possible combinations in Group 1

Table 20.1 Possible Rankings and Their Sum from First of Two Groups of Three Scores Each

	[,1]	[,2]	[,3]	[,4]	[,5]	[,6]	[,7]	[,8]	[,9]	[,10]	[,11]	[,12]
[1,]	1	1	1	1	1	1	1	1	1	1	2	2
[2,]	2	2	2	2	3	3	3	4	4	5	3	3
[3,]	3	4	5	6	4	5	6	5	6	6	4	5
Sum	6	7	8	9	8	9	10	10	11	12	9	10

	[,13]	[,14]	[,15]	[,16]	[,17]	[,18]	[,19]	[,20]
[1,]	2	2	2	2	3	3	3	4
[2,]	3	4	4	5	4	4	5	5
[3,]	6	5	6	6	5	6	6	6
Sum	11	11	12	13	12	13	14	15

are shown in Table 20.1. (I don't have to worry about Group 2, because those ranks would just be the ones that are left over.)

Four of those combinations have the sum of the ranks $<= 8$, which is the value of W_S. So if the data were distributed at random, which would be the case if the independent variable had no effect, then $4/20 = 20\%$ of the random samples would have a W_S less than or equal to the one that we obtained. So we would not reject the null hypothesis. Further, you can see that the only way we could declare a difference to be significant would be to have the smaller sum equal to six, which would occur with a probability of $1/20 = .05$ if treatments actually have no effect.

But what if we had many more scores? Could we run this test in the same way? In one sense the answer is yes. We would just make up a list of all possible random assignments to one of the groups and ask how many of those had the sum of the ranks less than or equal to the sum of the ranks for our experimental data. That is the way that Wilcoxon compiled his tables. However, there are often far more combinations of ranks than we care to deal with, which is why we go with his tables. We can take an example from a study of how children organize stories.

McConaughy (1980) argued that younger children organize stories in terms of simple descriptive ("and then . . .") models, whereas older children incorporate causal statements and social inferences. Suppose we asked two groups of children differing in age to summarize a story they just read. We then counted the number of statements in the summary that can be classed as inferences. The data are shown. The ranked values are shown in parentheses.

	Younger Children	Older Children
	12 (6)	6 (3)
	4 (2)	24 (12)
	8 (4)	14 (7)
	10 (5)	26 (13)
	2 (1)	18 (9)
	22 (11)	16 (8)
	20 (10)	28 (14)
SUM	39	66

The smaller sum of the ranks is therefore 39. The problem with this example is that there are $14!/(7!*7!) = 3,432$ possible arrangements of the data that we would have to consider. Do you really want to write down all of those combinations and sum the ranks of each? I don't. Fortunately Wilcoxon found a way to accomplish this task and created tables that we can use. You can find his table in the appendices. From that table we find that with seven scores in each group, a value of $W_S = 39$ would be significant in a one-tailed test at $\alpha = .05$. So we will reject the null hypothesis. The easy way to deal with this problem is to use something like SPSS. The results of using SPSS follow, and you can see that the one-tailed probability is .049, which is as close to .05 as we can get.

Wilcoxon-Mann-Whitney Test

		Ranks		
	VAR00001	N	Mean Rank	Sum of Ranks
VAR00002	1.00	30	26.77	803.00
	2.00	30	34.23	1027.00
	Total	60		

Test Statistics[a]	
	VAR00002
Mann-Whitney U	338.000
Wilcoxon W	803.000
Z	−1.662
Asymp. Sig. (2-tailed)	.097
Exact Sig. (2-tailed)	.098
Exact Sig. (1-tailed)	.049
Point Probability	.001

[a]Grouping Variable: VAR00001

Randomizing

Now suppose that we had data on two groups of 30 children each. Here we have a problem, because even if you didn't mind making up combinations, I doubt that you want to make up approximately $1.182646e+17 = 118,264,600,000,000,000$ of them, which is the number of combinations of 60 things taken 30 at a time. Here is where we start to move from rank tests to randomization tests. Staying with rank tests for a moment, it is clearly impossible to create all of those combinations, obtain their sums, and calculate p. So either we use a normal approximation to calculate p, or, for our purposes here, we randomize. What we will do is to sample randomly perhaps 10,000 combinations of those ranks and ask what percentage of those exceeds the value for our data. That will certainly be close enough for our purposes.

The code for doing such a procedure is below. You will see that out of 10,000 samples of data, the probability is reported as .047, which is very close to the .049 that SPSS produced.

```
### Wilcoxon Example

#These data have been created so that the one-tail p approx = .05
# SPSS gives it as .049
nreps = 10000
groups <- rep(c(1,2), each = 30 )

dv <- c(21, 28, 27, 22, 22, 18, 19, 15, 25, 37,28, 27, 17, 18, 21, 28,
27, 25, 27, 19, 21, 28, 27, 25, 22, 23, 18, 19, 15, 25, 25, 35, 34, 22,
21, 36, 23, 18, 15, 25, 35, 34, 22, 21, 36, 37, 28, 27, 17, 18, 35, 34,
22, 21, 36, 37, 28, 27, 17, 18)

result <- wilcox.test(dv ~ groups, alternative = "less")
print("The Wilcoxon test produces \n")
print(result)
dvr <- rank(dv)     #Rank the raw scores from low to high

W <- sum(dv[groups == 2])    # This is the sum of the ranks in Group 2
cat(" Wilcoxon's W = ", W)

sums <- numeric(nreps)  #Place to store sums
for (i in 1:nreps) {
  temp <- sample(dvr, 30)
  sums[i] <- sum(temp)
}
prob <- 1 - (length(temp[sums >= W])/nreps)
cat("The probability of a value of W equal to the one that we obtained
is = \n",prob)
_____

_____

The probability of a value of W equal to the one that we obtained is =
0.0473
```

I said that we were going to look closely at this test because it is a good introduction to randomization tests. The reason is that for randomization tests we are going to do the same thing that we did here, but we are going to use the raw scores instead of the ranks. When we have ranks, it is relatively easy to create tables like the one in the appendices. You know that if you have 15 observations, the ranks will always be 1–15, and that is relatively easy to work with. But when you have 15 raw scores, those scores can be literally any set of numbers. Computing the combinations of one set of scores tells you absolutely nothing about the combinations of another set. That is where Fisher and Pitman ran into a wall. They knew what they wanted (all combinations of the data) but they had no way to calculate that except for very simple cases. But your smart phone will probably do such a calculation now. We will come back to this problem shortly, but first I need to say something about other traditional nonparametric tests.

Wilcoxon's Matched-Pairs Signed-Ranks Test

While the Wilcoxon-Mann-Whitney rank sum test dealt with two independent groups, **the Wilcoxon Matched-pairs signed-ranks test** by Wilcoxon deals with paired samples. For continuity assume that the data in the previous example were collected a bit differently—from children when they were young and those same children when they were older. Here we have paired data, with the same means and medians as we had in the earlier example. I have simply rearranged the data within age condition to create some sort of correlation ($r = .63$) between the two conditions. That is what we would expect. If children received a high score when they were young, they probably also received a relatively high score when they were older. The same holds for children who received a low score when they were young. The data follow.

Younger Children	Older Children	Difference	Rank
12	18	−6	−3
4	16	−12	−6
8	24	−16	−7
10	6	4	2
2	13	−11	−5
22	25	−3	−1
20	28	−8	−4
T+ = 2	T − = 26		

For this test we calculate the differences between each child's younger and older score. Then we rank those differences without regard to the sign of the difference, and then assign those signs to the ranks. Finally we sum the positive and negative ranks separately to produce T+ and T−. Our test statistic will be the smaller of the absolute values of T+ and T−. These calculations are shown in the table.

Now we take our test statistic as T+ = 2. If you look in the appendices for the Matched-Pairs Signed-Ranks test with seven cases, you will see that the probability of T+ = 3 = .0391, and T+ = 4 is .0547. Our value of T+ = 2 is lower than that, so the probability of this result is significant at $p < .05$. We can reject the null hypothesis that there are no differences in the number of inferences given by children at different ages. Older children clearly give more inferences in talking about a story.

The results using SPSS and the R for these data follow. To use SPSS, I recommend choosing "**Nonparametric/Legacy/2 Related Samples.**" That approach will provide more complete results.

NPar Tests

	Descriptive Statistics				
	N	Mean	Std Deviation	Minimum	Maximum
Young	7	11.1429	7.55929	2.00	22.00
Old	7	18.5714	7.69972	6.00	28.00

Wilcoxon Signed-Ranks Test

		Ranks		
		N	Mean Rank	Sum of Ranks
Old–Young	Negative Ranks	1[a]	2.00	2.00
	Positive Ranks	6[b]	4.33	26.00
	Ties	0[c]		
	Total	7		

[a]Old < Young
[b]Old > Young
[c]Old = Young

Test Statistics[a]	
	Old - Young
Z	−2.028[b]
Asymp. Sig (2-tailed)	.043
Exact Sig. (2-tailed)	.047
Exact Sig. (1-tailed)	.023
Point Probability	.008

[a]Wilcoxon Signed-Ranks Test
[b]Based on negative ranks

```
### R Code for Wilcoxon Matched-Pairs Signed-Ranks

Young <- c(12, 4, 8, 10, 2, 22, 20)
Older <- c(18, 16, 24, 6, 13, 25, 28)
wilcox.test(x = Young, y = Older, alternative = "two.sided", mu = 0,
paired = TRUE,  exact = TRUE, conf.int = TRUE, correct = FALSE)


        Wilcoxon signed rank test

data:  Young and Older
V = 2, p-value = 0.04688
```

(continued)

```
alternative hypothesis: true location shift is not equal to 0
95 percent confidence interval:
 -13.5  -1.0
sample estimates:
(pseudo)median
        -7.75


cor(Young, Older)
[1] 0.6283273
```

Here, again, there is a significant difference in the number of inferences made by younger and older children.

Frank Wilcoxon (1892–1965)

Frank Wilcoxon is an interesting person in statistics for the simple reason that he was not really a statistician and didn't publish any statistical work until he was in his 50s. He was originally trained in inorganic chemistry and spent most of his life doing chemical research dealing with insecticides and fungicides.

Wilcoxon had been in a statistical study group with W. J. Youden, an important early figure in statistics, and they had worked their way through Fisher's very influential text (Fisher, 1935). But when it came to analyzing data in later years, Wilcoxon was not satisfied with Fisher's method of randomization of observations. Wilcoxon hit upon the idea of substituting ranks for raw scores, which allowed him to work out the distribution of various test statistics quite easily. His use of ranks stimulated work on inference based on ranks and led to a number of related statistical tests applied to ranks.

Wilcoxon officially retired in 1957, but then joined Florida State University and worked on sequential ranking methods until his death in 1965. His name is still largely synonymous with rank-based statistics. An interesting biography of Wilcoxon can be found at http://stochastikon.no-ip.org:8080/encyclopedia/en/wilcoxonFrank.pdf Retrieved 11/12/2015.

Kruskal-Wallis One-way Analysis of Variance

The Kruskal-Wallis test is simply an extension of the Wilcoxon-Mann-Whitney test to the case of three or more levels of the independent variable. I don't want to elaborate on this test because I am sure that you can imagine how it is carried out from a simple extension of the Wilcoxon-Mann-Whitney statistic. We simply rank the data without regard to group differences and then compute a statistic (H) which we can refer to tables produced by Kruskal and Wallis. H can be evaluated as a chi-square statistic on $k-1$ df, where k is the number of groups. The formula for H, (there referred to as K), can be found at http://en.wikipedia.org/wiki/Kruskal%E2%80%93Wallis_one-way_analysis_of_variance and the test is quite easy to run in SPSS and in R as the kruskal.test. The code for R follows, where the data are in three groups of seven, eight, and four observations.

```
# Kruskal-Wallis
group <- factor(c(1,1,1,1,1,1,1,2,2,2,2,2,2,2,2,3,3,3,3))
score <- c(55,0,1,0,50,60,44,73,85,51,63,85,85,66,69,61,54,80,47)
kruskal.test(x = score, g = group)
```

```
Kruskal-Wallis rank sum test
data:  score and group
Kruskal-Wallis chi-squared = 10.4, df = 2, p-value = 0.005496
```

Friedman's Rank Test for *k* Correlated Samples

The last traditional test to be discussed in this chapter is the distribution-free analogue of the one-way repeated-measures analysis of variance, **Friedman's rank test for *k* correlated samples**. It was developed by the well-known economist Milton Friedman—in the days before he was a well-known economist. This test is closely related to a standard repeated-measures analysis of variance applied to ranks instead of raw scores, though it is not exactly the same. It is a test on the null hypothesis that the scores for each treatment were drawn from identical populations, and it is especially sensitive to population differences in central tendency.

You would expect that if there are no systematic changes over a series of trials, some participants would have their best score on Trial 1, some would have their best score on Trial 2, and some on Trial 3. The same would hold for poorer scores. If that is the case, and if we created rankings for each participant on each trial, under the null hypothesis those rankings would be roughly random across trials. This is the basis for Friedman's test. He ranks the scores across trials separately for each participant, and then sums the ranking for each trial. If there is no effect due to trials, the sums would be expected to be about equal for each of the trials.

We will base our example on a study by Foertsch and Gernsbacher (1997), who investigated the substitution of the genderless word "they" for "he" or "she." With the decrease in the acceptance of the word "he" as a gender-neutral pronoun, many writers are using the grammatically incorrect "they" in its place. Foertsch and Gernsbacher asked participants to read sentences such as "A truck driver should never drive when sleepy, even if (*he/she/they*) may be struggling to make a delivery on time, because many accidents are caused by drivers who fall asleep at the wheel." On some trials the words in parentheses were replaced by the gender-stereotypic expected pronoun, sometimes by the gender-stereotypic unexpected pronoun, and sometimes by the neutral pronoun "they." There were three kinds of sentences in this study, those in which the expected pronoun was male, those in which it was female, and those in which it could equally be male or female. There are several dependent variables I could use from this study, but I have chosen the effect of seeing "she" when expecting "he," the effect of seeing "he" when expecting "she," and effect of seeing "they" when the expectation is neutral. (The original study is more complete than this.) The dependent variable is the reading time/character (in milliseconds). The data in Table 20.2 have been created to have roughly the same medians as the authors report.

Table 20.2   Data on Reading Times as a Function of Ponoun

Participant	1	2	3	4	5	6	7	8	9	10	11
Expect He/See She	50	54	56	55	48	50	72	68	55	57	68
Expect She/ See He	53	53	55	58	52	53	75	70	67	58	67
Neutral/See They	52	50	52	51	46	49	68	60	60	59	60

Table 20.3   Data on Reading Times as a Function of Pronoun

Participant	1	2	3	4	5	6	7	8	9	10	11	Sum = R_i
Expect He/See She	1	3	3	2	2	2	2	2	2	1	3	23
Expect She/ See He	3	2	2	3	3	3	3	3	3	2	2	29
Neutral/See They	2	1	1	1	1	1	1	1	1	3	1	14

Here we have repeated measures on each participant, because each participant was presented with each kind of sentence. Some people read anything more slowly than others, which is reflected in the raw data. The data are far from normally distributed, which is why I am applying a distribution-free test. If we were to rank within participants, the rankings would be those given in table 20.3.

Notice that the third category (See They) clearly has the lowest rankings, while Expect She/See He has the highest. Friedman calculated a statistic, shown below, on the sums for each row and referred that to the chi-square distribution on $k - 1$ df, where k is the number of trials per participant.

$$x_F^2 = \frac{12}{Nk(k + 1)}\sum R_i^2 - 3N(k + 1)$$

Where
  R_i = the sum of the ranks for the ith condition
  N = the number of participants
  K = the number of conditions
In our example, $X^2 = 10.36$ on 2 df, (p = .004), which is clearly significant.

20.2 Randomization Tests

To this point I have been discussing the traditional nonparametric tests because I think that you need to be aware of them. You will see them in papers and you will probably be expected to have some reasonable idea of what they do. But now I want to move on to a category of tests that are often called randomization tests. As the name and my earlier comments suggest, these tests work by creating random samples of data that would be expected to occur if the independent variable (e.g., treatments) has no effect. After creating many (perhaps 10,000) samples, we ask how often our obtained test statistic would occur in the set of samples based on a lack of effect.

Before I continue, notice that in the last paragraph I referred to "treatments having no effect." I did not use the phrase "null hypothesis," because we actually don't have a usual null hypothesis. A null hypothesis refers to population parameters (e.g., $\mu_1 = \mu_2 = \mu_3$), but randomization tests don't estimate population parameters. That is one of their strengths. In a way it is also a weakness. When we say that the scores in Treatment$_1$ could just as easily have landed in Treatment$_2$, we are saying that the two treatments are equivalent. When we run a standard t test, we make assumptions about variances and shapes, such that the only remaining way for groups to differ would be in terms of their means. But randomization tests don't make such assumptions, so it is possible that the groups would differ greatly in terms of variances, but we might miss that if your test statistic is a mean difference or some similar statistic. So we really need to be even more careful than usual in ensuring that the test statistic we use is a reasonable one.

The easiest way to see how these tests function is to examine an example of a test that might serve the same function as a one-way analysis of variance. I will use the data from Table 16.7 for an example. This is a study of maternal adaptation in three treatment groups. Group 1 was composed of mothers of low birth weight (LBW) infants who received an experimental intervention. Group 2 contained mothers of LBW infants who did not receive the intervention and Group 3 contained mothers of full-term infants who did not receive an intervention. When we analyzed these data in Chapter 16 we found that a standard analysis of variance produced $F = 5.53$, $p < .005$.

I use this example to show how a randomization test would work in this situation, but I think that once you see how it works, you can easily imagine how a variation on this test would work in a different situation (e.g., with two independent groups or even two related groups). The test statistic would be different, but the logic would be just the same; compute a test statistic on the original data and see how that compares to statistics based on randomized data. In discussing this test I will not present the underlying R code because that could confuse as much as it helps. I will speak in general terms, but the code for the analysis that I will discuss is available at the website for this chapter: https://www.uvm.edu/~dhowell/fundamentals9/Supplements/Chapter20R.html.

One of the mothers in that experiment had an adaptation score of 24. If the different treatment conditions had absolutely no effect on mothers' behavior, that 24 could equally well have come from any of the three conditions. The same goes for each of the other scores. The first thing that we will do is to calculate our test statistic on the experimental data. This test statistic should be some statistic that reflects the differences between groups. If we wish, we could compute a standard F statistic, but I am going to compute just the $SS_{between}$. As long as we will be randomizing data, the F and the $SS_{between}$ will be perfectly correlated, and $SS_{between}$ is a bit quicker to calculate. Then we will set that statistic aside for the moment, perhaps named SS.bet.obt.

Now we will start our randomization process. We will use the R command **sample(matadapt.data, size = 93, replace = FALSE)**. That will cause R to arrange randomly our 93 observations. We will assign the first 29 observations to the first group, the next 27 observations to the second group, and the final 37 observations to the third group. We will then calculate $SS_{between}$ for these three groups. In the case of random assignment, there will be no systematic differences between the groups we create. We will store that statistic away and repeat the whole process another 999 times. When we are done with looping through this process 1,000 times, we can ask what value of the randomized statistic cuts off the upper 5% of the distribution of randomized statistics. If our obtained SS.bet.obt is greater than that, we can reject the null hypothesis at $\alpha = .05$. Alternatively, and preferably, we could simply ask what percentage of the randomized values exceeds the obtained value, and that would give us the nearly exact probability. In our case the probability of our SS.bet.obt is .00493 when compared against the randomized samples.

Alternative Experimental Designs

I have just discussed the case of a one-way analysis of variance with three groups. If we had the equivalent of a *t* test on independent groups, we could do exactly the same thing because that would be just an analysis of variance with two groups. If, however, we didn't have independent measures, but rather had repeated measures, we would draw randomized samples by simply randomizing the order of scores within each participant. The same would hold for a *t* test for two related samples. Finally, if we were dealing with the correlation of two variables, we could hold the scores for one variable constant and randomize the scores on the other variable. This would amount to randomly pairing the scores.

The important point that was illustrated in the previous paragraph is that the entire procedure is nearly the same for each case. We simply change the way that we randomize data, and that method is based on what we would expect if there is no treatment effect or no correlation.

20.3 Measures of Effect Size

Measures of effect size are difficult to find with distribution-free statistical tests. (Conover(1980) discusses the use of confidence intervals for traditional nonparametric tests, but we are not going to cover that here.) An important reason for the difficulty is because many of our effect size measures are based on the size of the standard deviation, and if the data are very badly (nonnormally) distributed, a standard deviation loses much of its meaning for this purpose. If we know that data are normally distributed, and we know that the mean for one group is a standard deviation above the mean for another group, we can estimate that about two-thirds of the participants in the second group outscore the mean of the first group. But if our data are badly skewed we lose that kind of interpretation of the effect size. Similarly, even if we don't standardized the difference between means on the basis of a standard deviation, with badly skewed data we still do not have a good understanding of what it means to say that the median of group 1 is 15 points above the median of group 2.

One effect size measure that you could use is to count directly, in your sample, the number, or better yet the percentage, of one group that outscored those in another group. For example, suppose we found that the median birth weight for those who received prenatal care in the first trimester was 3245 grams, but for those who did not receive it until the third trimester, the median weight was 2765.5 grams. This difference would be statistically significant. We might find that nearly all mothers in the first trimester group had infants who weighed more than the median of the third trimester mothers. (Or, to put it in the reverse, perhaps only one mother in the third trimester group gave birth to an infant who was over the median weight of the first trimester group.) Reporting an effect size in this way may not be as satisfying as reporting effect sizes using $\hat{d}$ or a related statistic, but it is certainly more informative than simply reporting that the difference was significant.

20.4 Bootstrapping

I want to speak very briefly about a concept called "bootstrapping," because you are almost certain to see references to it. Bootstrapping is another example of a randomization procedure, but its purpose is usually different from what we have just been discussing. It is used primarily to obtain estimates of population characteristics such as a mean or standard deviation. The most obvious difference is that for bootstrapping we sample with replacement, whereas with our randomization tests we have been sampling without replacement.

Suppose that I have a set of data with a very nonnormal distribution. I would like to estimate the mean of the population from which those scores came. In the case of bootstrapping I will take my obtained data and treat them as an exact (small) copy of the parent population. Then I will draw a sample from those data, but this time I will sample with replacement. That means that a particular score could be drawn two or three times, or it might never be drawn. From that random sample I will compute a test statistic; perhaps the mean. Then I will repeat the process over and over again, each time computing the sample mean. When I am done, the mean of those sample means will be my estimate of the population mean. In addition, I could determine what means cut off the upper and lower 2.5% of the sample means, and those points would give me my confidence interval.

I have simplified this process a bit too much because it is better to make a slight adjustment to the mean of means, but the process is essentially as I laid it out. The corrections for bias are slight compared to the answer my process would give, and you can understand bootstrapping without my spelling out those corrections. The most important work on bootstrapping was done by Efron and Tibshirani (1993) and their book is reasonably readable. That is where I would recommend that you go if you want to know more. Alternatively, a search of the Web will bring up many useful sources.

20.5 Writing Up the Results of the Study of Maternal Adaptation

I gave an example of writing up the results of the maternal adaptation study in Chapter 16, and much of that summary is appropriate here. The important change would be to replace reference to an analysis of variance by saying that the data were analyzed using a randomization test on three independent groups. We need not report a test statistic such as F, or even mention that we used $SS_{between}$ as our test statistic, but we should mention that our test was particularly sensitive to means. We should then go on to point out that the test was significant at $p < .005$ when compared to randomized distributions. When we have a reasonable estimate of the size of an effect, we should be sure to cite that.

20.6 | Summary

This chapter summarized briefly two types of procedures that require far fewer restrictive assumptions concerning the populations from which our data have been sampled. We first covered the traditional nonparametric tests because students need to know about them. Each of these tests involves converting raw scores to ranks and working with those ranks. We then went on to randomization tests because they are playing a larger and larger role in research and are very powerful with few assumptions. What all of these tests have in common is that they ask how the scores (or ranks) would be distributed if the null hypothesis were true. To do so they look at all possible randomizations of the scores (or ranks) across groups. (That is why they are often called "randomization" tests, or "rank randomization" tests, respectively.) They then reject the null if the obtained pattern of results is too extreme. These tests are all nonparametric or distribution-free tests because they make many fewer assumptions about the shape of the distribution and do not rely on unknown parameters such as the population mean (μ) or variance (σ^2).

Finally we looked at bootstrapping techniques. These are used primarily for estimating population parameters. They differ from other randomization procedures by assuming that the obtained data is an accurate reflection of the shape of the population, and use sampling with replacement to generate multiple samples from that population.

Key Terms

Parametric tests, 524	Wilcoxon-Mann-Whitney test, 526
Nonparametric tests (distribution-free tests), 524	Wilcoxon's matched-pairs signed-ranks test, 530
randomization tests, 525	Kruskal-Wallis one-way analysis of variance, 532
permutation tests, 525	
Rank-randomization tests, 525	Friedman's rank test for k correlated samples, 533

20.7 | A Quick Review

A. A distribution-free test makes _____.
Ans: less severe assumptions about the distribution of the data in the population

B. Why are the tests discussed in the first half of this chapter often referred to as "rank randomization" tests?
Ans: They operate on what the distribution of their statistic would be if the data were converted to ranks and then randomized (or permuted) in all possible ways.

C. How does the null hypothesis tested by the Wilcoxon-Mann-Whitney test differ from the one tested by a standard independent groups t test?
Ans: It tests the null hypothesis that the groups were drawn from identical populations, not just populations with the same mean.

D. Randomization tests are replacing traditional nonparametric tests because
   Ans: they are a more direct test of the underlying hypothesis and have no assumptions about the underlying populations.

E. Randomization tests that are roughly equivalent to Wilcoxon's test use _____ as the test statistic.
   Ans: the t statistic or the mean of the differences

F. Randomization tests are more popular than they used to be because of _____.
   Ans: the availability of very fast software

G. The Kruskal-Wallis one-way analysis of variance is a simple extension of the _____.
   Ans: Mann-Whitney test

H. The major purpose of bootstrapping is to _____.
   Ans: estimate population parameters

20.8 Exercises

In these exercises I frequently ask you to use SPSS or R to solve a problem. You should have no problem with SPSS if you stick with the "Legacy" analyses. You should be able to use R by modifying the code that I give on the Web page for this chapter: http://www.uvm.edu/~dhowell/fundamentals9/Supplements/Chapter20R.html

20.1 Kapp, Frysinger, Gallagher, and Hazelton (1979) have demonstrated that lesions in the amygdala can reduce certain responses commonly associated with fear (e.g., *decreases* in heart rate). If fear is really reduced by the lesion, it should be more difficult to train an avoidance response in those animals because the aversiveness of the stimulus will consequently be reduced. Assume two groups of rabbits: One group has lesions in the amygdala, and the other is an untreated control group. The following data represent the number of trials to learn an avoidance response for each animal.

Group with Lesions	Control Group
15	9
14	4
8	10
7	6
22	6
36	4
19	5
14	9
18	9
17	
15	

a) Analyze the data in SPSS or R using the Wilcoxon-Mann-Whitney test (two-tailed).
b) Reanalyze those data using the randomization test for independent samples—it can easily handle only two groups and can be found on the chapter's website.
c) What can you conclude from these analyses?

20.2 Repeat the analysis in Exercise 20.1 using the appropriate one-tailed test.

20.3 Nurcombe and Fitzhenry-Coor (1979) have argued that training in diagnostic techniques should lead a clinician to generate and test more hypotheses in coming to a decision about a case. Suppose we take 10 psychiatric residents who are just beginning their residency and use them as participants. We ask them to watch a videotape of an interview and to record their thoughts on the case every few minutes. We then count the number of hypotheses each resident includes in his or her written remarks. The experiment is repeated with the same residents at the end of the residency with a comparable videotape. The data are given.

Participant										
	1	2	3	4	5	6	7	8	9	10
Before	8	4	2	2	4	8	3	1	3	9
After	7	9	3	6	3	10	6	7	8	7

a) Analyze the data using Wilcoxon's matched-pairs signed-ranks test.
b) What would you conclude?

20.4 Referring to Exercise 20.3,

a) Repeat the analysis using a suitable randomization test.
b) How well do the two answers agree? Why don't they agree exactly?

20.5 It has been argued that first-born children tend to be more independent than later-born children. Suppose we develop a 25-point scale of independence and rate each of 20 first-born children and their second-born siblings using our scale. We do this when both siblings are adults, thus eliminating obvious age effects. The data on independence are as follows (a higher score means that the person is more independent):

Sibling Pair	First-Born	Second-Born
1	12	10
2	18	12
3	13	15
4	17	13
5	8	9
6	15	12
7	16	13
8	5	8
9	8	10
10	12	8
11	13	8
12	5	9
13	14	8
14	20	10
15	19	14
16	17	11
17	2	7
18	5	7
19	15	13
20	18	12

a) Analyze the data in SPSS or R using Wilcoxon's matched-pairs signed-ranks test.
b) What would you conclude?

20.6 Repeat the analysis with a randomization test.

20.7 The results in Exercise 20.5 are not quite as clear-cut as we might like. Plot the differences as a function of the first-born's score. What does this figure suggest?

20.8 What is the difference between the null hypothesis tested by the Wilcoxon-Mann-Whitney test and the corresponding t test?

20.9 What is the difference between the null hypothesis tested by Wilcoxon's matched-pairs signed-ranks test and the corresponding t test?

20.10 One of the arguments in favor of distribution-free tests is that they are more appropriate for ordinal scale data. (This issue was addressed earlier in the book in a different context.) Give a reason why this argument is not a good one.

20.11 Why is rejection of the null hypothesis using a t test a more specific statement than rejection of the null hypothesis using a traditional nonparametric test?

20.12 Three rival professors teaching English 1 all claim the honor of having the best students. To settle the issue, eight students are randomly drawn from each class and given the same exam. The exams are graded by a neutral professor who does not know from which class the students came. The data are shown.

Professor Li	Professor Kessler	Professor Bright
82	55	65
71	88	54
56	85	66
58	83	68
63	71	72
64	70	78
62	68	65
53	72	73

a) Use SPSS to run the Kruskal-Wallis test on these data.
b) Run the appropriate randomization test and draw the appropriate conclusions.

20.13 A psychologist operating a group home for delinquent adolescents needs to show that the home is successful at reducing delinquency. He samples 10 adolescents living in their own homes who have been identified by the police as having problems, 10 similar adolescents living in foster homes, and 10 adolescents living in the group home. As an indicator variable he uses truancy (number of days truant in the past semester), which is readily obtained from school records.

Use SPSS to run the Kruskal-Wallis test on these data.

Natural Home	Foster Home	Group Home
15	16	10
18	14	13
19	20	14
14	22	11
5	19	7
8	5	3
12	17	4
13	18	18
7	12	2

20.14 As an alternative method of evaluating a group home, suppose we take 12 adolescents who have been declared delinquent. We take the number of days truant during each of three time periods: (1) the month before they are placed in the home, (2) the month they live in the home, and (3) the month after they leave the home. The data are as follows:

Adolescent	Before	During	After
1	10	5	8
2	12	8	7
3	12	13	10
4	19	10	12
5	5	10	8
6	13	8	7
7	20	16	12
8	8	4	5
9	12	14	9
10	10	3	5
11	8	3	3
12	18	16	2

Use SPSS or *R* to run Friedman's test on these data.

20.15 What advantage does the study described in Exercise 20.14 have over the study described in Exercise 20.13?

20.16 For the data in Exercise 20.5 we could say that three out of 10 residents used fewer hypotheses the second time and seven used more. We could test this with χ^2. How would this differ from either Friedman's test or an appropriate randomization test applied to those data?

20.17 Compute a reasonable effect size measure for the data in Exercise 20.1. There are probably several different measures that you could come up with, so you should chose one that will give your reader a real sense of the role played by lesions to the amygdala.

20.18 One hundred years ago Bleuler (1911) described schizophrenia as being characterized by a lack of connections between associations in memory. Suddath, Christison, Torrey, Casanova, and Weinberger (1990) ran an interesting study on this hypothesis. The hippocampus has been suggested as playing an important role in memory storage and retrieval, and it is reasonable to ask if differences in hippocampal structures (particularly size) could play a role in schizophrenia. Suddath obtained MRI scans on the brains of 15 schizophrenic individuals and their monozygotic (identical) twins. They measured the volume of each brain's left hippocampus. Suddath used monozygotic twin pairs in an effort to control as many variables as possible that influence the volume of cortical and subcortical structures. This, in turn, reduces the amount of variance to be explained. The results appear below as taken from Ramsey and Schafer (1997).

Pair	Normal	Schizophrenic	Difference
1	1.94	1.27	0.67
2	1.45	1.63	−.18
3	1.56	1.47	0.09
4	1.58	1.39	0.19
5	2.06	1.93	0.13
6	1.66	1.26	0.40
7	1.75	1.71	0.04

8	1.77	1.67	0.10
9	1.78	1.28	0.50
10	1.92	1.85	0.07
11	1.25	1.02	0.23
12	1.93	1.34	0.59
13	2.04	2.02	0.02
14	1.62	1.59	0.03
15	2.08	1.97	0.11
Mean	1.76	1.56	0.199
Median	1.77	1.59	0.110

If you plot the difference scores for these 15 twin pairs, as shown in Figure 20.1, you will note that the distribution is far from normal. Run a randomization test on the hypothesis that the volume of the hippocampus in the left hemisphere is the same for both conditions.

20.19 Write up a brief summary of the study in Exercise 20.10.

20.20 The history of statistical hypothesis testing really began with a tea-tasting experiment (Fisher, 1935), so it seems fitting for this book to end with one. (This is also a fitting ending because Fisher was one of the first to advocate randomization procedures, though he did not have the facilities to use them for larger problems.) The owner of a small tearoom doesn't think people really can tell the difference between the first cup made with a given tea bag and the second and third cups made with the same bag (which is why it is still a small tearoom). He chooses eight different brands of tea bags, makes three cups of tea with each, and then has a group of customers rate each cup on a 20-point scale (without knowing which cup is which). The data are shown here, with higher ratings indicating better tea:

Tea Brands	Cup		
	First	Second	Third
1	8	3	2
2	15	14	4
3	16	17	12
4	7	5	4
5	9	3	6
6	8	9	4
7	10	3	4
8	12	10	2

Using a randomization test, draw the appropriate conclusions.

## CHAPTER 21

Meta-Analysis

I n the previous 20 chapters we focused on individual studies, comparing group means, looking at correlation and regression models, analyzing contingency tables, and so on. Most of the time that is the bulk of what researchers in the behavioral sciences do. However, after we have a collection of similar studies on the same research question, we should ask how we can put these studies together and draw some general conclusions. One researcher may have studied avoidance behavior in mice following the administration of shock and found that avoidance increases with shock intensity. Another may have run a similar study and found no significant effect with, for example, a p value of 0.17. What are we to make of this? Does shock level really affect avoidance, does it not, does it affect avoidance under only limited conditions, or is this second study consistent with the first? Those are the kinds of questions we will look at in this chapter, though we will consider more than two studies at once.

CONCEPTS THAT YOU WILL NEED TO REMEMBER FROM PREVIOUS CHAPTERS

Effect size ($\hat{d}$):	Effect size measure usually of mean differences
r^2:	An effect size measure with correlational data
Risk Ratio–Relative Risk:	Ratio of two measures of risk—an effect size measure
Odds ratio:	Similar to risk ratio except using odds information

21.1 **Meta-Analysis**[1]

An excellent book on meta-analysis by Borenstein, Hedges, Higgins, and Rothstein (2009) begins by pointing to the fact that for many years Dr. Benjamin Spock, along with other pediatricians, counseled parents to lay their baby to sleep on its stomach. (If you don't know about Dr. Spock, and, no, he wasn't in *Star Trek*, your mother certainly does.) He probably had more effect on child rearing in this country during the last half of the 20th century than any other single person. His book (*Baby and Child Care*, 1946) went through many editions and was one of the best-selling books of all time. Also during those years more than 100,000 babies died of Sudden Infant Death Syndrome (SIDS)—many while sleeping on their stomach. During that time, evidence was accumulating about the dangers of this practice, but people never put all of the studies together until it was too late. When they finally did, SIDS deaths decreased dramatically when parents were instructed to place their infant on its back. (I am not trying to cast aspersions on Dr. Spock, who, after all, made a huge contribution to child rearing and was offering the same advice as his colleagues.)

Borenstein et al. used this as a simple but dramatic example of the need to confront all of the existing literature in a field and combine it into sensible conclusions. **Meta-analysis** is designed to do this. Meta-analysis has been a core feature of what is called Evidence-Based Medicine, and the Cochrane Collaboration has published literally thousands of such analyses in just about every area of medicine, much of it of direct relevance to behavioral scientists. We will use data from the Collaboration's collection in this chapter.

Meta-analysis has taken on much greater importance in recent years in light of the fact that many challenges to the use of traditional null hypothesis testing have focused on the unreliability of the results of single experiments. While I think that the challenges are often overblown, I certainly support basing our understanding of treatment differences on the results of multiple studies rather than just the one that we happened to publish yesterday.

Early attempts at consolidating evidence were based on what are called narrative studies. Here a researcher would read a large literature on a topic, make some subjective judgments about the studies he or she read, and then issue a conclusion. Such conclusions were highly subjective, weighting different studies in whatever way the researcher chose. Moreover, the approach was primarily limited to published literature, which, almost by its nature, focuses on statistically significant results. It ignored what Rosenthal (1979) called the **"file drawer problem,"** where negative results remained unpublished in someone's file cabinet. Rosenthal acknowledged that it is very likely that nonsignificant studies would be less likely to be published, thus biasing the published literature. He suggested a simple solution to this problem, which involved computing the number of null results that would have to be hiding in file drawers to increase our overall p level to nonsignificance. If only a few such studies would alter our conclusions, we should have less faith in our results.

A second problem that we need to address is the problem of imperfect studies. Although probably no study is perfect, some are more imperfect than others. For example, a failure to assign subjects randomly to groups can bias the results because

---

[1]I would like to thank Alan Mead of the Illinois Institute of Technology for a number of helpful suggestions for this chapter.

of extraneous variables that would be allowed to influence the outcome. We have no really good way of dealing with this. The suggestion has been made that we should record as many aspects of the studies we use as possible and later analyze to see if consideration of any of those variables would alter our conclusions. There are difficulties with this approach, especially because there may be few studies with any one imperfection, but we should at least try.

Put in its simplest terms, meta-analysis averages the results of many studies on a single topic. It is a very sophisticated averaging, beginning with effect sizes and weighting studies according to the precision of their results, but it is averaging nonetheless. The important point to keep in mind is that once you have your measure of effect size, whether it is d, or a risk ratio, or a correlation, the equations for combining and testing effect sizes are all the same. So when you see d in an equation, you could substitute Fisher's transformation of r, or $\log(RR)$, or some other effect size measure and simply carry on the calculations using those numbers.

I should mention at the beginning that a meta-analysis requires a fairly large amount of computation. I am not going to present most of the underlying formulae that are needed because I see no need for you to learn those here. My goal is to explain what meta-analysis is and how it is used. You need to have some idea of the kinds of computations that go into the analysis, but it is not necessary that you become proficient in carrying out those computations. If you want to conduct a meta-analysis in the future, you should go to several sources to understand the process more completely. Somewhat more extensive coverage can be found in Howell (2012), Chapter 17, and the Borenstein et al. reference mentioned previously is excellent, as is the book by Cooper, Hedges, and Valentine (2009).

21.2 | A Brief Review of Effect Size Measures

Suppose that you and I and some other people all run studies that are roughly equivalent. They don't need to be exact replications, but they need to address the same general question. Although in many research areas the same general class of tests, for example, t tests on means or chi-square on contingency tables, is used in most studies, that is certainly not always the case. Your study may end up with an odds ratio, mine might involve a t test between two group means, and another study might calculate a correlation coefficient in some way. In an ideal world we might all come to a statistically significant result, and we could happily say that when examined from a variety of directions the results are consistent and support the phenomenon under study. But we don't live in an ideal world, and we need to confront inconsistent, and often statistically nonsignificant, results. But how do we add together a t statistic, a χ^2, and a correlation coefficient and then divide by 3? The simple answer is that we can't. We need some common metric to put the studies on the same scale. It turns out that the effect size measures that we have seen throughout this book are ideally suited to this task. A major reason for this is that we know how to convert from one effect size to another.

Because we will be focusing on effect size measures, I need to digress and briefly review those measures. We have seen these in separate chapters, and it makes sense to bring them all together. The following section is not exhaustive, but it does cover the most important measures. Although there are a lot of formulae in this section, they are mainly for review and future use, and can be circumvented with good online effect size calculators, so read them over to remind yourself what they are all about, but don't feel that you need to memorize them.

Measures on Means

I will consider several measures on means. They are all a form of Cohen's d, although Hedges' correction known as g applies to all of them.

■ **Two Independent Groups—Treatment and Control**

    o Pooling variances

$$d = \frac{\overline{X}_1 - \overline{X}_2}{s_{pooled}} \quad s_d = \sqrt{\frac{n_1 + n_2}{n_1 n_2} + \frac{d^2}{2(n_1 + n_2)}}$$

    o Standardizing on standard deviation of Control group[2]

$$d = \frac{\overline{X}_1 - \overline{X}_2}{s_C} \quad s_d = \sqrt{\frac{n_1 + n_2}{n_1 n_2} + \frac{d}{2n_1}}$$

■ **Paired Measurements**

    o Standardizing on average standard deviation

$$d = \frac{\overline{X}_{post} - \overline{X}_{pre}}{s_p} = \frac{\overline{X}_{post} - \overline{X}_{pre}}{s_{diff}/\sqrt{2(1-r)}} \quad s_d = \sqrt{\left(\frac{1}{n} + \frac{d^2}{2n}\right) \times 2(1-r)}$$

    where r is the correlation between pre- and posttreatment scores.

    o Standardizing on s_{diff}—rarely recommended

$$d = \frac{\overline{X}_{post} - \overline{X}_{pre}}{s_{diff}}$$

■ **Multiple Independent Groups**
It generally makes sense to calculate treatment effects on two groups or two sets of groups, so I will skip formulae for effects of several groups.

■ **Hedges' g**
To this point we have used d as our standardized mean difference, and for this chapter we will continue to do so. This is essentially Cohen's d, although the idea of dividing by the standard deviation of the control group rather than a pooled standard deviation was first proposed by Glass. The problem with d is that it is slightly biased and tends to overestimate δ when the sample size is small.

    Hedges (1981) proposed a minor modification that involves solving for a correction factor

$$J = 1 - \frac{3}{4df - 1}$$

---

[2]On either of the Web pages that I will refer to shortly you can force the result to be based on the standard deviation of the control group by entering that value in both places that ask for a standard deviation.

and multiplying both d and s_d by J.

$$g = d \times J$$

$$s_g = s_d \times J$$

This would give us Hedges' g, and we then could continue to work with g in exactly the same way we will work with d. I'll stick with d for this example, but the point is important. Once we have our effect sizes it doesn't matter if they are d, g, or some other effect size such as a log(risk ratio). The mathematics from then on is the same.

Effect Sizes Based on Contingency Tables

Assume the following summary table

Condition	Recovered	Died	N
Treated	A	B	A + B
Control	C	D	C + D

■ Relative Risk = Risk Ratio

$$RR = \frac{A}{A + B} \bigg/ \frac{C}{C + D} = \frac{A(C + D)}{B(A + B)}$$

However, we generally deal with risk ratios on a logarithmic scale. Then

$$LogRiskRatio = \ln(RR) \qquad\qquad s_{LogRiskRatio} = \sqrt{Var_{LogRiskRatio}}$$

$$Var_{LogRiskRatio} = \frac{1}{A} - \frac{1}{A + B} + \frac{1}{C} - \frac{1}{C + D} \qquad CI_{\ln(RR)} = LogRiskRatio \pm 1.96 \times s_{LogOddsRatio}$$

We carry out our calculations of effect sizes and their confidence intervals using these statistics, but then convert the mean and confidence limits back to the original metric by

$$Mean = e^{\ln(RR)}$$

$$Lower = e^{lower_{LogRiskRatio}}$$

$$upper = e^{upper_{LogRiskRatio}}$$

Where e is the base of the natural number system, which is 2.71828.

■ Odds ratios

$$OR = \frac{A/B}{C/D} = \frac{A \times D}{B \times C}$$

Here again we normally work with the log of odds ratios, in which case

$$LogOddsRatio = \ln(OR) \qquad\qquad s_{LogOddsRatio} = \sqrt{Var_{LogOddsRatio}}$$

$$Var_{LogOddsRatio} = \frac{1}{A} - \frac{1}{B} + \frac{1}{C} - \frac{1}{D} \qquad CI_{\ln(OR)} = LogOddsRatio \pm 1.96 \times s_{LogOddsRatio}$$

As with risk ratios, we carry out all of our calculations with the log values, but then convert the final result back to odds ratios by

$$Mean = e^{\ln(OR)}$$

$$Lower = e^{lower_{LogOddsRatio}}$$

$$upper = e^{upper_{LogOddsRatio}}$$

You might ask why we operate on a logarithmic scale for both *RR* and *OR*. The primary reason is that the distribution of each is bounded by 0 at the lower end but is unbounded at the upper end, thus having a positively skewed distribution. By taking the log of either ratio we have a statistic that is more nearly normally distributed.

Effect Sizes with Correlations

Correlation coefficients are often used as measures of effect size, but, as we have seen earlier, their distribution is skewed unless the population parameter is 0. For this reason we use Fisher's transformation, which I have called r'.

$$r' = 0.5 \times \ln\left(\frac{1 + r}{1 - r}\right) \qquad s_{r'}^2 = \frac{1}{n - 3} \qquad s_{r'} = \sqrt{\frac{1}{n - 3}}$$

Here again we base our calculations in the meta-analysis on the transformed values, but then transform the result back to the original uses.

$$r = \frac{e^{2r'} - 1}{e^{2r'} + 1}$$

Converting among Measures of Effect Size

It is relatively easy to go from one effect size measure to another. Table 21.1 shows how to make several of these conversions. If there is a conversion that you need that is not included in this table, a quick search on the Internet will provide one.

Online Calculators

Instead of pulling out pencil and paper, you can calculate effect sizes, and move back and forth between them, using effect size calculators that can easily be found online. An excellent calculator for computing and converting effect size measures, created by David Wilson at George Mason University, is available at http://www.campbellcollaboration.org/resources/effect_size_input.php. This is the most complete online source that I have found, and will calculate just about anything.

Table 21.1   Converting among Effect Size Measures

LogOddsRatio to *d*

$$d = LogOddsRatio \times \frac{\sqrt{3}}{\pi} \qquad var(d) = var(LogOddsRatio) \times \frac{3}{\pi^2}$$

r to *d*

$$d = \frac{2 \times r}{\sqrt{1 - r^2}} \qquad var(d) = \frac{4 \times var(r)}{(1 - r^2)^3}$$

Table 21.2	Sentencing as a Function of the Race of the Defendant (the Victim Was White)		
Defendant's Race	Death Sentence		
	Yes	No	Total
NonWhite	33 (22.72)	251 (261.28)	284
White	33 (43.28)	508 (497.72)	541
Total	66	759	825

A simpler, but less complete, calculator, by Paul Ellis, is available at http://www.polyu.edu.hk/mm/effectsizefaqs/calculator/calculator.html. I strongly urge you to look at this website. Read the remarks in little tiny print near the bottom of the page and go to at least one of those links. You will be surprised how much useful information and online resources you will find there.

As an example of how to use these calculators, assume that you were conducting a meta-analysis on the sentencing of defendants depending on the race of the victim. You would come across a study by Unah and Borger (2001) that you would certainly want to include. Their data are shown in Table 21.2.

For these data $\chi^2 = 7.71$ and $N = 825$. You can go to Wilson's page, select Standardized Mean Difference (d), assuming that d will be our measure of effect size. Then select "chi-square," enter $\chi^2 = 7.71$, $N = 825$, and click on Calculate. You will find that $d = 0.1943$ and that the confidence limits for d are 0.0571 and 0.3341. That's not too difficult a task. If you would rather work in terms of relative risk (RR), choose that option from the opening menu, enter the cell frequencies, and click "Calculate." It's as easy as that.

21.3 | An Example—Child and Adolescent Depression

Rather than spend much of my time on actual calculations, I think that you will learn more about meta-analysis by looking at a number of examples. There is software out there to do the actual calculations for us beyond what the calculators I have just referred to will do, but the simple stuff won't load on my computer (the software is too old), and learning to use the available software is something that you would want to do if you were actually running a meta-analysis, but not if you are just trying to understand what it is.

Depression in children and adolescents has long been a concern in our society, and there have been many efforts to institute prevention programs to lower its incidence. Some of these are "universal" programs that are administered to all members of some target population. For example, a school district may introduce assemblies or changes in curriculum to affect all students in the district. A few of these programs are "selective," that is, aimed at smaller groups of students who are deemed to be at risk for depression. And a third category of programs, classed as "indicated" interventions, are aimed at children who are already displaying subclinical symptoms.

Horowitz and Garber (2006) conducted a meta-analysis of such intervention programs, asking whether intervention in general was effective and whether effectiveness varied across classes of programs. They first searched the PsychINFO database using "depression" and "prevention" as search terms. This search included dissertations so as to minimize publication bias. They then manually searched 15 journals over a 30-year span, looking for any additional studies. The point of this intensive journal search was to catch as many studies as possible so as to minimize bias. They found 30 studies that they could use. Each of these studies contained a treatment and a control condition.

Although I will not focus on the data collection phase, there is a large and important literature on the mechanics of meta-analysis, and anyone planning to conduct such a study needs to examine that literature. Cooper (2009) provides a thorough coverage of the process, as opposed to the statistics, of meta-analysis, and anyone planning a meta-analysis should consult that reference or a similar one before beginning. Other references that are helpful are Borenstein et al. (2009) and Cooper, Hedges, & Valentine (2009).)

Having collected all available studies, the Horowitz and Garber categorized them by author, target (Universal, Selective, and Indicated), sample size, mean age, percent female, length, effect size at post-intervention and follow-up periods, and a summary of the intervention. Such classification is routine in most meta-analyses. For our purposes we will focus on the effect sizes. I discussed effect size measures for studies with two groups in Chapter 7 and considered alternative ways of defining the standardizing measure (the standard deviation). Horowitz and Garber chose to calculate the effect size as the difference between the treatment and control mean depression scores at posttest divided by the standard deviation of the control group.

$$d = \frac{\overline{X}_{Control} - \overline{X}_{Treatment}}{s_{Control}}$$

As I said earlier, we often call this Cohen's d, with apologies to Glass who actually proposed it. The results of the analysis are given in Table 21.3. Each study contained a treatment and a control group. (One study is omitted from that table because it was not possible to compute an effect size measure.) They did not give the sample sizes for each group, so I am acting as if the cases were evenly split between the two conditions. (Data in that table that are entered as NA are missing values, and you may need to use a different notation depending on your software.) The first effect size measure (d_1) was taken at the end of intervention. The second measurement (d_2) was taken as close to six months after the end of the intervention as possible. The last column is the effect size at last follow-up, which may also be the six-month follow-up score. Eight studies were missing an effect size at the six-month follow-up (d_3).

I am interested in performance at the six-month follow-up because I want to know if a program is going to have some long-term effect. Therefore, we will analyze the results for the 21 studies with data on that dependent variable (d_2).

From Table 21.3 you can see that most of the effect sizes at six months are positive, but some are very small. The table does not show a significance test, but we will have that in a moment when we compute confidence limits on effect sizes. The fact that so many are positive would lead me to suspect that intervention has a positive

Table 21.3   Results from Horowitz and Garber (2006)

Author	Target	N	d_1	d_2	d_3
Clarke1	U	662	0.06	−.06	−.06
Clarke2	U	380	0.09	0.14	0.14
Kellam	U	575	−.01	NA	NA
HainsEllman	U	21	0.36	−.04	−.04
Cecchini	U	100	0.11	−.15	−.15
Petersen	U	335	−.12	NA	NA
Pattison	U	66	−.01	0.40	0.40
Lowry-Web	U	594	0.17	NA	NA
Shochet	U	260	0.39	0.25	0.25
Spence	U	1,500	0.29	0.03	0.03
Merry	U	364	0.02	−.13	0.05
Gwynn-	S	60	1.37	NA	NA
Roosa	S	81	0.41	NA	NA
Sandler	S	72	0.24	NA	NA
Wolchik	S	94	−.06	NA	NA
Beardslee	S	52	0.20	0.42	0.42
Seligman	S	235	0.32	0.12	0.25
Quayle	S	47	−.62	0.62	0.62
Cardemil1	S	49	0.99	1.24	1.24
Cardemil2	S	106	0.16	0.31	0.31
Jaycox	I	143	0.18	0.32	0.20
Clarke3	I	150	0.31	0.07	0.01
Reivich	I	152	0.12	0.40	0.22
Lamb	I	41	0.70	NA	NA
Forsyth	I	59	1.51	1.95	1.95
Clarke4	I	94	0.41	0.47	0.04
Yu-Selig	I	220	0.23	0.30	0.30
Freres1	I	268	−.06	0.16	0.03
Freres2	I	74	0.07	0.56	0.56

effect overall, though we will have to wait to see if it is more effect in some type of interventions than in others.

Forest Plots

A very simple way to examine these results is in terms of what is called a **forest plot**. Each study is plotted on a separate line, indicating its effect size and the confidence interval on that effect size. You can see this plot in Figure 21.1. The dashed vertical line represents an effect size of 0, so we want to see our effect sizes to its right. The values on the far right are the effect size and confidence limits on that effect size

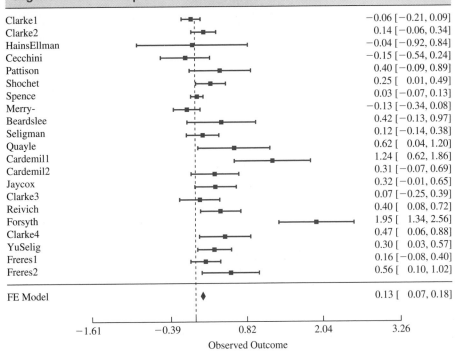

Figure 21.1   Forest plot for Horowitz and Garber's data

for each study. The plot was created using the metafor library in R, but any software for meta-analysis will give similar plots.

The square boxes represent the point estimate from the study in question. You will notice that each box has confidence limits associated with it. It should be obvious that the narrower the interval the more confident we are in our estimates. In general the width of the interval is also associated with the size of the sample, so that large samples lead to more precision. You will also note that the boxes vary in size. That variability is also directly related to the precision of the estimate.

You might find this figure disappointing. Many of those studies have confidence limits that cross 0.0, which means that a significance test on the differences in means would fail (be nonsignificant) in more than half of the studies. That is discouraging. But notice that most values of d, indicated by the small squares, are positive. At least that is encouraging. If we compute the probability of 17 or more studies out of 21 being on the same side of 0, which is the probability under the null hypothesis, that probability is .004, which is even more encouraging. Even that rough form of significance test tells us that the interventions seem to be working. But we want much more information than just a simple probability.

Calculating the Overall Effect

I indicated earlier that our overall effect is going to be a weighted average of the individual d values. It is reasonable to think that if a study had a very small computed standard error of d (s_d), we will be pretty confident that our d was measured with little error and we will have a good bit of confidence in that value. On the other hand, if the standard error of d is quite large, we have much less faith in our estimate. Thinking along those lines, we compute our overall effect size by weighting each d by the inverse of its standard errors ($W_i = 1/s_{d_i}^2$). The more confident we are in a particular study, the more weight we give our result in computing the average.

We will begin by looking at all 21 studies. We have defined d as

$$d = \frac{\overline{X}_{Control} - \overline{X}_{Treatment}}{s_{Control}}$$

and the variance of d and its standard error as

$$s_d^2 = \frac{n_1 + n_2}{n_1 n_2} + \frac{d^2}{2(n_1)}$$

$$s_d = \sqrt{s_d^2}$$

As I mentioned, Figure 21.1 shows us the values of d and the confidence limits on d for each study separately. The confidence limits are computed as $CI_{.95} = d \pm 1.96 s_d$.

Having computed d and its standard error for each study, we will now weight each effect size by the inverse of its variance, which will give greater weight to effects having greater precision.

$$W_i = \frac{1}{s_d^2}$$

We will then compute the mean treatment effect (d_i), and its standard error ($s_{\bar{d}}$) across all 21 studies.

Because we weight each study using W_i, the mean of d is found as $d = \Sigma W_i d_i / \Sigma W_i$ and the standard error of d is $s_{\bar{d}} = \sqrt{1/\Sigma W_i}$. For this meta-analysis the mean value of d is 0.128 and the standard error of $s_{\bar{d}}$ is 0.028. Thus the confidence limits on the corresponding parameter (δ), the true effect size in the population, are

$$CI = \bar{d} \pm 1.96(s_{\bar{d}})$$

$$CI_{lower} = 0.128 - 1.96(0.028) = 0.073$$

$$CI_{upper} = 0.128 + 1.96(0.028) = 0.183$$

$$0.073 \leq \delta \leq 0.183$$

Below the individual studies you will see a small, diamond-shaped figure. This represents the combined effect size from all 21 studies. The label on its left, "FE Model," stands for the effect size with a fixed model. In a fixed effect model, we assume that there is an underlying "true" effect and that all differences in the effects we see are due to sampling error. On the right you can see that the overall effect had $d = .13$ with confidence limits of 0.07 and 0.18. Notice that the confidence interval does not include 0, so the overall effect is significant. That is not a huge effect, but it is real.

Heterogeneity of Effect Sizes

Now that we have the mean and confidence limits of d across all studies, we want to look more closely at the data to determine if the effect size estimates are heterogeneous, suggesting that not all studies are estimating the same true effect. The data could be heterogeneous for two different reasons. It could be that the three target audiences respond differently to the intervention, so that differences among studies are really due to differences among targets. If so, that is something worth our attention. Alternatively there may be differences in the estimated parameters even among studies within the same set of targets. Or perhaps it is a mixture of both. Techniques exist for testing for variables that moderate our results, although we will not consider those here.

Skipping over a great deal of computation, we will define our weights for individual studies as W_i, as before, and compute a quantity called Q, which is a measure of the average deviation of individual values of d for all studies from the grand mean of d. If all of the studies were estimating the same effect size, the d_i should be roughly equal. Q is defined as

$$Q = \sum_{i=1}^{k} W_i (d_i - \bar{d})^2$$

For our meta-analysis $Q = 82.52$. The nice thing about Q is that under the null hypothesis of no differences in effect sizes it is distributed as χ^2 on $k - 1$ df where k is the number of studies. With 21 studies, $\chi^2_{.05}(20) = 31.41$. Because $82.52 > 31.41$ we can reject the null hypothesis and conclude that the studies are not all estimating the same true effect.

From here we could go on to compute a mean d for each subgroup of the target audience and draw conclusions about the effectiveness of treatment for each target audience. I will not do that here because I don't want to bury you in computations, but you can think of Q as being roughly analogous to the overall F in the analysis of variance, which simply tells us that not all means are equal, and subsequent analyses on the individual target differences as being analogous to analyzing multiple comparisons of means. It would be important to know if intervention is effective for all types of children, or if it really is only effective once the child has been identified as having a problem.

21.4 A Second Example—Nicotine Gum and Smoking Cessation

Psychologists have long been interested in helping people to quit smoking, and in the last 20 years we have seen the widespread use of nicotine gum and patches for this purpose. A very large meta-analysis of the effectiveness of such aids was published in the Cochrane database, referred to earlier, by Stead, Perera, Bullen, Mant, and Lancaster (2008). They examined 132 different studies, 53 of which compared nicotine gum to a control condition. We are going to use about half of those studies just to save space, but our results will be essentially the same as theirs. The data for 26 studies comparing gum with a control are shown in Table 21.4. (SuccessT and TotalT stand for number of successful attempts to stop smoking and the total number of cases in the treatment condition, and Success C and Total C are labels for the Control condition.)

The forest plot for the data is shown In Figure 21.2. (Notice that the effect sizes given on the right of Table 21.4 and in the forest plot are the log risk ratios rather than the risk ratios themselves.) You will note that almost every study had an effect size that was greater than 1.0 (for the risk ratio) or greater than 0 (for the log risk ratio). This strongly suggests that nicotine gum is effective in helping people to quit smoking and not to relapse.

Table 21.4 Data on Nicotine Gum as an Aid in Stopping Smoking

Study	Year	SuccessT	TotalT	SuccessC	TotalC	RR	Log$_{RR}$
Ahluwalia	2006	53	378	42	377	1.23	0.20
Areechon	1988	56	99	37	101	1.35	0.33
Blondal	1989	30	92	22	90	1.25	0.22
BrThorSociety	1983	39	410	111	1,208	1.03	0.03
Campbell	1987	13	424	9	412	1.39	0.33
Campbell	1991	21	107	21	105	0.98	−.02
Clavel	1985	24	205	6	222	3.98	1.38
Clavel-Chapelon	1992	47	481	42	515	1.18	0.17
Cooper	2005	17	146	15	147	1.13	0.12
Fagerstrom	1982	30	50	23	50	1.19	0.17
Fagerstrom	1984	28	96	5	49	2.44	0.89
Fee1982	1982	23	180	15	172	1.41	0.35
Fortmann	1995	110	552	84	522	1.20	0.18
Garcia	1989	21	68	5	38	2.03	0.71
Garvey	2000	75	405	17	203	2.02	0.70
Gilbert	1989	11	112	9	111	1.19	0.18
Gross95	1995	37	131	6	46	1.91	0.65
Hall85	1985	18	41	10	36	1.40	0.34
Hall87	1987	30	71	14	68	1.74	0.55
Hall96	1996	24	98	28	103	0.92	−.08
Harackiewicz	1988	12	99	7	52	0.91	−.09
Herrera	1995	30	76	13	78	1.98	0.68
Hjalmarson	1984	31	106	16	100	1.64	0.50
Huber88	1988	13	54	11	60	1.25	0.23
Hughes	1989	23	210	6	105	1.83	0.60
Hughes	1990	15	59	5	19	0.97	−.03

Although we are working with risk ratios rather than standardized mean differences, there are only minor changes in our calculations. In the first place we immediately convert the risk ratios to log risk ratios. We will then work with the logarithmic values until the end, when we will convert back to the standard metric.

The risk ratio is defined as

$$RiskRatio = \frac{SuccessT/TotalT}{SuccessC/TotalC}$$

$$LogRiskRatio = \ln(RiskRatio)$$

The variance and standard error, to a close approximation, are given by

$$Var_{LogRiskRatio} = \frac{1}{SuccessT} - \frac{1}{TotalT} + \frac{1}{SuccessC} - \frac{1}{TotalC}$$

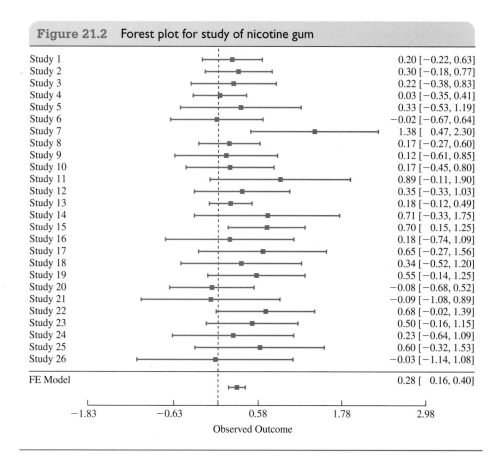

Figure 21.2 Forest plot for study of nicotine gum

$$s_{LogRiskRatio} = \sqrt{Var_{LogRiskRatio}}$$

Finally, the weights, $W_i = 1/s^2_{LogRiskRatio}$

We do not bother to calculate the variance and standard error of the risk ratio itself because we will never need them.

We still need to calculate summary statistics for the mean risk ratio and its confidence limits. To do so we work with the logarithmic values. We use the same basic formulae that we did before, except that we substitute the log risk ratio for d. I show the calculations simply to illustrate the similarities to what we did with d. You do not need to learn them.

$$Mean_{LogRR} = \frac{\sum(W_i LogRR_i)}{\sum W_i} = \frac{73.766}{267.416} = 0.276$$

$$Var_{LogRR} = \frac{1}{\sum W_i} = \frac{1}{267.416} = .0037$$

$$SE_{LogRR} = \sqrt{Var_{LogRR}} = \sqrt{.0037} = .06$$

$$CI = mean_{LogRR} \pm 1.96(SE_{LogRR}) = .276 \pm 1.96(.06) = .276 \pm 0.118$$

$$CI_{lower} = 0.158$$

$$CI_{upper} = 0.394$$

$$\exp(mean) = \exp(.276) = 1.32$$

$$\exp(CI_{lower}) = \exp(0.158) = 1.17$$

$$\exp(CI_{upper}) = \exp(0.394) = 1.48$$

The last step converted the logarithmic values back to the original metric of the risk ratio. Therefore we can write the confidence interval on the risk ratio as

$$1.17 \leq RiskRatio \leq 1.48$$

Our risk ratio is significantly greater than 1, indicating that the likelihood of a successful outcome is greater in the group that used nicotine gum, and the lower bound of the interval reflects about a 20% higher chance of success for that group.

There is far more that we could cover on meta-analysis, but what we have here should be sufficient to make you feel comfortable going to the literature. You know the methods of calculating a mean effect size and its standard error, whatever your measure, and you can set confidence limits on that effect size. You can interpret a forest plot and see how various studies stand with respect to each other even if they have been based on different test statistics. Collecting all of the data to do a meta-analysis is the really hard part. You have a good handle on the rest. There are certainly a lot of formulae, but if you work through them systematically they are not complicated, and no one would expect you to remember them all. (I assure you that I could not write them down from memory.) Each of the sources cited above is excellent and provides the information you need. There are also software programs that will not only carry out the calculations, but will allow you to organize the data about each study and examine the question of whether effect sizes are dependent on other variables such as gender or age. One of the best packages is the Comprehensive Meta-Analysis (CMA) package, developed by Borenstein, Hedges, Higgins, and Rothstein. It is not freeware, but you can hope that your university has a license for it. In addition, the Cochrane Collaboration has developed software named RevMan, which is free, and will do just about everything you would want and more. William Shadish keeps a list of available meta-analysis software at http://faculty.ucmerced.edu/wshadish/Meta-Analysis Software.htm. It contains links to many programs. Finally, R has at least three packages for meta-analysis, of which "metafor" is my favorite.

Key Terms

Meta-analysis, 545

Forest plot, 552

File drawer problem, 545

21.5 | A Quick Review

A   What is evidence-based medicine?
Ans: It is practice and advice based on the results of a meta-analysis on multiple studies.

B.   What is the "File Drawer Problem"?
Ans: This refers to the fact that many nonsignificant studies go unpublished and are hidden away where they do not contribute to final decisions about effects.

C.   Why do we use effect sizes rather than means or mean differences in our meta-analysis?
Ans: By using effect sizes we can convert whatever statistic we have to that measure and put all studies on an equal scale.

D.   What is a forest plot?
Ans: It is a graphic that puts all effect sizes on a single plot, showing their confidence intervals, and showing an overall effect size with its confidence interval.

E.   In combining studies we weight them in proportion to _____.
Ans: the standard error of their effect sizes

F.   Having shown from the meta-analysis that there is an overall true effect of an intervention, where do we go from there?
Ans: We would carry out further analyses to determine if the different categories of targets show more or less benefit. We would also want to know if even programs aimed at large groups of children are effective.

G.   When working with relative risk, or risk ratios, we generally transform the effect size with _____.
Ans: a logarithmic transformation

21.6 | Exercises

Mazzucchelli, Kane, and Rees (2010) examined studies of behavioral activation as a way to improve feelings of subjective well-being. (They defined behavioral activation as "intentional behavioral, cognitive, or volitional activity … intended to cultivate positive feelings, behaviors, and/or cognitions.") They report data on 11 studies comparing treatment and control groups. These data are broken down by those who showed minimal symptoms of depression and those who showed elevated symptoms. The results follow.

Author	Subgroup	n_E (est.)	n_C (est.)	Hedges' g	Standard error
Barlow86a	Elevated	12	12	−.134	0.523
Besyner79	Elevated	14	16	0.675	0.423
Lovett88	Elevated	33	27	0.204	0.305
Stark	Elevated	10	9	0.043	0.439
Van den Hout	Elevated	15	14	0.644	0.371
Weinberg	Elevated	10	9	0.976	0.467
Wilson	Elevated	9	11	1.466	0.524
Barlow86b	Minimal	12	13	0.133	0.352
Fordyce77	Minimal	50	60	0.609	0.195
Fordyce83	Minimal	40	13	1.410	0.483
Reich81	Minimal	49	49	0.378	0.179

21.1   Create a forest plot of these data.

21.2   Calculate a mean effect size and its standard error.

21.3   Calculate confidence limits on the mean effect size computed in the previous exercise.

Bloch et al. (2009) conducted a meta-analysis on the treatment of Attention-deficit/hyperactivity disorder. There have been reports that psychostimulant medications given to children with ADHD who have a history of Tourette's syndrome can increase the severity of tics. The authors found (among other studies) four studies that compared methylphenidate derivatives against placebo-controlled condition by rating scales for tic and ADHD severity. The results of these four studies for presence and frequency of tics are shown here. (The standard errors of d were estimated from the published results.)

Study	n	d	CI	s_d
Gadow92	11	0.11	−0.55 − 0.77	0.336
Castellanos	20	0.29	−0.18 − 0.76	0.240
TSSG	103	0.64	0.27 − 1.00	0.184
Gadow07	71	0.06	−0.17 − 0.29	0.117

21.4   Calculate the mean effect size estimate and its confidence limits for the data in this table.

21.5   Create a forest plot for the data in Bloch's study.

21.6   For the Bloch et al. study what would you conclude about the risk of increasing tic behavior using methylphenidate?

21.7   Three of the studies referred to in the previous exercises also looked at differences in ratings of ADHD severity as a dependent variable. These results are shown below.

Study	n	d	CI	s_d
Gadow92	11	1.11	0.44 − 1.77	0.341
TSSG	103	0.56	0.19 − 0.92	0.189
Gadow07	71	0.76	0.53 − 0.99	0.117

a)   Compute the mean effect size from these studies.
b)   Compute confidence limits on the mean effect size.

21.8   Create a forest plot for these results.

21.9   Why does it make little sense to look for heterogeneity of effect sizes in this example?

21.10   Bauer and Döpfmer (1999) examined the efficacy of lithium as an augmentation to conventional antidepressants. They found nine placebo-controlled studies testing lithium for those cases that did not respond to other antidepressants. The data, as estimated from their paper, follow:

Study	n	d	s_d	CI
Stein	34	−0.30	0.82	−1.10 − 0.50
Zusky	16	0.19	0.86	−0.65 − 1.03
Katona	61	0.50	0.51	0.02 − 1.02
Schopf	27	1.36	1.39	0.05 − 2.77
Baumann	24	0.97	0.99	0.09 − 1.85
Browne	17	0.51	0.87	−0.34 − 1.36
Kantor	7	0.51	1.55	−1.01 − 2.03
Heninger	15	1.33	1.38	−0.02 − 2.68
Joffe	33	0.76	0.70	−0.02 − 1.36

Create a forest plot for these results.

21.11   Compute the mean effect size and its confidence limits.

21.12   Kapoor et al. (2011) collected data on the treatment of myeloma, which is a cancer of the blood. (You may think that this has little to do with psychology, but I have myeloma, and I take a thalidomide derivative, so I have a particular interest in the results.) Rajkumar found four studies since 2007 that compared a standard chemotherapy treatment for myeloma with the same treatment that also included thalidomide. (Thalidomide was a drug prescribed as a sedative to pregnant women in the 1950s and was then found to create truly horrible problems with birth defects and was immediately withdrawn, but not until after causing 10,000–20,000 birth defects worldwide. It has recently been found to be an excellent treatment for some forms of cancer, though it is used with a great deal of caution.) The following table presents the results of the four studies. The cell entries are the number of cases.

Study	Success Thalidomide	Total Thalidomide	Success Control	Total Control
Palumbo	21	129	5	126
Facon	16	125	4	198
Hulin	8	113	1	116
Hovon	3	165	1	108

Compute risk ratios for each study as well as log risk ratios.

21.13 Compute the weighted mean risk ratio across the four studies.

21.14 Compute confidence limits on the mean risk ratio and draw the appropriate conclusions.

21.15 Can we conclude that thalidomide is beginning to redeem its awful reputation?

21.16 Why might it not make much sense to examine the results for heterogeneity of effects?

21.17 Bisson and Andrew(2007) conducted a meta-analysis of cognitive behavior therapy (CBT) as a treatment for posttraumatic stress disorder (PTSD). They found 14 studies for which they had clinicians' ratings of PTSD symptoms in both a CBT-focused condition and a wait list/usual care condition. The results are presented here.

Study	CBT			Control		
	N	Mean	St. Dev.	N	Mean	St. Dev.
Kubany1	45	15.80	14.40	40	71.90	23.80
Foa1	45	12.60	8.37	15	26.93	8.47
Kubany2	18	10.10	19.30	14	76.10	25.20
Resick	81	23.00	19.92	40	69.73	19.19
Cloitre	22	31.00	25.20	24	62.00	22.70
Foa2	10	15.40	11.09	10	19.50	7.18
Keane	11	28.80	10.05	13	31.90	31.90
Ehlers	14	21.58	28.56	14	74.55	19.12
Vaughan	13	23.00	10.20	17	28.50	8.90
Brom	27	56.20	24.10	23	66.40	24.30
Blanchard	27	23.70	26.20	24	54.00	25.90
Fecteau	10	37.50	30.40	10	74.60	24.70
Gersons	22	3.00	10.00	20	9.00	13.00
Rothbaum	20	21.25	22.50	20	64.55	19.87

Apply a meta-analysis to these data and draw the appropriate conclusions.

Appendix A

Arithmetic Review

Standard Symbols and
Basic Information

Addition and Subtraction

Multiplication and Division

Parentheses

Fractions

Algebraic Operations

The following is intended as a quick refresher of some of the simple arithmetic operations you learned in high school but probably have not used since. Although some of what follows will seem so obvious that you wonder why it is included, people sometimes forget the most obvious things. A more complete review can be found at http://www.uvm.edu/~dhowell/fundamentals9/ArithmeticReview/review _of_arithmetic_revised.html and I recommend that anyone who is not sure of the arithmetic skills should look at that.

One of the things that students never seem to learn is that it is easy to figure out most of these principles for yourself. For example, if you can't remember whether

$$\frac{18.1}{28.6 + 32.7} \quad \text{can be reduced to} \quad \frac{18.1}{28.6} + \frac{18.1}{32.7}$$

(it cannot, but it is one of the foolish things that I can never keep in my head), try it out with very simple numbers. Thus,

$$\frac{2}{1 + 4} = \frac{2}{5} = .4$$

is obviously not the same as

$$\frac{2}{1} + \frac{2}{4} = 2.5$$

It is often quicker to check on a procedure by using small numbers than by looking it up.

Standard Symbols and Basic Information

Numerator	The thing on the top
Denominator	The thing on the bottom
a/b	a = Numerator; b = Denominator
+, −, ×, ÷ (or /)	Symbols for addition, subtraction, multiplication, and division; called *operators*
$X = Y$	X equals Y
$X \approx Y$ or $X \simeq Y$	X approximately equal to Y
$X \neq Y$	X unequal to Y
$X < Y$	X less than Y (*Hint:* The smaller end points to the smaller number.)
$X \leq Y$	X less than or equal to Y
$X > Y$	X greater than Y
$X \geq Y$	X greater than or equal to Y
$X < Y < Z$	X less than Y less than Z (i.e., Y is between X and Z)
$X \pm Y$	X plus or minus Y
$\lvert X \rvert$	Absolute value of X—ignore the sign of X
$\dfrac{1}{X}$	The reciprocal of X
X^2	X squared
X^n	X raised to the nth power
$\sqrt{X} = X^{1/2}$	Square root of X

Addition and Subtraction

$8 - 12 = -4$	To subtract a larger number from a smaller one, subtract the smaller from the larger and make the result negative.
$-8 + 12$ $= 12 - 8 = 4$	The order of operations is not important.

Multiplication and Division

$2(3)(6)$
$= 2 \times 3 \times 6$

If no operator appears before a set of parentheses, multiplication is implied.

$2 \times 3 \times 6$
$= 2 \times 6 \times 3$

Numbers can be multiplied in any order.

$\dfrac{2 \times 8}{4}$

$= \dfrac{2}{4} \times 8$

$= 2 \times \dfrac{8}{4}$

$= \dfrac{16}{4} = 4$

Division can take place in any order.

$7 \times 3 + 6$
$= 21 + 6 = 27$

Multiply or divide *before* you add or subtract the result. But for the same operators, work from left to right [e.g., $8 \div 2 \div 4 = (8 \div 2) \div 4$, not $8 \div (2 \div 4)$].

$2 \times 3 = 6$

$(-2)(-3) = 6$

$\dfrac{6}{3} = 2$

$\dfrac{-6}{-3} = 2$

Multiplication or division of numbers with the *same* sign produces a positive answer.

$(-2)3 = -6$

$\dfrac{-6}{3} = -2$

Multiplication or division of numbers with *opposite* signs produces a negative answer.

$(-2)(3)(-6)(-4)$
$= (-6)(24)$
$= -144$

With several numbers having different signs, work in pairs to get the correct sign.

Parentheses

$2(7 - 6 + 3) =$
$2(4) = 8$

When multiplying, either perform the operations inside parentheses before multiplying, or multiply *each* element within the parentheses and then sum.

or

$$2(7) + 2(-6) + 2(3)$$
$$= 14 - 12 + 6 = 8$$

$$2(7 - 6 + 3)^2$$
$$= 2(4)^2 = 2(16)$$
$$= 32$$

When the parenthetical term is raised to a power, perform the operations inside the parentheses, raise the result to the appropriate power, and then carry out the other operations.

Fractions

$$\frac{1}{5} = .20$$

To convert to a decimal, divide the numerator by the denominator.

$$\frac{4}{3}$$

The reciprocal of $\frac{3}{4}$. To take the reciprocal of a fraction, stand it on its head.

$$3 \times \frac{6}{5} = \frac{3 \times 6}{5}$$
$$= \frac{18}{5} = 3.6$$

To multiply a fraction by a whole number, multiply the numerator by that number.

$$\frac{3}{5} \times \frac{6}{7} \times \frac{1}{2}$$
$$= \frac{3 \times 6 \times 1}{5 \times 7 \times 2}$$
$$= \frac{18}{70} = .26$$

To multiply a series of fractions, multiply numerators together and multiply denominators together.

$$\frac{1}{3} + \frac{4}{3} = \frac{5}{3} = 1.67$$

To add fractions with the *same* denominator, add the numerators and divide by the common denominator.

$$\frac{1}{6} + \frac{4}{3} = \frac{1}{6} + \frac{8}{6} = \frac{9}{6}$$
$$= 1.5$$

To add fractions with *different* denominators, multiply the numerator and the denominator by a constant to equate the denominators and follow the previous rule.

$$\frac{8}{13} + \frac{12}{25}$$

This is a more elaborate example of the same rule.

$$= \left(\frac{25}{25} \times \frac{8}{13} \right) + \left(\frac{13}{13} \times \frac{12}{25} \right)$$

$$= \frac{200}{325} + \frac{156}{325}$$

$$= \frac{356}{325} = 1.095$$

$$\frac{8}{1/3} = 8\left(\frac{3}{1}\right) = 24$$ To divide by a fraction, multiply by the reciprocal of that fraction.

Algebraic Operations

Most algebraic operations boil down to moving things from one side of the equation to the other. Mathematically, the rule is that whatever you do to one side of the equation you must do to the other side.

Solve the following equation for X:

$$3 + X = 8$$

We want X on one side and the answer on the other. All we have to do is to subtract 3 from both sides to get

$$3 + X - 3 = 8 - 3$$
$$X = 5$$

If the equation had been

$$X - 3 = 8$$

we would have added 3 to both sides:

$$X - 3 + 3 = 8 + 3$$
$$X = 11$$

For equations involving multiplication or division, we follow the same principle:

$$2X = 21$$

Dividing both sides by 2, we have

$$\frac{2X}{2} = \frac{21}{2}$$
$$X = 10.5$$

and

$$\frac{X}{7} = 13$$

$$\frac{7X}{7} = 7(13)$$

$$X = 91$$

Personally, I prefer to think of things in a different, but perfectly equivalent, way. When you want to get rid of something that has been added (or subtracted) to (or from) one side of the equation, move it to the other side and reverse the sign:

$$3 + X = 12 \qquad \text{or} \qquad X - 7 = 19$$

$$X = 12 - 3 \qquad\qquad X = 19 + 7$$

When the thing you want to get rid of is in the numerator, move it to the other side and put it in the denominator:

$$7.6X = 12$$

$$X = \frac{12}{7.6}$$

When the thing you want to get rid of is in the denominator, move it to the numerator on the other side and multiply:

$$\frac{X}{8.9} = 14.6$$

$$X = 14.6(8.9)$$

Notice that with more complex expressions, you must multiply (or divide) everything on the other side of the equation. Thus,

$$7.6X = 12 + 8$$

$$X = \frac{12 + 8}{7.6}$$

For complex equations, just work one step at a time:

$$7.6(X + 8) = \frac{14}{7} - 5$$

First, get rid of the 7.6:

$$X + 8 = \frac{14/7 - 5}{7.6}$$

Now get rid of the 8:

$$X = \frac{14/7 - 5}{7.6} - 8$$

Now clean up the messy fraction:

$$X = \frac{2 - 5}{7.6} - 8 = \frac{-3}{7.6} - 8 = -.395 - 8 = -8.395$$

Appendix B
Symbols and Notation

Greek Letter Symbols

α	Level of significance—probability of a Type I error (alpha)
β	Probability of a Type II error (beta); standardized regression coefficient
δ	Effect size combined with sample size to compute power (delta)
η^2	Eta squared
μ	Population mean (mu)
$\mu_{\overline{X}}$	Mean of the sampling distribution of the mean
ρ	Population correlation coefficient (rho)
σ	Population standard deviation (sigma)
σ^2	Population variance
Σ	Summation notation (uppercase sigma)
ϕ	Phi coefficient
χ^2	Chi-square
χ^2_F	Friedman's chi-square
ω^2	Omega squared

English Letter Symbols

a	Intercept; number of levels of variable A in analysis of variance
b	Slope (also called regression coefficient)
CI	Confidence interval
cov_{xy}	Covariance of X and Y

$\hat{d}$	Effect size estimate
df	Degrees of freedom
E	Expected frequency; expected value
F	F statistic
H	Kruskal–Wallis statistic
H_0; H_1	Null hypothesis; alternative hypothesis
MS	Mean square
MS_{error}	Mean square error
n, n_i, N_i	Number of cases in a sample
$N(0, 1)$	Read "normally distributed with $\mu = 0$, $\sigma^2 = 1$"
O	Observed frequency
p	General symbol for probability
Q	Weighted sum squared of $(d_i - \bar{d})$ deviations
r, r_{XY}	Pearson's correlation coefficient
r_{pb}	Point biserial correlation coefficient
r_S	Spearman's rank-order correlation coefficient
R	Multiple correlation coefficient
s^2, s_X^2	Sample variance
s_p^2	Pooled variance
s, s_X	Sample standard deviation
s_D	Standard deviation of difference scores
$s_{\bar{D}}$	Standard error of the mean of difference scores
$s_{\bar{X}}$, $s_{\bar{X}_1 - \bar{X}_2}$	Standard error of the mean; standard error of difference between means
$s_{Y - \hat{Y}}$	Standard error of estimate
SS_A	Sum of squares for variable A
SS_{AB}	Interaction sum of squares
SS_{error}	Error sum of squares
SS_Y	Sum of squares for variable Y
$SS_{\hat{Y}}$	Sum of squares of predicted values of Y
$SS_{Y - \hat{Y}}$	Error sum of squares = SS_{error}
t	Student's t statistic

$t_{.025}$	Critical value of t
T	Wilcoxon's matched-pairs signed-ranks statistic
T_j	Total for group j
W_i	Weighting factor in meta-analysis
W_S, W_S'	Mann–Whitney statistic
X or X_{ij}	Individual observation
$\overline{X}$ or $\overline{X}_{GM}$	Grand mean
$\overline{X}, \overline{X}_i, \overline{X}_{A_i}$	Sample mean
$\overline{X}_h$	Harmonic mean
$\hat{Y}, \hat{Y}_i$	Predicted value of Y
z	Normal deviate (also called standard score)

Appendix C

Basic Statistical Formulae

Descriptive Statistics

Variance (s^2)

$$s^2 = \frac{\Sigma(X - \overline{X})^2}{N - 1} = \frac{\Sigma X^2 - (\Sigma X)^2/N}{N - 1}$$

Standard deviation (s)

$$s = \sqrt{s^2}$$

Median location

$$\frac{(N + 1)}{2}$$

Hinge location

$$\frac{\text{Median location} + 1}{2}$$

General formula for z score

$$\frac{\text{Score} - \text{Mean}}{\text{Std. deviation}} \quad \text{or} \quad \frac{\text{Statistic} - \text{Parameter}}{\text{Std. error of statistic}}$$

z score for an observation

$$z = \frac{X - \overline{X}}{s}$$

Tests on Sample Means

Standard error of the mean ($s_{\overline{X}}$)

$$\frac{s_X}{\sqrt{N}}$$

z for $\overline{X}$ given σ

$$z = \frac{\overline{X} - \mu}{\sigma_{\overline{X}}}$$

t for one sample

$$t = \frac{\overline{X} - \mu}{s_{\overline{X}}} = \frac{\overline{X} - \mu}{\dfrac{s}{\sqrt{N}}}$$

Confidence interval on μ $$CI = \overline{X} \pm t_{.05}(s_{\overline{X}})$$

t for two related samples $$t = \frac{\overline{D}}{s_{\overline{D}}} = \frac{\overline{D}}{s_D/\sqrt{N}}$$

t for two independent samples (unpooled) $$t = \frac{\overline{X}_1 - \overline{X}_2}{s_{\overline{X}_1 - \overline{X}_2}} = \frac{\overline{X}_1 - \overline{X}_2}{\sqrt{\dfrac{s_1^2}{N_1} + \dfrac{s_2^2}{N_2}}}$$

Pooled variance (s_p^2) $$s_p^2 = \frac{(N_1 - 1)s_1^2 + (N_2 - 1)s_2^2}{N_1 + N_2 - 2}$$

t for two independent samples (pooled) $$t = \frac{\overline{X}_1 - \overline{X}_2}{s_{\overline{X}_1 - \overline{X}_2}} = \frac{\overline{X}_1 - \overline{X}_2}{\sqrt{\dfrac{s_p^2}{N_1} + \dfrac{s_p^2}{N_2}}} = \frac{\overline{X}_1 - \overline{X}_2}{\sqrt{s_p^2\left(\dfrac{1}{N_1} + \dfrac{1}{N_2}\right)}}$$

Confidence interval on $\mu_1 - \mu_2$ $$CI = (\overline{X}_1 - \overline{X}_2) \pm t_{.05}\, s_{(\overline{X}_1 - \overline{X}_2)}$$

Power

Effect size (one sample) $\quad d = (\mu_1 - \mu_0)/\sigma$

Effect size (two samples) $\quad d = (\mu_1 - \mu_2)/\sigma$

Delta (one-sample t) $\quad \delta = d\sqrt{N}$

Delta (two-sample t) $\quad \delta = d\sqrt{\dfrac{N}{2}}$

Correlation and Regression

Sum of squares $$SS_X = \Sigma(X - \overline{X})^2 = \Sigma X^2 - \frac{(\Sigma X)^2}{N}$$

Sum of products $$\Sigma(X - \overline{X})(Y - \overline{Y}) = \Sigma XY - \frac{(\Sigma X \Sigma Y)}{N}$$

Covariance $$cov_{XY} = \frac{\Sigma(X - \overline{X})(Y - \overline{Y})}{N - 1} = \frac{\Sigma XY - \dfrac{\Sigma X \Sigma Y}{N}}{N - 1}$$

Correlation (Pearson)	$r = \dfrac{\text{cov}_{XY}}{s_X s_Y}$
Slope	$b = \dfrac{\text{cov}_{XY}}{s_X^2}$
Intercept	$a = \dfrac{\Sigma Y - b\Sigma X}{N} = \overline{Y} - b\overline{X}$
Standard error of estimate	$s_{Y-\hat{Y}} = \sqrt{\dfrac{\Sigma(Y - \hat{Y})^2}{N - 2}} = \sqrt{\dfrac{SS_{\text{error}}}{N - 2}}$ $= s_Y\sqrt{(1 - r^2)\dfrac{N - 1}{N - 2}}$
SS_Y	$\Sigma Y^2 - \dfrac{(\Sigma Y)^2}{N}$
$SS_{\hat{Y}}$	$\Sigma \hat{Y}^2 - \dfrac{(\Sigma \hat{Y})^2}{N}$
$SS_{Y-\hat{Y}}$	$SS_Y - SS_{\hat{Y}} = SS_{\text{error}}$
SS_{error}	$SS_Y(1 - r^2)$
SS_{total}	$\Sigma(X - \overline{X})^2 = \Sigma X^2 - \dfrac{(\Sigma X)^2}{N}$
SS_{group} (one-way)	$n\Sigma(\overline{X}_j - \overline{X}_{GM})^2$
SS_{error} (one-way)	$SS_{\text{total}} - SS_{\text{group}}$
SS_{rows} (two-way)	$nc\Sigma(\overline{X}_{r_i} - \overline{X}_{GM})^2$
SS_{col} (two-way)	$nr\Sigma(\overline{X}_{c_j} - \overline{X}_{GM})^2$
SS_{cells} (two-way)	$n\Sigma(\overline{X}_{ij} - \overline{X}_{GM})^2$
$SS_{R \times C}$ (two-way)	$SS_{\text{cells}} - SS_{\text{rows}} - SS_{\text{col}}$
SS_{error} (two-way)	$SS_{\text{total}} - SS_{\text{rows}} - SS_{\text{col}} - SS_{R \times C}$ or $SS_{\text{total}} - SS_{\text{cells}}$
Protected t (Use only if F is significant.)	$t = \dfrac{\overline{X}_i - \overline{X}_j}{\sqrt{\dfrac{MS_{\text{error}}}{n_i} + \dfrac{MS_{\text{error}}}{n_j}}}$
Eta squared	$\eta^2 = \dfrac{SS_{\text{group}}}{SS_{\text{total}}}$

Omega squared (one-way) $$\omega^2 = \frac{SS_{\text{group}} - (k - 1)MS_{\text{error}}}{SS_{\text{total}} + MS_{\text{error}}}$$

Chi-Square

Chi-square $$\chi^2 = \Sigma \frac{(O - E)^2}{E}$$

Distribution-Free Statistics

Mean and standard deviation
(large sample) for
Mann–Whitney statistic
$$\text{Mean} = \frac{n_1(n_1 + n_2 + 1)}{2}; \quad s = \sqrt{\frac{n_1 n_2(n_1 + n_2 + 1)}{12}}$$

Mean and standard deviation (large
sample) for Wilcoxon's statistic
$$\text{Mean} = \frac{n(n + 1)}{4}; \quad s = \sqrt{\frac{n(n + 1)(2n + 1)}{24}}$$

Kruskal–Wallis H statistic $$H = \frac{12}{N(N + 1)} \Sigma \frac{R_j^2}{n_j} - 3(N + 1)$$

Friedman's chi-square statistic $$\chi_F^2 = \frac{12}{Nk(k + 1)} \Sigma R_j^2 - 3N(k + 1)$$

Meta-Analysis

Weighting factors for averaging d value $\quad W_i = 1/s_{d_i}^2$

Q statistic for variability in effects $\quad Q = \Sigma W_i(d_i - \bar{d})^2$

Appendix D

Data Set

Howell and Huessy (1985) reported on a study of 386 children who had, and had not, exhibited symptoms of attention deficit disorder (ADD)—previously known as hyperkinesis or minimal brain dysfunction—during childhood. In 1965 teachers of all second-grade school children in a number of schools in northwestern Vermont were asked to complete a questionnaire for each of their students dealing with behaviors commonly associated with ADD. Questionnaires on these same children were again completed when the children were in the fourth and fifth grades and, for purposes of this data set only, those three scores were averaged to produce a score labeled ADDSC. The higher the score, the more ADD-like behaviors the child exhibited. At the end of ninth grade and again at the end of 12th grade, information on the performances of these children was obtained from school records. These data offer the opportunity to examine questions about whether later behavior can be predicted from earlier behavior and to examine academically related variables and their interrelationships. A description of each variable follows.

ADDSC	Average of three ADD-like behavior scores
GENDER	1 = male; 2 = female
REPEAT	1 = repeated at least one grade; 0 = did not repeat
IQ	IQ obtained from a group-administered IQ test
ENGL	Level of English in ninth grade: 1 = college prep; 2 = general; 3 = remedial
ENGG	Grade in English in ninth grade: 4 = A, etc.
GPA	Grade point average in ninth grade
SOCPROB	Social problems in ninth grade: 1 = yes; 0 = no
DROPOUT	1 = dropped out before completing high school; 0 = did not drop out

The data are available at http://www.uvm.edu/~dhowell/fundamentals9/DataFiles/Add.dat

ADDSC	GENDER	REPEAT	IQ	ENGL	ENGG	GPA	SOCPROB	DROPOUT
45	1	0	111	2	3	2.60	0	0
50	1	0	102	2	3	2.75	0	0
49	1	0	108	2	4	4.00	0	0
55	1	0	109	2	2	2.25	0	0
39	1	0	118	2	3	3.00	0	0
68	1	1	79	2	2	1.67	0	1
69	1	1	88	2	2	2.25	1	1
56	1	0	102	2	4	3.40	0	0
58	1	0	105	3	1	1.33	0	0
48	1	0	92	2	4	3.50	0	0
34	1	0	131	2	4	3.75	0	0
50	2	0	104	1	3	2.67	0	0
85	1	0	83	2	3	2.75	1	0
49	1	0	84	2	2	2.00	0	0
51	1	0	85	2	3	2.75	0	0
53	1	0	110	2	2	2.50	0	0
36	2	0	121	1	4	3.55	0	0
62	2	0	120	2	3	2.75	0	0
46	2	0	100	2	4	3.50	0	0
50	2	0	94	2	2	2.75	1	1
47	2	0	89	1	2	3.00	0	0
50	2	0	93	2	4	3.25	0	0
44	2	0	128	2	4	3.30	0	0
50	2	0	84	2	3	2.75	0	0
29	2	0	127	1	4	3.75	0	0
49	2	0	106	2	3	2.75	0	0
26	1	0	137	2	3	3.00	0	0
85	1	1	82	3	2	1.75	1	1
53	1	0	106	2	3	2.75	1	0
53	1	0	109	2	2	1.33	0	0
72	1	0	91	2	2	0.67	0	0
35	1	0	111	2	2	2.25	0	0
42	1	0	105	2	2	1.75	0	0
37	1	0	118	2	4	3.25	0	0
46	1	0	103	3	2	1.75	0	0

ADDSC	GENDER	REPEAT	IQ	ENGL	ENGG	GPA	SOCPROB	DROPOUT
48	1	0	101	1	3	3.00	0	0
46	1	0	101	3	3	3.00	0	0
49	1	1	95	2	3	3.00	0	0
65	1	1	108	2	3	3.25	0	0
52	1	0	95	3	3	2.25	1	0
75	1	1	98	2	1	1.00	0	1
58	1	0	82	2	3	2.50	0	1
43	2	0	100	1	3	3.00	0	0
60	2	0	100	2	3	2.40	0	0
43	1	0	107	1	2	2.00	0	0
51	1	0	95	2	2	2.75	0	0
70	1	1	97	2	3	2.67	1	1
69	1	1	93	2	2	2.00	0	0
65	1	1	81	1	2	2.00	0	0
63	2	0	89	2	2	1.67	0	0
44	2	0	111	2	4	3.00	0	0
61	2	1	95	2	1	1.50	0	1
40	2	0	106	2	4	3.75	0	0
62	2	0	83	3	1	0.67	0	0
59	1	0	81	2	2	1.50	0	0
47	2	0	115	1	4	4.00	0	0
50	2	0	112	2	3	3.00	0	0
50	2	0	92	2	3	2.33	0	0
65	2	0	85	2	2	1.75	0	0
54	2	0	95	3	2	3.00	0	0
44	2	0	115	2	4	3.75	0	0
66	2	0	91	2	4	2.67	1	1
34	2	0	107	1	4	3.50	0	0
74	2	0	102	2	0	0.67	0	0
57	2	1	86	3	3	2.25	0	0
60	2	0	96	1	3	3.00	1	0
36	2	0	114	2	3	3.50	0	0
50	1	0	105	2	2	1.75	0	0
60	1	0	82	2	1	1.00	0	0
45	1	0	120	2	3	3.00	0	0
55	1	0	88	2	1	1.00	0	1
44	1	0	90	1	3	2.50	0	0

A D D S C	G E N D E R	R E P E A T	I Q	E N G L	E N G G	G P A	S O C P R O B	D R O P O U T
57	2	0	85	2	3	2.50	0	0
33	2	0	106	1	4	3.75	0	0
30	2	0	109	1	4	3.50	0	0
64	1	0	75	3	2	1.00	1	0
49	1	1	91	2	3	2.25	0	0
76	1	0	96	2	2	1.00	0	0
40	1	0	108	2	3	2.50	0	0
48	1	0	86	2	3	2.75	0	0
65	1	0	98	2	2	0.75	0	0
50	1	0	99	2	2	1.30	0	0
70	1	0	95	2	1	1.25	0	0
78	1	0	88	3	3	1.50	0	0
44	1	0	111	2	2	3.00	0	0
48	1	0	103	2	1	2.00	0	0
52	1	0	107	2	2	2.00	0	0
40	1	0	118	2	2	2.50	0	0

Appendix E
Statistical Tables

Table E.1 Upper Percentage Points of the χ^2 Distribution

df	.995	.990	.975	.950	.900	.750	.500	.250	.100	.050	.025	.010	.005
1	.00	.00	.00	.00	.02	.10	.45	1.32	2.71	3.84	5.02	6.63	7.88
2	.01	.02	.05	.10	.21	.58	1.39	2.77	4.61	5.99	7.38	9.21	10.60
3	.07	.11	.22	.35	.58	1.21	2.37	4.11	6.25	7.82	9.35	11.35	12.84
4	.21	.30	.48	.71	1.06	1.92	3.36	5.39	7.78	9.49	11.14	13.28	14.86
5	.41	.55	.83	1.15	1.61	2.67	4.35	6.63	9.24	11.07	12.83	15.09	16.75
6	.68	.87	1.24	1.64	2.20	3.45	5.35	7.84	10.64	12.59	14.45	16.81	18.55
7	.99	1.24	1.69	2.17	2.83	4.25	6.35	9.04	12.02	14.07	16.01	18.48	20.28
8	1.34	1.65	2.18	2.73	3.49	5.07	7.34	10.22	13.36	15.51	17.54	20.09	21.96
9	1.73	2.09	2.70	3.33	4.17	5.90	8.34	11.39	14.68	16.92	19.02	21.66	23.59
10	2.15	2.56	3.25	3.94	4.87	6.74	9.34	12.55	15.99	18.31	20.48	23.21	25.19
11	2.60	3.05	3.82	4.57	5.58	7.58	10.34	13.70	17.28	19.68	21.92	24.72	26.75
12	3.07	3.57	4.40	5.23	6.30	8.44	11.34	14.85	18.55	21.03	23.34	26.21	28.30
13	3.56	4.11	5.01	5.89	7.04	9.30	12.34	15.98	19.81	22.36	24.74	27.69	29.82
14	4.07	4.66	5.63	6.57	7.79	10.17	13.34	17.12	21.06	23.69	26.12	29.14	31.31
15	4.60	5.23	6.26	7.26	8.55	11.04	14.34	18.25	22.31	25.00	27.49	30.58	32.80
16	5.14	5.81	6.91	7.96	9.31	11.91	15.34	19.37	23.54	26.30	28.85	32.00	34.27
17	5.70	6.41	7.56	8.67	10.09	12.79	16.34	20.49	24.77	27.59	30.19	33.41	35.72
18	6.26	7.01	8.23	9.39	10.86	13.68	17.34	21.60	25.99	28.87	31.53	34.81	37.15
19	6.84	7.63	8.91	10.12	11.65	14.56	18.34	22.72	27.20	30.14	32.85	36.19	38.58
20	7.43	8.26	9.59	10.85	12.44	15.45	19.34	23.83	28.41	31.41	34.17	37.56	40.00
21	8.03	8.90	10.28	11.59	13.24	16.34	20.34	24.93	29.62	32.67	35.48	38.93	41.40
22	8.64	9.54	10.98	12.34	14.04	17.24	21.34	26.04	30.81	33.93	36.78	40.29	42.80
23	9.26	10.19	11.69	13.09	14.85	18.14	22.34	27.14	32.01	35.17	38.08	41.64	44.18
24	9.88	10.86	12.40	13.85	15.66	19.04	23.34	28.24	33.20	36.42	39.37	42.98	45.56
25	10.52	11.52	13.12	14.61	16.47	19.94	24.34	29.34	34.38	37.65	40.65	44.32	46.93
26	11.16	12.20	13.84	15.38	17.29	20.84	25.34	30.43	35.56	38.89	41.92	45.64	48.29
27	11.80	12.88	14.57	16.15	18.11	21.75	26.34	31.53	36.74	40.11	43.20	46.96	49.64
28	12.46	13.56	15.31	16.93	18.94	22.66	27.34	32.62	37.92	41.34	44.46	48.28	50.99
29	13.12	14.26	16.05	17.71	19.77	23.57	28.34	33.71	39.09	42.56	45.72	49.59	52.34
30	13.78	14.95	16.79	18.49	20.60	24.48	29.34	34.80	40.26	43.77	46.98	50.89	53.67
40	20.67	22.14	24.42	26.51	29.06	33.67	39.34	45.61	51.80	55.75	59.34	63.71	66.80
50	27.96	29.68	32.35	34.76	37.69	42.95	49.34	56.33	63.16	67.50	71.42	76.17	79.52
60	35.50	37.46	40.47	43.19	46.46	52.30	59.34	66.98	74.39	79.08	83.30	88.40	91.98
70	43.25	45.42	48.75	51.74	55.33	61.70	69.34	77.57	85.52	90.53	95.03	100.44	104.24
80	51.14	53.52	57.15	60.39	64.28	71.15	79.34	88.13	96.57	101.88	106.63	112.34	116.35
90	59.17	61.74	65.64	69.13	73.29	80.63	89.33	98.65	107.56	113.14	118.14	124.13	128.32
100	67.30	70.05	74.22	77.93	82.36	90.14	99.33	109.14	118.49	124.34	129.56	135.82	140.19

(*Source:* The entries in this table were computed by the author.)

Table E.2 Significant Values of the Correlation Coefficient

df	Two-Tailed Tests			
	p = .10	**p = .05**	**p = .025**	**p = .01**
3	.805	.878	.924	.959
4	.729	.811	.868	.917
5	.669	.755	.817	.875
6	.622	.707	.771	.834
7	.582	.666	.732	.798
8	.549	.632	.697	.765
9	.521	.602	.667	.735
10	.498	.576	.640	.708
11	.476	.553	.616	.684
12	.458	.533	.594	.661
13	.441	.514	.575	.641
14	.426	.497	.557	.623
15	.412	.482	.541	.605
16	.400	.468	.526	.590
17	.389	.455	.512	.575
18	.379	.444	.499	.562
19	.369	.433	.487	.549
20	.360	.423	.476	.537
21	.351	.413	.466	.526
22	.344	.404	.456	.515
23	.337	.396	.447	.505
24	.330	.388	.439	.496
25	.323	.381	.431	.487
26	.317	.374	.423	.478
27	.311	.367	.415	.471
28	.306	.361	.409	.463
29	.301	.355	.402	.456
30	.296	.349	.396	.449
40	.257	.304	.345	.393
50	.231	.273	.311	.354
60	.211	.250	.285	.325
120	.150	.178	.203	.232
200	.116	.138	.158	.181
500	.073	.088	.100	.115
1000	.052	.062	.071	.081

(*Source:* The entries in this table were computed by the author.)

Table E.3   Critical Values of the *F* Distribution: Alpha = .05

Degrees of Freedom for Numerator

	1	2	3	4	5	6	7	8	9	10	15	20	25	30	40	50
1	161.4	199.5	215.8	224.8	230.0	233.8	236.5	238.6	240.1	242.1	245.2	248.4	248.9	250.5	250.8	252.6
2	18.51	19.00	19.16	19.25	19.30	19.33	19.35	19.37	19.38	19.40	19.43	19.44	19.46	19.47	19.48	19.48
3	10.13	9.55	9.28	9.12	9.01	8.94	8.89	8.85	8.81	8.79	8.70	8.66	8.63	8.62	8.59	8.58
4	7.71	6.94	6.59	6.39	6.26	6.16	6.09	6.04	6.00	5.96	5.86	5.80	5.77	5.75	5.72	5.70
5	6.61	5.79	5.41	5.19	5.05	4.95	4.88	4.82	4.77	4.74	4.62	4.56	4.52	4.50	4.46	4.44
6	5.99	5.14	4.76	4.53	4.39	4.28	4.21	4.15	4.10	4.06	3.94	3.87	3.83	3.81	3.77	3.75
7	5.59	4.74	4.35	4.12	3.97	3.87	3.79	3.73	3.68	3.64	3.51	3.44	3.40	3.38	3.34	3.32
8	5.32	4.46	4.07	3.84	3.69	3.58	3.50	3.44	3.39	3.35	3.22	3.15	3.11	3.08	3.04	3.02
9	5.12	4.26	3.86	3.63	3.48	3.37	3.29	3.23	3.18	3.14	3.01	2.94	2.89	2.86	2.83	2.80
10	4.96	4.10	3.71	3.48	3.33	3.22	3.14	3.07	3.02	2.98	2.85	2.77	2.73	2.70	2.66	2.64
11	4.84	3.98	3.59	3.36	3.20	3.09	3.01	2.95	2.90	2.85	2.72	2.65	2.60	2.57	2.53	2.51
12	4.75	3.89	3.49	3.26	3.11	3.00	2.91	2.85	2.80	2.75	2.62	2.54	2.50	2.47	2.43	2.40
13	4.67	3.81	3.41	3.18	3.03	2.92	2.83	2.77	2.71	2.67	2.53	2.46	2.41	2.38	2.34	2.31
14	4.60	3.74	3.34	3.11	2.96	2.85	2.76	2.70	2.65	2.60	2.46	2.39	2.34	2.31	2.27	2.24
15	4.54	3.68	3.29	3.06	2.90	2.79	2.71	2.64	2.59	2.54	2.40	2.33	2.28	2.25	2.20	2.18
16	4.49	3.63	3.24	3.01	2.85	2.74	2.66	2.59	2.54	2.49	2.35	2.28	2.23	2.19	2.15	2.12
17	4.45	3.59	3.20	2.96	2.81	2.70	2.61	2.55	2.49	2.45	2.31	2.23	2.18	2.15	2.10	2.08
18	4.41	3.55	3.16	2.93	2.77	2.66	2.58	2.51	2.46	2.41	2.27	2.19	2.14	2.11	2.06	2.04
19	4.38	3.52	3.13	2.90	2.74	2.63	2.54	2.48	2.42	2.38	2.23	2.16	2.11	2.07	2.03	2.00
20	4.35	3.49	3.10	2.87	2.71	2.60	2.51	2.45	2.39	2.35	2.20	2.12	2.07	2.04	1.99	1.97
22	4.30	3.44	3.05	2.82	2.66	2.55	2.46	2.40	2.34	2.30	2.15	2.07	2.02	1.98	1.94	1.91
24	4.26	3.40	3.01	2.78	2.62	2.51	2.42	2.36	2.30	2.25	2.11	2.03	1.97	1.94	1.89	1.86
26	4.23	3.37	2.98	2.74	2.59	2.47	2.39	2.32	2.27	2.22	2.07	1.99	1.94	1.90	1.85	1.82
28	4.20	3.34	2.95	2.71	2.56	2.45	2.36	2.29	2.24	2.19	2.04	1.96	1.91	1.87	1.82	1.79
30	4.17	3.32	2.92	2.69	2.53	2.42	2.33	2.27	2.21	2.16	2.01	1.93	1.88	1.84	1.79	1.76
40	4.08	3.23	2.84	2.61	2.45	2.34	2.25	2.18	2.12	2.08	1.92	1.84	1.78	1.74	1.69	1.66
50	4.03	3.18	2.79	2.56	2.40	2.29	2.20	2.13	2.07	2.03	1.87	1.78	1.73	1.69	1.63	1.60
60	4.00	3.15	2.76	2.53	2.37	2.25	2.17	2.10	2.04	1.99	1.84	1.75	1.69	1.65	1.59	1.56
120	3.92	3.07	2.68	2.45	2.29	2.18	2.09	2.02	1.96	1.91	1.75	1.66	1.60	1.55	1.50	1.46
200	3.89	3.04	2.65	2.42	2.26	2.14	2.06	1.98	1.93	1.88	1.72	1.62	1.56	1.52	1.46	1.41
500	3.86	3.01	2.62	2.39	2.23	2.12	2.03	1.96	1.90	1.85	1.69	1.59	1.53	1.48	1.42	1.38
1000	3.85	3.01	2.61	2.38	2.22	2.11	2.02	1.95	1.89	1.84	1.68	1.58	1.52	1.47	1.41	1.36

Degrees of Freedom for Denominator (row labels)

(*Source:* The entries in this table were computed by the author.)

Table E.4 Critical Values of the F Distribution: Alpha = .01

	\multicolumn{17}{c}{Degrees of Freedom for Numerator}
	1	2	3	4	5	6	7	8	9	10	15	20	25	30	40	50
1	4052	5000	5403	5624	5764	5859	5928	5981	6022	6056	6151	6209	6240	6260	6287	6303
2	98.50	99.00	99.17	99.25	99.30	99.33	99.36	99.37	99.39	99.40	99.43	99.45	99.47	99.48	99.48	99.59
3	34.12	30.82	29.46	28.71	28.24	27.91	27.67	27.49	27.34	27.23	26.87	26.69	26.58	26.51	26.41	26.36
4	21.20	18.00	16.69	15.98	15.52	15.21	14.98	14.80	14.66	14.55	14.20	14.02	13.91	13.84	13.75	13.69
5	16.26	13.27	12.06	11.39	10.97	10.67	10.46	10.29	10.16	10.05	9.72	9.55	9.45	9.38	9.29	9.24
6	13.75	10.92	9.78	9.15	8.75	8.47	8.26	8.10	7.98	7.87	7.56	7.40	7.30	7.23	7.14	7.09
7	12.25	9.55	8.45	7.85	7.46	7.19	6.99	6.84	6.72	6.62	6.31	6.16	6.06	5.99	5.91	5.86
8	11.26	8.65	7.59	7.01	6.63	6.37	6.18	6.03	5.91	5.81	5.52	5.36	5.26	5.20	5.12	5.07
9	10.56	8.02	6.99	6.42	6.06	5.80	5.61	5.47	5.35	5.26	4.96	4.81	4.71	4.65	4.57	4.52
10	10.04	7.56	6.55	5.99	5.64	5.39	5.20	5.06	4.94	4.85	4.56	4.41	4.31	4.25	4.17	4.12
11	9.65	7.21	6.22	5.67	5.32	5.07	4.89	4.74	4.63	4.54	4.25	4.10	4.01	3.94	3.86	3.81
12	9.33	6.93	5.95	5.41	5.06	4.82	4.64	4.50	4.39	4.30	4.01	3.86	3.76	3.70	3.62	3.57
13	9.07	6.70	5.74	5.21	4.86	4.62	4.44	4.30	4.19	4.10	3.82	3.66	3.57	3.51	3.43	3.38
14	8.86	6.51	5.56	5.04	4.69	4.46	4.28	4.14	4.03	3.94	3.66	3.51	3.41	3.35	3.27	3.22
15	8.68	6.36	5.42	4.89	4.56	4.32	4.14	4.00	3.89	3.80	3.52	3.37	3.28	3.21	3.13	3.08
16	8.53	6.23	5.29	4.77	4.44	4.20	4.03	3.89	3.78	3.69	3.41	3.26	3.16	3.10	3.02	2.97
17	8.40	6.11	5.18	4.67	4.34	4.10	3.93	3.79	3.68	3.59	3.31	3.16	3.07	3.00	2.92	2.87
18	8.29	6.01	5.09	4.58	4.25	4.01	3.84	3.71	3.60	3.51	3.23	3.08	2.98	2.92	2.84	2.78
19	8.18	5.93	5.01	4.50	4.17	3.94	3.77	3.63	3.52	3.43	3.15	3.00	2.91	2.84	2.76	2.71
20	8.10	5.85	4.94	4.43	4.10	3.87	3.70	3.56	3.46	3.37	3.09	2.94	2.84	2.78	2.69	2.64
22	7.95	5.72	4.82	4.31	3.99	3.76	3.59	3.45	3.35	3.26	2.98	2.83	2.73	2.67	2.58	2.53
24	7.82	5.61	4.72	4.22	3.90	3.67	3.50	3.36	3.26	3.17	2.89	2.74	2.64	2.58	2.49	2.44
26	7.72	5.53	4.64	4.14	3.82	3.59	3.42	3.29	3.18	3.09	2.81	2.66	2.57	2.50	2.42	2.36
28	7.64	5.45	4.57	4.07	3.75	3.53	3.36	3.23	3.12	3.03	2.75	2.60	2.51	2.44	2.35	2.30
30	7.56	5.39	4.51	4.02	3.70	3.47	3.30	3.17	3.07	2.98	2.70	2.55	2.45	2.39	2.30	2.25
40	7.31	5.18	4.31	3.83	3.51	3.29	3.12	2.99	2.89	2.80	2.52	2.37	2.27	2.20	2.11	2.06
50	7.17	5.06	4.20	3.72	3.41	3.19	3.02	2.89	2.78	2.70	2.42	2.27	2.17	2.10	2.01	1.95
60	7.08	4.98	4.13	3.65	3.34	3.12	2.95	2.82	2.72	2.63	2.35	2.20	2.10	2.03	1.94	1.88
120	6.85	4.79	3.95	3.48	3.17	2.96	2.79	2.66	2.56	2.47	2.19	2.03	1.93	1.86	1.76	1.70
200	6.76	4.71	3.88	3.41	3.11	2.89	2.73	2.60	2.50	2.41	2.13	1.97	1.87	1.79	1.69	1.63
500	6.69	4.65	3.82	3.36	3.05	2.84	2.68	2.55	2.44	2.36	2.07	1.92	1.81	1.74	1.63	1.57
1000	6.67	4.63	3.80	3.34	3.04	2.82	2.66	2.53	2.43	2.34	2.06	1.90	1.79	1.72	1.61	1.54

Degrees of Freedom for Denominator

(*Source:* The entries in this table were computed by the author.)

Table E.5   Power as a Function of δ and Significance Level (α)

δ	Alpha for Two-Tailed Test			
	.10	**.05**	**.02**	**.01**
1.00	.26	.17	.09	.06
1.10	.29	.20	.11	.07
1.20	.33	.22	.13	.08
1.30	.37	.26	.15	.10
1.40	.40	.29	.18	.12
1.50	.44	.32	.20	.14
1.60	.48	.36	.23	.17
1.70	.52	.40	.27	.19
1.80	.56	.44	.30	.22
1.90	.60	.48	.34	.25
2.00	.64	.52	.37	.28
2.10	.68	.56	.41	.32
2.20	.71	.60	.45	.35
2.30	.74	.63	.49	.39
2.40	.78	.67	.53	.43
2.50	.80	.71	.57	.47
2.60	.83	.74	.61	.51
2.70	.85	.77	.65	.55
2.80	.88	.80	.68	.59
2.90	.90	.83	.72	.63
3.00	.91	.85	.75	.66
3.10	.93	.87	.78	.70
3.20	.94	.89	.81	.73
3.30	.95	.91	.84	.77
3.40	.96	.93	.86	.80
3.50	.97	.94	.88	.82
3.60	.98	.95	.90	.85
3.70	.98	.96	.92	.87
3.80	.98	.97	.93	.89
3.90	.99	.97	.94	.91
4.00	.99	.98	.95	.92
4.10	.99	.98	.96	.94
4.20	...	.99	.97	.95
4.30	...	.99	.98	.96
4.40	...	.99	.98	.97
4.50	...	.99	.99	.97
4.60	...	...	.99	.98
4.70	...	...	.99	.98
4.80	...	...	.99	.99
4.90	...	...	...	.99
5.00	...	...	...	.99

(*Source:* The entries in this table were computed by the author.)

Table E.6 Percentage Points of the t Distribution

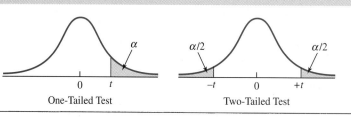

One-Tailed Test   Two-Tailed Test

	Level of Significance for One-Tailed Test								
	.25	**.20**	**.15**	**.10**	**.05**	**.025**	**.01**	**.005**	**.0005**
	Level of Significance for Two-Tailed Test								
df	**.50**	**.40**	**.30**	**.20**	**.10**	**.05**	**.02**	**.01**	**.001**
1	1.000	1.376	1.963	3.078	6.314	12.706	31.821	63.657	63.662
2	.816	1.061	1.386	1.886	2.920	4.303	6.965	9.925	31.599
3	.765	.978	1.250	1.638	2.353	3.182	4.541	5.841	12.924
4	.741	.941	1.190	1.533	2.132	2.776	3.747	4.604	8.610
5	.727	.920	1.156	1.476	2.015	2.571	3.365	4.032	6.869
6	.718	.906	1.134	1.440	1.943	2.447	3.143	3.707	5.959
7	.711	.896	1.119	1.415	1.895	2.365	2.998	3.499	5.408
8	.706	.889	1.108	1.397	1.860	2.306	2.896	3.355	5.041
9	.703	.883	1.100	1.383	1.833	2.262	2.821	3.250	4.781
10	.700	.879	1.093	1.372	1.812	2.228	2.764	3.169	4.587
11	.697	.876	1.088	1.363	1.796	2.201	2.718	3.106	4.437
12	.695	.873	1.083	1.356	1.782	2.179	2.681	3.055	4.318
13	.694	.870	1.079	1.350	1.771	2.160	2.650	3.012	4.221
14	.692	.868	1.076	1.345	1.761	2.145	2.624	2.977	4.140
15	.691	.866	1.074	1.341	1.753	2.131	2.602	2.947	4.073
16	.690	.865	1.071	1.337	1.746	2.120	2.583	2.921	4.015
17	.689	.863	1.069	1.333	1.740	2.110	2.567	2.898	3.965
18	.688	.862	1.067	1.330	1.734	2.101	2.552	2.878	3.922
19	.688	.861	1.066	1.328	1.729	2.093	2.539	2.861	3.883
20	.687	.860	1.064	1.325	1.725	2.086	2.528	2.845	3.850
21	.686	.859	1.063	1.323	1.721	2.080	2.518	2.831	3.819
22	.686	.858	1.061	1.321	1.717	2.074	2.508	2.819	3.792
23	.685	.858	1.060	1.319	1.714	2.069	2.500	2.807	3.768
24	.685	.857	1.059	1.318	1.711	2.064	2.492	2.797	3.745
25	.684	.856	1.058	1.316	1.708	2.060	2.485	2.787	3.725
26	.684	.856	1.058	1.315	1.706	2.056	2.479	2.779	3.707
27	.684	.855	1.057	1.314	1.703	2.052	2.473	2.771	3.690
28	.683	.855	1.056	1.313	1.701	2.048	2.467	2.763	3.674
29	.683	.854	1.055	1.311	1.699	2.045	2.462	2.756	3.659
30	.683	.854	1.055	1.310	1.697	2.042	2.457	2.750	3.646
40	.681	.851	1.050	1.303	1.684	2.021	2.423	2.704	3.551
50	.679	.849	1.047	1.299	1.676	2.009	2.403	2.678	3.496
100	.677	.845	1.042	1.290	1.660	1.984	2.364	2.626	3.390
∞	.674	.842	1.036	1.282	1.645	1.960	2.326	2.576	3.291

(*Source:* The entries in this table were computed by the author.)

Table E.7   Critical Lower-Tail Values of *T* (and Their Associated Probabilities) for Wilcoxon's Matched-Pairs Signed-Ranks Test

Nominal Alpha (One-Tailed)

n	.05 T	α	.025 T	α	.01 T	α	.005 T	α
5	0	.0313						
	1	.0625						
6	2	.0469	0	.0156				
	3	.0781	1	.0313				
7	3	.0391	2	.0234	0	.0078		
	4	.0547	3	.0391	1	.0156		
8	5	.0391	3	.0195	1	.0078	0	.0039
	6	.0547	4	.0273	2	.0117	1	.0078
9	8	.0488	5	.0195	3	.0098	1	.0039
	9	.0645	6	.0273	4	.0137	2	.0059
10	10	.0420	8	.0244	5	.0098	3	.0049
	11	.0527	9	.0322	6	.0137	4	.0068
11	13	.0415	10	.0210	7	.0093	5	.0049
	14	.0508	11	.0269	8	.0122	6	.0068
12	17	.0461	13	.0212	9	.0081	7	.0046
	18	.0549	14	.0261	10	.0105	8	.0061
13	21	.0471	17	.0239	12	.0085	9	.0040
	22	.0549	18	.0287	13	.0107	10	.0052
14	25	.0453	21	.0247	15	.0083	12	.0043
	26	.0520	22	.0290	16	.0101	13	.0054
15	30	.0473	25	.0240	19	.0090	15	.0042
	31	.0535	26	.0277	20	.0108	16	.0051
16	35	.0467	29	.0222	23	.0091	19	.0046
	36	.0523	30	.0253	24	.0107	20	.0055
17	41	.0492	34	.0224	27	.0087	23	.0047
	42	.0544	35	.0253	28	.0101	24	.0055
18	47	.0494	40	.0241	32	.0091	27	.0045
	48	.0542	41	.0269	33	.0104	28	.0052
19	53	.0478	46	.0247	37	.0090	32	.0047
	54	.0521	47	.0273	38	.0102	33	.0054
20	60	.0487	52	.0242	43	.0096	37	.0047
	61	.0527	53	.0266	44	.0107	38	.0053
21	67	.0479	58	.0230	49	.0097	42	.0045
	68	.0516	59	.0251	50	.0108	43	.0051
22	75	.0492	65	.0231	55	.0095	48	.0046
	76	.0527	66	.0250	56	.0104	49	.0052
23	83	.0490	73	.0242	62	.0098	54	.0046
	84	.0523	74	.0261	63	.0107	55	.0051
24	91	.0475	81	.0245	69	.0097	61	.0048
	92	.0505	82	.0263	70	.0106	62	.0053
25	100	.0479	89	.0241	76	.0094	68	.0048
	101	.0507	90	.0258	77	.0101	69	.0053
26	110	.0497	98	.0247	84	.0095	75	.0047
	111	.0524	99	.0263	85	.0102	76	.0051
27	119	.0477	107	.0246	92	.0093	83	.0048
	120	.0502	108	.0260	93	.0100	84	.0052

Nominal Alpha (One-Tailed)

n	.05 T	α	.025 T	α	.01 T	α	.005 T	α
28	130	.0496	116	.0239	101	.0096	91	.0048
	131	.0521	117	.0252	102	.0102	92	.0051
29	140	.0482	126	.0240	110	.0095	100	.0049
	141	.0504	127	.0253	111	.0101	101	.0053
30	151	.0481	137	.0249	120	.0098	109	.0050
	152	.0502	138	.0261	121	.0104	110	.0053
31	163	.0491	147	.0239	130	.0099	118	.0049
	164	.0512	148	.0251	131	.0105	119	.0052
32	175	.0492	159	.0249	140	.0097	128	.0050
	176	.0512	160	.0260	141	.0103	129	.0053
33	187	.0485	170	.0242	151	.0099	138	.0049
	188	.0503	171	.0253	152	.0104	139	.0052
34	200	.0488	182	.0242	162	.0098	148	.0048
	201	.0506	183	.0252	163	.0103	149	.0051
35	213	.0484	195	.0247	173	.0096	159	.0048
	214	.0501	196	.0257	174	.0100	160	.0051
36	227	.0489	208	.0248	185	.0096	171	.0050
	228	.0505	209	.0258	186	.0100	172	.0052
37	241	.0487	221	.0245	198	.0099	182	.0048
	242	.0503	222	.0254	199	.0103	183	.0050
38	256	.0493	235	.0247	211	.0099	194	.0048
	257	.0509	236	.0256	212	.0104	195	.0050
39	271	.0492	249	.0246	224	.0099	207	.0049
	272	.0507	250	.0254	225	.0103	208	.0051
40	286	.0486	264	.0249	238	.0100	220	.0049
	287	.0500	265	.0257	239	.0104	221	.0051
41	302	.0488	279	.0248	252	.0100	233	.0048
	303	.0501	280	.0256	253	.0103	234	.0050
42	319	.0496	294	.0245	266	.0098	247	.0049
	320	.0509	295	.0252	267	.0102	248	.0051
43	336	.0498	310	.0245	281	.0098	261	.0048
	337	.0511	311	.0252	282	.0102	262	.0050
44	353	.0495	327	.0250	296	.0097	276	.0049
	354	.0507	328	.0257	297	.0101	277	.0051
45	371	.0498	343	.0244	312	.0098	291	.0049
	372	.0510	344	.0251	313	.0101	292	.0051
46	389	.0497	361	.0249	328	.0098	307	.0050
	390	.0508	362	.0256	329	.0101	308	.0052
47	407	.0490	378	.0245	345	.0099	322	.0048
	408	.0501	379	.0251	346	.0102	323	.0050
48	426	.0490	396	.0244	362	.0099	339	.0050
	427	.0500	397	.0251	363	.0102	340	.0051
49	446	.0495	415	.0247	379	.0098	355	.0049
	447	.0505	416	.0253	380	.0100	356	.0050
50	466	.0495	434	.0247	397	.0098	373	.0050
	467	.0506	435	.0253	398	.0101	374	.0051

(*Source:* The entries in this table were computed by the author.)

Table E.8 Critical Lower-Tail Values of W_S for the Mann–Whitney Test for Two Independent Samples ($N_1 \leq N_2$)

n_2	$n_1 = 1$							$n_1 = 2$							n_2
	.001	.005	.010	.025	.05	.10	$2\bar{W}$	.001	.005	.010	.025	.05	.10	$2\bar{W}$	
2							4						⋮	10	2
3							5						3	12	3
4							6					⋮	3	14	4
5							7					3	4	16	5
6							8					3	4	18	6
7							9				⋮	3	4	20	7
8						⋮	10				3	4	5	22	8
9						1	11				3	4	5	24	9
10						1	12				3	4	6	26	10
11						1	13				3	4	6	28	11
12						1	14			⋮	4	5	7	30	12
13						1	15			3	4	5	7	32	13
14						1	16			3	4	6	8	34	14
15						1	17			3	4	6	8	36	15
16						1	18			3	4	6	8	38	16
17						1	19			3	5	6	9	40	17
18				⋮		1	20		⋮	3	5	7	9	42	18
19					1	2	21		3	4	5	7	10	44	19
20					1	2	22		3	4	5	7	10	46	20
21					1	2	23		3	4	6	8	11	48	21
22					1	2	24		3	4	6	8	11	50	22
23					1	2	25		3	4	6	8	12	52	23
24					1	2	26		3	4	6	9	12	54	24
25	⋮	⋮	⋮	⋮	1	2	27	⋮	3	4	6	9	12	56	25

n_2	$n_1 = 3$							$n_1 = 4$							n_2
	.001	.005	.010	.025	.05	.10	$2\bar{W}$	.001	.005	.010	.025	.05	.10	$2\bar{W}$	
3					6	7	21								3
4				⋮	6	7	24			⋮	10	11	13	36	4
5				6	7	8	27		⋮	10	11	12	14	40	5
6			⋮	7	8	9	30		10	11	12	13	15	44	6
7			6	7	8	10	33		10	11	13	14	16	48	7
8		⋮	6	8	9	11	36		11	12	14	15	17	52	8
9		6	7	8	10	11	39	⋮	11	13	14	16	19	56	9
10		6	7	9	10	12	42	10	12	13	15	17	20	60	10
11		6	7	9	11	13	45	10	12	14	16	18	21	64	11
12		7	8	10	11	14	48	10	13	15	17	19	22	68	12
13		7	8	10	12	15	51	11	13	15	18	20	23	72	13
14		7	8	11	13	16	54	11	14	16	19	21	25	76	14
15		8	9	11	13	16	57	11	15	17	20	22	26	80	15
16	⋮	8	9	12	14	17	60	12	15	17	21	24	27	84	16
17	6	8	10	12	15	18	63	12	16	18	21	25	28	88	17
18	6	8	10	13	15	19	66	13	16	19	22	26	30	92	18
19	6	9	10	13	16	20	69	13	17	19	23	27	31	96	19
20	6	9	11	14	17	21	72	13	18	20	24	28	32	100	20
21	7	9	11	14	17	21	75	14	18	21	25	29	33	104	21
22	7	10	12	15	18	22	78	14	19	21	26	30	35	108	22
23	7	10	12	15	19	23	81	14	19	22	27	31	36	112	23
24	7	10	12	16	19	24	84	15	20	23	27	32	38	116	24
25	7	11	13	16	20	25	87	15	20	23	28	33	38	120	25

(*Source:* Table 1 in L. R. Verdooren, Extended tables of critical values for Wilcoxon's test statistic, *Biometrika*, 1963, 50, 177–186.)

Table E.8   *Continued*

			$n_1 = 5$							$n_1 = 6$			
n_2	.001	.005	.010	.025	.05	.10	$2\overline{W}$	.001	.005	.010	.025	.05	.10	$2\overline{W}$	n_2
5		15	16	17	19	20	55							
6		16	17	18	20	22	60	...	23	24	26	28	30	78	6
7	...	16	18	20	21	23	65	21	24	25	27	29	32	84	7
8	15	17	19	21	23	25	70	22	25	27	29	31	34	90	8
9	16	18	20	22	24	27	75	23	26	28	31	33	36	96	9
10	16	19	21	23	26	28	80	24	27	29	32	35	38	102	10
11	17	20	22	24	27	30	85	25	28	30	34	37	40	108	11
12	17	21	23	26	28	32	90	25	30	32	35	38	42	114	12
13	18	22	24	27	30	33	95	26	31	33	37	40	44	120	13
14	18	22	25	28	31	35	100	27	32	34	38	42	46	126	14
15	19	23	26	29	33	37	105	28	33	36	40	44	48	132	15
16	20	24	27	30	34	38	110	29	34	37	42	46	50	138	16
17	20	25	28	32	35	40	115	30	36	39	43	47	52	144	17
18	21	26	29	33	37	42	120	31	37	40	45	49	55	150	18
19	22	27	30	34	38	43	125	32	38	41	46	51	57	156	19
20	22	28	31	35	40	45	130	33	39	43	48	53	59	162	20
21	23	29	32	37	41	47	135	33	40	44	50	55	61	168	21
22	23	29	33	38	43	48	140	34	42	45	51	57	63	174	22
23	24	30	34	39	44	50	145	35	43	47	53	58	65	180	23
24	25	31	35	40	45	51	150	36	44	48	54	60	67	186	24
25	25	32	36	42	47	53	155	37	45	50	56	62	69	192	25

			$n_1 = 7$							$n_1 = 8$			
n_2	.001	.005	.010	.025	.05	.10	$2\overline{W}$	.001	.005	.010	.025	.05	.10	$2\overline{W}$	n_2
7	29	32	34	36	39	41	105							
8	30	34	35	38	41	44	112	40	43	45	49	51	55	136	8
9	31	35	37	40	43	46	119	41	45	47	51	54	58	144	9
10	33	37	39	42	45	49	126	42	47	49	53	56	60	152	10
11	34	38	40	44	47	51	133	44	49	51	55	59	63	160	11
12	35	40	42	46	49	54	140	45	51	53	58	62	66	168	12
13	36	41	44	48	52	56	147	47	53	56	60	64	69	176	13
14	37	43	45	50	54	59	154	48	54	58	62	67	72	184	14
15	38	44	47	52	56	61	161	50	56	60	65	69	75	192	15
16	39	46	49	54	58	64	168	51	58	62	67	72	78	200	16
17	41	47	51	56	61	66	175	53	60	64	70	75	81	208	17
18	42	49	52	58	63	69	182	54	62	66	72	77	84	216	18
19	43	50	54	60	65	71	189	56	64	68	74	80	87	224	19
20	44	52	56	62	67	74	196	57	66	70	77	83	90	232	20
21	46	53	58	64	69	76	203	59	68	72	79	85	92	240	21
22	47	55	59	66	72	79	210	60	70	74	81	88	95	248	22
23	48	57	61	68	74	81	217	62	71	76	84	90	98	256	23
24	49	58	63	70	76	84	224	64	73	78	86	93	101	264	24
25	50	60	64	72	78	86	231	65	75	81	89	96	104	272	25

continued

Table E.8 *Continued*

			$n_1 = 9$								$n_1 = 10$				
n_2	.001	.005	.010	.025	.05	.10	$2\bar{W}$	.001	.005	.010	.025	.05	.10	$2\bar{W}$	n_2
9	52	56	59	62	66	70	171								
10	53	58	61	65	69	73	180	65	71	74	78	82	87	210	10
11	55	61	63	68	72	76	189	67	73	77	.81	86	91	220	11
12	57	63	66	71	75	80	198	69	76	79	84	89	94	230	12
13	59	65	68	73	78	83	207	72	79	82	88	92	98	240	13
14	60	67	71	76	81	86	216	74	81	85	91	96	102	250	14
15	62	69	73	79	84	90	225	76	84	88	94	99	106	260	15
16	64	72	76	82	87	93	234	78	86	91	97	103	109	270	16
17	66	74	78	84	90	97	243	80	89	93	100	106	113	280	17
18	68	76	81	87	93	100	252	82	92	96	103	110	117	290	18
19	70	78	83	90	96	103	261	84	94	99	107	113	121	300	19
20	71	81	85	93	99	107	270	87	97	102	110	117	125	310	20
21	73	83	88	95	102	110	279	89	99	105	113	120	128	320	21
22	75	85	90	98	105	113	288	91	102	108	116	123	132	330	22
23	77	88	93	101	108	117	297	93	105	110	119	127	136	340	23
24	79	90	95	104	111	120	306	95	107	113	122	130	140	350	24
25	81	92	98	107	114	123	315	98	110	116	126	134	144	360	25

			$n_1 = 11$								$n_1 = 12$				
n_2	.001	.005	.010	.025	.05	.10	$2\bar{W}$	.001	.005	.010	.025	.05	.10	$2\bar{W}$	n_2
11	81	87	91	96	100	106	253								
12	83	90	94	99	104	110	264	98	105	109	115	120	127	300	12
13	86	93	97	103	108	114	275	101	109	113	119	125	131	312	13
14	88	96	100	106	112	118	286	103	112	116	123	129	136	324	14
15	90	99	103	110	116	123	297	106	115	120	127	133	141	336	15
16	93	102	107	113	120	127	308	109	119	124	131	138	145	348	16
17	95	105	110	117	123	131	319	112	122	127	135	142	150	360	17
18	98	108	113	121	127	135	330	115	125	131	139	146	155	372	18
19	100	111	116	124	131	139	341	118	129	134	143	150	159	384	19
20	103	114	119	128	135	144	352	120	132	138	147	155	164	396	20
21	106	117	123	131	139	148	363	123	136	142	151	159	169	408	21
22	108	120	126	135	143	152	374	126	139	145	155	163	173	420	22
23	111	123	129	139	147	156	385	129	142	149	159	168	178	432	23
24	113	126	132	142	151	161	396	132	146	153	163	172	183	444	24
25	116	129	136	146	155	165	407	135	149	156	167	176	187	456	25

			$n_1 = 13$								$n_1 = 14$				
n_2	.001	.005	.010	.025	.05	.10	$2\bar{W}$	.001	.005	.010	.025	.05	.10	$2\bar{W}$	n_2
13	117	125	130	136	142	149	351								
14	120	129	134	141	147	154	364	137	147	152	160	166	174	406	14
15	123	133	138	145	152	159	377	141	151	156	164	171	179	420	15
16	126	136	142	150	156	165	390	144	155	161	169	176	185	434	16
17	129	140	146	154	161	170	403	148	159	165	174	182	190	448	17
18	133	144	150	158	166	175	416	151	163	170	179	187	196	462	18
19	136	148	154	163	171	180	429	155	168	174	183	192	202	476	19
20	139	151	158	167	175	185	442	159	172	178	188	197	207	490	20
21	142	155	162	171	180	190	455	162	176	183	193	202	213	504	21
22	145	159	166	176	185	195	468	166	180	187	198	207	218	518	22
23	149	163	170	180	189	200	481	169	184	192	203	212	224	532	23
24	152	166	174	185	194	205	494	173	188	196	207	218	229	546	24
25	155	170	178	189	199	211	507	177	192	200	212	223	235	560	25

Table E.8 *Continued*

n_2	.001	.005	.010	.025	.05	.10	$2\overline{W}$	.001	.005	.010	.025	.05	.10	$2\overline{W}$	n_2
				$n_1 = 15$							$n_1 = 16$				
15	160	171	176	184	192	200	465								
16	163	175	181	190	197	206	480	184	196	202	211	219	229	528	16
17	167	180	186	195	203	212	495	188	201	207	217	225	235	544	17
18	171	184	190	200	208	218	510	192	206	212	222	231	242	560	18
19	175	189	195	205	214	224	525	196	210	218	228	237	248	576	19
20	179	193	200	210	220	230	540	201	215	223	234	243	255	592	20
21	183	198	205	216	225	236	555	205	220	228	239	249	261	608	21
22	187	202	210	221	231	242	570	209	225	233	245	255	267	624	22
23	191	207	214	226	236	248	585	214	230	238	251	261	274	640	23
24	195	211	219	231	242	254	600	218	235	244	256	267	280	656	24
25	199	216	224	237	248	260	615	222	240	249	262	273	287	672	25

n_2	.001	.005	.010	.025	.05	.10	$2\overline{W}$	.001	.005	.010	.025	.05	.10	$2\overline{W}$	n_2
				$n_1 = 17$							$n_1 = 18$				
17	210	223	230	240	249	259	595								
18	214	228	235	246	255	266	612	237	252	259	270	280	291	666	18
19	219	234	241	252	262	273	629	242	258	265	277	287	299	684	19
20	223	239	246	258	268	280	646	247	263	271	283	294	306	702	20
21	228	244	252	264	274	287	663	252	269	277	290	301	313	720	21
22	233	249	258	270	281	294	680	257	275	283	296	307	321	738	22
23	238	255	263	276	287	300	697	262	280	289	303	314	328	756	23
24	242	260	269	282	294	307	714	267	286	295	309	321	335	774	24
25	247	265	275	288	300	314	731	273	292	301	316	328	343	792	25

n_2	.001	.005	.010	.025	.05	.10	$2\overline{W}$	.001	.005	.010	.025	.05	.10	$2\overline{W}$	n_2
				$n_1 = 19$							$n_1 = 20$				
19	267	283	291	303	313	325	741								
20	272	289	297	309	320	333	760	298	315	324	337	348	361	820	20
21	277	295	303	316	328	341	779	304	322	331	344	356	370	840	21
22	283	301	310	323	335	349	798	309	328	337	351	364	378	860	22
23	288	307	316	330	342	357	817	315	335	344	359	371	386	880	23
24	294	313	323	337	350	364	836	321	341	351	366	379	394	900	24
25	299	319	329	344	357	372	855	327	348	358	373	387	403	920	25

n_2	.001	.005	.010	.025	.05	.10	$2\overline{W}$	.001	.005	.010	.025	.05	.10	$2\overline{W}$	n_2
				$n_1 = 21$							$n_1 = 22$				
21	331	349	359	373	385	399	903								
22	337	356	366	381	393	408	924	365	386	396	411	424	439	990	22
23	343	363	373	388	401	417	945	372	393	403	419	432	448	1012	23
24	349	370	381	396	410	425	966	379	400	411	427	441	457	1034	24
25	356	377	388	404	418	434	987	385	408	419	435	450	467	1056	25

n_2	.001	.005	.010	.025	.05	.10	$2\overline{W}$	.001	.005	.010	.025	.05	.10	$2\overline{W}$	n_2
				$n_1 = 23$							$n_1 = 24$				
23	402	424	434	451	465	481	1081								
24	409	431	443	459	474	491	1104	440	464	475	492	507	525	1176	24
25	416	439	451	468	483	500	1127	448	472	484	501	517	535	1200	25

n_2	.001	.005	.010	.025	.05	.10	$2\overline{W}$
				$n_1 = 25$			
25	480	505	517	536	552	570	1275

Table E.9 Table of Uniform Random Numbers

68204	38787	73304	44886	92836	43877	61049	49249	66105
61010	78345	75444	91680	33003	24128	97817	77562	62045
04604	93468	78459	27541	19672	14220	25102	42021	19252
36021	25507	64060	72923	58848	10374	63102	41534	92884
28129	43470	94097	16753	56425	75299	93688	75569	52067
09406	06584	46324	13981	06449	42604	13372	69040	95955
86423	81835	64226	20398	65772	91052	73496	14451	95967
13249	58525	81893	32894	68627	75644	45848	61511	90232
75454	17352	56548	39618	86705	50783	48388	82047	14660
06260	46176	99237	69874	84180	32005	66130	18055	99748
38507	92795	80672	00102	22980	69115	95653	05231	94996
03917	26795	59832	19014	96206	45413	76624	71219	65855
17927	32368	08177	31236	45401	26731	92256	99530	43998
26811	88937	37187	39762	29942	40091	65731	95955	23368
18480	28160	81908	30456	22462	15677	55642	67383	86884
37589	91842	76351	90585	45588	42858	37806	67969	50621
79903	34187	26952	75820	96335	90281	04269	85202	94965
46155	30200	75000	28570	47516	06744	72193	01258	85047
60916	73212	15853	28398	04721	69363	47071	65568	88519
34419	82840	88235	61966	86517	23966	45764	42177	17269
08692	26667	12941	14813	30815	26633	68184	80721	80505
92851	44185	90848	18341	77915	00177	64014	35490	02937
97909	07280	72167	10002	27374	92880	60055	94168	30742
28437	22027	07739	30905	33151	73567	82960	50104	67005
48165	28174	17909	11230	00929	54604	32435	54120	85199
99891	30913	06315	30201	72073	39589	62868	66339	15850
98022	13010	67970	99203	12536	88149	44387	20250	50798
91292	54688	47029	38970	77880	77295	11887	17628	93802
89081	34643	12988	12971	87742	57720	24438	64088	49496
32527	74239	20056	46668	94561	70111	92537	83562	11306
01870	21584	48574	09871	74453	24812	45770	95667	52377
84011	87542	96564	64256	64653	90025	61613	94168	83254
01568	29682	67489	62984	51901	30716	24513	46678	67991
40360	19206	40321	16004	64481	16130	03904	15811	19369
09392	39926	79590	23991	82492	13032	67337	54322	06058
77323	20500	52466	33008	84211	26357	79006	41178	35169
47590	01007	65376	18189	84040	39476	25383	45398	64917
29321	65783	71403	32894	32627	39067	47985	51485	27415
09530	05358	58722	31912	73356	65884	12883	36242	29646
65612	06843	72233	73352	66600	23237	71759	76881	19652
40355	85067	40788	40148	46099	48056	27858	58365	30202
24963	49571	82377	08687	73448	95484	15155	41780	71951
87273	44050	71961	48464	84084	65225	62846	11634	04853
31643	44756	12493	09024	74204	69949	67842	36141	08477
58326	55342	31419	80776	64028	59957	52969	71997	71477
02327	00460	39178	09511	92688	88585	99257	98752	39623
19377	49122	60591	79773	66289	89650	49298	13499	53623
95046	30203	47493	74395	45213	66739	45097	91670	62152
65013	71958	48360	70885	60313	44241	18740	05705	07488
86032	89018	97117	35656	20401	86438	87250	04717	67726
11799	15777	11548	45918	45706	88554	75315	70233	72575
17843	64809	00390	11980	66129	07197	36712	55062	61191
42770	65397	45010	06463	86242	06361	14293	36343	97628
02410	96933	57864	93197	88227	57139	66382	95768	60660
70939	20457	62468	68698	74875	61111	59083	09152	93625
85616	15100	26242	28677	74655	05679	56676	67224	75318
85515	33174	05496	78789	81297	73985	82120	94070	20529

Table E.9   *Continued*

73466	06254	88113	98367	22018	99372	70171	52705	61202
72255	50729	05681	37216	09363	02385	93098	09502	92589
08121	48330	86725	52922	90349	81934	14849	68005	06791
94005	85164	22994	58921	85943	67506	79730	85382	61568
09108	52299	25991	00940	22493	60987	93573	79469	97147
85687	31723	67907	55306	71748	85048	17690	04784	98470
26190	02164	95889	89712	89795	73001	82210	39357	23867
34208	07539	60907	60693	01965	43492	46688	28891	23410
13032	78798	21733	35703	71707	11931	93513	78339	74754
16801	05582	47975	25046	59220	08275	67901	94954	36662
88735	91500	41654	97225	61188	24527	35220	99794	56097
82127	17594	94217	55324	06134	25207	26758	08687	06929
29284	42271	45833	19481	56972	99042	45304	39832	40188
56300	60964	13751	72385	91180	42371	55924	95783	33096
33132	33229	39955	16779	99286	23392	24255	90856	60004
65296	94444	32091	90681	95823	73091	92912	85979	30232
11069	52931	26381	71830	50467	47783	25223	81796	97745
06720	69637	99670	58392	57943	75965	14740	74814	75598
62719	14295	16605	13146	36992	50560	50121	90278	98283
95556	36672	87202	92730	81961	38894	61358	44519	71529
12490	12304	28804	42772	27104	35518	67361	84159	52442
29865	28847	70904	96638	54226	44701	67589	27352	81078
74486	63507	92193	65022	09583	43615	59910	05301	69347
01878	56351	68618	84432	30948	65180	75446	95963	75619
65405	25720	09364	51333	03752	65756	51967	92469	47296
31711	35173	45290	49326	50368	63829	05640	26675	27367
41028	50367	01904	68068	02324	58723	96333	77032	47878
76916	55336	48767	76915	79711	05182	70489	10244	45078
16404	93068	91519	85895	34872	24701	60932	91141	33252
06776	51133	76482	14812	19777	19614	51100	52943	04068
76818	05839	26058	80972	43337	24203	72345	37967	88138
16916	64028	38968	02783	63049	12261	89587	88988	88834
33696	41621	16648	11837	08094	38217	32919	16625	91567
00143	56431	90537	95332	29879	29363	48055	86410	10594
15932	59628	00086	74633	81208	05470	56385	23601	70545
86111	14530	39958	36155	60613	73849	74842	31030	30448
46218	36313	62063	59326	93522	48983	50335	30178	42755
84153	32199	77166	63912	07984	55369	56520	14633	00252
81439	35471	29742	57110	13710	21351	29816	32783	69004
92339	82043	80136	97269	28858	03036	01304	51363	40412
78421	33809	92792	96106	95191	43514	08320	25690	76117
44265	86707	80637	44879	81457	06781	11411	88804	62551
89430	51314	76126	62672	31815	12947	76533	19761	93373
36462	19901	02919	29311	31275	83593	34933	95758	63944
55996	59605	51680	27755	06077	12797	67082	12536	64069
69338	43838	06320	63988	16549	27931	27270	94711	47834
40276	17751	72508	23027	70257	42812	87319	09160	02913
67834	93014	07816	93085	14552	10115	87740	44125	51227

(*Source:* The entries in this table were computed by the author.)

Table E.10 The Normal Distribution (z)

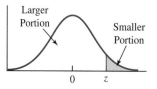

z	Mean to z	Larger Portion	Smaller Portion	z	Mean to z	Larger Portion	Smaller Portion
.00	.0000	.5000	.5000	.40	.1554	.6554	.3446
.01	.0040	.5040	.4960	.41	.1591	.6591	.3409
.02	.0080	.5080	.4920	.42	.1628	.6628	.3372
.03	.0120	.5120	.4880	.43	.1664	.6664	.3336
.04	.0160	.5160	.4840	.44	.1700	.6700	.3300
.05	.0199	.5199	.4801	.45	.1736	.6736	.3264
.06	.0239	.5239	.4761	.46	.1772	.6772	.3228
.07	.0279	.5279	.4721	.47	.1808	.6808	.3192
.08	.0319	.5319	.4681	.48	.1844	.6844	.3156
.09	.0359	.5359	.4641	.49	.1879	.6879	.3121
.10	.0398	.5398	.4602	.50	.1915	.6915	.3085
.11	.0438	.5438	.4562	.51	.1950	.6950	.3050
.12	.0478	.5478	.4522	.52	.1985	.6985	.3015
.13	.0517	.5517	.4483	.53	.2019	.7019	.2981
.14	.0557	.5557	.4443	.54	.2054	.7054	.2946
.15	.0596	.5596	.4404	.55	.2088	.7088	.2912
.16	.0636	.5636	.4364	.56	.2123	.7123	.2877
.17	.0675	.5675	.4325	.57	.2157	.7157	.2843
.18	.0714	.5714	.4286	.58	.2190	.7190	.2810
.19	.0753	.5753	.4247	.59	.2224	.7224	.2776
.20	.0793	.5793	.4207	.60	.2257	.7257	.2743
.21	.0832	.5832	.4168	.61	.2291	.7291	.2709
.22	.0871	.5871	.4129	.62	.2324	.7324	.2676
.23	.0910	.5910	.4090	.63	.2357	.7357	.2643
.24	.0948	.5948	.4052	.64	.2389	.7389	.2611
.25	.0987	.5987	.4013	.65	.2422	.7422	.2578
.26	.1026	.6026	.3974	.66	.2454	.7454	.2546
.27	.1064	.6064	.3936	.67	.2486	.7486	.2514
.28	.1103	.6103	.3897	.68	.2517	.7517	.2483
.29	.1141	.6141	.3859	.69	.2549	.7549	.2451
.30	.1179	.6179	.3821	.70	.2580	.7580	.2420
.31	.1217	.6217	.3783	.71	.2611	.7611	.2389
.32	.1255	.6255	.3745	.72	.2642	.7642	.2358
.33	.1293	.6293	.3707	.73	.2673	.7673	.2327
.34	.1331	.6331	.3669	.74	.2704	.7704	.2296
.35	.1368	.6368	.3632	.75	.2734	.7734	.2266
.36	.1406	.6406	.3594	.76	.2764	.7764	.2236
.37	.1443	.6443	.3557	.77	.2794	.7794	.2206
.38	.1480	.6480	.3520	.78	.2823	.7823	.2177
.39	.1517	.6517	.3483	.79	.2852	.7852	.2148

Table E.10   *Continued*

z	Mean to z	Larger Portion	Smaller Portion	z	Mean to z	Larger Portion	Smaller Portion
.80	.2881	.7881	.2119	1.29	.4015	.9015	.0985
.81	.2910	.7910	.2090	1.30	.4032	.9032	.0968
.82	.2939	.7939	.2061	1.31	.4049	.9049	.0951
.83	.2967	.7967	.2033	1.32	.4066	.9066	.0934
.84	.2995	.7995	.2005	1.33	.4082	.9082	.0918
.85	.3023	.8023	.1977	1.34	.4099	.9099	.0901
.86	.3051	.8051	.1949	1.35	.4115	.9115	.0885
.87	.3078	.8078	.1922	1.36	.4131	.9131	.0869
.88	.3106	.8106	.1894	1.37	.4147	.9147	.0853
.89	.3133	.8133	.1867	1.38	.4162	.9162	.0838
.90	.3159	.8159	.1841	1.39	.4177	.9177	.0823
.91	.3186	.8186	.1814	1.40	.4192	.9192	.0808
.92	.3212	.8212	.1788	1.41	.4207	.9207	.0793
.93	.3238	.8238	.1762	1.42	.4222	.9222	.0778
.94	.3264	.8264	.1736	1.43	.4236	.9236	.0764
.95	.3289	.8289	.1711	1.44	.4251	.9251	.0749
.96	.3315	.8315	.1685	1.45	.4265	.9265	.0735
.97	.3340	.8340	.1660	1.46	.4279	.9279	.0721
.98	.3365	.8365	.1635	1.47	.4292	.9292	.0708
.99	.3389	.8389	.1611	1.48	.4306	.9306	.0694
1.00	.3413	.8413	.1587	1.49	.4319	.9319	.0681
1.01	.3438	.8438	.1562	1.50	.4332	.9332	.0668
1.02	.3461	.8461	.1539	1.51	.4345	.9345	.0655
1.03	.3485	.8485	.1515	1.52	.4357	.9357	.0643
1.04	.3508	.8508	.1492	1.53	.4370	.9370	.0630
1.05	.3531	.8531	.1469	1.54	.4382	.9382	.0618
1.06	.3554	.8554	.1446	1.55	.4394	.9394	.0606
1.07	.3577	.8577	.1423	1.56	.4406	.9406	.0594
1.08	.3599	.8599	.1401	1.57	.4418	.9418	.0582
1.09	.3621	.8621	.1379	1.58	.4429	.9429	.0571
1.10	.3643	.8643	.1357	1.59	.4441	.9441	.0559
1.11	.3665	.8665	.1335	1.60	.4452	.9452	.0548
1.12	.3686	.8686	.1314	1.61	.4463	.9463	.0537
1.13	.3708	.8708	.1292	1.62	.4474	.9474	.0526
1.14	.3729	.8729	.1271	1.63	.4484	.9484	.0516
1.15	.3749	.8749	.1251	1.64	.4495	.9495	.0505
1.16	.3770	.8770	.1230	1.65	.4505	.9505	.0495
1.17	.3790	.8790	.1210	1.66	.4515	.9515	.0485
1.18	.3810	.8810	.1190	1.67	.4525	.9525	.0475
1.19	.3830	.8830	.1170	1.68	.4535	.9535	.0465
1.20	.3849	.8849	.1151	1.69	.4545	.9545	.0455
1.21	.3869	.8869	.1131	1.70	.4554	.9554	.0446
1.22	.3888	.8888	.1112	1.71	.4564	.9564	.0436
1.23	.3907	.8907	.1093	1.72	.4573	.9573	.0427
1.24	.3925	.8925	.1075	1.73	.4582	.9582	.0418
1.25	.3944	.8944	.1056	1.74	.4591	.9591	.0409
1.26	.3962	.8962	.1038	1.75	.4599	.9599	.0401
1.27	.3980	.8980	.1020	1.76	.4608	.9608	.0392
1.28	.3997	.8997	.1003	1.77	.4616	.9616	.0384

continued

Table E.10 Continued

z	Mean to z	Larger Portion	Smaller Portion	z	Mean to z	Larger Portion	Smaller Portion
1.78	.4625	.9625	.0375	2.28	.4887	.9887	.0113
1.79	.4633	.9633	.0367	2.29	.4890	.9890	.0110
1.80	.4641	.9641	.0359	2.30	.4893	.9893	.0107
1.81	.4649	.9649	.0351	2.31	.4896	.9896	.0104
1.82	.4656	.9656	.0344	2.32	.4898	.9898	.0102
1.83	.4664	.9664	.0336	2.33	.4901	.9901	.0099
1.84	.4671	.9671	.0329	2.34	.4904	.9904	.0096
1.85	.4678	.9678	.0322	2.35	.4906	.9906	.0094
1.86	.4686	.9686	.0314	2.36	.4909	.9909	.0091
1.87	.4693	.9693	.0307	2.37	.4911	.9911	.0089
1.88	.4699	.9699	.0301	2.38	.4913	.9913	.0087
1.89	.4706	.9706	.0294	2.39	.4916	.9916	.0084
1.90	.4713	.9713	.0287	2.40	.4918	.9918	.0082
1.91	.4719	.9719	.0281	2.41	.4920	.9920	.0080
1.92	.4726	.9726	.0274	2.42	.4922	.9922	.0078
1.93	.4732	.9732	.0268	2.43	.4925	.9925	.0075
1.94	.4738	.9738	.0262	2.44	.4927	.9927	.0073
1.95	.4744	.9744	.0256	2.45	.4929	.9929	.0071
1.96	.4750	.9750	.0250	2.46	.4931	.9931	.0069
1.97	.4756	.9756	.0244	2.47	.4932	.9932	.0068
1.98	.4761	.9761	.0239	2.48	.4934	.9934	.0066
1.99	.4767	.9767	.0233	2.49	.4936	.9936	.0064
2.00	.4772	.9772	.0228	2.50	.4938	.9938	.0062
2.01	.4778	.9778	.0222	2.51	.4940	.9940	.0060
2.02	.4783	.9783	.0217	2.52	.4941	.9941	.0059
2.03	.4788	.9788	.0212	2.53	.4943	.9943	.0057
2.04	.4793	.9793	.0207	2.54	.4945	.9945	.0055
2.05	.4798	.9798	.0202	2.55	.4946	.9946	.0054
2.06	.4803	.9803	.0197	2.56	.4948	.9948	.0052
2.07	.4808	.9808	.0192	2.57	.4949	.9949	.0051
2.08	.4812	.9812	.0188	2.58	.4951	.9951	.0049
2.09	.4817	.9817	.0183	2.59	.4952	.9952	.0048
2.10	.4821	.9821	.0179	2.60	.4953	.9953	.0047
2.11	.4826	.9826	.0174	2.61	.4955	.9955	.0045
2.12	.4830	.9830	.0170	2.62	.4956	.9956	.0044
2.13	.4834	.9834	.0166	2.63	.4957	.9957	.0043
2.14	.4838	.9838	.0162	2.64	.4959	.9959	.0041
2.15	.4842	.9842	.0158	2.65	.4960	.9960	.0040
2.16	.4846	.9846	.0154	2.66	.4961	.9961	.0039
2.17	.4850	.9850	.0150	2.67	.4962	.9962	.0038
2.18	.4854	.9854	.0146	2.68	.4963	.9963	.0037
2.19	.4857	.9857	.0143	2.69	.4964	.9964	.0036
2.20	.4861	.9861	.0139	2.70	.4965	.9965	.0035
2.21	.4864	.9864	.0136	2.71	.4966	.9966	.0034
2.22	.4868	.9868	.0132	2.72	.4967	.9967	.0033
2.23	.4871	.9871	.0129	2.73	.4968	.9968	.0032
2.24	.4875	.9875	.0125	2.74	.4969	.9969	.0031
2.25	.4878	.9878	.0122	2.75	.4970	.9970	.0030
2.26	.4881	.9881	.0119	2.76	.4971	.9971	.0029
2.27	.4884	.9884	.0116	2.77	.4972	.9972	.0028

Table E.10   *Continued*

z	Mean to z	Larger Portion	Smaller Portion	z	Mean to z	Larger Portion	Smaller Portion
2.78	.4973	.9973	.0027	2.94	.4984	.9984	.0016
2.79	.4974	.9974	.0026	2.95	.4984	.9984	.0016
2.80	.4974	.9974	.0026	2.96	.4985	.9985	.0015
2.81	.4975	.9975	.0025	2.97	.4985	.9985	.0015
2.82	.4976	.9976	.0024	2.98	.4986	.9986	.0014
2.83	.4977	.9977	.0023	2.99	.4986	.9986	.0014
2.84	.4977	.9977	.0023	3.00	.4987	.9987	.0013
2.85	.4978	.9978	.0022	⋮	⋮	⋮	⋮
2.86	.4979	.9979	.0021	3.25	.4994	.9994	.0006
2.87	.4979	.9979	.0021	⋮	⋮	⋮	⋮
2.88	.4980	.9980	.0020	3.50	.4998	.9998	.0002
2.89	.4981	.9981	.0019	⋮	⋮	⋮	⋮
2.90	.4981	.9981	.0019	3.75	.4999	.9999	.0001
2.91	.4982	.9982	.0018	⋮	⋮	⋮	⋮
2.92	.4982	.9982	.0018	4.00	.5000	1.0000	.0000
2.93	.4983	.9983	.0017				

(*Source:* The entries in this table were computed by the author.)

Glossary

Abscissa   Horizontal axis

Additive law of probability   The rule giving the probability of the occurrence of two or more mutually exclusive events

Alpha (α)   The probability of a Type I error

Alternative hypothesis (H_1)   The hypothesis that is adopted when H_0 is rejected. Usually the same as the research hypothesis

Analysis of variance (ANOVA)   A statistical technique for testing for differences in the means of several groups

Analytic view   Definition of probability in terms of analysis of possible outcomes

Bar graph   A graph in which the frequency of occurrence of different values of X is represented by the height of the bar

Beta (β)   The probability of a Type II error

Between-subjects designs   Designs in which different subjects serve under the different treatment levels

Bias   A property of a statistic whose long-range average is not equal to the parameter it estimates

Bimodal   A distribution having two distinct peaks

Bonferroni correction   A multiple comparison procedure in which the familywise error rate is divided by the number of comparisons

Box-and-whisker plot   A graphical representation of the dispersion of a sample

Boxplot   A graphical representation of the dispersion of a sample

Carry-over effect   The effect of previous trials (conditions) on a subject's performance on subsequent trials

Categorical data   Data representing counts or number of observations in each category

Cell   The combination of a particular row and column; the set of observations obtained under identical treatment conditions

Central Limit Theorem   The theorem that specifies the nature of the sampling distribution of the mean

Central t distribution   The sampling distribution of the t statistic when the null hypothesis is true

Central tendency   A measure of the center of a distribution. Often the mean, median, or mode

Chi-square test   A statistical test often used for analyzing categorical data

Conditional probability   The probability of one event *given* the occurrence of some other event

Confidence interval   An interval, with limits at either end, with a specified probability of including the parameter being estimated

Confidence limits   The endpoints of the confidence interval

Confounded   Two variables are said to be confounded when they are varied simultaneously and their effects cannot be separated

Constant   A number that does not change in value in a given situation

Contingency table   A two-dimensional table in which each observation is classified on the basis of two variables simultaneously

Continuous variables   Variables that take on *any* value

Control group   A group that receives either no treatment or the standard treatment against which other groups are to be compared

Correlation (r)   Measure of the relationship between variables

Correlation coefficient   A measure of the relationship between variables

Count data   Data which consist of the counts (frequencies) of the occurrence of some events

Counterbalancing   An arrangement of treatment conditions designed to balance out practice effects

Covariance (s_{xy} or cov_{xy})   A statistic representing the degree to which two variables vary together

Criterion variable   The variable to be predicted

Critical value   The value of a test statistic at or beyond which we will reject H_0

Curvilinear relationship   A situation that is best represented by something other than a straight line

d-family measures   Measures of the size of an effect that depend directly on differences between means

Decision making   A procedure for making logical decisions on the basis of sample data

Decision tree   Graphical representation of decisions involved in the choice of statistical procedures

Degrees of freedom (df)   The number of independent pieces of information remaining after estimating one or more parameters

Delta (δ)   A value used in referring to power tables that combines gamma and the sample size

Density   Height of the curve for a given value of X closely related to the probability of an observation in an interval around X

Dependent variables   The variable being measured. The data or score

df_{error} Degrees of freedom associated with $SS_{error} = k(n - 1)$

df_{group} Degrees of freedom associated with $SS_{group} = k - 1$

df_{total} Degrees of freedom associated with $SS_{total} = N - 1$

Dichotomous variables   Variables that can take on only two different values

Difference scores   The set of scores representing the difference between the subjects' performance on two occasions. Also known as "gain scores"

Directional test   A test that rejects extreme outcomes in only one specified tail of the distribution

Discrete variables   Variables that take on a small set of possible values

Dispersion   The degree to which individual data points are distributed around the mean

Double-blind study   A study in which neither the participant nor the experimenter knows which treatment is being given

Effective sample size   The sample size associated with the power of a study

Effect size (δ)   The difference between two population means divided by the standard deviation of either population

Effect size (δ)   The difference between two sample means divided by the standard deviation of either sample

Error bars   In a graphic, these are the bars drawn about a mean or other statistic usually representing one standard error above and below that statistic

Error variance   The square of the standard error of estimate

Errors of prediction   The differences between Y and $\hat{Y}$

Eta squared (η^2)   A measure of the magnitude of effect. Also known as the correlation ratio

Event   The outcome of a trial

Exhaustive   A set of events that represents all possible outcomes

Expected frequencies   The expected value for the number of observations in a cell if H_0 is true

Expected value   The average value calculated for a statistic over an infinite number of samples

Experimental hypothesis   Another name for the research hypothesis

Exploratory data analysis (EDA)   A set of techniques developed by Tukey for presenting data in visually meaningful ways

F statistic   The ratio of MS_{group} to MS_{error}

Factorial design   An experimental design in which every level of each independent variable is paired with every level of each other independent variable

Factors   Another word for independent variables in the analysis of variance

Familywise error rate   The probability that a family of comparisons contains at least one Type I error

File drawer problem   Nonsignificant results are often not reported, so what you see in the published literature is likely biased toward those studies that found significant effects

Fisher's exact test   A test on a contingency table that assumes fixed marginal values. A substitute for the chi-square test

Fisher's Least Significant Difference Test (LSD)   A multiple comparison technique that requires a significant overall F, and that involves standard t tests between pairs of means. Also known as the "protected t test"

Forest plot   A graphic that puts all effect sizes on a single plot, showing their confidence intervals, and showing an overall effect size with its confidence interval

Frequency distribution   A distribution in which the values of the dependent variable are tabled or plotted against their frequency of occurrence

Frequency data   Data representing counts or number of observations in each category

Frequentist view   A view of probability based on the relative frequency of occurrence of different outcomes

Friedman's rank test for k correlated samples   A nonparametric test analogous to a standard one-way repeated measures analysis of variance

Gain scores   The change in a person's score from the pretest measure to the posttest measure

Goodness-of-fit test   A test for comparing observed frequencies with theoretically predicted frequencies

Grand mean (GM)   The mean of all of the observations

Heterogeneity of variance   A situation in which samples are drawn from populations having different variances

Heterogeneous subsamples   Data in which the sample of observations could be subdivided into two distinct sets on the basis of some other variable

Histogram   Graph in which rectangles are used to represent frequencies of observations within each interval

Homogeneity of variance   The situation in which two or more populations have equal variances

Hypothesis testing   A process by which decisions are made concerning the values of parameters

Independent events   Events are independent when the occurrence of one has no effect on the probability of the occurrence of the other

Independent variables Those variables controlled by the experimenter

Interaction A situation in a factorial design or contingency table in which the effects of one independent variable depend on the level of another independent variable

Intercept The value of Y when X is 0

Intercorrelation matrix A matrix (table) showing the pairwise correlations between all variables

Interquartile range The range of the middle 50% of the observations

Interval estimate A range of values estimated to include the parameter

Interval scale Scale on which equal intervals between objects represent equal differences—differences are meaningful

Joint probability The probability of the co-occurrence of two or more events

Leading digits Generally the left-most digit

Leading digits (most significant digits) Leftmost digits of a number

Least squares regression Regression of Y on the basis of X where we minimize the squared deviations of predicted scores from obtained scores

Leaves Horizontal axis of stem-and-leaf display containing the trailing digits

Less significant digits Generally the digit to the right of the most significant digit

Linear relationship A situation in which the best-fitting regression line is a straight line

Linear transformation A transformation involving addition, subtraction, multiplication, or division of or by a constant

Line graph A graph in which the Y values corresponding to different values of X are connected

Magnitude of effect A measure of the degree to which variability among observations can be attributed to treatments

Main effect The effect of one independent variable averaged across the levels of the other independent variable(s)

Marginal totals Totals for the levels of one variable summed across the levels of the other variable

Matched samples An experimental design in which the same subject is observed under more than one treatment

Mean The sum of the scores divided by the number of scores

Measurement The assignment of numbers to objects

Measurement data Data obtained by measuring objects or events

Median (Med) The score corresponding to the point having 50% of the observations below it when observations are arranged in numerical order

Median location The location of the median in an ordered series

Meta-analysis A procedure for collecting together many studies on a specific topic and combining their results to draw overall conclusions

Midpoint Center of interval—average of upper and lower limits

Modality The term used to refer to the number of major peaks in a distribution

Mode (Mo) The most commonly occurring score

Monotonic relationship A relationship represented by a regression line that is continually increasing (or decreasing), but perhaps not in a straight line

Most significant digits Also known as the leading digits

MS$_{between groups}$ (MS$_{group}$) Variability among group means

MS$_{treatment}$ The mean squares for differences between treatments

MS$_{within}$ (MS$_{error}$) Variability among subjects in the same treatment group

Multicollinearity A condition in which a set of predictor variables are highly correlated among themselves

Multiple comparison techniques Techniques for making comparisons between two or more group means subsequent to an analysis of variance

Multiple correlation coefficient (R$_{0.123...p}$) The correlation between one variable (Y) and a set of p predictors

Multiplicative law of probability The rule giving the probability of the joint occurrence of independent events

Mutually exclusive Two events are mutually exclusive when the occurrence of one precludes the occurrence of the other

Negative relationship A relationship in which increases in one variable are associated with decreases in the other

Negatively skewed A distribution that trails off to the left

Nominal scale Numbers used only to distinguish among objects

Noncentrality parameter A measure of the degree to which the mean of the sampling distribution under the alternative hypothesis departs from the mean of the sampling distribution under the null hypothesis

Nondirectional test A test that rejects extreme outcomes in either tail of the distribution

Nonparametric tests Statistical tests that do not rely on parameter estimation or precise distributional assumptions

Normal distribution A specific distribution having a characteristic bell-shaped form

Null hypothesis (H$_0$) The statistical hypothesis tested by the statistical procedure; usually a hypothesis of no difference or no relationship

Observed frequencies The cell frequencies that were actually observed—as distinguished from expected frequencies

Odds   The frequency of occurrence of one event divided by the frequency of occurrence of another event

Odds ratio   The ratio of two odds

Omega squared (ω^2)   A less biased measure of the magnitude of effect

One-tailed test   A test that rejects extreme outcomes in only one specified tail of the distribution

One-way ANOVA   An analysis of variance where the groups are defined on only one independent variable

Order effect   The effect on performance attributable to the order in which treatments were administered

Ordinal scale   Numbers used only to place objects in order

Ordinate   Vertical axis

Outlier   An extreme point that stands out from the rest of the distribution

p value   The probability that a particular result would occur by chance if H_0 is true. The exact probability of a Type I error

Parameters   Numerical values summarizing population data

Parametric tests   Statistical tests that involve assumptions about, or estimation of, population parameters

Pearson product-moment correlation coefficient (r)   The most common correlation coefficient

Percentile   The point below which a specified percentage of the observations fall

Phi(Φ)   The correlation coefficient when both of the variables are measured as dichotomies

Point-biserial correlation (r_{pb})   The correlation coefficient when one of the variables is measured as a dichotomy

Point estimate   The specific value taken as the estimate of a parameter

Pooled variance   A weighted average of the separate sample variances

Population   Complete set of events in which you are interested

Population correlation coefficient rho (ρ)   The correlation coefficient in the population

Population variance (σ^2)   Variance of the population—usually estimated, rarely computed

Positively skewed   A distribution that trails off to the right

Post-hoc power   The power of a future study computed on the basis of the parameter estimates in a study you have already run

Power   The probability of correctly rejecting a false H_0

Predictor variable   The variable from which a prediction is made

Prospective study   A study in which you select participants on the basis of some current condition (e.g., a drug) and follow them into the future

Protected t   A technique in which we run t tests between pairs of means only if the analysis of variance was significant. Also known as Fisher's LSD test

Quantitative data   Another term for measurement data

Quartile location   The location of a quartile in an ordered series

r-family measures   Measures of the size of an effect that resemble the correlation between the dependent and the independent variable

Random assignment   The allocation or assignment of participants to groups by a random process

Random sample   A sample in which each member of the population has an equal chance of inclusion

Randomization tests (permutation tests)   Tests of hypotheses that base rejection of the null hypothesis of no difference between groups on the results of many random permutations of the data

Range   The distance from the lowest to the highest score

Range restrictions   Refers to cases in which the range over which X or Y varies is artificially limited

Ratio scale   A scale with a true zero point—ratios are meaningful

Real lower limit   The points halfway between the bottom of one interval and the top of the next

Real upper limit   The points halfway between the top of one interval and the bottom of the next

Regression   The prediction of one variable from knowledge of one or more other variables

Regression coefficients   The general name given to the slope and the intercept (most often refers just to the slope)

Regression equation   The equation giving the regression line

Regression line   The line of best fit drawn through a scatterplot

Regression to the mean   A (false) believe that over time all observations shall move toward the mean

Rejection level   The probability with which we are willing to reject H_0 when it is in fact correct

Rejection region   The set of outcomes of an experiment that will lead to rejection of H_0

Related samples   An experimental design in which the same subject is observed under more than one treatment

Relative risk   The risk under one condition relative to the risk under another condition

Repeated measures   Data in a study in which you have multiple measurements for the same participant

Repeated-measures designs   An experimental design in which each subject receives all levels of at least one independent variable

Research hypothesis (H_1)   The hypothesis that the experiment was designed to investigate

Residual   The difference between the obtained and predicted values of Y

Residual variance   The square of the standard error of estimate

Retrospective power   The power of a study in which you select participants on some criterion and then look back at their behavior in the past

Retrospective study   A study in which you select participants on some criterion and then look back at their behavior in the past

Risk   The number of occurrences on one event divided by the total number of occurrences of events

Risk difference   The difference in risk under two different conditions

Risk ratio   The ratio of two risks

Sample   Set of actual observations. Subset of the population

Sample statistics   Statistics calculated from a sample and used primarily to describe the sample

Sample variance (s^2)   Sum of the squared deviations about the mean divided by $N-1$

Sample with replacement   Sampling in which the item drawn on trial N is replaced before the drawing on trial $N + 1$

Sampling distribution   The distribution of a statistic over repeated sampling

Sampling distribution of differences between means   The distribution of the differences between means over repeated sampling from the same population(s)

Sampling distribution of the mean   The distribution of sample means over repeated sampling from one population

Sampling error   Variability of a statistic from sample to sample due to chance

Scales of measurement   Characteristics of relations among numbers assigned to objects

Scatterplot (Scatter diagram, Scattergram)   A figure in which the individual data points are plotted in two- dimensional space

Sigma (Σ)   Symbol indicating summation

Significance level   The probability with which we are willing to reject H_0 when it is in fact correct

Simple effect   The effect of one independent variable at one level of another independent variable (also known as simple main effects)

Skewness   A measure of the degree to which a distribution is asymmetrical

Slope   The amount of change in Y for a one-unit change in X

Spearman's correlation coefficient for ranked data (r_s)   A correlation coefficient on ranked data

Squared correlation coefficient   This is simply the square of the correlation coefficient

SS$_{cells}$ The sum of squares assessing differences among cell totals

SS$_{error}$ The sum of the squared residuals; the sum of the sums of squares within each group

SS$_{group}$ The sum of squares of group totals divided by the number of scores per group minus $\Sigma X^2/N$

SS$_{total}$ The sum of squares of all of the scores, regardless of group membership

Standard deviation   Square root of the variance

Standard error   The standard deviation of a sampling distribution

Standard error of differences between means   The standard deviation of the sampling distribution of the differences between means

Standard error of estimate   The average of the squared deviations about the regression line

Standard error of the mean   The standard deviation of a distribution of means

Standardization   Scaling a variable by subtracting the mean and then dividing by the standard deviation

Standard scores   Scores with a predetermined mean and standard deviation

Standard normal distribution   A normal distribution with a mean equal to 0 and variance equal to 1. Denoted $N(0, 1)$

Standardized regression coefficient (β)   The regression coefficient that results from data that have been standardized

Statistics   Numerical values summarizing sample data

Stem   Vertical axis of display containing the leading digits

Stem-and-leaf display   Graphical display presenting original data arranged into a histogram

Stepwise procedures   A set of rules for deriving a regression equation by adding or subtracting one variable at a time from the regression equation

Student's t distribution   The sampling distribution of the t statistic

Subjective probability   Definition of probability in terms of personal subjective belief in the likelihood of an outcome

Sums of squares   The sum of the squared deviations around some point (usually a mean or predicted value)

Symmetric   Having the same shape on both sides of the center

T-scores   A set of scores with a mean of 50 and a standard deviation of 10

Test statistics   The results of a statistical test

Trailing digits (least significant digits)   Rightmost digits of a number

Trimmed means   The mean of a distribution from which we have removed a particular percentage of the scores from either end of the distribution

Trimmed statistics   Statistics calculated on trimmed samples

Trimmed samples   Samples with a percentage of extreme scores removed

Tukey's test   A multiple comparison procedure for making pairwise comparisons among means while holding the familywise error rate at α

Two-tailed test   A test that rejects extreme outcomes in either tail of the distribution

Two-way factorial design   An experimental design involving two independent variables in which every level of one variable is paired with every level of the other variable

Type I error   The error of rejecting H_0 when it is true

Type II error   The error of not rejecting H_0 when it is false

Unconditional probability   The probability of one event *ignoring* the occurrence or nonoccurrence of some other event

Unimodal   A distribution having one distinct peak

Variability   The degree to which multiple scores on a variable differ from each other

Variables   Properties of objects that can take on different values

Variance Sum Law   The rule giving the variance of the sum (or difference) of two or more variables

Weighted average   The mean of the form: $(a_1X_1 + a_2X_2)/(a_1 + a_2)$ where a_1 and a_2 are weighting factors and X_1 and X_2 are the values to be averaged

Whiskers   Lines drawn in a boxplot from hinges to adjacent values

Wilcoxon's matched-pairs signed-ranks test   A non-parametric test for comparing the central tendency of two matched (related) samples

Wilcoxon-Mann-Whitney rank-sum test   A nonpara-metric test for comparing two independent groups

Winsorized mean   The mean of a trimmed sample where the trimmed scores have been replaced by the highest (and lowest) remaining values

Winsorized standard deviation   The same as a trimmed mean except that the calculated statistic is a standard deviation rather than a mean

Winsorized variance   The same as a trimmed mean except that the calculated statistic is a variance rather than a mean

Within-subjects designs   Experimental designs in which each participant produces multiple scores

$\hat{Y}$ The predicted value of Y

z-score   Number of standard deviations above or below the mean

References

Achenbach, T. M. (1991). *Integrative Guide for the 1991 CBCL/418, YSR, and TRFProfiles*. Burlington, VT: University of Vermont Department of Psychiatry.

Achenbach, T. M., Howell, C. T., Aoki, M. F., & Rauh, V. A. (1993). Nine year outcome of the Vermont Intervention Program for low birth weight infants. *Pediatrics, 91*, 45–55.

Adams, H. E., Wright, L. W., Jr., & Lohr, B. A. (1996). Is homophobia associated with homosexual arousal? *Journal of Abnormal Psychology, 195*, 440–445.

Agresti, A. (2002). *Categorical Data Analysis* (2nd ed.). New York: Wiley.

American Psychological Association. (2010). The Publication Manual of the American Psychological Association (6th ed.). Washington, DC: ISBN 978-1-4338-0562-2

Aronson, J., Lustina, M. J., Good, C., Keough, K., Steele, C. M., & Brown, J. (1998). When white men can't do math: Necessary and sufficient factors in stereotype threat. *Journal of Experimental Social Psychology, 35*, 29–46.

Associated Press. (Dec. 13, 2001) Study: American kids getting fatter at alarming rate.

Bauer, M., & Dopfmer, S. (1999) Lithium augmentation in treatment-resistant depression: meta-analysis of placebo-controlled studies. *Journal of Clinical Psychopharmacology, 19*, 427–434.

Bisson J, & Andrew, M. (2007) Psychological treatment of post-traumatic stress disorder (PTSD).*Cochrane Database of Systematic Reviews*, Issue 3.

Blanchard, E. B., Theobald, D. E., Williamson, D. A., Silver, B. V., & Brown, D. A. (1978). Temperature biofeedback in the treatment of migraine headaches. *Archives of General Psychiatry, 35*, 581–588.

Bleuler, E. (1950). *Dementia Praecox or the Group of Schizophrenias* (H. Zinkin, Trans.). New York: International Universities Press. (Original work published 1911)

Bloch, M. H., Panza, K. E., Landeros-Weisenberger, A., & Leckman, J. F. (2009). Meta-analysis: treatment of attention-deficit/hyperactivity disorder in children with comorbid tic disorders. *Journal American Academy of Child and Adolescent Psychiatry, 48*, 884.

Boos, D. D., & Stefanski, L. A. (2011). p-value precision and reproducibility. *The American Statistician, 65*, 213–218.

Borenstein, M., Hedges, L. V., Higgins, J. P. T., & Rothstein, H. R. (2009). *Introduction to meta-analysis*. Chichester: John Wiley & Sons, Ltd.

Bradley, J. V. (1963, March). *Studies in Research Methodology: IV. A Sampling Study of the Central Limit Theorem and the Robustness of OneSample Parametric Tests*. AMRL Technical Documentary Report 63–29, 650th Aerospace Medical Research Laboratories, Wright Patterson Air Force Base, OH.

Brescoll, V. L. & Uhlman, E. L. (2008). Can an angry woman get ahead: Status conferral, gender, and expression of emotion in the workplace. *Psychological Science, 19*, 268–275.

Brooks, L., & Perot, A. R. (1991). Reporting sexual harassment. *Psychology of Women Quarterly, 15*, 31–47.

Chernick, M. R., & LaBudde, R. A. (2011). An Introduction to Bootstrap Methods with Applications to *R*. Hoboken, NJ: Wiley.

Chicago Tribune. (July 21, 1995). Girl finds salary gap could begin at home.

Christianson, M. K., & Leathem, J. M. (2004). Development and standardization of the computerized finger tapping test: Comparison with other finger tapping instruments. *New Zealand Journal of Psychology, 33*, 44–49.

Clark, K. B. & Clark, M. K. (1947). Racial identification and preference in Negro children. In E. E. Maccoby, T. M. Newcomb, & E. L. Hartley (Eds), *Readings in Social Psychology* (pp. 602–611). New York: Holt, Rinehart, and Winston.

Cochrane, A. L., St. Leger, A. S., & Moore, F. (1978). Health service "input" and mortality "output" in developed countries. *Journal of Epidemiology and Community Health, 32*, 200–205.

Cohen, J. (1968). Multiple regression as a general data-analytic system. *Psychological Bulletin, 70*, 426–443.

Cohen, J. (1969). *Statistical Power Analysis for the Behavioral Sciences*. Hillsdale, NJ: Lawrence Erlbaum Associates.

Cohen, J. (1988). *Statistical Power Analysis for the Behavioral Sciences* (2nd ed.). Hillsdale, NJ: Lawrence Erlbaum Associates.

Cohen, J. (1990). Things I have learned (so far). *American Psychologist, 45*, 1304–1312

Cohen, J. (1992). A power primer. *Psychological Bulletin, 112*, 155–159.

Cohen, P. (2005). Jacob Cohen. In B. E. Everitt & D. C. Howell (Eds), *Encyclopedia of Statistics in Behavioral Science* (pp. 318–319). London: Wiley.

Cohen, S., Kaplan, J. R., Cunnick, J. E., Manuck, S. B., & Rabin, B. S. (1992). Chronic social stress, affiliation, and cellular immune response in nonhuman primates. *Psychological Science, 3,* 301–304.

Compas, B. E., Worsham, N. S., Grant, K., Mireault, G., Howell, D. C., & Malcarne, V. L. (1994). When mom or dad has cancer: I. Symptoms of depression and anxiety in cancer patients, spouses, and children. *Health Psychology, 13,* 507–515.

Conover, W. J. (1980). *Practical Nonparametric Statistics* (2nd ed.). New York: John Wiley & Sons.

Conover, W. J., & Iman, R. L. (1981). Rank transformations as a bridge between parametric and nonparametric statistics. *American Statistician 35 (3): 124–129.* doi:10.2307/2683975. JSTOR 2683975.

Conti, L., & Musty, R. E. (1984). The effects of delta9tetrahydrocannabinol injections to the nucleus accumbens on the locomotor activity of rats. In S. Aquell et al. (Eds), *The Cannabinoids: Chemical, Pharmacologic, and Therapeutic Aspects.* New York: Academic Press.

Cooper, H. M. (2009). *Research Synthesis and Meta-Analysis: A Step by Step Approach.* Thousand Oaks, CA: Sage

Cooper, H. M., Hedges, L. V., & Valentine, J. eds. 2009. *The Handbook of Research Synthesis and Meta-Analysis, 2nd Edition.* New York: The Russell Sage Foundation..

Crawford, J. R., Garthwaite, P. H., & Howell, D. C. (2009). On comparing a single case with a control sample: An alternative perspective. *Neuropsychologia, 47,* 2690–2695.

Crawford, J. R., & Howell, D. C. (1998). Comparing an individual's test score against norms derived from small samples. *The Clinical Neuropsychologist, 12,* 482–486.

Cumming, G., & Finch, S. (2001). A primer on the understanding, use and calculation of confidence intervals based on central and noncentral distributions. *Educational and Psychological Measurement, 61,* 530–572.

Dabbs, J. M., Jr., & Morris, R. (1990). Testosterone, social class, and antisocial behavior in a sample of 4462 men. *PsychologicalScience, 1,* 209–211.

Damisch, L., Stoberock, B., &Mussweiler, T. (2010). Keep your fingers crossed!: How superstition improves performance. *Psychological Science, 21,* 1014–1020.

Darley, J. M., & Latané, B. (1968). Bystander intervention in emergencies: Diffusion of responsibility. *Journal of Personality and Social Psychology, 8,* 377–383.

Diener, E., & Diener, C. (1996). Most people are happy. *Psychological Science, 7,* 181–185.

Dieter, R. C. (1998). The death penalty in black and white: Who lives, who dies, who decides. Retrieved June 6, 2006, from http://www.deathpenaltyinfo.org/article.php?scid=45&did=539.

Dracup, C. (2005). Confidence Intervals. In B. Everrit & D. C Howell *Encyclopedia of Statistics in Behavioral Sciences.* Chichester: John Wiley and Sons, Ltd.

Duguid, M. M., & Goncalo, J. A. (2012). Living large: The powerful overestimate their own height. *Psychological Science, 23,* 36–40.

Efron, B., & Tibshirani, R. J. (1993). *An Introduction to the Bootstrap.* New York: Chapman and Hall.

Ellis, P.D. (2009), "Effect size calculators," website *http://www.polyu.edu.hk/mm/effectsizefaqs/calculator/calculator.html* accessed on July 12, 2012.

Epping Jordan, J. E., Compas, B. E., & Howell, D. C. (1994). Predictors of cancer progression in young adult men and women: Avoidance, intrusive thoughts, and psychological symptoms. *Health Psychology, 13,* 539–547.

Everitt, B. (1994). Cited in Hand et al. (1994), p. 229.

Eysenck, M. W. (1974). Age differences in incidental learning. *Developmental Psychology, 10,* 936–941.

Faul, F., Erdfeldr, F., & Buchner, A. (2007). Statistical power analysis using GPower 3.1. *Behavior Research Methods, Instruments, & Computers, 41,* 1149–1160.

Fell, J. C. (1995). What's new in alcohol, drugs, and traffic safety in the U.S. (Paper presented at the 13th International Conference on Alcohol, Drugs, and Traffic Safety, Adelaide, Australia.)

Field, A. (2009). *Discovering Statistics Using SPSS.* Los Angeles, Sage.

Fisher, R. A. (1935). *The Design of Experiments.* Edinburgh: Oliver & Boyd.

Foa, E. B., Rothbaum, B. O., Riggs, D. S., & Murdock, T. B. (1991). Treatment of posttraumatic stress disorder in rape victims: A comparison between cognitive behavioral procedures and counseling. *Journal of Consulting and Clinical Psychology, 59,* 715–723.

Foertsch, J., & Gernsbacher, M. A. (1997). In search of gender neutrality: Is singular *they* a cognitively efficient substitute for generic *he*? *Psychological Science, 8,* 106–111.

Fombonne, E. (1989). Season of birth and childhood psychosis. *British Journal of Psychiatry, 155,* 655–661.

Froelich, A. G., & Stephenson, W. R. (2013). Does eye color depend on gender:? It might depend on who or how you ask. *Journal of Statistics Education [online], 21(2),* www.amstat.org/publications/jse/v21n2/froelich_ds.pdf.

Gardner, M. J., & Altman, D. G. (2002) Confidence intervals rather than p values. In D. G. Altman, D. Machin, T. N. Bryant, & M. J. Gardner. *Statistics with Confidence, 2nd ed.* BMJ Books.

Garland, C. F., Garland, F. C., Gorham, E. D, Lipkin, M., Newmark, H., Mohr, S. B., & Holick, M. F. (2006). The role of vitamin D in cancer prevention. *American Journal of Public Health, 96,* 252–261.

Geller, E. S., Witmer, J. F., & Orebaugh, A. L. (1976). Instructions as a determinant of paper disposal behaviors. *Environment and Behavior, 8*, 417–439.

Gentile, D. (2009). Pathological video-game use among youth ages 8 to 18. *Psychological Sciences, 20*, 594–602.

Geyer, C. J. (1991). Constrained maximum likelihood exemplified by isotonic convex logistic regression. *Journal of the American Statistical Association, 86*, 717–724.

Giancola, P. R., & Corman, M. D. (2007). Alcohol and aggression: A test of the attention-allocation model. *Psychological Science, 18*, 649–655.

Glass, G. V., McGaw, B., & Smith, M. L. (1981). *Meta-Analysis in Social Research*, Newbury Park, CA: Sage.

Good, P. I. (2001). *Resampling Methods: A Practical Guide to Data Analysis*. Boston: Birkhäuser.

Grambsch, P. (2008). Regression to the mean, murder rates, and shall-issue laws. *The American Statistician, 62*, 289–295.

Greenhouse, S. W., & Geisser, S. (1959). On methods in the analysis of profile data. *Psychometrika, 24*, 95–112.

Grissom, R. J., & Kim, J. J. (2012). *Effect sizes for Research: Univariate and Multivariate Applications*. New York: Routledge.

Gross, J. S. (1985). Weight modification and eating disorders in adolescent boys and girls. (Unpublished doctoral dissertation, University of Vermont, Burlington.)

Guber, D. L. (1999). Getting what you pay for: The debate over equity in public school expenditures. *Journal of Statistics Education, 7* (2).

Hand, D. J., Daly, F., Lunn, A. D., McConway, K. J., & Oserowski, E. (1994). *A Handbook of Small Data Sets*. London: Chapman & Hall.

Harris, R. J. (2005). Classical statistical inference: Practice versus presentation. In B. E. Everitt & D. C. Howell (Eds.), *Encyclopedia of Statistics in Behavioral Science* (pp. 268–278). London: Wiley.

Hart, V., Nováková, P., Malkemper, E. P., Sabine, C., Begall, S., Hanzal, V., Ježek, M., Kušta, T., Němcová, N., Jana Adámková J., Benediktová, K., Cervený, J., Burda H. (2013), Dogs are sensitive to small variations of the Earth's magnetic field. *Frontiers in Zoology, 10* (1), 80.

Hedges, L. V. (1981). Distribution theory for Glass's estimator of effect size and related estimators. *Journal of Educational Statistics, 6*, 107–208.

Hoaglin, D. C., Mosteller, F., & Tukey, J. W. (1983). *Understanding Robust and Exploratory Data Analysis*. New York: John Wiley & Sons.

Hoenig, J. M., & Heisey, D. M. (2001). The abuse of power: The pervasive fallacy of power calculations for data analysis. *American Statistician, 55*, 19–24.

Horowitz J., & Garber J. (2006). The prevention of depressive symptoms in children and adolescents: A meta-analytic review. *Journal of Consulting and Clinical Psychology, 74*, 401–415.

Hout, M., Duncan, O. D., & Sobel, M. E. (1987). Association and heterogeneity: Structural models of similarities and differences. In C. C. Clogg, Ed., *Sociological Methodology, 17*, 145ff.

Howell, D.C. (2005). Florence Nightingale. In B. S. Everitt, & D. C. Howell, (Eds.), *Encyclopedia of Statistics in Behavioral Science* (pp. 1408–1409). Chichester, England: Wiley.

Howell, D. C. (2012). *Statistical Methods for Psychology* (8th ed.). Belmont, CA: WadsworthPress, A Cengage Imprint.

Howell, D. C., & Gordon, L. R. (1976). Computing the exact probability of an R X C contingency table with fixed marginal totals. *Behavior Research Methods and Instrumentation, 8*, 317.

Howell, D. C., & Huessy, H. R. (1985). A fifteen year followup of a behavioral history of Attention Deficit Syndrome (ADD). *Pediatrics, 76*, 185–190.

Hraba, J., & Grant, G. (1970). Black is beautiful: A reexamination of racial preference and identification. *Journal of Personality and Social Psychology, 16*, 398–402.

Huynh, H., & Feldt, L. S. (1976). Estimation of the Box correction for degrees of freedom for sample data in the randomized block and split plot designs. *Journal of Educational Statistics, 1*, 69–82.

Jones, L. V., & Tukey, J. W. (2000). A sensible formulation of the significance test. *Psychological Methods, 5*, 411–414.

Kapoor, P., Rajkumar, S. V., Dispenzieri, A., Gertz, M. A., Lacy, M. Q., Dingli, D., Mikhael, J. R., Roy, V., Kyle, R. A., Greipp, P. R., Kumar, S., Mandrekar, S. (2011). Melphalan and prednisone versus melphalan, prednisone and thalidomide for elderly and/or transplant ineligible patients with multiple myeloma: A meta-analysis. *Leukemia 25* (4), 689–696.

Kapp, B., Frysinger, R., Gallagher, M., & Hazelton, J. (1979). Amygdala central nucleus lesions: Effects on heart rate conditioning in the rabbit. *Physiology and Behavior, 23*, 1109–1117.

Katz, S., Lautenschlager, G. J., Blackburn, A. B., & Harris, F. H. (1990). Answering reading comprehension items without passages on the SAT. *Psychological Science, 1*, 122–127.

Kaufman, L., & Rock, I. (1962). The moon Illusion. I. *Science, 136*, 953–961.

Kline, R. B. (2004). *Beyond Significance Testing*. Washington, D.C.: American Psychological Association.

Krantz, J. H. Cognitive Laboratory Experiments. Available at http://psych.hanover.edu/JavaTest/CLE/Cognition/Cognition.html

Landwehr, J. M., & Watkins, A. E. (1987). *Exploring Data: Teacher's Edition*. Palo Alto, CA: Dale Seymour Publications.

Langlois, J. H., & Roggman, L. A. (1990). Attractive faces are only average. *Psychological Science, 1*, 115–121.

Latané, B., & Dabbs, J. M., Jr. (1975). Sex, group size, and helping in three cities. *Sociometry, 38,* 180–194.

Leerkes, E., & Crockenberg, S. (1999). The development of maternal self-efficacy and its impact on maternal behavior. Poster presentation at the Biennial Meetings of the Society for Research in Child Development, Albuquerque, NM, April.

Lenth, R. V. (2001). Some practical guidelines for effective sample size determination. *American Statistician, 55,*187–193.

Lenth, R. V. (2011). Java Applets for Power and Sample Size [Computer software]. Retrieved *June19, 2012,* from http://www.stat.uiowa.edu/~rlenth/Power.

Levine, R. (1990). The pace of life and coronary heart disease. *American Scientist, 78,* 450–459.

Levine, R. V., & Norenzayan, A. (1999). The pace of life in 31 countries. *Journal of Cross-cultural Psychology, 30,* 178–205.

Liberman, M. (2007). Thou shalt not report odds rations. Retrieved March 9, 2015 from http://itre.cis.upenn.edu/languagelog/archives/004767.html

Liddle, B. J. (1997). Coming out in class: Disclosure of sexual orientation and teaching evaluations. *Teaching of Psychology, 24,* 32–35.

Lord, F. M. (1953). On the statistical treatment of football numbers. *American Psychologist, 8,* 750–751.

Magan, E., Dweck, C. S., & Gross, J. J. (2008). The hidden-zero effect. *Psychological Science, 19,* 648–649.

Malcarne, V., Compas, B. E., Epping, J., & Howell, D. C. (1995). Cognitive factors in adjustment to cancer: Attributions of selfblame and perceptions of control. *Journal of Behavioral Medicine, 18,* 401–417.

Mann-Jones, J. M., Ettinger, R. H., Baisden, J., & Baisden, K. (2003). Dextromethorphan modulation of context-dependent morphine tolerance. Retrieved December7, 2009, from www.eou.edu/psych/re/morphinetolerance.doc

Markon, J. (2008). Two justices clash over race and death penalty. Retrieved from at http://www.washingtonpost.com/wp-dyn/content/article/2008/10/20/AR2008102003133.html March 9, 2015.

Martin, J. A., Hamilton, B. E. , Osterman, M. J. K., Curtin, S.C. & Mathews, T. J. (2012). Births: Final data for 2012. National Vital Statistics Reports, 62, 9. U. S. Department of Health and Human Services.

Mazzucchelli, T., Kane, R.T., & Rees, C. S. (2010). Behavioral activation interventions for well-being: A meta-analysis. *Journal of Positive Psychology, 5, 105–121.*

McClelland, G. H. (1997). Optimal design in psychological research. *Psychological methods, 2,* 3–19.

McConaughy, S. H. (1980). Cognitive structures for reading comprehension: Judging the relative importance of ideas in short stories. (Unpublished doctoral dissertation, University of Vermont, Burlington.)

Meier, B. P., Robinson, M. D., Gaither, G. A., & Heinert, N. J. (2006). A secret attraction or a defensive loathing? Homophobia, defense, and implicit cognition. *Journal of Research in Personality, 40,* 377–394.

Mireault, G. C. (1990). Parent death in childhood, perceived vulnerability, and adult depression and anxiety. (Unpublished master's thesis, University of Vermont, Burlington.)

Moran, P. A. P. (1974). Are there two maternal age groups in Down's syndrome? *British Journal of Psychiatry, 124,* 453–455.

Nolen-Hoeksema, S., & Morrow, J. (1991). A prospective study of depression and posttraumatic stress symptoms after a natural disaster: The 1989 Loma Prieta earthquake. *Journal of Personality and Social Psychology, 61,* 115–121.

Nurcombe, B., & Fitzhenry-Coor, I. (1979). Decision making in the mental health interview: I. An introduction to an education and research program. (Paper delivered at the Conference on Problem Solving in Medicine, Smuggler's Notch, VT.)

Nurcombe, B., Howell, D. C., Rauh, V A., Teti, D. M., Ruoff, P., & Brennan, J. (1984). An intervention program for mothers of low birth weight infants: Preliminary results. *Journal of the American Academy of Child Psychiatry, 23,* 319–325.

OECD Health Statistics. (2013). downloaded 3/10/2015 from http://www.oecd.org/health/health-systems/health-at-a-glance.htm

Peterson, W. P. (2001). Topics for discussion from current newspapers and journals. *Journal of Statistics Education, 9.*

Pliner, P., & Chaiken, S. (1990). Eating, social motives, and selfpresentation in women and men. *Journal of Experimental Social Psychology, 26,* 240–254.

Pugh, M. D. (1983). Contributory fault and rape conviction: Loglinear models for blaming the victim. *Social Psychology Quarterly, 46,* 233–242.

Radelet, M. L., & Pierce, G. L. (1991). Choosing those who will die: Race and the death penalty in Florida. *Florida Law Review, 43,* 1–34.

Ramsey, F. L., & Schafer, D. W. (1997). *The Statistical Sleuth.* Belmont, CA: Duxbury Press.

Read, C. (1997). *Neyman.* New York: Springer.

Reynolds, C. R., & Richmond, B. O. (1978). What I think and feel: A revised measure of children's manifest anxiety. *Journal of Abnormal Child Psychology, 6,* 271–280.

Robinson, D. H., & Wainer, H. (2001) On the past and future of null hypotheses significance testing. Unpublished research report of Educational Testing Service (RR-01-24). Available at https://www.ets.org/Media/Research/pdf/RR-01-24-Wainer.pdf accessed on May 29, 2012.

Rogers, R. W., & PrenticeDunn, S. (1981). Deindividuation and anger mediated aggression: Unmasking regressive racism. *Journal of Personality and Social Psychology, 41,* 63–73.

Rosa, L., Rosa, E., Sarner, L., & Barrett, S. (1998). A close look at Therapeutic Touch. *Journal of the American Medical Association, 279,* 1005–1010.

Rosenthal, R. (1979). The file drawer problem and tolerance for null results. *Psychological Bulletin, 86,* 638–641.

Rosenthal, R. (1994). Parametric measures of effect size. In H. Cooper & L. Hedges (Eds.), *The Handbook of Research Synthesis.* New York: Russell Sage Foundation.

Rosenthal, R., Rosnow, R. L., & Rubin, D. B. (2000). *Contrasts and Effect Sizes in Behavioral Research: A Correlational Approach.* New York: Cambridge University Press.

Ryan, T., Joiner, B., & Ryan, B. (1985). *Minitab Student Handbook.* Boston: Duxbury Press.

Sackett, D. L., Deeks, J. J., & Altman, D. G. (1996). Down with odds ratios! *Evidence-Based Medicine, 1,* 164–166.

SaintExupery, A. de (1943). *The Little Prince.* (K. Woods, Trans.). New York: Harcourt Brace Jovanovich. (Original work published in 1943.)

Seligman, M. E. P, NolenHoeksema, S., Thornton, N., & Thornton, C. M. (1990). Explanatory style as a mechanism of disappointing athletic performance. *Psychological Science, 1,* 143–146.

Sethi, S., & Seligman, M. E. P. (1993). Optimism and fundamentalism. *Psychological Science, 4,* 256–259.

Sgro, J. A., & Weinstock, S. (1963). Effects of delay on subsequent running under immediate reinforcement. *Journal of Experimental Psychology, 66,* 260–263.

Siegel, S. (1975). Evidence from rats that morphine tolerance is a learned response. *Journal of Comparative and Physiological Psychology, 80,* 498–506.

Simon, J. L., & Bruce, P. (1991). Resampling: A tool for everyday statistical work. *Chance: New Directions for Statistics and Computing, 4,* 22–58.

Smithson, M. (2000). *Statistics with Confidence.* London: Sage.

Sofer, C., Dotch, R., Wigboldus, D. H. J., & Todorov, A. (2015). What is typical is good: The influence of face typicality on perceived trustworthiness. *Psychological Science, 26,* 39–47.

Spatz, C. (1997). Basic *Statistics: Tales of Distributions.* Pacific Grove, CA. Brooks/Cole.

Spilich, G. J., June, L., & Renner, J. (1992). Cigarette smoking and cognitive performance. *British Journal of Addiction, 87,* 1313–1326.

Spock, B. (1946). *Baby and Child Care,* New York: Duell, Sloan, and Pearce.

St. Lawrence, J. S., Brasfield, T. L., Shirley, A., Jefferson, K. W., Alleyne, E., & O'Brannon, R. E., III (1995). Cognitive behavioral intervention to reduce African American adolescents' risk for HIV infection. *Journal of Consulting & Clinical Psychology, 63,* 221–237.

St. Leger, A. S., Cochrane, A. L., & Moore, F. (1978). The anomaly that wouldn't go away. *Lancet, ii,* 1153.

St. Leger A. S., Cochrane A. L., & Moore F. (1979). Factors associated with cardiac mortality in developed countries with particular reference to the consumption of wine. *Lancet, i,* 1017–1020.

Stead, L. F., Perera, R. Bullen, C., Mant, D., & Lancaster, T. (2008). Nicotine replacement therapy for smoking cessation. *Cochrane Database of Systematic Reviews, 2009,* Issue 1, Art. *No. CD00146.* DOI: 10.1002/14651858. CD0146. Pub 3.

Stevens, S. S. (1951). Mathematics, measurement, and psychophysics. In S. S. Stevens (Ed.), *Handbook of Experimental Psychology.* New York: John Wiley & Sons.

Stigler, S. M. (1999). *Statistics on the Table: A History of Statistical Concepts and Methods.* Cambridge, MA: Harvard University Press.

Strough, J., Mehta, C. M., McFall, J. P., & Schuller, K. L. (2008). Are older adults less subject to the sunk-cost fallacy than younger adults? *Psychological Science, 19,* 650–652.

Suddath, R. L., Christison, G. W., Torrey, E. F., Casanova, M. F., Weinberger, D. R. (1990). Anatomical abnormalities in the brains of monozygotic twins discordant for schizophrenia. *New England Journal of Medicine, 322,* 789–794.

Thomas, M. H., & Wang, A. Y. (1996). Learning by the keyword mnemonic: Looking for long-term benefits. *Journal of Experimental Psychology: Applied, 2,* 330–342.

Thompson, B. (2000). A suggested revision of the forthcoming 5th edition of the APA *Publication Manual.* Retrieved from http://people.cehd.tama.edu/~bthompson/apaeffec.htm accessed on July 1, 2011.

Trzesniewski, K. H., Donnellan, M. B., & Robins, R. W. (2008). Do today's young people really think they are so extraordinary? *Psychological Science, 19,* 181–188.

Trzesniewski, K. H., Donnellan, M. B. (2009). Reevaluating the evidence for increasingly positive self-views among high school students: More evidence for consistency across generations (1976 – 2006). *Psychological Science, 20,* 920–922.

Tufte, E. R. (1983). *The Visual Display of Quantitative Information.* Cheshire, CT: Graphics Press.

Tukey, J. W. (1977). *Exploratory Data Analysis.* Reading, MA: AddisonWesley.

Twenge, J. M. (2006). *Generation Me: Why Today's Young Americans are More Confident , Assertive, Entitled—and More Miserable Than Ever Before.* New York: Free Press.

Unah, I., & Boger, J. (2001). Race and the death penalty in North Carolina: An empirical analysis: 1993–1997. Retrieved October 23, 2009 from http://www.deathpenaltyinfo.org/article.php?did=246&scid=

U.S. Department of Commerce. (1977). *Social Indicators, 1976.* Washington, D.C.: U.S. Government Printing Office.

U. S. Department of Justice, Bureau of Justice Statistics, *Prisoners in 1982*. Bulletin NCJ-87933. Washington, D.C.: U.S. Government Printing Office, 1983.

Utts, J. M. (2005). *Seeing Through Statistics* (3rd ed.). Belmont, CA: Brooks Cole.

Verdooren, L. R. (1963). Extended tables of critical values for Wilcoxon's test statistic. Biometrika, 50, 177–186.

Visintainer, M. A., Volpicelli, J. R., & Seligman, M. E. P. (1982). Tumor rejection in rats after inescapable or escapable shock. *Science, 216*, 437–439.

Vul, E., & Pashler, H. (2008). Measuring the crowd within: Probabilistic representations within individuals. *Psychological Science, 19*, 645–647.

Wagner, B. M., Compas, B. E., & Howell, D. C. (1988). Daily and major life events: A test of an integrative model of psychosocial stress. *American Journal of Community Psychology, 61*, 189–205.

Wainer, H. (1984). How to display data badly. *The American Statistician, 38*, 137–147.

Wainer, H. (1997). Some multivariate displays for NAEP results. *Psychological Methods, 2*, 34–63.

Walsh, T. B., Kaplan, A. S., Attia, E., Olmsted, M., Parides, M., Carter, J. C., Pike, K. M., Devlin, M. J., Woodside, B., Roberto, C. A., & Rockert, W. (2006). Fluoxetine after weight restoration in anorexia nervosa. *Journal of the American Medical Association, 295*, 2605–2612.

Weinberg, C. R., & Gladen, B. C. (1986). The beta-geometric distribution applied to comparative fecundability studies. *Biometrics, 42*, 547–560.

Weinstein, N., Ryan, W. S., Dehaan, C. R.,Przybylski, A. K., Legate, N., Ryan R. M., (2012). Parental autonomy support and discrepancies between implicit and explicit sexual identities: Dynamics of self-acceptance and defense. *Journal of Personality and Social Psychology. 102*, 815–832.

Weiss, S. (2014) The fault of our stats. *Observer, 27*, 29–30.

Welkowitz, J., Cohen, B. M., & Ewen, R., (2006). *Introductory Statistics for the Behavioral Sciences* (6th ed.). New York: John Wiley & Sons.

Werner, M., Stabenau, J. B., & Pollin, W. (1970). TAT method for the differentiation of families of schizophrenics, delinquents, and normals. *Journal of Abnormal Psychology, 75*, 139–145.

Wilcox, R. R. (2003). *Applying Contemporary Statistical Techniques*. New York: Academic Press.

Willer, R., Rogalin, C., Conlon, B., & Wojnowicz, M. T. (2013). Overdoing gender: A test of the Masculine overcompensation thesis. *American Journal of Sociology,* 118, 980–1022.

Williamson, J. A. (2008). Correlates of Coping Styles in Children of Depressed Parents: Observations of Positive and Negative Emotions in Parent-Child Interactions. Honors thesis, Vanderbilt University.

Winer, B. J., Brown, D. R., & Michels, K. M. (1991). *Statistical Principles in Experimental Design*. New York: McGraw-Hill.

Wong, A. (2008). Incident solar radiation and coronary heart disease mortality rates in Europe. *European Journal of Epidemiology, 23*, 609–614.

Young F. W. (2001). An explanation of the persistent doctor-mortality association. *Journal ofEpidemiology and Community Health, 55*, 80–84.

Zuckerman, M., Hodgins, H. S., Zuckerman, A., & Rosenthal, R. (1993). Contemporary issues in the analysis of data. *Psychological Science, 4*, 49–53.

Zumbo, B. D., & Zimmerman, D. W. (2000). Scales of measurement and the relation between parametric and nonparametric statistical tests. In B. Thompson (Ed.), *Advances in Social Science Methodology*, Vol. 6. Greenwich, CT: JAI Press.

Answers to Exercises

(I have not provided graphs where those are called for because of the amount of space they require and the cost of preparation. I have also left out a few answers that would require an inordinate amount of space. These items are included in both the Instructor's Manual and the Student's Manual. The Student's manual is available at

www.uvm.edu/~dhowell/fundamentals9/

In early chapters there is often close correspondence between these answers and the answers in the Student's Manual. This is much less true in later chapters, where the problems are more computational.)

CHAPTER 1

1.1 A good example is the development of tolerance to caffeine. People who do not normally drink caffeinated coffee are often startled by the effect of one or two cups of regular coffee, whereas those who normally drink regular coffee see no such effect. To test for a context effect of caffeine, you would first need to develop a dependent variable measuring the alerting effect of caffeine, which could be a vigilance task. You could test for a context effect by serving a group of users of decaffeinated coffee two cups of regular coffee every morning in their office for a month, but have them drink decaf the rest of the time. The vigilance test would be given shortly after the coffee, and tolerance would be seen by an increase in errors over days. At the end of the month they would be tested after drinking caffeinated coffee in the same and in a different setting.

1.3 Context affects people's response to alcohol, to off-color jokes, or to observed aggressive behavior.

1.5 The sample would be the addicts that we observe.

1.7 Not all people in the city are listed in the phone book. In particular, women and children are underrepresented. A phone book is particularly out of date as a random selection device with the increase in the use of cell phones.

1.9 In the tolerance study discussed in the text we really do not care what the mean length of paw-lick latency is. No one would be excited to know that a mouse can stand on a surface at 105° for 3.2 seconds without licking its paws. But we do very much care that the population mean of paw-lick latencies for morphine-tolerant mice is longer in one context than in another.

1.11 I would expect that my mother would continue to wander around in a daze, wondering what happened.

1.13 Three examples of measurement data: Performance on a vigilance task, typing speed, blood alcohol level.

1.15 Relationship: the relationship between stress and susceptibility to disease, the relationship between driving speed and accident rate.

1.17 You could have one group of mice trained and tested in the same condition, one group trained in one condition and tested in the other, and a third group given a placebo in the training context but given morphine in the testing condition.

1.19 This is an Internet search exercise with no fixed answer.

CHAPTER 2

2.1 Nominal: names of students in the class; Ordinal: the order in which students hand in their first exam; Interval: a student's grade on that first exam; Ratio: the amount of time that a student spent taking the exam.

2.3 If the rat lies down to sleep in the maze after performing successfully for several trials, this probably says little about what the animal has learned in the task, but more about motivation.

2.5 We have assumed the following at the very least (and I'm sure that I left some out):

1. Mice are adequate models for human behavior.
2. Morphine tolerance effects in mice are like heroin effects in humans.

3. Time on a warm surface is in some way analogous to a human response to heroin.
4. A context shift for mice is analogous to a context shift for humans.
5. A drug overdose is analogous to pain tolerance.

2.7 The independent variables are the gender of the subject and the gender of the other person.

2.9 The experimenter expected to find that women would eat less in the presence of a male partner than in the presence of a female partner. Men, on the other hand, were not expected to vary the amount that they ate as a function of gender of their partner. (They're kind of clueless.)

2.11 We would treat a discrete variable as if it were continuous if it had many different levels and were at least ordinal.

2.13 When I drew 50 numbers three times I obtained 29, 26, and 19 even numbers, respectively. The last time only 38% of my numbers were even, which is probably less than I might have expected—especially if I didn't have a fair amount of experience with similar exercises.

2.15 Eyes level condition:

(a) $X_3 = 2.03$; $X_5 = 1.05$; $X_8 = 1.86$
(b) $\Sigma X = 14.82$
(c) $\sum_{i=1}^{10} X_i = 14.82$

2.17 Eyes level condition:

(a) $(\Sigma X)^2 = (14.82)^2 = 219.63$;
   $\Sigma X^2 = 1.65^2 + \cdots + 1.73^2 = 23.22$
(b) $\Sigma X/N = 14.82/10 = 1.482$
(c) This is the mean, a type of average.

2.19 Putting the two sets of data together:

(a) XY = 2.854 1.06 4.121 1.750 0.998
   1.153 2.355 3.218 2.543 2.699
(b) $\Sigma XY = 22.7496$
(c) $\Sigma X \Sigma Y = (14.82)(14.63) = 216.82$
(d) $22.7496 \neq 216.82$
(e) 0.1187

2.21 Show $\Sigma(X + C) = \Sigma X + NC$

X   5 7 3   6 3 $\Sigma X = 24$

X + 4 9 11 7 10 7 $\Sigma(X + 4) = 44 = (24 + 5 \times 4)$

2.23 In the text I spoke about room temperature as an ordinal scale of comfort (at least up to some point). Room temperature is a continuous measure, even though with respect to comfort it only measures at an ordinal level.

2.25 Beth Peres

(a) In the Beth Peres story the dependent variable is the weekly allowance, and the independent variable is the gender of the child.
(b) We are dealing with a selected sample—the children in her class.
(c) The age of the students would influence the overall mean. The fact that these children are classmates could easily lead to socially appropriate responses—or what the children deem to be socially appropriate in their setting.
(d) At least within her school Beth could randomly sample by taking a student roster, assigning each student a number, and matching those with the numbers drawn from a random number table. Random assignment to Gender would obviously be impossible.
(e) I don't see negative aspects of the lack of random assignment here because that is the nature of the variable under consideration. It might be better if we could randomly assign a child to a gender and see the result, but we clearly can't.
(f) The outcome of the study could be influenced by the desire of some children to exaggerate their allowance or to minimize it so as not to appear too different from their peers. I would suspect that boys would be likely to exaggerate.
(g) The descriptive features of the study are her statements that the boys in her class received $3.18 per week in allowance, on average, whereas the girls received an average of $2.73. The inferential aspects are the inferences to the population of all children, concluding that boys get more than girls.

2.27 I would record the sequence number of each song that is played and then plot them on a graph. I can't tell if they are *truly* random, but if I see a pattern to the points I can be quite sure that they are not random.

CHAPTER 3

3.1 (b) There is too little data to say much about the shape of this distribution.

3.3 I would use stems of 3*, 3., 4*, 4., 5*, and 5. for this display.

3.5 Compared to those who read the passages:

(a) Almost everyone who read the passages did better than the best person who did not read them. Certainly knowing what you are talking about is a good thing (though not always practiced).

(b) **stem.leaf.backback(x = NoPassage, y = Passage)**
(c) It is obvious that the two groups are very different in their performance. We would be worried if they were not.
(d) This is an Internet question with no fixed answer.

3.7 The following is a plot (as a histogram) of reaction times collapsed across all variables.

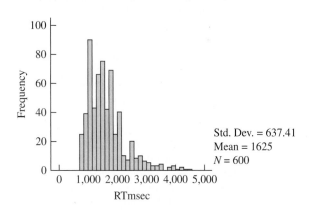

Std. Dev. = 637.41
Mean = 1625
N = 600

3.9 Histogram of GPA:

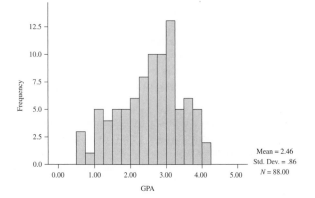

Mean = 2.46
Std. Dev. = .86
N = 88.00

3.11 (1) Mexico has very many young people and very few old people, whereas Spain has a more even distribution. (2) The difference between males and females is more pronounced at most ages in Spain than it is in Mexico. (3) You can see the high infant mortality rate in Mexico.

3.13 The distribution of those whose attendance is poor is far more spread out than the distribution of normal attendees. This is expected because a few very good students can score well on tests even when they don't attend, but most of the poor attendees are generally poor students who would score badly no matter what. The difference between the average grades of these two groups is obvious.

3.15 As the degree of rotation increases, the distribution of reaction time scores appears to move from left to right—which is also an increase.

3.17 The data points are probably not independent in that dataset. At first the subject might get better with practice, but then fatigue would start to set in. Data nearer in time should be more similar than data further apart in time.

3.19 The amount of shock that a subject delivers to a White participant does not vary as a function of whether that subject has been insulted by the experimenter. However, Black participants do suffer when the subject has been insulted.

3.21 Wikipedia gives an excellent set of data on HIV/AIDS prevalence at

http://en.wikipedia.org/wiki/List_of_countries_by_HIV/AIDS_adult_prevalence_rate

3.23 *R* code to reproduce figures in 3.21

```
### Households headed by women
percent <- c(.085, .088, .102, .108, .117,
.117, .116, .117, .118)
year <- c(1960, 1970, 1975, 1980, 1985,
1987, 1988, 1989, 1990)
famsize <- c(3.33, 3.14, 2.94, 2.76, 2.69,
2.66, 2.64, 2.62, 2.63)
par(mfrow = c(2,1))
plot(percent ~ year, type = "l", ylim =
c(.08, .12), ylab = "Percentage", col =
"red", lwd = 3)
plot(famsize ~ year, type = "l", ylim =
c(2.6, 3.4) ylab = "Family Size", col =
"blue", lwd = 3)
```

3.25 There is a tremendous increase in Down syndrome in children born to older mothers. This increase doesn't really take off until mothers are in their 40s, but with parents delaying having children, this is a potential problem.

3.27 Data on birth month and psychiatric diagnosis:

(a) You would have to transform the data to percentages/month to put them on the same scale.
(b) All three sets of data can be plotted together.

(c)

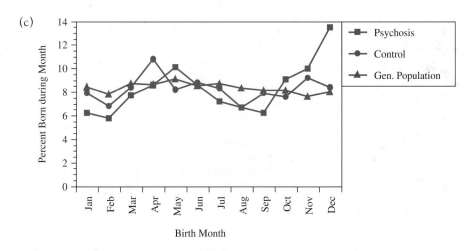

(d) There is a lot more variability in the psychosis group, but they have a much smaller sample than either of the other conditions, so that would be expected. The psychosis group is higher than the general population in the last three months of the year, but lower in the first three. I would need a statistical test (to be discussed in Chapter 19) to feel comfortable about saying that there are seasonal variations that are associated with psychosis.

(e) The control group allows us to compare two groups of people who have been referred for some sort of treatment. They would allow us to eliminate referral as an explanation. Notice that they stick closer to the general population than do the psychosis group, but the sample size for the control group is quite large.

(f) The most that I can conclude was already stated in (d).

3.29 Birth weight as a function of smoking behavior

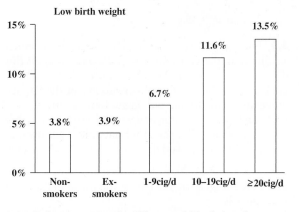

3.31 Life expectancy for White and Black females.

White females have a longer life expectancy than Black females, but the difference has shrunk considerably since 1920, though recent changes have been modest.

3.33 Plot of draft lottery data

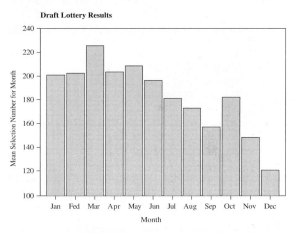

There is a clear drop in the mean lottery number across the year. The officials in charge hypothesized that there was probably insufficient mixing of the batches of numbers, which were put into the barrel a month at a time.

3.35 back to back stemplots

```
### Creating back to back stem-and-leaf
  displays.  Not covered in text.
library(aplpack)
grades <- read.table("http://www.uvm.
edu/~dhowell/methods9/DataFiles/Fig2-9.
dat", header = TRUE)
attach(grades)
males <- Grade[Sex == 1]
females <- Grade[Sex == 2]
stem.leaf.backback(males,females, m = 2)
# m controls bin size
```

CHAPTER 4

4.1 Mode = 72, Median = 72, Mean = 70.18

4.3 Even without reading the passage, students are still getting about twice as many items correct as they would by chance. This suggests that the test, which tests reading comprehension, is also testing something else. I am not surprised at these results because most students can guess at better than chance levels.

4.5 The mean falls above the median.

4.7 Rats running a straight-alley maze:

$$\Sigma X = 320; \overline{X} = \frac{\Sigma X}{N} = \frac{320}{15} = 21.33; \text{Median} = 21$$

4.9 Multiplying by a constant (5):

Original data   8   3   5   5   6   2   Mean = 4.833
Revised data   40   15   25   25   30   10   Mean = 24.17
                                          = 5 × 4.833

4.11 Measures of central tendency for ADDSC and GPA:

     ADDSC
         Mode = 50
         Median = 50
         Mean = 4629/88 = 52.6
     GPA
         Mode = 3.00
         Median = 2.635
         Mean = 216.15/88 = 2.46

4.13 The means are nearly the same for both conditions (Mean for Mirror = 1.6251 and mean for Same = 1.6269)

4.15 The only measure that is acceptable for nominal data is the mode, because the mode is the only one that does not depend on the relationships among the points on the scale.

4.17 Class attendance:

Regular attendees: Mean = 276.417; Median = 276
Poor attendees: Mean = 248.333; Median = 256

The two groups were 20 points apart in terms of the medians, and about 25 points apart in terms of means. Clearly those students who come to class do better.

4.19 This is an Internet activity for which there is no fixed answer.

4.21 This requires using the results of an Internet search.

4.23 The male optimists had a mean of 1.016 while the male pessimists had a mean of 0.945. This difference is reliable.

4.23 Trimmed mean

(a)

```
data <- read.table("Fig4-1.dat", header =
TRUE)
> attach(data)
> names(data)
[1] "NotRead"
> mean(NotRead)
[1] 46.57143
> mean(NotRead, trim = .1)
[1] 46.66667
```

(b)

```
errors <- c(10, 10, 10, 15, 15, 20, 20,
20, 20, 25, 25, 26, 27, 30, 32, 37, 39,
42, 68, 77)
mean(errors)
mean(errors, trim = .1)
hist(errors)

mean = 28.4
trimmed mean = 25.187
```

(c)   The second distribution is very skewed, as you can see from the histogram.

4.25 The Male Optimists had a mean of 1.016, while the Male Pessimists had a mean of 0.945. This difference is very reliable.

CHAPTER 5

5.1 Variability of NoPassage group:

       Range = 57 − 34 = 23
    Std. Dev. = 6.83
     Variance = 46.62

5.3 The variability of the NoPassage group is much smaller than the variability of the Passage group. If this difference turns out to be reliable, it could possibly be explained by the fact that the questions for the Passage group are asking for more than guessing and test-taking skills, and there may be greater variability due to variability in knowledge. On the other hand, it is not uncommon to find one standard deviation equal to two or three times another in small samples.

5.5 Percentages within two standard deviations in Exercise 5.2:

s = 10.61
$\overline{X} \pm 2(10.61) = 70.18 \pm 21.22 = 48.96 − 91.40$
16 scores (or 94%) lie within two standard deviations of the mean.

5.7 Multiplying or dividing by a constant:

Original	2	3	4	4	5	5	9	$\overline{X}_1 = 4.57$	$s_1 = 2.23$
$X \times 2$	4	6	8	8	10	10	18	$\overline{X}_2 = 9.14$	$s_2 = 4.45$
$X/2$	1	1.5	2	2	2.5	2.5	4.5	$\overline{X}_3 = 2.29$	$s_3 = 1.11$

5.9 Because adding or subtracting a constant will not change the standard deviation but will change the mean, I can subtract 3.27 from every score for X_2 in Exercise 5.8, making the mean 0 and keeping $s_2 = 1.0$. The new values are

$$-0.889 \quad 0.539 \quad -1.842 \quad 0.539 \quad -0.413 \quad 1.016$$
$$1.016 \quad \overline{X}_1 = 0 \; s_1 = 1.0$$

5.11 Boxplot for Exercise 5.1:

Median location = $(N + 1)/2 = 29/2 = 14.5$
Median = 46
Hinge location = (Median location + 1)/2
$\quad = 15/2 = 7.5$
Hinges = 43 and 52
H-spread = 52 − 43 = 9
Inner fences = Hinges ± 1.5 × H-spread = Hinges
$\quad \pm 1.5 \times 9$ = Hinges ± 13.5 = 29.5 and 65.5
Adjacent values = 34 and 57

5.13 Boxplot for ADDSC:

Median location = $(N + 1)/2 = 89/2 = 44.5$
Median = 50
Hinge location = (Median location + 1)/2
$\quad = 45/2 = 22.5$
Hinges = 44.5 and 60.5
H-spread = 60.5 − 44.5 = 16
Inner fences = Hinges ± 1.5 × H-spread = Hinges
$\quad \pm 1.5 \times 16$ = Hinges ± 24 = 20.5 and 85.5
Adjacent values = 26 and 78

5.15 The new variance is $(1 − 1/N)$ times the old variance.

5.17 Angle of rotation:

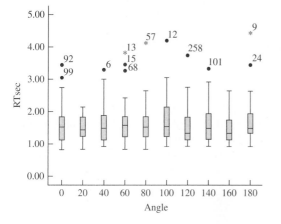

Stimulus: Mirror

5.19 The vertical bars lie at those points that cut off the minimum, the lowest 10%, the lowest 25%, the 50% point, the lowest 75%, the lowest 90%, and the maximum score. The diamond delineates the mean and a region around that mean that we will later identify as the 95% confidence interval. The mean is at the tallest point of the diamond. That is a lot of information for one simple graphic.

5.21 Treatment of anorexia:

I hypothesize that the two treatment groups will show more of a weight gain than the control group, but I have no reason to predict which treatment group would do better.

	Cognitive Behavior Therapy	Control	Family Therapy
Mean	3.01	−0.45	7.26
Median	1.40	−0.35	9.00
Std. Dev.	7.31	7.99	7.16

If we look at the changes from Before to After it appears that the Control group stayed about the same, but the two experimental groups increased their weight. This is true whether we look at means or medians. Notice that the standard deviation in the two experimental groups was noticeably higher after treatment, whereas the standard deviation of the Control actually decreased slightly. This suggests that some participants were helped more than others by the therapies.

5.23 For data on Cognitive Behavior Therapy

		Descriptive Statistics				
	N	Min-imum	Max-imum	Mean	Std. Deviation	Vari-ance
COGBEHAV	29	−9.10	20.90	3.0069	7.30850	53.414
Trim	19	−1.40	11.70	1.8000	3.04211	9.254
Winsor	29	−1.40	11.70	2.9552	4.88851	23.898
Valid N (listwise)	19					

Notice that the Winsorized variance is considerably greater than the trimmed variance, as it should be. However, it is lower than the variance of the original data, reflecting the fact that the extreme values have been replaced. Cognitive behavior scores were positively skewed, with several quite high values and one or two low values. Trimming and Winsorizing reduced the influence of those values. This causes the Winsorized variance to be considerably smaller than the original variance. The trimmed mean is considerably smaller than the original mean, but the Winsorized mean is only slightly smaller.

CHAPTER 6

6.1 Distribution of original values

For the first distribution the abscissa would take on the values of

| 1 | 2 | 3 | 4 | 5 | 6 | 7 |

For the second distribution the values would be

| −3 | −2 | −1 | 0 | 1 | 2 | 3 |

For the third distribution the values would be

| −1.90 | −1.27 | −0.63 | 0 | 0.63 | 1.27 | 1.90 |

6.3 Distribution of grades:

   (a) .6826
   (b) .5000
   (c) .8413

6.5 Katz's study:

   (a) 84.6
   (b) 80.0625
   (c) 25.65
   (d) I would conclude that they were not guessing.

6.7 Reading scores

   (b) 15.87%
   (c) 30.85%

6.9 A T score of 62.8 is the score that cuts off the top 10% of the distribution and is therefore a diagnostically meaningful cutoff.

6.11 (b) The probability of $z \geq 2.57 = .0051$. This is such a small probability that we will probably conclude that the student just made up the data rather than collecting them honestly.

6.13 (b) The easiest way to find the cutoff for the lowest 10% is to take the sample data and count them, empirically finding the point with 10% of the scores below it. Sometimes the simplest way is the best.

6.15 R code for above plot

```
y <- dnorm(seq(0,5, .1), mean =
mean(RTsec), sd = sd(RTsec))
x <- seq(0,5,.1)
hist(RTsec, breaks = 15, xlim =
c(0,5),ylim = c(0,.8), freq = FALSE)
par(new = TRUE)
plot(y~x, xlim = c(0,5), ylim = c(0,.8),
xlab = "", ylab = "", type = "l")
```

6.17 Identifying the highest 2% of Behavior Problem scores:

   The upper 2% is cut off by $z = 2.05$

$$2.05 = \frac{X - 50}{10}$$
$$2.05 \times 10 + 50 = X = 70.5$$

The critical cutoff is a score of 70.5.

6.19 The statisticians were upset because, by defining "overweight" as weighing more than 95% of peers (i.e., above the 95th percentile), the article seemed to be suggesting that there were 22% of children in the top 5%. Moreover, the article says that in 1986 only 8% of children were in the top 15%. That is just silly—it is analogous to "all of the children are above average." I assume that they meant to say that 22% (etc.) were above what the 95th percentile was some years ago, but that is a different thing. Even if that is the case, the results still look too extreme to be likely.

6.21 Histogram of combined data on emotional stability

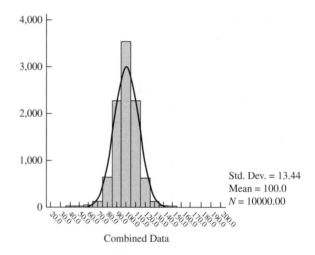

Notice that we have combined two normal distributions with the same mean, but the resulting distribution is not normal, as can be seen by comparing it to the superimposed normal curve. If the means were very different the distribution would become bimodal.

6.23 There are many out there. One is at http://davidmlane.com/hyperstat/z_table.html. An iPhone app named StatsMate will also work.

CHAPTER 7

7.1 Views of probability:

   (a) Analytic: If two tennis players are exactly equally skillful so that the outcome of their match is random, the probability is .50 that Player A will win the upcoming match.

   (b) Relative Frequency: If in past matches Player A has beaten Player B on 13 of the 17 occasions they have played, then Player A has a probability of $13/17 = .76$ of winning the upcoming match.

(c) Subjective: Player A's coach feels that she has a probability of .90 of winning the upcoming match with Player B.

7.3 More raffle tickets:

(a) .001
(b) .000001
(c) .000001
(d) .000002

7.5 Part (a) of Exercise 7.3 dealt with conditional probabilities.

7.7 An example of a conditional probability is the probability that you will go to see tonight's fireworks, given that the forecast is for rain.

7.9 $p(\text{mom looking}) = 2/13 = .154$; $p(\text{baby looking}) = 3/13 = .231$; $p(\text{both looking}) = 2/13 \times 3/13 = .154 \times .231 = .036$.

7.11 It would appear that having a message on a flyer increases the probability of proper disposal.

7.13 A continuous variable that is routinely treated as if it were discrete is children's learning abilities, where placement in classes often assumes that the child falls within one category or another.

7.15 The probability of admission is .02.

7.17 The probability associated with $z = -.21$ is .5832.

7.19 $p(\text{dropout} \mid \text{ADDSC} \geq 60) = 7/25 = .28$.

7.21 Conditional and unconditional probability of dropping out:

$p(\text{dropout}) = 10/88 = .11$
$p(\text{dropout} \mid \text{ADDSC} \geq 60) = .28$

Students are much more likely to drop out of school if they score at or above ADDSC = 60 in elementary school.

7.23 If there is no discrimination in housing, then a person's race and whether or not that person is offered a particular unit of housing are independent events. We could calculate the probability that a particular unit (or a unit in a particular section of the city) will be offered to anyone in a specific income group. We can then calculate the probability of that person being shown the unit, *assuming independence*, and compare that answer against the actual proportion of times a member of an ethnic minority was offered such a unit.

7.25 The data again would appear to show that the U. S. Attorneys are more likely to request the death penalty when the victim was White than when the victim was nonWhite. (This finding is statistically significant, though we won't address that question until Chapter 19.)

7.27 In this situation we begin with the hypothesis that African Americans are fairly represented in the population. If so, we would expect 0.43% of the pool of 2,124 people from which juries are drawn are African American. That comes out to be an expectation of 9.13 people. But the pool actually only had four African Americans. We would not expect exactly nine people—we might have seven or eight. But four sounds awfully small. That is such an unlikely event if the pool is fair that we would probably conclude that the pool is not a fair representation of the population of Vermont. An important point here is that this is a conditional probability. *If the pool is fair* the probability of this event is only .05—an unlikely result.

CHAPTER 8

8.1 Last night's hockey game:

(a) Null hypothesis: The game was actually an NHL hockey game.
(b) On the basis of that null hypothesis, I expected that each team would score somewhere between zero and six points. I then looked at the actual points and concluded that they were way out of line with what I would expect if this were an NHL hockey game. I therefore rejected the null hypothesis.

8.3 A Type I error would be concluding that I was short-changed when, in fact, I was not.

8.5 The rejection region is the set of outcomes for which we would reject the null hypothesis. The critical value would be the minimum amount of change below which I would reject the null. It is the border of the rejection region.

8.7 There really isn't anything to show here—either it works or it doesn't.

8.9 Guessing the height of the chapel.

(a) The null hypothesis is that the average of two guesses is as accurate as one guess. The alternative hypothesis is that the average guess is more accurate than the single guess.
(b) A Type I error would be to reject the null hypothesis when the two kinds of guesses are equally accurate. A Type II error would be failing to reject the null hypothesis when the average guess is better than the single guess.
(c) I would be tempted to use a one-tailed test simply because it is hard to image that the average guess would be *less* accurate, on average, than the single guess.

8.11 A sampling distribution is just a special case of a general distribution in which the thing that we are plotting is a statistic that is the result of repeated sampling.

8.13 Magen et al. (2008) study

(a) The null hypothesis is that the phrasing of the question will not affect the outcome—the means of the two groups are equal in the population. The alternative hypothesis is that the mean will depend on which condition the person is in.
(b) I would compare the two group means.
(c) If the difference is significant I would conclude that the phrasing of the choice makes a real difference in the outcome.

8.15 Rerunning Exercise 8.14 for $\alpha = .01$:

We first have to find the cutoff for $\alpha = .01$ under a normal distribution. The critical value of $z = 2.33$ (one-tailed), which corresponds to a raw score of 42.69 (from a population with $\mu = 59$ and $\sigma = 7$).

We then find where 42.69 lies relative to the distribution under H_1:

$$z = \frac{X - \mu}{\sigma} = \frac{42.69 - 50}{7} = -1.04$$

From the appendix we find that 85.08% of the scores fall above this cutoff. Therefore $\beta = .851$.

8.17 To determine whether there is a true relationship between grades and course evaluations, I would find a statistic that reflected the degree of relationship between two variables. (You will see such a statistic, r, in the next chapter.) I would then calculate the sampling distribution of that statistic in a situation in which there is no relationship between two variables. Finally, I would calculate the statistic for a representative set of students and classes and compare my sample value with the sampling distribution of that statistic.

8.19 Allowances for fourth-grade students:

(a) The null hypothesis in this case would be the hypothesis that boys and girls receive the same allowance on average.
(b) I would use a two-tailed test because I want to reject the null hypothesis whenever there is a difference in favor of one gender over the other.
(c) I would reject the null hypothesis whenever the obtained difference between the average allowances was greater than I would be led to expect if they were paid the same in the population.
(d) I would increase the sample size and get something other than a self-report of allowances.

8.21 Hypothesis testing and the judicial system:

The judicial system operates in ways similar to our standard logic of hypothesis testing. However, in a court we are particularly concerned with the danger of convicting an innocent person. In a trial the null hypothesis is equivalent to the assumption that the accused person is innocent. We set a very small probability of a Type I error, which is far smaller than we normally do in an experiment. Presumably the jury tries to set that probability as close to 0 as they reasonably can. By setting the probability of a Type I error so low they knowingly allow the probability of a Type II error (releasing a guilty person) to rise because that is thought to be the lesser evil.

CHAPTER 9

9.1 The two outliers would appear to have a distorting effect on the correlation coefficient. However, if you replot the data without those points the relationship is still apparent and the correlation only drops to –.54.

9.3 With 24 degrees of freedom, and two-tailed test at $\alpha = .05$ would require $r > \pm .388$.

9.5 We can conclude that infant mortality is closely tied to both income and the availability of contraception. Infants born to people living in poverty are much more likely to die before their first birthday, and the availability of contraception significantly reduces the number of infants put at risk in the first place.

9.7 Because both income and contraception are related to mortality, we might expect that using them together would lead to a substantial increase in predictability. But note that they are correlated with each other, and therefore share some of the same variance.

9.9 Psychologists have a professional interest in infant mortality because some of the variables that contribute to infant mortality are behavioral ones, and we care about understanding, and often controlling, behavior. Psychologists have an important role to play in world health that has little to do with pills and irrigation systems.

9.11 R Code Taken from chapter

```
DownData <-
read.table("http://www.uvm.edu/~dhowell/
fundamentals8/DataFiles/Ex9-10.dat",
header = TRUE)
attach(DownData)
pctDown <- Down/Births
plot(Age,Births)
plot(Age, pctDown)
ranks <- rank(pctDown)
plot(Age, ranks)
cor(Age, ranks)
```

9.13 If you convert the dependent variable to ranks (or if you convert it to logs), the relationship becomes much more linear because you have reduced the influence of the higher incidence rates. The relationship has gone from exponential to nearly linear, although I don't know what you have really gained in explanatory power over what you see in the figure above.

This is not a Spearman correlation because we have only ranked one of the variables.

9.15 The relationship between test scores in Katz's study and SAT scores for application purposes is a relevant question because we would not be satisfied with a set of data that used SAT questions and yet gave answers that were not in line with SAT performance. We want to know that the tests are measuring at least roughly the same thing. In addition, by knowing the correlation between SATs and performance without seeing the questions, we get a better understanding of some of what the SAT is measuring.

9.17 Correlation for the data in Exercise 9.14:

SAT: mean = 598.57 $\quad \Sigma X = 16760$ $\quad$ Std. Dev. = 61.57
Test: mean = 46.21 $\quad \Sigma Y = 1294$ $\quad$ Std. Dev. = 6.73

$$COV_{YX} = \frac{\Sigma XY - \dfrac{\Sigma X \Sigma Y}{N}}{N-1}$$

$$= \frac{780500 - \dfrac{16760 \times 1294}{28}}{27} = 220.3175$$

$$r = \frac{cov_{YX_1}}{s_Y s_{X_1}} = \frac{220.3175}{61.57 \times 6.73} = .53$$

With 26 *df* we would need a correlation of .374 to be significant. Because our value exceeds that, we report that there is strong evidence that relationship between test scores and the SAT is reliably different from 0.

9.19 When we say that two correlations are not significantly different we mean that they are sufficiently close that they could both have come from samples from populations with exactly the same population correlation coefficient.

9.21 The answer to this question depends on the student's expectations.

9.23 It is sometimes appropriate to find the correlation between two variables even if you know that the

relationship is slightly curvilinear. A straight line often does a remarkably good job of fitting a curved function provided that it is not too curved.

9.25 The amount of money that a country spends on health care may have little to do with life expectancy because to change a country's life expectancy you would have to change the health of a great many people. Spending a great deal of money on one person, even if it were to extend his or her life by dozens of years, would not change the average life expectancy in any noticeable way. Often the things that make a major change in life expectancy, such as inoculations, really cost very little money.

9.27 Extremely exaggerated data on male and female weight and height to show a negative slope within gender but a positive slope across gender:

Height	68	72	66	69	70
Weight	185	175	190	180	180
Gender	Male	Male	Male	Male	Male

Height	66	60	64	65	63
Weight	135	155	145	140	150
Gender	Fem.	Fem.	Fem.	Fem.	Fem.

9.29 We have confounding effects here. If we want to claim that red wine consumption lowers the incidence of heart disease, we have a problem because the consumption of red wine is highest in those areas with the greatest solar radiation, which is another potential cause of the effect. We would have to look at the relationship between red wine and heart disease controlling for the effects of solar radiation.

9.31 This is an Internet question with no fixed answer.

9.33 Using R is tricky because you need to install the MBESS package and the gsl package. The easier way is to computer the correlation (.3805) and use the package that I refer to in the question. The result will be

| r = | .3805 | Reset |
| n = | 50 | Calculate |

0.95 and 0.99 Confidence Intervals of rho

	Lower Limit	Upper Limit
0.95	0.115	0.595
0.99	0.025	0.65

CHAPTER 10

10.1 $\hat{Y} = 0.0689X + 3.53$

10.3 The predicted percentage of LBW infants would be 8.35.

10.5 I would be more comfortable speaking about the effects on Senegal because it is already at approximately the mean income level and we are not extrapolating for extreme values of X.

10.7 $\hat{Y} = 109.13$

10.9 Subtracting 10 points from every X or Y score would not change the correlation in the slightest. The relationship between X and Y would remain the same—only the intercept would change.

10.11 Diagram to illustrate Exercise 10.10:

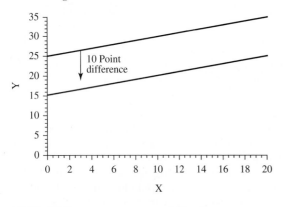

10.13 Adding a constant to each Y value:

(a) Adding 2.5 to Y simply raised the regression line by 2.5 units.
(b) The correlation would be unaffected.

10.15 $\hat{Y} = -0.0426X + 4.699$

10.17 The correlation dropped to $-.478$ when I added and subtracted .04 from each Y value. This drop was caused by the addition of error variance.

One way to solve for the point at which they become equal is to plot a few predicted values and draw regression lines. Where the lines cross is the point at which they are equal. A more exact way is to set the two equations equal to each other and solve for X.

$$0.9X + 31 = 1.5X + 18$$

Collecting terms we get

$$31 - 18 = 1.5X - 0.9X$$

$$13 = 0.6X$$

$$X = 13/0.6 = 21.67$$

To check this, substitute 21.67 in both equations

$$0.9 \times 21.67 + 31 = 50.503 = 1.5 \times 21.67 + 18$$

10.19 Weight as a function of height for males:

(b) $\hat{Y} = 4.356\ Height - 149.93$ The intercept is -149.93, which has no interpretable meaning with these data. The slope of 4.356 tells us that a one-unit increase in height is associated with a 4.356 increase in weight.
(c) The correlation is .60, telling us that for females 36% of the variability in weight is associated with variability in height.
(d) Both the correlation and the slope are significantly different from 0 as shown by an $F = 31.54$ and an (equivalent) t of 5.616.

10.21 $\hat{Y} = 4.356 \times 68 - 149.93 = 146.28$

(a) The residual is $Y - \hat{Y} = 156 - 146.28 = 9.72$.
(b) If students who supplied the data gave biased responses, then, to the degree that the data are biased, the coefficients are biased and the prediction will not apply accurately to me.

10.23 12.28 pounds

10.25 $\hat{Y} = -0.014 \times Trial + 67.805$

The slope is only -0.014 and it is not remotely significant. For this set of data we can conclude that there is not a linear trend for reaction times to change over time. From the scatterplot we can see no hint of a nonlinear pattern either.

10.27 The evils of television:

(b) Boys: $\hat{Y} = -4.821X + 283.61$
Girls: $\hat{Y} = -3.460X + 268.39$

The slopes are roughly equal given the few data points we have, with a slightly greater decrease with increased time for boys. The difference in intercepts reflects the fact that the line for girls is about nine points below that for boys.
(c) Television cannot be used as an explanation for poorer scores in girls, because we see that girls score below boys even when we control for television viewing.

10.29 Dropping pencils:

(a) As you move the pencil vertically you are changing the intercept.
(b) As you rotate the pencil you are changing the slope.
(c) You can come up with a very good line simply by rotating and raising or lowering your pencil so as to make the deviations from the line as small as

possible. (We really want to minimize squared deviations, but I don't expect that anyone's eyes are
good enough to notice the difference.)

10.31 Galton's data

(a) The correlation is .459 and the regression equation is $\hat{Y} = .646 \times$ midparent $+ 23.942$. (Remember to weight cases by "freq".)

(b) I reran the regression requesting that
SPSS save the unstandardized prediction and
residual.

(d) The children in the lowest quartile slightly
exceed their parents' mean (67.12 versus 66.66)
and those in the highest quartile average
slightly shorter than their parents (68.09 versus
68.31).

(e) It is easiest if you force both axes to have the
same range and specify that the regression line is
$\hat{Y} = 1 \times X + 0$. (If you prefer, you can use an intercept of 0.22 to equate the means of the parents
and children.)

(c)

Descriptives

		N	Mean	Std. Deviation	Std. Error	95% Confidence Interval for Mean Lower Bound	Upper Bound	Minimum	Maximum
Child	1.00	392	67.1247	2.24664	.11347	66.9017	67.3478	61.70	72.20
	2.00	219	68.0196	2.24030	.15139	67.7213	68.3180	61.70	73.20
	3.00	183	68.7055	2.46458	.18219	68.3460	69.0649	63.20	73.70
	4.00	134	70.1776	2.26850	.19597	69.7900	70.5652	61.70	73.70
	Total	928	68.0885	2.51794	.08266	67.9263	68.2507	61.70	73.70
Midparent	1.00	392	66.6633	1.06808	.05395	66.5572	66.7693	64.00	67.50
	2.00	219	68.5000	.00000	.00000	68.5000	68.5000	68.50	68.50
	3.00	183	69.5000	.00000	.00000	69.5000	69.5000	69.50	69.50
	4.00	134	71.1791	.78617	.06791	71.0448	71.3134	70.50	73.00
	Total	928	68.3082	1.78733	.05867	68.1930	68.4233	64.00	73.00

CHAPTER 11

11.1 Predicting quality of life:

(a) All other variables held constant, a difference
of +1 degree in Temperature is associated with a
difference of −.01 in perceived Quality of Life. A
difference of $1000 in median income, again with
all other variables held constant, is associated with
a +.05 difference in perceived Quality of Life. A
similar interpretation applies to b_3 and b_4. Because
values of 0 cannot reasonably occur for all predictors, the intercept has no meaningful interpretation.

(b) $\hat{Y} = 5.37 - 0.01(55) + 0.05(12)$
$+0.003(500) - 0.01(200) = 4.92$

(c) $\hat{Y} = 5.37 - 0.01(55) + 0.05(12)$
$+ 0.003(100) - 0.01(200) = 3.72$

11.3 Religious Influence and religious Hope contribute significantly to the prediction, but not religious
Involvement.

11.5 I would have speculated that religious Involvement
was not a significant predictor because of its overlap with

the other predictors, but the tolerances kick a hole in
that theory to some extent.

11.7 $R = .173$

$$R^{*2} = 1 - \frac{(1 - R^2)(N - 1)}{(N - p - 1)}$$

$$= 1 - \frac{(1 - .173)(14)}{(15 - 4 - 1)} = -.158$$

Because a squared value cannot be negative, we will declare it undefined. This is all the more reasonable in light
of the fact that we cannot reject $H_0: R^* = 0$.

11.9 The multiple correlation between the predictors
and the percentage of births under 2,500 grams is .855.
The incidence of low birth weight increases when there
are more mothers under 17, when mothers have fewer
than 12 years of education, and when mothers are unmarried. All of the predictors are associated with young
mothers. (As the question noted, there are too few observations for a meaningful analysis of the variables in
question.)

11.11 The multiple correlation between Depression and the three predictor variables was significant, with $R = 0.49$ [$F(3, 131) = 14.11$, $p = .0000$]. Thus approximately 25% of the variability in Depression can be accounted for by variability in these predictors. The results show us that depression among students who have lost a parent through death is positively associated with an elevated level of perceived vulnerability to future loss and negatively associated with the level of social support. The age at which the student lost his or her parent does not appear to play a role.

11.13 The fact that the frequency of the behavior was not a factor in reporting is an interesting finding. My first thought would be that it is highly correlated with Offensiveness, and that Offensiveness is carrying the burden. But a look at the simple correlation shows that the two variables are correlated at less than $r = .20$.

11.15 The multiple correlation for *my* data was .739, which is astonishingly high. Fortunately the *F* test on the regression is not significant. Notice that we have only twice as many subjects as predictors.

11.17 Predicting weight:

Coefficients[a]

		Unstandardized Coefficients		Standardized Coefficients		
Model		B	Std. Error	Beta	*t*	Sig.
1	(Constant)	−204.741	29.160		−7.021	.000
	height	5.092	.424	.785	12.016	.000
2	(Constant)	−88.199	43.777		−2.015	.047
	height	3.691	.572	.569	6.450	.000
	sex	−14.700	4.290	−.302	−3.426	.001

[a]Dependent Variable: weight

11.19 The weighted average is 3.68, which is very close to the regression coefficient for Height when we control for Gender.

11.21 Gender is important to include in this relationship because women tend to be smaller than men, and thus probably have smaller (though not less effective) brains. We probably don't want that contamination in our data. However, note that Gender was not significant in the previous answer, though the sample size (and hence power) is low.

11.23 A nuisance variable is usually a variable that confuses the relationship between other variables. It is not necessarily an unimportant variable, and the choice of name is not a good one.

11.25 The correlation between our best estimates of Distress2 and the actual values of Distress2 is .434, which is the multiple correlation.

CHAPTER 12

12.3 Mean = 4.1, standard deviation = 2.82. These are reasonably close to the parameters of the population for which the sample was drawn. The mean of the distribution of means is 4.28, which is somewhat closer to the population mean, and the standard deviation is 1.22

(a) The Central Limit Theorem predicts a sampling distribution of the mean with a mean of 4.5 and a standard deviation of $2.6/\sqrt{5} = 1.16$.
(b) These values are close to the values that we would expect.

12.5 If you had drawn 50 samples of size 15 the mean of the sampling distribution would still approximate the mean of the population, but the standard error of that distribution would now be only $2.6/\sqrt{15} = 0.689$.

12.7 First, these students scored better than we might have predicted, not worse. Second, these students are certainly not a random sample of high school students. Finally, there is no definition of what is meant by "a terrible state," nor any idea of whether the SAT measures such a concept.

12.9 Unlike the results in the two previous questions, this interval probably is a fair estimate of the confidence interval for P/T ratio across the country. It is not itself biased by the bias in the sampling of SAT scores.

12.11 $t = 2.22$, $p < .05$. Reject the null hypothesis and conclude that the girls gained weight at better than chance levels in this experiment.

12.13 The data are all over the place, with some gains as large as 20.9 lbs and some as low as −9.1. I suspect that we have an effect that works for some participants but not for others.

12.15 The best measure of effect size is to report the result in pounds gained, which is 3.01. However for those who want a more involved measure we can calculate

$$\hat{d} = \frac{\overline{X}}{s} = \frac{3.01}{7.3} = 0.41.$$

The problem with this measure is that it uses the standard deviation of gain scores, which is not a very satisfying metric.

12.17 I needed to solve for *t* instead of z because I did not know the population variance.

12.19 $t = -3.50$. With 35 *df* the critical value of *t* at $\alpha = .05$ is ± 2.03. We can reject H_0 and conclude that children under stress show significantly lower levels of anxiety than children in the general population.

12.21 The results in Exercise 12.18 are consistent with the *t* test in Exercise 12.17. The *t* test showed that these children showed lower levels of anxiety than the normal population, and the confidence interval did not include the general population mean of 14.55.

CHAPTER 13

13.1 $t = -0.48$. Do not reject the null hypothesis. This is a matched-sample t because responses came from married couples. We would hope that there is some relationship between the sexual satisfaction of one member of the couple and the other, but perhaps that is asking too much.

13.3 This analysis finally addresses the degree of compatibility between couples. The correlation is significant, but it is not very large.

13.5 The most important thing about a t test is the assumption that the mean (or difference between means) is normally distributed. Even though the individual values can range only over the integers 1 – 4, the mean of 91 subjects can take on any number of values between 1 and 4. It is a continuous variable for all practical purposes and can exhibit substantial variability.

13.7 We used a paired t test because the data were paired in the sense of coming from the same subject. Some subjects showed generally more beta-endorphins at any time than others, and we wanted to eliminate this subject-to-subject variability.

13.9 If we look at the actual numbers given in Exercise 13.6 we would generally be led to expect that whatever was used to measure beta-endorphins was accurate only to the nearest half unit. But then where did 5.8 and 4.7 come from?

13.11 You would not want to use a repeated-measures design in any situation where the first measure will "tip off" or sensitize participants to what comes next.

13.13 How many participants do we need?

First of all, in Exercise 13.6 we had 19 participants, giving us 18 df. This means that for a one-tailed test at $\alpha = .01$ we will need a t of at least 2.552 to be significant. So we can substitute everything we know about the data except for the N and then solve for N. $N = 4.481^2 = 21$ participants.

13.15 As the correlation between the two variables increases, the standard error of the difference will decrease and the resulting t will increase.

13.17 Student's $t = -0.319$. Notice that this is the same t as we had in Exercise 13.12. This is because there is a perfect linear relationship between first, second, and average guesses. (If you know the first guess and the average, you can compute what the second guess must have been.)

13.19 If I subtracted the Before scores from the After scores I would simply change the sign of the mean difference and the sign of t. There would be no other effect.

13.21 There is no answer I can give for this question because it asks the students to design a study.

CHAPTER 14

14.1 $t = -0.40$. We can conclude that we have no reason to doubt the hypothesis that males and females are equal with respect to sexual satisfaction.

14.3 The difference between the t in Exercises 13.1 and 14.1 is small because the relationship between the two variables was so small.

14.5 Random assignment plays the role of ensuring (as much as possible) that there is no systematic difference between the subjects assigned to the two groups. Without random assignment it might be possible that those who signed up for the family therapy condition were more motivated or had more serious problems than those in the control group.

14.7 You cannot use random assignment to homophobic categories for a study such as this because the group assignment is the property of the participants themselves.

14.9 In Exercise 14.8 it could well have been that there was much less variability in the schizophrenic group than in the normal group because the number of TATs showing positive parent–child relationships could have had a floor effect at 0.0. This did not happen but it is important to check for it anyway.

14.11 Experimenter bias effect:

$$t = 0.587 \; [t_{.05}(15) = \pm 2.131]$$

Do not reject the null hypothesis. We cannot conclude that our data show the experimenter bias effect.

14.13 Effect size for Ex14.11

$$d = \frac{\overline{X}_1 - \overline{X}_2}{s_p} = \frac{1.153}{\sqrt{16.359}} = \frac{1.153}{4.045} = 0.285$$

14.15 Comparing GPA for those with low and high ADDSC scores:

$t = 3.77$. Reject H_0 and conclude that people with high ADDSC scores in elementary school have a lower grade point average in ninth grade than people with lower scores.

14.17 The answer to 14.15 tells you that ADDSC scores have significant predictability of grade point average several years later. Moreover the answer to Exercise 14.16 tells you that this difference is substantial.

14.19 Anger with a reason is just fine.

$$s_p^2 = 5.9466; t = 3.01$$

The critical value is approximately 2.00, so we will reject the null hypothesis and conclude that when given a reason for a woman's anger, she is given more status than when no reason was given for the anger.

(c) We certainly would appear to have a double standard.

14.21 If the variances are equal they will also be equal to the pooled variance.

14.23 *R* on Ex14.8

```
data
<- read.table("http://www.uvm.edu/~dhowe
ll/fundamentals9/DataFiles/Ex14-8.dat",
header = TRUE)
attach(data)
Group = factor(Group)
t.test(Number ~ Group, alternative =
c("two.sided"), var.equal = TRUE)
_____

Two Sample t-test
data:  Number by Group
t = 2.662, df = 38, p-value = 0.01132
alternative hypothesis: true difference in
means is not equal to 0
95 percent confidence interval:
0.3472894 2.5527106
sample estimates:
mean in group 1 mean in group 2
          3.55            2.10
```

CHAPTER 15

15.1 Power using Lenth's program.

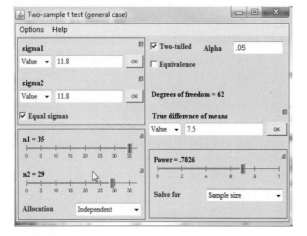

15.3 Power for socially desirable responses:

Assume the population mean = 4.39 and the population standard deviation = 2.61.
   (a) Effect size = 0.20
   (b) Delta = 1.20
   (c) Power = .22

15.5 Sample sizes (before rounding):

   156.25, 196.00, and 264.06

15.7 Diagram of Exercise 15.6:

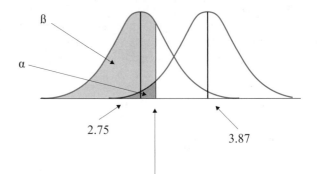

$$2.987 = 3.87 - 2.03 * 2.61 / \sqrt{36}$$

15.9 Avoidance behavior in rabbits using a one-sample *t* test:

   (a) For power = .50, $N = 15.21 = 16$
   (b) For power = .80, $N = 31.36 = 32$

15.11 With $\delta = 1.46$, power = .31.

15.13 Modifying Exercise 15.12:

   (a) Power = .22
   (b) $t = -1.19$. Do not reject the null hypothesis.
   (c) The *t* numerically equals δ, although *t* is calculated from statistics and δ is calculated from parameters. In other words δ is equal to the *t* we would get if the sample means and standard deviations were equal to the corresponding parameters.

15.15 The result with the smaller sample size impresses me more because it generally takes a larger effect to find significance with a smaller sample size.

15.17 Assuming equal standard deviations, the high-school dropout group of 25 would result in a higher estimate of δ and therefore a higher level of power.

15.19 Total Sample Sizes Required for Power = .60, $\alpha = .05$, Two-Tailed ($\delta = 2.20$)

Effect Size	γ	One-Sample t	Two-Sample t (per group)	Two-Sample t (overall)
Small	0.20	121	242	484
Medium	0.50	20	39	78
Large	0.80	8	16	32

15.21 The mean under H_1 should fall at the critical value under H_0. The question implies a one-tailed test. Thus the mean is 1.645 standard errors about μ_0, which is 100. Power $= \beta$ when $\mu = 104.935$.

15.23 Power $= .75$.

15.25 I will use R to solve Exercise 15.3, but the rest of the solutions can follow using modifications of this same code.

```
### The following is the important infor-
mation from the help file for pwr.t.test.
#pwr.t.test(n = NULL, d = NULL, sig.level
= 0.05, power = NULL,
      type = c("two.sample", "one.sample",
"paired"), alternative = c("two.sided",
      "less","greater"))
#Arguments
#n   Number of observations (per sample)
#d   Effect size
#sig.level      Significance level (Type I
error probability)
#power   Power of test (1 minus Type II
error probability)
#type          Type of t test : one- two- or
paired-samples
#alternative   a character string speci-
fying the alternative hypothesis, must be
one of "two.sided" (default), "greater" or
"less"

# First I will calculate the effect size
for Ex15.3
mu1 = 4.39
mu0 <- 3.87
sp <- 2.61
d <- (mu1 - mu0)/sp
pwr.t.test(n = 36, d = d, sig.level =
.05, type = "one.sample")

One-sample t test power calculation
          n = 36
          d = 0.1992337
  sig.level = 0.05
      power = 0.2135633
alternative = two.sided
```

CHAPTER 16

16.1 Analysis of Eysenck's data:

(a) The analysis of variance:

Source	df	SS	MS	F
Treatment	1	266.45	266.45	25.23*
Error	18	190.10	10.56	
Total	19	456.55		

* $p < .05$

(b) $t = 5.02$. Reject the null hypothesis.

16.3 Expanding on Exercise 16.2:

(a) Combine the Low groups together and the High groups together:

Source	df	SS	MS	F
Treatment	1	792.10	792.10	59.45*
Error	38	506.30	13.324	
Total	39	1298.40		

* $p < .05$

We have compared recall under conditions of Low versus High processing and can conclude that higher levels of processing lead to significantly better recall. (b) The answer is still a bit difficult to interpret because both groups contain both younger and older participants, and it is possible that the effect holds for one age group but not for the other.

16.5 η^2 and ω^2 for the data in Exercise 16.1:

$\eta^2 = .58$ and $\omega^2 = .55$.

16.7 Foa et al. study:

Source	df	SS	MS	F
Treatment	3	507.84	169.28	3.04*
Error	41	2279.07	55.59	
Total	44	2786.91		

* $p < .05$

(c) It would appear that the more intervention-ist treatments lead to fewer symptoms than the less interventionist ones, although we would have to run multiple comparison tests to tell exactly which groups are different from which other groups.

16.9 R code for Ex16.7

This code generates random data, so the means and standard deviations will not be exact. But the set.seed(3086) should produce a result that is significant.

```
# Generate data
set.seed(3086)
ST <- round(rnorm(14, 11.07, 3.95), digits
= 2)
PE <- round(rnorm(10, 15.40, 11.12), dig-
its = 2)
SC <- round(rnorm(11, 18.09, 7.13), digits
= 2)
WL <- round(rnorm(10, 19.5, 7.11), digits
= 2)
dv <- c(ST, PE, SC, WL)
group <- factor(a <- rep(c(1,2,3,4), c(14,
10, 11, 10)))
model <- lm(dv ~ group)
anova(model)
```

16.11 If the sample sizes in Exercise 16.7 were twice as large, that would double the SS_{treat} and MS_{treat}. However it would have no effect on MS_{error}, which is simply the average of the group variances. The result would be that the F value would be doubled.

16.13 R code for analysis of Exercise 16.2

```
#Ex16.13
data <- read.table("https://www.uvm.
edu/~dhowell/fundamentals9/DataFiles/
  Tab16-1.dat", header = TRUE)
attach(data)
group <- factor(group) # IMPORTANT! Spec-
ify that group is a factor
model1 <- lm(dv ~ group) # Calculate the
linear model of dv predicted from group
anova(model1)
16.13  Effect size for tests in Exercise
16.10.
```

16.15 Effect size for tests in Exercise 16.10. It only makes sense to calculate an effect size for significant comparisons in this study, so we will deal with SIT *versus* SC.

$$\hat{d} = \frac{\overline{X}_{SC} - \overline{X}_{SIT}}{\sqrt{MS_{error}}} = \frac{18.09 - 11.07}{\sqrt{55.579}} = \frac{7.02}{7.455} = 0.94$$

The SIT group is nearly a full standard deviation lower in symptoms when compared to the SC group, which is a control group.

16.17 ANOVA for ADDSC data

Source	df	SS	MS	F
Treatment	2	22.50	11.25	22.74*
Error	85	42.06	0.49	
Total	87	64.56		

* $p < .05$

16.19 Darley and Latané study:

Source	df	SS	MS	F
Treatment	2	0.854	0.427	8.06*
Error	49	2.597	0.053	
Total	51	3.451		

* $p < .05$

We can reject the null hypothesis and conclude that subjects are less likely to summon help quickly if there are other bystanders around.

16.21 Bonferroni test on data in Exercise 16.2:

For Young/Low versus Old/Low $t = -0.434$

For Young/High versus Old/High $t = 6.34$

There is clearly not a significant difference between young and old subjects on tasks requiring little cognitive processing, but there is a significant difference for tasks requiring substantial cognitive processing. The probability that *at least* one of these statements represents a Type I error is at most .05.

16.23 Comparison of WL and SIT:

$\hat{d} = 1.18$. The two groups differ by more than a standard deviation.

16.25 Spilich et al. study:

Source	df	SS	MS	F
Treatment	2	2643.38	1321.69	4.74*
Error	42	11700.40	278.58	
Total	44	14343.78		

* $p < .05$

Here we have a task that involves more cognitive involvement, and it does show a difference due to smoking condition.

16.27 Spilich et al. data on driving simulation:

Source	df	SS	MS	F
Treatment	2	437.64	218.82	9.26*
Error	42	992.67	23.64	
Total	44	1430.31		

* $p < .05$

Here we have a case in which the active smokers again performed worse than the nonsmokers, and the differences are significant.

16.29 Analysis of Langlois & Roggman:

(a) The research hypothesis would be the hypothesis that faces averaged over more photographs would be judged more attractive than faces averaged over fewer photographs.

(b) $F = 3.134$

(c) The group means are significantly different. From the descriptive statistics we can see that the means consistently rise as we increase the number of faces over which the composite was created.

16.31 Analysis EX.27 using R

```
data16.27 <- read.table("http://www.uvm.
edu/~dhowell/fundamentals9/DataFiles/Ex16-
25.dat", header = TRUE)
attach(data16.27)
Smkgrp <- factor(Smkgrp)
model2 <- lm(Errors ~ Smkgrp)
anova(model2)
```

```
Analysis of Variance Table
Response: Errors
        Df Sum Sq Mean Sq F value    Pr(>F)
Smkgrp 2  437.64 218.822 9.2584 0.0004665 ***
Residuals 42 992.67   23.635
```

```
16.32 Probability value for Ex16.31
prob <- 1-pf(9.258, df1 = 2, df2 = 42)
prob
[1] 0.000466617
```

CHAPTER 17

17.1 Thomas and Wang study:

(a) This design can be characterized as a 3×2 factorial, with three levels of Strategy and two levels of Delay.

(b) I expect that recall will be better when participants generate their own key words, and worse when participants are in the role-learning condition. I also expect better recall for a shorter retention interval.

(c)

Strategy	Delay	Mean	Std. Dev.	Cases
Gen.	5 min	14.92	5.33	13
Gen.	2 day	4.00	2.52	13
Prov	5 min	20.54	1.98	13
Prov.	2 day	2.00	1.47	13
Rote	5 min	15.38	5.45	13
Rote	2 day	12.77	6.80	13

17.3 Analysis of variance:

Source	df	SS	MS	F
Strategy	2	281.26	140.63	7.22*
Delay	1	2229.35	2229.35	114.53*
S × D	2	824.54	412.27	21.18*
Error	72	1401.54	19.47	
Total	77	4736.68		

* $p < .05$

There are significant differences due to both Strategy and Delay, but more importantly, there is a significant interaction.

17.5 Bonferroni test of data in Exercise 17.4:

For Data at five-minute delay:

Gen. versus Prov. Gen. versus Rote Prov. versus Rote
  $t = -3.15$ $t = -.26$ $t = 2.89$

For Data at two-day delay:

Gen. versus Prov. Gen. versus Rote Prov. versus Rote
  $t = 1.19$ $t = -5.24$ $t = -6.43$

For six comparisons with 36 df the critical value of t is 2.80.

For the five-minute delay the condition with the key words provided by the experimenter is significantly better than both the condition in which the participants generated their own key words and the rote learning condition. The latter two are not different from each other.

For the two-day delay the rote learning condition is better than either of the other two conditions, which do not differ from each other.

We clearly see distinct patterns of differences in the two delay conditions. The most surprising result is the superiority of rote learning with a two-day delay.

17.7 The results in the last few exercises suggest to me that if I were studying for a Spanish exam I would fall back on rote learning, painful as it sounds and as much against common wisdom as it is.

17.9 In this experiment we have as many primiparous mothers and multiparous ones, which certainly does not reflect the population. Similarly, we have as many LBW infants as full-term ones, which is not a reflection of reality. The mean for primiparous mothers is based on an equal number of LBW and full-term infants, which we know is not representative of the population. Comparisons between groups are still legitimate, but it makes no sense to take the mean of all primiparous moms combined as a reflection of any meaningful population value.

17.11 Simple effects versus *t* tests for Exercise 17.10.

(a) If I had run a *t* test between those means my result would simply be the square root of the $F = 1.328$ that I obtained.

(b) If I used MS_{error} for my estimated error term it would give me a *t* that is the square root of the *F* that I would have had if I had used the overall MS_{error}, instead of the MS_{error} obtained in computing the simple effect.

17.13 Analysis of variance for Exercise 17.12:

Source	df	SS	MS	F
Task	2	28,661.53	14,330.76	132.90*
Smokegrp	2	354.55	177.27	1.64
T × S	4	2728.65	682.16	6.33*
Error	126	13,587.20	107.84	
Total	134	45,331.93		

* *p* < .05

The main effect of Task and the interaction are significant. The main effect of Task is of no interest because there is no reason why different tasks should be equally difficult. We don't care about the main effect of Smoking either because it is created by large effects for two levels of Task and no effect for the third. What is important is the interaction.

17.15 Simple effects to clarify the Spilich et al. Example.

We have already seen these simple effects in Chapter 16, in Exercises 16.18, 16.19, and 16.21.

17.17 Further analysis of Exercise 16.3:

Source	df	SS	MS	F
Age	1	115.60	115.60	17.44*
HiLo	1	792.10	792.10	119.51*
A × H	1	152.10	152.10	22.95*
Error	36	238.60	6.63	
Total	39	1298.40		

* *p* < .05

We have a significant effect due to age, with younger subjects outperforming older subjects, and a significant effect due to the level of processing, with better recall of material processed at a higher level. Most importantly, we have a significant interaction, reflecting the fact that there is no important difference between younger and older subjects for the task with low levels of processing, but there is a big difference when the task calls for a high

level of processing—younger subjects seem to benefit more from that processing (or do more of it).

17.19

Source	df	SS	MS	F
E (Education)	1	67.69	67.69	6.39*
G (Group)	2	122.79	61.40	5.80*
EG	2	20.38	10.19	<1
Error	42	444.62	10.59	
Total	47	655.48		

* *p* < .05

(b) The program worked as intended and there was no interaction between groups and educational level.

17.21 $\hat{d}$ for level of processing study

$$\hat{d} = 3.46 \text{ (Using } MS_{error})$$

This is a very large effect size, but the data show an extreme difference between the two levels of processing

17.23 No main effects but interaction:

Cell means:

8	12
12	8

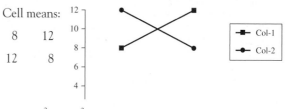

17.25 η^2 and ω^2

Strategy	$\eta^2 = .06$	$\omega^2 = .05$
Delay	$\eta^2 = .47$	$\omega^2 = .46$
S × D	$\eta^2 = .17$	$\omega^2 = .16$

17.27 Calculation of magnitude of effect for Exercise 17.13

Task	$\eta^2 = .63$	$\omega^2 = .63$
Smoke	$\eta^2 = .04$	$\omega^2 = .04$
T × S	$\eta^2 = .03$	$\omega^2 = .02$

17.29 The two magnitude of effect measures (η^2 and ω^2) will agree when the error term is small relative to the effect in question, and will disagree when there is a substantial amount of error relative to the effect. To some extent, all other things equal, the two terms will be in closer agreement when there are several degrees of freedom for the treatment effect.

17.31 You should restrict the number of simple effects you examine to those in which you are particularly interested (on *a priori* grounds), because the familywise error rate will increase as the number of tests increases.

CHAPTER 18

18.1 Study of migraines: (Results taken from SPSS)

Descriptive Statistics					
	N	Minimum	Maximum	Mean	Std. Deviation
WEEK1	9	7.0	30.0	20.778	7.1725
WEEK2	9	4.0	33.0	20.000	10.2225
WEEK3	9	5.0	14.0	9.000	3.1225
WEEK4	9	1.0	12.0	5.778	3.4197
WEEK5	9	4.0	17.0	6.778	4.1164
Valid N (listwise)	9				

18.3 I would have liked to collect data from students on the use of pain killers and other ways of dealing with migraines. I might also like to have data on stress levels over time so that I could possibly rule out the effects of stress.

18.5 Analysis of data in Exercise 18.4:

Source	df	SS	MS	F
Subjects	8	612.00		
Weeks	1	554.50	554.50	14.42*
Error	8	302.00	37.75	
Total	17	1159.70		

* $p < .05$

There is a significant increase in decrease in severity over time. $F = t^2 = 3.798^2 = 14.424$.

18.7 Effect size for Exercise 18.4:

We will use the square root of MS_{error} as our estimate of the standard deviation, because this is a standard deviation corrected for any differences due to subject effects.

$$\hat{d} = \frac{\overline{X}_0 - \overline{X}_3}{\sqrt{MS_{error}}} = 3.44$$

The decrease in severity from baseline to training is a reduction of approximately three-and-one-half standard deviations.

18.9 I would standardize the difference in means using the square root of the average of the variances of the two baseline measures. This gives us a denominator of 8.83.

$$\hat{d} = \frac{\overline{X}_{baseline} - \overline{X}_{training}}{s} = 1.49$$

On average, the severity of headaches decreased by nearly 1.50 standard deviations from baseline to training.

18.11 R analysis of Exercise 18.10

```
data.BST <- read.table("http://www.uvm.
edu/~dhowell/fundamentals9/DataFiles/Ex18-
10.dat", header = TRUE)
attach(data.BST)
dv <- c(Pretest, Posttest, FU6, FU12)
time <- rep(1:4, each = 10)
subject <- rep(1:10, 4)
time <- factor(time)
subject <- factor(subject)
cat("\nTrial Means \n")
tapply(dv, time, mean)
cat("\nSubject Means \n")
tapply(dv, subject, mean)
BSTmodel <- aov(dv ~ time + Error(subject/
time))
print(summary(BSTmodel))
```

Result

```
Error: subject
          Df Sum Sq Mean Sq F value Pr(>F)
Residuals  9   3318   368.7

Error: subject:time
      Df Sum Sq Mean Sq F value Pr(>F)
time   3  186.3   62.09   1.042   0.39
Residuals 27 1609.0   59.59
```

18.13 It would appear that without the intervention, condom use would actually have declined. This suggests that the intervention may have prevented that decline, in which case that nonsignificant result is actually a positive finding.

18.15 Bonferroni tests on data in Table 18.1:

We can use a standard *t* test because the error term has been corrected by the repeated-measures analysis of variance, which has already removed between-subject variability.

Paired Samples Test

| | Paired Differences | | | | | | | |
| | | | | 95% Confidence Interval of the Difference | | | | |
	Mean	Std. Deviation	Std. Error Mean	Lower	Upper	t	df	Sig. (2-tailed)
Pair 1 WEEK0–WEEK6	−2.680	2.6727	.5345	−3.783	−1.577	−5.014	24	.000
Pair 2 WEEK0–WEEK12	−3.040	2.9928	.5986	−4.275	−1.805	−5.079	24	.000
Pair 3 WEEK3–WEEK12	−1.600	2.8868	.5774	−2.792	−.408	−2.771	24	.011

The Bonferroni alpha level would be $.05/3 = .01667$

We will reject all of the null hypotheses because each p value is less than .0167.

18.17 SPSS analysis of data in Table 18.2

Tests of Within-Subjects Effects

Measure: MEASURE_1

Source		Type III Sum of Squares	df	Mean Square	F	Sig.
Time	Sphericity Assumed	962.450	3	320.817	2.411	.077
	Greenhouse-Geisser	962.450	2.424	397.003	2.411	.091
	Huynh-Feldt	962.450	2.985	322.482	2.411	.077
	Lower-bound	962.450	1.000	962.450	2.411	.138
Time × Group	Sphericity Assumed	1736.300	3	578.767	4.350	.008
	Greenhouse-Geisser	1736.300	2.424	716.210	4.350	.014
	Huynh-Feldt	1736.300	2.985	581.772	4.350	.008
	Lower-bound	1736.300	1.000	1736.300	4.350	.052
Error(Time)	Sphericity Assumed	7184.250	54	133.042		
	Greenhouse-Geisser	7184.250	43.637	164.636		
	Huynh-Feldt	7184.250	53.721	133.732		
	Lower-bound	7184.250	18.000	399.125		

Tests of Between-Subjects Effects

Measure: MEASURE_1

Transformed Variable: Average

Source	Type III Sum of Squares	df	Mean Square	F	Sig.
Intercept	29414.450	1	29414.450	46.795	.000
Group	168.200	1	168.200	.268	.611
Error	11314.350	18	628.575		

CHAPTER 19

19.1 $\chi^2 = 11.33$. We will reject the null hypothesis and conclude that students do not enroll at random.

19.3 $\chi^2 = 2.4$. Do not reject the null hypothesis that my daughter's sorting behavior is in line with my theory.

19.5 $\chi^2 = 29.35$. We can reject H_0 and conclude that the children did not choose dolls at random, but chose White dolls more often than Black.

19.7 $\chi^2 = 34.184$. Reject the null hypothesis and conclude that the distribution of choices between Black and White dolls was different in the two studies. Choice is *not* independent of the study and could easily be related to the time at which the studies were run. We are no longer asking whether one color doll is preferred over the other color, but whether the *pattern* of preference is constant across studies. In analysis of variance terms we are dealing with an interaction.

19.9 There are several ways that this study could be modified. We could simply rerun the present analysis by defining smokers and nonsmokers on the basis of the partner's smoking behavior. Alternatively, we could redefine the Smoker variable as "neither," "mother," "father," or "both."

19.11 $\chi^2 = 5.38$. We can reject the null hypothesis and conclude that achievement level during high school varies as a function of performance during elementary school.

Analysis using R

```
data.Add <- matrix(c(22, 187, 19, 74), by-
row = TRUE, ncol = 2)
result <- (chisq.test(data.Add, correct =
FALSE))
print(result)
print(1-pchisq(result$statistic, df = 1))
- - - - - - - - - - - - - - - - - - - - -
- - - - - -
        Pearson's Chi-squared test

data:  data.HH
X-squared = 5.3804, df = 1, p-value =
0.02036
```

19.13 A one-way chi-square test on the data in the first column of Exercise 19.12 would be asking whether the students are evenly distributed among the eight categories. What we really tested in Exercise 19.12 is whether that distribution, *however it appears*, is the same for those who later took remedial English as it is for those who later took nonremedial English.

19.15 $\chi^2 = 8.85$. The ability to reject a tumor is affected by the shock condition.

19.17 This is another place where we see the important relationship between sample size and power.

19.19 Dabbs and Morris study:

(a) These results show that there is a significant relationship between the two variables. $\chi^2 = 15.57$
(b) Testosterone levels in adults are related to the behavior of those individuals when they were children.
(c) This result shows that we can tie the two variables (delinquency and testosterone) together historically. I would assume that people who have high testosterone levels now also had high levels when they were children, but that is just an assumption.

19.21 Odds ratio for Ex19.19

$$OR = (80/366)/(462/3554) = 0.217/0.130 = 2.67$$

The odds of a history of childhood delinquency with high testosterone are about 2 2/3 higher for those with high testosterone.

19.23 We could ask a series of similar questions, evenly split between "right" and "wrong" answers. We could then sort the replies into positive and negative categories and ask whether faculty were more likely than students to give negative responses.

19.25 Racial differences in desired weight gain.
For White females, the odds of wishing to lose weight were $352/183 = 1.9235$, meaning that White females are nearly twice as likely to wish to lose weight as to stay the same or gain weight. For African American females, the corresponding ratio is $47/52 = .9038$. The odds ratio is $1.9235/.9038 = 2.1281$. This means that the odds of wishing to lose weight were more than twice as high among White females as compared to African American females.

19.25 Unah and Borger study
Chi-square = 7.71. The chi-square statistic is clearly significant. NonWhite defendants are sentenced to death at a significantly higher rate than White defendants.

CHAPTER 20

20.1 Amygdala lesions and fear responses (Kapp, Frysinger, Gallagher, & Hazelton, 1979):

(a) Analysis using the Mann-Whitney test:

The test run the traditional way

$$W_s = 53 \qquad W_s' = 2\overline{W} - W_s = 189 - 53 = 136$$

$W_{.025}(9,11) = 68 > 53$ $W_s < W's$ so use W_s in Appendix E. Double the probability level for a two-tailed test.

(b) Reject the null hypothesis and conclude that subjects in the Lesion group take longer to learn the task, as the theory predicted.

20.3 Nurcombe et al. study:

(a) $T = 8.5$; $T_{.025} = 8$. Do not reject H_0.

(b) We cannot conclude that we have evidence supporting the hypothesis that there is a reliable increase in hypothesis generation and testing over time. (This is a case in which alternative methods of breaking ties could lead to different conclusions.)

20.5 Independence of first-born children:

Hypothesis Test Summary

	Null Hypothesis	Test	Sig.	Decision
1	The median of differences between First and Second equals 0.	Related-Samples Wilcoxon Signed Rank Test	.027	Reject the null hypothesis.

Asymptotic significances are displayed. The significance level is .05.

(b) We can reject the null hypothesis and conclude that first-born children are more independent than their second-born siblings.

20.7 Data in Exercise 20.7 plotted as a function of the first-born's score:

The scatterplot shows that the difference between the pairs is heavily dependent upon the score of the first-born.

20.7 First-born children's independence:

(a) $T = 46$; $T_{.025}(20) = 52$

(b) We can reject the null hypothesis and conclude that first-born children are more independent that second-born children.

20.9 Wilcoxon's matched-pairs signed-ranks test tests the null hypothesis that paired scores were drawn from identical populations or from symmetric populations with the same mean (and median). The corresponding t test tests the null hypothesis that the paired scores were drawn from populations with the same mean and assumes normality.

20.11 Rejection of the null hypothesis by a t test is a more specific statement than rejection using the appropriate distribution-free test because, by making assumptions about normality and homogeneity of variance, the t test refers specifically to the population means—although it is also dependent on those assumptions.

20.13 $H = 6.757$. We can reject the null hypothesis and conclude that placement of these adolescents has an effect on truancy rates.

20.15 It eliminates the influence of individual differences (differences in overall level of truancy from one person to another).

20.17 One way to represent how effectively lesions to the amygdala interfere with fear responses is to report the percentage of lesioned animals who take longer to learn an avoidance task than any (or the median) control animal. In our case, the median number of trials to learn the avoidance was six trials for the control group. All (100%) of the lesioned group took more trials than this. Another way to represent the effect is to say that only two out of the 11 subjects in the lesioned group learned the task in fewer trials than the worst subject in the control group.

20.19 As a test of Bleuler's (1911) hypothesis that schizophrenia relates to a lack of connections in cortical locations dealing with memory, Suddath et al. (1990) compared the volume of the left hippocampus in 15 schizophrenic individuals and their monozygotic twin brothers. For these cases, the normal twins differed from their schizophrenic twin by a mean of .199 units, with larger volumes favoring the normal twin. A randomization test on this difference showed a probability value of .0031 on the hypothesis that twins did not differ in hippocampal volume. This study strongly supports the hypothesis that hippocampal volume is related to schizophrenia.

20.21 $\chi^2_F = 9.00$. We can reject the null hypothesis and conclude that people don't really like tea made with used tea bags.

CHAPTER 21

21.1 Mazzucchelli et al. (2010) study

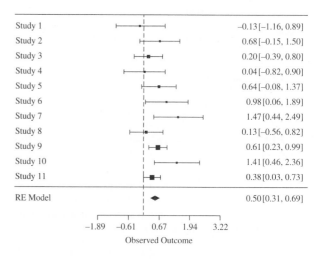

Study 1	−0.13[−1.16, 0.89]
Study 2	0.68[−0.15, 1.50]
Study 3	0.20[−0.39, 0.80]
Study 4	0.04[−0.82, 0.90]
Study 5	0.64[−0.08, 1.37]
Study 6	0.98[0.06, 1.89]
Study 7	1.47[0.44, 2.49]
Study 8	0.13[−0.56, 0.82]
Study 9	0.61[0.23, 0.99]
Study 10	1.41[0.46, 2.36]
Study 11	0.38[0.03, 0.73]
RE Model	0.50[0.31, 0.69]

−1.89 −0.61 0.67 1.94 3.22

Observed Outcome

21.2–21.3

Author	SubGrp	n1	n2	g		sg^2	weight	Wg	W*g^2	W^2	W(gi-gbar)^2	
Barlow86a	E	12.00	12.00	−0.134		0.2740	3.6496	−0.489	0.066	13.320	1.461	
Besyner79	E	14.00	16.00	0.675		0.1790	5.5866	3.771	2.545	31.210	0.174	
Lovett88	E	33.00	27.00	0.204		0.0930	10.7527	2.194	0.447	115.620	0.934	
Stark	E	10.00	9.00	0.043		0.1930	5.1813	0.223	0.010	26.846	1.076	
VanDenHaut	E	15.00	14.00	0.644		0.1380	7.2464	4.667	3.005	52.510	0.153	
Weinberg	E	10.00	9.00	0.976		0.2180	4.5872	4.477	4.370	21.042	1.045	
Wilson	E	9.00	11.00	1.466		0.2750	3.6364	5.331	7.815	13.223	3.403	
SUM		103.00	98.00				40.6402	20.173	18.258	273.772		
Barlow86a	M	12.00	13.00	0.133		0.1240	8.0645	1.073	0.143	65.036	1.078	
Fordyce77	M	50.00	60.00	0.609		0.0380	26.3158	16.026	9.760	692.521	0.320	
Fordyce83	M	40.00	13.00	1.41		0.2330	4.2918	6.052	8.533	18.420	3.564	
Reich81	M	49.00	49.00	0.378		0.0320	31.2500	11.813	4.465	976.563	0.455	
SUM		151.00	135.00				69.9222	34.963	22.900	1752.540		
GrandSum		254.00	233.00				110.5623	55.136		2026.311	13.663	
						Mean g =	0.499		Q =	13.663	which is chi.sq on 10 *df*	
						se(Mean g) =	0.095				*p* = .189	
						CI-lower =	0.312		C =	92.235		
						CI-upper =	0.685					
									Tau =	0.199		

21.4 The following results are from *R* using library (metafor)

Fixed-Effects Model (k = 4)

Test for Heterogeneity:
Q(df = 3) = 7.2655, p-val = 0.0639

Model Results:

estimate	se	zval	pval	ci.lb	ci.ub	
0.2274	0.0881	2.5813	0.0098	0.0547	0.4001	**

Signif. codes: 0 '***' 0.001 '**' 0.01 '*' 0.05 '.' 0.1 ' ' 1

21.5

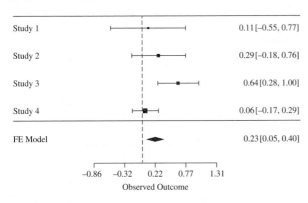

21.6 The confidence interval does not include 0, and we can safely reject the null hypothesis and conclude that methylphenidate does increase the severity of tics in these children.

21.7–21.9

Fixed-Effects Model (k = 3)
Test for Heterogeneity:
Q(df = 2) = 2.1121, p-val = 0.3478

Model Results:

estimate	se	zval	pval	ci.lb	ci.ub	
0.7364	0.0955	7.7109	<.0001	0.5492	0.9236	***

Signif. codes: 0 '***' 0.001 '**' 0.01 '*' 0.05 '.' 0.1 ' ' 1

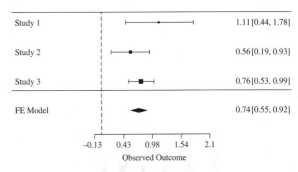

Again we have too few studies to look at heterogeneity seriously.

21.10–21.11

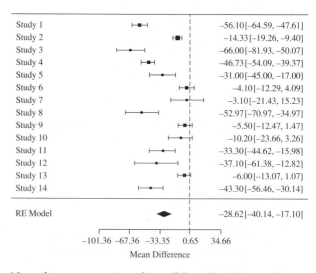

Fixed-Effects Model (k = 9)
Test for Heterogeneity:
Q(df = 8) = 2.1826, p-val = 0.9749
Model Results:

estimate	se	zval	pval	ci.lb	ci.ub	
0.5239	0.2826	1.8542	0.0637	–0.0299	1.0777	.

Signif. codes: 0 '***' 0.001 '**' 0.01 '*' 0.05 '.' 0.1 ' ' 1

21.12–21.16 Kapoor, Rajkumar et al. (2011)
The risk ratios and log risk ratios are
Risk Ratio
4.102326 6.336000 8.212389 1.963636
Log Risk Ratio
1.411554 1.846248 2.105644 0.674798

Mean Risk Ratio and confidence limits

Log Risk Ratio

Estimate	se	zval	pval	ci.lb	ci.ub
1.5747	0.3277	4.8055	<.0001	0.9324	2.2170

Risk Ratio	**CI_{lower}**	**CI_{upper}**
4.8293	2.5406	9.1798

Even at the low end of the confidence interval the addition of thalidomide increases the chances of success to 2.5 times the chance of success in the control group.

21.17 Random effects model for Bisson and Martin (2009) study

Random-Effects Model (k = 14; tau^2 estimator: REML)

tau^2 (estimate of total amount of heterogeneity): 438.6370 (SE = 189.2833)

tau (sqrt of the estimate of total heterogeneity): 20.9437

I^2 (% of total variability due to heterogeneity): 94.80%

H^2 (total variability / within-study variance): 19.24

Test for Heterogeneity:
Q(df = 13) = 236.1772, p-val < .0001

Model Results:

estimate	se	zval	pval	ci.lb	ci.ub
–28.6212	5.8774	–4.8697	<.0001	–40.1407	–17.1017

***

Note that we can reject the null hypothesis in our test for heterogeneity, though we have no specific variable that might explain that variability. We can also conclude that VBT is a more effective treatment than the Control treatment.

Index

List of Applications